W9-CND-684

THE AMERICAN ALPINE
JOURNAL
2008

Tatsuro Yamada tun-
neling up Memorial
Gate, north face of
Mt. Church
[pp. 42–47]
Yusuke Sato

Marko Prezelj and Vince Anderson on the corniced ridge during the first ascent of K7 West [pp. 72–79]. *Steve House*

CONTENTS

Members of the Gangwon University
team on a new route up the south ridge
during the second ascent of Varaha
Shikhar (The Fang, 7,647m)
[pp. 385–386]. *Lee Young-jun collection*

CLIMBS AND EXPEDITIONS

Submission Guidelines are at www.americanalpineclub.org/AAJ.

Corporate Friends

of the

AMERICAN ALPINE JOURNAL

*We thank the following for their generous financial
support of the 2008* AMERICAN ALPINE JOURNAL

SUMMIT PARTNER

patagonia®

BENEFACTORS

PATRONS

MOUNTAIN GEAR

Sunset on K7 West (6,858m) in Pakistan's Charakusa Valley [pp. 72–79]. *Steve House*

Friends
of the
AMERICAN ALPINE
JOURNAL

We thank the following for their generous financial support.

BENEFACTORS:
Yvon Chouinard
H. Adams Carter American Alpine Journal Fund

PATRONS:
Dr. Gordon Benner, Bishop Family Foundation
Ann Carter, Richard E. Hoffman, M.D.
John G. McCall, M.D.*
In memory of Charlie Fowler & Randall Grandstaff

Peter D. McGann, M.D., Edith Overly
Mark A. Richey, Dr. Louis F. Reichardt

SUPPORTERS:
Bill Archer, Jim Edwards & Michele Mass, John Harlin III
Jack Heffernan, William R. Kilpatrick, M.D.
Samuel C. Silverstein, M.D.

SPECIAL THANKS TO:
Margot Bias, William A. Burd, Robert J. Campbell
Neale E. Creamer, Z. Wayne Griffin, Jr., David Harrah
Michael John Lewis, Jr., Glenn E. Porzak, Steven Schwartz
William R. Stall, Mark Tache

THE AMERICAN ALPINE JOURNAL, 710 Tenth St. Suite 100, Golden Colorado 80401
TELEPHONE: (303) 384-0110 FAX: (303) 384-0111, E-MAIL: AAJ@AMERICANALPINECLUB.ORG
www.americanalpineclub.org

ISBN 978-1-933056-07-4
© 2008 The American Alpine Club. Printed in Canada. All rights reserved.

Felix Frieder on the first ascent of
Manara-Potsiny on Tsaranoro Be,
Madagascar [pp. 292–293].
Toni Lamprecht

The American Alpine Journal

John Harlin III, *Editor*

Advisory Board
James Frush, *Managing Editor*
Rolando Garibotti, Mark Jenkins
Mark Richey

Senior Editor
Kelly Cordes

Associate Editors
Lindsay Griffin
Dougald MacDonald

Art Director
Adele Hammond

Photo Doctor
Dan Gambino

Contributing Editors
Steve Roper, *Features*
Joe Kelsey, *Climbs & Expeditions*
David Stevenson, *Book Reviews*
Cameron M. Burns, *In Memoriam*
Frederick O. Johnson, *Club Activities*

Cartographer
Martin Gamache, Alpine Mapping Guild

Translators

Bean Bowers   Molly Loomis
Adam French   Henry Pickford
Rolando Garibotti   David Trippett
Caroline George

Indexers
Ralph Ferrara, Eve Tallman

Regional Contacts
Lowell Skoog and Matt Perkins, *Washington Cascades*; Drew
Brayshaw and Don Serl, *Coast Mountains, BC*; Raphael
Slawinski, *Canadian Rockies*; Antonio Gómez Bohórquez and
Sergio Ramirez Carrascal, *Peru*; Daniel Seeliger, *Cochamó*;
Rolando Garibotti, *Patagonia*; Damien Gildea, *Antarctica*;
Malcolm Bass, *Scotland*; Harish Kapadia, *India*; Elizabeth
Hawley, *Nepal*; Tamotsu Nakamura, *Japanese expeditions*; Anna
Piunova, *CIS expeditions*; Servei General d'Informació de
Muntanya, *Spanish expeditions*; Mark Watson, *New Zealand*;
Lindsay Griffin, *Earth*

With additional thanks to
Barry Blanchard, Carlo Caccia, Tommy Caldwell & Beth
Rodden, Jeremy Frimer, Nacho Grez, Colin Haley, Steve
House, Tsunemichi Ikeda, Pavle Kozjek, Elena Laletina, Jim
Logan, Nacho Morales, *Northwest Mountaineering Journal*
Anna Piunova, Joe Puryear, Denys Sanjines, Marcelo Scanu
John Scurlock, Steve Swenson, Mark Westman

Andrej Gmorvsek climbing Lufoo La
on Castle Peak in India's Miyar Valley
[pp. 366–368]. *Tanja Gmorvsek*

THE AMERICAN ALPINE CLUB

OFFICIALS FOR THE YEAR 2008
*Directors ex-officio

EXECUTIVE COMMITTEE

HONORARY PRESIDENT	PRESIDENT	VICE PRESIDENT
William Lowell Putnam	Jim Donini*	Steve Swenson*

HONORARY TREASURER	SECRETARY	TREASURER
Theodore (Sam) Streibert	Charles B. Franks*	Charlie Sassara*

DIRECTORS

TERMS ENDING 2009	TERMS ENDING FEBRUARY 2010	TERMS ENDING FEBRUARY 2011
Ellen Lapham	Cody J. Smith	Charlotte Fox
Greg Miller	A. Travis Spitzer	George Lowe
Conrad Anker	Danika Gilbert	Aimee Barnes
Jack Tackle	Mark Kroese	Doug Walker
John R. Kascenska	Paul Gagner	

SECTION CHAIRS

Alaska – Harry Hunt
New England – William C. Atkinson
Central Rockies – Majka Burhardt
Southeast – David Thoenen
Northern Rockies – Brian Cabe
Blue Ridge – Simon Carr

New York – Philip Erard
Sierra Nevada – Dave Riggs
Cascade – Al Schumer
Oregon – Mike Volk
Southwest – Linh Nguyen
Midwest – Benjamin A. Kweton

EDITORS

THE AMERICAN ALPINE JOURNAL	ACCIDENTS IN NORTH AMERICAN MOUNTAINEERING	THE AMERICAN ALPINE NEWS
John Harlin III	John E. (Jed) Williamson	Dougald MacDonald

STAFF

Executive Director – Phil Powers
Director of Operations – Penn Burris
Controller – Jerome Mack
Marketing Director – David Maren
Development Director – Cheryle Wise
Technology Manager – Craig Hoffman
Outreach Manager – Dana Richardson
Executive Assistant – Janet Miller

Grants Manager – Janet Miller
Membership Data Administrator – Emily Kreis
Events Coordinator – Brittany Griffith
Library Director – Gary Landeck
Preservation Librarian – Beth Heller
Ranch Manager – Drew Birnbaum
Ranch Assistant – Drew Kroft

PREFACE

The first ascent of K2's west face earned "best climb of 2007" status from many observers around the world. It is undoubtedly the most difficult route on the world's second-highest peak, and it required remarkable effort, skill, and persistence from the large team that completed it. Yet, despite devoting several pages to the ascent in the Climbs and Expeditions section of this year's *American Alpine Journal* [p. 339], we have chosen not to highlight K2's west face as one of our featured stories.

Although the K2 ascent involved a large team and traditional siege tactics, with more than 50 ropes strung up the steepest part of the face, this is not fundamentally what drove our decision to downplay the ascent. Like all climbers, we have personal preferences for styles of climbing, and we admire certain ascents more than others. But that's not the fundamental issue either, because we believe that as long as mountaineers climb in a way that doesn't destroy a future climber's ability to experience the route in its substantially natural state, they should be free to enjoy the mountains however they want. Pull on protection or climb all free? Use oxygen or suck wind? We may not admire some choices, but when climbers are honest about what they do and don't ruin the place for everybody else, we have no objections to anyone following their own lights. The route is still there for us to climb in our preferred style.

Style choices cross the line into ethical decisions when they directly affect other people—for example, when a climber decides to permanently alter the mountain environment. The team on K2 was free to climb its route in whatever style it chose. Certainly there are some inevitable impacts, such as the occasional rappel anchor. However, we feel it was unethical to abandon thousands of feet of rope and hundreds of pounds of equipment and provisions on K2's slopes. Turning a beautiful mountain face into a private junkyard is not a fair price for its initial "conquest." A climber does not establish ownership over a route simply by being there first. In our modern era, we recognize that mountains are public places where each visitor is obligated to respect the rights of future visitors.

Ultimately, style and ethics often converge. In choosing a climbing style, we also choose our impact on the environment and on other climbers. Deciding to drill holes for a sport climb. Choosing a large team and siege tactics over a small group and an alpine-style ascent. Using siege tactics to push so close to the edge on a difficult and dangerous route that it's nearly impossible to clean the mountain before leaving it. On these issues, the *AAJ* and the world climbing community are increasingly guided by one principle: the lower a climb's impact, the higher its achievement. In this sense, and perhaps only this sense, style truly matters.

THE EDITORS

Dave Turner's foot during his 34 days alone on the first ascent of Taste the Paine, Patagonia. Turner's ascent was made in extremely clean style. See his article starting on page 24.
Dave Turner

The American Alpine Club
2007–2008

The American Alpine Club is larger than ever, with more than 8,000 members, and has embarked on a broad range of new initiatives alongside its vital traditional programs, which include the 79th year of the *American Alpine Journal*.

In early 2008 the AAC, Colorado Mountain Club, and National Geographic Society completed and opened the Bradford Washburn American Mountaineering Museum in Golden, Colorado. The first of its kind in the United States, the museum offers a unique opportunity to explore climbing history and mountain culture and conservation, and includes numerous interactive exhibits. The museum website is www.bwamm.org.

The AAC also has increased its commitment to conservation of mountain environments. With the help of a $150,000 grant from the Argosy Foundation, the AAC's Alpine Conservation Partnership (ACP) with the Mountain Institute has ramped up preservation and restoration efforts in Nepal, Peru, and Tanzania. The ACP's focus has expanded to include documenting and mitigating the effects of climate change in alpine environments, through a program called Climbatology. In another conservation initiative, the AAC and Patagonia Inc. have undertaken a project to improve trails and campsites in Los Glaciares National Park in Patagonia. The club also has spearheaded human waste–management programs in Indian Creek, Utah; Rocky Mountain National Park, Colorado; and Grand Teton National Park, Wyoming.

The AAC is working hard to expand the availability of its knowledge resources online. The entire collection of the *American Alpine Journal*, from 1929 through 2007, is now available at www.americanalpineclub.org. AAC members also have online access to the this year's edition, and can browse the new *AAJ* Topos section, which contains dozens of topos, maps, and photos from climbs featured in the *AAJ*. The Henry S. Hall Jr. American Alpine Club Library is also moving forward in the digital world, with numerous electronic initiatives, including digitization of the Lt. Nawang Kapadia Himalayan Library collection of more than 1,250 photos.

Mountaineers and researchers benefit from the generosity of AAC members through the support of numerous grant programs. Nearly $40,000 in annual AAC grants support cutting-edge alpine climbs (Lyman Spitzer and McNeill-Nott awards), young climbers (Mountain Fellowships), climber/humanitarians (Zack Martin grant), and conservationists and scientists doing work in and about climbing environments. A list of recent grants may be found at page 453.

In addition to operating the Grand Teton Climbers' Ranch, a favorite base camp for climbers, the club is involved in joint ventures to build badly needed climbers' campgrounds near the Shawangunks cliffs in New York and the New River Gorge in West Virginia. In October 2008, in Colorado, the club will launch the first annual Craggin' Classic, a major new climbing festival.

Building relationships with climbers elsewhere in the world, the AAC hosted the first half of the Chinese-American Ladies' Climbing Exchange in June 2008, with the second half slated for October in China. Also in October 2008, the first International Climbers' Meet will be held at Indian Creek, Utah, with more than 55 climbers attending from two dozen countries. Shortly thereafter, the editors of the *AAJ* will host a "summit meeting" with 20 editors of mountaineering magazines and websites from a dozen different countries.

Everything the AAC does is designed to support, inspire, and unite the climbing community. By inviting your climbing partners to become members, you help strengthen our community and protect the places we climb. Learn more about the AAC, sign up a new member, or make a donation at www.americanalpineclub.org.

Imja
Glacier/Lake

1956
© Fritz Müller

2007
© Alton Byers

With the AAC's support, the Alpine Conservation Partnership has provided pioneering photographic documentation of glacial change around Mt. Everest. As glaciers have receded, 24 new lakes have formed in the region in the last decade. The lake at the base of the Imja Glacier (shown here) started forming in the 1970s and now holds 35 million cubic meters of water; it is considered a high risk for a glacial lake outburst flood, or GLOF. The Alpine Conservation Partnership is working to introduce solutions developed in Peru to help mitigate the danger.

Many milestones are being reached during the year 2008, including the opening of the Bradford Washburn American Mountaineering Museum (at left) in February. The museum contains priceless artifacts of American climbing history and many interactive exhibits. In October 2008, the AAC will launch the Craggin' Classic, a major new climbing festival in Colorado. *Jeremy Collins (above left); Dan Ham (left)*

THE ILLUSION OF CONTROL

Third time's the charm on Pumari Chhish South in Pakistan.

CHRISTIAN TROMMSDORFF

The south face of Pumari Chhish South (7,350m) above the Yutmaru Glacier, as seen from base camp at 4,500 meters. Yannick Graziani and Christian Trommsdorff climbed the face with four bivouacs. Khunyang Chhish East (7,400m, to the left) and the 6,890-meter peak to the right are both unclimbed. *Christian Trommsdorff*

Those who do not believe in God might reconsider their position when scanning through Shiro Shirahata's photographs of the Karakoram, especially if you are a mountain climber. At almost every page of *The Karakoram*, you will be impressed. Is the beauty of these high peaks only the result of pure geological randomness on the surface of our Mother Earth? I am not a follower of religion or of any system of belief, but when spending time in the higher Karakoram ranges I cannot help but feel deeply moved by the total wilderness of the environment. For alpinists who specialize in lightweight, high-altitude climbing, these high peaks are the ultimate on this planet.

Yannick Graziani and I couldn't have dreamt of a nicer reward for our 10th expedition together in 10 years than the successful ascent of what, in my view, was the most beautiful and majestic virgin peak above 7,000 meters in the world: Pumari Chhish South. Just have a look at page 45 of Shirahata's book!

In 2003, after seeing this photo and others of nearby peaks, I suggested to my friends and climbing buddies Yannick Graziani and Patrick Wagnon that we explore some of the glacier basins leading into the huge Hispar Glacier in the western Karakoram. We would hopefully also get a bit of climbing in.

Before that expedition, and despite an attempt to 8,200 meters on the south-southeast spur of K2 and a successful climb of Spantik's easy normal route with six clients, I clearly hadn't understood what climbing in lightweight style on the higher peaks of the Karakoram really meant. (As for Yannick, he had experienced being snowed in for weeks in his tent at the foot of Ultar's Hidden Pillar, without get-

Four previous attempts on Pumari Chhish South had been plagued by dangerous snow, but snow conditions were excellent during the 2007 climb, allowing rapid progress to the headwall at 6,400 meters. *Yannick Graziani*

ting the slightest weather window for any attempt.) The nine weeks we spent in the Hispar area from mid-April to mid-June 2003 would put me firmly in my place.

We came early, hoping for better weather than in summer, but it had been an extremely snowy winter, and several times we would experience what that meant on these mountains. During our first exploration in late April, we had to retreat at the junction of the Yutmaru and Hispar glaciers, at around 4,300 meters, after a massive overnight snow dump. During our retreat, we followed the tracks of a snow leopard—even it had decided to flee to lower altitudes.

We had been impressed by the massive, virgin south faces of Khunyang Chhish's main and east summits, but were also frustrated at not having seen Pumari Chhish's south face. As that first excursion had taken much longer than expected, and not having as much free time as us, Patrick decided to head home.

The upper south face as seen from near the first bivouac at 5,300 meters. From here the route reaches the prominent snow ramp that climbs from right to left, and then ascends a sustained mixed headwall from 6,400 to about 7,000 meters. *Christian Trommsdorff*

After a few days' rest in the marvelous haven of Karimabad village, Yannick and I agreed to go back to explore the hidden treasures of the Yutmaru basin. We hadn't been able to find any account of significant climbs or attempts there. [Editor's note: Julie-Ann Clyma and Roger Payne had made two attempts on Pumari Chhish South, in 1999 and 2000, reaching a high point of about 6,200 meters on the south face in very dangerous snow conditions.] A journalist friend accompanying us was designated expedition leader and sent back to Islamabad to obtain a permit for Khunyang Chhish Main from the Ministry of Tourism. In our minds, that permit would also do for Pumari Chhish South, since they were quite close together, and since the chances of making it above 6,500 meters on any of these peaks were very small (peaks below 6,500 meters were permit-free in Pakistan that year).

With a small team of porters from Hispar and lots of food this time, we made it back to the Yutmaru Glacier, where we had left all our equipment. Over a meter of snow covered the Yutmaru, so there was no chance for the lightly equipped porters to make it any farther. Luckily, we had brought skis and hired two strong high-altitude porters and guides, Qudrat and Bari, who had been with me on Spantik. During the following 10 days, while Yannick and I were exploring the neighborhood and trying to acclimatize, they skied back and forth to supply the base camp that we had established at around 4,500 meters, 10 kilometers up the Yutmaru Glacier. From base camp we had stunning views of Khunyang East, Pumari South, Yuksin Gardan, Kanjut Sar, Hispar Peak, and many unnamed 6,000ers.

Over three weeks we made three attempts to climb over 6,000 meters to acclimatize, but snow conditions were hopeless. We triggered several slab avalanches, and we even moved our base camp several hundred meters because huge avalanches were coming quite close, their blast sometimes smothering our mess tent with snow. The weather remained unstable, with regular and sometimes significant snowfalls, so without any chance of climbing higher we decided once again to go back for a rest in Karimabad. But we had fallen in love with the south face of Pumari Chhish South, and had forgotten all about Khunyang Chhish.

When we got back to base camp 10 days later, we declared ourselves sufficiently acclimatized for an attempt on our beloved face, although we guessed this was just wishful thinking. We hoped that since the face was very steep and faced exactly south, we would find better snow conditions.

On June 6, after a day of great weather that we spent watching avalanches purging the faces around us, we started off on our attempt. Given the frequent snowfalls, we couldn't expect to have more than three to four days for our ascent. Speed and therefore little weight in our packs would be the keys to success. The first day we started at 3 a.m. and had great snow conditions up to 5,400 meters. We could "run" up the first 300 meters, which were exposed to seracs sitting 2,000 meters higher.

Above, it was another story. It is hard to describe what it felt like on the huge ramp that crosses the face from right to left—to be stuck in waist-deep snow on a 55- to 60-degree slope with 1,500 meters of void below. Before reaching our first bivy, we took hours just to climb a hundred vertical meters. We had climbed 1,550 meters in 14 hours and were totally wasted. It took us another hour to cut a proper bivy platform on the ridge bordering the left side of the ramp.

The next morning we reached the top of the ramp after two hours, and then we made our way up almost two-thirds of the headwall, climbing well into the night. We couldn't find a proper place to bivy, and it had started snowing. Eventually we found a reasonable boulder—just large enough for two French asses—sticking out of the ice, fixed a net of rope under it for our feet, and sat down. That bivy was the kind you remember all your life. I got repeatedly covered by spindrift, and my chest started to get really cold. Meanwhile Yannick's bilious vomiting guaranteed us a show for most of the night. It was the usual Graziani altitude sickness, and I wasn't too worried because I knew how resilient he was.

The next morning, with all the fresh snow that had fallen, there was only one option: a Napoleonic "retreat from Moscow." After having survived this descent, in spindrift that became more and more like real avalanches as we got lower, the situation was clear for me: "E.T., go back to Karimabad, and then to France to enjoy the cherry season."

However, Yannick managed to convince me to stay for another try. On June 16, on the third day of our second attempt, we got hit with bad weather again. We had climbed a little further up this time, maybe to 6,850 meters, and on a different line in the upper part of the headwall. While rappelling, at around 6,500 meters, we witnessed a massive avalanche not far from us, triggered by a serac at our level. The bottom of our line got blown away, and our treasured approach skis with it. At base camp, four kilometers away from the bottom of our face, Qudrat and Bari experienced a 20-minute blizzard.

At least things were clear to both of us now: E.T.: go home!

In 2007 circumstances would turn out to be much more favorable, even though we hadn't organized a proper expedition. I had already planned a trip to Pakistan in the spring, taking some clients ski-touring in the Shimshal area, and then going to Kashmir to review the results of the emergency relief operation that we had set up following the disastrous earthquake of October 8, 2005. [See "A Note About the Author" for more about this relief operation.] As for Yannick, he had decided to ski some high peaks around Karimabad with his girlfriend, Caroline.

I left Chamonix a week before them, and just before my departure I managed to convince Yannick to go for yet another attempt on Pumari Chhish South. We both knew we wouldn't have the drive to stay for many weeks in the Yutmaru basin this time, and that acclimatizing elsewhere on more moderate peaks would be much easier. We agreed to meet on May 31, acclimatized and ready to give it another brief attempt. We allowed ourselves just two and a half weeks for the round trip from Karimabad.

In the end we actually acclimatized together, in fairly bad weather, spending just one night each on two different 5,800-meter peaks, during a six-day ski-touring trip in the Kunjerab Pass area with our girlfriends. Back in Karimabad, we took three days' rest. After five weeks of typical unstable Karakoram weather, we had almost lost hope. We scaled back any expectations. We would simply go and have a look.

An uneventful six-hour jeep ride brought us to Hispar village, where we hired friendly and efficient porters. We then trekked for three days to base camp, which this time we could set up on a beautiful grass meadow on a moraine, eight kilometers from the bottom of Pumari South (there was no snow this time, even at 4,500 meters). Fresh spring water was available nearby, and at each meal Ali, our favorite cook, treated us to some excellent cuisine.

On June 6 we made ourselves comfortable in base camp. That evening the weather cleared, and the next day was perfect. We got a forecast by satellite phone for at least six days of good weather. We couldn't believe our ears! Our packs were ready the next morning.

With the experience we had gained in 2003, and this longer window of good weather, we knew how to plan our first three climbing days. And things went as expected, except on day two, when we had to wait politely under an overhang at the bottom of the ramp for the wet snow slides to stop.

On day three, above the ramp, we once again climbed the first very hard section of mixed terrain on the face. Yannick led a 60-meter pitch up an overhanging, icy chimney—no place to fall! Then I took my turn on an easier but absolutely magnificent mixed line diagonalling up to the left.

We knew the fourth day would be D-day for our attempt. We would have to find the key passage through the top of the headwall, in unknown territory above the high point of 6,850 meters we had reached in 2003. We also knew we couldn't make it to the top from our third bivy at 6,600 meters, so we would have to climb with heavy sacks, and find a last bivy site above the headwall at around 7,000 meters.

One of the key pitches of the entire 2,700-meter face was just above our third bivy at 6,600 meters. In the late afternoon sun on day three, Yannick made an impressive lead up a slightly overhanging crack and chimney, then fixed it with one of our two 60-meter ropes.

That helped us a lot to get going the next day. We had known this section would be shady and very cold in the morning. Above the chimney, we decided to climb out toward the right side

Yannick Graziani leads beautiful mixed ground at about 6,700 meters during the fourth morning of climbing.
Christian Trommsdorff

Graziani traverses in high winds at about 7,100 meters, heading toward the summit. *Christian Trommsdorff*

of the headwall, a bit like we had done during our second attempt in 2003, but instinctively we took a somewhat different line. We climbed four pitches of superb mixed terrain on beautiful granite, then got stuck beneath the last 50 meters of the headwall.

On the left was another over-hanging chimney, which Yannick suggested climbing, but I refused, convinced it would cost us too much energy. After a very tense discussion about a possible pendulum to the left to look around the corner for easier terrain, I again refused, this time thinking it would be too risky. I remembered Doug Scott's accident in a similar situation high on the Ogre.

In the course of our "discussions," I dropped one my ice axes. We had finally agreed that I would do a diagonal rappel first, then Yannick would do his pendulum above me, with the rope held from below. But we managed to get our rope stuck when trying to rappel. While I was angrily tugging on the rope and trying to flip it around a corner, a loop that had got caught under my axe dislodged it. I eventually had to climb back up a bit until I could pull the rope from a more favorable angle, and then managed to join Yannick 15 meters above.

With all this maneuvering we had lost over an hour, and it was already late afternoon. However, when Yannick finally turned the corner to the left, I heard a cry of elation. It was one of those magic moments. From what we could see now, we knew that if the weather held we would have a real chance of making the top.

After seven or eight more mixed, then ice, then delicate snow pitches, we found a perfect bivy site at 7,000 meters, just 50 meters to the left of our line. It was now dusk and we had reached the edge of the high glacier basin between the Khunyang East, Pumari Main, and Pumari South summits. The slopes and ridges above us were much easier, although still at around 55 degrees. The weather remained excellent; the big uncertainty now was the snow conditions.

The next morning it took us four hours to climb the last 350 meters to the top. The snow got better as we climbed, as the slopes were more exposed to the high-altitude winds. However, when we were halfway up the wind suddenly got stronger, and about 100 meters from the top we were caught in 80 to 100 kph gusts.

Despite being very close to the summit, we began to doubt again. But then, as if by magic, the wind dropped a little. Had it not, we would have failed to make the summit once again!

Looking back at our 10 years of expedition climbing together, Yannick and I can feel a sense of fulfillment. Our passion for the high peaks is still intact, and we realize that the core values of our amateur climbing ethic have become clearer and sustainable over the years; these values are respect, friendship, spirit of discovery, beauty, ambition, progressive experience, high level of commitment, and maximal economy of means. They have led us to live extraordinary adventures that are hard to capture in photos, films, or words.

Four times in 10 expeditions, Yannick and I have failed to reach our objective, but experience and style come first for us. With Chomo Lonzo North and Central, and Pumari Chhish South, we have had the privilege of climbing three very beautiful and technical virgin 7,000-meter peaks. The climbing on Pumari Chhish last year went smoothly. We had been high on the mountain before, and this time we benefited from a great weather window. Still, the uncertainty of the key section of the headwall gave an incredible intensity to our fourth day on the mountain—a magic day we will never forget!

SUMMARY:

AREA: Hispar Muztagh, Karakoram, Pakistan

ASCENT: Alpine-style first ascent of Pumari Chhish South (7,350m) by the south face (2,700m, ABO 5.10 M6 A1), Yannick Graziani and Christian Trommsdorff, June 8–13, 2007. The two men climbed the face with four bivouacs, summiting at noon on June 12; they downclimbed and made approximately 35 rappels along the line of ascent over the next day and a half.

A shorter version of this article appeared previously in *Vertical.*

A NOTE ABOUT THE AUTHOR:

Born in 1964 in Grenoble, France, Christian Trommsdorf has completed more than 20 international expeditions. After a career as an electrical engineer, he became a UIAGM guide and has been based in Chamonix for the last decade.

After the October 2005 earthquake in Pakistan, along with Pierre Neyret (UIAGM guide) and François Carrel (journalist), Trommsdorff started a relief operation called Solidarité Alpes Cachemire in partnership with the French Alpine Club, and raised more than 150,000 euros that has been spent for emergency relief operations and lately for school reconstruction in four remote villages strongly affected by the quake. Trommsdorff is seeking funds to rebuild more schools with the help of a small, efficient team already in place in Pakistan. Contact: chris_trommsdorff @hotmail.com for details.

Battered by wind, sun, and altitude, Trommsdorff returns to the final bivouac. *Yannick Graziani*

TASTE THE PAINE

Thirty-four days alone on a big wall in Patagonia.

DAVE TURNER

Dave Turner contemplates the east faces of Cerro Escudo (right) and Fortaleza. Before Turner's solo new route in 2008, no one had climbed the east face of Escudo and then continued up the long, broken ridge to the peak's 2,450-meter summit. *Dave Turner*

Wiping the rime ice from my goggles, I could barely make out the glacier far below. I stepped higher in my aider, gaining a few inches onto the poor hook placement. "Don't blow it now," I thought. Just a little higher and…pop! The hook went and I went with it. Gold and gray rock accelerated in front of my eyes as I involuntarily headed back toward the belay. I heard the reassuring but somewhat scary sound of nylon ripping apart as a screamer clipped to a beak ripped open. The beak popped and I kept falling, now swinging wildly. Another screamer activated on the next beak placement, and then I rattled to a halt.

My belay anchor was just below. I debated ducking into the portaledge for a minute or two, to let a snow flurry pass and collect myself. It was my eighth day on the wall, and it obviously was going to be a long one. Instead I reached to the back of my harness for a jumar to go back up and finish the pitch. As I clipped the jumar to the rope, I noticed a squishy feeling inside my left glove. When I took it off, blood poured out. Apparently the hook had ripped open my knuckles when it sheared from the edge above. But the bleeding soon stopped, and I knew I could take care of it later; inside the por-taledge I had pain meds and stitch-ing materials, and later that night I could play doctor.

Turner's custom-made double-fly, triple-pole portaledge is a tiny dot in a sea of granite, one pitch above the big snow ledge near the bottom of the face. *Michael Rayner*

I started back up to finish the pitch, but after one move with the jumar the beak that had held my fall decided it had had enough and I crashed down against the portaledge. Shocked, I glanced over to the belay anchor, half expecting to find a partner to whom I could yell, "Did you see that?" But I was alone.

Sitting upstairs at Café Andino in the Peruvian town of Huaraz, sipping Americanos and browsing climbing mags, I came across an article about Cerro Escudo. Three Americans had climbed a route up the east face of this colossal peak in late 1994 and early 1995, and two other lines nearly reached the summit ridge, but no one had climbed the steep eastern and northern aspects all the way to the summit. Seeing the pics of the Americans in Gore-Tex suits and plastic boots, battling up this wall amid legendary Patagonian storms, I was hooked. I made plans that day to attempt this alpine big wall.

January 2007 saw me at the foot of Cerro Escudo. I had not come to climb; this was a reconnaissance trip to figure out the logistics and scope a new route on the east face. I found a potential line to the left of the American route: steep, beautiful gray and golden granite, and over 1,200 meters high. Just what I was looking for.

In November, I flew from my hometown of Sacramento to Buenos Aires, Argentina, paying $700 extra for all of my bags full of gear and supplies—everything I needed to stay in Patago-nia for four months and solo a big wall. In the terminal in Buenos Aires, I got into a dramatic fistfight when a man tried to rob one of my backpacks, but eventually I got the gear back and made my way to the Torres del Paine region of southern Patagonia.

Once I arrived at the park, the real work started. From the beginning I was against the idea of hiring horses or porters; I found it more rewarding to bring in everything alone. The approach to the wall was a 24-mile round trip from where the minibus drops you off. I made this approach 11 times, carrying gear, food, and fuel, for a total of more than 260 miles. But soon I was established at the base of the route, with a nice camp out on the middle of the glacier.

The climb started with a 150-meter slab that went pretty easily, mostly 5.6 and A2+, which brought me to a large, sloping snow ledge. It took almost two full days to haul all of the bags to this ledge, due to the heavy loads, bad weather, and a

Turner jugging low on the 1,200-meter wall. During most days, he felt lucky if he could lead and clean a single long pitch. *Dave Turner*

slight accident. As I was hauling the bags one by one, the sun made a rare appearance. All of a sudden the wall thawed and started to drop ice and stones all around me. I quickly made it back to the ground, unharnessed at the base, and walked to my glacier camp 10 minutes away. When the wall went into the shade two hours later, I returned to find that my gear deposit at the base had taken a direct hit from a large rock. My harness, aiders, daisies, jumars, Mini Traxion, and some biners were all destroyed or damaged. I had spares for everything except the harness. The swami belt was cut nearly halfway through, but luckily the Yates big-wall harness had so much remaining material that it seemed sufficiently strong. I daubed some Seam Grip over the cuts, sewed on some new gear loops, and called it good.

Once all the gear was on the big snow ledge, I blasted off on what was guaranteed to be the biggest adventure of my life. The next 1,000-plus meters would be steep and very difficult. The rock type and style of climbing seemed like a mix of El Capitan's Tempest and Zenyatta Mondatta routes, only much harder and longer. Most days, I would be lucky if I could climb a single long pitch, clean it, and prepare the rack and ropes for the next day. On average the leads took five to eight hours, as they usually were very long (65 to 70 meters) and the fierce weather made it difficult to climb quickly. Many times, wind and snow forced me back to the portaledge, which I almost always had set up and waiting. I had chosen to make this ascent starting in December, a bit earlier than most other big climbs in the park, so I would experience snow rather than rain. This way I would stay much drier, but it also was a lot colder. To me, the trade-off seemed good, as a vast majority of the climb was on direct aid and it doesn't make such a big difference if it is cold.

As I made my way up the wall, I usually moved my portaledge camp every two pitches. I

The 1,200-meter east face of Cerro Escudo, with routes and significant attempts marked. (1) Southeast couloir attempt (Banbolini-Jover, 1996), halted 200 meters below ridge. (2) Taste the Paine (VII 5.9 A4+, Turner, 2008), continued to summit of Cerro Escudo. (3) The Dream (VII 5.10 A4+, Breemer-Jarrett-Santelices, 1995), descended from ridge. (4) Via de los Invalidos (6c A3, German Alpine Club, 1994). (5) Et Si Le Soleil Ne Revenait Pas… (VI 5.10 A4, Nicolet-Zweiacker, 1997). (6) North ridge (5.10 A2, Gore-Perkins, 1992), 12 pitches of mixed climbing followed by 12 pitches on the north ridge, with a high point near the top of the Dream. *Dave Turner*

chose to climb the wall this way rather than to fix long strings of rope to the ground or between widely spaced portaledge camps. The camp-moving days were the most nerve-wracking parts of the ascent. I had so much equipment and weight, it would take me the better part of a day. The storms would come quick and strong, and I was very exposed to getting pounded while on the move. Setting up the next camp was always time-consuming and difficult. I used a Cliff Cabana ledge with a custom double-wall, triple-pole system, and I anchored this to three different points at all times. The updrafts on the wall were so severe they would lift even the haulbags, and I tied those down too. About half of my anchors used no bolts.

Inside my little home I had everything I would need for the climb and then some. I brought not only two rainflys, but also duplicate stoves, sleeping bags, Gore-Tex jacket/pants, sleeping pads, and just about every other essential item. Just getting everything in and out of the portaledge and the bags in the fierce winds was a mission.

Four pitches of difficult and increasingly steep climbing brought me to the first and only natural ledge above the big snow ramp near the ground. The afternoon I arrived there, the weather was quite unstable. At about 5 p.m. I decided to move everything up to the three-foot by eight-foot ledge. All went well while I hauled the bags, but by the time I started to break down the portaledge below, the storm was building at a pace that made me very uncomfortable. I sat in the portaledge for five minutes, debating whether to move it. I had only two hours before nightfall, which at that season and latitude is 11:30 p.m. I went for it—and paid for that decision.

Almost as soon as I lowered out the kit on the haul line, it started to snow and the wind picked up. It was blowing so hard it was almost funny. Even jumaring was difficult. At the ledge I fought to set up the Cabana; this was the biggest portaledge made, and it was like a giant sail. Once I got the portaledge set up, then came the crux: putting on the double rainflys. An expedition fly doesn't simply pull over the ledge like a tent fly. You have to open the fly and insert the ledge through the open door; if you don't get it just right, it won't fit together. Halfway through this stage, I heard an approaching gust of wind that sounded to me like it was ripping open the fabric of time. I had only one second to grab the corner of the ledge, and then I was airborne. The updraft picked up the portaledge and pulled me up with it until my feet were an honest two meters above the rock ledge. My daisies snapped up tight against the anchor, and the portaledge and I rode the wind for more than five seconds. I could not let go or the wind would beat the ledge against the rock and me until we were smashed to bits. So I just held on for the wild ride! After what seemed like an eternity, the gust passed and dropped us onto the ledge.

Over an hour later, I was safely inside the bivy. During the next two and a half days, three meters of snow fell and washed over the camp as Patagonia tried its best to remove me from the wall. After I made it through this I was quite content because I knew that my bivy system was sufficient for even the worst storms.

Pitch after pitch of long, thin, difficult cracks and seams presented themselves at just the right times. When the crack I was following would start to blank out, another was usually not far away. Most of the time I would pendulum to another crack just before I would have to drill. But, of course, sometimes rivets were needed: a time-consuming and mentally draining task, the dirty deed of big-wall climbing. Since most of the steep established routes that I'd done on El Cap and other walls had 100 to 200 holes, I carried more than 200 rivets. But in the end I drilled only 80 lead holes on the climb. In 25 pitches, I averaged only three to four holes per pitch. Nothing really blank stood in my way—a miracle, actually.

Near the middle of the route, I was climbing above my camp when a shower of small stones and ice bore down the wall, right at me. I tried to make my profile as small as possible and waited for it to come, watching intently. I dodged left and right as the volley went past, only to hear one large piece make a direct hit on the portaledge. After I finished the pitch, I returned to the belay to find a softball-sized rock had torn through the portaledge. Another session of sewing and gluing ensued, a constant task on a wall as pissed off as this one.

Once I had two pitches fixed above my highest hanging camp, I started thinking about my summit strategy. I loaded my alpine pack with ice tools, crampons, butane stove, bivy sack, and other gear. On day 33, I made my way up the two fixed ropes, intending to fix one last hard aid pitch, which would get me to an easier ramp that led to the summit ridge. An amazing, Shield Headwall–type pitch brought me to the ramp by 11 a.m. Early enough, I thought, to climb the two-pitch ramp and get a peek at the long summit ridge. Before long I was sitting in a notch atop the ridge, one leg draped over the east side of the massif, and the other over the west. A huge

A storm that dumped an estimated three meters of snow trapped Turner for several days at a camp more than 400 meters above the ground. *Dave Turner*

vertical tower blocked my view of the ridge ahead. It was still early, around 1 p.m., and a thought crossed my mind: Why not just go for it? I had not brought my pack with those essential items, food, or water. But I was excited and the weather seemed to be holding. I tied a 70-meter lead line onto my back, clipped some pro to my harness, and started free soloing.

On the ridge, the rock turned from beautiful, solid granite to loose, fractured metamorphic rock. Occasionally I self-belayed short sections with a loop of rope clipped to protection. I climbed up or around a seemingly endless series of towers and gendarmes, usually passing the steepest ones to the right (west). Eventually there was nothing higher, and my dream had come true. No, I made it come true. All of my experience, commitment, and drive had been focused over the previous years on this exact moment. I ducked back into a small notch directly below the summit and took some pics and video. I found a small trickle of water in the back of a crack that I could sip from. The weather was still good, but I was far from finished.

Almost as quickly as I had fallen into the magical summit mindspace, I returned to the reality of getting down. Without hesitation I turned my back on the summit and started soloing back down the ridge. I had to climb back up or around most of the towers I'd passed on my way up, making a few short rappels from slung horns. By 11 p.m. I was back in the ledge, stuffing my face with chocolate and hot drinks, with the iPod on full blast with my victory songs. The party didn't last long, but I remember waking up the next day with chocolate all over my face.

Remarkably the weather was still holding, and I started moving early to take advantage of it. I had 1,000 vertical meters to descend, and, believe me, rappelling an overhanging wall alone with about 250 pounds of gear is quite difficult.

First I would tie my four ropes together and down-swing and down-aid my way to the belay anchors, fixing a rope at each anchor. Then I would jug back up to the bags, removing all of the directionals except the belays. Back at the high anchor I would lower all of the bags onto my belay loop and then rappel with the bags down the four ropes. Finally I would jug back up, taking the low-

Although relentlessly steep, the wall was surprisingly well-featured, and Turner averaged only three to four drilled holes per pitch, far fewer than he had expected. *Dave Turner*

est rope with me, and then rappel again, pulling the ropes one by one as I made my way back down. I repeated this process for more than 18 hours straight, until I was headed down the last rope on the last set of rappels.

By this time the ropes were in bad condition, with numerous core shots and severe abrasions. About 60 meters above the glacier, one of these damaged sections passed through my specialized rappel system (a Grigri feeding a double-carabinered ATC extended from the harness), and suddenly the rope seemed to break. As the damaged rope hit the overheated ATC, the sheath either broke or burned, and I plunged the scariest two meters of my life. As the sheath stripped its way down the core, I started to smell burning nylon; the hot ATC was now beginning to burn through the core strands. I desperately reached to the back of my harness for my knife to cut away the heavy bags, but couldn't find it. So I just watched as the ATC burned its

Turner pauses for a photo just below the summit of Cerro Escudo. Leaving behind most of the gear he had planned to take to the top, Turner climbed the last three pitches of the wall and the shattered summit ridge, and then returned to his high camp, all in a single long day. *Dave Turner*

way into the core, until finally the device cooled sufficiently and stopped melting nylon. But now I was stuck. So much sheath had bunched up below the ATC that I couldn't budge it. Eventually I found my knife and cut my belay loop from my harness, freeing myself from the ATC. I dropped a bit onto the Grigri, which was now clipped to my two tie-in points, and then I pulled the handle as fast as I could and slid down the slab until my feet hit the glacier. I let out the biggest monkey call ever, and it echoed through the Valle del Silencio. A few other climbers who had been watching me for weeks started to flash their headlamps and holler from their high camp above the other side of the glacier. What a moment!

Unfortunately, that rope's core was so damaged that it would have been stupid for me to go back up to retrieve my ropes, and the other climbers and park guards talked me out of trying. I have been beating myself up over leaving this junk on the mountain; it was the one flaw in an otherwise perfect ascent. Many people believe the weather will remove the ropes, but I have a few rounds of drinks waiting for the next team (or soloist) who, when making the second ascent, cuts these ropes from the wall and piles them at the base for me to carry out.

SUMMARY:

AREA: Torres del Paine, Southern Patagonia, Chile

ASCENT: First ascent to the summit of Cerro Escudo by the east face, via a new route called Taste the Paine (VII 5.9 A4+); solo ascent by Dave Turner. The big-wall portion was 1,200 meters and 25 pitches, and the long summit ridge gained approximately 300 vertical meters with difficulties up to 5.9. Turner spent a total of about four days climbing the first 150 meters and hauling his equipment to a big snow ledge at that height. He left the snow ledge on December 23, 2007, and returned to the ground 34 days later, on January 25, 2008.

A NOTE ABOUT THE AUTHOR:

Dave Turner spent his 26th birthday on Cerro Escudo. Based in northern California, he has made more than a dozen solo ascents of El Capitan, including three solo new routes, and has completed five expeditions to South America. Turner thanks the American Alpine Club and Cascade Designs/MSR for generous support of this expedition through a Lyman Spitzer Cutting Edge Award.

THE MAGIC PILLAR

A pure alpine-style first ascent of the west ridge of Jannu in Nepal.

SERGEY KOFANOV

Jannu (Kumbhakarna) from the north. To reach the west ridge, Valery Babanov and Sergey Kofanov spent two and a half days climbing to the 6,350-meter saddle between Jannu and Sobithongie (6,652m). From there, it was 1,400 vertical meters and five days to the summit. *Valery Babanov*

The impossible is possible. There was a time when man thought that flying was impossible. There was a time when I thought it was impossible for two men to climb a new route in alpine style on Jannu's north side. But with his phone call in February 2007, Valery Babanov forced me to think hard about the possibility of the impossible.

Valery had called to discuss our planned expedition to Chomo-Lonzo in the fall. We talked about the dates of our flights, an approximate budget, equipment, and other matters. Somewhere in the middle of our conversation, Valery dropped a phrase along the lines of,

"Actually, Sergey, I've decided to change the goal for this climb. Let's go to Jannu. What do you think?" For about a second I matched the word "Jannu" with the image that was rising in my brain, and then I said, "Yes. Of course, yes!"

In fact, it was fundamentally unimportant for me where I would climb, so long as I was psychologically and physically prepared for any route and any mountain. The defining priorities were with whom and how I would climb. Valery could have suggested that I join him in climbing Olympus on Mars—I would have agreed without hesitation even to that.

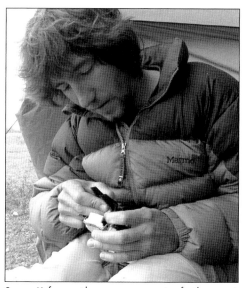

Sergey Kofanov at base camp, preparing for the ascent. For Kofanov, 29, the Jannu expedition was his seventh of the year. *Valery Babanov*

Jannu (Kumbhakarna) is rightly considered one of the most beautiful and difficult 7,000-meter peaks in the world. From the time of the first successful French expedition in 1962, not many alpinists have stood on her summit, and the reason for this is very simple: There are no simple routes. Even on the classical routes, to succeed it is necessary above all to change oneself, to switch one's consciousness onto a different plane. Only then will one acquire the resolve for this deed. But one must not construct such resolve on a foundation of anger. Rather, there should be a kind of commitment that borders on dispassion. In the mountains and in life in general, there are situations when one needs precisely this sort of dispassionate resolve, and yet it is very important to turn it on only at the most necessary moments. I call this the "syndrome of disconnecting the instinct for self-preservation."

Having resolved with Valery to put up a new route on Jannu, we both disconnected our instinct for self-preservation on the eve of our departure for Kathmandu. Or, rather, we tuned our internal clocks to turn off this instinct at the moment we started climbing in October.

I am certain that, from the moment of the conclusion of that telephone conversation with Valery, neither he nor I outwardly changed in the least; we continued to live as usual, though perhaps we did slightly more training. But inwardly we became different. Both of us understood that now we were and were not ourselves. We were other. No one, not even our closest friends, noticed anything. Only we sensed it. Only we knew that within us the clocks were already ticking, counting out the time from that moment when we'd made our decision.

Where there is comfort there is no energy—I needed more training, and I sacrificed much in order to find time for it. The expedition to Jannu was to be my seventh that year. Beforehand, there was Everest and Peak Communism, among others. In between expeditions I had breaks no longer than two weeks. In these intervals I trained more intensively, climbing in the gym and running laps on the track.

Kofanov in the glacial basin below Jannu's north face. After a rough night on the 45-degree ice slopes above Kofanov's right shoulder, the two men reached the col at 6,350 meters amid hurricane-force winds. *Valery Babanov*

In late spring Valery sent a letter posing a completely logical question: Would I be able to tolerate such a rhythm and still be ready for a difficult climb in the Himalaya? Insofar as I'd never had such a heavy season, I didn't know the answer. I laughed it off with a question of my own for Valery, then at the height of his guiding season in Chamonix: "And will you be ready after ten runs up Mont Blanc?"

On the 12th of September I was sitting in the airport in Qatar waiting for our connecting flight to Kathmandu. Next to me was the famous tennis player Marat Safin, who was flying with the climbing team of Sasha Abramov to Cho-Oyu. A girl approached and said, "Excuse me, are you Sergey Kofanov?" We conversed for a while; I gave her my card and autograph. Evidently, the result of specialization is that here, on the way to the Himalaya, Marat Safin is less well known than I am.

We arrived at base camp at the end of September. Over the next several days the wall was hidden by thick clouds. Finally the summit revealed itself, and for the first time we saw the wall in the flesh, not just in photos. For the first several hours, it simply took our breath away—the urge seized us to set off immediately and, if not begin climbing, at least touch the wall in order to convince ourselves that it actually existed, and wasn't merely a dream.

We studied the face and examined our options. There were only two: the western ridge

The first headwall on Jannu's west ridge climbs to about 7,200 meters. After a long snow ridge, difficult climbing resumes on the summit tower at about 7,400 meters. *Valery Babanov*

and a steep ramp well to the left of the "classic" Japanese route. We chose the ridge: It was very logical and beautiful, and, besides, a huge serac that was not visible in the photographs hung above the ramp option.

For acclimatization we slept at 6,200 meters, practically on the summit of Merra, not far from Jannu. We both understood that a preparatory ascent to this elevation was insufficient to climb in alpine style to 7,700 meters, but there was nothing to be done—there was nothing higher and relatively uncomplicated near Jannu. At night I couldn't sleep, so I read *My Way* by Tomo Cesen, where he recounts his new route on the northern wall of Jannu, which he did in 28 hours with two cans of sardines. Periodically I glanced outside the tent and looked at the northern wall illuminated by the moon—its appearance was simply unreal.

Our plan was to set out on October 14, even though the forecast predicted suitable weather for climbing only until the 16th. After that there would be snowfall and 80 to 100 kph winds on the ridge. We would have preferred to wait it out, but we couldn't wait because we didn't want to lose what little acclimatization we had.

Kofanov follows the spectacular snow arête above the first rock headwall. The summit of Sobithongie (6,652m) lies behind. *Valery Babanov*

We both understood that the advantage of alpine style and a two-man ascent is above all speed, and for that reason we tried to make our packs as light as possible. We packed dried food and fuel for approximately eight days, plus two cans of sardines. At the start our packs weighed 18 to 20 kilos, but the majority of this weight was equipment, which would hang from our bodies and harnesses while we climbed. We took a selection of slings, stoppers, and cams, about a dozen pitons, seven ice screws, two 60-meter ropes (one 5.5mm and the other 8.6mm), and a pair of ice tools for each of us. Our tent weighed less than a kilogram, and our sleeping bag, specially sewn to fit both of us, weighed only 900 grams.

Jannu's western ridge begins from a saddle at 6,350 meters between Jannu and Sobithongie (6,652 meters). During our first few days of climbing, approaching this col, we had to wander through a labyrinth of seracs along a huge glacier and climb ice-glazed rock and steep ice. On the 15th, we were forced to spend the night on an icy 45-degree slope. Before we were able to set up the tent, it took us almost two hours of chopping with our axes to remove about three cubic meters of ice. Even so, we weren't able to make room for our tent. Before sleeping we ate the last can of sardines. All night we tossed and turned—maybe as a result of the uncomfortable situation, or maybe the lack of acclimatization was beginning to take its toll.

But all this was just work and the mountain was not presenting us with unsolvable tasks. We knew the fundamental difficulties would begin above 7,000 meters, where our bodies would cease to renew themselves at night and the immovable burden of exhaustion would accumulate. Each of us had experienced similar moments more than once during other ascents, and so we knew what to expect.

Jannu's summit tower, as seen from the west ridge. Babanov and Kofanov followed the snow ridge to its high point below the tower, then angled up and right, and then back left, following snow ledges and steep mixed ground. This line on the summit tower had been climbed in 1981 and 1983 after an approach by the southwest spur; three French climbers reached the top by this route in 1983. *Sergey Kofanov*

Babanov begins the first lead on the summit tower: difficult mixed climbing at 7,400 meters. *Sergey Kofanov*

On the 16th we climbed almost seven rope lengths on very steep ice, two of which were at nearly 80 degrees. Toward lunch we reached the saddle, and Jannu's west ridge greeted us with hurricane winds, which forced us to curtail work on the route at noon and wait out the bad weather in our tent inside a crevasse.

In the morning we listened for a long time to the howling of the wind and debated whether it was worth crawling out of the tent. The wind, understanding that it wouldn't be easy to lure us out, got crafty; it let up for about an hour, waiting for the moment when we rolled up our tent, and then hurled itself upon us with redoubled force. We likewise decided to deceive the wind, and for about three hours we pretended to wallow through the snow in earnest, approaching the rocky part of the western ridge, but then unexpectedly we swung under a serac and set up a bivouac. The wind tried to rip our tent away over the next two hours, and then abated. This time, Valery and I were not fooled by this trick, and we didn't crawl out of the tent until the next morning. The forecast, which Valery's wife conveyed to us via radio, was for even stronger winds the next day, reaching 100 kph above 7,000 meters.

The next morning, October 18, we set off with the first rays of the sun—in those hours the wind was not yet so strong. At first we climbed about four pitches along steep ice. Then the ice gave way to rock, where Valery took the hardest sections. After this we belayed each other by turns. We met the sunset on a sharp, snowy knife-edge that was buffeted by the wind from two directions.

Working together, we struggled to blunt the firn-clad top of the knife in order to set up our tent on a well-formed platform. With the sun below the horizon, Valery removed his sunglasses, but this was a little premature. The wind whipped snow into our faces, covering our mouths and eyes. It wasn't possible to work without glasses, so Valery put his on again, but now they were frozen and filled with snow. He swung his axes blindly, periodically asking me

Kofanov belays at 7,500 meters, partway up the steep summit tower. Hoping to gain the summit and return to their equipment cache that same day, the two men could manage only 200 vertical meters before nightfall forced a bivouac at 7,600 meters. *Valery Babanov*

whether he was cutting in the right place. A few times he grazed his own head (thank god he was wearing a helmet), and he ripped the hood of his down parka. One time, I too fell under his busy hand, and a hole appeared in the sleeve of my parka. The wind happily snatched up the down and mixed it with the swirling snow, and we had to spit to clear our mouths because the down, though white as snow, did not melt in one's mouth.

After about an hour we crawled into the tent, which was beginning to remind us of a hen-house, with feathers swirling in the air. While I melted snow on the stove, Valery tried to use a bandage from the first-aid kit to prevent the last bits of down from escaping from his parka.

We passed that night in a half-delirious condition—neither Valery nor I could sleep at all. Therefore, we stirred ourselves long before light and set out with the sunrise. Now we were back on icy rocks; the leader climbed without a pack and hauled it up after each pitch. Near lunchtime the rocks ended and we climbed onto a relatively uncomplicated snow ridge, which led toward the summit tower. Valery's altimeter showed a height of 7,200 meters, and from this vantage point we could begin to see the other side of Jannu: huge snowfields extending to the south. We started the long climb toward the summit tower along snowy knife-edges. It seemed as if the tower was not far away, but night again found us still moving on the snowy ridge, between two gendarmes. Now used to swinging axes in the evenings, we chopped into the dense snow for two hours, and by the time the moon appeared we had crawled into the crookedly

Babanov below Jannu's 7,710-meter summit. The descent would require about 40 hours, concluding a 10-day round trip. *Sergey Kofanov*

erected tent. With a complete lack of appetite, we chewed on a piece of cheese and collapsed into half-conscious oblivion until morning.

Toward 11 a.m. on the morning of October 20, we reached the rocky summit tower, the base of which begins at 7,400 meters, according to Valery's altimeter. Only about 300 vertical meters remained before the summit. We decided to leave most of our things in the bergschrund, including the completely frozen digital camera, and continued upward with only the stove, a container of gas, our tent, and a film camera. In such a lightened state, we thought we should be able to climb to the summit and begin our descent that day—300 meters is not a lot, after all. But it soon became clear that we had underestimated the complexity of those final meters. For a few pitches we climbed at the edge of our abilities, expending large amounts of time.

Completely exhausted, we greeted nightfall among the steep pre-summit rocks at 7,600 meters. It was absolutely impossible to continue at night on such complex terrain, so we began swinging our hammers again, trying to cut something vaguely like a platform in the ice. We stopped when the axes began to strike sparks from the rocks; in order to cut deeper, we would have needed not ice tools but miners' picks.

For liabilities, we had one pick of Valery's Grivel bent to an improbable angle, and for assets we had a cubic meter of uneven platform space. It should have been clear to anyone that our tent wouldn't fit there, but in defiance of healthy common sense we nonetheless tried to squeeze it in. As a result, we broke one of tent poles, but we did not have the strength to repair it. We sat in the badly pitched tent as if we were sitting in a sack. All night we dangled our legs into the abyss, with no sleeping bag for warmth; parts of Valery lay on top of me because of lack of space.

To our delight, there was practically no wind—otherwise our chances of greeting the following morning in good health would have been severely diminished. Before crawling into the tent, we had beaten pitons into the icy wall and tied runners to them for anchors, lest by chance we fly downward with our tent during the night. Around 3 a.m. Valery asked me, "Seryoga, are you tied in?" I looked at my carabiners and said, "You know, I'm not." He said, "Me either." We'd already gone almost 24 hours without food and practically without water—if this wasn't the beginning of HACE, then we were very close to the edge of it.

The cold was cosmic. Sometimes we started up the stove in order to create the appearance of heat in the tent. The flame of the stove worked hypnotically upon my consciousness. I couldn't turn my gaze away from the fire; it simply bewitched me. It seemed that it drew the "I" out of me—in those moments I became an absolutely empty shell, and the entire surrounding world was concentrated in this stove, the flame of which filled me from within. Nothing existed except it. It was the pillar of the universe. At times it seemed that it was not me holding the stove, but the stove holding me, and then I would slip into half-sleep and the burning stove would fall out of my hands, sometimes onto me, sometimes onto Valery. This would call me back to this world, and for the next ten minutes I would come to my senses and begin to grasp who I was and where we were.

Around 4 a.m., after the regular awakening-by-stove, it occurred to both of us simultaneously that we had to do something. Otherwise we risked simply not waking up, remaining forever with the phantasmagoria raging within our brains. We forced ourselves little by little to stir ourselves, stuff our tent into our pack, fasten the pack to the pitons we'd pounded into the wall, and climb a little farther.

No more than 100 meters of altitude remained before the summit, but it took us three hours to cover this distance. At about 9 a.m. Valery shouted to me that he was on the summit and that he could see our base camp. I pulled out the camera and began to photograph him. Slowly I approached Valery while he dropped a few meters to one side to free up room for me on top. When I reached his level, he told me that we were not on the summit after all, and pointed to the continuation of the snowy ridge. We spent another half-hour crossing the 30 or 40 meters to the true summit, which was so pointed that only one person could straddle it at a time.

On top we both understood that something had changed. It was as if we had crossed an invisible border into a different world, in which the old sense of what was possible no longer applied. Until this moment the world—the mountain—had led us to feel at times strong and invincible, at other times helpless and weak. The world had forced us to adapt. Now we had forced a change upon the world, and we both knew it would never be the same as before.

SUMMARY:

AREA: Kumbhakarna Himal, Nepal

ASCENT: Alpine-style first ascent of the west pillar of 7,710-meter Jannu (3,000m, WI4+ M5 80°), October 14–23, 2007, Valery Babanov and Sergey Kofanov. The two approached the 6,350-meter col between Jannu and Sobithongie from the north. They followed the 1983 French route up Jannu's summit tower. Descent via the same route.

A NOTE ABOUT THE AUTHOR:

Sergey Kofanov was born in 1978 in Ekaterinburg, Russia, and now lives in Moscow. He has been climbing for more than 15 years and has extensive climbing and guiding experience in the Caucasus, Tien-Shan, and Pamir ranges, as well as the Himalaya.

Translated from the Russian by Henry Pickford.

Babanov (left) and Kofanov on top.

GORGE PLAY

Three first ascents in the Great Gorge of the Ruth Glacier.

TATSURO YAMADA

The zigzagging line of Seasons of the Sun, the new Japanese route up the southeast face of Mt. Bradley. The east buttress (Jöchler-Orgler, 1987) of Bradley is the right skyline. Several routes ascend the steep south face on the left. *Yusuke Sato*

In March 2007, Fumitaka Ichimura, Yusuke Sato, and I made a one-day ascent of a long, classic alpine route on Mt. Hotaka in Japan's Northern Alps, as preparation for a climbing trip to the Alaska Range that was near at hand. During this climb, I found my skills lacking and felt diffident about climbing with two of the greatest alpinists in Japan. As we hiked back to the parking lot in the twilight, I confessed that I had decided not to go to Alaska with them. Yusuke said, "Come on! Don't worry about such a stupid thing. Climbing with three people simply will be more fun than two. So, please, come with us!" Fumitaka agreed with nod. What lovely people they are! I felt my courage return, and my mind turned toward Alaska again.

On April 7 we flew into the Great Gorge of the Ruth Glacier with Talkeetna Air Taxi. We had become friends with pilot Paul Roderick during a trip the previous year to the Buckskin Glacier. Now he told us, "Mt. Church's north face is unclimbed. Someone has to do that…you guys should. We are watching what you do. Hah-hah-hah!" Then he flew away.

The Great Gorge is one of the deepest and narrowest valleys in North America, yet the glacier surface is vast. We put base camp in the very center of the gorge, and then started wandering around every clear day to check out virgin lines in the basin. Over the next several weeks, after two failures on the west face of Peak 7,400' and the north face of

Yusuke Sato leads the M6 second pitch of Season of the Sun on Mt. Bradley. The team fixed this pitch and returned two days later to climb the face in 15 hours. *Tatsuro Yamada*

Mt. Church, due to hard spindrift and the difficulty of the climbs, we made urgent attempts during any breaks in the bad weather and succeeded on Mt. Bradley, Mt. Church, and Mt. Johnson by new routes.

SEASON OF THE SUN

For hours we studied the southeast face of Mt. Bradley, clutching at straws. Finally we figured out one possibility on the east end of this massive, unclimbed mixed wall. Our line seemed to be a pretty complex but quite efficient way to reach the summit.

On April 20 we went to scout the initial Entrance Gully, which starts with a 300-meter snow slope. The gully ended with 60 meters of steep and thin ice along an overhanging rock corner. Yusuke cruised this M6 pitch, with a few good cam placements in a roof crack. We gained the top of the Entrance Gully, where it fuses into a ridge from the left. Then we fixed a rope on the M6 pitch below and headed back to our base camp for a rest day.

On April 22 we left base camp at 2:20 a.m., ran up the Entrance Gully, jumared our fixed line, and then jumped into the unknown. We snaked our way up the wall, trying to find the correct line by connecting snow patches on rock slabs, in order to reach an obvious couloir at one-third height. This long snow couloir led to the upper gully system much more easily than we'd expected from the bottom. We felt good about the weather. No cloud, no wind, and the southeast-facing wall received plenty of sunlight. We felt no cold as long as we kept moving, even with only an undershirt.

In the upper part of the face, the line got narrower and steeper, yet we kept up the speed. After negotiating a few technical pitches at M6R and WI4R, we were just below the summit cornice. We angled slightly to the right and found a single easy passage through the cornice. Right there was the summit. It was 6 p.m., the finish of a 15-hour climbing marathon. The pure pleasure of adventure filled our faces and minds.

Unlike in a real marathon, we still had to think about the descent. The route was too complex to rappel. So we descended the west ridge toward the other side of the mountain. Luckily it allowed us to walk most of the way, with only few rappels, down to a plateau of the Backside Glacier at midnight. The joy of climbing in Alaska is the very long daylight, although it squeezed all our energy. We had no strength to dig a bivy site. We nestled into our sleeping bags and just lay on the snow. *Zzzzz….*

On April 23 we walked a long way back to the Ruth Gorge by crossing 747 Pass between Mt. Dickey and

Fumitaka Ichimura leads a typical steep snow pitch on Memorial Gate, the first route up the north face of Mt. Church. See page 1 for a closer look at the difficulties on this route. *Tatsuro Yamada*

Mt. Bradley. The soft snow didn't allow us to go fast. We reached our base camp just before 6 p.m.

We were celebrating our first success on this trip, enjoying the taste of victory and sake, when someone called to us. I looked outside of our tent. A man was standing there, and he said in calm tone, "My partner died just now, so please lend me a radio to call for help." He pointed to the northeast buttress of Mt. Wake, next to Mt. Bradley. The victim was Lara-Karena Kellogg. We were not acquainted with her, but I believe that we shared a similar attitude about climbing, and so I knew I had the chance to fall into a similar tragedy. To carry on in my climbing life, I need to find a meaning for death in mountains. It's a part of climbing, also a part of life. After pondering this throughout the night, I felt more confident, inspired by Lara Kellogg's soul, which had never stopped climbing until the end.

MEMORIAL GATE

We wanted revenge on the central gully of Mt. Church's north face. It was obvious, beautiful, and, unbelievably, unclimbed, so it roused our enthusiasm. This time we had perfect weather, so we wouldn't be hit by spindrift. We knew everything about the route up to our retreat point. We left our base camp at 1:30 a.m. and ran through the crevassed glacier to base of the route. We deposited our snowshoes and started climbing at 3:30. We lunged straight into the narrowing gully, toward the steep part halfway up. Last time we had reached this part in heavy snowfall, and a wall of vertical soft snow had repelled Fumitaka's struggle. He confronted it three

The line couldn't be more compelling on the north face of Mt. Church, but unconsolidated snow and serious spindrift deterred previous attempts, including the Japanese team's first try in 2007. The peak was first climbed by the west ridge (right skyline) in 1977. *Tatsuro Yamada*

times, and each time he was thrown off, landing nicely on the soft snow slope five meters below.

This time it was my turn. I was eager at first, but soon was embarrassed because I didn't have a clue how to climb the deep, soft snow. I made up my mind to dig away all the snow until something hard appeared. Finally, I unearthed a ragged ice layer five meters up and put in some screws. Of course, they were not worth trusting, but they were better than nothing. I started to crawl up. My struggle to climb 20 meters of vertical snow stretched over two hours, but finally I won. Some cheers rose from my friends below, even though they must have been cold because I had kept them waiting for such a long time. Anyway, I was alive and over the crux. If someone said "do that pitch again," I doubt that I ever could.

Fumitaka then led two more very soft ice pitches. The angle eased and we seemed to have reached the middle of the route. From here we steered to the right to avoid the mixed headwall that waited at the top of the gully. Traversing along a snow band was more unstable than we had expected. The snow layer was quite thin, and our picks and front points scratched on the rock slab, making noises offensive to the ear. After two pitches of traversing, we emerged in the extensive upper snow slope. The summit cornice was close, so we were very excited, but soon we were reduced to torment by a 500-meter-long, snow-covered rock slab. Rarely could we find protection. We continued climbing without any belay, moving together and trying to always keep a few runners between each of us.

We were exhausted when we finally reached the overhanging cornice. Yusuke searched for a long time for a break in the wall, and Fumitaka and I froze as we belayed him. At last we heard Yusuke's laugh and followed his footprints into a hole in the cornice that he had excavated.

Sato begins the crux 5.10 A3 pitch on the west ridge of Mt. Johnson, after completing the Ladder Tube on Johnson's north face and intersecting the Elevator Shaft (Chabot-Tackle, 1995). See Climbs and Expeditions for a photo showing the location of both routes. *Tatsuro Yamada*

At the other side of the tunnel, we saw Yusuke smiling as he belayed. Released from the cold north face, we gained the summit ridge at 8:30 and enjoyed some warmth from the sinking sun. Two hundred meters of easy snow ridge led us to the summit. We stood on the beautiful pyramid at 9 p.m.

It's possible to walk all the way down this mountain by the west ridge, which was the route of the first ascent in 1977. Passing through the col between Mt. Church and Mt. Grosvenor, we arrived at the base of our route and picked up our snowshoes. It had been a 19-hour round trip.

THE LADDER TUBE

Now only seven days remained in our trip. We decided to throw everything into retracing a legend, the Elevator Shaft, Doug Chabot and Jack Tackle's route from 1995 on the north face of Mt. Johnson. However, when we visited the base of the wall for observation, we found a virgin line immediately right of the Shaft. "How lucky we are!" We changed our target at once.

On April 30 we left base camp at 9 a.m., very late because we were still fatigued from our last two climbs. We approached the base of Mt. Johnson's north face across a badly crevassed glacier. After depositing all our bivy gear, we started climbing our new line. It started with perfect alpine ice, thin but solid, with granite beside the gully to take protection. We enjoyed four nice pitches and then rappelled, fixing ropes on each of the pitches. We had a comfortable bivouac in a snow cave that we'd found during our scout in the bergschrund at the base of the Elevator Shaft.

On May 1 we started jumaring at 2:30 a.m. Yusuke had already started to climb the sixth pitch when the sun came up. Of course we didn't get any sunlight, but we were not cold because the climbing went so fast, following a continuous ice flow for the first 10 pitches. I worked on the 11th to 14th pitches. The ice got snowy and finally disappeared. Soon the gully ended with 10 meters of vertical rock in a corner without any ice. I dry-tooled it with well-placed cams for protection. I broke the snow mushrooms overhead and topped out on a shoulder of the west ridge, which we followed to the east. Soon the obvious crux of our climb appeared at the col where our route joined the Elevator Shaft. Above was a 100-meter, nearly vertical rock face. Yusuke blasted the first pitch (5.10R A3), and Fumitaka overcame bad snow on the mixed second pitch (5.7). We had just enough time to fix ropes on those pitches and arrange a comfortable bivy at the col before dark.

The next morning, after jumaring the two pitches in the dark, we walked up 400 meters of easy snow ridge to reach the summit by eight. We could see both Bradley and Church, and the other peaks all around the Gorge, an incredible playground. I couldn't believe that we made these three first ascents in just two weeks.

We spent the whole day descending our route, leaving two pitons and about 10 V-threads for rappels. We landed at the base at 3 p.m. and then won our final bet, passing through the icefall, which was like Russian roulette. Then we were back on flat ground, though we still had a long way back to base camp. As we walked, I silently thanked Fumitaka and Yusuke. By the grace of their invitation, I had experienced the pure fun of climbing in these mountains. I was like a kid playing in a park with big brothers, trying hard to be their equals. That effort had earned me some benefits, I think. As I trudged along the glacier, my steps were heavy but my mind was skipping toward the future.

SUMMARY:

AREA: Ruth Gorge, Alaska Range

ASCENTS: First ascent of the southeast face of Mt. Bradley (9,100') by Season of the Sun (1,400m, V WI4R M6R), April 22–23, 2007. First ascent of the north face of Mt. Church (8,233') via the central gully; the route is called Memorial Gate (1,100m, V AI4+R/X), April 26, 2007. First ascent of the Ladder Tube (1,000m, V 5.10R A3) on the north face and west ridge of Mt. Johnson (8,460'), April 30–May 2, 2007. All climbs were completed by Fumitaka Ichimura, Yusuke Sato, and Tatsuro Yamada.

A NOTE ABOUT THE AUTHOR:

Tatsuro Yamada was born in 1981 in Saitama, Japan. Since he started climbing in 2001, he has climbed in New Zealand, Canada, the United States, Europe, and Bolivia, where he completed a new route on the south face of Illimani with Yuki Satoh in 2006.

In May 2008 Yamada and Yuto Inoue disappeared during an attempt on the Cassin Ridge on Denali.

From left: Fumitaka Ichimura, Yusuke Sato, and Tatsuro Yamada atop Mt. Church. *Tatsuro Yamada*

THE FIN WALL

Exploring a little-known Alaskan giant.

FREDDIE WILKINSON

The Fin Wall in the distance, at the head of the upper Yentna Glacier. The federal wilderness boundary lies 12 miles from the wall, and planes may not land inside, so the team had to shuttle loads four miles to establish base camp. *Freddie Wilkinson*

Paul didn't even turn off the engine. The plane just sat there waiting, humming along in the silence of the Yentna Glacier. Ben Gilmore, Peter Doucette, and I stumbled around in the 50 mph backwash, awkwardly tossing duffle bags, skis, and tins of fuel into a pile on the wind-cupped glacier. When we were done we stepped back and raised our hands at the distant visage behind the Plexiglas window. If all went well, he would return in 20 days' time to retrieve us. The engine revved, the plane chattered forward, and a minute later we were alone. Fifteen miles up-valley, the Fin Wall waited.

For years I'd heard rumors from veteran Denali guides of a stunning alpine project that lurked just beyond the southern flanks of Mt. Foraker. I looked at the area on a map: It's a convoluted region, with broken glaciers that allow scant landing opportunities. Intrigued, I arranged a private fixed-wing tour of the area in 2006. After flying for three and half hours up and down the spine of the Alaska Range, I had confirmed two facts. One: The Fin Wall was some badass shit. Two: Accessing the wall was going to be a royal pain.

An impenetrable icefall six miles below the Fin Wall required a devious approach; the team ascended the couloir above the climbers, and then raced under a serac-topped wall to reach the upper glacier and the base of the Fin. *Ben Gilmore*

The Fin Wall sits at the head of the Yentna Glacier. The Denali National Park wilderness boundary, running a direct course from the summit of Mt. Russell to the summit of Mt. McKinley, bisects the Yentna approximately 12 miles below the wall, and commercial plane landings are prohibited inside this line. Six miles below the wall, a massive icefall rips across the glacier. Beyond, several miles of serac- and avalanche-threatened terrain must be crossed to reach the start of the climb. The wall itself comprises some of the most outrageous alpine topography I'd ever seen. Sandwiched between the southwest buttress of Mt. Foraker and the high ridgeline that separates the Yentna from the Lacuna Glacier, it is a tight alpine coliseum of 4,000-foot granite walls that converge at their base into an area about the size of a football field. A final colossal serac threatens this same area. A team must pass under this final danger and cross the bergschrund to reach the relative safety of the wall.

At first I was appalled by the approach. But the more you look at something, the more you appreciate its possibilities rather than its limitations. Climbing in the Alaska Range has changed over the past decade. With better communication, extensive air support, and several new guidebooks in print, there's been an increased interest in summits beyond Denali, and areas like the Ruth Gorge, the Tokositna Glacier, and Little Switzerland have exploded in popularity. These days there's a decidedly urban feel to climbing in the range. It's rare to have an area to yourself—normally there are friends to pass the time with in base camp, and accurate forecasts to decide when to launch on your climb. All this has helped make Alaska an accessible training ground for American alpinists, something we've historically lacked. But with the change, it's also important that we keep exploring. We need to find new venues—places that will remain wild for the next generation.

I drew in a proposed line and sent an application to the Mugs Stump grant committee, taking care to crop out that icefall in the bottom of the photo. If they really knew how dubious the approach was, I thought, they might not want to waste their money on us. Michael Kennedy's unexpected call arrived over the winter; now we were obligated to at least go take a look.

The trip was a chance to climb with two heroes of mine. I could only dream of doing a big Alaskan first ascent when I first met Ben Gilmore and Kevin Mahoney as a rookie guide in New Hampshire. When Kevin scaled back his expeditioning to concentrate on his guiding career and family, Ben and I made seasonal pilgrimages to Patagonia and Alaska. He's an utterly selfless individual, strong, quiet, and slightly prone to brooding: the perfect balance to my mouthy, wise-guy optimism. Kevin originally had planned to join us on the Yentna, but a ski guide's exam interfered. Because of the Fin's remote location and the complex glacier travel necessary to reach the wall, we knew we'd have to find a third partner. Enter Peter Doucette. Peter had never been on a major alpine climbing trip, but he has all the credentials of a New England hard man: born and raised in Whitefield, New Hampshire (north of the Notches), learned to climb on Cannon Cliff, and quietly tearing it up around the White Mountains since he was a kid. We knew he would be solid.

And now here we were, camped just before the wilderness boundary. The Yentna had an entirely different feel from any other spot I'd visited in the Alaska Range. Snaking moraine crests of sedimentary stone traced the boundaries of the valley. The frontier peaks to the west were cobbled together from a jaundiced yellow rock reminiscent of the Canadian Rockies or the Himalaya. The eastern ridgeline was snowier and composed of the more typical, battleship-gray granite of the Alaska Range. The next day, Ben, Peter, and I shuttled loads four miles up glacier and settled into a comfy base camp built into the lee of a moraine, about two miles below the icefall. Our elevation was 5,250 feet.

Ben was lying low with the flu, so Peter and I left in the morning with vague intentions of climbing the peak right behind base camp—the easiest, closest objective we could find. This unnamed summit was marked at about 8,900 feet on the Talkeetna D4 USGS map; having found no signs or record of a previous ascent, we took the liberty of dubbing it "Rogue Peak." The northeast face was mainly steep snow with a few rocky sections and one M5-ish chimney pitch. Descending a gully on the south face, Peter kicked off a captivating slab avalanche that prompted a quick tutorial in advanced alpine tactics.

Peter: "Err, this snow is pretty sketchy, maybe we should take our time and start rappelling?"

Me: "You're totally right, man, but if another one like that comes down on us in this tight gully, it'll kill us whether we're on rappel or not! Let's coil the ropes and downclimb—it'll get us out of here faster."

Peter good-naturedly shrugged, coiled the ropes, and began down-soloing without comment—proving just what a cool-handed fellow he is.

We arrived back in camp around suppertime and were pleased to discover that Mr. Gilmore was beginning to feel better. After a day of rest, the three of us left to explore the vast knife-edge ridge of summits that dominates the northwest fork of the Yentna, a group of peaks so inspiring and just plain manly that we had taken to calling them the "Mantoks." We followed a thin, aesthetic couloir up to the northernmost major summit (the north summit of Mantok 1, 9,300 feet). The terrain was relaxed and thoroughly enjoyable, with only a short mixed step that warranted breaking out the rope.

Of course, all three of us knew that we were just pud-knocking on these two climbs compared to our main objective. The day after we climbed Mantok 1, we went to take a serious look at the icefall. I wouldn't say that travel directly through the icefall is impossible, but it looked pretty dubious to us. The slopes on the right-hand (east) side of the icefall were even worse, with

multiple stacked serac features that were active daily. But there was a final option: the slopes to the left (west) side of the icefall. Though they would be highly avalanche-prone in bad weather, at least no major seracs loomed above. A rockband barred the way, but it looked like a hidden couloir might provide easy passage through it. Though the upper glacier looked as gnarly in person as it had in the photos, we had yet to see any catastrophic serac avalanches up there. Gradually, we convinced ourselves we could slip underneath the looming frozen sentinels. We packed food and fuel for four days and set the alarm for 3 a.m.

More by happenstance (read: laziness and poverty) then design, we had foregone carrying a sat phone and instead borrowed an FM aviation radio that was good for line-of-sight communication only. Ten days into the expedition we had yet to see or hear a single plane fly over the Yentna, despite perfect flying conditions. But even without a weather report, it was obvious that a system had moved in. When our alarm went off, it was socked in and snowing lightly. We went back to sleep.

At the base of the wall, rockfall penetrated the tent, prompting Ben Gilmore to don a helmet. Then spindrift from the concave face buried the team's shelter. They dug a snow hole and moved in, using the evacuated tent as a storm door, until it was time to climb. *Freddie Wilkinson (2)*

Muffled booms sounded in the valley above.

Twenty-four hours later, everything was cold and blue in the empty dawn light. We left camp unroped and followed our track to the first serious crevasse bridge at the edge of the icefall. From there we traversed the lower slopes of a 10,300-foot peak, alternatively skiing and cramponing across snowfields and then up a frozen snow couloir as we skirted the western edge of the

After an all-day approach and a bivouac, the team climbed the Fin Wall in 15 hours, then rappelled from the ridge as a storm approached. They reached base camp 24 hours after beginning the descent. *Freddie Wilkinson*

icefall. Above, we dropped back down to the glacier, put our skis back on, and began purpose-fully skinning toward the wall.

We had thought we might find a safe camp somewhere on this final stretch to the wall, but we didn't see any Holiday Inns up there—or even a spot where we would have been comfortable pitching a tent for the night. As it was, things were going smoothly and it was only late morning, so we continued skiing, moving closer to the final serac that guards the entrance to the face. We could see a few car-size blocks of debris lying in our path, but several feet of snow had accumu-lated on top of them. There were no signs of recent activity. After hastily stopping to cache our skis, we silently scurried under the serac and up to the bergschrund.

We stopped 50 meters past the 'schrund, kicked out a ledge for the tent, and climbed inside. Things were looking good: It was only midafternoon, and we had plenty of time to rest and psych up for a midnight departure for the virgin face above. While we lay in the tent, a thin mist curled up the valley and it started to snow, ever so lightly. Then it started to spindrift.

Snow began to accumulate between the tent and the inside wall of our chopped ledge with alarming speed. As if to accentuate our vulnerability, a small rock zinged a neat two-inch hole through the wall of our shelter. Soon it was necessary for one of us to be outside constantly, clear-ing away the spindrift. By now the sun was no longer visible through the clouds and it seemed to

Freddie Wilkinson leads the first pitch of the route: "a bit steeper and bit thinner then I'd expected." *Ben Gilmore*

be snowing harder. Not good. I grabbed the shovel and started digging a cave.

It was late evening by the time we had settled down in our new subterranean bivy. The forlorn tent, ripped and battered, hung over the entranceway to stop spindrift from entering our new home. It was obvious that bivying on the concave face above us would be a bad idea, so we'd have to go for it in a single day. I fell asleep half expecting and half hoping that the weather would still be unsettled in the morning, and then we could retreat.

"It's totally clear out there." Ben's voice stabbed through my damp sleeping bag and belay coat. A minute later I heard the rubberized squeak of the fuel bottle being pressurized, followed by the comforting roar of the stove. It was 4 a.m. We had gotten about five hours of fitful rest.

Buoyed by Ben's motivation, I readily agreed to take the first block. Our plan was to follow the path of least resistance, zigzagging up and right across the lower face to access a prominent couloir that dead-ended in a steep rockband halfway up. Once we had worked our way through this obvious crux, we planned to follow a hanging ramp up and right to access the final slopes that led to the summit ridge.

The first pitch was a wake-up call—a bit steeper and bit thinner then I'd expected. Above, I led four more pitches of moderate ice before handing over the rack to Peter. His block had some

"Full Gilmore." Ben Gilmore leads the crux pitch of the Fin Wall, after hanging his leader's pack to deal with unprotectable thin ice. *Freddie Wilkinson*

engaging routefinding over steep snow and the occasional rocky section. He efficiently led us right into the couloir, and then we simul-climbed into a daunting cul-de-sac ringed by 800-foot vertical cliffs. Miraculously, a perfect mixed chimney appeared in the back of the corner. Ben grabbed the rack and led off.

Ben had gotten injured the previous winter and had missed out on most of the New England ice season. Nevertheless, he swung his tools confidently and efficiently, as years of experience on this type of terrain in the Alaska Range took over. During the second pitch, he hung the leader pack before committing to a section of unprotectable thin ice. The third pitch featured 30 feet of vertical drytooling right off the belay. Taken together, Ben's block reminded us of Repentance or Remission, the classic chimney routes back home on Cathedral Ledge.

By the time we reached the beginning of the ramp, mild snow squalls were moving in and out. It was my turn to lead again, and I wearily kicked steps into the clouds. We were growing tired and needed to rest, but with the weather looking uncertain and the hour growing late, I decided to put my head down and punch it for the ridge. I'd focus on reaching the next rock, then catch my breath and begin again. The terrain unfolded slowly, up steep snow and then weaving through some fluted ribs. After a while I couldn't find reliable ice to place a screw, but we just kept simul-climbing up the steep, unending mountain.

Then I noticed that my posture had subtly changed. The angle of the slope was decreasing with each step. I crested onto the ridge at 9 p.m. In the distance a lenticular cap hovered over the summit plateau of Foraker, and a thick bank of clouds seethed to the south. To the northwest it was clearer and I could see the bloodshot Alaskan sun dipping toward the horizon. Ben and Peter joined me, and we put on our puffy pants and got the stove going.

Through the passing clouds, we could see the icefall and our base camp beyond. In the other direction, the summit was hidden from our view by an intermediate shoulder in the ridge. While I cooked, I listened to my two partners discussing the inevitable question of which way we should go.

Reaching the summit of the Fin unquestionably mattered to us. I gauged my weakened legs against the turning weather. I considered the prospect of reversing the approach in a whiteout, with the miles of avalanche terrain we would have to cross under. I thought about waiting out the storm in our snow cave at the base of the face while avalanches roared past, and the 20 or so rappels we would have to establish just to reach that tiny island of safety.

Summits do matter. But they don't matter that much—not to me. We downclimbed and rigged the first rappel.

We skied into base camp the next evening, 24 hours after leaving the ridge. By morning, two feet of snow had fallen on the glacier. It's tempting to believe that the storm confirmed our decision to turn back short of the summit. But who knows? Had we been a little bit fitter, perhaps we could have climbed faster and beat the weather. Maybe braver climbers would have pushed through the tempest and emerged unscathed. When we reached the wilderness boundary two days later, the Fin was still masked in clouds.

Each of us quietly carried impressions of what had happened. Ben confided in me that the expedition would always be a bittersweet experience for him. For Peter, who had had his first taste of hard alpine climbing, the trip was a watershed for previously unknown possibilities. And with some reluctance, after much soul searching, I admit that I am proud of what we did.

It's this uniquely human dimension to alpinism that draws me to the mountains. We'll rarely agree on what we do and why. Not in climbing, not in life. And I wouldn't have it any other way.

SUMMARY:

AREA: Yentna Glacier, Alaska

ASCENTS: First ascent of "Rogue Peak" (8,900'), via the northeast face (3,500', M5), Peter Doucette and Freddie Wilkinson. First ascent of "Mantok 1" (9,300'), via the east-facing All Talk Couloir (2,800', M5), Doucette, Wilkinson, and Ben Gilmore. See Climbs and Expeditions, later in this *Journal*, for photos of these peaks and a map showing their locations. First ascent of the Fin Wall, the south face of the Fin (3,800', Alaska Grade 6 NEI 5+), Doucette, Gilmore, and Wilkinson, May 3–5, 2007. The team climbed the wall to the crest of the southwest ridge of Mt. Foraker at ca 12,900 feet, retreating approximately 400 feet below the summit of the Fin.

A NOTE ABOUT THE AUTHOR:

Freddie Wilkinson lives with his girlfriend, Janet Bergman, in Madison, New Hampshire. He would like to thank the Mugs Stump Award for its support of this expedition.

THE TORRE TRAVERSE

A two-decade-old Patagonian dream is realized.

ROLANDO GARIBOTTI

The Torre Traverse follows the skyline from right to left (north to south), beginning at the saddle below Cerro Standhardt, in center right. Rolando Garibotti and Colin Haley traversed to Exocet, a chimney in the center of Standhardt's east face (marked with arrow), and then continued across the summits of Standhardt, Punta Herron, Torre Egger, and Cerro Torre. They descended Cerro Torre's southeast ridge, near the left skyline. In the background, across the ice cap, are Cerro Dos Cumbres (left) and Cerro Dos Cuernos. *Rolando Garibotti*

Twenty years ago, when I first hiked up the Torre Valley, the steep towers of the Cerro Torre massif loomed as if they were the cathedrals of a foreign religion. They looked distant, cold, and unattainable. Initially, merely hiking up the glacier seemed difficult, and although later during that visit I managed to climb nearly to Cerro Torre's summit I spent most of my time marveling at the mountains' majestic beauty.

During that first expedition to the Torre Valley, I became aware of the so-called Torre Traverse, a climbing line that crosses the skyline comprising Cerro Standhardt, Punta Herron, Torre Egger, and Cerro Torre, from north to south, with more than 2,000 meters of vertical gain. Back then, as a young climber from Bariloche, a town in northern Patagonia, it did not occur to me that I would ever try such a project, but as it turns out reality far surpasses imagination.

The traverse was the brainchild of Italians Andrea Sarchi, Ermanno Salvaterra, Maurizio Giarolli, and Elio Orlandi, who tried it on several occasions in the late 1980s and early '90s. The first real attempt was in 1991, when Salvaterra, with Adriano Cavallaro and Ferruccio Vidi, managed to climb as far as Punta Herron, completing what was likely the first ascent of that peak. Salvaterra climbed Herron via the north ridge, an aesthetic route called Spigolo dei Bimbi.

It wasn't until early 2005 that Salvaterra's "high point" was pushed farther, when German Thomas Huber and Swiss Andi Schnarf completed the Standhardt-to-Egger traverse. Having only intended to climb Standhardt, via the route Festerville, they decided on the summit to continue toward Egger. Moving light and fast they completed the first three peaks of the traverse in a 38-hour round trip, descending from Torre Egger via the Titanic route on the east ridge.

In late 2005 Salvaterra, Alessandro Beltrami, and I solved the last remaining puzzle of the traverse when we climbed Cerro Torre from the north via a new route, Arca de los Vientos. After this, the full traverse finally seemed plausible. Now, trying the traverse was not a choice for us; it was our fate. I knew I would never again have the chance to seriously attempt the first ascent of such an aesthetic line, and I decided to do everything within my reach to capture it. Since good weather periods in Patagonia seldom last longer than three days, we knew the traverse would require fast, efficient climbing, but, riding high on our Cerro Torre success, Ermanno, Ale, and I felt confident. Unfortunately, bad weather in 2006 prevented us from getting farther than Standhardt, and later that season a back injury kept me from further attempts.

Unfazed, Salvaterra returned in late 2007 with Beltrami, Mirko Masse, and Fabio Salvodei. On this attempt they climbed Standhardt via Ermanno's own Otra Vez, making the second ascent of this route, and continued to Herron and Torre Egger. They descended to the south, to the Col of Conquest, and climbed one pitch on Cerro Torre before retreating. During that same good weather window, Hans Johnstone and I began the traverse via Standhardt's Festerville, climbed Herron and Egger, and continued past the Col of Conquest, completing half of the upper tower of Cerro Torre before being turned back by a huge rime mushroom that proved impassable.

Having now done all the pieces of the traverse, I decided to stay in Chaltén for the remainder of the season to give it another try. Knowing every meter of the Torre Traverse changed my relationship with it. The original romance was replaced by a need for closure. I no longer felt like an artist but like a builder who needs to complete his contractual obligations, in this case obligations with myself, with my own dreams. I teamed up with a number of other partners, including Bruce Miller and Bean Bowers, but it was not until late January 2008, when I asked Colin Haley to join me, that a good weather window finally provided the opportunity for another attempt. At 23, Colin is one of the most active alpinists in North America; the previous January he had completed the much-tried link-up of Cerro Torre's À la Recherche du Temps Perdu with the upper west ridge, with Kelly Cordes. On scarcely a moment's notice, he put off a semester of university studies to stay in Patagonia and attempt the Torre Traverse with me. I had never roped up with him, but I knew him enough to appreciate his energy and sense of humor.

Ermanno Salvaterra and Alessandro Beltrami near the summit of Punta Herron during an attempt on the traverse in November 2007. In the background is the summit of Cerro Standhardt. *Rolando Garibotti*

On January 21 Colin and I climbed to the col north of Cerro Standhardt, ignoring the wind and clouds. When Hans and I retreated in November, it had been because we didn't have enough time to find a way around the humongous snow blob that blocked our way. This time, Colin and I decided to get a jump on the predicted good weather so we'd have an extra day on Cerro Torre if we needed it. Because it was still stormy, we chose to climb Standhardt via the route Exocet, which is well-protected from the wind. Colin led thin ice through the Exocet chimney, and we reached the summit sometime past midday, taking less than seven hours from the col to the summit.

Above the Col de Sogni, between Standhardt and Herron, rime coated much of the Spigolo dei Bimbi, our chosen route up Herron. For a moment I thought the conditions had once again made the traverse unclimbable. Partway up the second pitch, I placed two nuts, lowered about 60 feet, and pulled the rope. Colin worried that I might be giving up, but in fact I was searching for an alternate line. I had spotted a discontinuous crack system to the east while rappelling from Standhardt, and now I hoped this would allow us to avoid the rime-covered rock on Spigolo dei Bimbi. While the wind tried to strip me from the face, I smeared, crimped, and ran it out until I reached the alternate line, with which we bypassed the second, third, and fourth pitches of Spigolo del Bimbi.

Haley follows the second pitch on Punta Herron during the first day of the traverse in January. For several pitches the two men climbed about 20 meters left of their planned route, Spigolo dei Bimbi, to avoid rime-covered rock. *Rolando Garibotti*

Although the conditions were not great, we were willing to put up with them. I had been waiting for another try since November, and that translated into extra drive. This is not unusual. Often on trips I wait until shortly before I have to go home to put out my best effort. This same thing happens in many sports, not least in soccer, where the last few minutes of a game often are the most active.

All day we had fought the cold and wind, putting in one of the best efforts I can recall being part of. That night we spent an hour digging out a ledge below the Herron mushrooms, and then sealed ourselves against the wind inside our single bivy sack. We lit the stove and melted ice for a time. Then the stove fizzled out. A new canister didn't help, and our lighters didn't work either. Suddenly Colin said, "No oxygen!" He unzipped the bivy sack to flood our tiny home with fresh air.

On January 22, feeling unusually tired, likely because of our carbon monoxide poisoning, we climbed on in perfect weather. Colin led us up and over the Herron mushrooms, and from the summit a short rappel brought us to the Col de Lux, between Herron and Egger. Again, we found much more snow and rime than I had seen in November. After the first easy pitch, rime forced me to climb a couple of variations to the Huber-Schnarf line. Nevertheless, we soon reached the summit mushroom. Luckily, from this side the Egger mushroom is fairly easy, and Colin quickly led us to the summit.

Back in November I had been apprehensive about descending Torre Egger's south face.

Nobody had touched that face since the peak's first ascent in 1977. But now I knew the rappel line precisely, and it went smoothly. The face was entirely covered in rime, and so was the first pitch from the Col of Conquest up to a small pedestal where we joined El Arca's line.

Then, suddenly, it was too warm. Ice fell around us, crashing against the rock with the sound of waves. For the next two hours we climbed as fast as possible, ducking our heads, until we found a rock prow under which we could find shelter. It was only 5 p.m., but we decided to stop and bivy. Looking up we saw that the rime mushroom that had halted my attempt with Hans had fallen off. But El Arca did

Garibotti links flake systems to climb the Huber-Schnarf line on Torre Egger during the second day of the traverse. *Colin Haley*

not seem to be in great condition; there was much more ice than in 2005. I was eager to try a different line I had spied on the north face, but Colin cautioned against navigating uncharted terrain and convinced me that El Arca was the better option. It was this decision more than any other that ensured our success.

In the morning I charged up Cerro Torre's northwest face, leading pitches on El Arca that I had already climbed twice. In many places the cracks were choked with ice, and that slowed me considerably. Early in the season the lower temperatures seem to keep the melt-freeze cycle at bay on this face, so one can quickly clean off the rime and find clean cracks; in January the rising temperatures cause the rime to melt and refreeze deep in the cracks. At a key pendulum, another ice mushroom stood in the way. Unable to climb high enough, I took two 40-foot sideways falls. Tired and drained, I hooked a few moves and at last, sinking in shame, pulled courage out of my pack and drilled Arca's solitary non-belay bolt. Since El Arca was my own route I felt I had the "right" to drill, but I am less than proud of having done so.

(On the entire Torre Traverse there are five non-belay bolts: one on Spigolo dei Bimbi on Punta Herron, placed after the first ascent by an unknown party; three on the Huber-Schnarf route on Torre Egger; and my single new bolt on Arca. Considering the 2,050 meters of vertical gain, this is not a significant number, but given good conditions it should be possible to climb the traverse without using any of them.)

We turned onto the north face and found that the first three pitches were fairly clean of rime, but the last pitch was covered in ice, and I spent almost two hours climbing it. When I finally pulled up to the last belay on the north face at around 5 p.m., I breathed deeply with relief.

Haley silhouetted against Torre Egger. The Hielo Continental spreads to the west, with Volcan Lautaro in the distance. *Rolando Garibotti*

Colin led a short mushroom pitch, and then we lowered and downclimbed about 100 feet to join the 1974 Ferrari route on the west ridge. He then led two more pitches, climbing through natural rime tunnels, to reach the base of the final pitch. Both Colin and I had led this pitch before, but this time we discovered vertical rime as smooth as a pool table, devoid of any weaknesses.

It was 7 p.m. when Colin started his lead. The evening sunshine made the rime shine like gold and warmed it into a spongy, humid mess. For nearly two hours Colin dug and dug, burrowing a 40-foot vertical half-pipe. Then, too wet and tired to continue, he decided to retreat. The last time I'd climbed this pitch I had promised I would never lead it again, and I didn't offer to now. It was Colin's lead block, I rationalized, but I also was scared. We decided to bivy. After carving a small ledge out of rime, we lay down in a fantastic setting: We were 50 meters from the summit of Cerro Torre, with the enormous Southern Patagonia Ice Cap at our feet, and mountains and glaciers extended as far as we could see, from San Lorenzo in the far north to the Paine group in the distant south.

I lay awake most of the night, revisiting the 24 years of climbing that had brought me to this point. I thought back to my first visit to this massif in 1986, when, young and inexperienced, I'd needed three days to climb Agjua Guillaumet, one of the area's smallest spires. The experience then had been as rich as the Torre Traverse was now.

Colin had gotten soaked during his attempt on the final pitch, and it took him a long time to warm up in the morning. We didn't get moving until 9 a.m. Colin had none of his usual

Haley follows El Arca de los Vientos, high on Cerro Torre's north face. The two had previously descended Torre Egger's rime-covered south face, in the background. *Rolando Garibotti*

eagerness, but he geared up and started upward decisively. At the top of the half-pipe he'd carved the night before, instead of continuing to trench up the outer surface of the rime (which is what most leaders, including me, had done in the past), Colin brilliantly started digging a tunnel inside the rime wall. Progress was slow, but any progress at this point was welcome news. After more than three hours of methodic labor, he popped out 20 meters higher, climbed back into a higher natural tunnel in the rime, and emerged onto the summit plateau.

At midday we stood on top and linked into a long embrace. There was no sense of accomplishment or feeling of elation—there was still too much work ahead for that. I thought of Nadina, my four-year-old niece, and deflated like a punctured balloon. How could the rewards of this quest justify the risks I'd taken and the sacrifices I'd made? I'd seen my wife for only ten days in five months, and ignored my nephews and nieces for as long. The creative work behind the Torre Traverse had mostly ended before Colin and I even started; apart from a few variations forced by rime-covered rock, I'd climbed every meter of the traverse before. This time the greater challenges had been the complications of life itself: arranging enough free time, being injury-free and fit at the right moments, and finding a balance between desire and contentment. After so much recklessness, so much effort, so much time, I felt a crushing sense of responsibility to get myself down safely.

After a short rest we started the seemingly endless descent of the Compressor Route on Cerro Torre's southeast ridge. By evening, hungry and exhausted, we gratefully reached the glacier. As we slid and ran back to our camp, jumping over crevasses and crossing under seracs one last time, I broke into a grin, full of appreciation and eagerness for the challenges that lay below. Such a long and arduous journey to attain such a simple joy.

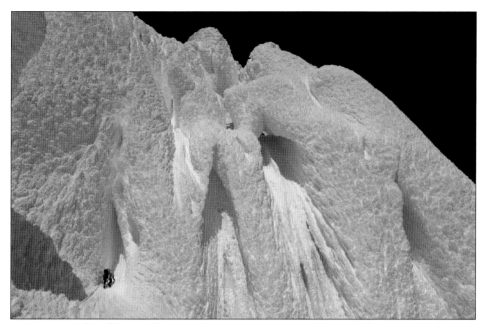

Haley begins the first of three mushroom pitches on Cerro Torre's west ridge. Natural rime tunnels led through these mushrooms, but Haley had to burrow his own tunnel through the final headwall. *Rolando Garibotti*

SUMMARY:

AREA: Cerro Torre Massif, Argentinean Patagonia

ASCENT: The first ascent of the "Torre Traverse," climbing Cerro Standhardt via Exocet (700m, VI 5.9 WI6), Punta Herron via Spigolo dei Bimbi (400m, VI 5.10 MI5), Torre Egger via the Huber-Schnarf route (250m, VI 5.10 MI3), and Cerro Torre via the upper portion of El Arca de los Vientos (700m, VI 5.11 A1 MI6), January 21-24, 2008, by Rolando Garibotti and Colin Haley. (Note: The MI grade stands for "mushroom ice.")

A NOTE ABOUT THE AUTHOR:

Rolando Garibotti has visited the Fitz Roy and Cerro Torre massifs more than 20 times, starting at age 15 when he climbed Aguja Guillaumet. His finest ascents in the area include the first complete ascent of the north face of Fitz Roy in 1995 and the first ascent of the north face of Cerro Torre in 2005, both alpine style. Born in Italy, raised in Argentina, and currently living in the United States, he considers himself a national of Bariloche, a town in the Lake District of northern Patagonia, as this is the place where he developed his passion for the mountains and where, one day, he hopes to enjoy his old age.

Haley (left) and Garibotti on the summit of Cerro Torre. *Rolando Garibotti*

THE SHAFAT FORTRESS

Avoiding conflicts with a new route in Kashmir.

JONNY COPP

Micah Dash starts the 1,000-meter east face of the Shafat Fortress with a 5.11 finger crack. The remains of a shrinking glacier cling to the face to his left. *Jonny Copp*

Over 500,000 troops are stationed along India's border with Pakistan in the disputed region known as Kashmir. Micah Dash and I traveled there to find an unclimbed mountain we had seen in a photo. Our journey took us from the peaceful town of Leh into the heart of the conflict zone, before dropping us south into the fairy-tale mountains of Zanskar. The Zanskar mountains are officially part of the Himalaya, but they buttress the Karakoram like a bridge between the world's two greatest ranges. The cultures there similarly fuse two major religions, Muslim and Buddhist.

Our directions and maps were poor. We were looking for a walled mountain somewhere in the Suru Valley. As we dropped south from Kargil, signs of the border dispute became less prevalent: no more foxholes and razor wire, though we did hear stories of hostage situations and even the killing of Buddhist monks in the area less than five years earlier. After two days of jeeping along the Indus River and then bouncing over hard rock roads up the Suru River Valley, we were still unsure how to find our destination. Nevertheless, we encouraged our jeep driver to forge ahead. By late afternoon on our second day of driving, the mountain we had seen only in a picture and thought about daily as our trip developed came into view. We were awed by its beauty and scale. We wanted to be the first to stand on its summit.

Our first problem was that we were on the wrong side of the river valley. "We're never going to make it across this river," Micah said as we stared across Class V white water. We walked upstream about a quarter mile to a section of the river that was wider and braided. The most promising stretch was roughly 160 feet across.

I agreed to swim for it. We were at 13,000 feet, and the turbid glacier water wasn't much warmer than the ice it had melted from. I ran a few hundred yards downstream to warm up before the plunge. Then I tied the rope around me, taped my sandals tight, and started in as Micah fed rope from a riverside belay.

The river was shallow for the first 15 feet, but this belied the crossing's seriousness. One more step and I was in over my head, swimming with all I had. At 150 feet I could see the last sandbar approaching, but I was fading. A few last desperate strokes got me there. I clawed and plunged my fingers into the sand until I was standing, and then bent over to recover my breath for a good five minutes. I crossed the smaller tributaries, and then Micah and I walked downstream with the rope to set up a tyrolean traverse. It took us all day to ferry our gear and food across.

We set up base camp in a grassy meadow between a few giant granite boulders. The area was pristine, with no marks of previous camps except for an old stone windbreak most likely built by horsemen years ago. Due to the Kashmir conflict, this area has been mostly off-limits since the '50s. Even as recently as the late '90s, there had been bloodshed in the nearest villages.

But now, to us, it was paradise. We settled into our new home, ate great food made by our friend and cook Phurtemba Sherpa, and acclimatized by bouldering on the fine blocks surrounding camp. We'd stare up at the mountain every few hours and watch the features change with the light. Over coffee we'd discuss the best potential route lines.

Each morning it rained or snowed for just an hour, and then the day would clear. The wall would be caked in rime ice and then melt. We were off exploring more boulders on our eighth day in camp when we saw a Kashmiri

To reach base camp, Jonny Copp had to swim the icy, surging Suru River. His ultimate objective rises overhead. *Micah Dash*

horseman in the distance. By his side was a brightly clothed European. We approached, somewhat shocked to see people in this area. Without much of a greeting, the European told us he was with an Italian team and that they (meaning not us) had the permit to attempt this peak. I let him know that we didn't need a permit for this peak in this region. I'd done my research. They walked off.

On our way back to camp, another man appeared. It was Dawa Sherpa, an old friend I'd met a few base camps ago on the other side of India. He has that good mountain spirit about him. We laughed a bunch. Then Phurtemba walked up and told us that many people were crossing the tyrolean we'd set up. Dawa, having been hired by the Italians, nodded an acknowledgment. We walked through the long, high-country grass and over to the river. Indeed, 10 people in logo-covered uniforms were moving their mountain of haulbags across. We tried to introduce ourselves, make small talk, and help, but they would have noth-

Dash (left) and Copp below the east face of the Shafat Fortress. *Jonny Copp*

ing of it. Across came tents, portaledges, hundreds of meters of fixing line, barrels of gear and bolts, and bags. We just sat and stared as their liaison officer let us know that he was fine with whatever we were doing, so long as the Italians OK'd it first. This made no sense to us. But, legally, we had to bow to his authority. After all, he could easily contact the nearest army outpost and have us apprehended.

We gave the Italians one more chance to tell us directly that we could not climb this mountain. As they walked by our camp we introduced ourselves again. The team leader was cordial, and he didn't say anything at that time about permits or problems. So we weren't going to wait for them to powwow and figure out a strategy to shut us down. We had just heard that two of their team were taking the jeep to the nearest police station to report us…for something. Decisive action was needed.

The rock face was not in great shape. Rime was still crumbling off, and meltwater was running down through major crack systems. But we had little choice. We decided to go for it. Climb now and deal with the consequences later was the idea. In retrospect, that's a theme that seems not too uncommon in our lives.

We quickly loaded our packs and started up the talus and glacial moraine without looking

Dash races to follow a 5.11 slab pitch toward the end of the first day of climbing. The two packed light, hoping to make it up and down the face in about three days. But the round trip extended to five days. *Jonny Copp*

back. As we walked, we talked in our best cowboy accents because we'd been reading Cormac McCarthy novels.

"I cain't believe them there Italianos," Micah said.

"I love them Italianos," I replied.

As we crested the first ice bulge in the glacier, we started chanting "I love the Italians, I love the Italians!" as a way to rid ourselves of the feelings of conflict. We didn't need any of that crap on our minds when facing the challenges ahead.

High clouds streaked across the sky the next morning, a sign that a storm might be on its way. But we were determined to start up the wall, rain or shine. We chose a beautiful finger crack to start, and that drove us into a six-pitch, left-facing corner. From there we beelined up a thin face with run-out 5.11 climbing. Then the line trended right into a leaning crack, bringing us to the base of some snow, ice, and exfoliating rock.

It was still my block of leads, so I traded out the rock shoes for crampons and ice tools. The next pitch had only one good piece of gear. I didn't want to clip the main line into all of the bad gear in deteriorating rock and ice because Micah would have ripped a lot of it while jumaring with the pack. This would have been dangerous. So I mostly used the tag line for protection. I cammed axe picks under loose fins of rock, chopped into snow blobs to gain some leverage for a move or two, placed cams between rotten rock and snow. I made it to the top of a small snow

The uncomfortable bivouac at the end of the first day of climbing. During the night, a storm moved in. *Jonny Copp*

cone below overhanging rock just as it was getting dark. We had no choice; this was our bivy.

We chopped the best ledges we could in the meager cone. Neither of our stances ended up as much more than sitting spots. We traded off our one sleeping bag throughout the night. Micah's leg cramped at one point, and he startled me awake with a howl. We talked about the practice of "onsighting" big mountain routes like this. We didn't know what was coming—the difficulties or how to get down. I like the gamesmanship of that cragging ethic. And throwing in all the objective hazards and variable conditions of alpine-style climbing on big peaks makes the game an even better mix of luck and skill.

We tried to sleep but checked our watches too frequently, longing for morning and the encouraging glow of the sun to bleed into the blackness. As soon as it did, we fired up the stove for coffee and stood up, careful not to collapse our stances. Within minutes of coffee hour, it had started snowing.

The cloud ceiling dropped. But we were not going down. We were not going to the Italian-occupied base camp, and we were not going to a Kashmiri police post. So we pendulumed out of our bivy and into a corner system. From there I led two mixed pitches into the cloud and found the best bivy site on the wall, big enough to pitch our small, single-wall tent. Like a big hold where you can shake out on a rock climb, this was the crucial rest spot for the second half of the wall. We poured hot soup down our throats and squeezed into our one sleeping bag with all of our clothes on—we had to dry out.

Dash follows a pendulum at the start of the second day. Two mixed pitches gained a comfortable ledge to sit out the storm. *Jonny Copp*

Waking at four the next morning, we decided to try for a push without bivouac gear. More mixed climbing brought us to the base of a gigantic offwidth system. It was time for Micah's block. As he cammed and grunted his body into the striking feature, I could see ice and water falling out of the crack.

Micah later recounted the epic pitch in an article in *Climbing*. "The first few pieces were solid, but soon the crack widened. Instinctually, I pressed myself into it, my right foot heel-toe-ing on the outside while my left side pressed against the icy, crumbly inside wall, which grew wetter by the minute. Soon, I was soaked from head to toe. My hands and feet were frozen, and hypothermia slowed my progress."

After an hour and a half, Micah had gained only 100 feet. I was looking at the watch but not saying a word. Except for the first few nut placements, his gear lay slotted between iced-over, loose blocks in the back of the crack, which was running with water.

"My brain would tell me to go, but 30 seconds would pass until I moved," Micah recalled. "I tried to weasel in a few pieces, but they were no good and merely slowed progress. Eventually, I settled for an ice screw in an aerated ice amoeba. Not far above, the rock looked as though it kicked back, so I punched it 25 feet above the screw to a point where the fissure pinched down. On the wall behind me, I spotted solid, though very wet, handholds…and maybe even some decent gear. 'Oh, my God, I need to switch sides!' I yelled to Jonny. But, 150 feet below and under a roof, he couldn't hear. Twenty minutes later, after tinkering in a small wire, I took a deep breath and switched sides, only to watch the Stopper pop out. I screamed aloud. Nothing felt solid except for my wooden fingers, but in an instant everything became crystal clear. Either I calmed down, relaxed, and climbed, or I fell off, took a 50-foot screamer onto the ice screw,

Dash à cheval on the summit of the Shafat Fortress (ca 19,500'). *Jonny Copp*

tore it, and likely fell to my death on the small ledge below."

After hours of belaying I heard a scream of true animal terror. I knew what it meant. I knew how it felt. And I knew all I could do was continue belaying. The rope inched out a few more feet, and I finally heard an exhausted "off belay." Micah had found a small stance and concocted an intricate nest of RPs and small TCUs. The pitch had absorbed almost three hours.

I jugged to the belay as quickly as possible. Then we climbed another short pitch. The day was half over and we still had at least 1,600 feet of hard climbing to make the 19,500-foot summit. Micah was soaked and going hypothermic. He'd done an outstanding job. But even if we warmed him up, facing an open bivy in these conditions would be dangerous. We made the tough decision to rappel to our bivy site and hope for the best for the next day.

We set up the tent and soaked up rest and hot fluids like sponges. We pulled our sleeping bag over us and all of our clothes, and settled in for a two-pigs-in-a-blanket snooze that lasted until one a.m., when the alarm went off again. We had our two ropes fixed above. Headlamps and stomachs bounced in the dark as we jumared, especially on the free-hanging 8mm tag line that ran over a roof.

It was now my block of leads. The wet corner above our high point was coated in verglas. In the dark I aided an overhanging section and then free-climbed, stemming around iced-up sections. Eventually the sun hit and lit up the vast, golden expanses of granite. The warmth was a blessing and a curse. I didn't want to get stuck in another waterfall. So we focused on climbing fast and efficiently. The higher we climbed, the colder it became.

One pitch climbed a Tuolumne-style arête to the right of the main corner. Another started in a right-facing rock corner and then turned to ice. Halfway through the pitch I hung on an iced-over chockstone, pulled up my boots, crampons, and ice tools, switched modes, and continued up beautiful mixed ground. Stretching the pitches to 200 feet was the system.

We weren't thinking about Italians anymore. We weren't thinking about world politics. We weren't thinking about paying bills, or relationships, or who's feeding the dog, or anything else except breathing hard in the thinner air and making the key movements and decisions necessary to go up. We were having fun.

If we kept pace we'd make the summit before sunset. Micah's last block of leads started at around 19,000 feet. He stood on a snow dollop and psyched up to pull on cold, wet rock shoes. "Grit your teeth, boy!" I hollered in my best cowboy impression.

Three pitches later I found myself gritting my own teeth. I was standing at a small stance and belaying Micah on a traverse when the lights went out with a bang. As I opened my eyes, shards of ice and snow crystals were still cascading around me and I was on my knees. I was looking straight down into a crack on the inside of the small ledge. I instinctively stuck my gloved fingers into the crack and held on until my wits came back. Then I heard Micah yelling to see if I was okay.

"Yeah, I think so," I yelled back.

A hunk of ice had slid off the summit. The end result was fairly minor: a cracked helmet and a solid headache for the duration of the route.

On August 11, an hour after the helmet cracking, we were on the summit. There had been real climbing all the way to the last five feet. We were elated. To the north we could see K2, Gasherbrum IV, and Broad Peak. And to the south we gazed into the Zanskar's forbidden areas, mountains still closed to Westerners but that should surely hold some world-class objectives.

Climb now and deal with the consequences later, I had said. In the end, after an initial awkward homecoming at base camp, we made friends with the Italians. We shared our rum. They shared their imported meats and cheeses. And Raju, their Krishna-like liaison officer, taught us to blow giant fireballs with kerosene (not recommended to those with a sensitive palate). Our trivial international conflict had been diffused with a good ol' party. Intoxicated, we wished the same for India and Pakistan.

SUMMARY:

AREA: Zanskar, India

ASCENT: First ascent of the Shafat Fortress (ca 19,500') via the east face, the Colorado Route (1,000m, VI 5.11 M6 C1), by Jonny Copp and Micah Dash, August 8–12, 2007.

NOTE ABOUT THE AUTHOR:

Jonny Copp is a climber, photographer, and founder of the Boulder Adventure Film Festival and Dirt Days Environmental Fair. He was born in Singapore in 1974 and has lived in Boulder, Colorado, for 15 years. He credits his best ascents to great partnerships and friends who can laugh in the midst of a great struggle.

The climbers are grateful for the American Alpine Club's Lyman Spitzer Cutting-Edge Awards and W.L. Gore's Shipton-Tilman Grant for making this trip possible.

The author. *Jonny Copp*

TWICE LUCKY

Ascents in the Charakusa Valley of Pakistan.

STEVE HOUSE

Previously unclimbed K7 West (6,858m) bristles with defenses. Two attempts have been made on the northwest ridge, near the left skyline in this photo. The secret to success lay in penetrating the rock pinnacles on the southeast side of the peak (at right). In the background are K7 (right, 6,934m) and unclimbed K7 Middle. The huge rock wall in the right center was climbed by a Belgian-Polish team in 2007 (see page 80). *Marko Prezelj*

The skin around Vince's eyes pinches into crows' feet of concentration. The first shadows of age. His mouth is drawn tight and square, cheeks flat against his face. He wears an expression of concentration, of joy.

Finding the cam he was seeking, he looks upward and reaches to place it. He is breathing roughly, noisily now. The ice is mostly trash, and he hacks at it before finding a solid placement. Then he moves like a spring; if I had looked away, I would have missed it. He is up and over the last few feet of steep ice and rock, and running up the gully, ropes flapping behind him.

The next day dawns gray and slowly. The wind blows doubt into our heads. We've climbed thousands of feet and a few dozen pitches to get here. It's a lot of effort to toss away at the first whiff of a squall. We pack for the day and I take off, leading as much to establish momentum as to climb.

I get it easy. Fun climbing, not too far out of our acclimatization. Vince gets it a bit tougher, climbing a few pitches interspersed with steep steps that get his lungs pumping. Marko gets sustained pitches of steep, brittle ice, 2,000 feet higher than we've yet been. Calves burn, tools feel heavy and dull.

When I take over the lead again in the early afternoon, I think I've got it made. We're on an easy snow ridge; just gotta head up and around to the summit. Wrong again.

Vince Anderson and Steve House on the summit of Naisa Brakk (previously called Nayser Brakk, ca 5,200m), on which the team completed the first ascent of the 3,000-foot southwest ridge (5.11-) during acclimatization. *Marko Prezelj*

First there is awe. Then the dawn of understanding. Then goals and the hard work of organizing, training, packing, saying good-bye. Sometimes there is achievement. Always there's the process. Going home is always harder than you think.

In August of 2007 I walk into Pakistan's Charakusa Valley for the fourth time, the valley still swarming with potential. In 2003 and 2004, my teammates and I had made seven new routes here. But there is more to be done. Two of the highest peaks in the region, the west summit of the K7 massif (6,858m) and the west summit of the K6 massif (7,200m) are still virgin. Marko Prezelj, Vince Anderson, and I want to be first to both summits.

Taking advantage of the varied terrain, we warm up with a relatively easy ascent of the northwestern couloir on Sulu Peak (ca 5,950m), camping just a couple of dozen yards below the summit. After resting a bit back in the idyllic meadows of base camp, we head up to climb the southwest ridge of Naisa Brakk (previously known as Nayser Brakk, ca 5,200m). The very strong rockclimbers Jeff Hollenbaugh and Bruce Miller had been turned back in 2004 by thin cracks and difficult protection. We bring pins and a rock hammer, allowing me to protect the pitch above their high point, and we are rewarded with fine 5.11a climbing on solid stone. It is a true and rare pleasure to do such clean and fantastic climbing on a first ascent.

The next day the pressure drops. No matter; we head up again, intent on another unclimbed jewel, Farol Peak. The following day we sit in the tent in the rain. Seeking more supplies to help us wait out the weather, I descend to base camp, returning with food and a bottle of Marko's homemade honey liqueur. Happily, we settle into the deluxe campsite that Marko and

The K7 group from the south. (1) The pillar climbed by Marko Prezelj and Maxime Turgeon. (2) The Anderson-House-Prezelj first ascent line on K7 West. *Marko Prezelj*

Vince have spent the day engineering out of the rubble heap of a moraine. After another day of lounging, however, we grow restless. Back to base camp.

The ensuing days are uninspiring. Cloudy and showery; we hardly ever see the peaks. One of our tents blows down in a gale, and the repair gives us welcome purpose. August 28 dawns brusquely, all gloom and despair. But by the time we've put away our morning tea and cakes, the sun is shining. Excitedly, we grab a rock rack and head out for an up-close view of our first big objective: K7 West.

In 2004, Marko, Doug Chabot, Bruce Miller, and Steve Swenson headed up to try this peak via a route from the glacier between K7 West and K7. The rock climbing near the bottom of their planned route turned out to be threatened by a serac. But Marko thought there was another way, a longer, less direct, but promising rock ramp well left of the serac danger. We would investigate.

Some easy scrambling brings us to the ramp, 150 feet wide and angling easily up and right in the direction of a splitter couloir that looks like it might deliver us, eventually, onto the summit. The climbing starts off well with a few 5.8 pitches on decent white granite. Then the wall steepens toward vertical and the crack pinches down. It's Vince's lead and his summer of guiding hasn't contributed to his forearm endurance. Suddenly he is off, the rope wrapping behind his leg on the way down. The resulting wound on his ankle will bother him the rest of the trip. The scrapes on his helmet make us all glad we are wearing them.

Back on the sharp end, Massive Vinny is out for blood; quickly he is on top of the 5.11a pitch. A couple more 5.10 pitches and we are on a broad shoulder looking directly at the couloir we want to climb. There is a huge place to camp here, room for hundreds of tents. We rap back

The climbers carried their heavy packs while following each pitch during the first day on K7 West. When a pitch was too hard for the leader to carry his own pack, one of the seconds would rappel and then reclimb the pitch with the leader's load. *Steve House*

down the ramp, gleeful about our discovery.

The last days of August are all gray. Someday, I think, I'll spend a summer someplace hot. A crag with a beer vendor near the base. Somewhere I'll beg for a break from the rays and cringe at my tanned hide. For now, though, I'm stuck in the Karakoram. My belly white. The sun only a rare guest.

The barometer creeps up; we pack. The packs feel light; I even decide to take our little video camera. The first day of September is absolutely flawless, the first such day since we arrived. We virtually float up the glacier and onto the base of the ramp.

Reclimbing the pitches we'd done earlier, each carrying a pack weighing 30 pounds, proves to be a lot of work. We're climbing in rock shoes, boots in the packs, which makes the rucks top-heavy and cumbersome. On the pitches too hard for the leader to climb with a full pack, one of us belays while the other raps down and climbs back up with the third load. Only the crux pitch doesn't yield to these tactics. Using a Tibloc and a prusik, Vince ascends the rope with the third pack on that pitch. We're glad to reach the spacious spot on the shoulder, where we pitch the tent near a protective rock wall and go to sleep by eight.

Day two brought splendid ice climbing in a narrow gully. *Steve House*

A day and a half later, it feels like we're getting close. Yesterday, after soloing 1,000 feet of moderate ground, we had climbed about a dozen pitches up the ice couloir and then chopped a ledge from the icy ridge for our second bivy. Today, we've each already led a block, with increasing difficulty, and now I lope up the summit ridge, anxious to beat an incoming storm. I round the first snow peak and am stopped dead. The gargoyle before me is ugly. Now, I've climbed some bad-looking snow and ice gargoyles. Taulliraju's summit ridge saw me in a slow-motion fall through snowy lacework before a firmer bit of the ridge lodged in my crotch and saved me from taking the big whip. Robson's got some infamous rime features, too. But this thing looks bad.

First I try the right side; if it is firm enough for me to climb 20 vertical feet to the top of the mushroom, I'll be able to happy-cowboy 100 or so feet to where the ridge looks more substantial. I plunge the shaft of an ice tool into the gargoyle's soft surface. It wouldn't hold a swallow's nest.

Mmmm. What about rapping down a few hundred feet, traversing underneath the mushroom, and climbing back up. I start to dig for an anchor. Nothing. Super-soft snow for miles.

That leaves the left side of the monster. Looks bad, I think, but I'd better check it out firsthand before I call this whole thing off.

As I start, Marko pops up behind me. We've been simul-climbing, and 50 meters of rope lie in the snow between us. He picks it up, worms his way down into the snow ridge, and puts me on belay. I chop and clean and kick, working down and behind a smaller, car-size chunk of the ridge. It's nice because I can lean back on it.

Day three on K7 West was snow-climbing day, and some of the fragile cornices and mushrooms were nearly impassable. *Steve House*

Once past this, I am urged on more by Marko's encouragement than by any sense of optimism. I swing and sweep and pull hard on the plunged shafts of my axes. Who thought snow climbing could be 5.11? I stem out left and start to wiggle between the ridge and a land yacht–sized chunk of snow that has split away and is leaning 15 degrees over the abyss to the south. It's like climbing horizontally through a crevasse. The snow on the ridge side is pretty hard, and I'm moving along, stemming the gap, tools stuck in the right side of the fissure, when it happens.

I feel movement, but snow compresses so I don't realize at first that the block I'm stemming against is falling away. By the time I do understand what is happening, my stemmed foot is swinging back in, throwing me off balance. I'm holding on for dear life, and my tools stay put in the harder snow of the ridge. Then the noise comes. Loud. Booming. Then rolling away. What thunder would sound like if you were inside the cloud. The massive block hits the slope a few hundred feet below me and is atomized.

Marko is yelling something. I'm yelling, "I'm okay, I'm okay!" Not so much because I'm okay—I'm scared shitless—but I'm not dead, and right now anything other than dead is okay, so I keep yelling as the sound falls away.

Marko understands, and I resume climbing. What other choice do I have? A few yards farther along, the snow gives off the blue tint of ice. Well, almost ice. Where the big block split off from the wall, the cold heart of the gargoyle is exposed. I turn a few screws into the beast and belay Marko and Vince to me.

The next couple of pitches are slow and insecure. But I've seen worse, so it's just a matter of keeping my concentration and not screwing up. At the top of the second pitch the angle eases and I crest the ridge. It's as wide as Fifth Avenue and only slightly steeper. I walk till the rope comes tight and then keep walking.

It's stormy now—hoods up, walking with a shoulder into the wind, yelling from six inches apart to communicate, barely a rope length's visibility. The ridge peaks and tilts downward. I stop and pull in the ropes. There is hugging. Posed photos. I get out the video camera and the Pakistani flag that I took to K7's main summit during the second ascent of that peak three years earlier. In the midst of our celebration, the clouds blow apart for a few seconds and everything stops. We aren't on the summit.

The summit of K7 West...or is it? The team reached what they thought was the top in a whiteout, only to see a higher peak during a brief clearing. They quickly climbed to the true summit, where a cornice collapse nearly proved disastrous. *Steve House*

But it's close. So we toss everything back into the packs. By the time I've stowed the video, Marko is tugging at me with the rope. I scramble to catch up, gasping at the effort. The clouds close back in. I lose sight of Marko 100 feet in front of me. Suddenly his rope stops. I pause for a few moments. Some of his rope slides back down the hill out of the cloud. Then it gets pulled in quickly. He's on top.

Quickly I join him. He's wide-eyed. Excitedly quiet. It's too windy to talk, so he gestures at a crack right by his last tracks, a few yards higher. I understand: We're on top of the corniced summit, and the cornice had cracked right between his feet when he groped upward the last few feet. We're twice lucky.

I back away from the summit and pull in Vince's rope. When he arrives I explain what happened; he looks at Marko knowingly. Marko shrugs. No celebration is forthcoming. Vince spins and starts down.

At base camp it snows each day for the next six days. On September 11 it clears enough to start to dry out some things. The next day we head out across the wet meadows and climb a long, rambling rock ridge behind Naisa Brakk. The views are painful. What are we doing rock climbing when we should be starting up K6 West? In my mind I know Marko's right. The last storms must have deposited many feet of snow on the big mountains, leaving our intended route dangerous for days as it avalanches and cleans itself. But in my heart, where decisions are made, I am in anguish.

I don't enjoy the ridge climb and am almost relieved when we find slings on the first summit. It justifies my feelings that we're wasting time; we're not even getting an FA.

The next day at breakfast I announce: "I'm going to check out K6. Anyone want to come with me?" Of course they do. We have five days before the porters come to pick us up and start us

The approach to K6 West. Two icefalls bar the way to the peak's west face. The team made it through the first icefall (center), but not the second. *Marko Prezelj*

on our trip home. The next day at noon, still under a blue sky, we head off.

Up close we can all see that the mountain is lying under a deep blanket of white. The ice we'd hoped to climb isn't even visible. We pitch the tents in the only safe spot, between two icefalls, and Marko and I head off to try to find a way through the second icefall.

I like it when failure is unequivocal. Nothing short of a high-altitude helicopter would get us through that icefall. Every option is totally blocked. As if to illustrate the point, after we descend to Vince at the bivy tent, the left side of the upper icefall collapses in a solid whump, right where we had considered climbing.

In the morning we sleep late, watch the sun come up on the mountains around us, and enjoy the place. Slowly, we pack and start down the glacier. The next day, Vince and I pack while Marko joins Maxime Turgeon for a final rock climb. They rap off the summit of a fine little rock spire an hour after dark. Their route would be a classic Grade V anywhere else. It's like a 25-meter sport climb compared to the still-unclimbed monsters looming above. We'll be back.

SUMMARY

AREA: Charakusa Valley, Pakistan

ASCENTS: Northwest face of Sulu Peak (ca 5,950m) via a probable new route up a couloir (950m, 60°), August 18–19, 2007. First ascent of the southwest ridge of Naisa Brakk (ca 5,200m), with about 900 meters of rock climbing up to 5.11-, August 21, 2007. First ascent of K7 West (6,858m) via the southeast face (2,000m, 5.11a WI5), September 1–4, 2007. All ascents by Vince Anderson, Steve House, and Marko Prezelj. Prezelj and Maxime Turgeon also climbed a rock spire (900m, 5.11 A0) on the east side of the south face of K7 West on September 18.

A NOTE ABOUT THE AUTHOR:

Steve House has completed nine climbing expeditions in Pakistan. This year he plans to try his luck in the Nepal Himalaya, with a post-monsoon attempt on Makalu's west face. House, 37, is pleasantly ensconced in Terrebonne, Oregon, near Smith Rock, where he did his first multipitch climb and where the sport climbing is a pleasant antidote to alpinism.

Steve House. *Marko Prezelj*

HANDHOLDS TO HEAVEN

Hard free-climbing on the rock walls of Pakistan's Charakusa Valley.

NICOLAS FAVRESSE

Sean Villanueva (left) and Olivier Favresse prepare to climb the final headwall cracks on Badal, a 26-pitch mostly free climb on the west flanks of K7 West. *Adam Pustelnik*

B eep, beep, beep…. It's one a.m. I wake in the middle of one of those dreams where nothing makes sense. It seems as though I've barely fallen asleep; but, no, it's already time to get up. I'm warm in my sleeping bag, and the thought of having to get out reminds me of those rough mornings before school the day after a mega climbing session with my friend Sean Villanueva. We were so motivated that we would end our sessions at home with pull-ups and weighted hangs, filling our climbing packs with bags of potatoes and bottles of olive oil; we would continue until we had drained ourselves of all our energy, nearing masochism, beyond midnight. The next day, getting out of bed was a piece of work, and thinking in school was even harder. But climbing was our passion!

Now I'm on an expedition in an isolated region of Pakistan: the Charakusa Valley. The big walls are all around us. It takes me a few minutes to come back to reality, and then I recall the magnitude of the day ahead. I close my eyes one last time and think about the gigantic needle we hope to climb, its beauty, the pleasure it will provide, the place where we are. That's it! I feel ready. All my anxieties about this attempt vanish, giving way only to positive thoughts. I get out of my sleeping bag and start to get dressed, respecting meticulously the layering that I had decided on the night before. The full moon is out, so powerful that we can barely see the stars. The weather forecast seems accurate: The sky is completely clear. Sean is already up, busy making porridge. He tells me he wasn't able to sleep; he was too excited.

The Belgian-Polish team stopped climbing when the line of Badal reached lower-angle rock and snow. Although they had hoped to reach the summit of the "Badal Wall" formation, about 300 meters higher, lack of food and a forecast for eight days of bad weather convinced them to descend. *Nicolas Favresse*

Sean Villanueva, my brother Olivier Favresse, and I (all members of the Belgian Alpine Club Rock Climbing Team), and Adam Pustelnik from Poland (Hi-Mountain Team) have traveled to the Charakusa Valley to free-climb new routes on steep rock faces in the best style we can. We had known this was a great area for traditional alpine climbing, but it wasn't clear whether we would find the steep faces of good granite we were looking for. What kept us going was our faith in a few statements by previous explorers, mentioning the great rock climbing potential.

It's our first time in Pakistan, and we are extremely impressed by the kindness of the local people. A week after our arrival in Islamabad, we reach K7 base camp (4,200 meters) in the Charakusa Valley, after three casual days of trekking from the village of Hushe. We set up camp along a stream next to a moraine in a grassy field full of beautiful granite boulders. The bouldering here is top-class, with plenty of problems of all difficulties.

None of us has had much experience with such altitude; three of us have never been above 3,500 meters. Acclimatizing feels like we're getting spanked at first. It doesn't help that we're underestimating these walls' size by a factor of three. Near our camp is a crack-covered cliff called the Iqbal Wall that looks perfect for an "easier" adventure day. We estimate the wall at 150 meters high. It turns out to be about 400 meters.

We decide to split into two teams for two different lines on the Iqbal Wall. Olivier and Adam go for a beautiful dihedral on the left side of the wall, while Sean and I head for some thin cracks through the steepest part. We feel very sure of ourselves—it should be casual to put up two new routes in one day! But we quickly learn our lesson. Sean and I bail at a free-climbing dead end at the top of our fourth pitch, completely exhausted by the altitude.

Villanueva scopes the route ahead. *Adam Pustelnik*

Meanwhile, Olivier and Adam have a much worse experience. On the sixth pitch of their dihedral, Olivier detaches a fridge-sized rock despite hardly touching it. He tries to hold the rock in place, but it's way too heavy. The huge rock rolls over his back while Olivier manages to hang on, and then it bounces down the dihedral and glances off Adam's foot—and fortunately just his foot! His heel is completely cut open in the Achilles area.

In normal conditions, such a cut would have healed after 10 days, but at this altitude everything heals slower and hygiene is harder to maintain. During the whole expedition, Adam's wound will never recover completely, and he won't be able to wear his climbing shoes or do any free-climbing. Despite his ugly wound, however, he joins us on all of our projects and strongly contributes to the success of the expedition.

After unsuccessful lightweight attempts on two different faces, we reconsider our strategy. Right in front of our base camp, along the west side of K7 West, is a major wall, some 1,200 meters high. After asking local people about it and looking at our notes, we are surprised to learn that probably no one has climbed or even attempted this face. For this huge objective we pack about 20 days worth of food, aiming to stay on the wall either until there isn't any more food or the summit is made. Going big-wall-style seems like a good way to get our bodies acclimatized to this altitude.

Sean and Adam do a day of reconnaissance on the first eight pitches, and then we launch. Once on the wall we climb capsule-style; we fix rope above our camps until we find a well-protected ledge, and then move our camp upward. During the climb we establish three camps.

The first seven pitches follow a steep dihedral leading to a snow patch, our first camp. Up to pitch 11 the best route is easy to follow, with straight-up crack systems. But on pitch 12 the path becomes much trickier. I am not an aid climbing expert, so I have to spend six hours aid-climbing the line, with many hook moves and beak placements. But even though the aid climbing is quite difficult (I'm guessing around A3+), we find a way to free-climb the pitch using small crimpers on pre-fixed, run-out gear, at a difficulty of around 7c (5.12d).

Beautiful cracks take us up the wall past two more camps, at pitch 14 and pitch 20. Above the 16th pitch are amazing cracks on a steep headwall. And after 15 days (seven of them stuck in snowstorms) and 26 long pitches of sustained and steep climbing (all free except for five meters of icy crack on pitch 24 that would not be an issue to free in good conditions) we reach the top of the rock face at an altitude around 6,000 meters.

Unfortunately, the forecast calls for eight days of bad weather. We no longer have enough food to wait for good conditions to climb snow to the real summit, about 300 meters higher. Anyway, the rock and the free climbing are what we've really come for. But we have to admit that topping out would have been icing on the cake.

Nicolas Favresse leads the crux 12th pitch of Badal. The first ascent of this pitch required six hours of aid climbing, with many hook and beak placements, and the free climbing went at 5.12+, with just one bolt. *Adam Pustelnik*

Back in base camp we quickly refill our empty reserves with some actual cake and whiskey. We call our new route Badal, which, according to our guide, Raja Nafees, means "mix cloudy" in Urdu. We had thought "mix cloudy" meant good weather for climbing, but in the end we've found it means mostly bad.

Deep up the valley is a beautiful needle detached from the south side of K7. To us it seems like the nicest feature in the area for free climbing. The quality of the granite is excellent, and the wall magically appears to have splitter cracks all over it. After studying past expeditions' accounts, we learn that climbers had tried the left side of this feature in big-wall style, but didn't succeed. It's almost like a dream to find this virgin piece of rock.

Early in our expedition, we tried to climb the longest and most obvious line on this needle, the south ridge. But we were exhausted from not being well acclimatized, and we reached a free-climbing dead end about 10 pitches up. Thirty days later, after

Villanueva leads the icy final pitch of Badal before reaching low-angle rock and snow patches. This pitch went free, with boots and ice tools, but an icy crack two pitches below required five meters of aid. *Nicolas Favresse*

climbing Badal, we couldn't be better acclimatized, and after scoping the wall we decide to try again, following a slightly different crack system. Our strategy is to go light and fast, with no bivy gear. We pack a stove for melting snow, four bolts, and about 10 pitons.

At two a.m. we leave base camp without headlamps in a mystical light created by the moon. All the summits are visible. I can hear only our shoes crushing the ice. We are dumbfounded by the lunar ambience. Stopping by a water-filled crevasse, we try to drink as much as possible, but it is so cold that my teeth freeze each time I swallow. We'll have to make do with three liters of water until we find snow to melt on the route. We can't waste any time!

Around 4:30 a.m. we reach the foot of the needle. It is so big and beautiful that it is hard to look away. We put on crampons and climb up a gully threatened by hanging glaciers. I feel so vulnerable, but reason reassures me, reminding me that conditions are good. We reach a little ledge, sheltered from the seracs, and now we only have to overcome an ocean of granite to reach the summit. Without wasting a second, I put on my climbing shoes and am warmly welcomed by a beautiful offwidth. It's only the beginning and I am already fighting with all my might. "Off belay—blue rope coming up—rope, Adam, fixed!" There we go, we're on it. We have thought so much about this route that we are like preprogrammed machines. I look around me and the sun is already lighting up the summit of Kapura.

Sean, Olivier, and I share the leading, and we follow most pitches free. Adam jugs up with

Nafees' Cap stands below K7 (right) and K7 Central, with the line of Ledgeway to Heaven marked. The four men climbed the 28-pitch route all free at 5.12+ in a 40-hour round trip from base camp. At least one team had previously attempted the left side of the formation. *Olivier Favresse*

a huge pack because he still can't put on his climbing shoes. The altitude and the hygiene didn't help his healing, but his mind has remained strong, which impresses us a lot. He makes our task much easier by carrying lots of gear, which enables us to move faster.

Below the fourth pitch, no cracks are visible ahead. The only way is to climb an unprotectable ridge. During our first attempt on this spire, we had wondered if we would have to place a protection bolt here. It didn't look too hard, but the climbing was delicate, not allowing for any mistakes. It was Sean's turn to lead. The rock was lightly covered with green lichen, not helping Sean with his confidence, especially considering that a fall could be lethal. I could barely look. Sean made some progress, but then hesitated. Once he committed to this crux, retreat would likely have been impossible. He tried the moves a few times, then he looked at me with an expression of regret and said, "Give me the hand drill!" I opened my pack to find the gear, but before I could send it up to him I realized that, without a word, he was going for it!

Demonstrating total mental control, he was quickly through the hardest part. A climb like this feels like a big video game, where each pitch represents a unique test that we have to pass in order to continue to the next level. Now, during our second attempt on the route, this test is much easier, since we know what is coming.

Offwidths, chimneys, finger cracks, dihedrals—we quickly link the pitches. Sean sends a superb pitch, worthy of the most beautiful leads on the Nose in Yosemite, and then comes the big question mark. It's our 12th pitch, and we're near the dead end we had encountered during our previous attempt. This time we'll either follow a thin, oblique crack, or attempt a traverse farther left toward a bulge, without knowing what lies beyond. After some hesitation I climb up the thin crack. Then, looking to the left, I change my mind and attempt the traverse. I fall. I try again, but it's very hard. The smooth wall has barely any holds, but I feel drawn to it like a magnet. I try to traverse higher, lower, then a hold breaks. With every try, my heart races and I am completely out of breath. Last try, because time is precious. I rub my shoes and go for it, as confidently as I can. In the middle of the crux, I realize that my sequence will not work. I change plans instantly and throw myself into a battle with fingernail crimpers. And…yes! It works! Behind the corner, I find another crack system that puts us back on track. Now the summit

Brothers Olivier Favresse (top) and Nicolas Favresse follow the second pitch (5.11+) of Ledgeway to Heaven. "No one wants to jug on such beautiful pitches!" *Sean Villanueva*

seems to be reflecting in my shining eyes.

Soon we reach a lower-angled section. It's around two p.m., and we are about a third of the way up the face. We have already been climbing for nine hours. Now we are able to move faster for about 300 meters, with four people simul-climbing, but fatigue and the altitude are starting to take over.

My brother Olivier has major stomach problems. He offers to go down alone with one rope or to wait for us on a ledge until we come down. But we insist on sticking together, whether we go up or down. We agree to keep moving and see how it goes. By dusk we are still far from the summit and Olivier's state is not improving. At the end of each pitch he is completely exhausted, and on each ledge he falls asleep. During a pendulum, he retches. We have to watch him carefully to make sure he doesn't make a foolish mistake. But we don't want to turn around, now that we are so far up. We each help Olivier as much as we can, and Adam heats water for tea whenever we find snow on ledges. All night we keep climbing. Each time we think we are at a dead end, a little miracle happens.

Around seven a.m. we all arrive on the summit of the needle. A magnificent sunrise lights up K7, K6, and Kapura—an amazing range of incredible summits surrounding us. Olivier tells us he is feeling better and thanks us for having pulled him up there.

The descent is long because we have to build every rappel anchor, but the nice weather stays with us. At dusk we set foot on the glacier, and around 8:30 p.m. we reach our base camp, more than 40 hours after leaving. Our guide has prepared an amazing dinner. Yes, it is only rice with corn and a few green beans, and yet it seems to be filled with the lingering flavor from our new route, which I consider the most beautiful I have ever climbed.

We decide to name the climb Ledgeway to Heaven because it offers superb, comfortable ledges between the hard climbing, and we name the needle Nafees' Cap, in honor of our excellent guide.

A few days before our departure, Sean and I, along with Jerzy "Juras" Stefanski, a Polish climber in the area, return to the Iqbal Wall for some unfinished business. Our route follows an obvious oblique crack on one of the steepest parts of the wall. This time the climbing goes smoothly—completing a new route in a day on this formation now seems reasonable. We have come full circle.

SUMMARY:

AREA: Charakusa Valley, Pakistan Karakoram

ASCENTS: Capsule-style first ascent of Badal (1,200m, 5.12+ A1) on the west side of K7 West, all free except for five meters of icy cracks, by Nicolas and Olivier Favresse, Adam Pustelnik, and Sean Villanueva. The team reached the top of the rock wall at ca 6,000 meters on July 24, 2007, after 15 days on the face. They descended the next day. They fixed eight pitons and 12 bolts: six bolts to hang portaledges, four to reinforce belays, and two to protect free climbing. Single-push first ascent of Nafees' Cap, a spire at the base of K7's south face, by Ledgeway to Heaven (1,300m, 5.12+), Nicolas and Olivier Favresse, Adam Pustelnik, and Sean Villanueva, late July 2007. The climbers left one bolt and one piton on the route. All 28 pitches were led free, and most were followed free by at least one climber. First ascent of the Ski Track (400m, 5.11) on the Iqbal Wall, Nicolas Favresse, Jerzy Stefanski, and Sean Villanueva, early August 2007.

A NOTE ABOUT THE AUTHOR:

From the smallest boulder to the highest mountain, Nicolas Favresse likes everything about climbing. Born in Brussels, Belgium, in 1980, he is a full-time climber, and home is two vans on two different continents. Favresse notes: "We were extremely disappointed to see that other expeditions had left trash near their base camps. We came down with two full trash bags of other people's garbage. How is it possible that people come to this beautiful setting without respecting it?"

The team, from left: Raja Nafees, Olivier Favresse, Sean Villanueva, Nicolas Favresse, and Adam Pustelnik. *Olivier Favresse*

Portions of this article previously appeared in the journal of the Brabant section of the Belgian Alpine Club and were translated from the French by Caroline George.

SIULÁ CHICO

The first ascent of a huge ice wall in the Cordillera Huayhuash of Peru.

JORDI COROMINAS

Outside in the urban night it is snowing. The cold wind howls intensely off the port. After dinner, without the help of either drink or smoke, our conversation wanders, ideas going in all directions, minds expanding. Enveloped in the aroma of the café, Manel de la Matta brings up his old idea for a journey across the sea for six months—at last he is to realize it. As if revealing a map to some long-lost treasure, he hands around a photograph of the west face of Siulá Chico.

Years later, I carry out my own dream of crossing the ocean to Siulá Chico, the first of three trips to this mountain. Following in the footsteps of the conquistadors, we arrive in the land of El Dorado. Here the locals cast dark glances at us (or so we imagine), their weapons glinting in the night. In any foreign land, how are we to know our friends from our enemies? Then again, do we even know this at home?

We encounter a tavern where we seek information: El Vagamundo. Nearly ensnared by the pungent fumes of pisco and the alcoholic confusion of the bartender, we are saved by a charming waitress who directs us to the guesthouse of a friend. Here we find ourselves among other treasure hunters, and in no time we are able to negotiate some muleteers who will take us from the city at dawn, toward the mountain. On the trail we ponder what drove the conquistadors, in their shining suits of iron, to push on across this high plain, beneath a punishing sun, with nothing but snowy peaks on the horizon. Perhaps they were simply seeking the most distant place imaginable? Perhaps we are continually doing the same thing?

May 2007, Cutatambo. Two families living in shacks of corrugated tin receive us warmly, inviting us in for the local staple of cheese and potatoes. We decide to camp beneath the open mouth of the abandoned lead and silver mine of San Martín, named for the general who liberated much of Latin America from the oppressive colonial rule of the Spanish. We pitch our tent among some more recent ruins, dating to when the glacial lake beneath Nevado Sarapo was drained in order to avoid the possibility of a catastrophic flood, like the ones that have devastated entire villages in the adjoining Cordillera Blanca. These mountains are alive, or at least more alive than our own lands. Once in awhile they convulse, hurling on the valley below everything they can shake loose. In the moraine we play gold prospectors, collecting brilliant rocks to bring back home.

We spend several days carrying loads along the dusty trail of the lateral moraine called Bomb Alley by Joe Simpson after his epic on Siulá Grande, and through the stony moraine where Simpson somehow crawled his way back to life to the tune of that horrid song—*a brown girl in the ring, tra la la la la*. No science can tell us where that fine thread hangs between living and letting go. Finally we are in position to attempt the ascent of the west face of Siulá

Chico, called "the little one" because it is just a bit lower than Siulá Grande, but by no means because it is small.

On May 20 we leave base camp in splendid weather. On this attempt—my third on the face in five years—Oriol Baró accompanies me. Oriol is 20 years younger than me, but he shares my goals and ethics in the climbing realm, demonstrating that the basic essence of alpinism endures through the years despite all the excuses that we look for to climb mountains in other ways.

Early the next morning we access the Siulá Glacier. Although not large, the glacier begins as a labyrinth and soon becomes heavily crevassed, with enormous holes lurking. We would move closer to the base of Siulá Grande, but we shy away from it because every so often a piece of cornice breaks loose and sweeps down the gullies of the face, tumbling out onto the glacier we are crossing.

Oriol Baró and Jordi Corominas climbed the west face of Siulá Chico (6,265m) in six days. They carried a portaledge and haul bag but climbed alpine-style, placing no bolts. *Oriol Baró Collection*

We pitch the tent in a flat spot that doesn't appear too exposed, just far enough away, we hope, from the crevasses and avalanches. While we climb, we'll leave our small home of yellow nylon standing, hoping that from the wall it will offer the illusion that amid this vast cirque of mountains—Yerupaja, the Siulás, and Sarapo—we are not alone.

The imposing west face of Siulá Chico is hidden by the fame of Siulá Grande, and this is what has protected it until now from the ravenous view of almost all other alpinists. Even though it does not yet have a route on it, in Huaraz they joke that I'm opening a sport climbing area on its flanks because I've returned so many times. In 2003 Jordi Tosas and I were completely mistaken in our tactics on the mountain. On that occasion we attempted a line of frozen waterfalls on the left side of the wall, linked by a pitch of aid on horrible rock. The aid climbing required us to back-clean our pitons in order to stretch our gear for use higher up. We both remember this line having the most difficult ice climbing either of us had ever done. We completed around 600 meters of the route up to a shoulder. There, weak from both physical and psychological fatigue, we had to retreat.

The problem was that we hadn't known how to read the wall. Once committed to it, there are no ledges where one can sleep, and everything is more vertical than it appears from below. Even the fields of snow turned out to be sheets of ice where we couldn't fashion any platform.

That first attempt, we bivouacked coiled up among the stalactites of ice behind frozen cascades. Since then, we've carried a hammock and haul bag, so that at least we could sleep.

The west face is guarded halfway up by a long row of giant snow mushrooms. After midday, the sun hits this part of the wall and the *apus*, as the locals call the mountain spirits, begin to play, aiming their lances of ice at the impudent humans that have dared to enter their domain. For this reason, it is necessary to find a protected spot by noon to wait out the bombardment.

In 2007, as we did in 2005, we start the route in the center of the wall, following a series of steepening icefields under some overhangs that offer a bit of protection from above—a good thing since as soon as we pass

Corominas leads steep ice during the fourth day on Siulá Chico's west face. *Oriol Baró*

the bergschrund there is a small avalanche of ice. Beyond the overhang, two short pitches of either aid or mixed climbing—the manner of passage depending on the condition of the snow and the efforts that one can muster—lead to a bivy site exposed to everything that falls. Just above this, a long traverse across thin ice leads toward the right side of the wall, making for quite a challenge in dealing with the haul bag. Our attempt in 2005 ended after a bad blow from a fall on this traverse. This time we finish the traverse just a bit bruised from the falling projectiles.

At our second bivouac we spend two nights. The weather has changed, and it snows constantly through the night and during the following day. The vertical nature of the wall keeps the snow from accumulating, and we endure constant washing by spindrift but no big avalanches. We try to doze as much as possible to avoid eating. While climbing you don't think so much of food, but trapped here for an entire day we end up seeing barbequed chickens circling around our heads.

Oriol wonders aloud what the Brits must be made from that allowed them to endure a sitting bivouac on this wall's tiny, exposed ledges. [Mick Fowler and Simon Yates attempted the left side of the west face in 1998, climbing 10 pitches over two days before retreating in the face of rock and ice fall.] At least the canopy of our hammock protects us somewhat from the spindrift. Later in the season, on Huascarán Sur, we will test what Oriol calls the "Fowler style" of bivouacs, but that is another story. For the rest of the climb the weather remains unsettled, with clouds rolling in each afternoon and dumping a bit of snow. During our final bivouac, on our way down, we'll have an electric party to celebrate our summit, replete with thundering drums.

From the central snowfield, we pick our way up a line of gullies, waterfalls, and sheets of thin and poorly protected ice. What slows us down most is building belay anchors. The rock is compact limestone with few cracks, the ice is often too soft or too thin, and we place no bolts

Baró heads toward a difficult step during the final day of climbing on Siulá Chico. *Jordi Corominas*

on the face. Even after finishing our strange and extensive triangulations, which are far from "by the book," we pray to the *apus* that the leader will find a good piece as quickly as possible. I tell Oriol after one pitch, "I thought about untying because I knew that if you fell the belay would fail. But after thinking it over I realized that that would only leave me alone in this place without a rope. So I kept belaying but stopped watching."

After a number of pitches of authentic north face–style alpinism, we arrive on a shoulder of sugary meringue, where finally we can scratch out a ledge big enough for us both to stand flat-footed and dance on top of the clouds.

From here we cross to the other side of the mountain, via a kind of "Traverse of the Gods," with the void sucking at our heels. This leads to another pitch of excellent thin ice, and finally we reach the vertical flutings of unconsolidated snow for which these mountains are infamous, with only two pickets to help us overcome our fears. Luckily the ropes are long and the simul-climbing is brief, and we find a smear of ice for anchoring ourselves.

And the summit? A mound of soft snow, fog, cornices, and a mountain that drops to the other side; this is not a summit so much as a story that has just finished. All this means is that another story begins, and that the infernal cycle of stories will continue so long as we have strength.

SUMMARY:

AREA: Cordillera Huayhuash, Peru

ASCENTS: First ascent of the west face of 6,265-meter Siulá Chico (900m, ED+ VI AI5+ A2) by Oriol Baró and Jordi Corominas, May 2007. The two men carried a portaledge and haul bag, and they bivouacked five times during the ascent and once during the descent. They used no bolts. After this climb, Baró and Corominas completed a new route on the northeast face of Huascarán Sur, and Baró, Corominas, and Enrique Muñoz climbed a new route on the south face of Nevado Copa. Details of these climbs in the Cordillera Blanca are found in the Climbs and Expeditions section.

A NOTE ABOUT THE AUTHOR:

Jordi Corominas was born in Barcelona in 1958, and lives in Benasque, a small town in the Pyrenees. He works as a mountain guide.

Translated from the Spanish by Adam French, with additional translation by Molly Loomis and Bean Bowers.

82 x 4,000

All of the Alps' highest peaks in a single winter season.

Tomaz Jakofcic climbing the Schreckhorn in the Bernese Oberland of Switzerland. Miha Valic and Jakofcic linked the Lauteraarhorn and Schreckhorn for one of Valic's more difficult days in the Alps. *Miha Valic*

Situated in the very center of Western civilization, the Alps are criss-crossed by roads, tunnels, lifts, ski trails, and passes. Despite all that, these mountains remain one of the rare places in Europe where we can still escape from our fast-paced everyday lives, appreciate the sun rising, and enjoy the silence and solitude—all the things we sorely miss in the urban jungle.

Besides being the refuge of the modern man, the Alps also are the most climbed mountains in the world, thus giving their name even to the activity itself: Alpine climbing. Good road connections, mountain huts, and excellent rescue services mean climbers can focus exclusively on what they enjoy most: climbing. All the logistical issues we have to deal with on other continents do not exist here. In the Alps, the climbing is always close.

This level of popularity also means that new challenges are hard to find. There are of course still demanding virgin ascents and repetitions of difficult ones, and lately there has been a boom of multiday enchainments. Other adventures include traversing the Alps on skis, climbing all the major faces in one season, and speed records on individual routes. Another such idea is to climb all Alpine peaks over 4,000 meters in a limited period of time.

In the summer of 1993, English climbers Martin Moran

Blaz Stres (left) and Miha Valic on the summit of Mont Blanc in mid-March, on the 81st day of Valic's campaign. On this day, Valic and Stres bagged five 4,000-meter peaks via the Brouillard Ridge. *Miha Valic*

and Simon Jenkins climbed 75 4,000-meter summits of their choice in 52 days. A year later the international mountaineering organization UIAA created an "official" list of the major peaks that surpass the 4,000-meter level. It includes 82 peaks and is based on the importance, individuality, altitude difference from neighboring peaks, and, to a point, the popularity of the individual summit. Eleven years later, in 2004, two French climbers, Patrick Berhault and Philippe Magnin, decided to try to climb all 82 peaks in 82 days. They began their project in the spring, but the tragic death of Patrick Berhault stopped their endeavor after 65 successfully climbed peaks. In the spring of 2006, Italian climbers Franz Nicolini and Michele Compagnoni tried their luck, but had to give up the marathon after 25 summits because of bad weather.

I had been thinking of a similar climbing challenge for a while. After researching different possibilities, I decided to try my luck in winter, a step forward from the other attempts, and from Moran and Jenkins' success in summer. I would try to make my project as simple as possible, with no support team. While thinking about all this, an autumn expedition I had planned to join in the Indian Himalaya was cancelled, and suddenly I was free to pursue my project that winter.

Several things had to be considered before I could embark. The most important was the schedule and the route: which peaks should be linked together, which were the fastest climbing routes, which summits could be climbed even in bad weather, avalanche risk, or right after snowfall—these were just some of the questions I had to answer. I was not familiar with most of the peaks, so climbing guidebooks became my best friends.

Another important consideration was money. Three months of living in France, Switzerland, and Italy meant a big financial burden. To cut down on costs, I bought a second-hand van and used it as my home. Only occasionally did I splurge on a hotel room to dry out and enjoy the full luxury of a bathroom. With some notable exceptions I did not manage to get any big sponsors for my project. I was surprised by the complete indifference of the majority of Slovenian companies that produce and sell climbing gear. In the end, the project could be carried out only with a great deal of help from acquaintances, my local alpine club, individual sponsors, and a large personal investment.

Finding a single climbing partner with enough experience and climbing skills, not to mention three months and lots of money to spare, was a lost cause from the start. I decided to carry

With little money to spare for more than three months in the Alps, Valic and his companions slept in a second-hand van. *Miha Valic*

out the project alone, despite the fact that having a companion would have made many things a lot easier. But I would not always be climbing alone—several friends offered their company, and together we laid out a schedule. Without their support in time and money, this project would have been doomed from the start.

All the little things to be sorted out meant that sometimes I could barely find the time for training. But a project of such scale of course requires extensive mountaineering experience, which I had been gathering since childhood. My first guides in the Alpine world were my parents and my scout group; later I began learning about climbing in the Alpine school, followed by 11 years as qualified Alpine climber, and lately as an internationally licensed mountain guide.

Right after Christmas the weather forecast looked promising and the conditions favorable, so Rok Blagus and I headed toward Courmayeur. The Aosta Valley route is always long and boring, and it seems to go on forever when you are driving on a three-lane motorway with a 20-year-old van that won't go faster than 100 kph, while you're trying to catch the last lift to Helbronner.

As my first tour I chose what looked to be the most technically demanding ascent, the traverse of the Aiguilles du Diable to the summit of Mont Blanc du Tacul. Thus, on the 27th of December I was standing on the top of the first peak on my list, Corne du Diable. With plastic boots on our feet and heavy bivouac gear on our back, we progressed slowly. The climbing was not easy either (grade five), and the descents quite exposed. The sun set behind Mont Blanc before four p.m., and we were forced to bivy on a snow ledge just under the summit of Pointe Médiane (our third peak over 4,000 meters that day) until eight the following morning. It was difficult to crawl out of the sleeping bag again and get back to the rock after such a long night. After two more aiguilles and a traverse of the snowed-up ridge, we were on the top of Mont Blanc du Tacul. We made a quick descent and managed to catch the last cable car from the Aiguille du Midi to Chamonix.

With our first climb over, the project was under way, and it set a routine that went on for the next three months. After every ascent and descent, I sat down to write a short description for my website, checked and cleaned my gear, checked the weather forecast I was receiving daily from Gregor Sluga, and decided on a plan for the next couple of days. I tried to eat and sleep as

Blaz Grapar near the top of the Aiguille du Jardin, a satellite of the Aiguille Verte, Mont Blanc Massif, France.
Miha Valic

Valic on the summit of Les Droites on April 7, the final day of his quest. *Blaz Grapar*

much as possible to get enough strength for the exhausting days in the mountains. Despite the warmest winter in recent years, freezing cold swept through the valleys at times. The temperatures hit record lows at the end of January, when even the village of Chamonix was shivering at 14 degrees (C) below freezing. On that day everything in my unheated van froze: water, milk, cans, pasta sauce, and even the dishwashing liquid.

The days in the mountains felt incredibly similar. Early-morning rising, melting the snow for breakfast and drinking water, a walk in the dark, the sunrise, then hiking or climbing for a whole day, followed by an evening routine of yet more snow melting, cooking dinner, drinking lots of liquids, and sleeping. Day in, day out. More important than the difficulty of the routes were the conditions, as even the easiest of the ascents suddenly became very demanding after heavy snow, or in fog or wind. In summer the standard routes to the more popular peaks over 4,000 meters are full of people, but in winter everything is different. All the mountain huts are unattended, the routes are more difficult because of the snow, the day is short, and the cold, strong winds and lack of human presence give these summits a feeling of being somewhere in the great mountain ranges of other continents.

In all, I did around 55 to 60 days of climbing. On non-climbing days, when the weather or conditions were too bad, I just waited, checking the weather forecast every 10 minutes and window shopping. Those were very long days.

None of the individual climbs I did could be listed as top Alpine ascents, although some of the ridge traverses were definitely challenging winter routes. Among those were especially the Aiguilles du Diable traverse, the Rochefort–Grandes Jorasses ridge traverse, the traverse of the Mischabel Group, the Schreckhorn-Lauteraarhorn ridge traverse, and the Brouillard Ridge of

Mont Blanc. But perhaps the most demanding, although nothing exceptional in a technical sense, was my ascent of the eastern ridge of the Weisshorn. Despite a favorable forecast, the weather suddenly changed for the worse, with snow falling all day. The snow gave way under my feet, and the rocks were covered with virgin powder. I had to cover 3,100 meters of altitude from my starting point. Upon my descent into the valley, I was completely wasted.

Ultimately, the most challenging part of the project was persevering with it until the end, finishing all 82 peaks, covering 60 kilometers of vertical distance, and holding on for 102 days. This was difficult in several ways: logistically, motivationally, physically, and, above all, mentally.

The weather was good at the beginning of winter, with great conditions, and I could follow my plan precisely. I managed to climb 46 peaks in the first 41 days, but then long spells of bad weather began. Despite doing my best to take advantage of any day with at least acceptable weather conditions, sometimes even stubbornly pushing up the hill in weather that usually would have kept me safely at home, I could only make it to the top of seven mountains between mid-February and mid-March. Luckily, the weather turned for the better at the end of winter, and I climbed 20 summits in nine days, thus at least partially catching up. By March 18, the planned deadline of my project, I had ticked 74 Alpine peaks in 82 days. I wasn't going to make it during the calendar winter, but I decided to finish my endeavor and climbed the remaining eight peaks by April 7, in a total of 102 days.

This project never would have been possible without great help from 15 friends climbing by my side (in order of participation): Rok Blagus, Alenka Klemencic (three times), Blaz Grapar (two times; also my webmaster), Luka Kronegger, Boris Lorencic, Gasper Rak, Tina DiBatista, Miha Lampreht, Matevz Kramer, Tadej Debevec, Vesna Niksic, Miha Macek, Blaz Stres, Klemen Gricar, and Tomaz Jakofcic.

I tried to summit all 82 peaks in 82 days, and I did not succeed, but instead did the last few peaks in calendar spring. Doing a continuous traverse in winter, when all the huts are closed, would of course be a step forward. But there are many other mountain ranges in the world, still waiting for traverses, where you can experience a complete lack of civilization. For me, these other ranges are waiting!

Summary:

Area: European Alps

Ascents: Miha Valic climbed all 82 of the "official" 4,000-meter peaks in the Alps, alone or with various partners, in 102 days, from December 27, 2006, through April 7, 2007.

Portions of this story previously appeared in the Spanish magazine *Desnivel.*

A Note about the Author:

Born in 1978, Miha Valic lives in Ljubljana, Slovenia, and works for the Slovenian Police Force's sports unit, and sometimes as a UIAGM mountain guide. In the last decade he has frequently joined international expeditions, establishing new routes in Bolivia, Nepal, and Pakistan. When he's not working or climbing, Valic dedicates much of his time to training his golden retriever, Uka, as a search and rescue dog.

LIGHTNING STRIKE

The first ascent of the north face of Arwa Tower in India.

STEPHAN SIEGRIST

Hauling loads toward advanced base camp below the north face of Arwa Tower (6,352m). The new route Lightning Strike climbs the face above the upper figure, starting with the obvious zigzagging cracks. The northern flank of Arwa Crest is to the left. *Visual Impact/Heinz Aemmer*

Mick Fowler and Steve Sustad were the first foreign mountaineers to see Arwa Tower, hidden between two lines of ridges above the remote Arwa Valley, in a restricted zone near India's border with China. Fowler's photos from the first ascent of the peak in 1999 made their way around the world, and the *American Alpine Journal* used one on its cover in 2000. I saw this photo in the climbing library of an American friend, and I was so fascinated by the beautifully formed mountain that I kept taking pictures of the journal's cover. However, attempting the peak would have to wait. I still had other projects in mind, and the cost of a permit in this military zone would have burst my budget at the time.

Finally the Indian authorities reduced the immense cost of the permit, and thus it became clear that the time had come to take on the challenge. In addition to Fowler and Sustad's route up the northwest face, a French expedition had climbed two new routes up Arwa Tower in 2002, on the south face and northwest buttress. Later that year, a Swiss expedition climbed a couloir left of the north face to the east ridge and then on to the summit. But the main north face was untouched.

The meticulous planning and preparation for our expedition took up a lot of time. Once the team was assembled, permits received, gear shipped, and the last bits and pieces cleared up, on April 28, 2007, we flew from Zürich to India. After several days on bumpy roads we reached Badrinath, and from there we and our porters carried our luggage to base camp at 4,350 meters, which we reached on May 5. Although we had a lot more information than Mick Fowler did, we still weren't even sure if this was the best place to start up the mountain.

In any case, first we had to deal with other problems. We were divided into two groups: a women's team made up of Ines Papert and Anita Kolar, who wanted to attempt the French route on the northwest buttress, and our group of Thomas Senf, Denis Burdet, and me, who had our eye on the compact granite of the unclimbed north face. Our first evening in base camp was not quiet. Anita was in the early stages of pulmonary edema, and her condition worsened so much that we decided to put her on heavy medication and transport her to a lower camp. We packed her into a large haul bag and pulled and carried her for six hours through the night, down to a military camp in Gastoli, which is empty in spring; here we spent the rest of the night. Thanks to the support of our accompanying film crew and a friend, we managed this exertion without getting altitude sickness ourselves. Moving lower worked wonders on Anita's condition, and she and Ines continued down to Mana and on to Josimath to recover.

However, we were not done with health issues. After we returned to base camp, all of us suffered from stomach problems. Denis was so sick that he had to stay put while Thomas and I went out to look for a suitable advanced base camp. After a few hours of searching for the right route, we reached a small pass that led us into the "Lost Valley" and finally gave us an unobstructed view of the mighty Arwa Tower. We both stood there gaping at the face, mouths wide open, like children who have received a much-wanted Christmas present. At the foot of the imposing north face, at 5,300 meters, we found a suitable place for our camp on a huge glacial table.

It was the 18th of May when we hauled the last gear to advanced base camp on skis and plastic sleds. It was backbreaking work, especially because we did not have any porters to help us. But we were eager to get started. We had studied the face and agreed on climbing possibilities and style, as well as the most logical and safest route: a zigzagging line through the compact granite, resembling a bolt of lightning. (The route was later christened Lightning Strike.) We would be somewhat protected from falling ice by overhanging rock, and we hoped to find good cracks.

Quickly, however, we discovered that nothing would come easily on this route. On the second rock pitch we had to wield a shovel to free the cracks of snow cornices that had been formed by strong winds under an overhang. This required seemingly endless work just to win a few meters. The cracks soon became so big that even our largest Camalot no longer fit. Thus on the third pitch we had to move onto the smooth, polished wall. Luckily we had packed our climbing shoes and some bolts, but we soon discovered that the rock features we'd studied in Fowler's pictures were unusable for free climbing. The compact, icy rock forced us into difficult

Thomas Senf belays Stephan Siegrist on the last pitch of the slabby lower half of the face. Ice-glazed rock made for slow progress, and the team averaged little more than two pitches a day. *Visual Impact/Denis Burdet*

and time-consuming aid. We felt like nanosurgeons on these icy slabs, working with birdbeaks instead of scalpels. Without "birdies," we would not have stood a chance of moving forward. We knew this north face would be a huge challenge, but not in our wildest dreams did we imagine we would have to fight so hard in the first few meters. We managed only two rope lengths on this day, not a lot on a 900-meter rock wall!

In Sanskrit Arwa means "horse," and this horse did not want to be tamed. On our second day on the wall it began to snow. At first it was only light flurries, but then it became stormy and the snow fell continuously. On the fourth day it was really blustery, and we could hardly set up our portaledge. That night small avalanches kept sliding down the wall. As I lay in the hammock underneath our portaledge, Thomas and Denis had to continually shake snow off the fly above us. The weight of the wet snow strained our little home, and the seams of the canopy began to tear. After a long night, we found ourselves encased in snow and ice, just like the face. Since it was still snowing continuously, we decided to rappel and fix our lead and haul ropes from our portaledge camp to the ground. We hoped to return in better conditions.

Over the next few days it snowed so heavily in base camp that the kitchen tent and three other tents collapsed under the weight. We tried to imagine what the face might look like! The weather improved on the 26th and so did our moods. Two days later we finally got back up to

Denis Burdet getting organized at Camp 2, above the 12th pitch of the route, after yet another snowstorm. *Visual Impact/Stephan Siegrist*

ABC, where we planned to spend the night before returning to the face in the early morning. Because of the new snow the climbing appeared unstable, but we hoped the morning would reveal to us how we should proceed. However, that evening Thomas shook with a high fever. This lean, tough figure who never complains had been quiet during the ascent, and we had not known he was ill. He did not want to ruin our chances. But we had no choice but to go back down to base camp.

With little time left on our permit, we would have to start soon if we wanted a chance at the summit. Although Thomas was stlll feeling ill, we returned to advanced base camp on May 30. That evening it began to snow again, but when we crawled out of our tents at midnight a wonderful full moon lit up the mountain. I knew our chance had come.

The morning sun warmed us as we reached the top of the ropes we had left. Above, the terrain remained demanding, and we hoped it would ease farther up. All day we struggled to reach a somewhat protected bivy site at around 6,000 meters, and in the last light of the day we set up our portaledge.

The next morning I was startled to hear Denis yell "merde!" He had been struck by a rock on the shoulder, but thankfully the straps of his backpack had absorbed much of the impact and no bones were broken. Still, he would have to rest in the portaledge all day. Too bad, I

Siegrist starts pitch 18 on the fourth day of the second attempt. *Visual Impact/Thomas Senf*

thought—it had been his turn to lead the next block! In spite of everything, this was our record day: Thomas and I managed four short rope lengths before evening.

On June 3 it snowed again nonstop. We used this break to recover. Fortunately, Denis' shoulder proved to be "just" bruised and Thomas, who was still getting over his cold, seemed to be convinced that if he gave his germs to me he would get better faster. We spent the day downing aspirin and antibiotics. The summit was still far off, even if it seemed to be dancing in front of our noses. We passed the time with our national card game, Jass, which helped distract us from the continuous questions: What would happen next? Have we got enough gas? When is it going to get easier? You can make yourself crazy with these questions.

During the day it was pleasantly warm, but the nights were uncomfortable. In the cold of the night, the urine bottle was coveted. Lying in my sleeping bag, I would call to Denis, "Tu peux me passer le piss bottle," and this precious container would be passed down to the lower floor. The contents may have smelled strange, but the bottle was very warm.

The portaledge had to be kept closed the whole night because of spindrift. As a result, the oxygen inside was reduced through our breathing and cooking; the lighter only spat small sparks at the cooker, and it took ages to get it going. The lack of oxygen also meant we suffered from headaches, and when the alarm went off at 4:30 a.m. we could not get rid of the feeling of fatigue. We felt like factory workers. Getting up was horrible, and it was always the same routine: cooking, eating, drinking, and then trying to force yourself into clothing, shoes, and harnesses. Each day Denis reminded us, "Pas toucher le tente!" If we touched the nylon tent a layer of ice that had built up overnight from our body vapor would fall on us like snow. Every evening we had the same thought: "Tomorrow is summit day!" And then, once again, it wasn't. The ramp system we'd seen in Fowler's pictures, which looked easy from below, proved to be rounded and covered with icy snow; we had to dig to find tiny cracks for protection, and we could only manage two rope lengths a day. We were so tired that it was hard to concentrate, and

Siegrist on the summit of Arwa Tower. The final passage was a "proper two-meter boulder problem." *Visual Impact/Denis Burdet*

we were dropping too much gear. Time, gas, and food were running out.

On the seventh of June the morning was extremely cold and accompanied by a lot of wind. We cut through a gap to the northwest face and then continued through deep snow to the western ridge, and then we were nearly there. The top was a proper two-meter boulder at 6,350 meters. "Allez! Allez!" We egged each other on like little kids. A few hard breaths and we each could take our turn on the summit—there was only space for one person at a time. After a week of utmost concentration, exertion, doubt, belief, joy, pain and hope, we sat on top in calm sunshine!

At four in the afternoon we began to rappel. We had to spend one more night in the portaledge, and then, at first light, we crawled out, packed everything up, and continued rappelling toward the foot of the wall, reaching advanced base camp early in the afternoon. Time was running out, and the porters were waiting below. Thus we continued down with all our gear to base camp, where we were received with beaming faces and a big summit cake. Five days later we were flying back to Switzerland, where it was already time to begin preparing for the next goal.

SUMMARY:

AREA: Garhwal Himalaya, India

ASCENT: Capsule-style first ascent of the north face of Arwa Tower (6,352m) via the route Lightning Strike (900m, VI M5 5.9 A3), by Denis Burdet, Thomas Senf, and Stephan Siegrist, May 31–June 8, 2007. Earlier in the expedition, the team climbed seven pitches over four days, leaving three ropes fixed for their final push.

A NOTE ABOUT THE AUTHOR:

Born in 1972, Stephan Siegrist works as a mountain guide and expedition climber. He has climbed new routes in Patagonia, on Thalay Sagar in India, and on the north face of the Eiger, not far from his home in Interlaken, Switzerland. His website is www.stephan-siegrist.ch.

Thomas Senf, Denis Burdet, and Stephan Siegrist (left to right) on the summit. *Visual Impact/Denis Burdet*

GROWING UP

On the south face of Half Dome, Yosemite.

DOUG ROBINSON

Half Dome's south face is a mile wide and 2,000 feet high. The routes near Growing Up: (1) Lost Again (5.10 A3+, Eric Kohl solo, 1992); (2) Growing Up (5.13a A0, Sean Jones et. al., 2007); (3) South Face (5.8 A3, Harding-Rowell, 1970); (4) Southern Belle (5.12d with 5.11X, Schultz-Shipley, 1987; FFA: Cosgrove-Schultz, 1988). Based on route lines by Clint Cummins. *Shawn Reeder*

Scaling an icon is tricky. You have to climb through legend to grasp the stone itself. It took me years to see beyond the in-your-face northwest wall of Yosemite's greatest icon, Half Dome. Sean Jones, though, is so over it he calls the northwest face "the dark side."

This is really Sean's story, his stellar new route. But I got deeply involved, maybe over my head. We had both noticed the potential, and been drawn to a new free climb. I set out to film Sean on it, and even before my film ran out of support, I had come under the spell of this bright wall and couldn't walk away. A lot of virtual ink has been spilled over this climb already, if you count more words than *War and Peace* on the internet (www.supertopo.com/climbing/thread.html?topic_id=566859). The controversy hinged on our decision to rap in from the summit to find a climbable line on the upper wall, and then to put in protection bolts from our rap line. Some climbers got very offended, since Yosemite has always had a staunchly ground-up tradition.

Here in the *American Alpine Journal* climbers usually write their own spray. Even though Sean led the climbing, I'll lay down a few words. For one thing, it gives me a chance to brag about my friend, since Sean flies under the radar in the Valley. Yet he has a remarkable eye for a good line, and more first ascents here (91) than anyone, ever. And I'd like to explain why we bent the Valley's traditional rules along our way up Half Dome's south face.

Over on the dark side, the Regular Northwest Face Route, even though streaked with black, still shines. In 1957 it became the first Grade VI in America. "Never had the slightest doubt we'd make it," Jerry Gallwas said last summer during a gathering to mark the fiftieth anniversary of that ascent. He and Don Wilson stood shoulder to shoulder with Royal Robbins at the Yosemite Lodge

Sean Jones, committed on the crux tips lieback moves on pitch 10, 5.13a. *Shawn Reeder*

celebration. Jerry showed off part of their secret: a rack of handmade hard-steel pitons. Fun-loving guys and robust, they have all moved on to big lives beyond climbing.

How many of us have romped up the Northwest Face in their footsteps? Maybe ten thousand. We're the lucky ones. Along the way came all the big-wall firsts. In-a-day: 1966. Solo: same year. All free: '76. And Dean Potter dropped our jaws by soloing with the rope coiled on his back in 2002. I got to join that parade in 1973 for the first hammerless ascent. At that time it was shocking to climb with just stoppers and hexes, but it's boringly normal now (with cams). Still, our first clean ascent slam-dunked a revolution. Environmental action has often been sparked by climbers. John Muir's impetus to make Yosemite a park is an outstanding example. The movement to preserve the rock by climbing clean was interesting because it appealed to climbers not so much as a moral imperative but as an intriguing challenge. It was just plain fun.

As for most of us, the NW Face was my first Grade VI. Always more of a free climber than a wall guy, I felt most proud of leading the Robbins Chimney, flaring, runout, and scary. The

Sean works thin face climbing that hopscotches the porcelain wall right above the lip of the great arch, pitch 15. *Shawn Reeder*

climbing itself is always more core than whatever gets done about protecting it. And free climbing already loomed as the future of our stony practice.

Come around into the southern light; the backside glows. It's a very different wall here. The south face is a mile wide, smooth, and blank. A few dikes crawl down but don't reach the ground. Two arches crack the mirror front and center, hook left and vanish into glass.

Warren Harding first attacked the main arch in 1966, but the eventual first ascent took five tries over half a decade, a trial even for Harding's legendary tenacity, and for the sorcerer's most eager apprentice, Galen Rowell. (Galen loved being "a former second of Warren Harding and Fred Beckey.") Rowell's beginner's camera caught Harding struggling to escape the arch out a double-overhanging corner, "his most strenuous lead" (*Vertical World of Yosemite*). Faced with undulating blankness above, Harding came up with the innovation of bat-hooking: balancing on a filed-down hook in a shallow drilled hole. On one of their attempts, the October surprise of a fierce snowstorm led to the first-ever big wall rescue, when Royal Robbins spun down out of the summit clouds with a hot thermos and a rope to help Harding and Rowell escape the iced-up face.

In the end their climb left a trail of drilled holes to the summit. Was big-wall climbing growing up or losing its innocence? The drill has, for half a century and more, been the hinge of doubt in climbing. Certainly there would be more drilling, and more ropes from above.

The bright wall's big promise was still to come, because this wall's potential is in free climbing, as one generation's blank face becomes a featured playground for the next. It was well into the 1980s before free climbing made serious inroads onto the main south face. Autobahn (5.11+R, Charles Cole, John Middendorf, and Rusty Reno, 1985) was the opening move. Like the half-dozen climbs that soon followed, it was a bold statement on exceptional stone.

"Playground," however, turned out to be far too optimistic. Every one of the new free routes proved hard, sketchy, and serious—R rated at least. Even now they are rarely repeated. Crowning the development, Karma, and the queen of the south face lines, Southern Belle, both crossed the final frontier of boldness to become X-rated. Karma (Jim Campbell, Dave Schultz, and Ken Yager, 1986) has not attracted a second attempt, and the trickle of interest in Southern Belle (established in 1987 by Dave Schultz and Walt Shipley, freed by Schultz and Scott Cosgrove in 1988) has only built its fearsome reputation.

By the time Sean stepped up to the south face in 2007, a deathly calm had settled over the wall; free climbing on it had essentially stopped in 1994. Here was one of the biggest and most beautiful stretches of stone in all of the Valley, and it was just sitting there, ignored. Sure it was a long approach walk, and half hidden. But "out of sight, out of mind" was not the main reason for the quiet. Blame it on the runouts. You could say that the story of free climbing on the backside of Half Dome hinged not on the boldness of its first ascents, but on a July day in 1994, the day Hank Caylor took his sick fall. He dropped 70–80 feet off Southern Belle's eighth pitch. Such a long fall might be okay on steeper rock. Chris Sharma, for instance, has taken many plummets that long on his limestone cave project out in the Mojave. But he falls into space. Even El Cap is steep enough for clean drops. But this face is only 75 degrees. That's pretty stout for smearing, but hideously slabby to fall on. Somewhere on his descent Hank's foot caught on the wall and stopped. When his leg kept going, something had to give. Other foot, other leg too. Imagine rapping out of there on your knees, dangling ankles that crackled. He touched the ground gingerly and started to crawl.

Had boldness on the south face crossed a line and become plain stupid? Both the guys who put up Karma say there is no way they would ever go back. Dave Schultz, forging the FA of Southern Belle with Walt Shipley, led that infamous runout eighth pitch. Returning to free it with Scott Cosgrove, he didn't want that lead again. Cosgrove stepped up to his proudest lead, but says he'd never go back. John Bachar and Peter Croft both turned around below that point. The Belle waited 18 years for a successful second ascent, by Leo Houlding and Dean Potter. Potter later told me he had been scared. Certainly no offense to any of them, then, if some of us find it a waste of a big swath of lovely stone. Maybe there's another way….

Boldness is something I've always admired and often pushed. Just the other day in Bishop I heard that someone had backed off one of my runout leads from 1970, Smokestack on the Wheeler Crest. Sean, too, had put up a 5.11 slab route with a scrape-off-all-your-skin, 100-foot runout—on a slab across the San Joaquin River from Balloon Dome. But then he thought better of what he'd done, and he went back to retro-drill a few more bolts onto his route for the benefit of future climbers.

But we're getting ahead of the story here, talking about the golden headwall high on the south face. Lets return to the ground, back to early spring 2007, crunching over a ribbon of snow along the base of the wall. Back to Sean's vision of an all-new, all-free line up the south face. Back to searching for a first step up onto the Dome. It wasn't obvious where to start. First try, he got 60 feet up slabs and then shut down. Sean's second try freed five beautiful pitches up Harding and Rowell's classic aid line before hitting a pitch that was grainy and way harder—if it could be freed at all.

Pause to glance at the guidebook. A route line on a photo turns out to be misplaced. Walk in under that main arch. It's huge in there, and complex with three major crack systems.

Southern Belle starts up the right one. The central cracks are the original South Face Route. The left system, in spite of being fingered by the misplaced ink, was unclimbed. What a gift. Sean headed up that line of stark and wonderful cracks, where the giant arch meets the main wall of the Dome.

The climbing was as clean as it gets. No munge, no grass, no grit. Just polished, flinty, square-cut corners that gradually leaned left, pressing harder on his right shoulder the higher he went. This was the business; the climbing seemed to run about 5.12 on every pitch. Finally, with the crack closing down to a tips layback, the corner leaning terminally outward at its arched top, and the slab dropping oddly away underfoot, the route cruxed on its tenth pitch at 5.13a.

With the arch now a looming overhang and the crack pinched out, serendipity struck. A few feet down an easy ramp led to a dike. The dike was burly at 5.11+, but kept going for two pitches (with a spot of A0), clear out past the end of the arch. Three months into his south face project, Sean was finally poised on the brink of the golden headwall. This was both a celebration and a problem.

Spending so long up there, Sean ran through many loyal partners. Robbie Borchard, Jake Jones, and Ben Montoya all worked hard on the wall before being recalled to their lives below. I had my own problems. By the time summer rolled around my movie project had fizzled and tendonitis in an elbow reduced my wall time to drill-monkey status. Now we were squarely confronted, not only by the headwall itself, its stone scalloped into shallow dishes rather than edges, but by the beyond-bold climbing ethos that held a stranglehold on the entire south face.

Our next move has been debated hotly and endlessly, in Yosemite and on the Web. Partly because Half Dome is an icon, and its history matters. Partly because we were up-front about what we'd done. But ropes have been dropping in from above on Valley walls for decades, especially on El Cap ever since the free-climbing gold rush began there in the 1990s. Coming in from above is a handy tactic, after all, for spying on free climbing potential, and maybe for slipping in some pro that would be useful later. In many ways, Growing Up just became a lightning rod for a lot of half-hidden behavior that had actually been skulking around our beloved gulch for decades. We poked at the campfire, squirmed in our beach chairs, popped another set of beers, and dove back into discussing our thorny predicament. First of all, we didn't have a clue which direction to climb. Crack systems lead you clearly, but hard slabs confuse, because sometimes you can't see the next move even when it's in front of your face. We had already been confronted by the tendency of this wall to blank out, beginning with Sean's first foray off the ground. By now we had seen it so often we were starting to call it "the fortress effect." So we hesitated to simply forge out onto the upper slabs, which risked putting up a route that blanked out in a sea of porcelain: bolts to nowhere.

If you could even get in a bolt. As slab climbing goes, this wall is way steep and way slippery. It's hard to find a stance to drill from, and even hook placements to aid the drilling (hooks have been considered acceptable style ever since the Bachar-Yerian in Tuolumne) were rare on this scalloped terrain lacking in edges. All this had already been highlighted by the existing routes—and by how few routes actually existed.

We flatly rejected putting up another near-death runout like the other routes on the wall to date. That's a dead end. With no one willing to accept such a mortal gauntlet, climbing on this great wall would continue to wither away to nothing. Sean had a better idea, one that has opened the beauty of the south face to be climbed a little more often, as it deserves. But it would

High on the golden headwall, Sean enjoys easier climbing with killer views of Little Yosemite Valley and the Clark Range. *Shawn Reeder*

require a change in ethos, an evolution in style, which is a bitter pill in a Valley steeped in tradition. Including a thousand feet of it, freshly climbed beneath our heels.

Finally, we sighed, loaded our packs with fixed rope, hiked to the top, and dropped in to find the line, and then to drill the bolts. And what a sweet line we found! At times there were barely a scattering of holds weaving through the porcelain. Especially traversing right, above the lip of the arch, where sometimes a divot broken out of mirrored polish formed the tenuous line onward. That stretch came in at 5.11c. Even so, it demanded another 60 feet of A0. We were thankful that we explored, because it saved us from bolting our original vision of where the route would go, one that fizzled out after two pitches. That would have left the pollution of a line of bolts to nowhere.

On a wall loaded with dikes, we found only one on this upper slab, but it's such a beauty we started calling that pitch the "Mini-Snake Dike." It was surprisingly moderate at 5.10c. The climbing stayed consistently good, and consistently hard with sustained 5.10 and 5.11, leading to a 5.11d move that turned out to be the crux of the upper slabs. There's more noticeable texture up high, but it's hard to grasp, and would have been daunting to try to drill from stances.

Sarah Watson became Sean's final partner on the route. Sarah had only been climbing two years, but the former gymnast went hard-core desert rat and hung out for weeks at a time in Indian Creek, honing her jamming skills. Her first day on Half Dome, Sarah led hard 5.11 pitches down under the arch. Then a sprained ankle confined her to couch surfing while Sean

Sarah Watson romps up the Mini Snake Dike pitch, 5.10c. This 200-foot dike was the only clear feature on the thousand-foot upper headwall. *Shawn Reeder*

and I hand-drilled on the upper wall. But with the ankle fully taped, she joined Sean for the final send on July 28.

This Valley has a staunch trad history. I like that, have loudly upheld it, and contributed my share. But it's also a tradition that has been breached many times over recent decades, first by sport climbs on short cliffs, and lately on nearly every newly freed line on El Cap Done, but not much talked about. Somehow, by just plainly saying what we were up to, we became the whipping boys for shadowy behavior by most of the leading activists. Suddenly I went from the father of clean climbing to an evil rap-bolter. I don't mind drawing the heat, but a lot of folks see only black and white. Growing Up is not an ideological repudiation of ground-up style, not open season to grid-bolt the Valley. Rather, it came from listening to the stone itself, taking a cue from the can't-stance-to-drill-and-can't-even-hook nature of this particular piece of terrain.

Have I mentioned that it's drop-dead gorgeous up there? And private? Even hanging out in the ponderosa forest at the base. A mile east of the south face, hundreds of people a day went up the cables on the east shoulder. Half a mile west they cue up for the Snake Dike on the west shoulder. On the south face, though, we didn't see a single visitor in four months of coming and going. Up on the wall there is a spread-eagle view of the high country. The rock is oh-so-clean. Squeaky clean. Slippery polished crystalline clean. It's a brilliant surface to be poised upon, and it had been locked away from the common enjoyment for too long.

I'm sorry to take up so much of this good community's time and attention talking about ropes from above and how bolts get placed. It distracts our attention from the climb itself, which in the end is what really matters. This whole dispute over how bolts are placed is badly skewed, as if the experience of the first ascent party matters more than how it feels for the thousands who come along after. But Sean and I would rather focus on these people, the ones who will actually climb the route. As an example, take the proud and wonderful Snake Dike around the corner. There is no counting how many people have romped up its unlikely dike, generously littered with holds, which offers the only reasonable climbing on the face—come to think of it, it's the only popularly accessible free climbing on the entire monolith of Half Dome. Surely hundreds of thousands of us have climbed it. My life is richer for having climbed Snake Dike, and I've spewed about how cool the moves are to hundreds of people. Does it really matter how it was for those guys who put up this route back in the Iron Age? Growing Up opens a similar experience to a lot of climbers. Sure, it's far harder, but times change. Evolution happens.

I get increasingly anti-elitist about climbing. It is such a profound experience—changing my life over and over—that I believe more climbers climbing more will help tilt our troubled planet in a better direction. In that context, a bit of crowding on occasional routes is hardly worth whining about. We're not going to have a planet to quibble about saving unless a few more people start having the experiences that motivate us to love this fragile skim of life cling-ing to our stony sphere, and to help preserve it. Maybe this is a way for climbing to actually become less of a selfish, elitist pastime. Not that selfish is bad. It's actually essential. The pursuit of such intense personal experience is at the heart of our solitary transformations. And only by such growing up as individuals can we come together into a more profound environmental force.

Growing Up: the line speaks for itself. Go climb it. And then, if you feel slighted, tell us it's not worth it. Sean calls this the finest climb he's ever established. I think even among the modern standards being forged on El Cap, this is Yosemite's climb of the year. Now it's your turn. Climb it if you can, or even rap in from above to sample some of the final slabs. The climbing up there is not like anything else in the Valley or in Tuolumne. It's hard, beautiful stone. And it's accessible: runout beyond sport climbing but definitely not a death route. In the end, bucking tradition seemed worth it to us. But the resulting line is what matters. The route belongs to you now. You decide. As Dylan Thomas said, "The function of posterity is to look after itself." The matter is out of our hands.

SUMMARY

AREA: California, Yosemite Valley.

ASCENT: Half Dome, south face, Growing Up (21 pitches, VI, 5.13a, A0). Sean Jones, Rob-bie Borchard, Jake Jones, Ben Montoya, Sarah Watson, April–July, 2007.

A NOTE ABOUT THE AUTHOR:

Doug Robinson has seen plenty of revolutions in 50 years of climbing. Called the father of clean climbing, he also assisted Yvon Chouinard's ice climbing revolution, and co-wrote Climbing Ice. *His route Dark Star is the longest alpine climb in the Sierra. He was the founding president of the Amer-ican Mountain Guides Association, and he likes to challenge clients. Doug's book* A Night on the Ground, A Day in the Open *has been called "John Muir meets Jack Kerouac," and his video* Moving Over Stone *became the best-selling "rock video" of all time. Doug's Half Dome movie still awaits funding.*

EMERGING FROM THE MISTS

The sublime alpine peaks of Sikkim, India.

BY ROGER PAYNE

The south face of Rathong, as seen from the north-northwest ridge of Koktang during Roger Payne and Julie-Ann Clyma's 2006 expedition. *Roger Payne*

The former Himalayan kingdom of Sikkim is one of the most varied, beautiful, and compact regions of the Himalayas. Now a state in the northeast corner of India, Sikkim pokes northward like a thumb jammed between Nepal and Bhutan, with Tibet to the north. From its western border it is a mere 70km to Sikkim's eastern border with Tibet and Bhutan.

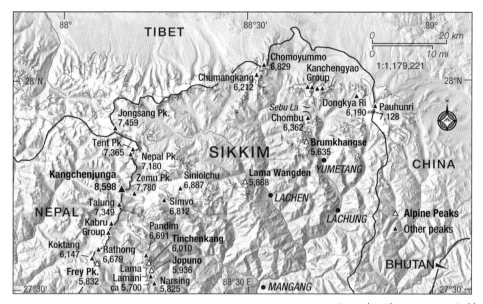

Martin Gamache, Alpine Mapping Guild

Trapped within this diminutive 7,096-square-kilometer landmass is perhaps the greatest vertical differential in the world. The high point is 8,598m, on the summit of Kangchenjunga, the third highest mountain in the world. The low point is less than 300m above sea level, where the Tista River leaves the steep tropical forests for the plains of West Bengal in the south, a region once legendary for malaria. Meanwhile, just over 100km to the north, drivable roads climb to more than 5,000m to reach the arid Tibetan Plateau. The culture and people of Sikkim are also diverse and extremely friendly. There can be few if any other places with such variety in altitude, climate, flora, and fauna in such a small and accessible region.

For climbers, Sikkim is a paradoxical paradise. My preconceptions about the difficulty of access to peaks and the high costs were completely overthrown when I first visited in October 2004—everything was much more accessible and easy to arrange than I had believed. This is why Julie-Ann Clyma and I have returned for three subsequent climbing trips and are currently planning another. There are countless rock walls, winter icefalls in high forests and mountain valleys, many interesting unclimbed 5-6,000m+ peaks, a clutch of virgin 7,000m peaks, and the world's longest unclimbed high-altitude ridge. A very welcome addition is new regulations for "Alpine Peaks," which means small teams can easily obtain permission and at modest cost. We had an input into these new and improved regulations, which is welcome evidence of a state government that is open-minded and committed to sustainable development in mountain regions.

The climbing paradox is that despite a long history of mountain exploration, Sikkim does not have a reliable up-to-date record of first ascents. Some successful ascents have not been clearly recorded, some ascents have been claimed but may not have been climbed, and some summits have been reached but not recorded at all. I have had the strange experience of reading in a Sikkim newspaper about someone's "first" ascent of a summit that I had previously climbed myself (and that as a third ascent). Given this unusual and somewhat confusing background, and all that is recorded in the *Himalayan Journal* and elsewhere, this article is not an attempt to clear and correct the historical record, but merely to highlight selected achievements and some of the excellent climbing opportunities that exist in Sikkim.

BACK IN THE MIST

The original inhabitants of Sikkim were the Lepchas, who were food gathering people speaking a language of uncertain origin. They worshipped the spirits of nature and mountain summits, and had an oral history. The first major in-migration of Tibetan and Bhutanese (Bhutia) people occurred during the fifteenth century. Then, toward the end of the nineteenth century, major migration from Nepal led to increased cultivation. The relatively easy-to-cross mountain passes between Sikkim and Tibet gave it great strategic significance during the British Indian period, and in 1817 Sikkim became a protectorate of Britain, a responsibility assumed by India in 1947. During the Sino-Indian border conflicts and the era of the Cold War, the passes were closed and turned into major tension points between India and China; both sides of the border were heavily militarized. In 1975 Sikkim became the 22nd State of India (the smallest except for Goa). Today, Sikkim is an integrated multicultural society, and India and China have given each other mutual recognition on the status of Sikkim and Tibet. Despite continued heavy military presence on the border, the Natu La—one of the main passes between Sikkim and Tibet—is now open for limited local trade and may soon open for tourism.

Sikkim's known climbing history begins in the British period. In two remarkable journeys, in 1848 and 1849 the legendary naturalist Sir Joseph Hooker climbed several 5,000m peaks, attempted some 6,000m peaks, and almost completed a circuit of Kangchenjunga, thus launching a "golden age" of mountain exploration in Sikkim that lasted almost a century. John Claude White, the Political Officer to Sikkim and later Bhutan (1887–1908), was another early seminal figure. White introduced protected status to vast areas of Himalayan forest, and created a remarkable personal collection of photographs of his travels on the northeast frontier and in Tibet. In 1899 came Douglas Freshfield's famous expedition around Kangchenjunga that included Vittorio and Erminio Sella, who also took some fine photographs, including of the striking Siniolchu—once vaunted as the most beautiful mountain in the world. And because the high passes of Sikkim comprised the eastern gateway to the Tibetan Plateau, Francis Younghusband crossed this way on his historic "Lhasa Mission" of 1904. So did all the early expeditions to the north side of Everest.

The most prolific early climber was Dr. Alexander Kellas, who made several visits to Sikkim between 1907 and 1921. He climbed many peaks, mostly with local companions, and in 1910 made ten ascents including Chomoyummo (6,829m) and Pauhunri (7,128m). Kellas wrote several important papers on the effects of altitude, but sadly, he wrote very little about his extensive climbing experiences. Kellas wondered if Everest could be climbed without supplementary oxygen, and because of his experience and knowledge, he was selected for the first Everest expedition in 1921. Unfortunately, after crossing from Sikkim to the Tibetan Plateau he became seriously unwell and died of a heart attack at Kampa Dzong.

The "golden age" of mountain exploration that began with Hooker in 1848 arguably reached its zenith on the peaks around the Zemu Glacier in the 1930s. Continuing the lightweight alpine-style approach that was established early on, in 1936 Paul Bauer, Adi Göttner, Karl Wien, and Günther Hep made the first ascent of Siniolchu (6,887m) and Simvo (6,812m). The era perhaps ended in 1939 with the ascents of Tent Peak (7,365m) and Nepal Peak (7,180m) by the Swiss-German party of E. Grob, H. Paidar, and L. Schmaderer. Other influential people during this pre-World War Two period were Marco Pallis, Freddy Spencer Chapman, G. O. Dyrenfurth, C.R. Cook, John Hunt, and Eric Shipton. When Himalayan mountaineering resumed after the interruption of the Second World War the spotlight was on a different style of climbing and the 8,000m peaks. In the case of Kangchenjunga, the focus turned to the Nepal side of the mountain.

ABOVE THE MISTS

Unlike some of the world's highest mountains, Kangchenjunga is easily visible from the lowlands and populated areas. It is an amazing sight from hill towns like Pelling and Darjeeling. Given its dominant size and shape, and its magnificent appearance in early morning and evening light, it is hardly surprising that it has long been an object of worship to locals and an inspiration to climbers. The remarkable first ascent in 1955 was from the Nepal side of the mountain. However, the Sikkim side had seen two determined attempts on the northeast spur in 1929 and 1931 by strong groups led by Paul Bauer. This dangerous and difficult route was eventually completed in 1977 by an Indian Army expedition led by the redoubtable Col. Narinder "Bull" Kumar, which was the second expedition to succeed in climbing Kangchenjunga.

The ongoing history of climbing on Kangchenjunga has mostly been on the Nepal side of

Kangchengjunga (8,598m) at sunrise. The third tallest mountain in the world is also Sikkim's highpoint and its western border, with Nepal. The line of shadow and light marks the south ridge (Prezelj and Stremfelj, 1991) the right-hand skyline is the formidable unclimbed east-southeast ridge and Zemu Peak (7,780m). *Roger Payne*

the mountain. This includes the remarkable alpine-style ascent of Kangchenjunga's south summit by the south ridge (which marks the border between Nepal and Sikkim), which was climbed in 1991 by Andrej Stremfelj and Marko Prezelj from Slovenia.

In 1991 the State Government of Sikkim classified the main, south, and west summits of Kangchenjunga as sacred, and banned the "scaling of the sacred peaks." This has been taken to mean that all climbing attempts on the Sikkim side of Kangchenjunga are prohibited. However, it may be possible to obtain permission from the Sikkim authorities to climb Kangchenjunga if the sacred peak restriction is respected and the actual summits remained untrod by climbers originating in Sikkim. If so, this would open up the possibility of a traverse of Kanchenjunga's formidable unclimbed east-southeast ridge, which includes Zemu Peak (7,780m). This is without doubt one of the major high-altitude mountaineering challenges.

IN THE WEST

South along the border from Kangchenjunga is Talung (7,349m) and at least three 7,000m summits in the Kabru group. In 1883 William Woodman Graham claimed an ascent of Kabru, but later this was dismissed and it was thought he was on some other mountain. Kabru North (7,338m) was climbed in 1935 (C.R. Cooke and G. Schoberth) and Talung from its Nepal side in 1964 (F. Lindner and T. Nindra). Kabru Dome (6,600m) and the North and South summits of Kabru are classified as sacred. However, this has not prevented recent ascents by Indian and foreign groups, although it is not clear if the groups concerned had the permission of the authorities in Sikkim.

Farther south again is Rathong (6,679m) and Koktang (6,147m), which offer interesting

Kangchengjunga (far right) climaxes a string of 7,000m peaks, including the Kabru group and 7,349m Talung, the highest of this collection. *Roger Payne*

The south face of Rathong (6,679m) rising above the East Rathong Glacier. The col at the head of the glacier was crossed for the first ascent by the southwest flank and west ridge. The southeast ridge drops from the summit toward the camera, and was attempted in 2006 by Clyma and Payne. *Roger Payne*

Frey Peak is the rocky summit on the left, while Koktang (6,147m) is the snow-clad high peak, whose true summit may still be virgin. *Roger Payne*

The west face of Narsing (5,825m) seen during the first ascent of Lama Lamani. Apparently the first ascent of Narsing was by Kellas in 1921 before he joined the Everest team in Darjeeling. Currently Narsing is designated a sacred peak, and thus off limits. *Roger Payne*

Along Sikkim's most popular trek, from the village of Yuksom, rise from left to right: Tinchenkang (6,010m)., Jopuno (5,936m), Lama Lamani (ca 5,700m), unknown, and Narsing (5,825m). *Roger Payne*

opportunities for alpine-style first ascents. Julie-Ann and I explored in this area in autumn 2006 when we climbed some adjacent 5,000m summits. According to the Alpine Club's on-line Himalayan Index, Koktang has been climbed twice (via the southwest face in 1982 and via the northeast face and north ridge in 1991), and Rathong has had two ascents (in 1964 and 1987 via the West Rathong Glacier and icefall). The steep mixed south face of Rathong looks interesting, but has some serac hazards, and the southeast ridge is a technical challenge we tried, but

During the third ascent (first in alpine style) of Tinchenkang, in 2005. Tinchenkang is designated an "Alpine Peak."
Roger Payne

Pandim (6,691m) has been attempted several times, but is currently designated sacred. However, the peak has multiple summits, and it may be possible to get permission to climb a lower highpoint. *Roger Payne*

we ran out of weather and time. Koktang has a long corniced summit ridge and, according to the great chronicler of Himalayan ascents Harish Kapadia, "the true high point, lying at the northernmost end, remains to be climbed." Having climbed quite a bit of new ground, we made some progress on the northwest-north ridge of Koktang, but deep cold snow and unstable cornices stopped us. This route would probably be a more reasonable undertaking in the pre-monsoon spring period.

Jopuno (5,936m) is designated an "Alpine Peak," which makes it easy and economical to get permission to climb. The only ascents have been by the right-hand skyline and the spur descending left of the summit. *Roger Payne*

Near the snout of the Rathong Glacier is the mountain base camp for the Himalayan Mountaineering Institute in Darjeeling. Groups from the HMI Darjeeling train on the glaciers and peaks thereabouts, including the technical Frey Peak (5,830m), which has had numerous ascents with the aid of fixed ropes. This is one of the peaks designated by the Government of Sikkim as an "Alpine Peak." In 2004 two Spanish climbers, Alain Anders and Garo Azuke, were active in this area and climbed two technical routes on peaks they referred to as Tieng Kg (ca 6,000m) and Phori (5,837m) (see p. 385, *AAJ 2004*).

Running parallel and to the east of the above peaks is the route of Sikkim's most popular trek: a five-day journey from the historic village of Yuksom to the Gocha La (Heaven's Gate). As you ascend, you get excellent views of Kangchenjunga, and to your east a group of fine-looking alpine-scale peaks. The first of real note is the technical-looking Narsing (5,825m), which is another "Sacred Peak." However, just north of this is Lama Lamani (ca 5,700m), Jopuno (5,936m), and Tinchenkang (6,010m), the latter two being "Alpine Peaks," for which it is easy to obtain permission. In spring 2005 with Sagar Rai and Kunzang Bhutia (friends of ours in the Sikkim Amateur Mountaineering Association), we made the first ascent of Lama Lamani, then made the third ascent (and first alpine-style ascent) of Tinchenkang (see p. 400, *AAJ 2006*). Jopuno has just had its 2nd ascent (Sam Gardner and team, spring 2008). These peaks offer good medium-grade alpine ascents, and are destined to become classic climbs of the Eastern Himalaya.

Farther north again is the dramatic peak of Pandim (6,691m), which attracted the attention of the early explorers, and more recently has had some confusingly reported attempts. Pandim has a superb-looking technical west ridge, but is another sacred summit. It is actually a group of summits, so perhaps in the future it may be possible to climb one of the lower peaks.

Indian mountaineers have been especially active in West Sikkim. Members of the Himalayan Club, instructors from the mountaineering institutes, and military groups have all made important climbs. Some ascents have been accurately documented in the *Himalayan*

Journal, the *AAJ*, and elsewhere, while others are less well recorded, and some were not recorded for security reasons. If Sikkim ever receives a definitive guidebook of climbs, it will be the
outcome of some very diligent research.

ALONG THE BORDER, NORTH AND EAST

North of Kangchenjunga is Jongsang (7,459m), which sits at the junction of the borders
between Nepal, Tibet, and Sikkim. Its first ascent came in 1930 via its north ridge, by G. O.
Dyrenfurth's international expedition to Kangchenjunga. The Sikkim-Tibet border follows the
watershed over high peaks and passes to Pauhunri (7,125m) (first ascent in 1910 by Kellas) in
Sikkim's northeast corner. Just south of Pauhunri are two virgin 7,000m summits, then a ridge of
unnamed 6,000m summits. Farther south again, the peaks become lower and lead to the historic
passes of Natu La (between Gangtok and Yatung in Tibet) and Jelep La (between Kalimpong
and Yatung).

Permission to access the peaks and passes along the Sikkim-Tibet border has been
extremely limited ever since the start of the Sino-Indian border conflict of 1962. However, you
can pick almost any mountain along the Sikkim-Tibet border and find an interesting climbing
objective. In September 2004, a strong team organized by the Indian Mountaineering Foundation (IMF) in New Delhi attempted the border peak of Chomoyummo (6,829m). The leader
was the highly respected and hugely experienced Dr. P. M. Das, a vice president of the IMF. The
attempt ended in tragedy when Das and four others were killed in an avalanche.

Peaks along the Sikkim-Tibet border, including Chumangkang (6,212) on the left and Chomoyummo (6,829m) on
the right, as seen from below the northeast ridge of Chombu. *Roger Payne*

At some stage access to the peaks on the Sikkim-Tibet border will become easier, which could launch a new "golden age" of first ascents and new routes in this part of the Himalaya. Meanwhile, just away from the border is a ring of peaks that are easier to access, and offer very interesting climbing potential from the valleys of Lachung and Lachen.

WITHIN THE BORDER

During World War Two, British climbers were able to take leave in the region of Lachung and Lachen, and members of the Himalayan Club including Trevor Braham explored the area. It is a fascinating journey up from the steep forested slopes of the Lachung Valley, to reach open plains typical of the Tibetan Plateau around Yume Samdong, and then cross the Sebu La down into the open part of the Lachen Valley, to then descend back south to steep valleys and forests. Such was the interest in making this journey that the Himalayan Club built huts on either side of the Sebu La (both of which are now in ruins).

After the Sino-Indian conflict broke out in 1962, this area was closed apart from military expeditions. Then in 1976 Harish Kapadia and Zerksis Boga obtained permission to do the Sebu La trek. Twenty years later, in 1996, an expedition led by Doug Scott (including Lindsay Griffin, Julian Freeman-Attwood, Skip Novak, Mark Bowen, Paul Crowther, Michael Clark, Col. Balwant Sandhu, and Suman Dubery) obtained permission for Gurudongmar (6,715m) and Chombu (6,362m).

Gurudongmar and the other peaks in the Kangchengo group have steep southern aspects;

Looking northeast from the open plains of Yume Samdong (4,624m), which is now a popular day trip by jeep from Lachung. The track at left is heading towards the Dongkya La (5,495m) above which is the technical-looking Dongkya Ri (6,190m). The other peaks are 6,233m, 6,346m, 6,517m, and 6,626m; concealed behind these is the border with Tibet and Pauhunri (7,125m). *Roger Payne*

Looking down toward Sebu Cho. At the extreme left is Yulhekang (6,429m), then Gurudongmar West (6,630m), Gurudongmar Main (6,715m), and Sanglapu (6,224m). These peaks in the Kangchengyao group have steep southern aspects, but are approached more easily from the north, where the ascents are shorter. *Roger Payne*

they are approached more easily from the north and have shorter ascents. While returning from the 1936 Everest expedition by crossing the Naku La, Shipton, Warren, Kempson, and Wigram made the first ascent of Gurudongmar. However, having read their account, I feel it is more likely that the summit they reached was Gurudongmar West (6,630m), which would make the first ascent of the main peak in 1980 (by the Assam Rifles led by Norbu Sherpa).

Chombu was described by Doug Scott as "the Matterhorn or the Shivling-like peak of Sikkim." It was explored in the 1940s and 50s by members of the Himalayan Club. Apparently,

Brumkhangshe (5,635m). This Alpine Peak has only one recorded route, on the right-hand skyline. *Roger Payne*

there was an attempt in 1961, but according to Harish Kapadia, "A definite ascent of this peak is yet to be established."

A large part of Scott's article "Exploration and Climbs in Northeast Sikkim" (p. 53, *Himalayan Journal*, 1997) concerns the difficulty, high cost, and uncertainty of obtaining permission for the peaks. The team members were enterprising in their explorations in what was then a high-security area, but somewhat thwarted by bad weather and heavy snow on their

The glacier camp on the descent from Brumkhangshe, looking across to Pauhunri (7,125m) in the distance and unclimbed peaks along the border with Tibet. *Julie-Ann Clyma*

Looking south toward Julie-Ann Clyma and a cloud inversion in the Lachung Valley from the northeast ridge of Chombu. Rising to the left from the crevassed area of the Rula Kang Glacier is the lower part of the southwest ridge of "Eagle Peak" (ca 5,540m). On the skyline to the right is Brumkhangshe (5,635m). *Roger Payne*

The east face of Chombu and the upper Rula Kang Glacier. *Roger Payne*

Roger Payne on a rock step on the excellent southwest ridge of "Eagle Peak" in 2007. *Julie-Ann Clyma*

efforts to climb Gurudongmar and Chombu. As an indication of how things have changed since 1996, the expedition's base camp at Yume Samgong (4,624m) is now a very popular day trip by jeep from Lachung. On one day in October 2007—a public holiday—93 tourist jeeps and one motorcycle registered with the last police post to drive up to Yume Samgong (or "Zero Point" as it is usually called locally).

Above Yumtang in the Lachung valley members of the Sikkim Amateur Mountaineering Association and groups from the Sonam Gyatso Mountaineering Institute have made a number of ascents. In the winter of 2004, the Lachung Valley experienced its first modern icefall climbing. Richard Durnan and friends from Colorado, Canada, and Austria climbed many easy-to-access routes up to 180 meters long and up to WI5 and M5 in difficulty (see p. 384, *AAJ 2004*). As Durnan wrote, "There is great potential for further development of ice climbing in this area."

Julie-Ann and I first tried to visit North Sikkim in 2006 to attempt Gurudongmar (6,715m), but we could not get all the necessary clearances. However, in the autumn of 2007, we got permission for Brumkhangshe (5,635m), which is one of the two "Alpine Peaks" in North Sikkim (the other being Lama Wangden, 5,868m, in the Lachen Valley).

With help from Sikkim Holidays in Gangtok and the Sikkim Amateur Mountaineering Association, we found the registration with police and army posts very straightforward, and the police and military personnel were friendly and helpful. We situated our base camp by the road close to the police post at Shiv Mandir (marked at 3,905m on the Swiss map of Sikkim Himalaya). We arrived in low cloud and rain, and hence it appeared a rather miserable spot. However, our moods improved as the weather lifted and the peaks and nearby cliffs revealed themselves.

The north ridge of Brumkhangshe turned out to be an easy and very good snow climb, which gave excellent views of many peaks of a similar altitude on both sides of the Lachen Valley. We explored the unnamed glacier to the north of Brumkhangshe, which has a number of peaks around it (which are presumably unclimbed). We also took a close look at Chombu, but found the east face high in objective danger and the northern aspects under too much "interesting" snow (the north ridge of Chombu could be a good route in the pre-monsoon season, and the west face offers a worthy challenge).

There are many peaks around the Rula Kang Glacier under Chombu's east face. Instructors from the Sonam Gyatso Mountaineering Institute have apparently climbed Pheling (ca 5,500m— easy snow climb), which is just south along the ridge from Chombu "East" (5,745m), which Doug Scott and team climbed in 1996 (crux of V with limited protection). Immediately east of Chombu's northeast ridge is what we called "Eagle Peak" (ca 5,540), which has a very good mixed southwest ridge and from the summit awesome views of the peaks in the Kangchengyao group.

INTO THE LIGHT

The future for mountaineering and climbing in Sikkim looks very promising. The State Government has made it easier for foreign visitors to get access to some interesting peaks that are

Evening light on Kangchengya (6,889m), Yulhekang (6,429m), Gurudongmar West (6,630m), and Gurodongmar (6,715m), as seen from a camp below the northeast ridge of Chombu. *Roger Payne*

away from the borders. Meanwhile, the border areas are becoming less sensitive, and hopefully in the future tourism and mountain recreation can resume there as well. The tourism service providers in the capitol Gangtok are friendly and reliable, and are being supported by the Ministry of Tourism and the Sikkim Amateur Mountaineering Association (SAMA). Together, they are expanding their capacity to provide services to international tourists and mountain recreationists, and at the same time promoting sustainable development in mountain regions. Hence, climbers and mountaineers in Sikkim are developing local skills and knowledge, helping with local guide training, and giving opportunities to young people in Sikkim to enjoy climbing and mountaineering. With limited resources, SAMA has been doing an excellent job.

In the past Sikkim has been enveloped in the mists of border tensions and access restrictions. Happily, the sublime mountains of Sikkim are now very definitely emerging from those mists, and the future looks bright.

The "Alpine Peaks" of Sikkim are:

West Sikkim
Frey Peak, 5,830m (Chaunrikiang valley)
Tinchenkang, 6,010m (Thansing valley)
Jopuno, 5,936m (Thansing valley)

North Sikkim
Lama Wangden, 5,868m (Lachen)
Brumkhangse, 5,635m (Yumthang)

The regulations for the Alpine Peaks of Sikkim are included in the Sikkim Government Gazetteer, No 83, 29 March 2006 (http://sikkim.gov.in/asp/Miscc/sikkim_govtgazettes/GAZ/GAZ2006/gaz2006.pdf; scroll to page 90). This is a very large file, but the Alpine Peaks section alone can be found at www.AmericanAlpineClub.org/AAJ.

A NOTE ABOUT THE AUTHOR:

Expedition reports for Julie-Ann Clyma and Roger Payne's trips to Sikkim can be found at http://www.rogerpayne.info/climbing.htm. Roger, 52, is a Brit with decades of new-routing experience in Asia, Europe, and one long new route in the Grand Canyon of Arizona. He and Julie-Ann live in Leysin, Switzerland, where they work as Alpine guides. They would like to thank all the organizations that supported their explorations in Sikkim, including the Government of Sikkim, Sikkim Amateur Mountaineering Association, Sikkim Holidays, British Mountaineering Council, Mount Everest Foundation, UK Sport, Beal, DMM, Julbo, Lyon Equipment, MACPAC, Outdoor Designs, Petzl Charlet, Rab, Terra Nova and The Mountain Boot Company.

Roger Payne and Julie-Ann Clyma on Rathong in 2006.

CLIMBS AND EXPEDITIONS
2008

Accounts from the various climbs and expeditions of the world are listed geographically from north to south and from west to east within the noted countries. We begin our coverage with the Contiguous United States and move to Alaska in order for the climbs in Alaska's Wrangell Mountains to segue into the St. Elias climbs in Canada.

We encourage all climbers to submit accounts of notable activity, especially long new routes (generally defined as U.S. commitment Grade IV—full-day climbs—or longer). Please submit reports as early as possible (see Submissions Guidelines at www.americanalpineclub.org/AAJ).

For conversions of meters to feet, multiply by 3.28; for feet to meters, multiply by 0.30.

Unless otherwise noted, all reports are from the 2007 calendar year.

CONTIGUOUS UNITED STATES

Washington

Washington, summary of activity. 2007 was not particularly rainy, but the Cascades never saw the usual settled periods in late winter or the typical eight or more weeks of summer sunshine. Even worse, dry weather invariably seemed to come midweek, frustrating for those of us who hold steady jobs. However, it was far from a shutout for Washington climbers.

In January Colin Haley and Mark Bunker traversed the three peaks of Mt. Index in a day, making remarkable time on a great outing that rarely sees repeats. The first new alpine accomplishments of the year were reported in April. Ski mountaineers, who in years past have made exciting first descents mid-winter, reported several new lines in the Olympic and Cascade mountains; they appear at www.nwmj.org. At the end of April, Haley and Dylan Johnson climbed an ice-and-mixed line on the northeast face of Mt. Stuart, linking various parts of existing routes with two new ice pitches. They called their line the Lara Kellogg Memorial Route (IV WI6 A0).

One leftover item from 2006: a previously unreported route put up by Chris Greyell and friends. Flight of the Falcon (III 5.10b or 5.9 A0) ascends the south face of Salish Peak, near Darrington on the west slope of the Cascades. The two longest new climbs in 2007 took place deep in the heart of the range. Blake Herrington and Dan Hilden made a mid-season traverse of the Gunsight Peaks, and Herrington and Sol Wertkin climbed the long east ridge of Goode Mountain in late August [both ascents reported below].

New routes closer to the road but still in alpine settings include Matt Alford and Darin Berdinka's rock route, the Northwest Arayette (III 5.9), on the northwest pillar of Mt. Shuksan. They climbed the route, which rises above the east edge of the White Salmon Glacier, in August. In September Wayne Wallace and Mike Layton established the Southwest Ridge (III 5.8) of Mt. Triumph.

The Southwest Ridge of Mt. Triumph. Inset: Layton psyching-up at base camp before the climb. *Mike Layton*

By far the greatest concentration of new route activity took place in and around Washington Pass. In June Larry Goldie and Scott Johnston climbed the North Buttress (III 5.9) of Varden Creek Spire, a satellite of Silver Star Mountain. Bryan Burdo teamed-up with Johnston to establish a new rock climb on the southeast face of South Early Winter Spire. Hitchhiker (IV 5.11 A0 [or 5.10 A1]) took three visits, spread over two months, from July to September. The route, which starts 100 yards right of Passenger, has one 5.9 pitch, six of 5.10, and two of 5.11. The pair equipped it with good belays, and it should attract repeat attention.

In late season a small cadre established four new crag climbs by nearby Cutthroat Creek. On the Snout, Blake Herrington and Jason Kilgore put up Deviated Septum (III 5.10b), and Kilgore and Eric Gratz climbed Smelling Salts (III 5.10). On Cutthroat Wall, Max Hasson and Herrington climbed The Perfect Crime (III, 5.9), and Herrington and Dan Hilden climbed Easy Getaway (III 5.10-).

Fall came early with a stormy October and huge early season snowfall that produced unstable conditions, leading to several avalanche fatalities in Washington. Climbers showed caution, and activity in the 2007-08 winter season was less than normal. Thanks are due the Northwest Weather and Avalanche Center (www.nwac.us) for their fine efforts at publicizing the danger and producing accurate hazard assessments.

Washington continues to see overall wilderness usage decrease, while certain destinations see distinct spikes. Part of this trend may be due to washed-out access roads (the 2003 floods) remaining closed, but climbers generally seem to be making fewer extended wilderness outings. Climbers' attention continues to be focused by "select" guidebooks and Internet discussions. For example, rangers report that the Terror Creek Basin in the Southern Pickets is seeing increased visitation, and the classic Ptarmigan Traverse remains popular, despite now requiring several miles of roadway hiking due to the 2003 washout of the Suiattle River road. Meanwhile, other areas are overlooked, and even the ever-popular Forbidden Peak area is seeing a slight decline in climber interest. Similarly, rangers at Mt. Rainier report that all but the most popular routes are largely neglected. Near Leavenworth climbers are flocking to Prusik Peak, Dragontail, and Mt. Stuart, while many surrounding objectives see little traffic.

Matt Perkins, *Northwest Mountaineering Journal, AAC*

The Gunsight Peaks. Gunrunner starts slightly down and left of the arrow, out of view, and climbs over the Northeast, North, Middle, and South peaks. *John Scurlock*

Gunsight Peaks Traverse, Gunrunner. Tales of white granite and striking crack systems on the Gunsight Peaks have intrigued climbers for years, but the two-day approach and notoriously unstable weather have kept the number of actual visits low. On July 9 Dan Hilden and I crossed onto the Chickamin Glacier at Blizzard-Gunsight Col and carefully traversed north on icy slopes beneath the four major peaks of the Gunsight group. At the ridge's northern end we began climbing a corner and face on clean granite. We followed the crest for seven pitches to a cavernous chimney below the summit of the misnamed Northeast Peak (which is actually NNW of the North and Middle Peaks). Dan led up under a large roof, which capped the chimney, and emerged out of a hidden escape hatch hole at the top. We continued along the crest, simul-climbing a couple of pitches and making one short pendulum (A1) on the North Peak, which can be easily avoided by future parties. From the namesake Gunsight Notch, we reached the Middle Peak via a 5.9 dihedral on the east side of the crest, above the Blue Glacier. As twilight faded, we picked up the pace. After topping a penultimate gendarme, Dan led the final pitches to the South Peak by moonlight. We did the rappel descent to the Blue Glacier in total darkness, with just enough starlight reflecting off the snow and white granite to display the gaping moat that we carefully avoided.

Gunrunner (IV 5.10 A1) covered mostly new ground; I think only four of the 18 pitches had been previously climbed. Since the north end of the ridge starts considerably lower, the route felt more upward than traversey, with 12 of the first 13 pitches being up pitches. The route gains approximately 1,500 vertical feet.

The day before Gunrunner, we did a three-pitch new route on the steep east face of South Gunsight Peak, Accidental Discharge (5.10), which varied from rad 5.10 hands to horrifyingly bad rock. The day after Gunrunner, we made the second ascent of Middle Gunsight's East Face (7 pitches, III 5.10d), which is an immaculate route, as good as it gets.

Photos: www.cascadeclimbers.com/forum/ubbthreads.php/ubb/showflat/Number/702676

BLAKE HERRINGTON

Megalodon Ridge, the long left-hand skyline rising to the summit of Goode Mountain. *Blake Herrington*

Goode Mountain, Megalodon (east) Ridge. After speaking with alpinists who had eyed or attempted Goode's east ridge, and after finding recent bail slings on an attempt myself, I couldn't get the climb out of my mind. I described the monster to Sol Wertkin, also from Bellingham, and we approached the peak from Rainy Pass on September 5. Sol dubbed the route "Megalodon Ridge," paying homage to a long-extinct sea-monster with curving fins and sharp teeth. After hiking nine miles on the Pacific Crest Trail and two more up the North Fork of Bridge Creek, we left the trail at an obvious clearing before Grizzly Creek and climbed to the toe of a clean-looking arête that descends northeast from the main ridge. We scrambled up a pitch of 5th-class at dusk and settled down for an exposed bivy on a bench below the technical climbing.

The next morning we began simul-climbing the arête. After two hours we surmounted the 8,200' tower where the arête joins the southeast extension of the ridge (labeled Memaloose Ridge on the USGS topo). We made a 50m rappel from a nut we placed near the top. From there Sol and I swapped leads and did running belays along the crest, encountering climbing up to 5.8. As we neared the headwall of the Southeast Peak, the rock steepened abruptly. The direct line on the crest yielded two pitches of 5.10 crack climbing and an exciting bit of stemming on tenuous blocks. From the Southeast Peak we skirted the icy moat to the final gendarmes. The crux came when we attempted to descend into Black Tooth Notch, the last major gap before the summit. Sol down-led an overhanging pitch of 5.10 above the Goode Glacier, which I had dismissed as an option that "would not go." Using beta that Sol shouted across, I reached his belay alcove, and after a few more pitches of easier climbing we reached the summit (IV+ 5.10). We bivied atop the peak that night and the next day descended to Park Creek and hiked back to our car, arriving thoroughly thrashed, yet satisfied.

Photos: www.cascadeclimbers.com/forum/ubbthreads.php/ubb/showflat/Number/721583

BLAKE HERRINGTON

California

YOSEMITE VALLEY

Half Dome, Growing Up. In July Sean Jones and Sarah Watson completed Growing Up (5.13a A0), a 21-pitch new route up the center of the largely overlooked south face of Half Dome. The route begins with the last unclimbed crack line in the Great Arch, and then face climbs the upper headwall. Jones worked the route for several months with various partners, including the prolific Doug Robinson, who made, among other great climbs, the historic first clean ascent of Half Dome's Northwest Face route in 1973. "I liken the climbing to Astroman meets Crest Jewel, on steroids," says Robinson. See his feature earlier in this *Journal*.

Yosemite National Park, various ascents. [Below we present some of the significant long-route news from 2007, compiled from a variety of different sources.] Tommy Caldwell continued his unprecedented Valley free-climbing accomplishments, starting at the end of May when he and his wife Beth Rodden made a team free (and second free overall) ascent of El Corazon (35 pitches, 5.13b), on El Capitan in a seven-day ground-up push. After a whopping two days of rest, Caldwell then freed Golden Gate (41 pitches, 5.13a) in 20 hours. Two falls ruined Caldwell's onsight attempt (onsight on the independent pitches, that is; the route shares some pitches with El Corazon), but his redpoint was still the route's first one-day free ascent. In October Caldwell made the long-awaited second free ascent, and first one-day free ascent, of the Direct Northwest Face route on Half Dome, originally freed by Todd Skinner over an extended period in 1992 and rated 5.13d. Caldwell linked two of the crux 88° slab pitches to bump up the difficulty to 5.14a.

After three years of work, during a seven-day push in May Rob Miller and Justen Sjong freed the 30-pitch Muir Wall on El Cap via a new five-pitch variation to the Shaft variation. Miller and Sjong's variation includes a new crux, at 5.13d.

El Cap's Freerider (37 pitches, 5.12d) continued its incredible popularity, seeing a record number of free ascents in 2007, including its first rope-solo free climb, by Canadian Stephane Perron over seven days in the spring.

The bold, talented youngster Alex Honnold free-soloed Astroman (10 pitches, 5.11c) and the North Face of the Rostrum (8 pitches, 5.11c) in a day in September, becoming the first to repeat Peter Croft's 1987 feat. On El Cap, Honnold made a one-day free ascent of Freerider and freed the Salathe (35 pitches, 5.13b/c).

On the speed-racer front, in October Alexander and Thomas Huber set a new record on El Cap's Nose route, coming in at a jaw-dropping 2:45:45, a little over three minutes faster than the now, like, totally slowpoke old record set by Yuji Hirayama and Hans Florine in 2002. A few days before their undisputed record, the Hubers ran up the route in a time so close to the then-existing record that they were unsure whether they'd set a new record, reportedly due to uncertainty over whether the stopwatch should stop at the final chain anchors or the large tree beyond, and whether it stops when the leader or the second reaches the aforementioned finish line. So they returned a few days later to huck another, faster lap. It now appears that, in fact, both of their ascents had broken the old record.

In addition to Growing Up, Sean Jones put up an eight-pitch 5.11c wide-crack line, called Laid to Rest, up the major corner system on the far right side of Half Dome's south face.

El Capitan, Dawn Direct. In September I embarked on another solo mission to climb new terrain on El Capitan. I had scoped this line on the southeast face since I climbed Mescalito in 2004, enabling me a good up-close look at the features. The route starts about 25m right of Mescalito, and has about 500m of new climbing.

I intended to connect to the Wall of Early Morning Light in a more direct and natural fashion than Warren Harding took in his controversial ascent of that route back in the day. His route took him and Dean Caldwell almost a month to establish, and they received harsh criticism for excessive use of bolts and rivets. The first half of their route contained the highest concentration of drilled placements, and wandered all over the lower part of the wall, making large traverses to the left to hit the main dihedral coming down from the Wino Tower ledge.

My intent was simple: to climb a 500m direct plumb line start to this dihedral, using far fewer bolts and rivets than they did. WEML has more than 300 bolts, with approximately 200 on the first half. In covering the same vertical gain (to just over halfway up the wall) on my direct-start route, I drilled only 66 holes

The route (Dawn Direct, VI 5.8 A4-) was difficult right off the ground, but most of the climb was steep, clean, and beautiful. The crux came at pitch seven, where a nice dihedral of 14 consecutive birdbeak and copperhead placements greeted me right off the belay. My line crossed Mescalito, Adrift, and the Reticent Wall on its direct path to WEML. I spent 16 days creating this line, my third solo FA on the Captain, and joined the Harding route for the upper 450m to the summit.

DAVE TURNER, *California, AAC*

Half Dome, Arcturus, first free ascent. In June Rob Pizem and I free-climbed (5.13) the 22-pitch Arcturus on the northwest face of Half Dome. Originally climbed by Dick Dorworth and Royal Robbins way back in 1970, the route had been forgotten by Yosemite climbers, who apparently suffer from long-hike-aphobia. The route had some loose rock here and there, but not more than I would expect from a grade VI wall. To quote Robbins' *AAJ 1971* report, "We placed some bolts, but I cannot remember how many." And so it goes. The route is mostly excellent and would make a nice alternative to the polished cracks of the regular route, but I reckon it will slide back into obscurity for another 40 years.

MICHAEL ANDERSON, *AAC*

SIERRA NEVADA

Incredible Hulk, Eye of the Storm. In August Brent Obinger and I completed a new free line on the Incredible Hulk. Jonny Copp and I had started this line in July 2006, but had had to turn back slightly below mid-height due to incipient seams and no bolt kit.

Amazingly, with all the activity on the Hulk in the last five years, this line is completely independent except for the first pitch and the ridge pitches.

Our route starts where the Moynier guide indicates, incorrectly, the start to Positive Vibrations. Our first pitch is the right-hand border of the triangular slab, and the standard way to start Positive Vibrations is on the left side of the triangular slab. The original (Bard-Harrington) Positive Vibes start is somewhat right of the triangular slab, and left of the red dihedral, on 3rd-class ledges. So, in essence our first pitch is shared, but with what, I'm not sure.

After a rope-stretching first pitch, the second pitch begins by climbing right out of the left-facing corner and traversing a short slab face to gain a hanging crack system. The third pitch climbs a short, bouldery corner and then steps left to gain an obvious hanging splitter. This is one of the route's cruxes. Pitch 4 deposits the climber on the "midway" ledge (which is really only at about one-third height). Here the route crosses Astrohulk and Tradewinds. A long easy ramp leads up and right to an obvious stance with a bolted anchor. From here it's hard to get lost, as the system is all alone in the middle of the broad west face, rising and gently traversing right to finish on the ridge approximately 80' left of the Red Dihedral.

Our route, Eye of the Storm (12 pitches, V 5.12) takes the longest line on the west face of the Hulk, and has quality, sustained climbing from bottom to top. True to the Hulk, this route climbs more like Yosemite Valley than the High Sierra. It has a great variety of corner and splitter climbing, with technical faces connecting features.

NILS DAVIS

Brent Obinger finishes the crux 8th pitch of Eye of the Storm. The pitch climbs the paralleling seam and dihedral below until joining the arching corner (which then dies out and requires a committing throw to finish). *Nils Davis*

Incredible Hulk, Solar Flare. I spotted the line from Blowhard, which takes the left edge of the west face. Just when the sun came 'round and kissed the face I saw a line of featured but very shallow corners, between the Polish Route and Sunspot, leading two-thirds of the way up the cliff. After that, a big question mark: maybe a bit of blankness into a corner that led left into Escape from Poland or, if I was lucky, the stunning orange arête that takes the left edge of Sunspot. This big reddish square is an anomaly on this vast white wall, like a creepy birthmark, and is the distinguishing feature of the Sunspot route, which takes the prominent dihedral up the birthmark's right side.

I started this route with Eli Stein, climbing a couple of pitches on a semi-rest day. I came back with Kevin Calder and again with Nils Davis, exploring higher. It really came together when Conrad Anker came out to play in late August. Jimmy Chin and Jimmy Surette also came as cameramen to make us feel important, or just self-conscious. Fresh from Everest, Conrad immediately showed that wallowing up snow hummocks is excellent training for fingery granite. After a couple of days of exploratory flailing Conrad and I climbed Solar Flare (V 5.12+) with storm clouds moving in, cameras rolling, and me climbing embarrassed in skin-tight long johns (the warmest pants I had).

Although this route follows disconnected corners, it consists mostly of face climbing, the first of its kind on the Hulk. About 60 feet up the first pitch of Sunspot—where that route cuts right—we climbed straight up on a crack and then a face for a couple of 5.10 pitches that turned to 5.11 as the wall steepened. Conrad led the fifth pitch, the first of the 5.12s, pitching off a few times on the delicate stemming corner, while I shivered in my puffy jacket at the belay. Higher, spicily runout stemming led to a bouldery traverse that brought us to a belay under the orange arête. This is the coolest pitch on the route: pimping and high-stepping up the edge— white granite on the left wall of the arête and orange on the right. After that, Conrad led one more 5.12 stemming pitch, just as the first rain fell, and we scooted up the 10th and last pitch to the ridgecrest. Rain mixed with sleet induced us to rationalize about how we'd done all the new climbing and that the remaining ridge climbing was easy (although we didn't become so delusional as to say that summits don't count), and we decided to rap. So, depending on how high your horse is, we succeeded on a great new route or wimped out when push came to shove. Either way, we cut it close. If we had taken the time for one more bowl of cereal at camp, we wouldn't have gotten that far. Next morning dawned beautiful, however, and all four of us succumbed to summit fever and chased each other up the classic Positive Vibes, putting whipped topping on top of an already great trip.

PETER CROFT, *AAC*

Lone Pine Peak, South Corner. On May 26–27 Miguel Carmona and I established the South Corner (V 5.9 C1) on Lone Pine Peak. Our route takes the most direct line to the area where all of the routes on this part of the south face (Direct South Face, Winter Route, Land of Little Rain, Summer Ridge, Windhorse, Pathways Through To Space) intersect, climbing 12 pitches before joining the Direct South Face (Beckey Route) for its last six pitches to the summit plateau. It is the obvious huge left-facing corner just left of the start of the gully of the Beckey Route and right of Pathways Through to Space. Our climb follows the corner to its top, joining the Beckey Route at a prominent pine tree below the Eye of the Needle.

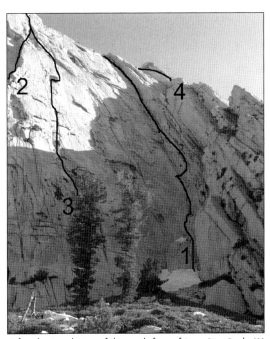

A foreshortened view of the south face of Lone Pine Peak: (1) South Corner (Carmona-LeMay, 2007). (2) Windhorse (Bindner-Holland, 1999). (3) Pathways Through to Space (Nelson-Quale, 2004). (4) Direct South Face (Beckey-Bjornstadt, 1970). *Joe LeMay*

Miguel and I made four trips in 2006 to see if the route would go, pushing up to pitch 9, where climbing difficulty and a lack of wide gear stopped us. Then in 2007 we made it to our high point, and spent the rest of the day aiding through the crux. The wall was near vertical there with a 6" wide, slightly overhanging corner crack. Aid gear was 2"x3" pieces of wood, cut on lead. We then retreated to a cave at the start of pitch 8, which provided a cramped bivy spot. The next morning, we climbed to pitch 12, where we joined the Beckey Route just below the Eye of the Needle and the Sandy Ledges. We rappelled from there, as we'd previously climbed the easier remaining six pitches of the Beckey Route that continue to the summit plateau.

The route starts on 3rd-class ledges that lead into the corner. Climb the corner to a sloping platform, and after a ropelength, traverse right into a big open chimney. Continue up on face holds and wide cracks to a platform with a pin. Up wide cracks, then up the corner. Continue to a foot-wide ledge. To the right of the ledge is the bivy cave where we spent a night. Climb the dirty corner over grass steps and brush to a belay, then up the brushy corner, then aid (C1) the corner (up to 9" wide) past a bolt, and continue on difficult terrain to a ledge. Continue up the brushy corner over sustained terrain to a platform and cave. Climb in the chimney, out past a bolt, then left out the roof to a big platform. An easy pitch leads to the tree at the intersection with the Beckey Route.

JOE LEMAY, *AAC*

Lone Pine Peak, Winter Chimney, first winter ascent. On March 11 Scott Nelson and I made the first winter ascent of the Winter Chimney (Carmona-LeMay, July 2005) on the south face of Lone Pine Peak (12,994'). The route starts up the classic Winter Route (Jones-Rowell, 1970) before branching off right up a steep east-facing corner system leading directly to the summit plateau. The Winter Chimney is somewhat of a Sierra oddity in winter and spring because it presents

The south face of Lone Pine Peak, showing the Winter Route (left) and Winter Chimney. *Charles Ince*

many pitches of excellent mixed climbing high on a 3,000' south face. The route features memorable chimneys, steep snow chutes, rock, and ice, culminating in a spectacular alpine experience.

We completed our ascent in a near 24-hour push from the stone house in the Tuttle Creek drainage, directly below the massive south face. A complicated approach and decent frame the climbing, which was relatively moderate: 5.7 M3 WI3. Under winter-like conditions the climb offers Grade V commitment, with few retreat options once you are established on the face.

CHARLES INCE

Scotty Nelson on pitch 4 of the Winter Chimney during the route's first winter ascent. *Charles Ince*

Idaho

Chockstone Peak, Beggars Can't Be Choosers. In mid-August, Elisif Harro and I completed a nine-pitch route, Beggars Can't Be Choosers (1,800', III+ 5.9+), up the north ridge to the west face of Chockstone Peak in the Sawtooth. The route features good rock and good protection. It begins at the lowest point of the granite dome that lays against Chockstone Peak, and the first five pitches of the route ascend this dome. From the top of the dome scramble around to the west face of the upper tower and the obvious ski-track hand cracks. Follow these up the west face to the summit.

NICK DOLECEK

Utah

Devil's Castle: (1) Horns of Satan (5.10c, Garrett-Smoot, 2003). (2) Black Streak (5.10b, Garrett-Garrett, 1988). (3) Evil Eye (5.11a, Henshaw-Smoot-Smoot, 2001). (4) Shadow of the Blade (5.10d, Cabe-Smoot, 2007). (5) Gothic Miller ([white line], 5.11c, Miller-Smoot, 2004). (6) Gothic Pillar (5.11b, Garrett-Smoot, 2002). (7) Portable Darkness (5.9+, Cabe-Scullion, 2007). *Brian Smoot*

Devil's Castle, new routes. Devil's Castle is the beautiful, rocky, majestic mountain above Albion Basin, located near Alta ski resort in the Wasatch Mountains. At nearly 11,000', the 700-800' north face remained unclimbed until 1988 when James and Franziska Garrett first ventured onto it. Until that time, the questionable rock and lack of clean, continuous crack systems deterred climbers from venturing onto the Rockies-like limestone. They began by following a prominent black streak on the lower half of the face. From a midway ledge, they encountered challenging route-finding and loose rock. They made their way up to the rocky summit in seven pitches, placing no bolts. Their route, the Black Streak (5.10), became popular. In 2001 I had a look at the half-mile-wide wall to the right. In two attempts Jonathan Smoot, Glen Henshaw, and I established the second route on the wall in eight pitches (5.11). We narrowly escaped disaster when hikers above started knocking down loose rocks.

Five more routes have since been done, two of them in 2007 (Shadow of the Blade, 5.10d, Brian Cabe and I; Portable Darkness, 5.9+, Cabe and Matt Scullion). Because of loose-rock danger, all of the routes have pitches that were retrofitted with bolts or were rappelled and drilled. Much cleaning has helped improve the quality of the climbing. These adventurous routes attract traditional climbers longing for cool summer temperatures, the beautiful alpine setting, and the mental challenge of multi-pitch route-finding. Pitches range from typical runout limestone face climbing to overhanging, bolt-protected pump fests. Quiche eaters need not apply. The easiest route, Portable Darkness, is 5.9+. All of the routes are well worth doing.

BRIAN SMOOT

The Colossus of Cannonville, first ascent, Nonplussed on Dust on Crust. This tower is located just outside Kodachrome Basin State Park, a few miles southeast of Bryce Canyon. Access is through the state park, where rock climbing is not allowed, but the tower itself is on BLM land. The rock is dusty shale, as soft as it can be and still be climbable with standard aid gear. It looks like early 1970s Yes record-cover album art rearing out of an overgrazed plain.

The first attempt, in January 2006 with Strappo Hughes, ended after two days and 220'. At a ledge 180' up, my old Bosch drilled belay bolt holes in the mud too fast; after finishing each hole, I let the drill run for longer in midair, so Strappo would assume the rock was more solid. Another 40' up we hit a "this is death, we can't go this way" shoulder that had looked really easy from the ground.

On a second visit with Strappo, later that spring, my three-day hangover prevented us from leaving the ground.

I returned with my wife, Fran Bagenal,

The Colossus of Cannonville, showing Nonplussed on Dust on Crust. *Crusher Bartlett*

for a romantic Thanksgiving getaway in November 2006. Fran belayed me for three days on the 200' first pitch, lying in one pile of dust while being pelted with rocks and ordered to send up more gear. Atop the pitch I fixed ropes from three six-inch-long bolts, and we left.

Chip Wilson and I returned in March and spent five days finishing the route, which we called Nonplussed on Dust on Crust (450', 4 pitches, A3). I don't think there was a single free move on it. The aid bolt count was 14 in the pitches, and belays are bolted, bringing the total to roughly 26 bolts. We called the tower The Colossus of Cannonville and reached the summit on March 9, after a total of 11 days of climbing spread over four visits to this little-explored area. A fuller account of this climb can be found here:

www.alpinist.com/doc/ALP19/newswire-bartlett-mud-tower-utah

STEVE "CRUSHER" BARTLETT, *AAC*

ZION NATIONAL PARK

The Bishoprics, first ascent. Over three days in April, without sleeping bags or a water filter-pump, David Everett and I did the first ascent of the Bishoprics, as labeled on the Zion National Park topographic map.

The Bishoprics are a group of formations in a remote setting that is difficult to reach. Reaching the Bishoprics is like reaching the Sun Dial or the Altar of Sacrifice; these formations all sit atop large plateaus. Once on these plateaus you walk to the base of the formations, where technical climbing begins—usually 1,000 feet or more of it to the summit. Successes lie not in climbing hard but in finding creative passages and strategizing. The difficulty lies more in the committing approaches and descents than the climbing.

Short of putting up a major aid line on the thousand-foot cliffs below the Bishoprics plateau, we took what appears to be the only way to reach them. We hiked the West Rim Trail from Angel's Landing and rappelled into the Phantom Valley. We then skirted the east side of the Inclined Temple, climbed out of a slot canyon, and traversed around to the Bishoprics. We got lost, really lost. Originally we were headed toward a different formation. On day two David thought we should look for a way out, but I convinced him that as long as we were there, we should climb the Bishoprics.

Once we reached the plateau, the climbing on the Bishropics was not difficult (south face, 5.5/5.6) but the white-cap sandstone is extremely rotten, like sand cakes on a beach. Protection was minimal and from small, tied-off, drought-stricken bushes—Zion ridge climbing at its best.

From the Bishoprics plateau, the only practical descent to terra firma is to follow the ridge southwest until it is not possible to traverse any farther, and then rappel into the valley of Coal Pits Wash. We did more than 1,200' of rappels, and we had not planned to come out the way we did. We hiked Coal Pits Wash for several miles to the highway and hitchhiked back to Springdale, a long way from where we started at Angel's Landing, inside the park.

DAN STIH

Abraham, the Connoisseur's Variation. In April, Dave Littman and I climbed the south face of Abraham in The Court of the Patriarchs. Dave had started planning during the preceding winter, and luck was on my side because I was his only available partner between February and April.

Abraham's south face is unforgettable, and I didn't want to miss the opportunity. We spent four days hauling loads and fixing ropes. Our route began in the gully on the east side of the south face. This gully is the starting point for the Radiator, the John Wilkes Booth Memorial

Buttress, and possibly the Lowe route. We followed the Radiator for a couple of loose gully pitches and then moved onto some more serious climbing on JWBMB. This entire adventure was characterized by wild, loose, and difficult climbing, and the JWBMB was no exception. Several cracks on the headwall appeared to be cam cracks, as seen from the ground through binoculars. Closer investigation revealed their true identity: butt cracks with beak seams in the back. Four pitches of thin, intricate climbing brought us to the top of the first headwall crack system. A couple of hooks, a bolt, and a pendulum brought us to virgin territory. We climbed two beautiful previously unclimbed pitches to reach our high camp on a huge ledge, where we rejoined JWBMB. From there the route completely changed character, thankfully allowing our pace to improve. The angle of the cliff kicked back, but we were leaving vertical, clean, thin splitters for choss-filled cracks and gullies. For the next 50' we were on JWBMB, and then I led out an unclimbed roof to join up with Dr. Thunder, a route climbed in 1999 or 2000. We followed Dr. Thunder for a pitch and a half to gain the exit chimney of the Lowe route. The Lowe boys climbed some extremely loose choss in their mountaineering boots. Dave and I were impressed. The top of the chimney is also the top of the vertical rock and the point where all routes intersect, climbing white slabs to the summit. On the second lead up the slabs I found a lone empty drilled angle hole where I was feeling the stress of runout Zion slab climbing, so I attempted to pound a stopper into the hole with my nut tool (it didn't really work). We had left the heavy iron gadgets down at the high camp, so the stopper in the hole was all I got. We summited late in the afternoon, finding no sign of human traffic but a couple of water-filled potholes in which we happily washed our dirty faces. We descended by reversing our route back to high camp without mishap. Dave and I spent one last night on the wall drinking cocktails and trying to consume the rest of our food. Over the previous four days we had successfully linked every known route on the mountain and added three new pitches. We climbed a total of 17 pitches and named our adventure The Connoisseur's Variation (VI 5.10 A3+).

BRYAN BIRD

Various first free ascents. In February Brian Smoot, Colby Wayment, and I free climbed The Locksmith Dihedral (IV, previously 5.11 C1), located on the wall to the left of the Watchman. This formation was dubbed "The Gatekeeper Wall" by Dave Jones, though locals had been calling it G-1 [Peak 6,482']. The first four pitches are excellent, and would make a great half-day outing at a very attainable difficulty of mostly 11+, with one short section of 12-. The upper pitches have sections of loose and/or sandy rock, which must be weighed against summit fever. The entire route can be rappelled with two ropes.

The very next day I walked up to the Apex Wall (erroneously also called the "Angelino Wall") with Eric Coleman to try Hello Mary Lou, which came highly recommended by its first ascensionist Dave Jones. Despite a valiant effort, the route did not succumb within our time frame. Eric then remained in town to woo a cute local, while I returned home to work and family. In March we freed the route (V 5.12+/13-). The first pitch is the technical crux, falling somewhere in the 12+ to 13- range, depending on finger size, ape index, and astronomical sign. Nevertheless, less quantifiable challenges await higher on the route. I learned to be cautious with recommendations from Jones.

A week later I returned to climb the Silmaril with Brian. Another Jones route, it is located on the Watchman and had been repeated a few times. Brian had spotted a promising three-pitch variation around an A2 pin crack, so we went for a free ascent. The variation climbs a major left-facing dihedral 100 feet left of the original start. I was nearly stymied by the first pitch, which recent rains had coated in a layer of fine sand, but we succeeded (V 5.12R) and found enjoyable 5.11 corners above. The key to the free ascent was a critical ledge that allowed us to regain the original route, and the Incredible Hand Crack on Steroids pitch six was a highlight.

MICHAEL ANDERSON, *AAC*

Arizona

Vermilion Cliffs, More Sand Than Stone. Climbing.com and Alpinist.com reported that, in March, Fitz Cahall, James Q Martin, and Albert Newman made the first free ascent of the 1,600-vertical-foot Tooth Rock in Arizona's remote Vermilion Cliffs. More Sand Than Stone (V 5.11) climbs a prominent 600' dihedral on the south-southwest face, before traversing left to an arête and eventually finishing on the final six pitches of the Lost Love route. We were unable to get a first-hand report, but hope to provide one in the future.

Montana

Mt. Siyeh, Upward Descent. Glacier National Park is home to many alpine faces, but there is one that stands above the rest: the north face of Mt. Siyeh. We knew little about this face; allegedly it had only been climbed once, back in the 70s by Dirty Sox Club members Terry Kennedy and Jim Kanzler. I then found out, though, that my friend Justin Woods climbed it with Ben Smith in 2005. Ryan Hokanson and I were on our summer "Tour de Crap," having just finished long limestone routes on Howse and Alberta in the Canadian Rockies, so we figured we were ready.

When we saw the face after the one-hour approach, it didn't appear any worse than others we'd climbed. In fact, it looked less sustained. Having no idea where the other routes were, Ryan and I decided on what appeared to be the most obvious line: a prominent spine on the left side of the face that went directly to the skyline.

On September 6 we started simul-soloing up the low-angle flanks, quickly finding that

Upward Descent on the towering pile of choss otherwise known as the north face of Mt. Siyeh. Three routes are known to exist on the face. *Ryan Hokanson*

Glacier's rock was indeed much worse than that of the routes we had done in the Canadian Rockies. Within a few hundred feet we roped up for a steep bulge, and kept simul-climbing. The climbing remained easy, but was too loose to safely free solo. Ropelengths disappeared below us, and we found ourselves part way up the headwall.

It was my lead. I began looking for a weakness through a crux, but every path proved to be some of the worst rock I had ever tried to climb. Eventually I passed the lead to Ryan. He repeatedly tried, but every time was turned back by terrifying rock quality. After hours of effort, we accepted defeat.

Knowing that our light rack and single rope were inadequate for rapping 2,500' the way we came, we searched for another way off. The only way seemed to be a mile-long ledge that led to a huge choss gully far away.

With one rappel and a short bit of downclimbing, Ryan and I made it to the ledge. The day was ending, so we made haste and started our mile-long traverse off the mountain. A few hundred meters of traversing to the east granted us a new view. Ryan spied what he thought was a weakness above. With the remaining rays of light, we scrambled to the base of the head wall and spent the night.

Out of water and with only dry food, we suffered a night of agony. Desperate for water, we racked up and began climbing. Immediately we knew this weakness would take us to the top of the face. The line was loose but manageable. After some 4th-class, then six or seven pitches of delicate 5.9, I chimneyed up a gash onto the summit ridge.

The summit was a short distance away, and melting snow shimmered in the sunlight. After much-needed water, Ryan and I were standing on the summit. (Upward Descent, 750m, V 5.9)

CHRIS GIBISCH

Wyoming

GRAND TETON NATIONAL PARK

Mt. Moran, South Buttress Houdini. In three days in October, Hans Johnstone and I fixed some protection and opened the beautiful corner system 15m right of South Buttress Right. The first two pitches are 5.11 classic corners with excellent protection and strenuous, cryptic, Houdini moves. We crossed South Buttress Right at its crux pitch and continued directly up and left. Two more quality pitches, including a nice 5.11 roof, led into a left-leaning weakness that took us all the way to the top of the South Buttress Drifter route, where we rappelled from its fixed anchors.

The most dangerous passage came on our late night return across Leigh Lake. A strong, windy tempest surfed our canoe east, down cold, foamy faces and through deep black troughs. We fought a final crossing to Boulder Island as waves broke over the bow, reaching String Lake in record time.

We recommended our route, South Buttress Houdini (V 5.11d), as a direct start to the South Buttress Right, but lots of Teton 5.10R traversing keeps us from recommending its top half 'till we straighten it out.

Also of note is the May FFA of Death Canyon's O-Mega Crack (III 5.12). O-Mega Crack has had several repeats from well-traveled climbers, who have compared it to the best granite classics of its grade.

GREG COLLINS, *AAC*

WIND RIVER MOUNTAINS

South Continental Tower, Continental Drifters. From the idyllic upper meadows of the Little Sandy Valley, the South Continental Tower consists of a lower west-facing wall separated from the freestanding summit pinnacle by a large talus bench. In 1994 Joe Kelsey and Paul Horton scaled the lower wall via the northwest arête, continued up the west ridge of the summit pinnacle, and were surprised to encounter ancient soft-iron pitons. Apparently, an unknown party bypassed the lower wall via a talus gully to the southwest and made the first ascent of the South Tower via the west ridge of the summit pinnacle.

On August 11 Nick Stayner and I established an excellent new route up the west face of the lower wall. We began a couple of hundred feet right of the northwest arête and linked dihedral systems for five pitches, before joining the northwest arête for the sixth pitch, which

The Continental Towers (north, main, south) from the Little Sandy Valley. (1) Aristeia (III 5.9R, Bowman-Stayner, 2001) and (2) North Ridge (II 5.8, Horton-Kelsey, 1994), with scrambling until the solid lines. (3) East Chimney (III 5.7 A2, Beckey-Stevenson, 1967) finishes from the southern notch, with most of the lower gully and climb hidden. (4) Northwest Arête (III 5.8, Horton-Kelsey, 1994) finishes on (6), where Horton and Kelsey found pre-Chouinard-era pitons in the final pitches (5.3 and 5.7) of the summit tower. This final section, above the broad shoulder, can be approached by scrambling up the descent gully (off-frame to the right), as the pair did two days later to retrieve part of their rack that they forgot on the summit. "The next morning, when we were racking for the main Tower [route (2)], we found the rack to be surprisingly skimpy," Kelsey said. (5) Continental Drifters (IV 5.11a, Bowman-Stayner, 2007). (6) Upper West Ridge (5.7, Unknown). *Nick Stayner*

reaches the talus bench. We then scaled the obvious crack cleaving the center of the south face of the summit pinnacle in a 70m pitch. Continental Drifters (IV 5.11a) provides 1,100' of stellar rock and engaging climbing. Unfortunately, the 5th pitch crux finger crack is rather gritty, and was aided on lead and freed on second. It awaits a free lead, and should clean up nicely if it receives a few more ascents.

TREVOR BOWMAN

Lost Eagle Pinnacle, Jenkins-Fleming Direct. On July 1 Patrick Fleming and I, both secret members of the notorious Wyoming Alpine Club, whined our way up a new route on the northwest face of Lost Eagle Pinnacle. Beginning at dawn we headed for a left-leaning, left-facing dihedral, found another one a few pitches up, moved back right, ascended a chimney choked with ice, then continued up the middle of the face to the summit. Descending the opposite side (south face), we spilled down five 200' raps to reach the top of a high gully, and walked west and then north down scree. We were back in time for dinner, with hair-raising stories of friable rock, freaky runouts, and a fridge-sized boulder that we pulled down on ourselves while rapping. Don't believe any of it. Gorgeous adventure: 13 pitches, 5.9R.

MARK JENKINS, *AAC*

The Jenkins-Fleming Direct on Lost Eagle Pinnacle. *Mark Jenkins*

Colorado

Grizzly Creek, Mudflap Girl and Mudwall. Unreported from 2005, in the Grizzly Creek drainage of Glenwood Canyon, Chris Kalous and I established Mudflap Girl (700', IV 5.10), the first new route on the wall since Layton Kor's explorations in the 1960s. Several climbers not present on the final ascent began work on the route in fall 2002. Mudflap Girl ascends the tall buttress on the north end of the Grizzly Creek Wall, mostly via gear-protected climbing, with some bolts and fixed pins. The hardest climbing is well protected, but there are runout sections and route-finding challenges throughout. Though still a big adventure, this is probably the most user-friendly route on the wall.

In April 2007 Tony Angelis and I completed an old Layton Kor project, Mudwall (600', IV 5.10+), in the same drainage. The line follows a cryptic path up the obvious, continuously overhanging sector, with few discernable features. It was attempted twice by Kor in the

Get there early, beat the crowds. The Grizzly Creek Wall, from left to right: Mudwall (2007), Culp-Kor (early '60s), Bear Paw (Dalke-Kor, mid '60s), Mudflap Girl (2005). *Jeff Achey*

Jeff Hollenbaugh lost in a sea of mud on an earlier attempt at Mudwall. *Jeff Achey*

mid-1960s. On the first attempt he and Bob LaGrange managed, by Kor's account, "75' of direct aid on terribly rotten rock." Kor returned with Huntley Ingalls, his partner for the first ascent of the Titan in Fisher Towers, and they managed only another 75', reaching, "a section of even worse rock, where we could find placements for neither pitons nor expansion bolts." Ingalls promptly declared the rock nothing "like the Dolomites," replaced Kor's proposed moniker "Cima Fantissima" with the unarguably apt "Mudwall," and refused to return. The line stood idle for 40 years until a spontaneous, rainy day assault on the appalling overhangs in June 2005 yielded an intriguing 60' of progress.

Despite the enthusiasm of that day, I was apparently the only one with enduring curiosity about the blocky overhanging expanses that continued above. I experienced the same difficulty Kor reported in finding partners, but recruited Tony Angelis, a talented ice climber and peak-bagger with some rock experience. My fondness for less-than-bullet stone, Angelis's near-complete naivete, and our mutual need for distraction from personal concerns proved a potent mix. In four early season visits in 2007 we pushed Kor's neglected brainchild to the top of the crag.

Memorable passages included the 30' of gently overhanging sand that had finally thwarted Kor and Ingalls, overcome in a flurry of desperate free-climbing (this section later cleaned up into 5.9+), handlebar-like rails that allowed the wildly overhanging White Dihedral to go all free on-sight, the tottering pillars and improbable blank bulges (and four-hour belay session) of the Wonder Wall, and the unexpected, uncalled-for, Birdbeak-protected crux on the "only vertical" last pitch. Excluding the challenges we encountered with layers of grit, mobile blocks, route finding, establishment of protection, and continuous anxiety that the entire escarpment might somehow collapse, most pitches failed to surpass mid-5.10 in difficulty, offering large holds, dramatic, exposed positions, and good belay ledges on which to recover.

We placed bolts only at belays, but with an eye toward posterity we equipped the route with a generous number of Dolomites-style soft-iron pitons (from a retired climber's collection that we had acquired in trade for tequila). We used some aid to establish many of the pitches, but on our final push we climbed the route all free. We did extensive cleaning during our several rappels and re-climbs of the pitches, and it would be a shame if this spectacular route was not recommendable to someone. Alas, imagination fails me as to whom.

JEFF ACHEY

Capitol Peak, the Crystal Dragon. In October, when fall storms lashed the high peaks of Colorado's Elk Range with almost daily fronts of freezing rain and snow, a thin ribbon of water ice breached the 800' lower granite buttress guarding the steep couloirs and rock bands of Capitol Peak's (14,130') north face. When the weather broke Kevin Dunnett and I rounded up our gear and a couple of mules to ease the approach, and headed in.

The Crystal Dragon on Capitol Peak. *Royal Laybourn*

We agreed that the opportunity to climb this type of ephemeral, almost mythical, line trumped all obligations. Five years and four attempts on this face, with a cast of strong and talented companions, had only whetted my desire. As I age and the years pass (47, 48, 49, 50…), a deep internal debate has questioned the strength of my desire, the strength of my arms, the depth of my endurance, and the intrinsic value of the rewards.

Even from our camp at the bottom of the face, we weren't sure there was enough ice. Scoping the line through our binoculars offered no encouragement. We headed off predawn to flounder through frozen boulders and snowfields up to the base of the face. The overlaps were loaded with icy daggers and narrow bands of water ice, with a constant shower of spindrift. Solid tool placements and excitement at finding quality ice allowed me to move quickly through the roofs without placing much gear. The first and second pitches held the thickest ice, averaging 3-4", although much better bonded than in previous years. Kevin's lead on the second pitch required crossing difficult vertical rock bands to connect isolated plaquettes of ice. His hanging

Kevin Dunnett leaving the bomber belay on pitch 4 of the Crystal Dragon. *Royal Laybourn*

belay stance in a narrow chimney offered no protection from falling ice or the pounding spindrift from the upper snowfields. On pitch three I delicately balanced up narrow seams of ice and vertical rock, fighting to create placements and calling on all the resources gained in over 30 years of ice climbing. Though I was immersed in waves of billowing spindrift, the intensity warmed me with euphoria. At another semi-hanging belay 600' up with only marginal gear, including the pick of my axe driven deep into a crack, the angle lessened. If we were to tread the summit ridge far above without a bivouac, we would have to move quickly. Kevin arrived, grinning and bloodied, and started with an exposed tension traverse to reach another ice runnel, less than a foot wide. A couple of barn-door moves and some strenuous pulls got him to good anchors and the top of the first buttress.

We climbed the remaining 1,800' to the summit ridge in three blocks, through steep unconsolidated powder snow alternating with desperate, marginally protected face climbing across blank rock. Loose, overhanging rock on the summit headwall and the burning daylight convinced us to do a series of rising leftward traverses to join the standard Knife-Edge route (northeast ridge) at the base of the summit pyramid.

As the sun slipped below the horizon, since we were tired but happy, we forewent the summit. Pleased with our success on what we called the Crystal Dragon (IV M7 WI5), we headed unroped down the Knife-Edge. Darkness fell as we soloed down the last technical moves. Hours of post-holing by headlamp through the steep boulder fields finally led us back to the tent around midnight.

ROYAL LAYBOURN

BLACK CANYON OF THE GUNNISON NATIONAL PARK

North Chasm View Wall, the Black Sheep. On April 22 Mike Pennings and I finished our long-term project on the western edge of the North Chasm View Wall. The route tackles an obvious dihedral system located 200 yards up the narrow, choss-capped gully between the Plunge Pillar formation and the "Pig Routes" buttress. Mike dubbed the route the Black Sheep in keeping with the farm theme for route names in the area. Although it felt good to have finally completed the route, 30' of pesky aid remained. Over the next five weeks I invested many days on this difficult section and finally succeeded in redpointing the line (IV 5.13b) on May 30. The climb tackles seven excellent pitches, and can be climbed at a high-quality and reasonable 5.12- A0. A good topo and further details can be found at the North Rim Ranger Station and in *Rock and Ice* #166.

JOSH WHARTON, *AAC*

North Chasm View Wall, Air Guitar. In May Jared Ogden and I redpointed Air Guitar (V 5.12+), a 17-pitch line on good rock up the middle of North Chasm View Wall. For several years we poked around before sorting out the line that begins right of the Diagonal and follows an obvious, clean, right-facing corner system to join High and Dry, for a couple of pitches, where it crosses the Diagonal. Our route then veers left on steep rock for several pitches, to join the last few pitches of Air City through the big roofs near the top.

The climb has some of the most memorable pitches in the Canyon, including the Great Roof for Dads, a 60' roof traverse that looks like 5.13+ but goes at 5.10, the pumpy, spicy High and Dry pitch off the Diagonal, the final Air City roof, Devils Tow-eresque corner cracks, and some Eldorado-quality face climbing on natural gear. It is mostly 5.11 and 5.12 and took us two days

North Chasm View Wall, home to more than a dozen routes, with the Black Sheep (left) and Air Guitar. *Topher Donahue*

for the redpoint. There are a few good ledges, but a one-day ascent would be a good time. The redpoint of Air Guitar was about the most fun I've ever had climbing.

TOPHER DONAHUE

South Chasm View Wall, Dry Rubbed. In May Mike Pennings and I dropped into the South Chasm View Wall after hunting for a cup of coffee and bacon in Montrose. We were fired up for a new line we had eyed from the north side over the years.

Considering our late start, we were happy to make it back to the rim by dusk. The route climbs about 1,200', taking a line to the right of the Kor-Dalke and to the left of the Falcon Wall. The most significant features are a series of tiered roofs that angle up and right, looking more like waves than 90° roofs. We encountered serious climbing up to 5.11+. We named the route Dry Rubbed after the brand of bacon we found. Warning: some loose rocks encountered.

JONATHAN COPP

The Northwest Face route on Apache Peak. *Dougald MacDonald*

ROCKY MOUNTAIN NATIONAL PARK

Apache Peak, Northwest Face; Shoshoni Peak, Mass Wasting. Indian Peaks guidebook author Gerry Roach describes the northwest face of 13,441' Apache Peak as "steep, broken, and uninteresting." Maybe so in summer, but in the spring, with lots of snow and some ice, it becomes an attractive alpine route. Greg Sievers and I made the probable first ascent of this face on June 3. From the closed gate on the Brainard Lake Road, east of the mountain, we rode mountain bikes to the Long Lake trailhead, then walked through snow to Isabelle Glacier. We climbed one of the southwest couloirs on Shoshoni Peak to reach the plateau west of Shoshoni, at about 12,800'. From there we headed northwest to a steep couloir and descended about 2,000 vertical feet to a camp at Triangle Lake, just east of Lone Eagle Peak. This took most of a day.

The next morning we followed the line of least resistance on Apache's main northwest face. We started with a 750' gully (containing the route's mixed and water-ice cruxes), then a pitch of steep rock (5.7). Easy mixed ground led to a long traverse to the right (south) to skirt a blank headwall. After turning a prominent see-through buttress, we climbed steep snow and easy ice bulges to rock ledges 100' below the summit. We measured 2,000 vertical feet from the start of roped climbing to the summit. We did 10 pitches with a 70m rope, plus 750' of simul-climbing: IV 5.7 WI3 M4+, with lots of 40° to 60° snow. In a snowstorm we downclimbed the steep Apache Couloir to the east to return to our cached snowshoes and eventually our bikes.

Harder mixed lines on Apache might come into condition in late spring or early fall, but the face is well-hidden, and aspirants will have to risk the long approach to see if anything is there.

During our approach to Apache, Sievers and I had spotted a steep rock line on Shoshoni Peak, and on August 19 we returned and climbed Mass Wasting (III 5.10b). This five-pitch route climbs the steep west face of the eastern of Shoshoni's two buttresses, right above the trail to Isabelle Glacier. Jeff Lowe once soloed a route on this buttress, somewhere to the right of our line.

DOUGALD MACDONALD, *AAC*

Alaska

ALASKA RANGE

Geographical note: While the well-known peaks in Denali National Park are often called "The Alaska Range," these peaks form just one part of the immense Alaska Range, which contains many significant subranges, including the Hayes and Delta ranges, and the Revelation, Kichatna, and Tordrillo Mountains.

HAYES RANGE

Special Olympics, south ridge. My wife Anna Liljedahl, Andy Stern, and I flew into the Hayes Range from the Denali Highway with Gracious Air on June 8. The short, relatively inexpensive flight landed us on a fish-filled pristine lake a day's hike from the Nenana Glacier. We made a barefoot base camp on lush tundra on the north bench of the Nenana Glacier. Our objectives were three: collect rocks for my Ph.D. dissertation on the tectonic history of the Alaska Range, climb as many untouched granite peaks as time and food allowed, and avoid the permit hassle and buzz that Denali Park offers to the west. The granite was a tad shattered, but Andy and I climbed peak 8,060' (the glacier is at 4,000') via the south ridge (4th-class mixed, 75° slush, knife-edge straddling). We egotistically assume the peak hadn't been climbed before and named it Special Olympics (SO) in reference to both Andy and I having suffered life-changing injuries. Though an occasional tourist helicopter ruined one nap, I recommend the area for those looking for an alternative to the flash and dash of the central Alaska Range. The geology we did has actually caused a paradigm shift in Alaska geology, but, like climbing, the doing is more interesting than the telling.

JEFF APPLE BENOWITZ

DENALI NATIONAL PARK

Denali National Park and Preserve, summary. The 2007 climbing season began with the first solo winter ascent of Mt. Foraker, by the renowned Japanese climber Masatoshi Kuriaki. This "Wind Warrior" of the Alaska Range posted the only successful ascent of Foraker out of 21 attempts this season [reported in the *2007 AAJ*—Ed.].

We conducted 19 search and rescue missions, involving five fatalities, reminding us again how fragile life is in

Special Olympics peak, showing the south ridge route. *Jeff apple Benowitz*

the Alaska Range. These incidents involved climbing falls, crevasse falls, rappel failure, snow blindness, an avalanche, altitude sickness, and other medical problems. Along with numerous medical transports of patients from the 14,200' camp on Denali, the NPS-contracted Lama Helicopter, flown by pilot Jim Hood, performed two operational short-haul rescues this season in terrain outside our typical focus area, including a day-hiker on Mt. Healy near park head-quarters and a distressed hiker in Wrangell-St. Elias National Park.

Congratulations go to Denali Pro Award winners Heidi Kloos and Robert Durnell, guides for Mountain Trip International, for their selfless assistance to other climbers during a particu-larly grueling rescue mission.

The South District staff continued to investigate and penalize businesses offering unauthorized commercial services within the park, both in the aviation and mountain-guiding realms. This year, working with the United States Attorney's Office, we conducted two undercover investigations. One of these investigations led to the execution of a search warrant, and charges are pending in the case. The other investigation resulted in the cancellation of climbing permits for illegally guided clients. This past season the National Park Service cancelled over one hundred registrations for climbers involved—knowingly or unknowingly—with illegal businesses.

Quick Statistics—Mt. McKinley and Mt. Foraker:

Mt. McKinley: Average trip length: 16.8 days. Average trip length for groups that summited: 17.6 days. Busiest summit day: June 12, with 77 summits. Summit breakdown by month: June (379), May (177), July (15). Average age: 37. Women constituted 12% of all climbers.

Forty-five nations were represented on Mt. McKinley and Mt. Foraker, including U.S. (729 climbers), U.K. (64), Canada (50), Germany (39), and Spain (36).

McKinley was attempted by 1,218 climbers, with 47% reaching the summit; 1,099 attempted the West Buttress, with 47% summiting. Twenty-one climbers attempted Mt. Foraker, with only Masatoshi Kuriaki summiting.

The complete Mountaineering Summary can be found at www.nps.gov/dena/planyourvisit/summaryreports.htm

Summarized from the DENALI NATIONAL PARK & PRESERVE ANNUAL MOUNTAINEERING SUMMARY

Other notable ascents (in addition to individual reports below). British climbers Jon Bracey and Andy Houseman made the long-awaited second ascent of the French Route on Mt. Hunter's North Buttress in early May. Since the 1984 first ascent, the sustained and intimidating route had shut down many strong parties. Bracey and Houseman climbed the 6,000' vertical to the summit and descended the West Ridge, taking four days total.

On June 9 Pierre Darbellay and Raphael Slawinski climbed a new line to the summit ridge of Kahiltna Queen. Their Le Voyage au Bout de La Nuit (Journey to the End of the Night, 450m, WI4+ R) climbs a prominent gully immediately right of the West Face route.

In mid-June Colin Haley and Mark Westman made an impressively fast ascent (less than two days to the summit) of the difficult 7,800-vertical-foot Denali Diamond on Denali's steep southwest face. This was the route's fifth ascent.

On Denali in June the three south-facing couloirs in the black rock, which are obvious from the 17,200' camp on the West Buttress, descending from the North Peak, were skied for the first time, by a group that included Adam Clark, Greg Collins, Chris Davenport, Nick Davore, Clark Fines, and Kirsten Kremer.

The Fin, Fin Wall to summit ridge; Rogue Peak, first ascent, northeast face; Mantok 1, first ascent, All Talk Couloir. In early May on the northeast fork of the Yentna Glacier, Peter Doucette, Ben Gilmore, and Freddie Wilkinson climbed the remote and previously untouched south-facing Fin Wall (3,800', AK Grade 6, NEI 5+) on a ca 13,300' peak informally known as "The Fin," located along the Southwest Ridge of Mt. Foraker, about four horizontal miles southwest of Foraker's summit. The team climbed the impressive wall and retreated from the ridge at ca 12,900', approximately 400' below The Fin's summit. Reaching the face involved a long and

Mantok 1, showing the All Talk Couloir and descent. *Ben Gilmore*

The route climbed on the northeast face of Rogue Peak. *Ben Gilmore*

adventurous approach up the complex icefall in the right-hand fork at the head of the Yentna's northeast fork. They also made the first ascents of two peaks in the left-hand split of the Yentna's northeast fork: ca 8,900' "Rogue Peak" via the northeast face (3,500', M5, Doucette-Wilkinson), and ca 9,300' "Mantok 1" via the east-facing All Talk Couloir (3,500', M5, Doucette-Gilmore-Wilkinson). See Wilkinson's feature earlier in this *Journal*.

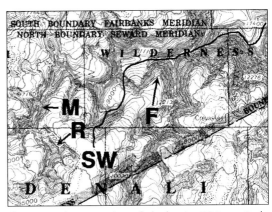

The Yentna Glacier's northeast fork, showing (R) Rogue Peak, (M) Mantok 1, (F) Fin Wall—see Freddie Wilkinson's feature earlier in this *Journal*. For reference, the Southwest Ridge of Mt. Foraker (SW) is also indicated. From Talkeetna D-3 and D-4 maps, courtesy *www.topozone.com*

The Throne, Swisser than Swiss Chocolate; Royal Tower, Got Lucky to summit slopes. Where in Alaska would two Swiss go to climb but Little Switzerland? On May 16 Lucas Iten and I landed on the Pika Glacier and quickly got to work. Most of the rock was still covered in snow, but we warmed up by repeating The Lost Marsupials (10 pitches, ca 5.8) on The Throne (7,390') in alpine boots. A few days later we donned our climbing shoes and climbed The Throne again, this time via an excellent 12-pitch route, which at the time we believed to be new but later learned had previously been climbed. The route, mostly 5.9-10, with one 5.10+ crux (FA unknown) starts near the right side of the South Face Gully, just left of the noticeable orange-stained rock.

American Jack Sasser, who would join us later in the trip, had been a volunteer ranger on the Pika the previous summer with NPS ranger Gordy Kito, and they had drawn up a list of the most attractive unclimbed lines in the area. Three days after our previous Throne outing we climbed a new route, Swisser than Swiss Chocolate (10 pitches, 5.11+), on the steep west face of The Throne just right of a

Got Lucky, on the south face of Royal Tower, rising from the Crown Glacier. *Martin Gutmann*

massive rock scar and left of a giant roof. Pitch after pitch of 5.10-ish climbing over slabs, up offwidths, and past heavenly cracks led straight to the summit snow slopes. Lucas onsighted the crux pitch at 7a (approximately 5.11d). Since we had already been on the summit twice, we then rappelled a neighboring route.

On May 25 Jack arrived, and we immediately got drunk with the Alaskans camped next to us. The next day we didn't leave camp until noon for one of our main objectives: the giant unclimbed pillar on the south side of Royal Tower (8,130'). Unlike most routes on the Tower, which start from the Pika, this route begins from the Crown Glacier. Despite our wicked hang-overs, we experienced one of our most enjoyable days of climbing ever. We picked a route up the lowest rock band and climbed straight toward the pillar, finding pitch after pitch of perfect granite. Most pitches were in the 5.9-5.10 range with two 5.11 cruxes, one a slightly overhang-ing offwidth and the second a barely protectable stretch of face-climbing. After ending at the unstable summit snow slopes, we began rappelling Got Lucky (14 pitches, 5.11) at midnight, and arrived back at camp in time for another round of partying with our Alaskan campmates.

With terrible weather, we spent the next week and a half playing botchy ball, drinking Appenzeller (Swiss version of Jaegermeister), and trying to avoid the black bear that kept wan-dering through camp. We did make two unsuccessful attempts on unclimbed faces, one on Italy's Boot (ca 7,700') and another on Your Highness (ca 7,800').

MARTIN GUTMANN, *Swiss Alpine Club*

Mt. Grosvenor, West Ridge to summit gendarme, and various activity. Located west of the Great Gorge and unnamed on most maps, the Backside Glacier affords access to several large peaks by their comparatively tame western ramparts. The lower-angled glaciated slopes and sweep-ing ridgelines appeared the perfect venue for Alaska-sized ski mountaineering objectives.

On April 11 Paul Roderick of Talkeetna Air Taxi flew in Ben Traxler (Boulder, CO) and me. This being our first visit to the range, we were surprised and a little intimidated to learn that in the veteran pilot's many years of experience, we were the first party he'd delivered onto the Backside Glacier.

We spent our first several days exploring route options and evaluating the unstable snow at lower elevations and on the unnamed peaks to the west.

On our first objective, the west ridge of Mt. Wake, we climbed low-fifth-class and mod-erate rock and technical post-holing to 65°, before being thwarted by unstable snow and by rock with Butterfinger®-like characteristics in a prominent notch at 7,600', just below Mt. Wake's glaciated summit dome. Descending near our route of ascent, we discovered a more direct couloir up to 50° steep.

The following day we skied south toward "Backside Lake" and attempted the south face of Mt. Church in low visibility. After crossing several massive old wet slides, we skied to just below the prominent Church-Grosvenor col before retreating in inclement weather.

Making the most of several weather-induced "rest-days," we skied a few of the numerous east-facing couloirs, up to 50°, flanking the unnamed 6,500' summit bordering the west side of Backside Glacier. This summit is likely unclimbed and would make a nice short daytrip from base camp.

As high pressure took hold on April 21, we focused on the west ridge of Mt. Grosvenor and skied and climbed the snowy ridge (to 50°), before intersecting the striking summit

Mike Bromberg and Ben Traxler attempting the west ridge of Mt. Wake. *Mark Stadsklev, www.alaskaphotopilot.com*

pyramid. From here we climbed the southwest face via moderate rock and snow to 75° before intersecting the South Face route (Walsh-Westman, 2005) below the first of two prominent fingers near the summit. We turned around at a large gendarme about 50 vertical feet below the summit, unstable snow being the primary on our long list of perceived excuses. I suppose that makes this a (gasp) "modern route," or, more realistically, a steep ski adjoining the Walsh-Westman.

The West Ridge route on Mt. Grosvenor. *Ben Traxler*

We descended the route of ascent, encountering perfect ski conditions with brilliant exposure and striking views. We agreed that this elegant line is comparable in commitment to the West Face of Mt. Dickey and only slightly more technical.

We spent our last several days exploring and attempting lines on a peak we called "False Bradley," a prominent snow dome that dominates the head of the glacier in the 747 Pass area but is really only a false summit on the Mt. Bradley massif.

Overall, the Backside Glacier offers many possibilities for moderate ridge climbs in a superb, seldom-explored setting. Mid-April or earlier seems to be the most appropriate time to visit, as we experienced a significant shed cycle on solar aspects toward the end of our trip. The skiing possibilities remain limitless, although your safety in this area is entirely contingent on your ability to assess snow conditions, as most routes involve prime avalanche terrain.

Ben and I express our gratitude to the American Alpine Club's Mountain Fellowship Fund grant, without which our expedition would not have been possible.

MIKE BROMBERG, *Crested Butte, CO, AAC*

Mt. Dan Beard, Sideburn Rib. In April, Gareth Hughes and I made the trip across the Atlantic to attempt the unclimbed east face of Mt. Dan Beard. Bad weather thwarted an early reconnaissance, but early evening on the 12th we headed over. We chose a line on the far right that seemed elegant and sheltered, weaving up mixed ground before gaining a snow arête high on the face that leads to the summit seracs. We started up the face at 7 p.m., through steep and often waist-deep snow interspersed with short, moderately difficult, mixed steps on crumbly granite held together by ice. We reached the snow arête, from where interesting weaving through seracs gained us the summit at 3 a.m. An unnerving, not-recommended descent of the heavily seracked north face and a long powder trudge up and over the ridge leading to Point 8,245' finally got us back to the skis and then our base camp near the mountain house after a 24-hour round trip.

In keeping with the beard theme, we suggest the name "Sideburn Rib" (4,500', mixed to Scottish IV, serac pitches to 75°, 65° snow).

On the way to Sideburn Rib we spied a pair of superb-looking steep couloir lines tucked

Sideburn Rib on Mt. Dan Beard. *Vivian Scott*

away in the east face's huge rock buttress, to the left of our route. A week later we started up the right-hand line—a very deep couloir sporting two huge chockstones. A thousand feet of 50° snow took us to the bottom of the climbing, which started with a sustained pitch of WI5+ on slightly hollow ice. The next pitch sported an unratable overhanging ice offwidth—one of the most bizarre pitches either of us has climbed—which succumbed with arm-bars and other trickery. Above, easier ice led to the first chockstone. Passing it directly proved impossible, as the promising-looking pillars were unconsolidated snow, but a mixed pitch on the left wall let us outflank the chockstone at about M4. Above, two long pitches of 50° snow and a short 80° ice step put us beneath the second chockstone, where we ran out of luck. An unprotectable inch-thick 90° ice smear on the right, leading to a disintegrating hanging chandelier, was the only way up, and we decided the pitch was too dangerous. With fatter conditions the couloir will make a superb route. From a distance the remaining

Gareth Hughes breaking trail toward an unclimbed line on the east face of Mt. Dan Beard, attempted after the team's successful climb. Inset: Looking down the offwidth pitch on the attempt. *Vivian Scott*

pitch or two to the ridge looked relatively straightforward, though there may be a cornice to negotiate.

On our last day we skied up Dickey via Pittock Pass, enjoyed a superb decent, then headed for the bars in Talkeetna. A fantastic place—we'll be back!

VIVIAN SCOTT, *Edinburgh, U.K.*

Peak 8,010', A Fine Blend. Ryan Hokanson (Alaska) and I (Montana) headed to the Buckskin Glacier for a three-week adventure scampering trip, setting up camp just below the Moose's Tooth on May 3. Two meters of new snow and spindrift thwarted our five attempts on the east faces of the Moose's Tooth and Bear Tooth, but we managed a new route on Peak 8,010', a smaller summit at the head (western end) of the Buckskin. A beautiful gash-like corner system, which appeared to be nicely choked with ice, leads directly up the east face to the summit. Ryan and I figured it would be about six pitches and take part of a day, camp to camp—a perfect warm-up compared to the other routes we had attempted.

The east face of Peak 8,010'. A Fine Blend climbs the obvious cleft directly to the summit. *Gibisch-Hokanson collection*

On May 11 we left camp around 10 a.m. and, after a two-hour approach, reached the base of the face around noon. Ryan led first, onto good ice, and when the rope came tight we began simul-climbing. Early on, some short but steep ice caught me off guard. Pitch after pitch, the climbing got more technical and more poorly protected than we had anticipated.

Partway up, another storm socked the entire cirque. Snow blew directly up the gash, but spindrift wasn't cascading down. I climbed up to what appeared to be the crux, pounded some iron, and brought Ryan up. He led into a series of tricky, overhanging snow blobs devoid of usable ice. After 120' of brilliant climbing, Ryan found his first solid pro

Ryan Hokanson starting up A Fine Blend. *Chris Gibisch*

as the pitch eased off. A few more ropelengths led to a large snow-mushroom-encrusted chock-stone. After overhanging snow and a few mixed moves I was on 50° snow. Two more pitches, and we were standing on top.

It was 1:00 a.m. and snowing; visibility was less than 50m. We tried to rap off the north ridge to a pass separating the Ruth and Buckskin glaciers, but, after losing our way, we succumbed to a brief bivy and waited for more light. However, our proposed descent led to pow-der-covered granite slabs, so we descended our route. Ten rappels and a bit of downclimbing got us to our skis.

After leaving the range, we could find no reference to the line being climbed previously, nor did we find evidence of other climbers. It was a fine blend of climbing, which left a memo-rable impression on us. A Fine Blend (750m, IV AI6 M6+ 50°) is Peak 8,010's second recorded line, after the South Route (500', Allemann-Lotscher, 1968). Ryan and I found that obscure, shorter climbs are sometimes the scariest and most rewarding.

CHRIS GIBISCH

Bear Tooth, House of the Rising Sun to southwest ridge. In mid-April, Jared Vilhauer, Zach Shlosar, and I left our base camp and skied to our gear cache on the south fork of the Buckskin Glacier. We left our skis and headed for an untouched 3,200' line I had spied in March on the southeast face of the Bear Tooth. The climb started with an icefall and snow slope to reach the face. When we were four pitches up the polished icefall, the slopes above started sending down spindrift so persistent that our wait under an overhanging serac turned into a bivy. The night was clear and cold, and the morning the same. Zach led out and took us up the snowfield to the start of the technical portion of the route. We relaxed a little, glad to be out of the shotgun alley and at the base of a cool new route. Jared took the next block, climbing scratchy, thin, vertical ice with no pro for long stretches. Climbing and hauling each pitch took time. We stopped for the night on a small patch of 60° snow. Over an hour's worth of effort yielded two small ledges.

The southeast face of the Bear Tooth, showing House of the Rising Sun. *Jared Vilhauer*

We woke to a light snow falling, accompanied by spindrift slides. The terrain above was too steep to build up huge avalanches, though the small slides were intimidating. Slides would be more or less constant for the rest of our climb, as it snowed every day. I led out of the bivy ledge up a pitch of undulating AI4 until I ran out of rope. The next pitch was vertical bad ice with bad pro and took several hours, during which Zach and Jared were constantly bombed at their belay in the narrow couloir. As I pulled the crux, a big slide nailed me, packing the inside of my shell with snow. Exhausted, I offered the next pitch to Jared, who took it gladly. It ended up being creative A2. While Zach belayed, I

Jared Vilhauer on day 3 on the Bear Tooth. *Zach Shlosar*

dug our next cave behind a thin skin of ice. Soon Jared fixed the ropes and rappelled into bivy #3.

In the morning we ascended the lines. I took the next pitch; another protracted effort up vertical-to-overhanging snow/ice, but with good sticks and reasonable pro after much searching. The next portion of the climb kicked back a bit, and we moved together, with Zach leading over fun ice and snow. Zach brought us to the base of good ice, the quality of which had been improving as we gained altitude. Another pitch had us at what looked to be a terrifying steep, rotten couloir. We were being pummeled by larger and larger slides, so we exited the couloir to gain the ridge as quickly as possible. Two mixed pitches brought us to our high point, just below the southwest ridge (we didn't actually break through the cornice), as darkness fell and the weather worsened. We dug torture-tube bivies into a small snow spur, with huge exposure, where the left side of our couloir met the ridge, zipped our bivy sacks shut against the whirling snowstorm, and slept.

The next day the storm was the worst yet, so we rapped a half-pitch and dug a better cave to wait out the weather. We could hear avalanches hissing over the cave walls as the storm went on.

The next morning, our sixth on the route, our food was gone. We had finished our couloir (3,200', AK Grade V, AI6 A2) to the ridge. We did not make the summit but were happy to climb such an awesome feature on a beautiful mountain. Fourteen raps, much downclimbing, and a quick ski brought us back to the base. Because the southeast face caught only the early morning sun, we named the route House of the Rising Sun in the spirit of our friend Johnny Soderstrom. Johnny loved both exploratory climbing in Alaska and Bob Dylan. To finish with style, we skied the Buckskin to the Chulitna River and hiked to the road.

JESSE (BILL) BILLMEIER

Kichatna Spires, mystery routes. Widely reported, including to the *AAJ*, were that three presumably new ice/mixed/snow couloir routes were climbed somewhere in the Tatina Glacier area of the Kichatna Spires, by U.K. climbers Mike "Twid" Turner (leader), Simon Hitchens, and Phil Jeffery. Turner's report, however, included no information on the locations of the peaks or lines. In response to our requests for this information, Turner wrote, "Just tell folk that there was some nice climbs put up and if they go they will have a great time."

RUTH GORGE

Mt. Bradley, Season of the Sun; Mt. Church, Memorial Gate; Mt. Johnson, The Ladder Tube. Japanese climbers Fumitaka Ichimura, Yusuke Sato, and Tatsuro Yamada established three impressive new routes in the Ruth Gorge in April and early May. Season of the Sun (4,600', V WI4R M6R) climbs Mt. Bradley (9,100') via its southeast face; Memorial Gate (3,600', V AI4+R/X) climbs Mt. Church (8,233') via the central gully on its north face; and The Ladder Tube (3,000', V 5.10R A3 WI4+R M5) climbs Mt. Johnson (8,460') via the north face and west ridge. See Yamada's feature earlier in this *Journal.*

The north face of Mt. Johnson (1): The Elevator Shaft (Chabot-Tackle, 1995) and (2) The Ladder Tube (Ichimura-Sato-Yamada, 2007). The other routes by the 2007 Japanese team are shown in Yamada's feature article, earlier in this *Journal. Tatsuro Yamada*

The Stump, Choss-o-Licious. In a 17-hour round-trip from base camp on May 30 and 31, Joe Johnson, Steven Lucarelli, and I established this incredibly fine, choss-infested route. It basically starts on the southeast buttress of The Stump, atop a large scree slope to the left of black water streaks coming off the Wisdom Tooth, and 100 yards east of Game Boy. Our 10-pitch route consisted of several easy ascending traverses, a few good lines of beautiful solid rock, and a couple of difficult pitches made of choss.

JOHN PARNIGONI

The Stump and Eye Tooth, various new routes. At the end of June, Renan Ozturk and I landed on the Ruth Glacier. This marked the first leg of our "Alakastan 2007" expedition. Renan and I had both been training for the mission by dialing in Freerider on El Capitan in Yosemite Valley, which each of us freed just before leaving. Less than a week after our ascents, we watched the plane disappear down the majestic Ruth Gorge.

Our goal was single-push, all-free first ascents. To Renan and me a free ascent requires each of us to lead or follow every pitch free, which in the alpine setting is problematic because, to make it to the top, you have to lug mountain boots, ice axes, crampons, and water. The second would climb with a small pack, and we would simul-climb as much as possible.

My initial impression was that the 3,000' Eye Tooth, our main objective, looked ominous, pissed off, and ready to serve up a royal beat-down. The year before, Renan had made it nearly halfway up a first ascent on the Eye Tooth's "central pillar" feature all free, only to blow a tendon on a 5.12R pitch. Before that, Renan had made it 500' up an obvious unclimbed corner system on The Stump, to the right of Chris McNamara and Joe Puryear's beautiful 5.11 free route, Goldfinger, before being stormed off. The weather had been terrible before our arrival, but the

The west face of the Eye Tooth: (1) The Beholder (Ozturk-Wright, 2007). (2) Dream in the Spirit of Mugs (Bonapace-Haas-Orgler, 1994). (3) Austrian variation (probable line) (Fidi-Neumayer, 2002). (4) Ballad of a Dead Soldier variation (Ozturk-Wright, 2007). *Renan Ozturk*

Renan Ozturk on the "Point of No Return" pitch, traversing toward the upper pillar on The Beholder. *Cedar Wright*

sun had come out for our flight in and The Stump looked good to go.

The day after arriving on the glacier we went for it. For some reason Renan remembered the climbing to be mostly "casual" 5.10. Renan's memory isn't his strong point. It was muddy finger locks with no pro. It was heinous run out stemming. It was a total horror show. There were a few classic pitches so I wouldn't call it a pile…but it was close. We reached the summit of The Stump via the last few crux pitches of Goldfinger. We dubbed our new route Brownfinger (5.11 R/X) in honor of the muddy finger locks and as a playful dig at my buddy McNamara. We rappelled Goldfinger, returning to base camp 12 hours after we left.

The next day was painful. We weren't fully recovered from our El Cap adventures, Brownfinger had sapped us, and, worst of all, the weather was still sunny. The Eye Tooth still looked horrifying, so we opted for another line on The Stump, the next corner right of Brownfinger. Surprisingly the line followed very little of the actual corner, wandering to both sides, eventually leaving the corner altogether and forging up some high-quality featured face climbing with little to no protection. We dubbed this upper headwall "The Leap of Faith" because there was no obvious line but there was a path. This line was completely independent and had consistently good rock. We called it StumpJumper (5.11R), in honor of its improbable "jump-around" nature. Luckily we climbed fast because we topped out as it started to snow. We descended in mildly bad conditions, and got pretty wet.

Thank goodness for a couple of days of rain. Renan and I wanted to climb the Eye Tooth, but the central pillar looked real scary, so we opted for a direct finish variation to the Dream in the Spirit of Mugs route, which would go directly up the pillar, where the original route corkscrewed to the right. We established a 1,000' direct variant, and found the climbing to be ultra-classic, steep, and surprisingly no more difficult than the original line. Renan had done Dream… the year before and thought that this variant improves the climb. We called our line Ballad of a Dead Soldier (5.10+ R). It should be noted that descending Dream… involves 3,000' of sketch traversing and rappels with plenty of loose rock. Not over till it's over.

The weather again closed in, and we enjoyed a few rest days in the tent. Finally the weather cleared but still seemed iffy. One afternoon we established The Great Transformation, an ultra-mega-classic located on the southwest-facing rock buttress at the end of the long ridge that extends down and west-southwest from the West Summit of the Moose's Tooth. (This buttress borders the left-hand side of the entrance to the approach glacier that leads up to the Root

Canal.) The route climbs five pitches, including two of solid 5.12, to an obvious ledge. This was one of my best efforts in the mountains, as I just barely onsighted both crux pitches. The crux third pitch we dubbed "Indian Creek Trainer," as it was a splitter 180' mid-5.12 finger crack straight out of the Creek. This was one of the best routes I've ever done, and I hope it gets a repeat.

One rest day later, with one lead line still core-shot-free, we went for the central pillar of the Eye Tooth. We motored through the bottom section and raced across an avalanche gully, just barely making it across before the sun started thawing things and rocks started cutting loose. To get across the gully I led a horrifying 5.10+ X pitch with the best gear being an R.P. behind a loose flake and the anchor being a "bomber" double zero and zero TCU. The upper pillar was dreamy, sustained, high-quality 5.10 and 5.11, with only a few death blocks to stem past. As with our previous Eye Tooth climb, we finished on the highest rock point along the summit ridge, but didn't slog through the unconsolidated snow to the true summit. The Beholder (3,000', V 5.12 [5.10X]).

We descended Ballad…, as it is more direct (we recommend it), but we totally epiced, taking far longer than the climb. After we down-soloed 300' of easy fifth-class at the top, on the first rappel the middle of the lead line stuck in a crack, and we had to cut it in the middle. For 3,000' we passed a knot at every rappel. On the ski back to base camp, I broke the binding off a ski, Renan broke the tail off one, and we both post-holed like zombies back to camp.

Renan and I have the good fortune of being sponsored by The North Face. We could never have funded the Alaskastan Expedition on our own and are very thankful. A week later we were on the plane to Pakistan.

CEDAR WRIGHT

Sugar Tooth, Southeast Buttress. Over three-days in mid-June, Peter Haeussler and I (both of Anchorage) established a 20-pitch free climb on the Sugar Tooth. This was my third attempt at the route, the second with Peter, and the second ascent of the peak (Bonapace-Haas-Orgler made the first by the West Face in 1994).

On June 14 Peter and I landed at the Sheldon Amphitheater. Our approach took three days, due to rain, Peter's fall into a water-filled crevasse, and a spooky climb over Espresso Gap onto the north fork of the Coffee Glacier. On day three, the weather cleared, and we were treated to full-on views of the 3,000' southeast buttress.

We started climbing moderate ground left of where the low point of the buttress intersects the Coffee Glacier. The first day we climbed 15 pitches on solid, moderate rock. Our packs slowed us considerably, and we hauled them through a few short harder sections. Most of the pitches were lower-angled 5.6 and 5.7. The crux was a steep left-facing dihedral on pitches five through eight, with free climbing up to 5.10. Shortly after the sun left us, we encountered a long ledge system where we excavated a flat tent site, complete with snow for water.

The second pitch of day two was the most serious of the route, with a series of roofs that required much traversing and routefinding. Protection was sparse, and a 25-pound pack made every move harder. Pitch 17 brought us to a small pinnacle, which we named Sweet Tooth Spire. From here a horizontal ridge traverse led to the summit snow slopes. Peter then led a long pitch through bottomless wet snow. Soaked to the bone, we were grateful for the sun. Another pitch of steeper snow led to a spectacular summit ridge and our first glance at the Eye Tooth. Before

The Southeast Buttress route on the Sugar Tooth, with (E) indicating Espresso Gap. *Jay Rowe*

Jay Rowe leading pitch 8 on the Sugar Tooth. *Peter Haeussler*

the climb, we had kicked around the idea of trying to link together the Sugar Tooth and the Eye Tooth. It appeared to involve at least two long rappels to the Sugar Tooth-Eye Tooth notch, then another 8-10 pitches of challenging rock and snow to summit the Eye Tooth. It seemed a bit more than we were willing to bite off, so we dropped the packs and enjoyed the remaining knife-edge summit ridge.

Without packs, we felt like cats tiptoeing along the top of a fence. The exposure was incredible, and after three pitches the ridge culminated in a symmetrical pyramid-shaped summit. The final moves involved a dicey 5.8 friction layback in wet mountain boots to a summit so sharp I could hardly balance on it. The top was devoid of protection, so I downclimbed back to Peter, and he took his turn. We spent the rest of the day establishing a direct rappel line to pitch 15, where we spent a second night, and finished the rappels the next day.

The moderate grade (20 pitches, V 5.10, 50° snow), location, and spectacular summit made the route certainly worth three trips. The route is shorter and technically easier than the West Pillar (Dream in the Spirit of Mugs) of the Eye Tooth, and a competent party could climb it in a long day from the Ruth Gorge. An early start from just west of Espresso Gap would minimize the objective hazards traversing the Gap and have the team at the base of the route in around three hours. Carrying only shell gear, light boots, and one axe each, a party could climb and descend the route and get back over Espresso Gap before the sun hits the next day. The route topo is on file at the Denali Ranger Station.

JAY ROWE

Hut Tower, Tower Couloir to Werewolf-Hut Col. James Mehigan and I aren't keen on beach vacations, so we traveled to Alaska in April, just in time for the end of a two-month high-pressure spell. On the day we arrived the wind swung to the south, which, according to a local climber, brings two types of clouds: serious and accumulating.

We gave ourselves just two weeks to pull off the first ascent of the couloir leading to the col between the Werewolf and Hut towers (6,700' and 6,200'), but pulled it off in a 23-hour continuous push, battling subzero temperatures, falling snow, and marginal ice conditions.

The crux section of the climb involved a struggle with an overhanging chimney that was shrouded by a veil of vertical powder snow. Running through the powder snow, though, were four-inch-wide tentacles of semi-consolidated snow-ice that made the route possible. It included three pitches of stout Scottish Grade VII, with the second-from-last pitch being much like the moves out of the cave on Darth Vader (VII, 8) on Ben Nevis.

Tower Couloir, 500m, ED, Scottish VII, A1.

OLIVER METHERELL, *U.K.*

KENAI MOUNTAINS

Mt. Godwin, probable first ascent, West Ridge. In early April, my dad Harold Faust, George Peck, and I climbed the West Ridge (Alaska Grade 2) of Mt. Godwin in the Kenai Mountains, near Seward. At about 5,860', Mt. Godwin is not a tall peak, though it is the highest summit on the Godwin Glacier and does have 4,300' of prominence. We believe that ours was the first ascent. On March 31 we parked at Mile 13 of the Seward Highway and headed up the South Fork of the Snow River on snowshoes. We crossed the river several times, but with cold temperatures, there was only one open crossing. About seven miles up the river, we headed south into the mountains along the west side of the Kindling Glacier. Eventually we roped up and headed up the glacier to a pass between Mt. Godwin and Kindling Mountain at 4,350'. Here we set up camp. In the morning, we headed up the West Ridge of Godwin. Based on our observations from the day before, we believed the route would be nontechnical and brought little gear. Most of the ridge was a straightforward snow stomp, though a rock band at 5,300' ended up being the crux. Harold led through this section with exposed low-5th-class moves and the psychological

The West Ridge of Mt. Godwin. *Harold Faust*

belay of accessory cord. From the rock band the ridge continued steepening all the way to the summit; snow conditions were perfect for kick-stepping. We descended the route we climbed. Back in camp by mid-afternoon, we relaxed, ate, and explored the immediate area. The following day we headed down the Godwin Glacier to Fourth of July Creek, where we had parked a second truck.

MATT FAUST

ALASKA ST. ELIAS MOUNTAINS

Flight Path Peak, east ridge, and other routes. In May, John Durham, Bob Brownsburger, Bob Jacobs, and I spent a week of unusually fine and clear weather climbing peaks off a spur of the upper Baldwin Glacier in the St. Elias Mountains, near the Canadian border. According to our research and our pilot (Paul Claus), most of the peaks on the north side of the glacier we were on had been climbed. The prominent peak at the head of the glacier, to our south, had one ascent and was known to Paul as "Flight Path Peak" (ca 10,500'), due to its prominence as a landmark while flying in to Mt. Logan from his lodge. Paul made the first ascent of the peak in the late 90s, via easier snow slopes on the south side of the peak. We climbed the east ridge of Flight Path Peak, for its second ascent. Our 1,500' route involved a pitch of ice to 70°, half a dozen moderate rock pitches, and much 4th class on loose rock. We also climbed a snow, ice, and rock couloir on each of two unnamed 10,000' peaks on the north side of the glacier. We believe these to be new routes, though we could not confirm this.

VINCE ANDERSON, *AAC*

Canada

ST. ELIAS RANGE

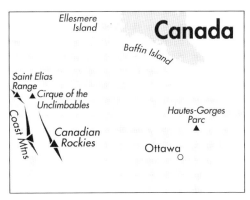

Kluane National Park and Reserve, summary. The weather in this region is generally unforgiving and unpredictable during the climbing season. High winds, thick clouds, and heavy snowfalls are the bane of pilots and climbers alike. In 2007 a steady cycle of low pressure cells, spinning off waves of cold, humid air, developed over the northern Gulf of Alaska. Most groups found themselves waiting for days for a clear break in the weather to fly the 100km to their base camp. No group was spared the experience of spending three, four, or five days at a time huddled in the tent, taking turns digging out spindrift before the tent walls collapsed.

This year there were a high number of failed attempts. Only one group, three Canadians, stepped onto the main summit of Mt. Logan, via the King Trench route. Several other groups fought their way through blizzards to the plateau and up minor peaks of Logan. All groups reported battling wave after wave of high winds and extremely cold temperatures.

Two climbers from the U.K. climbed Lowell Peak (3,630m), just west of Pinnacle Peak, via its west ridge. This may be a first ascent.

Attempts were also made on the North Ridge of Mt. Kennedy, the south face of Mt. Logan, the East Ridge of Mt. Logan, the Southeast Ridge of Mt. Steele, and unclimbed Mt. Saskatchewan in the Centennial Range. These expeditions all reported poor snow conditions as their main problem.

Despite poor weather and conditions, there were no serious accidents or search and rescues. One group reported a team member falling 10 feet, unroped, into a crevasse on the King Trench route. She was retrieved unscathed but shaken. Another climber was assisted down that route with undiagnosed chest pains. Several climbers, especially those who spent considerable time at high elevations, reported mild cases of frostbite to fingers and toes.

In 2007 there were 115 people in 33 mountaineering groups registered for the Icefield Ranges of Kluane. Eighty-two people were on the King Trench route of Mt. Logan. Only one pair of climbers attempted the East Ridge, and three people attempted a south face route on Mt. Logan. Twenty people participated in ski tours or were involved in glaciological or biological research within the Icefields.

Anyone interested in mountaineering in the Icefield Ranges of Kluane National Park and Reserve must register with the Kluane National Park Warden office. Call 1-867-634-7279 to speak to a warden, or check out our website at www.pc.gc.ca/pn-np/yt/kluane/.

ANDREW LAWRENCE, *Park Warden, Kluane National Park and Reserve*

Lowell Peak, West Ridge. Dave Hesleden and I visited the St. Elias Range planning to climb a route on either Pinnacle Peak (3,714m) or Lowell Peak (3,630m). We flew onto the Lowell Glacier from Kluane Lake on May 1 and made a camp at ca 2,000m, where we could easily access both mountains. Unusually high winter and spring snowfall meant that all aspects of all peaks were seriously avalanche-prone. We abandoned an attempt on the south pillar of Lowell Peak when the slope beneath us slid while we approached the berg-schrund.

Lowell Peak in the background, with the unclimbed south pillar dropping from the summit. Hesleden and Richadson's West Ridge is not visible. *Dave Hesleden*

By chance, a long ski tour the next day gave us a view of Lowell's west ridge, which is more of a pronounced rib. More to the point, it looked like a safe line, and, facing into the prevailing wind, there was less chance of windslab. We climbed it the day after (May 8) in a 12-hour roundtrip from base camp. There was 1,400m of ascent, initially on skis, then along a horizontal ridge carrying skis, then skiing across a snow bowl, and then climbing the rib itself. The climbing was straight-forward but hard work—initially 45° waist-deep snow, followed by Scottish III climbing on loose snow and rotten ice to the easier summit slopes. The weather then deteriorated and we continued to the corniced summit in a whiteout.

Lowell Peak was first climbed by Canadians Larry Stainier and Rodden McGowan on May 7, 1993, by the east face and north ridge (*AAJ 1994*, pp. 154-155). Like most parties climbing in this area, they were based on the South Arm of the Kaskawulsh Glacier, to the north of Pinnacle Peak. We believe ours was the second ascent of the mountain.

The south pillar of Lowell Peak remains a fine climbing target. There are numerous icy lines up the steep buttress rising to the summit or the runnels to its left. Our route of ascent would make the easiest descent back to the Lowell Glacier.

SIMON RICHARDSON, *Scotland, AAC*

BAFFIN ISLAND

Copier Pinnacle, A Little Less Conversation. On April 16, 2006, my best friend Hans Copier committed suicide. Two weeks after his death I, with Dutch climbers Roland Bekendam and Rens Horn, set out for the Stewart Valley, attempting to climb an unclimbed mountain via a vertical 800m rock face. I wished to place Hans' ashes on top of this mountain.

We struggled in cold and bad weather with loose rock and loneliness. After 50 days I came home having climbed less than 300m of the virgin wall. During the last day on the wall we left a small jar with the ashes on a tiny ledge, making it impossible for me to not return or to forget this climb. I stashed some gear in Stewart Valley and, once home, started looking for financial support and, most importantly, a climbing partner.

A Little Less Conversation, the route of first ascent on Copier Pinnacle. *Martin Fickweiler*

In early 2007, when I was thinking of returning alone, I found somebody who wanted to join me. Niels van Veen was an experienced climber, but not on the big stone. We entered Stewart Valley on May 6, having problems with just barely enough snow on the moraine for skidoo travel. After leaving us with food and fuel for almost five weeks, the Inuit left and loneliness surrounded me once again. There, above a 900m high slope stood the wall that made me travel here all over again. (Base camp at N 70°44' W 71°27'.)

Conditions were much colder than the year before, but we made good progress on the wall, aiding to A3 and free climbing the wider sections at 5.11a. We spent seven straight nights in our portaledge, fixing ropes as we went. On May 20 we arrived at the summit, exactly one year after I started the climb. There were no signs of earlier ascents, so we named the mountain Copier Pinnacle, in loving memory of Hans Copier. We made a small tower on the summit on which I placed the jar with ashes, feeling joy and sadness at the same time.

Two days later back at base camp, we discovered that our satellite telephone was blocked by the provider, and there was no way to communicate with the rest of the world. People at home would start to worry, and Levi, our outfitter, was waiting for confirmation to pick us up at Walker Arm.

Rens Horn jugging lines during the 2006 attempt on Copier Pinnacle. *Martin Fickweiler*

I remembered seeing three weeks earlier, when we were cruising the fjords on the back of a skidoo, a big base camp at Sam Ford Fjord, so we went there lightweight. It was odd to realize that nowadays men had to walk almost 90km to make a phone call. We found a team of six BASE jumpers, a luxurious base camp with lots of great food, and, I almost forgot, a telephone that put us in contact with the rest of the world.

We named the 800m high route A Little Less Conversation, a name that will always make me remember the old days.

MARTIN FICKWEILER, *Rotterdam, The Netherlands*

Kiguti on the left, rising among the walls of the Sam Ford Fjord. Inset: the Norwegian Route (Felde-Hetland-Lied-Nessa, 2007); Nirvana (Ascaso-Ballester-Chaverri, 1995) climbs the prow to the right. *Lars Nessa*

The new route on the right side of the Fin massif: Gud Har Ikkje Gløymt Oss, Han Gir Bare Faen. *Lars Nessa*

Kiguti, Norwegian Route; Fin massif, Gud Har Ikkje Gløymt Oss, Han Gir Bare Faen. In early April, Ole Lied, Sigurd Felde, Audun Hetland, and I left Norway for Sam Ford Fjord. We had seen pictures of the great wall of Kiguti from the Norwegian 2000 expedition to Baffin, so we wanted to have a closer look. We knew that the wall had been climbed but did not have any detailed information about the route(s). [In 1995, Spanish climbers Daniel Ascaso, Javier Ballester, and Pepe Chaverri made the first ascent of the wall via Nirvana (5.9 A3+) in eight days, climbing the prow on the right side. No other routes are thought to exist on this wall—Ed.]

After two days in Clyde, where Levi Palituq provided us with accommodations and other assistance, we headed out for Sam Ford Fjord. We established our camp in a sheltered bay between Kiguti and the Fin. We spent the next two days carrying gear and scrutinizing a possible route. There was one obvious, continuous line that caught our attention. Although the line looked attractive, we were afraid it had already been climbed, so we searched for a less conspicuous line. There was one that had the same start as the other, but after two or three pitches it headed slightly left through a compact slab. It reached a half-moon-shaped dihedral that continued up one-third of the wall. From the top of the dihedral, the line followed thin cracks through the steepest aspect of the face and continued to the very summit.

Two pitches of mixed climbing led to a big snow ledge under the main wall. From there aid climbing started, and after five or six days we fixed ropes all the way to a small ledge 300 vertical meters above the fjord. After 10 days the comfort of living on the fjord ended.

The first pitch above Camp 1 turned out to be the crux. We used peckers and heads in a thin crack, but in many places the face only allowed hooking. A great pendulum, the dihedral, and the ledge itself were hazards in case of a fall. The line offered many pitches of exquisite A2, only interrupted by A1 and A3 pitches in between. The rock was porous in places, because it was eroded by air and not by water. Many cracks were compact and shallow, which meant we often had to use a hammer.

Lars Nessa at a belay on the Norwegian Route. *Lars Nessa collection.*

The lower half of the wall was vertical and slabby, while the upper half overhung slightly. If a rock fell from the top of the route, it would free-fall for 12 seconds before hitting the big snow ledge—an observation of interest to BASE-jumpers visiting the fjord and, for us, a source of really exposed climbing.

After 15 days and 1,000m of climbing we reached the summit of Kiguti. The line was challenging to the very last pitch, but we had a nice time on the wall. We brought food for 16 days and two barrels (150kg) of ice from an iceberg, which was sufficient for the climb.

The Norwegian Route has 23 pitches and is graded VI 5[Norwegian] A3+.

After time skiing and reading, we looked for other routes. Audun and Sigurd wanted to try a 400m aid line on the Fin, but they gave up after three days because of strong, cold winds. Ole and I did an alpine line on the right side of the Fin, with 700m of continuous crack and dihedral climbing on a beautiful pillar. We named the route Gud Har Ikkje Gløymt Oss, Han Gir Bare Faen [rough translation: God Hasn't Actually Forgotten Us, He Just Doesn't Give a Damn]. It comprises 12 long pitches (60+m) and is graded 5.10 A0.

We had a great time on Baffin, enjoyed the spectacular walls, the harshness of nature, and got to know some great characters in the local communities.

LARS FLATØ NESSA, *Norway*

The Wall of Clouds, Nassariit, and other shenanigans. From May 1 to June 18 Sam Beaugey, Martial Dumas, Jean-Yves Fredricksen, Yann Mimet, and David Ravanel (and later Jean-Noël Itzstein, for jumps) made their first visit to Baffin to climb, ski, paraglide, and BASE jump. The original aim of the climbers was to visit the Stewart Valley and try a new route on Great Sail Peak. However, their equipment arrived late, so they undertook an easier approach and traveled to Scott Island (Piliktua in Inuit) at the mouth of Clark (also referred to as Scott) Inlet. Farther west the inlet splits into two fjords—Clark and Gibbs—that run north and south of Sillem Island.

The Wall of Clouds, showing Nassariit. The next formation to the right is The Raven. *David Ravanel*

After a reconnaissance of the walls on Scott Island, the French settled on a 650m face that in 1999 had been dubbed The Wall of Clouds, 1.5 km northwest of the Ship's Prow. Splitting into two groups, the French chose lines 150m right of Aularutiksanga (Sedeneyer-White, 1999) and spent six hours climbing the first 20m of their choices before deciding to concentrate on one. The left-hand line was technical and elegant, the one to the right loose and dangerous. Working in shifts, they began fixing the left-hand line. The first two pitches involved a lot of bat-hooking until reaching a decent crack. After four days they had only completed three pitches. Temperatures as low as -27°C caused problems for the belayer, who was sometimes immobile for up to eight hours. They decided the second should work from a portaledge with fly, where he was supplied with books. During days off from the wall, the climbers would sometimes plod up to a suitable summit and make a BASE jump or paraglider flight. After six days the high point was 350m above the ground. The team installed the first portaledge camp here, and all five members moved up with three ledges and 10 haul bags, for a continuous push to the summit. The climb took a left-facing dihedral and required difficult aid with beaks, copperheads, blades, and small camming devices. There was also the problem of expanding flakes and dangerous blocks. Leading one pitch, Fredricksen carefully tied off an 80 kg loose rock, perched above his head, and lowered it until his belayers could cut it loose for a seven-second flight to the fjord. After seven days on the wall and one more camp at 500m, they reached the summit and named their route Nassariit (650m, A4). Dumas, Fredricksen, and Ravanel rappelled with the breakables, the other bags were tossed down, and Beaugey and Mimet got in a fine BASE jump.

For the final 15 days the group moved back to Sam Ford Fjord, but not before a BASE jump off the Ship's Prow, which the French found was barely 500m high, not the 650m previously reported. Some also BASE jumped the 700m wall of The Beak and then turned to the huge 1,300m high wall on Polar Sun Spire, flying out from the great north face. Team members also made repeat ski and snowboard descents of the Polar Star Couloir (1,100m) on Mt. Beluga (also skied by members of a six-person French-Swiss team the day before), first climbed and skied in 2002 by Brad Barlage and Andrew McLean. While the others returned by conventional skidoo to Clyde River, Fredricksen returned by a solo, kite-assisted ski journey, covering the 160km of frozen water in less than two days.

LINDSAY GRIFFIN, *Mountain INFO, www.climbmagazine.com, AAC*

COAST MOUNTAINS

Coast Mountains, remote areas summary. [Note: In addition to mention in this summary, some of the routes have individual reports, below—Ed.] Summer 2007 never really set up on the coast, with only short intermittent periods of settled sunny weather, and mountaineering suffered. One group that did have a holiday full of innovative climbs were six Scots who based themselves just north of Mt. Geddes (3,227m) in the Frontier Group, 10km northwest of Mt. Waddington. Over a two week period they managed many new routes on both rock and ice, including two fine additions to the north face of Geddes.

Jay Burbee, Peter Hudson, Cam Shute, and Brock Wilson knocked off the long-talked-about second ascent of the beautiful, solid granite 350m southeast buttress of Mt. Queen Bess (3,298m), ticking the first free ascent in the process (about 5.10a).

The rest of the backcountry was quiet. I participated in two exploratory trips, which, while opening a bit of new territory, were modest technically. The first, with Markus Raschke, Peter Renz, and Mickey Schurr, explored remote, mostly untrod terrain in the far northwestern lobe of the Pantheon Range, 10km southwest of Klinaklini Lake, in unsettled weather. Jordan Peters and I also enjoyed a brief trip into the head of Beece Creek, east of Taseko Lake in the dry, sprawling south Chilcotin area. We climbed Mt. Vic (3,005m) from the west via the snowslopes of the upper northwest ridge, but an attempt on a new ice route on the superb, expansive north face of Beece Peak (ca 3,025m) had to be put off for another visit because of lack of time.

Paul Baker, Jesse Mason, and Jordan Peters climbed the 450m northwest buttress on Mt. Moe (2,664m), north of Wedgemount Lake in early September, finding decent rock at a 4th- to low 5th-class standard.

DON SERL, CANADA, *ACC, AAC*

Southwest British Columbia (southern Coast Mountains and Canadian Cascades). 2007 was lean for new routes in southwest B.C., continuing a trend of the last few years. In part this is attributable to a natural tailing off after the great burst of activity that followed the release of the *Alpine Select* guidebook in 2001, but this year's low level of new-routing can also be blamed on pernicious summer weather. By some accounts it rained every single weekend. Most new routes that were reported are from the drier inland portions of the range.

The season got off to a good start when Dave Bastercheea, Jack Hannan, and Jon Johnston, from the Whistler-Pemberton area, snowmobiled up the Lillooet River logging roads from Pemberton on March 31 and, taking advantage of a stable spring snowpack, made the second ascent and first ski descent of Beautiful Nightmare (1200+m, IV 60°) on the north face of Plinth Peak, at the edge of the Lillooet Icefields. The spring season was then uneventful.

While summer was largely rained out on the coast, a large party from the British Columbia

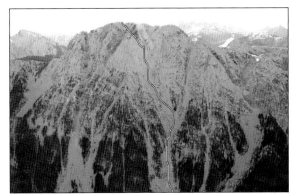

Graveyard Shift, on the north face of Mt. Brice. *Drew Brayshaw*

Mountaineering Club celebrated the 100th anniversary of the first ascent of Mt. Garibaldi by making an ascent of the Via Normale in period gear and clothing, the finding of which, from museums, old climbers' basements, and thrift stores, proved to be the crux.

As for new routes, in July Tyler Linn, Nick Elson, and Sarah Panofsky climbed the first buttress right of the South Buttress/Beckey Route on Matriarch Mountain in Cathedral Provincial Park, perhaps the last unclimbed buttress on the massif. The route gave eight pitches, mostly in the 5.7-5.8 range but with a distinctive slab-to-roof crux. The entire route, left unnamed, is worthy of III 5.11a. Also in the Cascades, in late summer Craig McGee, Andre Ike, and Brad White climbed a route on the Les Cornes formation in the Anderson River Range. The Gatekeeper (IV 5.12a or 5.11d A0) consists of eight rope-stretching new pitches on the leftmost edge of the buttress and then finishes on the upper pitches of the classic Springbok Arête.

Near Chilliwack, in September Jeremy Frimer and Sarah Hart claimed a new seven-pitch 5.10c A0 route on South Nesakwatch Spire, which they dubbed Hart of Starkness. However, the route is very close to a 2003 line, Bugaboo Crack, and portions of the earlier route or unreported variations since may intersect this newly claimed line. However, it seems that at least a portion of Jeremy and Sarah's route may be new because of the amount of crack-cleaning that was required to find pro on parts of the line.

Garibaldi Park saw another possible first ascent in September, when Jordan Peters, Jesse Mason, and Paul Baker climbed the northwest buttress of Mt. Moe (III low 5th-class) after finding the north face of Weart out of condition. This line had not seen any previously reported activity, but due to its relatively easy nature and proximity to popular peaks, it is possible that it may have previously been climbed and left unreported.

Finally, in early December, Jesse Mason, Graham Rowbotham and I took advantage of an unusual spell of cold weather to climb the north face of Mt. Brice in the Cascades. This massive face (1,200m valley bottom to summit) had, due to its obscurity and somewhat remote location, not been previously attempted. After a seven-hour bushwhack to the base, we climbed the central gully on the face for 1,000m, with nine pitches of water ice to WI3/3+ followed by endless snow to the summit and a long headlamp descent back to Skagit River. The 23-hour car-to-car time prompted the name Graveyard Shift (IV WI3 60° snow).

DREW BRAYSHAW, *Canada, AAC*

Bicuspid Tower, Life in the Fast Lane. On our first day on the Tiedemann Glacier, August 20, Graham McDowell, Ryan O'Connell, and I tried to navigate the maze into the Stiletto cirque and our objective, the majestic 2,000' unclimbed granite wall of the Blade. Late in the day a 40–60' wide crevasse, spanning the width of the glacier, stopped us. But we located a collapsed section of ice and snow that looked as if it could provide access to the other side. Dubbing the slender bridge Crunch Time, we descended to camp.

Several days later, after some storms, we crossed Crunch Time, but only a few hundred feet up the ice-coated face we retreated. With the remaining light we tried the southwest face of Bicuspid Tower, a nearly 1,000' bone-white granite peak with a twin summit. It

Ryan O'Connell in the Stiletto cirque, with the southwest faces of Dentiform (D) and Bicuspid Tower (B; its dual summits are in-line with the photo, thus not distinguishable). Inset: Life in the Fast Lane, on Bicuspid. *Ian Nicholson*

had been climbed a handful of times, but had countless promising corner systems. We climbed four long pitches until dead-ending at loose, blank rock.

The next three days stormed viciously, with high winds lifting our tents. Graham brought large rocks into his tent, but while moving one he hurt a muscle in his stomach. When he woke he could barely sit up. We later learned that he had torn a muscle in his abdomen, requiring surgery. However, he urged Ryan and me to try something without him.

When the storm passed, on September 1 Ryan and I quickly ascended the glacier and belayed across Crunch Time. We'd decided on another attempt at Bicuspid Tower. This time we chose a slightly different, more direct start, but rejoined our previous attempt at the top of the first pitch. Stellar jamming and a stem box made up the second pitch (5.10a). The third pitch started with a 40' splitter, 3" cupped hand-crack (5.10b) that led to a ramp and difficult face climbing. The face gave way to a long dihedral with a continuous 3"-7" crack system for 600'. We groveled up the off-widths, aiding and French-freeing the steeper sections. We reached the col between the two summits. My research indicated that the south summit, while slightly lower, had never been reached. This was reinforced by our finding no rappel slings or sign of previous passage. We summited at 8:00 p.m., 45 minutes before dark. We named our route Life in the Fast Lane (IV 5.10c C1) because of all the obstacles we encountered.

We descended into the night, and midway down the weather turned bad. When we hit the ground at 11:00 p.m., it was snowing as hard as ever. We rappelled over Crunch Time on an 11'-diameter snow bollard, due to the deep snow. We walked quickly down the glacier, though our fatigue was showing. We were tripping and falling on moderate terrain, and then, while downclimbing a section of ice, I caught my crampons on my pants and tumbled head over heels for 60'. Miraculously, I was unscathed.

We arrived at camp at 3:00 a.m. Graham was waiting and quickly made hot drinks. His abdomen was no better, so we flew out the next day.

IAN NICHOLSON, *AAC*

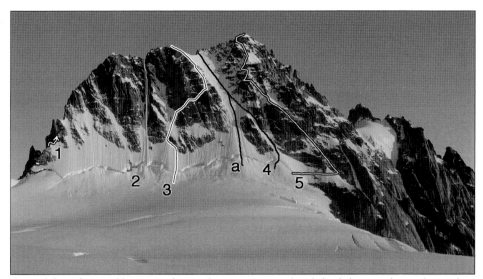

The north face of Mt. Geddes: (1) Northeast Ridge (starts on snowslope behind, then up ridge; Beebee-Beebee-Firey-Firey, 1972). (2) Bottleneck Couloir (Diedrich-Landreville-Paxson, 1991). (3) Central Buttress (Hamilton-Kennedy-Rubens, 2007). (4) Hourglass Face (Down-Howe, 1984). (4a) Direct Start (Diedrich-Landreville, 1991). (5) Caledonia (Kennedy-Rubens and McGougan-Ritchie, 2007). *Des Rubens*

Neil McCougan on Caledonia. *Des Rubens*

Frontier Group, various climbs. In the Frontier Group of the Waddington Range, Bob Hamilton, Billy Hood, Neil McGougan, Dave Ritchie, and we did several climbs, all except one of which (Bottleneck) we believe to be new. Our thanks to Don Serl and Simon Richardson for their generous advice.

Mt. Geddes, north face, Caledonia (550m, D+ 60° max, Kennedy-Rubens and McGougan-Ritchie, July 30). A fine mixed route, starting with an exposed rightward traverse well below the right-hand start of the Hourglass Face, ascending the slanting open couloir and snow arêtes right of the wide Hourglass Face couloir, and finishing directly to the main summit. Climbed in excellent snow/ice conditions. We rappelled the Hourglass Face in seven 60m raps.

Mt. Geddes, north face, Central Buttress (400m, TD- 65° max, Hamilton-Kennedy-Rubens, August 4). A good line on the rocky central buttress right of the Bottleneck Couloir. We crossed the bergschrund about 50m right of the foot of the Bottleneck Couloir and climbed steep snow, with short ice steps, to the top of the snow bay below a rock wall, moved up and right following the prominent snow ledges running across the buttress at around mid-height, and continued up the buttress. We finished just west of the central summit and rappelled the Hourglass Face.

Mt. Geddes, north face, Bottleneck Couloir (repeat). On August 4 McGougan and Ritchie attempted a steep snow-and-ice line slanting up left from about halfway up the Bottleneck Couloir, but retreated two pitches beyond the Bottleneck due to poor ice. They rappelled back into the Bottleneck Couloir and followed it to the top.

Mt. Haworth, South Ridge route (350m, 5.6, Hamilton-Hood, July 30). The rocky ridge starts from the col below the NE Ridge of Mt. Geddes. The initial section included a number of slabby rock pitches before the easier upper section. The route finished on the South Face route (which was used to descend) for the final bit to the summit.

Mt. Haworth, Whisky Galore (340m, 5.8, Hamilton-Kennedy, July 31). The most promi-nent line on the rocky southwest face, up a large right-facing corner that faces the glacier below the north face of Mt Geddes. Good rock quality, climbing corners and slabs to a knife-edge arête, then a steep, exposed wall, more slabs, and then the easier upper ridge to the summit. Descent by rappelling the route.

Polydactyl Ridge, East Pinnacle (ca 2,800m, GR 371029), East Ridge (120m, F, Hood-McGougan-Ritchie-Rubens, July 31). The eastmost and higher of the two rocky summits on the serrated east-west ridge. Access the peak via an easy scramble from a base camp under the west ridge of Mt. Haworth, on the north edge of the glacier north of Mt. Geddes. The adjacent west-most peak/pinnacle was climbed in 1964 by Culbert and Woodsworth.

Mam Beag (2,680m, GR 396031; for non-Gaelic speakers *Mam Beag* means "Small Breast"), SW Ridge (150m, F, Hamilton-Hood-Kennedy-McGougan-Ritchie-Rubens, August 1). The southeast ridge of Mt. Roovers culminates in a rounded snow dome (which we named Mam Beag) overlooking the Oval and Parallel glaciers. A nice snow arête led easily from the col between Roovers Glacier and Parallel Glacier (Propyleum Pass) up the southwest ridge to the summit.

Sgurr Hamilton (2,720m, GR 394034), SE Ridge (250m, AD 5.6, Hamilton-Kennedy-Rubens, August 1). The jagged southeast ridge of Mt. Roovers contains several rock pinnacles and towers, including the bulky Roovers Needle. Sgurr Hamilton, named in honor of the eld-est member of our party, is the first prominent, pointed tower seen when approaching from Mam Beag. It is near the eastmost end of the ridge and to the east of Roovers Needle.

Umbra Ridge (Point 2,477m, GR 418018), West Buttress (300m, AD 5.6, Hood-McGougan-Ritchie, August 1). We gained this route by climbing snow slopes above Parallel Glacier to an obvious col between Point 2,477m and a subsidiary peak to the west. From the col climb the cleanest slabs keeping to the crest of the buttress. Probably the first ascent of this sum-mit. Descend the same route.

STEVE KENNEDY *and* DES RUBENS, *U.K.*

Northern Pantheons, first ascents and exploration. On July 24 Markus Raschke, Mickey Schurr, Don Serl, and I flew from Bluff Lake to the northern Pantheons. Our pilot, Mike King of White Saddle Air, dropped Mickey, me, and the extra gear on a knob at 51° 43' 3" N, 125° 24' 7" W, ele-vation 2,250m. He dropped Don and Markus north of Demeter. They traversed Demeter north-to-south and explored south around the head of the valley, gaining our base camp on the 27th.

Mickey and I established camp and climbed Peak 2,543m on the 24th. We propose the name Friga (wife of Odin) for this peak. Our attempt on Dionysus (2,575m) on the 24th was blocked by a step broken by a wide crack, but on the 29th Don and Markus climbed it (at 5.8, with an aid move at the start), to make the first ascent of this peak. On the 27th Mickey and I

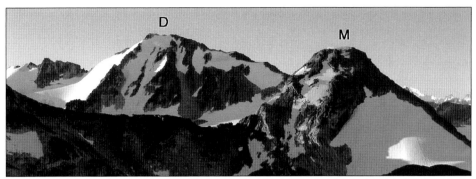

Durga and Mahisha from base camp. Renz and Schurr climbed the skyline ridges from right to left, though the back-side ridge connecting Mahisha to Durga is obscured in this angle. *Peter Renz*

climbed two peaks south-southeast of camp. We climbed the closest peak (2,350m, 2km distant) by its northwest ridge, and propose the name Mahisha (the buffalo demon). We climbed the farther peak (2,494m, 2.75km distant) by curving south and east around the cirque to a col and then to the summit by the west ridge. We propose calling this peak Durga (the slayer of Mahisha). On the 29th Mickey and I climbed the 2,477m peak just east of Friga, for which we propose the name Friga East. The morning of the 30th Mike King flew us out.

Aside from a cairn that Don and Markus found on Demeter, the area seemed untouched. Our base camp was comfortable, with nice views though with limited access to the peaks that Don and Markus scouted on their loop south from Demeter. More routes and peaks beckon.

PETER RENZ, *AAC*

BUGABOOS

The Real Mescalito, on North Howser Tower. Many routes exist on this face. The shorter tower to the right is Central Howser. *Marc Piché*

North Howser Tower, The Real Mescalito. In August, Crosby Johnston and I connected in the East Creek Basin. My schedule gave us only two days—the time it takes most parties just to make the approach and exit. We knew we'd have to light a fire under our asses to get out in time. We hiked up and over to the Pigeon-Howser Col that afternoon and restlessly tried to settle into our sleeping bags.

The line planned in my mind, sketched together from four previous trips to North Howser's west face, connected a lower corner system (The Shooting Gallery) to the Seventh Rifle gully and then upward into cracks in the vicinity of the fictitious line, Mescalito. The true Mescalito is on El Capitan and not North Howser Tower, a mistake made by editors and authors of the previous guidebooks. We hoped the new line would provide a free route straight up the middle of the face, filling in the gap on the topo where Mescalito had originally been drawn. Nervous anticipation settled in as we prepared and repackaged our gear for the next day, paring down in all ways possible: no bivy gear, light approach shoes, a single set of crampons, one ice tool, and one head lamp (I forgot mine).

Our 3 a.m. start on August 13 brought us to the base of the face after three hours of negotiating steep and tenuous conditions on the glacier. Going light always seems like a good idea until you end up descending 55° hard glacier ice with a single crampon and a shared headlamp.

Since I freed the Shooting Gallery section of the route the previous year, while establishing the fourth free route on the west face (Under Fire, 21 pitches, ED2 5.11), this variation has been climbed and cleaned twice more and offers moderate 5.10 climbing on clean splitter cracks and the best access to the upper face. We connected pitches and simul-climbed the first 500m, establishing ourselves on the upper part of the face by early afternoon. We crossed the Seventh Rifle gully and continued straight up the face for 200m of perfect fist jamming and stemming in a clean water-worn right-facing corner. Simon Meis and I had climbed this terrain the year before, but loose, wet and verglassed conditions above had turned us around. It looked like the upper pitches were going to be clean and steep, but getting to them would require several pitches of horrendously loose, wet and icicle-strewn granite. This section of the face was like a freezer box, with surface hoar covering the cavernous fissures and loose death flakes exfoliating off as we tiptoed by. Working our way up the right side of the upper corner systems, avoiding the center of the carnage, we found mostly clean and steep finger cracks. The climbing was sustained at solid 5.11 but required sections of aid to avoid dropping rocks onto the belayer. Dents in my helmet, scrapes on my shoulders, and one particularly disconcerting throbbing bruise on my inner thigh finally coerced us out of this gauntlet of death. We ended up diverting out of the main corner system, forgoing the continuous line we were following, and traversing left. The traverse avoided most of the loose rock on the upper wall. We then returned right into the obvious shaft for the final pitch. Crosby pushed the line up splitter cracks to the summit ridge, arriving in the early evening, with only 100m of scrambling to reach the summit.

Although a couple of quality steep pitches wove through this granite choss in the upper headwall, we came to the sad realization that no amount of cleaning would render this route a classic. Nevertheless, we were exhilarated to have completed our goal. Eleven-and-a-half hours after starting the climb, we had successfully completed a one-day first ascent of North Howser Tower's west face: The Real Mescalito (ED2 5.11+ C1, 18 pitches with lots of simul-climbing). We did not seize a free ascent, but there is always next year and many more cracks and corners strewn across the west face.

As daylight started to fade we tripped and stumbled back to the bivy, with the rush of the day's events still pulsating through our veins. We had added haste to our adventure, not because we had jobs to return to or appointments to keep but because we had become enamored of two beautiful and captivating women. Our continuous banter on sex, love, and relationships had acted like an IV, injecting an insatiable vigor into my body. My hands were bloody and my body swollen, but none of this mattered. I frantically packed my bags, hoping that I would be able to descend before dark (the only headlamp wasn't mine). As I walked away from the bivy, I looked back and saw Crosby already opening his sleeping bag and lining up his dinner celebration like a sheikh lining up his harem. I wanted to stay and celebrate with him but instead turned and trudged on, possessed by the blissful thoughts of soft skin and warm embraces.

JOSHUA LAVIGNE, *Canada*

CANADIAN ROCKIES

Summary. [Note: In addition to mention in this summary, several of the bigger routes have individual reports, below—Ed.] The 200-300m south face of Mt. Yamnuska (2,200m) is steeped in history as the birthplace of Rockies' rock climbing. For many years, even as sport climbing swept through the surrounding Bow River Valley, Yam remained a bastion of tradition and ground-up climbing. However, the

Goat Slabs, with Barbacoa (left) and Mix Meister. Many other routes climb this face. *Andy Genereux*

proliferation of bolts on routes new and old showed that Yam was not completely immune to change. The final step in this metamorphosis came in 2005, when longtime local new-route activist Andy Genereux installed the first entirely top-down route on the cliff: Rejection of the Faith (240m, 5.11c). Genereux's creations (he has since established more top-down routes on Yam), with their many bolts and emphasis on convenience and safety, have proved immediately popular. Not everyone agrees, however, with the direction of climbing on Yam. Allan Derbyshire, an English ex-pat, has been climbing on Yam since the seventies. In 2007, with Kevin Embacher and Choc Quinn, he established Faith (275m, 5.11b). With its ground-up style and bold climbing, Faith stands in stark contrast to nearby Rejection of the Faith.

2007 provided a similar study in contrasts on neighboring Goat Slabs. In July, Genereux and local legend Urs Kallen, author of the first guidebook to Yam, put up Mix Meister (720m, 5.10d). While established ground-up, Mix Meister, with its bolted stations and largely bolt-protected climbing, has a distinctly sport flavor. As a result it received quick repeats. Then in October visiting Americans John Harlin and Mark Jenkins put up Barbacoa (10 pitches, 5.9/5.10 R/X) nearby. Harlin summed up the dilemma of traditional new routing in the Canadian Chossies: "I don't think anyone will be in a rush to repeat this route. But we had a great time, because it was such a fun adventure."

Located a few km farther west up the Bow Valley, the Rimwall (2,685m) is impressive, easily accessible, and largely ignored. Until last year, only three routes ascended the kilometer-or-so long cliff. In August, Dana Ruddy and Raphael Slawinski tried to remedy this with Murder by Numbers (450m, 5.11). The route is a traditional affair, with five protection bolts in ten pitches, and features limestone of exceptional quality (by Rockies' standards).

Until last year what might be considered the Yam of Jasper, Roche Miette (2,377m), had only three major routes. Last summer Dana Ruddy, the resident Jasper hardman, and Matt Reynolds added a fourth line, up the north face of the formation. Like the other routes on Roche Miette, Grey Streaks (IV 5.11) has a distinctly traditional flavor, with only one or two protection bolts in its eight or so pitches.

The big alpine news of 2007 was a new route on the Emperor Face of Mt. Robson (3,959 m), one of the biggest faces of the Rockies [see below].

Though not in the same league as the Emperor Face, a few new routes and variations were completed during the summer. In August on the iconic Mt. Assiniboine (3,616m), Dana Ruddy and Steve Holeczi established the Northeast Face (IV M5), a significant variation to the popular North Ridge (II 5.5). The Northeast Face route climbs a triangular mixed face left of the ridge, joining the North Ridge above the Red Band.

The triple-summitted Mt. Bryce (3,507m) sits alone on the west side of the Columbia Ice-field. In September Cory Richards, Dana Ruddy, Raphael Slawinski, and Eamonn Walsh climbed the North Face Couloir (IV AI4) variation to the classic North Face (IV). Rather than ascend a uniform sheet of 55° ice, the variation climbs a deep gully to the right, with varied and enjoyable climbing. The drive, ascent, and descent fit comfortably into a two-day weekend, a testament to the mixed blessing of logging road access.

The following weekend Slawinski and Walsh went to Mt. Alberta (3,619m), where they established the obscure West Face route (V 5.10+) [see below]. Only a few weeks later, the ice season started with a bang. On the north face of Snow Dome (3,451m), around the corner from the famous Slipstream (925m, WI4+), a spectacular line formed, weeping from the serac bar-rier. A few years before, the north face of Snow Dome was the scene of an infamous Internet prank, whereby doctored photos of Ice Porn, a supposed giant new route, found their way into climbing news. But this time was no prank, and over two days in October, Cory Richards, Dana Ruddy, and Ian Welsted climbed and descended The Real Ice Porn (800m, V WI5+) [see below]. Only a few days later, visiting Swiss climbers Simon Anthamatten and Ueli Steck repeated the route and added another pitch through the serac barrier.

For the two Swiss this was only the start of an incredible rampage that included Rocket Baby (M8+ WI5+X), a four-pitch alternate start to the new-wave mixed testpiece Rocketman (350m, M7+ WI5+) on Mt. Patterson (3,191m). On the lower cliffs of Crowfoot Mtn. (3,055m) Anthamatten and Steck climbed an oft-eyed discontinuous series of drips to create four-pitch Cockfight (M9+ WI5+), one of the most technical multi-pitch mixed routes in the range.

In recent years the popularity of mixed climbing has inspired people to look above the mixed crags and below the big mixed faces. Mini-alpine routes, typically found during the shoulder seasons of spring and fall, often yield excellent mixed climbing. In that vein in Octo-ber, Rob Owens and Eamonn Walsh climbed the north face of a possibly unclimbed 2,680m outlier ("Mt. MOG") of Mt. Whymper (2,844m) in the Chickadee Valley. A few weeks later Owens and Steve Holeczi established Zeitgeist on the northwest face of nearby Mt. Bell [see below].

Activity on bigger routes ground to a halt with the end of November, as the short, cold days of winter descended on the Rockies. On the Stanley Headwall, Raphael Slawinski and friends climbed several new routes and variations. This classic ice and mixed venue might have been thought climbed out, yet some unusual ice formations yielded some interesting new pitches, all in a strongly traditional vein.

As the days got longer again, so did the routes being put up. In February 2008 Rob Owens and Jon Walsh ventured up a rock corner to the right of the Upper Weeping Wall. The corner Owens and Walsh headed for promised little more than snowed-up rock climbing, but they found plenty of thin ice. No Use in Crying (205m, M7) is likely climbable every winter, and deserves to become a classic.

Icefall Brook is a remote drainage on the west side of the Rockies, in winter accessible only by a long ski or, more conveniently, helicopter. In March the international team of Audrey Gariepy, Caroline George, Jen Olson, Ines Papert, and Jon Walsh spent ten days comfortably camped within striking distance of a multitude of unclimbed lines. During their stay they established seven WI5/6 routes and three mixed lines ranging from M5 to M12, up to 600m long.

While rich in ice- and mixed-climbing accomplishments, the winter of 2007–08 did not encourage alpine climbing. From November through February hardly a week went by without an avalanche incident. A number of these proved fatal.

By early March 2008 Raphael Slawinski, Eamonn Walsh, and Ian Welsted rationalized their choice of objective, the Northeast Buttress (a.k.a. the Greenwood-Jones route, summer V 5.9) on Mt. Temple (3,540m) as having essentially no avalanche hazard. Their calculations proved correct, and over three days they climbed and descended this, the last of the major north face routes to receive a winter ascent. In keeping with the modern ethos, they dry-tooled the entire route at M6. A few days later, visiting climbers Steve House and Roger Strong climbed the route in a continuous 25.5-hour round-trip push from a camp below the north face.

The action then shifted north to the great pyramid of Mt. Chephren (3,274m), where Pierre Darbellay and Raphael Slawinski established the Dogleg Couloir (V+ M7 A1) [see below].

Meanwhile, Vince Anderson and Steve House ventured to the formidable north face of Mt. Alberta and put up the Anderson-House (VI M8 WI5), a difficult line climbed in excellent style just outside of calendar winter, but in full-on winter conditions [see below].

The spring alpine season came to a close in early April with another big roadside line. Mt. Wilson (3,260m) is an ice-climbing mecca, with one of the greatest concentrations of waterfall ice in the Rockies. In recent years climbers have started taking some of these lines not only to the proverbial end of the difficulties (typically fairly low on the mountain), but all the way to the summit ridge. Raphael Slawinski and Jon Walsh established Dirty Love (V M7) up a giant corner/chimney system above the (unformed) Shooting Star (350m, WI6), climbing the route in a continuous 23-hour push car-to-summit. They downclimbed and rappelled a gully on the south face (which turned out to be the route Living In Paradise), taking a further eight hours. As with so many weekend alpine adventures, the crux came at the end: staying awake on the drive home.

RAPHAEL SLAWINSKI, *Canada, AAC*

Mt. Robson. Emperor Face, Haley-House. When I got the call, Joe Josephson was on the other end of the line. Joe and Barry Blanchard were looking for a third to join them on an attempt on the Emperor Face, and so began what we came to call "the annual attempt and failure to climb Mt. Robson." Over 10 days in March 1997, Barry, Joe, and I made two attempts on the face. Our first attempt, up the central gully, ended at one-third height by that favored climber's delusion, dry snow over steep rock. (Amazing how it looks climbable if you spend enough days staring at it.) Next we tried the largest gully system on the right side of the face. A couple of thousand feet up, we could traverse 80' to the Emperor Ridge and comfortable bivouac sites. There I discovered that I had somehow dropped a crucial part of the stove, rendering it inoperable. Rather than huck myself straight off the cliff, as was my initial inclination, we spent a dry, cold night. At sunup Barry calmly led us back down the Emperor Ridge, with a dozen rappels and much downclimbing.

For the next 10 years, every spring I went north for the month of March, hoping to climb the Emperor Face. In 2000 Barry, Joe, and I climbed to the same highpoint and descended the same way, thwarted by storm. Later a pair of young Slovenians climbed precisely the same terrain

Mt. Robson's (12,989') Emperor Face: (1) Logan-Stump (1978). (2) Cheesmond-Dick, (1981; finishes on the north face, to the right of the 1963 Callis-Davis route). Both routes were approached via the Mist Icefall, below. (3) Infinite Patience (Blanchard-Dumerac-Pellet, 2002). (4) Haley-House (2007; approached from above, with arrows showing the descent and the dotted black line showing the ascent). (ER) is the Emperor Ridge (Perla-Spencer, 1961), and the dashed line shows the 1974 Callis-Kanzler attempt (see note in text), which traversed off and descended the north face. Some of the lines, especially (1) and (2), have been wildly misdrawn in a variety of publications. Each Emperor Face line shown here was drawn by a member of the respective first ascent party. *John Scurlock*

and declared it a new route.

Barry and I didn't consider it done. Then, in October 2002 Barry climbed the route with Eric Dumerac and Philippe Pellet and named it Infinite Patience. In July 2001 I spent seven nights there in a tiny tent with Rolando Garibotti, and in March 2007 another nine days in the Hargreaves Shelter with Vince Anderson. In 1997 we'd helicoptered in and skied out. In 1998 we'd flown in and out. With Rolo and Vince I was determined to go by foot, but each time the weather window had closed by the time we had negotiated the 27km approach.

I had slept 35 nights below the face over a span of ten years. After the March '07 attempt I bookmarked all Internet weather forecasts for Jasper, Valemont, and McBride (Robson being roughly equidistant from these locales) and checked the forecasts religiously. I created a spreadsheet to track the forecasted and actual weather, to estimate their reliability. Finally, in late May the weather looked good, but Vince was in Alaska guiding.

Colin Haley is young and lucky and available. Good, too. So I drove to Seattle, bivied in Colin's parent's loft, and on May 24 we drove to Valemont, hired a helicopter, and flew to the Helmut-Robson col. The flying got us there within the forecasted three-day good weather period (we burned the first day driving and flying), and it allowed us a safe approach to the face by downclimbing the Mist Glacier to the start of the climbing. I had done the approach from Berg Lake and up through the dangerous Mist icefall four times, and my odds were not getting better.

We left the tent at 4:30 a.m. on May 25 and were climbing within an hour. Colin led the first block of seven pitches. We stretched the pitches by simul-climbing where reasonable, thus averaging 80m per pitch. At over half-height the wall gets steep, and my experience and familiarity with the terrain came into play. There is a steep corner system just left of the apex of the face. I headed for that, leading a block of seven excellent pitches with very good ice conditions. The last 30m through the headwall were exciting, steep M7 climbing that kept me on my arms.

Mt. Robson from the northwest, with Berg Lake in the foreground. *John Scurlock*

The rock varied from solid to suspect. The climbing was excellent, with technical moves protected by small cams and pins. But the greatest surprise was finding a tight Lost Arrow piton right at the exit move. The pin had to be from the '78 Jim Logan and Mugs Stump ascent (*AAJ 1979*, pp. 122-24). A few meters higher I found two more pitons that had obviously been someone's belay. The pitch overhung about six or seven meters in the last 30. At 10:30 p.m. we hacked out a sitting stance on an ice arête that appeared to be 300-400' of easier climbing below the Emperor Ridge cornices, covered ourselves with a lightweight tarp, and alternately dozed and drank warm water while waiting for sunup.

Illustrious oranges and dazzling reds made me feel like I was climbing out of a 70's Technicolor daydream as I led the final two moderate thin ice and mixed pitches. At the ridge we belayed down a hundred feet and started simul-climbing across the top of the south face before unroping. We aimed for the Wishbone Arête and soloed up it for a few hundred feet. The ice was spooky rime, so we brought out the rope. I went ahead, winding over, around, and through the incredibly wild formations.

As we started climbing down a rime lump, the wind whipped and seemed to tear a momentary hole in the clouds. We had just climbed over the summit. We headed down the Kain Route, which Colin had descended before. Our camp-to-camp time was approximately 36 hours.

After we got home Dougald MacDonald put me in touch with Jim Logan. Jim concluded our phone conversation by saying "I like the idea that somebody else has been there now. It's like Mugs and I knew what it was like up there. Now you guys know what it is like. It's kind of cool. Nobody else knows. I was getting to the point where I was wanting somebody to do that face. When you did, it made me really happy. I really liked it."

"Jim," I replied, "We liked it too."

STEVE HOUSE, *AAC*

Emperor Face, historical note. Nearly forgotten, in 1974 Pat Callis and Jim Kanzler made the first significant attempt at the then-unclimbed Emperor Face, climbing high on the face through a feature they called the "Jaws." Callis recalls their attempt:

Colin Haley leading on the lower half of the Haley-House route. *Steve House*

"It was a significant mountaineering experience at the time, involving four bivies, but we did not write it up because we did not go to the summit. We were escaping, having misjudged the nature of the upper wall as being ice. The lower part was great ice, and we did half the face in one and a half days but did not take enough rock gear and food for the rest of it.

"Ours was the first serious attempt, and it was in was in 1974, following two earlier explorations by me with Hank Abrons in '72 and Kanzler in '73. Also, we invited Jeff Lowe and Mike Weiss to go on another try in '75, but after hanging out at the base waiting for weather, we had to give it up.

"Kanzler deserves recognition for realizing the feasibility of the line through the Jaws in '74 and talking me into doing it. Although it was the line Abrons and I picked in '72, by '74 I was thinking of a more conservative route that went left up the snow ramp at the bottom before going directly up."

Mt. Alberta, Anderson-House. At 4:30 a.m. on March 26, 2008, in bitter cold, Steve House and I left the Lloyd McKay hut and approached the ridge leading to the rappel station down to the north face of Mt. Alberta. A harsh breeze made it was hard to fully appreciate the beauty of the aurora display on the northern horizon, dazzling and ominous at the same time. After rappelling onto the northern slopes, my losing and then finding one of my ice tools, sometime between 9 and 9:30 we arrived at the base of the north face, roped up, and started the real climbing.

We climbed what we may be the common approach pitches, probably M5, though photos in the guidebook seem to put the normal start farther right, and where we went did not feel that "climbed." Anyway, we reached the base of the ice (snow) field in three pitches. We put the ropes away and soloed the incredibly steep (for snow climbing) face, passing the occasional bare ice patch. Near the Yellow Band, the snow yielded to the typical steely, hard, gray ice you'd expect there. We got the ropes out again and did three easy but scrappy mixed pitches through the Yellow Band to the base of the steep, rock headwall. The weather deteriorated, and it started to snow and cloud over. We considered bailing to the Northeast Ridge, but continued,

Vince Anderson nearing the Yellow Band on the north face of Alberta, with the headwall rising above. Dashes: Anderson-House (2008), with bivy spot (B). Solid: Glidden-Lowe (1972). For an overview photo of the face see *AAJ 2007*, p. 191. *Steve House*

Anderson leading the third pitch of the second day. He dead-ended, came back left and took a crack straight up that offered two fantastic M7 pitches. *Steve House*

convincing ourselves that retreat would still be feasible from a short ways higher. We could see the start of the Glidden-Lowe route nearby, but found a crack system 60m right that looked like better climbing in these winter conditions. Two long, difficult pitches (M7 and M8R/X) of high-quality dry-tooling led up and left to intersect the G-L above its third pitch, in the snowy alcove described for that climb. Here the G-L angles up and right onto a buttress, but we found a steep, narrow ice pillar above. It was now about dark, probably 9 p.m., and we hoped to find a decent bivouac spot above the obvious ice. After an exhausting bout with this pitch (cold, black ice) and one more short pitch through snow mushrooms, we found a bivy spot between mushrooms that was somewhat protected from the now-frequent spindrift avalanches. We fixed 30' of the next pitch, and by 1 a.m. we were finally settled in and ready to try to sleep. The night was cold, but tolerable. Our down sleeping bags had gotten a little wet, but we hoped to avoid another night on the mountain.

We woke after 6 a.m. and slowly made our way out of our wet cocoons and back onto the climb. Steve had done the bulk of the hard leading the previous day, so I took the sharp end and started up a small ice corner to the end of the water ice. A small ledge system then traversed right, towards the G-L and the summit ice slopes. Deep snow covered the airy traverse, which required belly crawling and precarious tip-toeing to reach a niche with more moderate ground above. By now, most of our gloves were frozen hard and semi-useless from constant immersion in the snow, making it quite difficult to manipulate the gear. Another few pitches of good mixed climbing up flakes, corners, and slabs covered in thin névé (M7 and M6) brought us back to the G-L exit pitch. A short bit of moderate mixed terrain put us onto the upper slopes, from where we continued straight up on slabby mixed, because we thought the exit traverse onto the ice seemed convoluted.

The ground we climbed, however, would probably be less attractive in summer conditions. A 150m pitch put us onto the summit ridge and gave us our first glimpse of the sun in two days. At 5:45 p.m. we stopped briefly on top before heading down the corniced south ridge toward the Japanese Route.

Unsure of where to descend the east face, we guessed the wrong gully and spent a truly miserable night out, shivering in our frozen, useless sleeping bags, before brilliant morning sunshine greeted us on the 28th. By 10 a.m. we were safely in the flat basin and slogged back to the hut, where we could eat, drink, and rest a bit before heading out for Steve's truck.

VINCE ANDERSON, *AAC*

Mt. Alberta, West Face. I first saw a photo of the face in a 1989 *Climbing* magazine. A spectacular aerial shot showed a wall of black limestone topped by a dazzlingly white summit ridge, with a rare blue sky. A gothic flying buttress, rising gracefully to the summit icefield, jumped out at me. The caption read: "The unclimbed west face of Mount Alberta." At the time, given my abilities, the photo may as well have been of Olympus Mons on Mars, but I did not forget it.

Mt. Alberta's West Face route, viewed from the approach. *Raphael Slawinski*

One weekend in late July, Rich Akitt and I headed for the face, but, for reasons that escape me now, I thought we should traverse to it on one of the large scree ledges that girdle Alberta. We retreated, and the next day ran up the Northeast Ridge, descended the Japanese route, hiked out to the road, and drove back to Calgary, arriving shortly before dawn on Monday.

I thought I was done with Alberta for the season, but gradually I found myself thinking about it again. So on a heartbreakingly beautiful Friday afternoon in mid-September, Eamonn Walsh and I waded across the Sunwapta River and headed up Woolley Creek. The fresh snow plastering the peaks would not melt until spring, but ever the optimist, I figured the steepness and sunny aspect would mean it would still be in rock-climbing shape.

We skidded down rubble and jumped gritty crevasses toward Alberta, visible only as a hulking black shape against a star-filled sky. The moon was just past new and did not light our way like last time, but unlike

Eamonn Walsh on Mt. Alberta. *Raphael Slawinski*

last time I knew where to go. Staying low, we rounded the south end of the mountain and easily walked across a rocky plateau beneath the west face. At a shallow col that plunged into a deep, shadowed valley to the north, we stopped for a quick rest. A cold wind whipped across the saddle, and we were soon moving again, scrambling up scree and rock steps toward the vertical headwall capping the west face. We filled up on water where it trickled down an ice gully, keeping an eye out for falling stones. Where the gully opened into a snowfield, we donned crampons and traversed to the base of our chosen rib. A beautiful ribbon of ice cascaded down between the main wall and the lower part of the buttress. We were briefly tempted, but our having only one tool apiece and no screws convinced us to stick to the rock. Besides, we were freezing and could see the first rays of sunlight warming the crest.

At the top of the first pitch we found an old rappel station. And I do mean old: heavy, rusted pins stamped "Swiss made," connected with bleached goldline. In 1963 four Vulgarians had attempted the west face and nearly made it up before being forced down by electrical storms. We would be following in their footsteps most of the day. Changing into rock shoes, we continued up.

Crimping on crumbling edges, the last knifeblade a distant memory, I basked in my fear. At least once a year I find myself whimpering to my partner: "I do not want to be scared anymore." And yet perched on that flying buttress, high above empty, silent valleys, there was nowhere else I would rather have been.

As the afternoon wore on we were faced with a steep off-width crack, the only weakness in what looked to be the final steep step. Fortunately, the rock also took a turn for the better, and after some grunting and me sending a few volleys of stones down on Eamonn's head ("Dude, are you OK?" "I'm… not… sure…") we were up, and looking at what we hoped really was the final steep step. We snuck up it via an easy gully, the rock shoes and chalk bags went into the packs, out came boots and crampons. Under an intensely blue sky, more Karakoram than Canadian Rockies, we walked up the gentle snow slope to the summit and, without stopping, headed down the long south ridge.

Night fell as we completed the last rappel down the Japanese gully, below and upwind of the Elephants' Asses. But we knew where to go and so were spared sitting out a cold night. Plunging into the darkness, we downclimbed rock steps and surfed scree toward the distant creature comforts of the hut.

Mt. Alberta (3,619m), West Face (V 5.10+).

RAPHAEL SLAWINSKI, *Canada, AAC*

Snow Dome, The Real Ice Porn to serac band. On October 13 Dana Ruddy, Cory Richards, and I climbed a waterfall ice route (800m, WI 5+) on the north face of Snow Dome. It is the fifth route on Snow Dome, and the first on the north face proper, around the buttress from Slipstream. As with Dave Marra's route, For Fathers, we did not top out our route, which is guarded by a serac band. Dave, who had spotted the line, persuaded us before we ventured on the route that, from his experience, climbing blue seracs was not wise. A week after our ascent Ueli Steck and Simon Anthamatten climbed through the serac and added 50m to our effort, nonetheless not topping out, stopped by a huge cornice.

Some debate ensued as to what properly constitutes a FA. After discussion with a few respected locals, a consensus seemed to emerge that waterfall FAs do not have to top out, while

Snow Dome: (1) Borderline. (2) Aggressive Treatment. (3) Slipstream.
(4) The Real Ice Porn (ends at serac band; inset). *Cory Richards*

to claim an alpine FA one must top out on the mountain (Although certain prominent FA claims do not follow this rule). This, at least, is what some of us eager for the fame of FAs have agreed upon.

A good day was had by all on the route, marked by Dana-rope gunning all of the vertical ice, plus a bivy at 10,500' on the descent, thus bucking the trend to do routes in a rush.

IAN WELSTED, *Canada*

Mt. Chephren's northeast face, including the Wild Thing (left) and Dogleg Couloir, with the bivy at the square. *Raphael Slawinski*

Mt. Chephren, Dogleg Couloir. Our second night on Chephren sticks in my mind. A night spent surfing the line between control and chaos. The final rock band on the face festooned with obscene snow mushrooms, like a scene from a demented dream. But I am getting ahead of myself. I cannot recall when I first heard the line right of the Wild Thing on Chephren's northeast face referred to as the Dogleg, but the name was appropriate and it stuck. The line starts as a snow gully, then at two-thirds height abruptly bends left, culminating in a series of chimneys cutting through the rock bands guarding the summit.

On a crisp morning in early April 2007, with the first hint of dawn lighting the eastern sky, Dana Ruddy, Eamonn Walsh, and I were a few hundred meters up the initial gully when the sun hit the face. I never cease to be amazed at how quickly pleasure can turn to terror in the mountains. Slides came thundering down and we spent several hours hunkered under a rock outcrop. Once things quieted down, we got out as quickly as possible.

Less than twelve months later I was back, with Pierre Darbellay, enticed by a full moon and a good forecast. An avalanche tried to toss me down the giant snow cone below as I soloed the initial ice step, but it was the only one all day. We simul-climbed past our previous high point, through more ice steps, up a broad snowfield, and into a narrowing couloir. By mid-afternoon the couloir had steepened to a vertical corner. We pulled out the rest of the rack and the other rope, and got down to business.

The next two pitches, thinly iced, with decent rock gear, would have been fun had it not been for the overnight pack. But after some whining, I grunted onto the largest ledge girdling Chephren's summit block. A crater in the slope blasted out by a snow mushroom that had fallen from somewhere above helpfully exposed some choss into which to drive iron, lash it all together, and call it an anchor. The next rockband went easily, and it was time to find a bivy. We slept so well in our comfortable cave that we overslept the alarm. Outside, the clouds were barely above our bivy site. By mid-morning it started snowing, and suddenly the sky was full of rocks, and Pierre came hammering down the chimney. We found the tool he had lost during the fall, but his hip was bruised, and I went up to finish the pitch.

As he climbed past my stance, I remarked cheerfully that it looked like the angle eased above, the chimney turning into a snow gully. For the first but not the last time that day, I was right about the snow but wrong about the angle. Snow choked the overhanging chimney above, and two hard pitches later we emerged onto the snow ledge below the final rock band. By then the light snow had turned into a swirling mass of heavy flakes. With strange detachment I watched small slides start on the ledge and gather volume as they disappeared down the chimney, following the parallel lines of the ropes. Tools slid off of marginal edges, and crampons sparked on the smooth limestone, as I managed the next pitch without falling. Actually, that is not quite true. I was standing on a snow mushroom fiddling a nut into crack when I felt myself fall—and then stop. The umbilical on my tool had caught my plummet. While Pierre seconded the pitch, I tried to memorize the terrain above the belay in the fading light. The chimney system continued straight up, while off to the right weird snow blobs seemed to promise lower-angle terrain. I headed that way first, only to retreat below a blank wall. I was balancing between snow mushrooms, traversing back left above Pierre's stance, when overhanging rock and snow rushed upward. I bounced to a stop 10m lower, unharmed.

I yarded back up to the cam that had held me and that now became the anchor. Pierre came up and continued across the traverse that I had helped clear of treacherous snow formations. At 3 a.m. I started up what I hoped would be the last pitch. The keychain thermometer on my pack showed -15° C. Between the fatigue and the spindrift blowing from the summit ridge, it felt colder. My first charge, up the right-hand branch of the chimney, ground to a halt at an unprotected, overhanging offwidth. The left-hand branch did not look much more promising, but after trying to squeeze and then dry-tool my way up, I shamelessly hung from a few knifeblades to gain more reasonable ground above.

Wind gusted across the summit ridge as I struggled into my belay jacket and overmitts. I was too cold and tired to feel exultation, only relief. Pierre came up, somehow manhandling both our packs. As we traversed across the wind-scoured southern slopes, they slowly turned from black to gray. Day was breaking. Six hours later, after wading down avalanche slopes that thankfully stayed put, and post-holing to the ground with every step in the woods, we were back at the car. We had a bottle of single malt waiting for us, but were too dehydrated to celebrate. We brushed a thick layer of fresh snow from the roof of the car and drove off to find water.

Mt. Chephren, Dogleg Couloir (V+ M7 A1), March 22-24, 2008.

RAPHAEL SLAWINSKI, *Canada, AAC*

Mt. MOG, Owens-Walsh, and Mt. Bell, Zeitgeist. Alpine climbing—or perhaps "alpine cragging"—on lesser known, lower elevation peaks (but still with decent-sized faces) is catching on in the Canadian Rockies. This winter I enjoyed a number of great days on these sorts of objectives, including some new routes.

On October 26 Eamonn Walsh and I headed for the north face of an unnamed 2,680m peak in the Chickadee Valley, just on the B.C side of the Continental Divide, off the west side of Highway 93N, the Banff–Radium Hot Springs road. I first noticed this peak and its face while ski-touring the previous spring. A spring or winter ascent would have a lot more snow to deal with, and the result would be a different experience, to say the least.

Eamonn and I ended up having an awesome day. The route looked to be predominantly rock, but in fact ice was splattered on every pitch, though we used only two ice screws on the entire route. There were a couple of hard pitches, but lots of easier mixed (M4) in between, allowing us to get to the top and down in 16 hours.

We aided one short section to keep the pace. It would have gone free at a short but very physical M8-ish (overhanging, arcing roof-corner-crack, with decent gear but no feet to start).

Zeitgeist, on the northwest face of Mt. Bell. The right skyline is the North Ridge route. *Rob Owens*

The descent involved downclimbing and one rappel to the south side of the peak, and then down the drainage to the east (involving exposed downclimbing and one more short rappel). In retrospect, I think we should have gone down a couloir on the west side of the peak.

Rack: 6 pins (blades to baby angle), the upper two sizes of BD peckers (amazing in thin, ice-filled, or expanding cracks and flakes, my new favorite gear for Rockies alpine climbing), 8 nuts (full size range), cams from .5" to 3" (a #4 Camalot would be useful a couple of times, but we did without).

After considerable research, we don't think the peak had been climbed, so we called it Mt. MOG. MOG stands for Man of Girth, which Eamonn and I both are. Our route gains 600m in elevation and went at about IV+ M6+ A1. Worth Doing.

Two weeks later, on November 8, Steve Holeczi and I approached Mt. Bell via Taylor Lake (9km west of Castle Junction on Highway #1), taking 2.5 hours to the base

Mt. MOG and the Owens-Walsh route. *Rob Owens*

of the northwest face. This was our second attempt at the route, the first being two days earlier, and we were rewarded with high-quality quartzite mixed climbing. The feature we climbed is a sub-face of sorts and does not lead directly to the summit. The route reaches the North Ridge (5.3) of Mt. Bell at about two-thirds height. We decided not to head to the summit, as the North Ridge is quite different in character from the rest of our climb.

Zeitgeist (German for "The spirit of the times"; 530m, IV+ M7- WI5R) went in 10 pitches, with pitches 6, 7, and 8 having steep ice and dry-tooling, sustained mixed climbing, and awesome quality. We rappelled the route in 12 ropelengths off a mixture of ice and rock anchors.

Rack: 10 screws; a set of nuts; cams to 3" with double .75, 1, 2; 6 pins (mostly KBs); bird beaks/peckers/ice hooks; 12 draws.

ROB OWENS, *Canada*

Greenland

WEST COAST

Paddle to the Peaks Expedition, first ascents between Maniit-soq and the Evigkels Fjord. Althea Rogers, Kelly Ryan, and I spent 65 days exploring the magnificent region between Kangerlussuaq and Maniitsoq. Mountains here rise directly from the sea, the coast cut by countless fjords and inlets. We left Maniitsoq on the longest day of the year, our modes of transportation being limited to kayak and foot. This type of exploration is especially significant in such a remote region. About as "ground-upwards" as you can get, our holistic approach to climbing and exploration allowed us to gain a better knowledge of the area, as well as emphasizing the

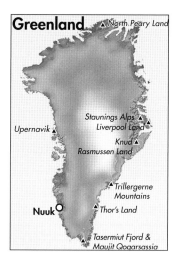

importance of the Leave No Trace ethic. We paddled through glassy waters reflecting the golden glow of the midnight sun, our routine for much of the expedition being to sleep during the height of the day and exploring in the twilight hours. As we moved through the fjords, we examined the glaciers, snowfields and ridges for feasible routes on towering peaks and, discovering a line that enticed us, hauled our boats out of the ocean and unpacked our climbing equipment. Abundant light meant we were able to climb 15 hours or more per day. As weeks disappeared into months, we honed our organization: packing and unpacking heavily loaded boats went from a messy jigsaw puzzle to a balanced routine, only occasionally thrown by a forgotten cooking pot or jacket. By the finish, we had summited 10 peaks. These are listed in chronological order.

Suilaarsarfik (1,326m), west ridge, June 26. We climbed 500m of seasonal snow to a saddle, then scrambled along the crest to the summit (easy 5th class). On the summit we found evidence of previous ascents.

Peak 839m, south couloir attempt, June 29. The snow couloir led to a notch on the southwest ridge, where we retreated. Southwest buttress attempt, June 30: 5.6 to the notch gained the previous day, at which point we again descended. North Couloir, July 2: AI 3 for 400m to a snow dome and the summit plateau.

Peak 850m, west face, probable first ascent, July 5. One pitch of AI 3 gave access to a broad ice shield, which gave AI 2 climbing to the top of the face, followed by 4th class scrambling to the summit. This peak may have been climbed previously, most likely via the ridge, which can be gained easily from a prominent heli-ski drop off-point between Peaks 850 and 1,038.

Peak 741m, north ridge, July 7. From the glacier we scrambled for 300m up the ridge west of the peak, to where it joins a summit block. The climbing then got challenging. A crack system to the left of a large detached pillar led to easier ground, above which two to three pitches of steep 5.8–5.10, followed by three pitches of 5.6 or so, led to the summit (IV 5.9+).

Qaqqarsuaralak (1,334m), south ridge, attempts, July 15 and 22. Multiple attempts on both good and bad rock taught us the art of climbing in pristine places. The hardest climbing was a section or two of 5.8 to gain the south ridge from the west. Once on the crest, the climbing was straightforward (5.6), until the ridge becomes a knife-edge and the rock quality seriously diminishes. It was here we chose to retreat. We don't know whether this peak has been climbed but suspect that it hasn't.

Peak 1,041m, southeast face, July 20. This gave us a reprieve from sitting out bad weather in the tent and proved to be an enjoyable climb. It could even be done in cloud. Third class scrambling up the face led to the ridge and the summit.

Qinnguata Qaqqai (1,216m), northwest ridge, August 4. Third class scrambling up slabs, followed by scree slopes. This peak had a cairn on the summit, but we believe it is popular with heli-skiers and may not have been climbed from the ground.

Peak 1,444m, east ridge, August 8. A long glacier approach and a steep scree valley led to the east col, above which we followed the ridge (3rd class) to a flat plateau surrounded by steep walls, which formed the summit.

Peak 1,775m, southeast ridge, August 13. This is a massive peak with a long, demanding glacial approach. Once on the southwest ridge, reaching the summit proved easy, but the late summer conditions made accessing the ridge difficult.

Peak 700m, southeast face, August 19. A glacier approach followed by 4th class scrambling to the summit. A great bang for the buck.

Brad Washburn Cabot, *AAC*

East Coast

Dronning Louise Land, various ascents. Gerwyn Lloyd, Tim Radford, and I, members of a North Wales-based mountain rescue team, visited the most northerly significant mountain range in Arctic East Greenland, an area known as Dronning Louise Land. Only two other expeditions had visited this region: a combined British Forces expedition, which traveled south through the area in 1953 for surveying, and a Tangent-organized team, which visited the western sector in 2000. We planned to visit the southeast, an area named The Fairytale Peaks by the 1953 expedition (so called because they did not reach it and said anything they recorded about it would be a fairy tale).

From Constable Point we flew north, refueling at Daneborg. We had requested the Twin Otter to land at N 75°57'59.23", W 25°8'16.30", but after much circling the pilot told us he could not land, due to extensive blue ice and crevasse fields. He flew northwest, looking for a safe landing site, finally dropping us on the edge of the ice cap at N 76°11'24.55", W 26°32'49.73", over 50km from our intended landing point. We estimated it would take us five or six days to reach our original destination, and as our pick-up point was well to the north, we decided it was unfeasible to visit the Fairytales and reluctantly changed our plans, deciding to follow the edge of the ice cap north to our intended pick-up point at N 76°28'8.64", W 26°11'36.48". The majority of peaks we passed along the way would still be unclimbed.

We had a secondary aim: Southwest Dronning Louise Land had been identified as a potentially good site for meteorite collection. Theoretically, any meteorite should be visible as a rock that was distinct from the other specimens in the debris field. Unfortunately and somewhat surprisingly, the geology was so diverse that every rock appeared distinct from every other, and this part of our scientific program was not successful. However, we tried to take a small rock sample from each peak visited, and these were later analyzed.

Arriving on May 13, we made eight camps on our ski journey, being flown out of the area

Seen from 2,048m Carnedd Môr Ladron, Y Lliwedd (2,052m) is the double-summited peak at the end of Iron Ridge. The 2007 Dronning Louise expedition traversed the ridge as far as the summit marked (L) but did not continue to the furthest point. The rocky slopes rise ca 800m to the crest of the ridge from the glacier to the left, and all peaks in the background are believed to be unclimbed. *Russ Hore*

on June 8. The sun never dipped less than 40° above the horizon, but sleep never seemed to be a problem. In total we skied ca 80km and ascended 19 peaks, of which 15 were first ascents. The changes to our intended route meant that the last part of the journey was through an area which had been visited by the 2000 Tangent Expedition, and a few of the peaks had already been climbed.

On May 15 we made the first ascent of Penderyn (2,143m, N 76°13'28.44", W 26°38'21.68"), naming it after a single malt Welsh whiskey. From our Camp 3 at 1,912m we made five first ascents: on the 19th Copa Rhosyn (2,067m, N 76°15'19.10", W 26°21'06.63") and Y Lliwedd (2,052m N 76°15'35.23", W 26°20'03.55"); on the 21st Cornucopia (1,996m, N 76°15'51.53", W 26°22'29.03"), Foel Fras (1,917m, N 76°16'30.00", W 26°24'33.72"), and Carnedd Môr Ladron (Pirate Peak, 2,049m N 76°15'40.32", W 26°22'35.51"). Farther north on the 23rd we made the first ascent of Bryn Poeth (2,084m, N 76°20'59.28", W 26°20'48.18") via snow slopes of about Scottish II and a splendid snow ridge. The name means "warm hill" in Welsh and reflected the temperatures on the day. On the 24th we made the second ascent of Softice (1,833m, N 76°19'52.65", W 26°19'53.72), a peak first climbed by the 2000 expedition, and on the following day the first ascent of Yr Esgair (The Staircase, 2,002m, N 76°17'55.08", W 26°32'58.38"), named for the shape of its east ridge, the upper section of which comprised fantastic evenly spaced slabs. After we moved north to Camp 5 on the 27th, overnight gale force winds eased during the following afternoon and allowed an ascent of the nearest peak, a flat-topped pyramid named Dickens Bjerg, (2,241m, N 76°23'41.30", W 26°21'09.11"). Ours was the second ascent. On the 31st the plan was to climb a peak near to our Camp 6 and then head for the pick-up point. We split up to make the second ascent of Falkonner Klippen (2,088m N 76°26'55.76", W 26°19'51.40") by two routes: one by a rotten, broken rock ridge and the second by a more direct line up an ice couloir. This peak was first identified by the 1953 team.

During our ski to Camp 7, we passed a tempting ridge on a small peak. Next day we attempted it. The ridge was easy to attain but soon reared up into a steep section, possibly Scottish III. Above a level section a sharp ridge led to a pleasant rock scramble and the summit. A rappel from a double Abalakov and a dodgy ice screw saw us back on safe ground: a fantastic route. We named the formation DB Ridge (1,941m, N 76°27'03.65", W 26°15'28.16"). The same day we made the first ascent of Dinky Do (1,904m N 76°27'17.04", W 26°07'48.66") and on June 2 In-Pin (1,980m N 76°26'21.96", W 26°16'38.58"). We also climbed Aonach Mor (1,941m N 76°26'08.16", W 26°12'43.86") on the 2nd, a second ascent. On the 3rd we moved our camp just over 1km to join an expedition led by Nigel Edwards, which was to be collected by the same Twin Otter. Due to mechanical failure and then poor weather, we couldn't be picked up immediately and in the meantime made first ascents of Carnedd y Genod (1,974m, N 76°27'16.62", W 26°04'59.22") and Mynydd Glaslyn (1,893m, N 76°28'10.32", W 26°00'58.14"), both on the 3rd, and Pod (N 76°29', W 26°16'; coordinates are approximate due to GPS failure) and Golden Dome (1,954m, N 76°27'19.74", W 26°07'0.36") on the 4th.

Southwest Dronning Louise Land is a beautiful part of the world. The mountain vistas rival any other, and with the serenity of the Arctic, they provide a magical and unique setting.

RUSS HORE, *U.K.*

Andrees Land, exploration and first ascents. Exercise Boreal Zenith was an Army Mountaineering Association exploratory expedition to Andrees Land that was organized to commemorate 50 years of British Army Mountaineering. The expedition took place from July 3–August 3. Members Sally Brown, Cath Davies, Keve Edwards, Beth Hall-Thompson, Ollie Noakes, Dave Stanley, Joe Williams, and I between us made 34 ascents, of which 29 were new. The climbs ranged from simple snow plods to steep north faces, mixed alpine ridges, and steep rock routes. Grades ranged from Alpine PD to D and up to British HVS on pure rock.

Andrees Land is located at N 73°35', W 26°00'in North East Greenland National Park, ca 800km north of the Arctic Circle. The closest permanent habitation is Scoresby Sund, 370km to the south. The area is mountainous and bounded on the south and east by fjords and on the west and north by the permanent ice cap. It is bisected from east to west by the Grejsdallen Valley. We could find only limited information on this region prior to our visit. The only documented mountaineering that we could find took place as long ago as 1950. However, geologists have been to this area more recently. Mountains reach a maximum altitude of 2,300m, mainly rising from glacier plateaus at ca 1,800m, giving ascents of up to 500m. Summits vary from rounded snow domes to small rocky spikes and generally consist of sedimentary rocks that tend to be shattered and loose. That said, we encountered a number of solid gendarmes and buttresses. There is also an area of granite, with large slabs that remain unclimbed, and a large, complex granite face on Lizard Peak that offers plenty of options for new routes.

The valleys are steep-sided and glacially eroded, ranging in altitude from sea level to ca 750m. Glaciers are dry below ca 1,600m. During July valley floors are free from snow, with an abundance of vegetation and wildlife. Andrees Land lies just outside an important polar bear denning area, but we had no encounters with the animals. We took simple camp precautions to avoid attracting their attention and carried rifles to protect against attack. However, musk ox are widespread throughout North East Greenland; these large herbivores were abundant in the Grejsdalen Valley.

During July the region has continuous sunlight and is dominated by relatively stable high-pressure systems, though occasional storms did occur. Temperatures ranged from -10°C at night to +10°C during the day. The Danish Geod tisk Institut produces the best mapping, at a scale of 1:250,000 with a contour interval of 50m; two map sheets cover the region.

It took 45 minutes to fly from Mestersvig to Andrees Land in a privately chartered Twin Otter, arranged through Air Iceland. This carried all expedition personnel, equipment, and freight, and constituted the bulk of our flight costs from the U.K. We established base camp in the Grejsdalen at N 73°35'22.6", W 26°01'23.1" and an altitude of 468m.

To single out a few of our first ascents, on July 11 we climbed Dionysus (2,180m) from the Monte Bello Glacier via the east ridge, 500m of good ice on the north face, finishing on the west ridge. It was a 15-hour day, at an alpine grade of AD. On the 15th we climbed Jacobis Bjerg (2,188m) via the south ridge. This involved first climbing 2,162m Idwal Tooth, a large tower on the ridge that we climbed via a wide central chimney (AD). The continuation to the summit of Jacobis Bjerg involved numerous gendarmes. The grade was again AD, and we descended by the northwest ridge. On the 22nd we climbed Lizard Peak (1,404m) via the north ridge—Golden Sunlight Buttress (AD). Once on the crest, we climbed a three-pitch pillar at British V Diff, after which easy scrambling led to the summit. The following day we climbed a rock spur to the left of the Lizard; Reptile Rib (D) gave 11 pitches on good granite, with two crux pitches of British VS 4c. On the 28th we returned to the Lizard to add The Fabulous Bakini Boys, a seven-pitch rock route with a fourth-pitch crux of British HVS 5a.

Despite the numerous ascents, our expedition only scratched the surface of mountaineering objectives in Andrees Land. During the flight out we noted that the area to the south and east of the Monte Bello Glacier contained a number of interesting looking peaks, some of which appeared to be guarded by multiple rocky gendarmes. There is a fork in the western end of the Grejsdalen; we did not explore the southerly branch, though we could see it during the ascent of an unnamed 1,948m summit close to Stenmanden (1,970m). It is extremely steep-sided and has the potential for significant mountaineering challenges. To the north and west of the Grejsdalen are numerous steep-sided peaks, a large lake, a further large valley (Eremitdal), and an area marked on the map as unexplored.

SAM MARSHALL, *Army Mountaineering Association, U.K.*

Central Staunings Alps, various first ascents. Laubie Laubscher, Mark Litterick, Ken Moore, Stephen O'Sullivan, Heike Puchan-Whitworth, Brian Shackleton, Brian Whitworth, and I comprised the Scottish Mountaineering Club expedition to Scoresby Land in North East Greenland National Park. We departed the U.K. on April 29 and were flown by a ski-equipped Twin Otter from a very warm Akureyri in Iceland on the 30th. Traveling via Constable Point to collect fuel and freight, we arrived at base camp early that afternoon, making an exciting landing on the huge Lang Glacier (Stor Gletscher on some maps) at 1,390m (N 71°59'43", W 24°48'44.2"). The nose wheel and skid buried themselves in the soft snow, so we disembarked from a jauntily-angled fuselage and were handed shovels for the excavation needed to free the plane.

On May 1 we climbed our first new peaks; Drumglas Beag (2,060m) via the north face

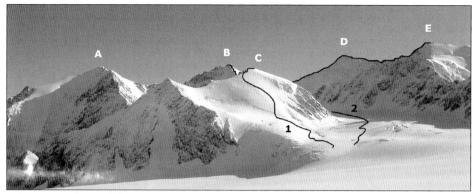

Looking more or less south from the upper Lang Glacier into the lower Wuss Glacier (right). (A) Margeretabjerge (2,430m). (B) Drumglas (2,330m). (C) Drumglas Beag (2.060m). (D) Cordulaspids (2,430m). (E) Jobjerge (2,330m). (1) North face of Drumglas Beag connecting to the north ridge (Biancograt) of Drumglas. (2) East ridge of Cordulaspids via the north face (250m, 60°) of LoLa col (hidden) leading to the southeast ridge of Jobjerge. All five peaks were climbed by the 2007 SMC expedition. *Colwyn Jones*

from the Lang Glacier at AD+, and the main peak of Drumglas (2,330m, N 71°58'41.5", W 24°52'49.5") via the north ridge at AD and descent of the west ridge. Snow and low cloud restricted activity from the 2nd to the 4th, but during this period four members did a 12-hour ski tour to dump half the food and fuel at Crescent Col, which they could reach avoiding avalanche-prone slopes. This cache was strategically placed for the return ski journey to the coast.

On the 5th we climbed a consolation peak close to camp on the west side of Lang Glacier, at F+, naming it Mollytinde (1,670m, N 71°59'21.1", W 24°50'47"). Next day we made ascents of Cordulaspitze, (2,430m, N71°58'41.9", W 24°54'28.1"), via the north face (AD) and east ridge from the Wuss Glacier, and of Jobjerg (2,330m, N 71°59'0.3", W 24°55'17.1") via its southwest ridge at AD. This crest is the continuation of Cordulaspitze's north ridge. We also climbed Juliasbjerge (2,058m, N 71°59'35.8", W 24°55'16.6") via its south ridge, approaching up a couloir on the west flank.

On the 7th we climbed Puchwhitstinde (2,339m, N 72°00'38.8", W 24°45'39.1") and Hasentinde (2,376m, N 72°01'24.5", W 24°47'08.4"), on the east side of the Lang glacier. We reached the col between the peaks, then climbed the north flank of Puchwhitstinde and the south ridge—Igel (Hedgehog) ridge—of Hasentinde. The following day a party repeated Puchwhitstinde, this time via the newly explored O'Sullivan-Moore Glacier and a couloir on the south face (Snowbunting Couloir, AD). That same day the dominant, shapely Margretabjerge (2,430m, N 71°58'34.7", W 24°50'58.0") was climbed by two different routes: the southeast flank and southwest ridge at PD and the southeast-facing Presidential Couloir (AD with an exciting exit) from the previously unnamed Witches' Cauldron Glacier.

On the 10th we crossed Crescent Col and relocated base camp in the upper reaches of the Gully Glacier, which lies in the real heart of the Staunings Alps. On our way we climbed Skartinde, to the east of Crescent Col. We ascended this 2,400m peak via the easy northwest flank (F). We believe the peak was first climbed in 1996 by a Norwegian expedition, but we think our ascent may have been only the second. The following day we climbed Himmelstinde (Heaven's Peak, 2,492m, N 72°04'51.8", W 25°05'22.5") via the south ridge (AD) and the col between it and adjacent Archangel Peak. On the 12th we retraced our steps to the col and made the first ascent of 2,558m Archangel (N 72°04'31.5", W 25°05'23.5"), following the east ridge at D+. We descended onto the glacier to the west; finding it very crevassed, we named it Devil's Own Glacier, and were forced to re-ascend to the summit and go back down our ascent route. That same day members of the expedition climbed Cold Shoulder (2,450m) by the west ridge (PD). This point lies on the west ridge of C.F. Knoxtinde. We also climbed the shapely Hjorne-spids (2,870m) by a new route, the 600m Laubscher–Litterick Gully on the southwest flank at a grade of D. We believe this to be the sixth overall ascent and fourth independent route on the peak.

Farther east we climbed An Caisteal (2,614m, N 72°03'31.9", W 24°59'52.6") by a face and gully on the east flank, then up north ridge at a grade of D/TD-. We climbed two other peaks on May 15th: Crescentinde (2,455m, N 72°03'38.0", W 24°57'15.0") via the northeast face at PD, and Ebensbjerg (2,510m, N 72°03'34.9", W 24°58'05.8") by its northeast face at AD. We think our route on Crescentinde is probably new, though the peak may have been climbed by the 1996 Norwegian team. Three members also made the probable third ascent of Skartinde, repeating the route of May 10.

On the 16th we moved our base camp to a stunning location at the top of Col Major and next day climbed the only true rock routes of the trip: the already established south ridge (British Mild VS) on Ian's Peak (2,607m, N 72°07'13.3", W 24°55'01.3") and a new variant to the ridge that we named Accessory Rib (British VS 4c). Our ascent of the original route on the south ridge is most likely the second, the first dating from 1960.

Moving down enormous Bersaerkerbrae Glacier on the 20th, we made the first ascent of Skotsketinde (Scotland's Peak (1,775m, N 72°07'36.6", W 24°45'20.4"), via the east ridge at PD+, and a summit noted on the map as Panoramic Peak. We climbed the latter, the most shapely of the surrounding peaks, via an avalanche-prone couloir on the southeast flank and the shattered south ridge to the summit pinnacles (PD+). We found a cairn on the lower pinnacle and constructed another on the higher. Altimeters showed 1,988m, considerably higher than given on the map. The following day we skied down the glacier and made a safe exit from the

One of many unclimbed peaks on the south side of MåL glacier, which flows east into the Lang (Stor) Glacier in the Staunings Alps. *Colwyn Jones*

snout. On the 22nd and 23rd we continued skiing to the coastal plain and over sea ice to the gravel airstrip at Mestersvig, where we were collected on the 25th. Apart from snow and poor visibility from the 2nd to 4th and again on the ski out from the Bersaerkerbrae, the weather was sunny and cold. Superficial frostbite was diagnosed in three members of the team. However, the expedition was very successful, climbing 16 new peaks and naming four new glaciers. All coordinates are GPS readings.

Of note is that three of our five MSR stoves did not work properly with Jet A1 fuel. These were the Whisperlite 600, a Whisperlite International, and a Dragonfly and cannot be recommended with this fuel, despite our carrying a full complement of different jets. Fortunately, two older MSR GSK II stoves worked very well. The expedition gratefully acknowledges the financial support received from the Mount Everest Foundation, the Gino Watkins Trust, The Mountaineering Council of Scotland, and SportScotland.

COLWYN JONES, *Scottish Mountaineering Club*

South Liverpool Land, Kronen northeast pillar (not to summit); Peak 800, south face to southeast ridge, first ascent. Climbing solo my goal was to make first ascents of mixed faces, ridges, and buttresses in the southern part of Liverpool Land, a little north of Scoresby Sund (often described as the largest fjord system in the world). The rock is friable and rotten, so although parties have traveled through it during the summer, and parts of Liverpool Land have been visited during the winter and spring for ski mountaineering (see *AAJ 2005*), little climbing has been achieved.

I was taken from the village of Ittoqqortoormiit, which has around 600 inhabitants, by a young Inuit hunter, Esajas Arqe, and his 10 dogs. On the sled we had all our provisions, camping and climbing equipment, plus a rifle to guard against polar bears. There was much fresh snow, which made it difficult for the dogs, particularly as we approached the mountains and the terrain became steeper. We only traveled 13–15km northwest from the village, but once at our destination it felt remote and isolated. Esajas stayed while I went climbing.

I went in April. May would probably be alright too for mixed climbs but June and July too warm. The temperature in the mountains was often -6 to -10°C dropping to -15 to -20°C during the night. On some days there were strong winds. Between the 13th and 23rd I made two climbs. The first was on the northeast pillar of Kronen (1,140m), which gave 50–60° snow/ice, UIAA IV rock and mixed climbing up to M3. I stopped on the top of the pillar after 500m and descended the way I had come, leaving one piton in place. The route, which I named Arctic Passion, starts from near the head of the Nissedal Valley.

The second climb was the south face and southeast ridge of unnamed Peak 800m, which is directly south of Kronen and northeast of the Tvaedal Valley. I climbed the middle of the south face for 350m, then trended right to the southeast ridge, where I followed the rocky crest to the summit. The total vertical gain was 500m and the difficulties UIAA IV+ M3 and 45-65° snow/ice. I left one piton in place at the end of the traverse. I called the route Light and Loneliness. From the summit I downclimbed the east face over 45° snow, ice and, rocky sections. I found no evidence of previous climbers during my visit but didn't feel there was much scope in this area for worthwhile mixed climbing, nor for routes much harder than I did.

EDUARD BIRNBACHER, *Germany*

Ren Land, exploration, science, and first ascents. Following a successful expedition to neighboring Milne Land in 2004, 50 members of West Lancashire County Scouts again left the U.K. in July for the Arctic. Our final destination was to be the rarely visited Ren Land, a mountainous, glaciated area attached to the mainland of East Greenland in the innermost depths of Scoresby Sund.

The main party arrived at Constable Point on July 20 by chartered flight from Iceland Air. Over the following two days, the main party traveled via Milne Land and on to Ren Land using Twin Otter aircraft, a helicopter, and six local speedboats. Base camp was at a height of 656m (GPS) on the north side of the Edward Bailey Glacier, which flows down to the Catalindalen.

Existing maps are based on aerial photography, with very little ground exploration. Collectively, the expedition explored almost 1,000 square miles of glaciated mountainous terrain in the center of Ren Land. This will improve knowledge and detail on the 1:50,000 maps prepared by a Network member of the expedition.

The area was a milieu of spires and minarets—

This slender granite spire is one of a number of Trango-like towers in Ren Land. This particular formation is nearly 500m in height and located ca 14km up the Apusinikajik Glacier from Skillebugt Inlet on the southeast coast. At least one other, located south of the terminal moraine of the Edward Bailey Glacier, was thought to be approaching 1,000m. *Dick Griffiths*

Southeast Ren Land. Looking east-southeast down the Edward Bailey Glacier from the top of Screeming Rib below the summit of Mt. Brassica (2,065m). The walls and pillars on the far side of the glacier are unclimbed. Even more interesting are the rock pillars and spires (mostly hidden) in the far right background, which lie around the head of the glacier—dubbed the Alpine Bowl. A few of these peaks were climbed by members of the West Lancashire County Scouts expedition. *Dick Griffiths*

far harsher than experienced in Milne Land in 2004. Despite this, we climbed 32 mountains— all of which were first mountaineering ascents and have been named, subject to confirmation. Most of these were two to four days from base camp. Challenging gullies and mixed routes were put up by several members of the expedition. We also identified major climbing objectives, particularly for those into big wall climbing; some were thought to be well in excess of 1,200m high.

During our time in East Greenland, the expedition also established neutron-sensing equipment for cosmic ray analysis on behalf of the University of Central Lancashire, caught seed bugs for the University of Stirling, and collected glacial rafted debris for the University of Lancaster. From comparison with the available aerial photographs (1987) we will be able to provide an indication of the rate of recession of the glaciers in the area.

The weather was fairly typical for the Arctic. Of the 32 days in East Greenland we experienced only two of low mist/light rain, 16 days of predominantly sunny weather, and for the remaining 14 wall-to-wall blue skies, 24 hours a day. We did many activities at night to take advantage of slightly firmer snow and less meltwater

We began on July 27 with an ascent of Commandment Peak (2,127m, 0527 1400 / 7891 1800) in the Alpine Bowl. Then came Missing Ring (2,110m, 0516 185 / 7901 744), a ski peak on the Main Ice Cap, July 28 (and again on August 10); Ren Land Icecap High Point (2,303m, 0513 634 / 7904 687), a ski peak on the Main Ice Cap, July 29; and Screening Rib (ca 1,500m, 0523 700 / 7901050) behind base camp, July 30. On July 31 two parties climbed Christmas Puderne (2,122m, 0518 637 / 7900 571), west of Watchtower Glacier, one via White Christmas Gully; Little Pudding (2,103m, 0517 907 / 7900 515), west of Watchtower Glacier; Consolation Point (1,914m, 5248.000 / 7894 800), south of Edward Bailey Glacier, across from base camp via Lost Valley Glacier and Prolapsed Gully; and Pourhelène (1,909m, 0519 119 / 7898 504), west of Base Camp. On August 1 we climbed Scout Centenary (2,016m, 0526 930 / 7902 263), EBG north side and east of base camp, via Mare de Glace; Dyb Dyb Dyb (2,100m, 0527 166 / 7902 638), EBG north side and east of Base Camp; Dob Dob Dob (2,167m, 0527 785 / 7903 385), EBG north side, east of base camp; Woggle (2,168m, 0527 810 / 7903 732), EBG north side, east of base camp; Bite of Trevor (2,146m, 0528 112 / 7904 342), EBG north side, east of base camp; Montane (2,201m, 0527 164 / 7906 576), EBG north side, east of base camp; Jamboree 2007 (2,055m, 0520 673 / 7907 082) north of EBG on main ice cap. More summits were ascended on August 4: Great Tower (1,802m, 0518 924 / 7905 223) above Ski Camp; Sea Kayaker's Enigma (2,007m, 05182 590 / 7905 850) on the main ice cap north of EBG; Mount Brassica (2,065m, 05229600 / 7901804) on the ice cap behind base camp, ascent via Screening Rib Extension and descent by Joe's Folly; St Pauls (2,185m, 0528710 / 7902790) on the north side of EBG, east of base camp; Passe På (2,013m, 0518 811 / 7893 517) at the corner of EBG and Catalindalen, via Afdintha Glacier; Kragenrede (2037m, 0518 556 / 7893 050) at the corner of EBG and Catalindalen; Twelfth Knight (2,055m, 0514 131 / 7893 539) on the south side of upper EBG. The next foray took place on August 7 when we climbed Badger (2,044m, 0510 148 / 7893580), on the south side of upper EBG; Bodger (1,954m, 0512 127 / 7894 800) on the south side of upper EBG; B2 (1,947m, 0511 999 / 7894 455) on the south side upper EBG; Unicorn (1,894m, 0526 313 / 7896 1) on south side of EBG, opposite base camp, via Pipe Dream Gully; SAC (2,063m, 0526 239 / 7894 070) on south side of EBG, opposite base camp, also via Pipe Dream Gully. On the 10th we climbed the Watchtower (1,859m, 0519 239 / 7905 169) a tower at the head of Watchtower Glacier; Fulfilment (2,101m, 0535 298 / 7892 167) in the Alpine Bowl overlooking Scoresby Sund; Trio Grande (2,185m, 0533 923 / 7893 061) in the

Alpine Bowl; Peak 2 (2,007m, 0534 068 / 7892 759) in the Alpine Bowl; Peak 3 (2,185m, 0534 389 / 7892 497) in the Alpine Bowl; Peak 4 (2,185m, 0535 020 / 7892 674) in the Alpine Bowl. Our last ascent was made on the 14th: Point 5P (2,185m, 5360 9000 / 7913 1500), a spur of Recce Peak at the head of Apusinikagik. Location coordinates were generally obtained using GPS, as per established UTM coordinates overlaid on our own 1:50,000 maps, prefixed by W 26°.

On August 9 a kayak group left base camp for the coast with a view to paddling out through Bear Islands to arrive on Milne Land by the 15th. Helicopters were used to take equipment from base camp to either the coast or Constable Point, after which all members walked out to the Ren Land coastal strip, arriving by the 14th, ready for collection by local speedboats, which would transfer them to Milne Land. From there it was a Twin Otter flight back to Constable Point. The expedition returned to Iceland on the 18th

DICK GRIFFITHS, *U.K.*

Orca as seen from the southwest. Base camp is at 400m, and the height of the wall is 1,250m. The highest point of the icecap has a spot height of 2,074m. Marked is the line climbed by Satoshi Kimoto, Taeko and Yasushi Yamanoi. The glacier runs left (northwest) a short distance to reach the Ikaasakajik Fjord, the narrow strip of sea separating the north coast of Milne Land from Ren Land (peaks in the distance are in Ren Land). *Manabu Hirose*

Milne Land, first ascent of Orca. Satoshi Kimoto, Taeko and Yasushi Yamanoi made the first ascent of a 1,250m-high big wall in northeast Milne Land. It took 17 days during August to complete the 40-pitch route, named Orca, at 5.10+ A2. Yasushi had discovered the wall during an aerial reconnaissance in May. Returning in July with Manabu Hirose, a TV producer from the Japan Broadcasting Corporation, Yasushi and his team used a helicopter to fly from Constable Point to Ittoqqortomiit and from there took a boat across Scoresby Sund to the east coast of Milne Land, in about eight hours. From there they again used a helicopter to fly west up a prominent glacier system and then north, toward the coast, down another glacier system to land at a suitable base camp (30–40 minutes flight). On the return they flew by helicopter from base camp to Constable Point (1.5 hours). The use of the helicopter was dictated by the large quantity of filming equipment. They established base camp on July 27 at a height of 400m on the glacier, just 30 minutes walk from the foot of the southwest-facing wall.

The shallow corner system taken by the Japanese route up the head-wall of Orca, northern Milne Land. *Yasushi Yamanoi*

The three began climbing the face on the 29th. The first 600m were rather slabby and straightforward, with most pitches 5.9 or less. On August 8 they established a high camp and began work on the headwall, a vertical face of 400m with good crack systems, followed by 250m of ridge. It took five days to climb the 400m, which was mainly crack- and face-climbing at 5.10. However, several loose sections forced the use of aid. On the 15th they placed a final camp on the ridge and the next day, traveling light, completed nine pitches to the summit. The team arrived on top at 11 p.m. after 15 hours climbing. They used 46 bolts. There is no previous report of big wall climbing in Milne Land, but the area has many steep rock walls and alpine faces.

MANABU HIROSE *and* YASUSHI YAMANOI, *Japan*

Sortebrae Mountains, seven ascents. Our eight-member expedition comprising Andy Garman, Alasdair Garnett, Rob Green, Clare O'Sullivan, Jonathan Philips, Tracey Quine, Malcolm Sloan, and I left the U.K. on June 2, bound for an unvisited glacier in the Sortebrae area. This is not the Sortebrae Glacier but an area of mountains to the west of that glacier, our chosen landing site being a little over one day's ski from the Borgetinde Massif to the southeast, and somewhat farther from Ejnar Mikkelsens Fjeld to the south. Our expectations were high, our minds full of unclimbed alpine peaks and what we would achieve. Achieve them we did, but there was an Arctic Odyssey awaiting us.

After a series of delays caused by mechanical failure and a long period of bad weather, an advance party left for our Greenland landing site almost a week late. The flight to Greenland was one that will live long in our memories. Words cannot do justice to the beauty of the ice-flecked sea, eventually meeting the mountains and the glaciers under a curtain of mist. The flight felt too short, too rushed to allow us to feast our eyes on the spectacle and drink in its beauty, its remoteness, its splendor. This was the Arctic, and it was everything we expected.

The reverie was broken when we landed at N 69°1.3', W 27°50.8' (1,552m). The plane stopped violently, as it encountered soft snow and buried itself in the glacier. Two days of digging with the help of a reinforcement of mechanics, sent by a coast guard helicopter, saw the plane back on the level, and it returned to Iceland for the second half of our party, who were

It took two days with the help of reinforcements flown in by a coastguard helicopter to dig out the Twin Otter, get it back on the level and prepare a runway for take off. The mountains of the Sortebrae cast a watchful eye over proceedings. *David Jakulis*

landed 40km from our position. Affecting a reunion filled the next few days.

We split into two parties and from the 14th–17th explored separate subsidiary glaciers for a route onto the icecap. The forays were successful, with both teams getting members onto the icecap, from where three new peaks were climbed. On the 16th Alasdair, Tracey and I climbed the 2,706m Pile of Stones (N 69°10.7', W 27 46.9') at PD and the same day made an ascent of Poacher's Peak (2,773m, N 69°9.6', W 27°43.9'), also at PD. During this period Clare, Jonathan, Malcolm, and Rob climbed an unnamed peak at Scottish II. All were first ascents. We returned in murky weather to find a fresh supra-glacial river cutting off our tents, necessitating a long detour. The following day we raced the sun for the snow bridge so we could move base camp to a safer position, the abnormally warm temperatures beginning to be a real concern.

The new position brought access to new peaks, and we attempted some fine mountains, black spires against a background of endless white glaciers. We generally avoided rock in favor of snow faces and ridges in incredible situations. We made ski descents from the base of some routes, on snow of varying condition. From a camp at 1,532m, Andy, Tracey, and I climbed Solstice Peak (2,222m, N 69°7.8', W 28°4.3') at PD on June 20 and the following day got to within 100m of the top of an unnamed peak at N 69°6.7', W 28 4.7'. The grade was PD to our high point at 2,285m; continuing to the summit would have involved rock at ca UIAA IV. At the same time another party retrieved the equipment a previous expedition had been forced to abandon, encountering crevasse falls and worryingly bad snow before returning with loaded pulks.

A realization that the Twin Otter would not return for us at our present position forced another move, this time heavily laden, to higher ground. The plane returned to collect the equipment belonging to the previous expedition, only to bury its nose in the glacier again, and

Beautiful unclimbed objectives in the Sortebrae Mountains to the north of Ejnar Mikkelsens Fjeld. *David Jakulis*

require our (now expert) extraction techniques. The situation was less serious than the first burial, and the plane was on its way in the early hours. The following day teams struck out for Borgetinde and two nearby unnamed peaks, one unclimbed. We skinned through alpine terrain made more serious, more beautiful, by the vastness and the silence of the Arctic, as we passed impressive seracs and the debris of huge avalanches.

Teams reached a high point on the Borgetinde summit tower. On the 26th Alasdair and Andy retreated from a sentinel peak at the mouth of the Borgetinde Glacier in bad snow. The following day Tracey and I reached the summit of a previously unclimbed peak of 2,842m (N 68°51.8', W 28°14.6') adjacent to Borgetinde, following a knife-edge snow arête with empty space on one side and the Borgetinde plateau shimmering below on the other (PD+). From the summit we could see the sea. The ski descent, believed to be the first from the Borgetinde plateau, was one of the best mountain experiences of my life. Floating down powder, gliding on névé, we passed under huge walls and between immense seracs and crevasses, carving the face of the mountain, the only sound the scrape of our skis in the vast silence of the Arctic mountainscape. There is something about the Arctic, something we glimpsed that day, which will be with me forever, calling me back.

Repeated plane burials meant Flugfelag would not land in our current position. We needed to move to a position on the edge of the icecap, over 30 km away, fully laden, in two days. This immediately after a 16-hour day on the mountain, in which we had covered 32 km. A routine of one-hour pulking, followed by five minutes rest, saw us there in time, passing through unvisited areas, climbing ever higher. On the 29th Jonathan and Malcolm climbed a snow peak on the ice cap at ca N 69°14.2', W°28 52', while Rob ascended a neighboring summit. There was little time for dwelling on the fact that our trip was coming to an end, and the arrival of the Twin Otter heralded a subdued atmosphere. We could have stayed much longer. Our expedition benefited from the kind support of the Arctic Club, the Alpine Ski Club, Andrew Croft Memorial Fund, Gino Watkins Memorial Fund, and the Mount Everest Foundation.

DAVID JAKULIS, *U.K.*

Editor's note: Ejnar Mikkelsens Fjeld and Borgetinde had two ascents each prior to 2007. The first ascent of the former, 3,308m peak was a tour de force and thought to be the highest unclimbed peak in Greenland at the time. In 1970 a British team led by Andrew Ross sailed down the coast from Scoresby Sund and trekked inland for over 70km to make a committing ascent of what some people consider to be one of the most impressive summits in East Greenland. It was not climbed again until 1998, when a Swiss team led by Roland Aeschimann repeated this south glacier route. Borgetinde is 3,338m and was first climbed in 1972 by Rod Brown and Nigel Soper from a Sheffield University expedition and again in 2000 by Nigel Edwards's British expedition (see AAJ *2001). Prior to 2007 another British team led by Bob Dawson had climbed peaks a little to the north of the 2007 British location, and in 2006 two Tangent-organized expeditions visited the northeastern sector bordering the icecap (see* AAJ *2007). Before the arrival of the British group in 2007 another group made the third ascent of Borgetinde but failed on Ejnar Mikkelsens Fjeld due to avalanche conditions. A second group, an all-women expedition, also climbed peaks in the Sortebrae, situated a couple of days travel from the British group.*

Schweizerland, Mt. Forel and Perfeknunatak, corrections. The route climbed on Mt. Forel by the Spanish team in 2006 was the northeast ridge and not the southeast as stated in *AAJ 2007* (pp. 204–5). Most likely this was a first ascent; the ridge seen on the right side of the picture on p. 204, the northwest ridge, was climbed by a Tangent expedition. Forel was first climbed in 1938, via a relatively straightforward snow route, by Andre Roch's Swiss expedition, which traveled through Schweizerland and climbed 13 other virgin peaks, including Laupers Bjerg, Rodeburg, and Rytterknaegten, the latter an impressive technical rock ascent. Forel did not receive a second ascent until 1966, when it was climbed by Japanese. However, it is more likely to have had 20 or so ascents, rather than a dozen as reported.

The Spanish also climbed the southwest ridge of Perfeknunatak via a line they named Al Tran-tran. Although the report states they weren't clear if the peak had been climbed before, it is actually located directly opposite Forel and was first climbed by Swiss in '38. Hans Christian Florian, Jens Jørgen Kjærgaard, and Martin Madsen climbed it on June 3rd, 2004, and discovered a fine cairn on the summit. They checked for messages and rebuilt it, and are surprised that it was not visible to the Spanish. The straightforward route to this summit is from the east, just out of the frame to the right on the p. 204 photo.

HANS CHRISTIAN FLORIAN, *Greenland*

Fox Jaw Cirque, six first ascents. In mid-June, Josh Beckner, Darcy Deutcher, Kadin Panagoulis, Jed Porter, Annie Trujillo, and I stepped off a boat and schlepped seven miles into the Fox Jaw Cirque in the Tasiilaq Fjord Area. First reports of climbing in this cirque stem from 1998, when Dave Briggs and Mike Libecki climbed a 360m gem on a formation dubbed the Molar. Dave and Mike bestowed the name "Fox Jaw" on the jagged granite cirque, after comparing it to the toothy jaw-line of a fox skeleton that they found during the approach. We took it as a totem of luck when we stumbled upon the same fox jaw during our hike to the area.

And what luck we had. It's possible that we had the best weather of any alpine climbing area in the world during our six-week stay: only seven days of lazy drizzle disrupted the continuous sunny weather. We climbed six new routes—five in the cirque and one on a peak to the east, which we named Ganesh. To say the least, the climbing was marvelous—thin granite

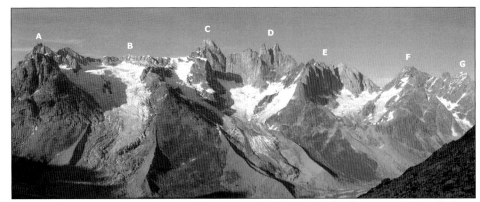

Looking east at the Trillingerne Group as seen across the Tasiilaq River valley from Ganesh. (A) Pikkelhuen (2,039m). (B) Pt. 1,842m. (C) Storebror (2,069m). (D) Trillingerne (northwest summit, 1,943m; southeast summit 1,965m). (F) Fox Jaw Cirque (highest point 1,684m). (G) Pt. 1,639m. (H) Pt 1,553m. The head of the Tasiilaq Fjord is off picture to the right. *Josh Beckner*

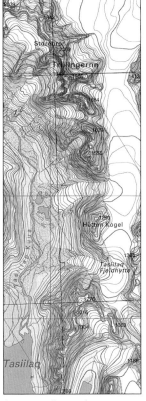

cracks with generous face holds kept the climbing moderate. There was much less loose rock than one might expect in an alpine environment. In fact, the climbing could be considered alpine-lite: the pleasure of alpine climbing with half the danger. The low elevation, pleasant temperatures, mega-daylight, splitter weather, and solid rock constantly put smiles on our faces.

A typical climbing day looked like this: We'd awake at 4 a.m., stuff some sort of Danish cereal into our mouths, slog up the moraine for two hours, hop onto the glacier for a bit, pick a line on one of the dozen or so buttresses, and start climbing. The height of the walls constantly surprised us—routes that we imagined would be eight pitches turned out to be 12 or so. Because of this the larger climbs often took two efforts. We'd get up part way and realize we didn't have the food/water/guts to complete it, so we'd come down and try again in a couple of days. We didn't place any bolts; the only gear we left was for rappel anchors.

Non-climbing days were spent hiking around the valleys, scrambling up non-technical peaks, racking, and preparing, or reading a book from our extensive library. The food available in Greenland, it should be said, wasn't ideal. We arrived a week before the first Danish re-supply boat of the season. Much of our food was expired "salami" and cheese that, while it didn't

The Trillingerne Group north of the head of the Tasiilaq Fjord in Schweizerland. This is a small part of a 1:100,000 color map named Kaarali Gletscher, which has been produced with 25m contours by Hans Christian Florian. It covers the area from the Tasiilaq river in the west to the Knud Rasmussen Glacier in the east, and from the 16th September Glacier in the north to the huge glacial lake of the Sermiligaq in the south. Available from Hans Christian Florian Sørensen, Sygehuset, DK-3913, Tasiilaq, Greenland; hcflorian@hotmail.com.

Schweizerland's Fox Jaw Cirque from the south. (A) Unnamed summit on the southwest ridge of Storebror. (B) Milk Tooth Spire (ca 1,100m). (C) Molar. (D) Storebror (2,069m). (E) Incisor. (F) Cavity Ridge. (G) Trillingerne northwest (1,943m). (H) Trillingerne southeast (1,965m). (I) Fang. (J) Left Rabbit Ear. (K) Right Rabbit Ear. Snaggletooth is off picture to the right. (1) Doublemint Direct (III 5.8, Lundin-Whorton, 2007). (2) Tooth Fairy (330m, III 5.8, American-Canadian team, 2007). (3) Descent used by Lundin and Whorton after Doublemint Direct. (4) Attempt on the Molar by Beckner, Furman and Panagoulis, 2007. (5) Tears in Paradise (ca 600m, V 5.11 A1, Libecki, 2001). (6) Descent route followed by Lundin and Whorton after their ascent of Right Rabbit Ear and the Fang. (7) Naeterqaabin-Jebbananee (550m, 13 pitches, IV 5.10, American-Canadian team, 2007). (8) Straight Up Now Tell Me (ca 550m, 16 pitches, V 5.9 A2, Lundin-Whorton, 2007). Not marked are: Gute Zeiten, Schlechte Zeiten (350m, 5.8, Leitner-Schöls, 2000) between 2 and 3; Southeast Buttress (330m, III 5.9, American-Canadian team, 2007) a little left of 3; Lovin' All the Right Places (465m, IV 5.10 A2+, Briggs-Libecki, 1998) on the Molar, probably right of 4; Beers in Paradise (600m, V 5.10+, A0 pendulum, American-Canadian team, 2007) starting to the left of 5; Swiss Route on Cavity Ridge (2000). Lines are approximate. *Erin Whorton*

give much intestinal crisis, was fairly hard to choke down without a grimace and a gag.

At the end of our trip we were very happy to meet Jessica Lundin and Erin Whorton, a climbing duo from the U.S. We only overlapped for a couple of days, but it was great to share each others' psyche, and try to overwhelm them with stories and beta. Spending time with them also reminded us of how weird we had gotten. Our trip was enriched with the camaraderie of each other's company, the stunning setting, and the interaction with local Inuit and Danes. We thank the National Outdoor Leadership School for their generous support. If you would like more information on climbing in the Fox Jaw, contact me at nathanfurman@yahoo.com.

Summary of first ascents: Tooth Fairy (III 5.8, 7 pitches, 330m) on Milk Tooth Spire (Baby Molar); Natural Mystic (V 5.10+, 17 pitches, 900m) on Snaggletooth; Naeterqaabin-Jebbananee (IV 5.10, 13 pitches, 550m) on Left Rabbit Ear; Beers in Paradise (V 5.10++, A0 pendulum, 14 pitches, 600m) on the Incisor (shares four pitches with the Libecki Route); Southeast Buttress (III 5.9, 7 pitches, 330m); on Milk Tooth Spire (Baby Molar); Ganesh (III 5.8, mixed snow and ice, 7 pitches, 330m).

NATHAN FURMAN, *AAC*

Fox Jaw Cirque, new routes. On July 18 Jessica Lundin and I arrived in Kulusuk, thrilled to be attempting new routes in the Arctic. We spent a week in Tasiilaq stocking up on provisions, scrambling up a few mountain ridges, and watching arch-shaped icebergs drift by. Anxious to get our hands on some granite, we were dropped off at the head of the Tasiilaq Fjord on July 25 and, schlepping three loads each, made a beeline for base camp.

The righthand (eastern) end of the Fox Jaw Cirque showing the line of Natural Mystic on Snaggletooth. This formation lies to the right of an area dubbed the Land of Towers by the 2007 American-Canadian team. *Josh Beckner*

The Milk Tooth Spire (1,100m) was our first climbing objective. On August 4 we began simul-climbing through 4th-class grassy and rock ledges, stopping occasionally to belay for short mid-5th class sections. We aimed for where the route steepened 500m above us. Eight pitches of clean rock put us on the summit, 24 hours after beginning the ca 900m, broad ridge. Our route, Doublemint Direct (III 5.8), follows the western skyline ridge of the most westerly peak in the cirque.

Feasting on wild blueberries for a few days, we rested and scouted our next objective, the unclimbed Right Rabbit Ear (RRE). On August 14 we picked our way across 780m of 5th-class slabs, stopping to pick up gear we had cached earlier that week. At first light we left our bivy site below the towers and started up the face of the RRE. Finishing with a two-pitch, splitter 5" crack, we reached the top of the tower at dusk on the second day. By mid-August the fabled midnight sun had given way to six-hour nights, so we waited before rappelling into the gully between the two Rabbit Ears. Early next morning we traversed to the Left Rabbit Ear and then climbed a few pitch-

Jessica Lundin jumaring during the first ascent of Straight up Now Tell Me. *Erin Whorton*

es to the summit of the Fang, which connects the two towers. We rappelled through the night, eventually reaching our bivouac gear for a much-needed snooze in the rain, before retracing our path across the slabs on August 19. The next day the storm moved back in, dusting our new 16-pitch route, Straight up Now Tell Me (V 5.9 A2), with snow. We are grateful for the grants provided by the AAC and Mountain Hardwear for making this trip possible.

General information: We flew via Reykjavik, Iceland, to Kulusuk, an island village of 300 people. Reversing this route is an excellent option, as thermal pools throughout Iceland offer a relaxing end to an Arctic trip. Icelanders especially love dirty climbers wading through their pristine pools in underwear that has been worn for six weeks. Kulusuk is a small fishing town, and food supplies are better obtained in nearby Tasiilaq, a town of 1,500 people and now the major center of the East Coast. Tasiilaq (also called by the Danish name Ammassalik) boasts two grocery stores, a hospital, a café, an Inuit history museum, and a lot of sled dogs. Although most Inuit are subsistence hunters, a variety of Danish food can be bought for modest prices at the grocery stores, depending on the time of year. Goods for the whole year are delivered in a huge cargo ship each summer, the timing determined by when the almost impenetrable shell of the sea ice breaks apart. Barren shelves greet the visitor who arrives before the ship. This year the cargo arrived in early July, and we had our choice of cheese, smoked meats, and many packets of dried sauce. A few kilos of butter proved a choice addition to the arsenal.

Many visitors intent on ski-mountaineering in Schweizerland arrive in April and May, while rock climbers are better served by the more stable weather patterns of June, July, and August, when the temperature is 40–50°F. In early summer the night is the gentle alpenglow of a 24-hour day, but by late August the six-hour nights are dark enough to prohibit climbing, and it is rather colder.

Once at Tasiilaq, the easiest way to get around is by motorboat. Dines Mikaelsen, the mayor's son, operates Mikaelsen Tours, and he gave us a lift to the head of the Tasiilaq Fjord, 60 miles to the north. Hotel Red House also organizes boat drop-offs and hosts a campground, where visitors can stay while organizing supplies. Many steep granite walls line the fjord and tempted us to change our plans. Beware these sirens' call. From the drop-off point we hiked eight miles northeast to establish base camp in the flat expanse between the chossy peaks that line the valley. A few sound pieces of rock poke out of the surrounding glaciers: the peaks of the Fox Jaw Cirque and the massive walls of Trillingerne and Storebror.

History of climbing in the Fox Jaw Cirque: In 1998 Dave Briggs and Mike Libecki opened up climbing on these spires, which they named after the pesky arctic fox that stole their food and because the spires looked like a row of teeth. During this expedition, Briggs and Libecki established the 465m route Lovin' All the Right Places (IV 5.10 A2+) on the Molar. Libecki returned alone in 2001 to establish the 550m Tears in Paradise (V 5.11 A1) on the Incisor. During the same summer another team, Katy Holm, Andrea Kortello, Karen McNeill, and Dave Thomson, arrived in style. Approaching by sailboat, they established two new routes on the Trillingerne Peaks and attempted the Left Rabbit Ear in the Fox Jaw. Meanwhile, the previous year, a Swiss party had climbed Cavity Ridge to the right of the Incisor, while Matthias Leitner and Wolfgang Schöls (Austria), on their way out to the fjord from the Tupalik Group, put up a direct route on the 350m south face of the Milk Tooth (Baby Molar): Gute Zeiten, Schlechte Zeiten (5.8). An American-Canadian team arrived in 2007; as reported above, this rock-star team made six first ascents in the Cirque and surrounding region during their month-long reign in the valley.

These ascents were on the Fox Jaw spires. For years many climbers have sought adventure on ski throughout the Schweizerland Mountains, and have found refuge in the Tasiilaq Mountain Hut, a fine structure built by Hans Christian Florian-Sorenson, a Danish physician and climber resident in Tasiilaq.

ERIN WHORTON, *AAC*

SOUTH COAST

CAPE FAREWELL REGION

Agdlerussakasit, Maujit Qoqarsassia, new route. On August 14 Eliza Kubarska and I, from Poland, finished our new route to the summit of 1,560m Maujit Qoqarassia [a subsidiary summit of 1,750m Agdlerussakasit, above the west bank of Torssukatak Sound—Ed]. The east face of this summit, which rises straight out of the fjord, has been called one of the tallest sea cliffs in the world and can only be reached by boat. Despite the fact our team was only two, we decided to travel by kayak; we were not only able to explore the cliffs but also have our full share of adventure. As usual we would have to overcome our fear of falling, but this time falling into water, where hypothermia would set in fast.

After traveling deep into the fjord, we established base camp on Pamiagdluk Island, 2km from the wall on the opposite side of the channel. Kayaking to the foot of the face was the only way to start the climb and unlike the other three parties that have climbed routes on this face, we had to work alone with no one left at base. Our first problem was finding a place we could safely leave kayaks, and get back to them after sending the route. We found a good spot but then had to make a traverse to our chosen line, and here we left a few fixed ropes.

After climbing the first 600m we reached spectacular overhangs, and found that aid would be necessary to circumvent them. However, our goal was free-climbing, so we rappelled two pitches (including a wonderful pitch of 7a) to a ledge and went looking for other possibilities. We found a line that avoided the roofs on the left. We were fortunate with bivouacs: each night, by luck, we found some sort of ledge.

Three days of climbing took us to a big terrace that cuts across the face. That same day the weather turned bad and, after spending the night under a big boulder in a storm, we decided to retreat by following the terrace left, traversing a system of ledges, and descending vertical grass to the snow couloir that borders the left edge of the face. Going down from here was rather dramatic. It was raining; the couloir was steep with 10m-deep breaks, and water thundered underneath. Having to negotiate this in approach shoes, with a hammer instead of an ice axe, totally psyched

On Pamiagdluk Island, the east face of (M) Maujit Qoqarassia rises some 1,500m from the Torssukatak Sound and can only be reached by boat. (T) is the slightly lower summit known as the Thumbnail. Marked is the new Polish route, Golden Lunacy. This is the fourth route on the face, the lines of the other three being visible in *AAJ 2004* p. 268. *David Kaszlikowski* us out. The rope wasn't proving much help, and our biggest fear was falling into a slot with the river below. We hadn't taken axes or crampons, because we didn't want to carry them on the face, and the couloir had looked easy in good weather.

Eventually we reached a 20m-high ice wall. On either side rose wet, vertical walls. Rivers cascaded around us, soaking everything except the jammed block on which we were standing. We were cold, our sleeves were wet, and our feet freezing. We took a minute to warm up, then began a rappel, praying that the rope wouldn't slip off the rock, in which case I'd probably drown in the waterfall. The haul bag turned me upside down but I managed to catch the first rock sticking out of the water and pull myself towards it. Thank God I didn't tie a prussic; being wet it would have almost certainly jammed. After six hours we reached the kayaks but it was too rough to paddle the fjord, so we spent another night in the rain, sitting on our ropes with plastic bags over our heads. Fortunately it was calm in the morning, and after 20 minutes paddling we were inside the tent.

It now rained for six days. When it stopped, we returned to the face, using rope left in place to speed our return up the tricky couloir to the terrace. After a bivouac we reached the top in 10.5 hours. This upper part was beautiful climbing on solid granite, with sections of 6c+. Some of the most interesting parts were terribly difficult, wet offwidths led by Eliza. The last

pitch to the summit was a 60m tower, at 6c+, with an amazing view. However, just after we topped out, clouds built over our heads, and soon we couldn't see farther then 100m. We rappelled late into the night from natural gear. The top section of our route may share common ground with Hidrofilia (6c+/7a A2+, 1,620m of climbing), completed by Cecilia Buil and Roberta Nunez in 2003. [There are two other routes to the right that lead to a slightly lower summit, dubbed The Thumbnail. One was climbed in 2000 at British E6 6b by Ben Bransby, Matt Dickinson, Ian Parnell, and Gareth Parry from the U.K, the other in 2003 by James Mehigan and Richard Sonnerdale at Brtiish E3 5c. Both have a vertical gain from the sea of 1,350m. The wall is around 1.5km wide—Ed.]

Our route, Golden Lunacy, was 1,500m high with maximum difficulties of 7a+. Apart from one pitch, where a rest point was used while drilling a bolt to pass a loose block, the route was free-climbed onsight, some pitches being climbed unroped. There are five bolts

David Kaszlikowski takes a tentative first few steps onto the 1,500m east face of Maujit Qoqarassia. Eliza Kubarska waits below. Behind are rocky spires on the northwest coast of Pamiagdluk Island. *David Kaszlikowski*

on the route: three on belays and two for protection. The granite was excellent throughout; we believe these fjords house some of the best granite climbing in the world, with unclimbed walls 700–900m high.

DAVID KASZLIKOWSKI, *Poland*

Tasermiut Fjord, Tininnertuup, northeast face, attempt. Sarah and Tony Whitehouse attempted a major variation to the unrepeated Rapakivi Road on the northeast face of Tininnertuup (1,725m), the 1,000m route (28 pitches,1,300m of climbing) put up in 2004 by Swedish climbers Martin Jacobsson and Ola Knutsson. Rapakivi Road takes the large, steep, inset slab to the left of the prow climbed in 2002 by a Norwegian-Swedish team to create Qivitooq (VI F7a A2, 1,000m, 26 pitches, Blixt-Krane-Massih, 2002). Based in the underdeveloped valley that lies between the Tininnertuup Qaqqat and the Hermelnbjerg, the British couple fixed ropes on the lower section, then attempted to climb the prominent left-facing corners above the point where the original route moves right. Bad weather prevented a completion, but the pair hopes to return in 2008 to this area, situated at the head of the Tasermiut, south of the Sermitsiaq.

LINDSAY GRIFFIN, *Mountain INFO, www.climbmagazine.com*

Tasermiut Fjord, Ketil, west face, first alpine-style ascent, correction. AAJ 2000 reported an ascent, thought to be the fourth, of the 1977 French Route on the west face of Ketil. The two climbers, Americans Jon Allen and Doug Byerly, believed they were making the first alpine-style ascent of the route, which they completed in two days to a bivouac that was 50m of easy scrambling below the summit ridge. Next day, ferocious winds forced them to retreat down the line of ascent without visiting the summit a short distance above. In fact, during July 1980 Erich Baud, Pierre Lainé, and I, from France, climbed the route over three days in alpine style. We reached the summit and descended the easy south face in perfect weather. We flew from France with only 20kg of baggage each, and on the climb had only one 90m rope, and traditional protection including a few pitons. On the first day we climbed 22 pitches to the first possible bivouac ledge, and on the second another 22. On day three we climbed five difficult pitches and then a further 14 of easy ground to the summit. Close to the top we realized that the south face looked far easier and safer than descending the 50-odd vertical pitches of the west face. We rappelled the south face in a day, bivouacked at the bottom, and hiked back to base camp in a further half day. This was the second overall and first alpine-style ascent of the route.

BRUNO CHRÉTIEN, *France*

Tasermiut Fjord, Nalumatorsoq, Stupid White Man. On July 20 Jørgen Becher, Steffen Laetsch, and I completed an ascent of Stupid White Man on the south-southwest face of the Left Pillar of Nalumatorsoq. The same team made an attempt on this line during August 2005, climbing the first four pitches, mostly free with a 6b offwidth. Bad weather meant that this was as high as we got. Returning in 2007 we started up the line on July 4. Above our previous high point the climbing is primarily in finger cracks, and we needed to do a considerable amount of gardening. Progress was slow, particularly as we were hand-drilling our bolt placements, about 40 in all. Due to our speed, we decided to climb the hardest parts on aid and free the whole route later. However, it took us 10 days, with seven nights spent on the wall, to complete the ascent. Our schedule meant that the last possible climbing day was the 20th, the day we reached the top, so we were unable to try a free ascent.

Two weeks later two Poles, Maciek Ciesielski and Wawrzyniec Zakrzewski, free-climbed most of the pitches on which we had used aid [see below]. However, they didn't reach the top, due to bad weather. They felt a free ascent would rate 7b, but we believe that to be an overestimate.

Stupid White Man starts up the first pitch of the 1996 Thomas–Turner route, Umwelten, then takes a crack line to the left to the top of pitch 12. Here it crosses Umwelten and climbs a dihedral-chimney system to the top of pitch 15, where we rejoined Umwelten at the belay. Here we replaced two old loose pegs with bolts. We then moved left, climbing just 5m left of Umwelten to the summit ridge. (At the top of our 16th pitch we saw a two-nut anchor just to the right.) Opened in capsule style with portaledge camps, the new route has seventeen 30–50m pitches and 640m of climbing. Most belays have two bolts, so it is possible to rappel the route. Difficulties are sustained at 6a–6b, with nine pitches requiring A1 aid.

The Left and Central Pillars on the south-southwest face of Nalumatorsoq (2,045m). The Right Pillar is the sharp spire visible in profile. (1) Stupid White Man (640m of climbing, 17 pitches, 6b A1, Bänsch-Becher-Laetsch, 2007). Shortly after this ascent two Poles climbed the first 10 pitches at 5.12b. (2) Nagguteeqqat (600m, 12 pitches, 6c A2, Hinarejos-Jareño-Martin-Martin-Palomares-Romero-Romero, 2007). The dotted line between the two is Umwelten (600m, British E5 A1, Thomas-Turner, 1996). For other routes on Nalumatorsoq see AAJ 2004 p. 263). *Jürgen Becher*

MICHAEL BÄNSCH, *Germany*

Tasermiut Fjord, Nalumatorsoq, Stupid White Man, attempt; Ulamertorssuaq, War and Poetry, attempt. Wawrzyniec "Wawa" Zakrzewski and I have climbed in Patagonia, Yosemite, and the Trango Tower area of Pakistan. Last year we visited Greenland, from late July till late August. Out of the 26 days that we spent in the Tasermiut, it rained on 20. Three times we attempted the new German route, Stupid White Man on Nalumatorsoq, but each time we were defeated by rain. The route is nice and follows a logical line up a continuous crack system. All pitches are difficult, and even the easiest involve offwidths. On our first attempt we climbed the first five pitches onsight, though the last, which we felt was 5.11+, we led with rest points. On our second attempt we climbed the first five pitches on our first try but only managed the sixth pitch on the fourth attempt. We felt this pitch to be 5.12b. The next two pitches we climbed onsight, but the ninth was very vegetated, and we spent three hours aiding and cleaning it, before making a redpoint at 5.12a. Once again we were forced down by rain. On our third and final attempt we climbed each of the initial nine pitches on our first try, and then continued up a straightforward 10th pitch before again being defeated by rain. We gave up and decided to go to Ulamertorssuaq.

On the big west face we climbed the first 16 pitches (the bolted ones) of War and Poetry onsight at 5.12b. However, the 17th pitch, rated 12c, we only got on our second go. We then climbed two more difficult offwidths before it got dark and from our high point made four rappels to the Black Heart Ledge, where we bivouacked. During the night it rained, so we bailed, rappelling to the ground in two hours. For our trip we used the services of Tierras Polares, by whom we were given considerable assistance. We really recommend this organization—great service at a great price.

MACIEK CIESIELSKI, *Poland*

Tasermiut fjord, Kirkespiret, Alpin Glow; Nalumasortoq, Nagguteeqqat. I first saw the granite walls of Tasermiut at a slide show in Murcia. After several years of climbing in the Alps and Yosemite, I was ready for them, but had done too much training and became bored by climbing. I needed a rest and turned to sailing. I bought a wreck and daydreamed about long voyages. I saw pictures of a French expedition that had traveled to South Georgia on a sailing boat and wondered, "Why not?" The answer came in the form of work, responsibilities, and lack of money. I modified my plans and decided to fly to Greenland and put up what I believed would be the first Spanish route on Nalumasortoq. Our Alicante team comprised Alberto Hinarejos, Hugo Jareño, Enrique Martin, Javier Martin, Javier Palomares, Jesus Romero, and I. However, not long before we were ready to leave, we discovered a Basque party had climbed a route on the far left side of the wall. However, we decided to go anyway.

We landed in Narssarssuaq on July 3 and next day set off for the Tasermiut in a fast boat, motoring among icebergs and through fjords and rain showers. On the way we collected our gear, which was sent by cargo ship at the start of April, and became stuck in sea ice two miles off Nanortalik. The closely packed sea ice also prevented us getting into the Tasermiut. It was decision time, and we opted to be dropped at the shore below the Nalunaq gold mine on the west side of the fjord and then try to contact a local fisherman, who might take us across to the opposite shore. On the approach we got a beautiful view of Kirkespiret. The staff from the mine helped carry our gear, and the next evening we were comfortably set up at their camp. The people were extremely polite in allowing us to stay and offered us maps, pictures, and, most important, hot water. We were surprised and pleased with such kindness and sincere help.

Next day three to four hours walk and scramble took us to an advanced base near a small stream at the snow line. A further hour put us under the north face of Kirkespiret. Directly opposite, on the far side of the fjord, we could see the huge walls of Ulamertorssuaq. It took our breath away, and we began to refer to it as El Bicho, which means it is not of this world.

We crossed the pass leading to the west face of Kirkespiret and on July 6 split into two parties and started up the wall. One team began close to the pass, while the other opted for a big 50m-long crack more to the right. I was part of the second group, with Alberto and Jesus. However, after two pitches everything was wet, so we abandoned our line and tried another. Meanwhile our friends had climbed quickly and were on a big ledge, two pitches and about one-third of the way up the face. We began another line just to the left of theirs. Both parties came down for the night, leaving ropes fixed.

Next day was beautiful and sunny. The weather was mild, the rock was dry, and we were motivated. Our friends ran up the wall and by midday were out of sight. We reached a big ledge and made a long traverse right, looking for a different line. Again we made a mistake, finding the rock extremely rotten and dangerous. After difficult downclimbing and rappelling we regained the ledge and descended. The other party continued through the night, completing the remaining 260m and arriving on the summit at 6 a.m. We reached the foot of the spire three hours later and helped them down after their 26 hours non-stop ascent.

The west face of Kirkespiret (ca 1,590m) above the Nalunaq gold mine in Tasermiut Fjord. Marked is the new Spanish route Alpin Glow. The lefthand line in the lower section is the variation start El Fari. *Juan Carlos Romero*

The route they named Alpin Glow (360m, 6c and A1+) was completed by Jareño, both Martins, and Palomares. We named our 100m variant start El Fari (5+ and A1, three pitches).

After this ascent we made contact with our boat and found that the sea ice had opened. We were picked up on the 9th and ferried to the base camp below Ulamertorssuaq. Next day we set up an advanced base and several of the team went up to the west face of Nalumatorsoq (2,045m), to start our intended new route on the left side of the central black streaks. Our line was just 30m to the right of what would become Stupid White Man, a route being opened by a German team. Working in shifts we overcame scary offwidths and poor weather to arrive at a long flat ledge we called "Chess ledge." We had fixed 250m of rope to this point, when bad weather moved in and confined us to base camp for three days. We then fixed a further 70m above the ledge and on the 18th set off for the top. After almost 24 hours of non-stop climbing three of us reached the top of the wall. It was 7 a.m. on the 20th. Everyone except our camera-man Enrique took part in opening the route, which we named Nagguteeqqat (6c and A2, 600m) after a popular bread eaten in Greenland. Thanks to our walkie-talkies we were all able to meet and carry the gear back to base camp.

JUAN CARLOS ROMERO, *Spain*

Mexico

Parque Nacional Barranca del Cobre, Dong Tower, the Main Vein. A bachelor expedition for John O'Connor brought five friends to the rim of Barranca del Urique, in Parque Nacional Barranca del Cobre, Chihuahua, from January 9-25. We originally intended to climb sport routes in the sun, but poor weather and rock quality shifted our focus.

Nine years ago Sam Shannon caught sight of a collection of 100+ towers, located four hours southwest of Creel. Rough roads and foot trails provided us access to the towers, where we found no evidence of outside climbers, though the local Tarahumara people had previously climbed some of the easier 5th-class towers.

Chris Dunbar and I climbed the obvious continuous crack up the center of the west face of the largest and most prominent free-standing tower, which we called Dong Tower. We climbed it in a day, after fixing the first pitch and waiting for a weather window. Sean Jordan accompanied us on the day of the ascent but bailed after the first pitch because of ominous rock quality, flora, and large beehives. Five pitches later we finished our route, the Main Vein (500', 5.9 A2+), and briefly stood on the summit before beginning a twilight descent. We placed bolts at belays, equipping them with rap rings on the descent. We also climbed two other towers and several cliffs near basecamp. We experienced a large, rugged canyon teeming with people who are truly living off the land.

IAN BARRETT, *Colorado*

Cañón de la Huasteca, Arte de Malaria and Parque Nacional Basaseachic, free repeat of Subiendo el Arcoiris. On March 13 Eliza Kubarska and I made a rare repeat of the free-climbing testpiece,

The towers by Barranca del Urique, with Dong Tower indicated (only the upper half is visible). Inset: The Main Vein, on Dong Tower. The initial 1²/₃ pitches are obscured in this view. *Ian Barrett*

Subiendo el Arcoiris (Climbing the Rainbow; 300m, 5.13b (8a) max), in Basaseachic National Park in Chihuahua. We climbed the route in redpoint style after a short preparation period. The climb has fragile rock, and some holds on the original line have broken off. We had to find detours on pitches 3, 4, and 7, but the climb is beautiful with a delicate breeze blowing from the waterfall, and we had a constant rainbow hanging behind our backs.

Also during the trip Curt Love (U.S.) and Laurent Antichant (France) almost freed the route, with only one fall, on the 5.12d second pitch.

Afterward we moved to the Guitarritas section of Cañón de la Huasteca, Monterrey, relatively close to El Potrero Chico, to find our own virgin wall in the place that the Huichol Indians consider the center of the universe. We opened a line that we called Arte de Malaria, in part because Eliza was hospitalized with malaria after a January trip in Chiapas, but also because everybody undergoes his own "malaria" to survive.

Bolting ground-up, we opened the line through eight days in March. Our route is 300m long, 5.12c (7b+) max, and 10 pitches: 5.10c, 5.11b, 5.12b, 5.9, 5.12b, 5.12b, 5.12a, 5.12c, 5.10c, 5.10c.

DAVID KASZLIKOWSKI, *Poland*

A close-up of Arte de Malaria. "Ugly, but the best wall in Guitarritas Huasteca canyons," according to the author. *David Kaszlikowski*

The Guitarritas area of Cañón de la Huasteca, showing Arte de Malaria. Although a sport climbing area exists nearby, this is likely the only long route in the photo. *David Kaszlikowski*

Peru

CORDILLERA BLANCA

Taulliraju, north face to final cornice. In late June
Micah Retz and I set off to the beautiful Taulliraju
(5,830m), wanting to climb a new route. After
watching the direct southwest face avalanche a few
times, we headed over the west col with a few days
of food and fuel. The remote and seldom-visited
north face had not been climbed by a new route
since 1979. We placed camp ten minutes' walk below
the face on the immense Taulliraju-Puchirca Glacier.

There are only two other routes on the north
side of the mountain, and only one climbs the
entire north face proper. The original Terray route
(500m, MD A1 60°, 1956) climbs the left side of the north face for a few hundred meters, then
quickly gains the northeast ridge. The Bajan-Busch route (600m, V 5.9 AI4 95°, 1979) roughly
starts on the original route, but takes a straight line to the summit on the left side of the face.

Looking at the face straight on, it was easy to decide where we would climb. A perfect ice
runnel at mid-height on the right side of the face ran for at least 400m. Guarding the bottom
of this runnel was a 60m vertical rock wall, and above the runnel were vertical and overhanging passages of water ice along the summit bulges.

We started at 7 p.m. to ensure good conditions, as we knew these upper ice sections
would be the crux. I took the
first block of climbing to about
mid-height, then Micah took
over to the top. I quickly
reached the crux rock band.
Difficult mixed climbing led to
a high-quality vertical granite
band that went at 5.10 and finished with a desperate mantel
in crampons. In the mixed
runnel, we switched leaders.
That section went quickly, as
we placed virtually no protection through the 70°-85° sn'ice.
We could usually belay from
rock anchors on either side of
the runnel. Little pro through
overhanging bulges of water
ice made the climbing bold as
well as difficult. Two pitches

Micah Retz doing battle on Taulliraju's summit mushroom. *David Turner*

below the summit the sun came out and complicated things greatly. The ice no longer was cold and hard, which made climbing and placing screws difficult. At the top, at 8 a.m., neither of us was willing to surf out onto the last few meters of the unstable cornice. We decided to rappel our ascent route, mostly on threads and pickets, instead of one of the unfamiliar lines. The descent took four hours.

The 650m route required 18 hours roundtrip from our glacier camp at 5,000m. The route went at 5.10 WI5 M6, but conditions change with Peruvian climbing, making grades difficult to peg. We were lucky to have a heavy snow- and ice-pack from the previous winter, as I have seen photos of this face when it was almost entirely rock.

We also attempted the first ascent of Taulliraju's corniced and highly technical west ridge. We believe this to be the first attempt. Although we climbed half of the ridge in one long day, we had to rap off due to dangerous snow conditions. At one point I punched through the ridge, and when I pulled my legs out of the holes, I could see blue sky beneath! This ridge will be climbable during a season with a low snowpack; the heavy winter, which enabled us to climb our north face route, shut us down on this one. Thanks to Black Diamond and Casa de Zarela of Huaraz for their help with this trip.

DAVID TURNER, *AAC*

Nevado Caraz I, Dos Gringos to summit cornices. On July 13, 2006, Slovenians Rok Stubelj and Arcon Jernej climbed the south face, to the right of the West Ridge, of Nevado Caraz I (6,025m), to directly beneath the summit. In nine hours they reached the summit cornices, which prevented them from reaching the West Ridge. They took six hours to descend in 15 rappels. They named what they climbed Dos Gringos (800m, TD 90° [max] 55°-65° [avg]).

ANTONIO GÓMEZ BOHÓRQUEZ (SEVI BOHÓRQUEZ), *Andesinfo, Spain, AAC*

Chacraraju Oeste, Bouchard-Meunier (with variations) to summit ridge, and Alpamayo, Chilean variation. On a July 19 acclimatization climb, Felipe González Donoso, Felipe González Díaz, and I made a Chilean variation (MD 90°) to the 1988 Cacha-Parent route on Alpamayo's southwest face. [Editor's note: Moraga originally reported that their variation was to the 2002 Escruela-Tain route (400m, ED 95°), as shown on pp. 138-139 of Cordillera Blanca scholar and *AAJ* correspondent Antonio Gómez Bohórquez's book, *Cordillera Blanca Escaladas*. Bohórquez reports, however, that he mistakenly credited Escruela and Tain in his book, and that the first ascent of this line belongs to Peruvian P. Cacha and Canadian S. Parent.] We attacked the wall by a runnel right of the Cacha-Parent and then traversed left over an arête to follow another runnel just below the huge snow cornice on the summit ridge that threatens the classic Ferrari route. We summitted Alpamayo (5,947m) after 6.5 hours.

On July 22, from high camp below Chacraraju Oeste (6,112m) Donoso, Juan Henríquez, and I reconned the approach to the intimidating south face and assessed the magnitude of the challenge. The wall only grew taller and more vertical as we came closer. We returned to camp to sleep for a few hours before the start of what would be the most demanding adventure of our lives.

The next day we started climbing in alpine style, with each of us leading three-pitch blocks, while the other two followed free climbing. We found mixed sections with thin ice

Chacraraju Oeste's south face, with the 1977 Bouchard-Meunier route (solid line) shown here as per original expedition routeline photo—some sources have mis-drawn this line. Dots represent the 2007 Chilean variations. Not shown is the 1983 French route (Desmaison-Arizzi-Chappaz-Fourque), which takes a runnel to the right and finishes via the ridge. The '77 and '83 routes are likely the only complete (to summit) routes on this face. *Armando Moraga*

plastered on the rock, inconsistent snow more than 80° steep, and sparse protection. At 8:00 p.m. we dug a small snow ledge, melted water, and ate before continuing at 2:00 a.m.

After 23 pitches (850m, ED+ 95°), by afternoon we reached the summit ridge at about 6,000m. Enormous ice mushrooms greeted us and proved impossible to overcome. We tried our best and even took three whippers in the process, but we could not find a way to the summit. Hopeless, we started the descent, which proved more difficult than the climb. We made 20 long, insecure rappels, eventually following the French Direct route.

We returned safely to the ground after a 50-hour round trip. At some point we all had thoughts that we may well have not made it, but indeed we were hiking back to camp, daydreaming, or rather, dreaming asleep as we hiked.

Editor's note: Though the Chileans thought they climbed new terrain between the '77 Bouchard-Meunier route and the '83 French Direct route, and Internet reports reported such, further research and comparisons of route lines reveals that they mostly climbed the 1977 route, with minor variations.

ARMANDO MORAGA, *Chile*

Nevado Yanapaccha Noroeste, Hay Que Ser Humildes. In mid-August Carlos Pineda and I climbed a direct line on the southwest face of Nevado Yanapaccha Noroeste (Noroeste I; 5,290m). This Nevado is situated southeast of well-known Nevado Chacraraju. Our base camp was at the abandoned Refugio Glaciar Broggi, next to Laguna Broggi. On August 14 we left our cozy camp early, reaching the base of the wall just after sunrise. Due to the chossy condition of this face, the route involves loose rock with poor protection. Rockfall is common, especially in the afternoon when the wall receives sun. The route starts to the left of a noticeable ice-water

runoff in the middle of the amphitheater that leads to the face. The first pitch was a spicy, verglas-covered 5.8. From there the route continued on a relatively easy slab to 150m of class 4. Nine more pitches of moderate climbing, with short sections up to 5.9+, put us on the summit ridge. Another 200m of loose class 4 and a short section on snow led to the summit. We descended the west ridge to the Laguna Glaciar Broggi and were back to camp 14 hours after leaving. We dubbed our route Hay Que Ser Humildes (550m, V 5.9+R), and I dedicate it to our fallen friends in the mountains. We have to keep in mind that, after all, the mountains always have the final say.

MAIKEY LOPERA, *Venezuela*

Hay Que Ser Humildes, the only known route on the southwest face of Nevado Yanapaccha Noroeste (a.k.a. Noroeste I; 5,290m). *Maikey Lopera*

Huascarán Sur, Turbera, and Nevado Copa, Mostro Africano to southwest ridge. Upon returning to Huaraz in June, after climbing Siulá Chico, Oriol Baró and I decided to attempt something more. Having spent six days on our previous route, we wanted something on which we could move fast, similar to what we might climb in the Alps.

In 2005 I climbed a line on Huascarán Norte that snaked around the French Route on the northeast face. The French Route follows the most vertical and safest part of the wall, but as I was climbing alone and as rapidly as possible, I sought out easier, though at times more exposed, passages. From this route I had the opportunity to see the north face of Huascarán Sur (6,768m), upon which I mentally traced a potential line of ascent.

Oriol and I needed to make this line a reality. We climbed the 1,200m-high north face in two days, with a bivouac spent sitting in the middle of the wall á la Mick Fowler. The route links huge snowfields on the right side of the rocky portion of the north-northeast face (just left of the hanging glaciated face) via short sections of rock. We bivouacked again near the northeast ridge, which completed our route, and then continued to the summit, which Oriol did not like because it required such a great deal of "walking." We bivied again while descending the normal route (La Garganta), which we were neither familiar with nor did we enjoy, due to its exposure to serac fall. Turbera (1,200m, MD+ M5 A1).

In 2003, at the end of a course for young alpinists held by the Spanish Federation of Mountain Sports and Climbing, three of the participants—Elena de Castro, Roger Ximenis, and Oriol—headed to the south face of Nevado Copa (6,188m) intending to climb a new route. However, the *apus*, or mountain spirits, hurled the mountain down upon them as they were preparing for bed. They escaped from the avalanche of rock and ice mostly unharmed but plenty shaken. They fled in the middle of the night, wearing boot liners and with a single headlamp between them. Finally, a potato truck carried them back to Huaraz.

Huascarán Sur with the Northeast Ridge route on the left, Turbera in the middle (dots indicate ascent bivies), and La Garganta on the right. Other routes exist left of Turbera. *Baró-Corominas photo*

Oriol's theory was that the mountain couldn't fall on him twice in the same place. Operating under this illusion we returned to the south face of Copa via the Quebrada Paccharuri [Ruripaccha on the latest Alpenverein-skarte map], accompanied by Enrique "Kikon" Munōz, a friend from Madrid who works as a mountain guide in South America. We climbed the 800m wall (Mostro Africano, ED V/6) in a day, with small packs. [The trio bivied on the summit ridge at ca 6,050m, from where they then descended.] Oriol, of course, had divided up the pitches so that the nicest one fell to him, but we didn't say anything, as it looked steep and difficult. It turned out to be one of the best pitches of ice that any of us had ever climbed, even with the packs and at altitude. One couldn't ask for more happiness.

JORDI COROMINAS, *Spain (translated by Adam French)*

Cajavilca III, Southeast Face, and Contrahierbas, attempt. John Pearson and I accessed the glacial basin below the east

Mostro Africano, on Nevado Copa's south face. *Baró-Corominas photo*

The unclimbed south face of Cajavilca I. *Anthony Barton*

Cajavilca III's Southeast Face route. *Anthony Barton*

faces of Nevados Contrahierbas and Cajavilca from the northeast, and I am pretty sure we were the first climbers to do so. It's actually very accessible due to the mining trail to Mina Cajavilca,

The unclimbed east face of Nevado Contrahierbas and the Arbulo-Barton highpoint. *Anthony Barton*

and then there is only one route leading into the upper basin.

On July 6 we climbed Cajavilca III's (5,419m) Southeast Face (550m, AD+). The route started easy, perhaps 40-45°, up to the gully through the lower rock wall. A short, steep step then gave access to the gully, and two 55-60° pitches led to a belay on an ice ridge. A three-pitch 50-55° snow face led to the next rock wall and gully. The gully to the right of this rock wall gave another two pitches, 50° initially but increasing to about 70°. The second of these two pitches led nearly to the summit.

I made a second trip to the Contrahierbas massif with Xabier Arbulo, and we made it to 5,650m on Contrahierbas' east face. It's a serious route, as you traverse above a 400m vertical rock wall. We started at night to avoid objective dangers, but a half-hour after sunrise, under a fair amount of stonefall, a rock hit Xabier, and he dropped his rucksack. Fortunately, clouds rolled in, allowing us to escape.

We were fortunate, but had it not been for the stonefall incident we would have made it, as the final part was straightforward and safe. We carried all of our kit, intending to descend by the mountain's easy western slopes, since a direct descent didn't seem possible, and the objective danger would make it extremely risky.

ANTHONY BARTON, *U.K.*

Apu Wall, Pararasapac Inti. In summer 2006 Odín Pérez noticed a big unclimbed granite wall in the Quebrada Ishinca. Back in Mexico he showed me pictures, and I was committed to climbing it.

We arrived in Huaraz on July 17 and soon established base camp right at the entrance of Huascarán National Park. Our unnamed wall was the second from the left (west) of four large rock buttresses that rise from the slopes of the north side of the canyon. The first wall when entering the canyon is unnamed, the second is what we ended up naming Apu, the third is Hatun Ulloc, and the fourth is Ishik Ulloc [see below report]. From base camp we cleared a trail up to the base of the wall at 4,100m. The approach takes 30 minutes.

On July 19 we started climbing. The lower headwall is characterized by discontinuous cracks that traverse under huge roofs. The lower pitches were the hardest of the route. During our first day on the wall, we opened two pitches. The first is a sparsely protected granite slab that led to the overhanging headwall. The second is a beautiful pitch that traverses up under huge roofs, and has the hardest free-climbing of the route. A small horizontal crack remained A2, because a key hold broke while I tried to free it. The rest of the pitch can be climbed at 5.12. The next two days we struggled to climb the third pitch, which goes under a roof to a ledge below an imposing black roof. This pitch remained unfinished as we left for a week on July 22 to climb Cruz del Sur on La Esfinge.

We returned on August 1. After another day on pitch 3, we finally reached the ledge. Pitch 3 combines run-out face climbing with overhanging crack climbing. Pitch 4 goes under a 10m black roof. We free-climbed the first part of the pitch but aided the upper part. I took a 15m fall while leading the A2+/A3 upper part, when a RURP's sling snapped and several knifeblades and Lost Arrows pulled.

Easier terrain above pitch 4 finished the headwall. After spending a night on the wall, we reached the summit in three long, exposed pitches, with some short aid sections, finishing with an amazing chimney that goes from one side of the wall to the other. Almost all the pitches are 40-50m long and R-rated, even though the route

Pararasapac Inti, the first route on Apu Wall. *Carlos Sandoval Olascoaga*

has high-quality climbing on good rock. After making the first ascent of the wall on August 5, we named it Apu (Quechua for "mountain guard"). We named our route Pararasapac Inti ("wall of light and shadows"; 310m, V 5.12R A2+/A3), because it's located on a south face and never receives sunlight below the summit.

CARLOS SANDOVAL OLASCOAGA, México

Quebrada Ishinca, rock climbs. In early July in the Quebrada Ishinca, German climbers Alexander Schmalz-Friedberger and Michael Zettelmeyer established Con Ojeras Debajo de Ojos Vidriosos (180m, 5.10+ C2) on the overhanging east face of Ishik Ulloc (Ulloc Chico), the next formation to the right (east) of Hatun Ulloc. The route finishes by climbing the chimney between Ishik Ulloc's twin summits, sharing the final pitch with the 2005 route, Lawak.

Around the same time, their teammates Hans-Martin Troebs and Marc Wolff climbed a new route in the middle of the east face of Hatun Ulloc. Compañia Vertical (200m, 7b, 6b obl.) is approached via the first three pitches of Karma de los Condores (Crill-Gallagher, 2004), on the south face, to the big ledge, before traversing around to the east face. The steep route includes four protection and 12 belay bolts (all placed by hand, on lead), and also makes for an excellent rappel route for parties who've climbed Karma de los Condores.

Compiled from reports from www.alpinist.com and ANTONIO GÓMEZ BOHÓRQUEZ

Chinchey Central, Directa Alberto Vittone. On May 19 Peruvian climbers Elias Flores, Michel Araya, Miguel Martinez, and Quique Apolinario, all Don Bosco de los Andes guides, started their journey from the town of Huantar to the Quebrada Rurichinchay, a deep valley with heavy vegetation from its start. A road does not exist to base camp.

They stayed at a moraine camp (4,950m) on May 23, trekked higher on unstable, serac-threatened ice, and established base camp at 5,400m. They prepared to climb the next day, but bad weather and avalanche danger caused them to wait in base camp for two more nights. On May 26 at 2 a.m. they started. It took two hours to reach the northeast face, where 60° to 65° ice made stakes and ice screws extremely useful. They climbed 60m pitches, and at 1 p.m. they finished climbing the wall and reached the final ridge, and then the 6,222m summit at 1:30, naming their route Directa Alberto Vittone (750m, D). They rappelled from Abalakovs down their line of ascent. Since the wall is in the sun all day, they recommend an evening descent.

SERGIO RAMÍREZ CARRASCAL, Peru

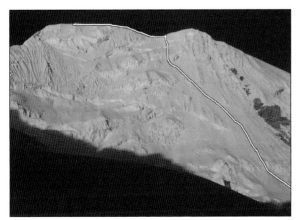

Directa Alberto Vittone, on Chinchey Central. *Quique Apolinario*

Yanamarey Sur, west ridge. On July 8 Chilean-North American Evelio Echevarría and Peruvian Alberto

Murguía approached via the Queracocha Valley and climbed the west ridge of Yanamarey Sur (5,220m). This may be a new route and the second ascent of the peak. It was first climbed from the south by Hartmann and Reiss in 1965. The summit height is given as 5,197m in the Peru ING.

ANTONIO GÓMEZ BOHÓRQUEZ (SEVI BOHÓRQUEZ), *Andesinfo, Spain, AAC*

CORDILLERA HUAYHUASH

Siulá Chico, west face. In May Spanish climbers Oriol Baró and Jordi Corominas made the first ascent of Siulá Chico's (6,265m) sustained, difficult west face (900m, ED+ VI AI5+ A2). The pair carried a portaledge and haul bag, placed no bolts, and bivouacked five times during the ascent and once during the descent. After this climb, they moved to the Cordillera Blanca and established new routes on Huascarán Sur and Nevado Copa, as reported above. See Corominas' Siulá Chico feature earlier in this *Journal.*

Pt. 5,740m ("Siula Antecima"), naming correction. In *AAJ 2007*, pp. 220-221, Lindsay Griffin provided information on an Italian team climbing a peak that they named "Siula Antecima." However, Lorenzo Festorazzi's photo with their ascent line clearly shows that they are referring to Pt. 5,740m on Alpenvereinskarte *Cordillera Huayhuash* 0/3c, which is the same as Jurau B (5,727m) in the Alpine Mapping Guild 2004 map and in other guides.

ANTONIO GÓMEZ BOHÓRQUEZ (SEVI BOHÓRQUEZ), *Andesinfo, Spain, AAC*

Quesillo, east ridge, Electric Lane, to near summit; Huaraca, North Ridge and Northeast Face. Between July 22 and August 12, Tom Bide, Martin Lane, Graeme Schofield, and I went to the southern spur of the Cordillera Huayhuash. First, and most eventfully, we went to Quesillo's east ridge (a.k.a. Electric Lane). This route had seen attempts by at least one party, with retreat in bad weather. Setting off early in the morning, we climbed in two pairs and had made good progress, soloing the easier initial sections of the ridge, when dawn broke. The crux was a 15m steep jam crack (UIAA 5+) to gain the top of one of many gendarmes on the lower ridge. But then a 55m rappel down the north face of the ridge, and a subsequent rising traverse around a 10m gap, slowed our progress. Further climbing along the easy rock ridge led to a slab pitch of UIAA 5. Soon we reached the snow ridge, which led to a rock band that we climbed by a short runnel (Scottish 3/4). The ridge remains 60° steep from here, and the snow deteriorated, allowing no worthwhile protection.

As we neared the summit, the weather rapidly deteriorated, and we heard thunder. Our initial plan was to descend the west ridge to the glacier; the climbing now became urgent. Approximately one rope length from the summit, the state of the remaining ridge looked too time-consuming and dangerous; a notch on the ridge 50m below the summit was our high point (grade TD-). We found an ice cave high on the north face and one-by-one climbed in. It was during this process that a lightning strike struck our entire four-man team. Martin was rendered unconscious for 30 seconds, before waking up disorientated, confused, and in a state of shock (much the same as normal, really).

"What's happened?" Martin asked.

"We've all been struck by lightning, mate" Graeme replied.

Huaraca, with the Northeast Face (left) and North Ridge routes. *Carl Reilly*

"Was it my fault?"

"No, I am pretty sure it wasn't," Graeme said, and he was pretty sure it wasn't.

We looked at Martin, who was still in the land of the fairies, and regrouped in the ice cave as the storm worsened. It would be impossible to descend that day.

Our poorly made snow-hole within the ice cave left our upper torsos and heads exposed, and the four of us lined up ala spoons. On a positive note, we could all fit in the hole, but on a negative note, it had no heat-retaining qualities whatsoever. While none of us are particularly huggy sorts, it is fair to say that nobody was trying to be the alpha male. Graeme even reports that he had never been so glad to be sandwiched between two strapping young men.

After we suffered 12 hours of utter misery, the sun began to creep over the horizon. Suddenly Martin seemed liveliest of all; clearly the lightning strike had charged him up. We descended the northeast face by a series of rappels and downclimbing.

After recovering from the electrifying experience, we put up two routes on the north side of Huaraca. Tom and Martin established the North Ridge route from the col between Huaraca and Jaurau. The route follows the narrow snow ridge, which is corniced in sections, through rock bands until an overhanging rock wall forced them into a series of gullies and slabs on the northeast face. These led to snow slopes and the summit. Grade: D (UIAA 4+).

Graeme and I climbed the Northeast Face route, starting from an obvious snow cone and following a right-trending but wandering line through a series of cracks and chimneys, leading to steeper chimneys, 45m left of the ridge, which we climbed to snow slopes and the summit. Grade: D (UIAA 5).

We all descended by downclimbing the east ridge for 100m, before making two rappels down the south face to reach the glacier between Huaraca and Quesillo.

CARL REILLY, *U.K.*

Trapecio, Los Viejos Roqueros Nunca Mueren, and tragedy. On August 2, 2006, José Manuel Fernández and Miguel Ángel Pita climbed the southeast face of Trapecio (5,653m) via the couloir systems to the right of the July 2005 route by Slovenians Pavle Kozjek, Miha Lampreht, and Branko Ivanek and Basque Aritza Monasterio (*AAJ 2006*, pp. 244-246). The Spanish pair climbed nine initial pitches, with 60m ropes, including a middle section of moving together for 150m and some 70m pitches. They overcame a frozen waterfall (70°, then 80°-85°) on the ninth pitch and then descended [highpoint unclear] after naming their climb Los Viejos Roqueros Nunca Mueren (Old Rockclimbers Never Die, ca 750m V/4+). See *Desnivel*, no. 51, 2007, p. 104.

They rappelled twice from rock pitons and once from a single camming device. On their fourth rappel, their snow stake pulled from the sugary snow and Fernández died in the fall. Pita bivouacked for 12 hours, sitting on a small ice ledge, before climbing unroped to the summit and descending via the northwest face.

ANTONIO GÓMEZ BOHÓRQUEZ (SEVI BOHÓRQUEZ), *Andesinfo, Spain, AAC*

Puscanturpa Este, Stonehenge. Grega Kresal and I, who climbed Chacraraju's 700m east face (VII A2) together in 1993, returned to Peru for the east face of Puscanturpa Este (5,410m). The peak is located in the extreme southeast corner of the Huayhuash, a great distance from the standard western approaches. Our new line, Stonehenge (600m, 10 pitches, VII+ 70° ice), ascends a wall that had not been attempted for over twenty years. In 1986 a set of loose blocks turned around Nixon and partner, the first and only team to attempt the face, only half a pitch up the ridge. (We found one of their abandoned carabiners 20m up.) Ours is likely the second ascent of the peak. We completed the climb in 14 hours roundtrip on July 6, in pure alpine style.

We drove 11 hours from Huaraz to Cajatambo, from where we trekked two long days to the south side of the peak. Here we established base camp. Starting at 4 a.m. on July 6, we made a one-hour approach to the base of the east face. We climbed 200m of moderate ice to reach the steep wall of lithic tuff, typical Puscanturpa rock. (Several rock routes have been established on the west face of Puscanturpa Norte.)

Climbing on volcanic rock was something special, with excellent friction, clean cracks,

Stonehenge, the only route on this side of Puscanturpa Este. *Pavle Kozjek*

Grega Kresal approaching the summit of Puscanturpa Este, with the summit ridge falling away behind him. *Pavle Kozjek*

and thin sharp edges that seemed made for boots (I had rock shoes with me, but kept them in my pack.) However, some sections of the climb were spiced with large, unstable blocks.

With a 60m rope we climbed 10 pitches on the face. The first two pitches (V, VI) worked up steep slabs and cracks to an obvious ledge. A system of cracks and corners followed. The fifth pitch (VII) offered perfect rock with few protection possibilities, and the sixth (VII+) began with the "Scary Corner," a loose 10m dihedral that moved so much it nearly crushed a Camalot. We then traversed right into another corner, and after more long pitches (VI, V) we reached the broken summit ridge from the north side. We summited early in the afternoon and cautiously rappelled the same line, because the normal route (West Ridge, 1986) was so broken and difficult, I was scared to descend it.

According to Jeremy Frimer's guidebook, which inspired me to attempt this wall, Stonehenge marks the peak's second ascent.

PAVLE KOZJEK, *Slovenia, AAC*

Historical note and correction. Several historical references to this mountain contain mistakes. Although the Slovenian route appears similar to route 328 on Puscanturpa Este drawings 157, 159, and 160 in Jan Kielkowski's impressive 1992 Cordillera Huayhuash guidebook (vol. 6, pp. 32-34; in Polish), this guidebook line is almost certainly misdrawn. The text accompanying route 328 refers to a climb on a different mountain: the June 20, 1963, climb of Puscanturpa Central (5,442m), by Julius Hensler and Pedro Baltazar (*AAJ 1964*). Perhaps line 328 drawn on Este was intended to represent what Kielkowski reports as an undescribed, unnamed British route established on August 12, 1985. This British ascent, however, is surely the August 11-13, 1986 (not 1985) Northwest Ridge route (*Alpine Journal 1987*, pp. 72-73), on the other side of the mountain. Plate 29 in the *AJ 1987* may have created the confusion, as the caption refers to the successful British climb (incorrectly placing it), but the photo is from the southeast—the complete opposite aspect of the mountain. Kielkowski's sketch is from virtually the same angle as this photo, and his line 328 matches the *AJ* caption mistake.

Regardless, Kielkowski's 328 route line on Puscanturpa Este does not exist as a route, even today—the Kozjek-Kresaj 2007 line is farther east. Kielkowski's 329 route line/arrow was likely intended to represent (though it's drawn too steep) the approach taken by Brits John Nixon and "Ian" (no last name given in *AJ 1987*; the pair was on the same trip as the Northwest Ridge Brits) on their August 11-12, 1986 attempt, which became the 2007 Slovenian route. Much of this history is accurately documented in Jeremy Frimer's extensively researched 2005 guidebook,

Climbs and Treks in the Cordillera Huayhuash of Peru.

Incomplete details and scant reporting in multiple languages often create difficulty in accurately deciphering information on climbs in this region. Thanks to Antonio Gómez Bohórquez, Jeremy Frimer, and Pavle Kozjek for this information and for translation help.

CORDILLERA APOLOBAMBA

Cordillera Apolobamba, various ascents. In July and August we did some climbs in a remote area of the Peruvian Apolobamba along the Peru-Bolivia border. Few climbers have visited this area. In 2004 Peter Butzhammer, Benjamin Reuter, Dr. Stepfan Fuchs, and I had already climbed in the Cordillera Vilcanota when we met Hermann Wolf, who invited us to explore the Quebrada Viscachani, in the Cordillera Apolobamba, with his expedition. His team also included Gerd Dauch, Manni Obermeier, and Otto Reus (who had been to the Apolobamba with Hermann in 1968).

In 2004 we did the following climbs:

July 10: Suchi I / Huejoloma I (5,361m), first ascent, north ridge, probably UIAA rock II (perhaps III); O. Reus, P. Butzhammer, B. Reuter, Bros Delgado (Peruvian).

July 13: Suchi III / Huejoloma III (5,243m), first ascent, from northwest, loose rock and sand, UIAA II near the summit; H. Wolf, O. Reus, M. Obermeier, A. Bayerlein, Andres Zevallos (Peruvian).

July 15: Chaupi Orco (6,059m), new route; first ascent from Peruvian side; from northwest via Glaciar Viscachani, difficult due to crevasses, camp at 5,450m, then up north ridge to the summit; Dr. S. Fuchs, B. Reuter, A. Bayerlein.

July 15: Suchi II / Huejoloma II (5,238m), first ascent, from northeast; H. Wolf, O. Reus, M. Obermeier, A. Zevallos (Peruvian).

July 18: Sorapata II

Chaupi Orco Norte, showing the new route on the west-northwest ridge. *Benjamin Reuter*

Yanaloma's southeast ridge. *Benjamin Reuter*

Chaupi Orco with the camp indicated, the 2004 route (north ridge) on the left, and the 2007 route (north face) on the right. *Benjamin Reuter*

(5,511m), first ascent, via Glaciar Sorapata parallel to Sorapata Crest, then up east ridge (snow, rock, ice), then becoming mainly rock to the summit; B. Reuter, A. Bayerlein.

We know of a German expedition made up of Ulrich Lossen, Thomas Drexler, Robin Groschup, and Thomas Raab that had been in the area in 2005 and made the probable first ascents of Sorapata III (5,440m, west ridge, after climbing over Sorapata II, Drexler-Groschup-Lossen) and Yanaloma (5,219m, north-northeast ridge, rock up to III+, whole team). We also heard that an international team failed to repeat our climb on Chaupi Orco.

In 2004 Benjamin and I saw an interesting gully in the Salluyo group, but unfortunately we didn't have time. In September 2006 I called Benjamin, and we began organizing our return.

In 2007 we made the following climbs (with, as above, new route and first ascent claims according to our research). Our base camp was in the Quebrada Viscachani at 4,635m:

Nevado Salluyo II (5,818m), new route; from camp at 5,315m, west gully (400m, TD-/TD 80° III [UIAA rock]); B. Reuter, A. Bayerlein.

Nevado Chaupi Orco Norte (5,958m [Jordan map], 6,025m [GPS]), new route and first ascent from this side; from camp at 5,365m, west-northwest ridge (650m, AD+ 70° III); Jan Eisenstein, Dr. S. Fuchs. FA of peak was in 1950s (Italians), second in 1960s (Hermann Wolf), both from the Bolivian side.

Campanane II (5,307m), probable first ascent, northeast ridge (mostly rock I and II, with some III); B. Reuter, A. Bayerlein.

Yanaloma (5,219m), new route and first ascent from this side, southeast ridge (450m, V- [mostly III and IV]); B. Reuter, P. Brosius.

Nevado Chaupi Orco (6,059m), new route; from camp at 5,450m, north face (500m, D-60°); J. Eisenstein, B. Reuter, M. Hoess, P. Brosius.

Nevado Sorapata IV (5,272m), first ascent, from base camp up the Sorapata Crest, then descend 50m, then south of the glacier between Sorapata II and III, then up again (some II rock) and across small glacier at ridge and more easy rock to summit (PD II); Dr. S. Fuchs, A. Bayerlein.

Caca Yuacho Cocho (5,557m), from northeast; J. Eisenstein, M. Hoess.

ANDREAS BAYERLEIN, *Germany*

CORDILLERA CARABAYA

Chichicapac, north ridge; Mamacapac, first ascent; Cornice, south ridge. Mike Cocker, Jonathan Preston, and I arrived in Peru on June 14 and spent a week acclimatizing and buying essentials before arriving at base camp (a four-hour walk with donkeys from the end of a dirt track) at beautiful Laguna Chambine on the south side of the little-visited Cordillera Carabaya.

We spent a few days on reconnaissance, including a look at the south face of Chichicapac (5,614m), our intended target. Unfortunately, though there was a good Scottish-type gully and a mixed line up the face, the lower half was threatened by huge cornices.

Instead, on June 29 we made the first ascent of the north ridge of Chichicapac, grading the route D. Starting from a bivy in the cirque west of the ridge, we followed an easy gully to a col, at 5,123m, with spectacular views to the northeast. We followed the ridge for five pitches on rock, the hardest of which was around MVS and rather friable. Above, easier snow climbing led to the summit. We descended the west ridge (the original route), thus making the first traverse of the peak.

On July 3 we ascended the glacier to the fine peak of Screwdriver (5,543m), to look at its unclimbed south face. However, no obvious line presented itself, so we turned to the nearby unclimbed and spectacular rock spire of Mamacapac (5,525m). We climbed it (PD) via a straightforward snowslope to a high col, from where three pitches of easy-angled but horrendously loose rock gained the summit. There is confusion over the naming of the peaks in this area, with at least one expedition map being wrong. We have tried to sort this out and believe we have the peak names correct.

On July 6 Jonathan and I (Mike dropped out, having sprained his wrist) made the first ascent of the spectacular south ridge of Cornice (5,710m). After an initial 250m of moving together, we climbed 13 excellent pitches of continually interesting and exposed mixed and ice/snow climbing, finishing at the marginally higher end of a severely corniced ridge. The mountain has only had one previous ascent, probably to the other end of this summit ridge, and it is not known if the ridge was traversed. We did the climb in one push from a bivouac on the moraine below the glacier, and descended by downclimbing and rappelling, largely in the dark. Grade D.

Our team disputes the assertion by John Biggar that the rock is akin to Galloway granite—or, while it may be, it is Galloway granite that has been through a mincer and scattered liberally over the crags! Otherwise it is a beautiful

Chichicapac from the west, showing the north ridge ascent and west face descent. The huge rock tower is unclimbed but appears rather loose. *Stephen Reid*

area with many possibilities for new routes.

On July 8, after ten days of perfect weather, we left base camp in a blizzard and spent several days trying to evade protests and riots to return to Lima. All major roads were blocked with rocks, the airport at Juliaca was overrun by demonstrators who smashed the landing lights, and transport was at a standstill. After two days of watching from our hotel roof as teargas-firing riot police battled with slingshot-wielding mobs, we got a bus to Arequipa, which dropped us and the other passengers at a cement works in the middle of the desert, 26 km from town, as the road ahead was blockaded. With a combination of lifts and shank's pony, and carrying 30+ kg of luggage apiece, we ran the gauntlet of stone-throwing hooligans and eventually made it to the town center. We finally left Peru three days later than scheduled.

We are grateful for the financial support from the MEF and the BMC.

Jonathan Preston on the south ridge of Cornice. *Stephen Reid*

STEPHEN REID, *U.K.*

Allincapac (5,780m), Twin Peaks (Ipsa Rita/Yspa Ritti) (5,721m), Cornice (5,710m), Chequilla (altitude unknown, probably unclimbed), Tower (given as 5,577m but perhaps 150m higher), Papacapac (altitude unknown, probably unclimbed), Screwdriver (5,543m), Mamacapac (5,525m). The lines of ascent on Cornice and Mamacapac are indicated. *Stephen Reid*

Venezuela

Acopan Tepui, Perdidos en Venezuela, and Piedra de Culimacare, Conio Crack. December 2007: Two weeks into the Venezuelan Amazon by bongo boat, Matt Othmer, Brazilian climbers Daniel Guimaraes and Eric Silvestrin, and I blazed a trail through dense virgin swamp with six indigenous Yanomamis, still days from the base of our objective, the striking unclimbed east face of Cerro Aratitiyope. The water level dropped six feet in two days, due to lack of rain, guaranteeing that further progress toward Aratitiyope would strand us in the dry season, weeks from civilization, up an Amazonian creek with no water. It was a sad but easy decision to turn back.

Perdidos en Venezuela, on Acopan Tepui. *Asa Firestone*

Tricky maneuvering got us back to bigger rivers, and we visited a smaller granite dome, Piedra de Culimacare, by the Casiquiare Canal. We put up Conio Crack (II 5.10+ A3-) on the steepest side of the dome, and then brought our beloved indigenous boat driver, Flaco, up the back side so he could get his first aerial view of the jungle canopy. Two weeks later we were back in Puerto Ayacucho. I came down with a terrible fever, but a simple (and free) malaria test came back negative. I soon recovered, and we were in motion on another epic 26-hour bus ride to the Gran Sabana, near Angel Falls.

In mid-January 2008 we hired a four-seat propeller plane in Santa Elena to fly us to Yunek, a remote indigenous village at the base of Acopan Tepui. After friendly negotiations with the Pemon people, more hacking through the jungle, a close encounter with a fer-de-lance (pit viper), and five long days on the wall itself, we reached the top of our new route, Perdidos en Venezuela (Lost in Venezuela; 1,300', V 5.11 C2+). We struggled through high winds, scorpion-infested cracks, loose rock, a sheared rope, and a fall logged while interviewing with National Geographic Radio. The climb turned out to be of the highest quality. At the summit the Amazonian sandstone had weathered into wild, soaring shapes preventing easy travel. The only way down was to rappel the route.

Perdidos ascends a dihedral system on the pillar above our base camp, ca 100m to the right of a prominent waterfall on the southeast prow of Acopan. It is just to the south (left) of the beautiful 2003 British route, Unate Arête. This zone is just left of Pizza, Chocolate y Cerveza (Arran-Arran-Rangel, 2003), which is left of the north pillar (home to Purgatory and the Dempster-Libecki variation; see *AAJ 2007*).

Our first three pitches involved tricky aid and free climbing to get on top of a small waterfall, around a roof, and to the dihedral system. Then came 1,000' of unbelievable free climbing. We climbed the route in 13 pitches, although we recommend 11. We placed two bolts at each anchor for rappels, and another five on the route itself. There are great bivy spots on top of pitches four and six, and most belays are also fairly comfortable.

ASA FIRESTONE, *AAC*

Brazil

Morro dos Cabritos, O Céu é o Limite. Brazil features several areas with routes up to 1,260m (4,000') long, especially in the states of Rio de Janeiro, Minas Gerais, and Espirito Santo, where there are an amazing number of towers and domes of granite and gneiss.

In 2006 Daniel Bonella and I opened O Céu é o Limite (5.11b), one of the longest free climbs in Brazil, on Morro dos Cabritos (1,850m), in Três Picos State Park, two hours' drive northeast of Rio de Janeiro city. The 950m route includes technical slab climbing, face climbing on small and big holds, layback cracks, and finger- and hand-jam cracks. The route consists of 24 pitches, with several technical moves of 5.11a and 5.11b. It took us nine days of climbing and drilling to place more than a hundred bolts on the face-climbing sections. Of course, the cracks are still clean for placing gear, which is an important ethic in the area.

The wall is mostly smooth, without good ledges for bivouacs, so we fixed ropes on the hardest pitches, nearly 300m of rope, and slept at the base. As placing bolts can be a dirty, exhausting job, we took breaks and went home between efforts, since it's only a couple of hours away. At the base of the mountain is a clean, warm river waiting for the fastest teams, or for lazy ones who turn back. It's especially a treat on hot summer days, when the temperature can reach 32°C (90°F) in the mountains. Several parties have now climbed O Céu é o Limite; the average climbing time is around 10 hours, not including the rappel and the approach, which takes only 15 minutes from the road.

The first time we went to Morro dos Cabritos was in October 2005, and we opened four pitches of easy slab. Later that month we returned and set three more pitches, with 5.10 moves. Because of the hot season (November to March), we took a break and started again in May

Mountains in Três Picos State Park: (A) Pico Maior de Friburgo (2,350m), (B) Pico Medio (2,300m), (C) Morro dos Cabritos (1,850m), (D) Pedra das Antas (2,000m). On Morro dos Cabritos: (1) Face Norte (5.11b A0), (2) O Céu é o Limite (5.11b), (3) Normal Route (and rappel route; 5.10a A0). Not shown is a route located somewhere between (2) and (3). *Antonio Paulo Faria*

2006, setting another three pitches one day, and fixing ropes on the hardest pitches. We went back six more times, for single days, in June, August, September, and finally October, when we finished the route.

Although there are three other long routes on this mountain, the biggest concentration of long routes in Brazil is on Pico Maior de Friburgo (2,350m) and Capacete (2,100m), also in Três Picos State Park. There are 50 routes on these mountains, ranging from 5.8 to 5.13a, some as long as 18 pitches or 700m. Some pitches are on vertical walls with huge feldspar crystals protruding from the many pegmatite dikes.

ANTONIO PAULO FARIA, *Brazil*

Bolivia

Silvio Neto climbing pitch 5 of O Céu é o Limite, on a 2007 repeat ascent. *Antonio Paulo Faria*

Khuchu Mocoya Valley, ascents and exploration. In early July, Hal Watts, Markus Roggen, Bernard Lam, Ben Withers, and I spent 23 days in the Khuchu Mocoya Valley in the northern Araca Group of the Cordillera Quimsa Cruz, where we climbed 11 routes, 10 of which we believe to be new. There is some confusion over peak names in the area; different maps have different names, and some peaks are known only by colloquial names. There are a few "well-known" landmarks, such as Pico Penis (a.k.a. El Obelisco), Cuernos del Diablo, and Nevada Saturno. These landmarks are generally consistently named, so routes can be located by their relative positions.

Our base camp was on the banks of the Rio Khuchu Mocoya, west of Laguna Blanca, and we spent several days looking for good lines on the faces to the east. We had come to the area hearing that it was a granite paradise, and there was certainly a lot of granite; however, most faces were shorter than we had expected, generally 150-300m high.

We climbed our first route, E-dirt (140m, E3 5c), on the slabs to the southwest of Nevada Saturno. The rock was good, but with a lot of vegetation in the cracks. We had bought a garden trowel in La Paz, which was useful for clearing dirt. Next we climbed a striking crack line on the slabs to the northeast of Laguna Blanca, a four-pitch E1 5b. We found evidence—two stuck nuts and a bolt—that this route had been previously climbed.

We then visited the next valley to the north (the Turaj Umaña River Valley, which some locals call the Torrini Valley) in search of more north, sunny faces (though the north side of the valley had numerous faces around 200-300m high, some with uninterrupted crack lines for their duration). This valley is home to an impressive northwest-facing formation, on the south side of the valley, that local climber and guide Gonzalo Jaimes had called Torrini (not to be confused with the Cerro Torrini on the HOJA maps, which is about 2.5km north of the Turaj Umaña Valley—outside the valley but close enough to confuse things). We later learned that this peak is Gross Mauer, at least as named by the German FA team. Gross Mauer means "Great/Big Wall" and is the formation where Lynnea Anderson and Donny Alexander established the AA Crack, up one of the most striking features on the peak, in 2002 [*AAJ 2003*, pp. 315-316]. We climbed on the peak briefly, but it was basically a bolted crag with almost no potential for new routes.

Mostly unnamed rock walls on the north side of the Turaj Umaña River Valley, the next valley north of the Khuchu Mocoya Valley in the northern Araca Group, showing the Gatt-Wutscher (1990) FA route on what they named Pico Horizonte. Some locals reportedly call this peak Las Tenazas. Other routes likely exist in this photo, but we were unable to track them down. *Virgil Scott*

On this same south side of the valley we found excellent sunny rock faces, 100-250m long. We climbed several routes in this area: three along the western end of the north faces framing the valley and two in an area to the east. In the western area, the routes were La Cueva Comoda (230m, E1 5b), Motivationsriss (120m, HVS 4c), and a 200m VS 4c. In the eastern area we climbed La Manera Dura (150m, E5 6b) and Lalilu (120m, E2 5c). We climbed all routes onsight except La Manera Dura.

During a snowy period Bernard and Ben climbed a mixed route (grade III/4) on the slabs near the col that leads to the next valley northwest of base camp.

Other new routes included a three-pitch 100m VS 4c in the Diablos area by Bernard and Markus; a long scramble to the northwest of Saturno (250m, AD-) by Bernard and Ben, and a long ridge traverse (PD+) by Ben, Bernard, and Markus.

We found one larger face (400-500m), which we nicknamed the "Big Wall," about 2km northwest of Laguna Blanca. [Not to be confused with the other "Big Wall," Gross Mauer, a.k.a. Torrini, albeit not the "real" Cerro Torrini on HOJA maps; according to Bolivian climber, guide, and guidebook author Denys Sanjines, this face that Scott is referring to is called La Gran Muralla, which, in English, means "The Great Wall," but, again, not to be confused with Gross Mauer, either Torrini, or other big and great walls—extremely confused Ed.] It was probably the most spectacular face we saw in the area, but unfortunately it was loose and steep. We spent four days attempting to climb it and made only 50m of progress. As far as we know this face has no routes, which Jaimes confirms. This seemed like one of the few, if not the only, unclimbed face of this size in the area and would make a great objective for a team that doesn't mind the cold and is willing to aid.

During our time in the Quimsa Cruz we found a lot more evidence of climbing than we had expected. For more information, see www.quimsacruz2007.co.uk.

VIRGIL SCOTT, *U.K.*

Argentina and Chile

CENTRAL ANDES, CHILE

Torres del Brujo, A Ultima Dama and other climbs. From January 10–22, 2008, Joao Cassol (Florianopolis, Brazil), Wagner Machado (Curitiba, Brazil), and I explored the seldom-visited Torres del Brujo. Located 120km south of Santiago, Chile, the area may best be described as a smaller version of its famous Patagonian neighbors to the south. The primary difference between the two regions is the likelihood of long periods of high pressure in the Torres del Brujo during the South American summer.

We set out from the trailhead under a deep blue sky, with two heavily laden and disagreeable mules. Our arrival two days later at the base of the towers went, more or less, according to plan, and we promptly set out to repeat one of the easier routes on the Aprendiz de Brujo, a 300m tower at the foot of 500m Brujo Falso, our main objective.

The day after our arrival, we climbed the classic Aprendiz route Uno Poco de Patagonia (300m, IV 5.10d) in a long day from our camp at the base of the glacier. During the course of

Torres del Brujo, with the arrow and inset indicating A Ultima Dama. *Joao Cassol*

this day, we realized that the glacier conditions were too poor to permit safe passage with the amount of equipment we needed to carry to Brujo Falso. We then set our sights upon the walls on the opposite side of the glacier from the Brujo Falso, walls that seemed conducive to a lighter style.

Joao Cassol, belayed by David Trippett in the chimney above, following the 65m first pitch of A Ultima Dama. *Wagner Machado*

On January 17, with ever-present high pressure, we found our way to a substantial wall that looked promising. The unnamed peak is adjacent to a tongue of glacial icefall that descends from the icecap above and east of the peak. Examination of the wall revealed two previously climbed lines, but farther up-glacier toward the icefall tongue we found a line that appeared unclimbed. Located on the very left side of the wall and threatened by seracs from the icefall, the line starts in the middle of a system of right-facing corners and can be distinguished by the presence of a short section of chimney 65m above the glacier, at the top of the first pitch. From here, the climb ascends a strenuous hanging flake above the chimney and continues in a fairly direct line, on crack and face features, to the top of the steep wall. This first part of the wall is characterized by steep, hard 5.10 crack climbing. After the steep section of the wall, the route changes to an alpine ridge climb. The final 150m is seldom more difficult than 5.9, and routefinding on the broad ridge never seemed difficult, with several logical options available to reach the summit. We completed our route in one long day from camp. Because it seemed to be the last unclimbed line available to our party, we named it A Ultima Dama (320m, IV 5.10+), Portuguese for "the Last Lady."

During our trip we also established several single-pitch routes from 5.10-5.11 in an area we dubbed Gato de Brujo (the Sorcerer's Cat), at the lower end of the same long rampart as our route. There was at least one other route there, likely done by Italians. (The bolts were Italian, anyway.)

DAVID TRIPPETT, *Vancouver, B.C., AAC*

CENTRAL ANDES, ARGENTINA

Aconcagua (6,962m), 2007–2008 season overview. This season 7,658 climbers and trekkers arrived at the provincial park, 345 more than last season (visitation grows yearly by about 5–10%). Of these, 4,548 had a climbing permit, 1,400 succeeded (about the normal 30% rate), 278 were evacuated, and a Romanian climber died.

A possible new route or variation was established on the west face by Czechs Josef Lukas and Leopold Sulovsky. American boy Jordan Romero, only 11 years old, broke Aconcagua's age record. There was controversy because the boy had a judge's permit; normally people younger than 14 aren't allowed on Aconcagua. Jordan asked for the seven summits as a gift at his ninth birthday party, and in 2006 he ascended Kilimanjaro and Elbrus.

Frenchman Francois Bon approached Aconcagua in early winter conditions. He then made a speed-flying (free skiing and high-speed paragliding) descent of the south wall in four minutes and 50 seconds. "With the altitude it goes so fast!" Bon said. "I fell from the sky along the walls." He has also descended Mont Blanc and the Eiger.

MARCELO SCANU, *Buenos Aires, Argentina*

Aconcagua, possible new route or variation. Various sources, including www.alpinist.com and www.czechclimbing.com, reported that Czechs Josef Lukas and Leopold Sulovsky climbed an alpine-style new route on Aconcagua's west face. The route is right of the Normal Route and left of the West Face (1965) route (which it crosses at the Gran Acarreo) but seems to climb substantial portions of other routes, particularly Guias Mendocinos (1992) and Flight of the Condor (2002). Exactly how much of the route is new remains

Aconcagua from the west, showing the Lukas-Sulovsky line, which shares substantial terrain with existing routes. The main summit (6,962m) is hidden from view, while what looks like the high point in this image is actually the south summit (6,930m). *Mauricio Fernández, www.summitediciones.com.ar*

unclear and, due to language barriers, getting information proved difficult. Regardless, Lukas confirmed the route line shown here and added, "We were on top on January 29, 2008, at 7 p.m. after three days of climbing. One day back to base camp. Our first camp was at 5,200m, second at 6,200m. Maximum UIAA 5. Bad rock with a lot of falling stones."

Thanks to Vlado Linek, Damian Benegas, and Mauricio Fernández (author of *Aconcagua, La Cima de América*) for information.

Mt. Tupungato, first winter ascent. Mt. Tupungato (6,570m) stands in front of Santiago, Chile, on the border with Argentina. It is famous for its bad weather, being swept every day by furious western winds, moistened by Santiago's smog.

After an investigation in both countries showed no previous winter ascents, we planned to go for it and film a documentary. The group was comprised of five Argentinians: Diego de Angelis, Fernando Garmendia, Guillermo Glass, Rolando Linzing, and me.

We approached Tupungato from Argentina, even though it demands crossing the Cordillera Frontal, a lower range directly to the east, then descending to the Tupungato Valley. On August 31 we departed from Refugio De la Plaza, a military post at 2,090m. Our backpacks weighed 45kg, as we needed to take filming and mountaineering gear, including glacier, skiing, and avalanche equipment, in complete self-sufficiency.

After some days acclimatizing in lower valleys, we followed the Las Tunas, Pabellón, and Grande rivers and crossed the Cordillera Frontal through the Portezuelo del Fraile col (4,746m). Then we followed the Tupungato Valley to its source at the mountain's southern glacier. A couple of stormy days followed, but on September 13 at 4:45 a.m. we left our last camp, pitched at 5,500m on the southern ridge, and starting climbing the southern route, a glacier up to 45°. At night the weather got stormy once more, and this time also very cold. We kept climbing and, at 10:30 p.m. Glass, Linzing, and I reached the main summit in a storm with -50°C temperatures, while DeAngelis and Garmendia reached the 7m-lower eastern summit.

Two days later we trekked to Tupungato's eastern glacier, where a plane disappeared in 1947 and was discovered by Garmendia and Pablo Reguera 51 years later, at 4,500m. Despite the amount of snow, we found a tire, still inflated.

We returned to Refugio de la Plaza 18 days after leaving it, having climbed 7,200m total and walking 95km.

DARIO BRACALI, *Argentina, CAB, AAC*

NORTHERN PATAGONIA, CHILE

Volcán Michinmahuida, West Face. The icy dome of Michinmahuida Volcano (8,071'), near the town of Chaiten in northern Chilean Patagonia, is rarely visited because of bad weather and a long approach trek through the cold jungle. In three days, finishing on Januray 16, 2006, Chileans Cristian Stephens, Juan Pablo Ortega, and I opened the West Face (PD). The route starts

The West Face route on Volcán Michinmahuida. *Rodrigo Ponce*

just left of the West Glacier and climbs moderate slopes through large crevasse fields. The crux of this route is finding the right way through the crevasses.

RODRIGO PONCE, *Club Andino Universitario, Santiago, Chile*

Cerro Pico Moro, first ascent, Normal Casanova. After my return from Cochamó, Jose Datolli, Felipe Opazo, and Marcelo Cortes organized an expedition to Cerro Pico Moro, near Palena, Chile. With the help of the Chilean Air Force and the Municipality of Palena, we embarked for this Patagonian city. From Palena we were transported to the nearby Valle el Azul, where Datolli and I set off without a stove or bivy gear for a trip that we supposed would take two days, up an unclimbed peak. After getting whipped by bad weather, we waited for the support of the rest of our team and some locals who were bringing in supplies for an advanced base camp. After a day of waiting for good weather, Datolli and I set off again without bivy gear, climbing three pitches and descending to a bivy at the base of the wall. Early the next morning we started again, freeing the first three pitches and continuing to the summit, which we reached at 2 p.m. By 4 p.m. we had returned to the base of the wall, where the rest of the team awaited us, and we all returned to advanced base camp.

Normal Casanova, the first route on Pico Moro. *Michael Sánchez Adams*

The route, Normal Casanova, climbs the southwest face in eight pitches, beginning with a finger and hand crack, which contains the only 5.10. From here to the top the climbing is relatively easy, but with a lot of loose blocks. Though we climbed in summer, mid-February, I recommend this part of Chilean Patagonia for winter [southern hemisphere winter] ascents. It is virtually unexplored and full of unclimbed glaciers and peaks.

MICHAEL SÁNCHEZ ADAMS, *Chile (translated by Adam French)*

COCHAMÓ

Summary. Cochamó's highest number of both international and Chilean climbers visited the area this season, and the number of new routes surpassed the last few combined. The spectrum grew to include not only big walls, short multi-pitch cracks, and sport routes, but deep-water soloing too. (Though at least 20 single-pitch routes went in, only the longer routes are reported here, to supplement the individual reports below.)

The Amfiteatro (Amphitheater), a gigantic granite bowl with almost a dozen big walls, received the newest and most classic big-wall ascents. Chilean Michael Sanchez and Germans Martin Waldhor and Achim Mink made several impressive climbs, reported below. Chilean Jose Ignacio Morales and Brazilian Roberto Sponchiado completed their 10-pitch La Hora Es Ahora (400m, 5.11b/c C1+) on the left side of El Espejo, in the Amfiteatro. "It has a little of everything," said Morales, "long cracks, technical faces, flakes, and dihedrals—varied and entertaining...over excellent rock."

Superb climbing on Excelente Mi Teniente, El Espejo. *Michael Sánchez Adams*

Later, Chilean brothers Javier and Jorge Durán opened the valley's easiest long climb, Espiral de Clavos (300m, 5.10a), up a huge face they called La Sombra. A great story exists behind the route name, tying together some generous Swiss climbers, a haul bag falling off a truck, Torres del Paine, an old Chilean lady, and La Hora Es Ahora.

Australian Anthony Schellens and I added the first color of climbing to the Arco Iris wall by opening its first completed route, Através del Iris (450m, 5.10c).

American Wes "Tomás" Thompson opened La Vaina Oscura (175m, 5.9+ A2+) in a way never seen before in the valley—a solo first ascent on a previously virgin wall to the right of the Arco Iris wall.

Americans Peter Fasoldt and Eli Simon found their Wicked Big Toddlah (150m, 5.10b), an obvious crack system on the right side of Milton Adams.

Spanish climbers Jose Miguel Diaz and Alejandro Puche climbed the center of La Junta Wall but stopped short a few pitches from the top when, as is so often is the case, the weather turned sour, and they ran out of time. They called their efforts Vivir para Trabajar (675m, 5.11c).

Americans Winter Ramos and Mateo Touchette also came close to the top of the right side of the huge wall Capicúa, as reported below.

Okay, that's it for this Radio Cochamó report, wishing you great climbing, over and out.

DANIEL SEELIGER, *www.cochamo.com, Bariloche, Argentina*

Cerro Noemi Walwalun and El Espejo, various ascents. In January 2008, Germans Martin Waldhor and Achim Mink, and I climbed up to the Junta Valley in search of new routes. A five-hour approach brought us to our familiar bivy site, from where we could access the walls of the Amphitheater area.

Cerro Noemi Walwalun, first free ascent (by variation) of Cien Años de Soledad (800m,

El Espejo's first three lines: (1) Cinco Estrellas. (2) La Hora Es Ahora. (3) Excelente Mi Teniente. *Jose Ignacio Morales*

ED- 6B A2+). In the first weeks of January, Jose Ignacio Morales, Mikel Martiarena, and I made serious attempts, and then on January 28 Waldhor, Mink, and I freed two alternate pitches to bypass the aid on this route.

El Espejo, Excelente Mi Teniente (14 pitches, 5.11a). This route follows a system of cracks through a pair of obvious roofs in the center of El Espejo's wall. The route climbs 14 pitches, with difficulties up to 5.11a and a number of pitches of 5.8 and 5.9. A vari-

Michael Sánchez Adams on an earlier attempt at the eventually successful free variation to Cien Años de Soledad. *Jose Ignacio Morales*

ety of climbing, from finger and hand cracks to off-width, along with the two roofs, makes this an interesting, athletic, and aesthetic line. Established ground-up on January 30, we placed 18 bolts, all on lead (14 of which were for rappels—in addition to some wedged knots). Our rack consisted of a set of Stoppers and a set of Friends, with doubles of #4.

El Espejo, Cinco Estrellas (400m, 5.10d). This route is located 15 minutes left of Excelente Mi Teniente. The nine-pitch route begins with a system of cracks and dihedrals to the left of an obvious pillar at the apex of the principal gully. The name, which is related to the rating scale for quality in the valley established by Daniel Seeliger, suggests that we think this route is of the highest quality and aesthetics (from the fifth pitch onward). The route was opened ground-up, with seven bolts placed on lead and the same rack as used on Excelente Mi Teniente. Descent was via Excelente Mi Teniente

Cerro Noemi Walwalun, lower wall, Sácalo pa'Entro Papá (ca 400m, 5.10b). Achim noted this system of cracks and dihedrals leading to the big ledge below the headwall on Cerro Noemi Walwalun. We climbed nine pitches, beginning in a system of somewhat dirty cracks. We used the same rack as on Excelente Mi Teniente and placed one bolt for a belay. From the ledge beneath the headwall, descent can be made via the rappels of Cien Años de Soledad.

MICHAEL SÁNCHEZ ADAMS, *Chile (translated by Adam French)*

Capicua, Gato Negro Lo Mejor Vino En Caja. Matt Touchette and I returned to paradise in January 2008 to try to find a route on the breathtaking, beautiful, serene Capicua, a 1,000m granite wall in Cochamó. There were two existing routes on the wall [photo p. 266, *AAJ 2006*], by a Catalan team and a German team, but both routes were 20 pitches, A4+, and called for 24 beaks. We wanted something more accessible and less intense, with less suffering.

Our discovery could not have been better. After some searching, we approached our line via two 30m pitches (dirty crack and moss, 5.10, then an easier second pitch) in the Mate Landia cragging area (below Capicua), which took one-tenth the time of the previous parties' vertical bushwhack, plus we got to climb. Another hour of scrambling over 4th class rocks and bushes then brought us to the base of Capicua, and we put up four pitches (25m 5.8, 60m 5.8 A0 [pendulum], 40m 5.9+, 30m 5.10) of beautiful free climbing at a moderate grade on a sunny morning. The first three pitches angle up right to the base of the big left-facing system. Work was slow but rewarding. Pounding in pitons (the route doesn't need many, and we left two fixed), hand-drilling bolts, and cleaning dirty cracks doesn't sound like fun to many people, but we were onto a soon-to-be classic Cochamó climb, and the feeling could not have been better. After our first day we came down to camp exhilarated, excited to jumar up our fixed ropes and continue in the morning.

Ignoring the constant buzz of the huge biting horse flies (*tabanos*) was difficult, but we thought of the welcoming people down in the valley and their positive energy. The brilliance of the jungle surrounded us. Atop our fixed ropes we climbed a beautiful, wet, mossy chimney pitch to an enormous ledge (25m, 5.9), then a crack system on the right (25m, 5.9), then a steep aid corner and a final pitch to a huge, prominent ledge with a waterfall pouring down to the right. We reached the ledge at dark, feeling satisfied, content, and exhausted. IV 5.10+ A1+, 10 pitches (including the two approach pitches). Gear: standard free rack with extra TCUs, plus a knifeblade and sawed-off baby angle for the aid corner.

Though the ledge marked the end of the corner system and seemed like a logical ending, there is potential for more climbing above. The terrain looks vague and would likely require more bolts, though, and the waterfall could get you wet and cold if it is flowing at high volume. We had planned to sleep on the ledge, until the winds picked up and drenched our minimal clothing. We brought out our Nalgene bottle filled with Gato Negro wine, hence the route name: Gato Negro Lo Mejor Vino en Caja (Black Cat the best wine from a box). We rested on the ledge for a bit and then rappelled in the dark to eat lentil soup with sausage.

WINTER RAMOS

CENTRAL PATAGONIA, CHILE

Cerro Largo, first ascent, northeast ridge; Cerros Hyades, Turret, and Escuela, first winter ascents. After making the first winter crossing of the Northern Patagonia Ice Cap in July 2006, we wanted to climb mountains on the northeast side of the Ice Cap, increase our knowledge of this vast glaciated area of Patagonia, and experience this unknown area in winter. Club Aleman Andino and Club Andino Universitario members Camilo Rada, Mauricio Rojas, Nicholas von Graevenitz, and I left Santiago on July 6 to enter the Lake Leones sector. After days of transport by horses and Zodiac, we reached the foot of the Leones Glacier, the easiest access to the northern sector of the Ice Cap. Three days later we gained Cristal Pass, the entrance to the plateau, where an intense storm, quite infrequent in winter, pinned us for

Cerro Largo's first ascent route, the northeast ridge. *Pablo Besser*

eight days in our igloo. We then enjoyed eight days of good weather, and traveled 12km on skis with pulkas, going past San Valentin and to the base of Cerro Hyades (3,100m). This colossus, the primary target of our trip, had only two ascents (New Zealanders in 1969 and 1973), neither in winter. From the north on July 29, half the time on skis, we climbed the 1969 route, mostly on the west face but spiraling around to the north and finishing from the northeast. Accompanied by the sun, and with the Pacific Ocean at our backs, everything seemed perfectly in place. We skied a great part of the descent, with the best snow but also some crevasses that forced to remain roped the whole way, limiting the pleasure of the ski.

The next day we left in the middle of a gale with zero visibility. After six hours—thanks purely to the GPS—we reached the foot of Cerro Largo (Long Mountain) and built another igloo—exhausting work that made us sweat, turning our layers to frozen armor under our parkas—rather than try to set up tents. Two days later, July 31, we left the igloo for snow-covered Orange Peak, a satellite of Cerro Largo, and skied up it, enjoying a golden sunset on the summit. We had an unforgettable ski down, not only due to the scenery but also the good snow.

Cerro Largo extends almost 15km from north to south, and was the highest unclimbed mountain on the northern Ice Cap. The only possible route seemed to be the northeast ridge, though it was guarded by huge overhanging seracs. Camilo and Nicholas left very early the next day, and after 10km of uphill they reached the mountain's first steep slopes. A few hours later they reached the huge overhanging serac, which had a solid 14m of glacier ice that overhung 40°. Camilo aided through it, using all of our screws. Nicholas jumarred, and after eight difficult hours (MD) they were the first to climb Cerro Largo (2,800m), and in winter—the most technical Chilean ascent in the Patagonia Ice Cap. They returned to the igloo late, as happy as exhausted.

Good weather followed, so the next day we all went to Cerro Turret (2,285m), ascended its small summit, and continued to nearby Cerro Escuela (2,100m), reaching its summit in late afternoon, both ascents from the north via easy terrain that was perhaps previously climbed. We returned to the igloo after more then 22km of travel and two first winter ascents in that long day. Two days later we descended the long and smooth Nef Glacier and camped by the impressive Cerro Cachet. At noon the next day we left the Ice Cap to enter the humid Patagonian forests of lengas and coigües trees.

We exited through the Soler River Valley, with three days travel, under heavy loads, bringing us to the shores of Plomo Lake and our boat ride to civilization. On August 12, after our 36-day expedition, a carnivorous dinner in Coyhaique marked the end of another Patagonian winter adventure.

Instead of the long days and nicer temperatures of summer, we prefer winter's predictable long spells of clear days with no wind. Although we have only nine hours of daylight, and temperatures sometimes to -30C°, in the long run we can climb a lot more. Also, the special winter light makes an unforgettable scene in this vast, unexplored area.

PABLO BESSER, *Club Aleman Andino and Club Andino Universitario*

Avenali Tower, first ascent, Avenali Avenue. The Avellano Towers are a remote, recently discovered group just northeast of Lago General Carrera in Chilean Patagonia. They comprise several low but rugged granite towers. The rock ranges from excellent to choss and, due to their proximity to the Northern Patagonia Ice Cap, the weather can be trying. In March 2004 a group of climbers led by Dave Anderson and Nacho Grez, after a two-day approach from the north, did a route on the northern-most tower ("Avellano Tower," *AAJ 2004*, pp. 307-308). The next year John Bragg, Wes Bunch, Angela Hawse, and Brenton Regan explored a southern approach from the small town of Bahia Murta. John broke his leg during the rugged approach, ending their attempt.

From our base at my new house on the shores of Lago General Carrera, Thom Engelbach and I used the Bragg approach in an attempt to reach the unclimbed, southernmost tower. We call this "Wild Patagonia" versus "Chamonix Patagonia," the Chalten area, where there are some of the best climbs in the world but no exploration.

Taking advantage of weather more Sierra-like than Patagonian, we left our cozy base on the morning of January 21, 2008, and drove to the trailhead at Bahia Murta. Seven hours of gnarly hiking got us to base camp in a beautiful cirque 2,000 vertical feet below, and west of, the tower. The next day we made an exploratory hike to the col south of the tower, scoping out a line rising from just down and east of the col, before depositing our technical gear and returning to base camp. After luxuriating in atypical sunshine on the morning of the 23rd, we left camp for the two-hour approach to a bivy at the col.

Aerial view from the east, showing (1) Avellano Tower (see *AAJ 2004*, pp. 307-308, and *AAJ 2006*, pp. 270-271) and (2) Avenali Tower. Everything else is likely unclimbed. *Rolando Garibotti*

Avenali Avenue, the line of first ascent on Avenali Tower. *Julie Maret*

The southern end of the Avellano chain from the west, with Avenali Tower rising above Thom Engelbach's head. Donini and Engelbach climbed the southeast ridge, out of view. *Jim Donini*

The next morning we left before dawn on a clear, windless day, scrambled down, and started climbing the broad southeast ridge. The climb felt more like an excursion into Rocky Mountain National Park than a Patagonian first ascent. About 500m of climbing in 16 pitches had us on the virgin, windless summit of what we called Avenali Tower, for our mentor Peter Avenali who was my inspiration for going to the area. [Editor's note: Some sources initially reported this as the tower immediately south of the northernmost tower climbed in 2004 (Avellano Tower), but it is actually farther south along the same group of towers (see photo). A natural barrier between Avellano Tower and Avenali Tower blocks the view from one tower to the other, and, though they are in the same chain of towers, they are approached via different valleys.] Our route, Avenali Avenue (V 5.11- R A0), has something for everyone. Rock ranging from sublime to shite, difficult routefinding, and some sketchy pro serve up climbing that will keep you on your toes. Eleven raps got us back to the col at midnight, culminating an 18-hour roundtrip.

This season, since Patagonian weather was so consistently good, I propose that all new routes receive an asterisk. They need to be done in more representative conditions before they get full value.

JIM DONINI, *AAC*

SOUTHERN PATAGONIA, ARGENTINA

CHALTEN MASSIF

Chalten massif, summary. Unprecedented amounts of good weather greeted climbers in the 2007–08 Patagonia season, resulting in numerous new routes and significant ascents. [Note: This summary supplements the individual reports, mostly of longer routes, below.]

On the southeast buttress of Bifida's south summit, American Crystal Davis-Robbins and Chilean Nico Gutierrez completed the second ascent, and first complete ascent (to summit) of Cogan (800m, TD 5.10 A1, Bruckner-Schorghofer, 1993), which originally ended 100m from the summit after joining Cheoma. Davis-Robbins and Gutierrez climbed a number of variations to the original route.

American Colin Haley and German Carsten von Birckhahn made the second ascent of the upper portion of Puerta Blanca (Huber-Walder, 2007) on Desmochada, climbing several variations along the way. They approached via the Desmochada-Poincenot gully, rather than climbing the rock buttress just left of Desmochada's west face, as did Huber and Walder.

Later in the season Haley and Rolando Garibotti completed the third ascent of the Afanasieff route (1,600m, TD 5.10) on the northwest ridge of Fitz Roy. They started from a camp in the Torre Valley and climbed up and over Hombre Sentado ridge, reaching a point seven pitches below the summit on their first day. After a cold sleeping-bag-less bivy they climbed to the summit and descended the Franco-Argentine route.

Earlier in the season, French climbers Aymeric Clouet and Christophe Dumarest established a new variation to the Afanasieff route, climbing the steep 400m buttress between the Supercanaleta and Afanasieff routes. They followed a series of steep cracks, with difficulties up to 7a and A2, that they christened Le Chercheur d'Absolu. Clouet and Dumarest traversed left at the top of the initial pillar to join the Afanasieff route, which they followed to the summit.

West face of St. Exupery: (1) Chiaro di Luna (Girodani-Manfrini-Valentini, 1987; finishes on other side). (2) Southwest "Austrian" Ridge (Barnthaler-Lidi, 1987). (3) Supertrek (Bowers-Nettle, 2003). (4) Brooks-Crouch (1999) to junction with (2); Bransby-Tresch (2004) to summit. (5) Last Gringos Standing (Grohne-Huey, 2008). *Jesse Huey*

A similar line had been previously tried by another French team in 2002 and 2003; they tried to continue upward, following the ridge crest, but were turned back 700m up by blank rock.

Also on Fitz Roy, but farther east, American Bean Bowers and Garibotti climbed an independent line to the top of the Goretta Pillar. Their route, Mate, Porro y Todo lo Demas, climbs a series of steep cracks on the northwest edge of the pillar (accessed by Paso Cuadrado). They took 10 hours to climb the twenty-some pitches to the top of the pillar, then descended via the Casarotto route to the col (Bloque Empotrado) north of the pillar, from where they rappelled west back to the base of the climb. In the upper third the route climbs a series of wide cracks, just left of the pillar's edge. The superb climbing went mostly free, with a short section of easy 5.11 and two 10-foot sections of A0 due to icy cracks. This route saw two repeats, by Brazilian and Argentine teams, both stopping at the top of the pillar as well. The buttress just left of the wide cracks on the upper third of Mate, Porro y Todo lo Demas, and right of Chimichurri y Tortas Fritas, was climbed as a variation to the Kearney-Knight variation to the Casarotto route by Americans Jesse Huey and Toby Grohne (Gringos Perdidos, 6–8 new pitches up to 5.11).

In November Italian Claudio Inselvini and Swiss Michi Lerijan climbed a major variation (No Brain, No Pain) to the Supercanaleta. After climbing 800m up the Supercanaleta gully, well below the Bloque Empotrado, they traversed right for 200m, across a series of ledges and easy slabs, crossing Ensueño to near the southwest ridge. They then climbed six to eight pitches, involving slabs and steep cracks on the north side of the ridge, to reach the upper portion of Tonta Suerte, before joining the upper ridge of Supercanaleta and eventually the summit.

On the east face of Fitz Roy, Americans Jimmy Haden and Mike Pennings made the first alpine-style ascent of Royal Flush (5.12 A1, Albert-Arnold-Gershel-Richter, 1995, to junction with El Corazon), and only the second complete ascent of the route to the summit (first complete ascent by Gäbel-Schafroth-Treppte, 1998, in three days roundtrip with fixed ropes). Haden and Pennings completed the 4,000' route in a 48-hour roundtrip from Paso Superior.

On the west face of St. Exupery, Huey and Grohne established Last Gringos Standing (V 5.11- C1), just left of the Southwest "Austrian" Ridge (Barnthaler-Lidi, 1987), over two days in early March 2008. Huey and Pennings spotted the route in February, and during a recon climbed three pitches of perfect 5.10 cracks to a dike, where they discovered enough holds to allow a 60' leftward traverse to a second crack system that promised to lead to the upper ridge. Huey returned with Grohne, free-climbing everything except one icy crack and joining the Austrian Ridge after seven pitches, along which they continued to a bivy at the notch between a false summit and the true peak, which they reached the following morning.

Unreported previously, in early 2007 Ariel Martorelo y Horacio Gratton climbed a five-pitch variation to the Rubio y Azul route on Aguja Media Luna. Their line climbs a crack system (5.11) on the steep prow left of Rubio y Azul, which it joins at the middle break on pitch six.

ROLANDO GARIBOTTI, *AAC*

Cerro Adela, Asamblea de Majaras. Alvaro Novellón, Oscar Perez, Santi Padrós, and I had hoped to climb Cerro Torre, going directly to the Col of the Hope via A la Recherche du Temps Perdu (Marsigny-Parkin) and continuing to the summit by the Ferrari West Face route, a link-up first completed by Colin Haley and Kelly Cordes in January 2007. Many parties other than Marsigny and Parkin had tried this link-up before, including Pepe Chavarri and I in 1995, Bruno Sourzac and Laurence Monoyeur in 1997, and Ermanno Salvaterra and a partner later. During our attempt to climb A la Recherche du Temps Perdu, while we were a little below halfway, two consecutive avalanches released from the serac above, urging us to retreat—luckily without serious consequences.

(S) Adela Sur: (1) Northeast Arête (Aikes-Monaco-Pellegrini, 1967), (2) Direttissima dei Seracchi (Grassi-Rossi, 1986). (A) Cerro Adela: (3) de la Cruz (1987), (4) Gringo en la Noche (Podgornik, 1991), (5) Asamblea de Majaras (both exits shown; Ascaso-Padrós and Novellón-Perez, 2007). (N) Adela Norte. (M) El Mocho. (CT) Cerro Torre. *Rolando Garibotti*

Alvaro Novellón near the top of Asamblea de Majaras, Cerro Adela. *Dani Ascaso*

After a day of rest we tried a new route on the east face of Cerro Adela. At 12:30 a.m. on October 10 we began walking in the dark from our snow cave on the glacier immediately below Adela's and Torre's south faces. By sunrise we had climbed 600m of ice with maximum steepness up to 85°. Later, with the sun warming up, we simul-climbed 200m of easy snow and mixed ramps.

When we arrived at the base of last the 200m steep step, we decided that each party would take a different line, so we would not have to wait for each other. Alvaro and Oscar climbed a line just left of the gully, while Santi and I climbed a more direct finish, which involved tenuous mixed climbing on bad rock. This final section was the crux of the climb, with poor rock and ice making us nervous. After 15 hours of climbing, we climbed the summit ridge and shortly after were on top of Cerro Adela.

For our descent, we did not know the terrain very clearly. We headed south along the ridge and then dropped east, toward the Torre Valley, via the col before Cerro Ñato. On the hanging glacier below Ñato we dug a hole inside a crevasse and spent the night. The following afternoon we arrived at El Chalten. The descent was not difficult but was fairly involved.

This expedition celebrated the 75th anniversary of the Peña Guara club of Huesca, to which Alvaro, Oscar, and I belong. Without its support this climb might not have been possible.

Asamblea de Majaras (1,000m, ED 95°[max] M5+).

DANI ASCASO, *Spain*

The Torre Traverse (Cerro Standhardt, Punta Herron, Torre Egger, and Cerro Torre). From January 21–24, 2008, Rolando Garibotti and Colin Haley made a phenomenal first enchainment of these towers in a continuous alpine-style push, climbing from north to south in a four-day roundtrip. The Torre Traverse had been coveted by leading Patagonian climbers for nearly 20 years. See Garibotti's feature earlier in this *Journal*.

Cerro Piergiorgio, La Ruta del Hermano to summit ridge. In early 2007 we fixed 400m of rope up Piergiorgio's 950m northwest face. We decided to use fixed ropes after hearing that a group of Germans climbers had tried the face with portaledges, only to have them shredded by the wind. On our last day of climbing we were forced down by a storm and had to leave the fixed ropes in place. Leaving the ropes motivated us to return to try again. We at least wanted to clean the ropes.

Early this year (2008) we returned to Chalten, and while we waited for Cristian Brenna and Mario Conti to arrive [Conti, a member of the 1974 Ragni di Lecco team that made the first ascent of Cerro Torre, was there as support, not part of the climbing team—Ed.], Giovanni Ongaro and Herve Barmasse reclimbed to our previous high point. Since many of the ropes were frayed, we had to reclimb the pitches. We did not have new fixed ropes, so we re-used the old ones, knotting over frayed sections. We fixed a further 60m from our high point, to a point at the base of a chimney, where during our first summit attempt Giovanni was hit by rockfall, hurting his hand, forcing him

Piergiorgio's northwest face: (1) Esperando la Cumbre (Giordani-Maspes, 1996), follows skyline to the leftmost summit. (2) Pepe Rayo (DalPra-Girardi-Nadali-Sarchi, 1996), stops at ridge. (3) La Ruta del Hermano (Barmasse-Brenna, 2008). (4) Greenpeace (Manica-Vettori, 1985) to a summit on the far right. (a) start of 1995 attempt (Giordani-Maspes) that retreated high on the wall. The narrow, rime-capped spire to the right is actually an in-line view, from north to south, of the Torre group. In front of the Torres, to the right of Piergiorgio, is Domo Blanco. The pillar just left of Piergiorgio is unclimbed. Left of it, going off-screen, is Cerro Pollone. *Martin courtesy Herve Barmasse*

to retreat and return to Italy. On our second attempt the wind forced us to retreat, and finally our third attempt was successful.

We, Christian and Herve, set off from our tents at 2 a.m. on February 7, jugged our fixed ropes [460m], and reached the summit ridge at 2 a.m. the following day, descending back to our tents at 11 a.m. in a blizzard. While descending in the middle of a storm, we were unable to retrieve our fixed ropes.

Our route climbs an inobvious line that is exposed to rockfall, as Giovanni's accident proves. In the first 600m the climbing is mostly aid, involving expanding flakes on dubious rock, with many blank sections that we overcame by drilling approximately 40 bat-hook holes. We climbed pitches on the second part of the route both aid and free. The majority of the belay stations have one bolt, while on the 29 pitches we placed six progression bolts. Our climbing style was not ideal, but not unlike the ascent of Cerro Murallon by Robert Jasper and Stefan Glowacz. [Glowacz and Jasper abandoned 500m of fixed rope on the wall—Ed.] We called our route "La Ruta del Hermano" and dedicated it to Agostino Rocca and his family, since they made this project possible. The route follows the 1995 Ragni di Lecco's attempt, led by Casimiro Ferrari,

A rare and complete view of the upper aspects of Cerro Torre from the north, showing the two significant attempts and the complete route, which was the key to Garibotti and Haley's Torre Traverse. From left to right: Burke-Proctor 1981 attempt (dots represent hidden portions), Ponholzer-Steiger 1999 attempt (high point is approximate), El Arca de los Vientos (Beltrami-Garibotti-Salvaterra, 2005; joins the upper Ragni di Lecco route in the huge mushrooms). The Col of Conquest is hidden, just below the foreground snow. This shot is a composite of three photos taken from the top of Torre Egger. *Rolando Garibotti* up the center of the wall and then angling left to the summit ridge. Due to rockfall, not much is left of the Ragni attempt—only three pitches. It was impressive to find 15m blank sections below old belay stations, where rock and cracks climbed years before had simply caved off.

Compiled from e-mails from CHRISTIAN BRENNA *and* HERVE BARMASSE, *Italy*

Care Bear Traverse (Guillaumet, Mermoz, and Fitz Roy); Guillaumet, The Lost Men; Fitz Roy, Hoser Chimney. Dana "Mad Dog" Drummond and I hit the soon-to-be-paved streets of Chalten on January 16, 2008. With a promising forecast, we quickly repacked and hiked in the next day to the Piedras Negras bivy on the north side of the Fitz Roy massif. Following a tip from Colin Haley, we headed for a new line on the west face of Guillaumet that Colin had attempted the week before. After a false start, we finally got going on the right line at 11 a.m. The climb went in eleven pitches, with a touch of 5.11 and a few aid moves around iced cracks. The highlight was undoubtedly the final two pitches, where Dana navigated us up the Fissure Mad Dog, a burly offwidth and squeeze chimney system that topped out only 15m south of Guillaumet's true summit. On the pitch above Colin's high point, we found a single European-style piton with sun-bleached bail tat tied to it. On the same pitch I noticed a German candy bar rapper, expiration date 1993, wedged into a crack. Perhaps we had joined with Padrijo, the only established route on the face (which was indeed established in 1993), although the topo and photo on www.climbinginpatagonia.freeservers.com shows Padrijo taking a crack system right of our line. A more likely scenario, given Padrijo's traversing nature, is that the team rappelled down our corner system. The last possibility, though the resident experts in Chalten have no record of it, is that this line received an undocumented ascent or attempt. Anyhow, we've named it The

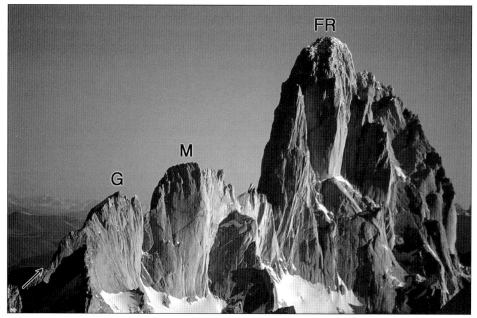

View from the northwest, with the Care Bear Traverse starting at the arrow and climbing the approximate skylines of Guillaumet (G), Mermoz (M), and Fitz Roy (FR). *Rolando Garibotti*

Lost Men (550m, 5.11a A0) in honor of these unknown soldiers. Perhaps someone out there will read this report and can shed light on the historical record.

The weather kept getting better, so we packed for the main attraction: Fitz Roy, the north face of course. Our vague plan was to investigate new terrain on or near Tehuelche. We left high camp at 3 a.m. on January 21, hoofed it over Paso Cuadrado, and dropped to the base of the face. In the predawn light, we failed to see any compelling lines on the lower face, and followed the starting pitches of Tehuelche to the Gran Hotel ledge. From here, we followed a chimney system up the prominent headwall right of Tehuelche. This portion of the climb was dripping wet and offered 5.10 adventure climbing at its finest, with a surprise M5 chockstone pitch at the top. We established about 10 new pitches before joining the Afanasieff Ridge just before dark. We brewed up, broke out our single sleeping bag, and spooned until dawn, then scrambled the final few hundred meters to the summit of Fitz Roy at 9:30 a.m. Our climb, Hoser Chimney (5.10 A1 M5), should be considered a minor variation rather than any sort of major new route. Still, we found it remarkable that such a long, complex face could be climbed at such a modest grade. After rappelling Tehuelche in the blistering afternoon sun, we made it back to Piedras Negras at dark. Several days later Crystal Davis-Robbins and Max Hasson established another line in the same neighborhood. With an independent start and harder, better climbing, I think their effort produced the finer line.

A week later Mad Dog and I onsight-freed the Red Pillar route (650m) on Mermoz. A few of the pitches were wet, but the coarse granite still provided enough friction. The route lived up to its reputation in terms of quality, though its technical grade is probably closer to Yosemite 5.11+. Potential suitors of this classic should note that we carried a single 70m rope, which worked perfectly for descending the anchor-bolt-equipped line.

Having climbed Guillaumet, Mermoz, and Fitz Roy, we considered linking them in a single skyline traverse. Down in Chalten we pored over photos on my computer of the gendarmed ridge that connects the summit of Guillaumet over Mermoz to the start of the Goretta (North) Pillar of Fitz Roy, identifying key features. We reckoned we'd need three days to pull of the enchainment, but the unsettled forecast called for two short 30-hour spells of high pressure, separated by a short wind storm with colder temps. Realizing that our only chance at the link-up was to sit out the unsettled weather somewhere in the middle of the traverse, we went a little heavy on bivy gear, borrowing a lightweight tent from our buddy Mark Postle. We made up for this extra weight by carrying no pins or bolts, just one axe, and a single pair of aluminum crampons.

The first day, February 5, we began climbing from Paso Guillaumet at 8 a.m. and linked Guillaumet's Brenner Ridge to the West Face of Mermoz. This enchainment is a fun objective in itself and had been done at least once before. The ridge connecting these two classics involved many 30m rappels and ledge traverses, with a few moderate "mountaineering pitches" mixed in. We reached the summit of Mermoz at 6:30 p.m. and, rather than press on, took time to build a protected bivy. As the wind increased that night, and an endless line of vaporous freight trains rolled by outside, we were thankful. The next day we waited until noon for the winds to abate before continuing. We wanted to reach the base of the Casarotto Route, on the Goretta Pillar, in time to rest and psyche up for the next day. This section of ridge hadn't been traversed before and in many ways seemed like it would be the crux of the link-up. We found lots of committing rappelling, ledge-shuffling, and moderate climbing, but amazingly encountered no stopper gendarmes or dead-end slabs. Whenever the route seemed to blank out, an appealing option waited on the other side of the ridge. We reached a talus slope 60m above the Bloque Empotrado at the start of the Casarotto route (Kearney-Knight variation) by 6 p.m. and excavated another bivy ledge.

Mad Dog and I had divided the leading duties according to our relative strengths. With more alpine routefinding experience, I had led the ridge traverse from the summit of Guillaumet to the start of the Casarotto. The next morning, February 7, I unleashed the Dog, who's spent the last two years living in Yosemite, on the splitter cracks of Fitz Roy. From my perspective, the next 10 hours passed in a blur of wind-sprint jugging, belaying, and fast action gear exchanges. It felt like I was the member of some bizarre alpine pit crew, as Mad Dog short fixed the entire route and delivered us onto the summit of Fitz Roy by 5:30 p.m. In a word: badass.

We had left our bivy gear at the base and were thus committed to rappelling the route. The weather threatened, then our ropes stuck, and I had to perform a mandatory "mystery jug" to free them. Why do descents always have to be so fucking dramatic in Patagonia? But just when it looked like we were on the verge of a full-blown epic, we reached the Bloque and dropped to the lee side of the ridge.

Throughout the day we had watched my girlfriend, Janet Bergman, and Zack Shlosar climb the Red Pillar. Now, we watched their headlamps as we simultaneously rappelled through the darkness. We touched down on the glacier at the same time, and shared a middle-of-the-night reunion before slogging back through Paso Guillaumet and down to Piedras Negras in the spitting rain. Mad Dog and I largely attribute our success on what we called the Care Bear Traverse (VI 5.11 A0) to our willingness to carry a comfortable bivy set up. Traditional bivies aren't stylish these days, but the extra comfort and rest they afforded us allowed us to chill out and then attack.

FREDDIE WILKINSON, *AAC*

Fitz Roy, El Flaco con Domingo. On January 26, 2008, I met Crystal Davis-Robbins; we were both without partners, and the weather continued to blow everyone's mind. I felt like I needed more rest, but there was no time for that.

We ran into Freddie Wilkinson and Dana Drummond on the hike up; they had just climbed the face that we were interested in, via the bottom half of Tehuelche and a new path to the summit ridge. The crux involved a mixed chimney that we hoped to avoid. Preferably we could find dry rock that would yield some quality free-climbing.

After scoping from the base, we started from a horizontal snow bench below and maybe 800' right of Tehuelche's landmark leaning spire. I led off the snow and found great cracks, followed by a bit of kitty litter and then a broad face with sporadic features. Our sixth pitch took a lot of my energy, as it traversed a ropelength to the left, toward Tehuelche. A few more pitches up a corner I found a good ledge for eating lunch and transferring the lead. Due to a surprisingly bulky backpack, the second jumared most of the climb. After three more pitches, while jugging I spotted a bolt to our left: we had found Tehuelche. Easier ground and simul-climbing on Tehuelche got us to the Gran Hotel, the ledge system that breaks the wall in half. We'd climbed about 15 long pitches. We slogged up dry talus to the apex of this ledge and found improved bivy spots and a wedge of icy snow for making water. The impressive Diedro di Marco (Tehuelche's notorious off-width) shot directly above us; the sun's rays transform this feature into a funnel for water and rock.

In the morning we climbed a right-facing crack system capped by an imposing roof. We

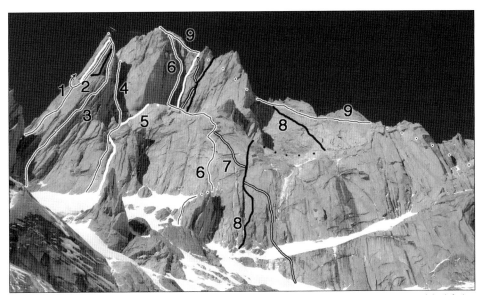

Fitz Roy from the northwest. (1) Kearney-Knight variation to the Casarotto route, which starts just around the left sky-line, out of view, and continues near the upper left skyline to the summit. (2) Chimichurri y Tortas Fritas. White line is the Young Jerkers variation (finishes on Casarotto), black line is Gringos Perdidos variation. (3) Mate, Porro y Todo lo Demas. The previous routes are on the Goretta Pillar formation. (4) Polish route. (5) French North Face (finishes on 9). (6) Tehuelche. (7) El Flaco con Domingo (finishes on 9). Upper black line is Hoser Chimney, which starts on 6 and summits on 9. (8) Ultimos Dias del Paraiso (finishes on 9). (9) Afanasieff route. *Rolando Garibotti*

later learned that Freddie and Dana had climbed a left-facing corner to the right (our corner and theirs basically form a big stem box, about 50' wide at its base). Our routes met at the roof, which turned out to be well-featured and relatively easy, and then shared maybe 20'-30' to the belay. Crystal led four spectacular pitches up to this point, and where the boys headed right toward their namesake chimney, Crystal went left around the corner and onto a small headwall. We switched leads one last time, and I climbed fun cracks with awesome exposure until

Crystal Davis-Robbins leading the first pitch off the Gran Hotel, on El Flaco con Domingo. *Max Hasson*

they petered out, forcing me left onto easier ground. Ten pitches off the Gran Hotel I crested the ridge and found signs of the Afanasieff route. Since we planned to rappel Tehuelche, we ditched the pack and simuled to the summit for a memorable sunset.

Darkness was coming, and the wind was picking up, so we started a long night of rappels that got us back to the bivy just before daybreak. The lower half went much faster in the sunlight, and after a long slog back to camp we gorged on pasta and slept well into the next day.

El Flaco con Domingo (1,500m [1,000m new], VI 5.11).

MAX HASSON, *AAC*

La Silla, El Bastardo. Stephan Siegrist, my brother Alexander, and I returned to Patagonia with the same ambitious target in mind: the traverse of the Cerro Torre massif. When we arrived in mid-January 2008 the Torres were completely covered in ice. But on the positive side, the weather forecast predicted no less than three consecutive days of good weather—that's what we need! There was only the problem that it would get really warm, which stands for extreme danger. Conditions under which we wouldn't attempt the traverse. [Rolando Garibotti and Colin Haley completed the Torre Traverse during this weather window—see Garibotti's feature earlier in this *Journal*—Ed.]

Instead we focused on the towers of the Fitz Roy group! The winds, coming from the Pacific across the Hielo Continental, unload most of their humidity on the first great barrier, the Torres. The Fitz Roy group gets a small fraction of the ice and snow, so you don't find the giant mushrooms and notorious rime ice that can make the Torres so dangerous. In the Fitz Roy group we even found an attractive target: the unclimbed west face of La Silla.

Alexander, with Mario Walder from East Tyrol, attempted this face last year, but this time it looked much better. With us again this year was Mario Walder, on stage to attack the west face of La Silla.

The weather is perfect, and on January 22 we climb the lower, not-so-steep part of the wall. The climbing never exceeds 5.10, and most parts are easier. Finally we arrive at the base of the 600m monolithic headwall, where we set up our bivouac. The next morning we start early, as we don't know what to expect. The first 300m are really steep, and the climbing is dominated by dihedrals and long off-widths. Most of it we could climb free, but due to icy conditions we have to aid short sections. After climbing 12 mostly long pitches we reach the distinctive

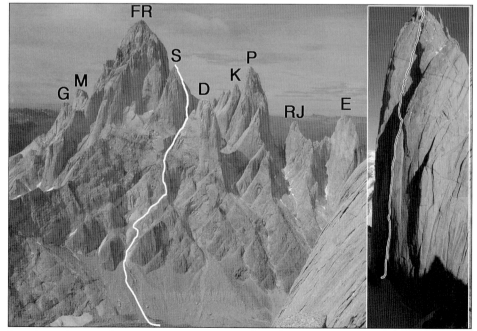

From the southwest: Guillaumet, Mermoz, Fitz Roy, La Silla (technical approach and route (inset) indicated), Desmochada, Kakito, Poincenot, Rafael Juarez, St. Exupery. *Martin Waldor.* Inset: *Sacha Friedlin*

double-summit of La Silla by early afternoon, realizing the first ascent of its west face—what a great climb!

The long rappel session has us back to the glacier late evening. The entire climb is done without any previous preparation. El Bastardo is the first route on that marvelous face. The name is the idea of Mario Walder, who wasn't baptized by his hometown priest because he was a bastard.

Later we enjoyed windows of good weather and climbed to some nice summits: Torre Egger, Cerro Standhardt, Aguja Rafael Juarez, St. Exupery, Aguja de la S, and El Mocho.

THOMAS HUBER, *Germany*

Poincenot, Banana Wall. After studying the region in hopes of opening a new route, we found a picture in the *AAJ* showing this magnificent north face with no line up the fractured center, between Old Smugglers (800m, 5.10+ A1/2, Crouch-Donini 1996) and the Potter-Davis (550m, 5.11 C1, 2001) lines. This was the start of our adventure, which brought us to climb those wonderful granite cracks.

After getting useful information in El Chalten, thanks to Carsten von Birckhahn, who showed us nice photos of the face and gave beta on the approach, Sacha Friedlin and I started on January 11, 2008, for a one-push attempt. After a 17-hour roundtrip in Canadian winter weather that slowed us, we climbed only four pitches of mixed climbing up the face after the long, snowy approach.

Five days later, on January 16, the forecast announced good weather coming the 18th. We didn't wait and started from Chalten at 7 p.m., slept at Agostini camp 10km farther, and started at 10 the next morning for the remaining four hours of approach. Under bad weather at 11 p.m., above the couloir between Aguja Kakito and Poincenot, we spent three hours chopping an ice ledge. The next day, after unsuccessfully trying to sleep through heavy spindrift, we climbed slowly up icy cracks to reach a good bivy site at the end of pitch 6, having fixed our two 60m ropes above. Perfect weather on the 19th allowed us to finish the wall (taking our ropes with us), continuing to summit, and then descending the Whillans-Cochrane route on the other side, in a 24-hour push.

We placed no bolts or pitons, so the route (800m, VI 5.11a M6+ C1) is free of gear, even at belays. It is very sustained, as nearly every pitch is in the 5.10 range, with a few cruxes of 5.11a. We French-freed in a few spots due to icy cracks—these sections would go free in warmer weather—and encountered mixed climbing on the first three pitches in the Aguja Kakito couloir and again on pitch 6. The M6+ mixed crux (pitch 3) involved unconsolidated vertical snow below overhanging rock passages, but could be avoided by climbing a one-rope-length direct line between pitch 2 and pitch 4, avoiding the unfriendly first bivy site. With that variation the next party would have to do mixed climbing only up to M4.

We named the route Banana Wall because of the curving geometry of its high-quality granite cracks that graced almost every pitch.

FRÉDÉRIC MALTAIS, *Québec, Canada*

Poincenot, complete west ridge (DNV Direct) and Blood on the Tracks, free ascent; Desmochada, variation to The Sound and the Fury. In 2007 I was in the Torre Valley with a large group of

Canadians. The weather was cold and dismal, making for less-than-ideal alpine climbing conditions. My stay was coming to a close when, through the swirling clouds, the west ridge of Poincenot caught my eye. My trip was done, but I vowed to return and try the line.

In mid-January 2008 I found myself in the Torre Valley again, this time with 20 year-old Jason Kruk. We are best friends and share a youthful enthusiasm about climbing and are alwa, s willing to get ourselves into some trouble. With a perfect three-day good weather forecast, I suggested the Poincenot line. Jason agreed.

The first day was mentally the toughest. It became obvious why the line had never been completed. The lower ramparts of Poincenot are composed of kitty-litter granite, Joshua Tree at its worst. By nightfall we neared the Fonrouge-Rosasco and Southern Cross routes. The next day we followed the Fonrouge-Rosasco to the summit and rappelled the Carrington-Rouse. We spent three days on Poincenot: two on the way up, one on the descent. About 30-40% of the route is new. The complete west ridge of Poincenot was originally attempted by a Polish party in 1986, the year I was born. We jokingly named the route the DNV Direct (1,500m, VI 5.11+ R/X A1) after the District of North Vancouver, the happy suburb where we grew up.

Poincenot's north face: (1) Northwest Pillar (1986). (2) Old Smugglers (Crouch-Donini, 1996). (3) Potter-Davis (2001; approaches from other side). (4) Banana Wall (Friedlin-Maltais, 2008). (K) is Aguja Kakito. *Mario Walder*

Next up was Desmochada. We hoped to climb something on the tower all-free on lead and second, without jumars. There is an enormous ledge at about ¼ height, clearly delineating the lower-angle climbing below from the steeper business above. On the ledge Jason and I scanned the terrain above, looking for the line most suited to free-climbing. We climbed a slight variation (700m, V+ 5.11+ A1) to The Sound and the Fury, a Freddie Wilkinson and Dave Sharratt route. We diverged from the original line, because it looked too thin to free. Our variation's crux involved a thin corner followed by a punishing finger crack. We took a couple of falls throughout the two-pitch variation, but restarted from a no-hands stance each time. At the top of the tower, Jason's leg cramped up in an offwidth and he hung on toprope. We topped out at dusk and rappelled through the night in a gathering storm, shivered for a few hours on the big ledge, then walked down a terrifyingly loose gully to camp, thoroughly wasted.

While on Poincenot, Jason and I spent time staring at the beautiful north face of Rafael Juarez. Freddie Wilkinson drew us up a topo for his route, Blood on the Tracks (600m, V 5.12), that he established with Taki Miyamoto, Dave Sharratt, and Paul Turecki. Sharratt and Wilkinson had freed every individual pitch at 5.12 but hadn't climbed the route free to the summit, in a push. [On their original complete ascent they used some aid. Miyamoto, Sharratt, and

Jason Kruk following the crux pitch of the team's variation to to The Sound and the Fury, on Desmochada. *Will Stanhope*

Wilkinson returned later and freed the individual pitches they'd previously aided—Ed.] Colorado hardman Mike Pennings joined us for our first attempt, but we were stormed off four pitches up. After a day of rest Jason and I tried again, this time freeing to the summit. I fell once on the crux pitch, pulled the rope, and sent second try. Jason followed clean, and the whole route was climbed free for both the leader and the second, without jumars.

For me this trip was a dream come true. There was a gung-ho crew of climbers from all over the world, always willing to roast a sheep and drink a few Quilmes cervezas. The weather was perfect, and the cracks were ice-free, perfect for free climbing. We tried hard, and we had fun.

WILL STANHOPE, *Canada*

SOUTHERN PATAGONIA, CHILE

TORRES DEL PAINE NATIONAL PARK

Cerro Escudo, Taste the Paine. In December 2007 and January 2008, with a minimum of rope fixing and no fixed camps, Dave Turner spent 34 continuous days on the east face of Cerro Escudo, soloing a new route (VII 5.9 A4+). Above the 1,200m wall, Turner continued up the technical, 300-vertical-meter ridge to the summit. In addition to impressive style and difficulty, Turner was the first to climb the face and continue to the summit. See Turner's feature earlier in this *Journal.*

Almirante Nieto, Calambrito, to sedimentary band. On January 31, 2008, Daniel Darrigrandi, Nacho Grez, and I approached the west face of Almirante Nieto from the Bader Valley, the most unknown big wall valley in Torres del Paine. Only a few expeditions have climbed routes in this valley, and many new routes and some first ascents await serious climbers.

Almirante Nieto is a huge mountain that has three west-facing walls, and we don't think any routes existed on the wall where we climbed. We departed base camp at 4 a.m. and took three hours to reach the base of the wall, heading up a slabby drainage with snowpatches to a prominent right-facing dihedral that looks like a banana. In the upper half, at the big roof we traversed to the right and continued to the base of the black rock. The climb ends where the sedimentary rock starts, as its poor quality makes it almost impossible and too risky to climb. We climbed six pitches (300m, 5.9+ R) on great granite, including finger cracks, offwidths and chimneys. It was a great climb, though many sections were unprotectable.

We descended by traversing right, and found a direct and easy way to rappel.

HERNAN JOFRE, *Chile*

Torre Central, El Gordo, el Flaco y el'Abuelito. Rolando Larcher, Elio Orlandi, and I climbed a direct new route on the east face of the Central Tower of Paine, between Magico Este and Riders on the Storm. The 1,250m route has 7a+ free climbing (6b+ obl.) and a short section of A3+, but the aid is only about 20% of the route. We climbed 23 pitches, capsule style, with many being 65m and 70m long. We climbed for three days (January 25–27, 2008), preparing the lower part, and then rested on January 28 as, despite a nice day, we were exhausted. The next day we attacked the wall, and on February 7 at 6 p.m. we summited the Central Tower. On the 8th, at 11 p.m. we reached the base after a romantic rappel.

FABIO LEONI, *Italy*

El Gordo, el Flaco y el'Abuelito, on Torre Central's east face, home to several other routes. *Fabio Leoni*

Hoja, Sangre de Condor. In the French Valley a Columbian-Venezuelan team climbed a new route on Hoja. Columbians Sergio Garcia and Sebastian Munoz and Venezuelans Manuel [last name unknown] and Jorge Guerra faced bad conditions for most of their climb, but finally summited on December 22. They think that their route, Sangre de Condor (6a+ A2) would go all free with good weather. Further details were unavailable.

STEVE SCHNEIDER, *AAC*

SOUTH OF PAINE

Cerro Ladrillero, from the northeast. In the austral extreme of the Americas, nature becomes savage, with steep geography that includes a labyrinth of islands, fjords and mountains, glaciers, deep forests of incredible colors, and land that's difficult to travel. Definitely an ecologically rich countryside, but also characterized by extremely unstable weather and high humidity, cold temperatures, and especially strong winds.

For these reasons, many mountains remain unclimbed, and information is scarce. Patagonia requires, as Eric Shipton said, a dose of stoicism, and also experience, time, and patience—a lot of patience.

For information on Cerro Ladrillero (1,705m [various reported altitudes]; first ascent from the south, see *AAJ 2005*, pp. 302-303) we visited the Instituto de la Patagonia de la Universidad de Magallanes and studied aerial photographs for possible route ideas.

The next step was to get there. Cerro Ladrillero is located in the western extreme of the sparsely populated Riesco Island, which has only one road. The road ends at the last remaining *estancia*, Estancia Rocallosa. There was more than 50km of inaccessible terrain between there and our base camp, a seashore on the inlet of Estero Riquelme, at the south end of Seno Skyring [Skyring Sound].

"Navigation is very difficult in this sea, Seno Skyring. The problems are the streams and the strong wind. Once I went to fish and remained there for ten days," said the first fisherman whose boat we tried to hire. Finally we hired someone with a Zodiac and courage to take us to

Estero Riquelme. On Thursday, November 13, after two hours of good sea conditions, the Zodiac dropped us on the beach.

Behind us was a deep, dense forest with wild animals and no passage made by human hand. Much reconnaissance was necessary to find the way, which we cleared with a machete. We headed southwest from the beach, eventually reaching the northeast part of the glacier.

A couple of exhausting days were necessary to carry our gear and reach our advanced camp, in the rocks below the glacier. We only needed one good day, with visibility, to face the enigmatic glacier and attempt the summit. Finally, on November 22 we got a spectacular view, verified our planned route, and started up the northeast slopes. Near the top we wrapped around to climb the final headwall from the east-southeast. The last part to the summit was 40°-50° and we fixed ropes. The climb—and the Patagonian wind—did not disappoint.

The last members of the group returned to base camp at midnight. We expected to leave the island the next morning, but the weather forecast was bad. The five members of our group who went in the first rotation spent 4.5 hours navigating a brave sea with strong winds. This compelled the others to remain on the island. Two days later we left base camp and returned to civilization.

We left a copy of Juan Ladrillero's navigation notes on the summit, and as we ventured again into Seno Skyring, leaving Cerro Ladrillero behind, we felt wonder and humility toward the great navigators who discovered these lands, and we felt satisfied with our achievement and our beautiful route. It's dedicated to Juan Ladrillero, and to all the explorers who tread on these wonderful lands.

LT. COL. ALBERTO AYORA HIRSCH, *Spanish Army Mountain Group*

TIERRA DEL FUEGO, CHILE

Iorana I and Iorana II, first ascents. Andy Parkin and I made the first ascents of two peaks at the head of Sena Pia in the Cordillera Darwin, after a drop-off from the yacht Iorana on March 6.

We approached the peaks by crossing glaciers and climbing through beech forests and snow-covered rock slabs to an ABC at 1,300m. We followed a ridge and glacier, and broke through serac bands, in climbing the south face of the smaller peak to access the southeast ridge of the higher one. Overall alpine grade AD. We named the peaks Iorana I (2,340m) and II (2,075m), reaching the summits on the 8th and getting picked up on the 9th.

SIMON YATES, *U.K*

Iorana I and II. After summiting II, Yates and Parkin traversed the connecting skyline ridge to I. *Simon Yates*

Antarctica

ELLSWORTH MOUNTAINS—
SENTINEL RANGE

Vinson Massif, summary and new normal route. A new record total of 157 people reached the summit of Vinson during the 2007-08 season, including at least 19 women. Most of the Vinson ascents were by a new variant to the normal route, detailed below. The most significant action on Vinson this season was by women. Maria Paz ("Pachi") Ibarra of Chile with

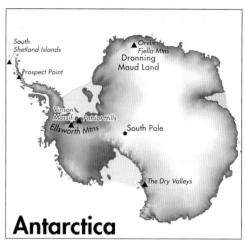

Slovakian/Australian Jarmila Tyrril climbed a new route on the west face. Norwegians Ine-Lill Gabrielsen and Rita Glenne climbed Vinson then skied straight to the South Pole from the mountain by a new route in fast time, and unsupported. A separate group, Randi Skaug and Kristin Moe Khron of Norway, with Anne Mette of Denmark, approached Vinson by skiing the 200km from Patriot Hills (as did one other group). Three women were working as guides— Patricia Soto of Chile, and Molly Loomis and Winslow Passey of the USA, with both Soto and Passey each summiting twice with clients. Dave Hahn bagged his 25th summit of Vinson. Two Vinson parties also climbed the normal southwest face route on Mt. Shinn (4,660m).

The climbing season started late, due to bad weather at Patriot Hills, but then kicked off with a week of brilliant, sunny blue skies. However after that it was all downhill, with only very short patches of good weather for the rest of the season—often only half a day—and none of the good multi-day spells traditional for the range. A severe storm hit around December 13, destroying or blowing away a number of tents at both high and low camps on Vinson, causing

more than a few desperate situations and several minor frostbite problems. (Tent sites at Low Camp should have high walls on all four sides to counter the changing direction of winds in such storms.) Though the major force of the storm came over the mountain from the east and down onto the tents, some subsequent blasts turned up-valley and hit Low Camp from the south, catching a number of teams unawares.

The "New" Normal Route: At the start of the season ALE staff fixed around 1,200m of rope up the slope just north of Low Camp, as an

The "new" Normal Route above the Low Camp on Mt. Vinson. *Damien Gildea*

The upper section of Mt. Vinson's "new" Normal Route, as seen from Mt. Shinn. *Damien Gildea*

alternative to the traditional route going around the corner and up the "headwall" to Goodge Col. This was done as there has been increasing serac fall into the cwm below the headwall in recent years, most of it coming from Mt. Shinn, but also some from the cliffs on Vinson. This new alternative, first suggested in the early 1990s by Roger Mear, then later proposed by Conrad Anker and Dave Hahn, proved very popular this season, though a few teams did use the old route. Using the new route puts one at the northern end of the crest of the west face, at the western edge of the high, broad valley normally followed by climbers on summit day. The presence of an ALE radio repeater with antenna at this point on the crest led to the nearby tent site being referred to as "Repeater Camp." Repeater Camp will likely become the new "'High Camp," while the older high camp on Goodge Col will be known as "Shinn Camp"—partially to prevent confusion over the radio. Though the slope of the new variant is not at all difficult, it is quite sustained at the angle, more so than the old route up the headwall. At approximately 3,900m the new camp is slightly higher than the old 3,700m camp (now Shinn Camp) on Goodge Col, meaning that summit day is slightly shorter and also that teams can see summit weather conditions sooner.

The ropes may not be absolutely necessary for the ascent, but they add an element of safety to the descent, particularly for tired climbers with a heavy load, even more so in bad weather. Currently, the ropes do not go right to the top of the face, nor all the way to the camp. They finish at a small flat area slightly off to the left, requiring a rising traverse right to reach Repeater/High Camp. There are some crevasses on this section, as there are lower down on the roped section of the slope. There are also crevasses on the section from Repeater/High Camp across to the line of the normal route in the upper cwm. Route finding on these two sections could be troublesome in bad weather.

DAMIEN GILDEA, *Australia*

The 1,200m Chilena-Slovak Route, by Maria Paz "Pachi" Ibarra and Jarmila Tyrill, climbs a previously untouched section of Mt. Vinson's west face, just north of the main wall. *Damien Gildea*

Vinson and Epperly, new routes; Tyree, attempts; Ryan, first ascent. This season, with the support of the Omega Foundation, I led my sixth expedition to the range in order to climb and resurvey the high peaks. With Chileans Camilo Rada and Maria Paz "Pachi" Ibarra, and Jarmila Tyrill, a Slovakian living in Australia, our main objective this year was ascents of both Mt. Epperly and Mt. Tyree, two of the most difficult high mountains in Antarctica, to run the GPS on top and ascertain more accurate heights for our new map. After a one-week delay in Punta Arenas we landed near the old (pre-1993) Vinson BC area on November 28th and set up camp in perfect weather. Over the following two weeks we made ascents of the pyramidal Schatz Ridge, moved camp closer to the range at 2,350m, climbed a direct line on the north face of Knutzen Peak (3,373m), recced the approach to the west face of Tyree, and climbed over the bergschrund on the south face of Epperly to recce our planned route above. We also climbed around the col leading into the Vinson normal route, and the other three climbed part-way up Vinson, all in the name of trying to get some acclimatization before attempting what we knew would be a long and difficult climb on Epperly.

In the first week of December the weather was perfect, but it gradually deteriorated and during the night of the 13th/14th a major storm hit the range. Both of our tents were damaged—poles broken, fly ripped—almost simultaneously by a particularly strong gust, and we both spent the following eight hours huddled in severely damaged and disintegrating tents, holding them up against the gale with our backs or feet, fully dressed ready to get out if necessary. Not that we had anywhere to run to. Fortunately the storm eased around 10:30 on the 14th and we spent the day recovering and rebuilding, making use of our smaller reserve tent and scavenging one damaged tent to repair the other. It stormed again that night, but on the 15th we were able to clean up once again and re-sort the remains. On the 16th we skied around to Vinson BC with sleds, both to get some replacement tents from ALE and to spend some time higher on Vinson to acclimatize. Arriving at Low Camp late on the 17th, we spent two days in poor weather before heading up Vinson on the 20th in slightly better weather. Camilo and I climbed up by the ropes of the new "normal" route from Low Camp to Repeater Camp in three hours, but the girls had headed for a new line they had been eyeing over the previous weeks.

As one moves north, the main part of the west face of Vinson ends with a very faint rocky buttress. Just north of this is a smaller rocky face, cobwebbed with snow and ice lines, that had not been climbed. Jarmila and Pachi chose a line up the right-hand side of this face and crossed the bergschrund around 3,000m at 17:00. Climbing about 1,200m of moderate mixed terrain with some steeper, awkwardly sloping rock, in worsening weather, they topped out on the face at 23:30. From here they crossed into the upper cwm on Vinson to the normal route taken on

The south face of Mt. Epperly, one of the most difficult high peaks in Antarctica, showing the new line taken by Damien Gildea and Camilo Rada. *Damien Gildea*

The final four-meter pillar atop Mt. Epperly, which has only been climbed by Erhard Loretan, in the mid 1990s. *Damien Gildea*

summit day. At this point they met Camilo, who had been patiently waiting for them. In such poor weather Camilo and I had elected to stop moving up around 4,200m, from where I descended back to Low Camp. In a brief clearing of the weather the three decided to continue to the summit, though by the time they reached it at 05:00 on the 21st, visibility was minimal and they descended in whiteout using GPS, getting back to Low Camp just over five hours later. The women named their route the Chilena-Slovak Route. It is the first new route climbed on Vinson by an all-female team.

Late on the 22nd we left Low Camp and descended back to our camp beneath Epperly via the col between Knutzen and Shinn ("Sam's Col") that had been part of the pre-1993 normal route. Whilst very easy on the eastern "inside" slope, the western "outside" slope has become steeper and icier over the intervening years and is not recommended.

A short-lived period of good weather at high camp on Mt. Tyree, shortly before things changed for the worse. *Damien Gildea*

Our route of descent took the mixed snow and rock slopes to the southwest of the col, requiring a descending traverse with some concrete-hard ice near the bottom, unpleasant with heavy loads. The following days were mixed weather.

The 27th looked like good weather, so Camilo and I set off for Epperly at 15:30. A rising traverse on the lower slopes led us up a snow ice face, which we mostly climbed on the left through rockier ground, as the snow was now quite deep and soft. The face narrows into a couloir higher up, before ending in a steeper rock wall some distance below Epperly's summit plateau. The route to this point was mostly steep snow climbing, some easy ice, but with steeper steps of around 65° climbed through the mixed sections on bad, gravelly rock. We climbed all this unroped. By this stage we had been in radio contact with the women in camp and told them to start climbing. Thinking the upper couloir would dead-end in difficult rock, Camilo and I exited the couloir on steeper ground and wasted nearly two hours climbing loose rock and soft snow up a small rib forming the upper left wall of the couloir. This turned out to be unnecessary, as the couloir did in fact end in a body-width snow chute to top out at the base of the upper rock wall—a more sensible exit used by the women a day later.

Epperly was supposed to be 4,359m, but our altimeters showed we were at that height already, though we could see we were still some distance from the summit. We melted ice for drinks before heading east across some easy slopes toward the daunting summit pyramid of Epperly. This we climbed directly up its west face, scrambling over easy rock to a point beneath the cornices atop the face. However, upon climbing onto the highest cornice we faced the problem we had known about long before. The actual highest point of Epperly is a slightly detached, steep pillar of rock, draped in thin ice, the top of which was about 4m above us. The side facing us looked difficult to climb, but possible if we could reach it. The pillar to the left and right was vertical to overhanging rock, with a 2,000m drop below. We could see a piton, with webbing attached, low down in a crack on the pillar, no doubt left by Erhard Loretan—the only other person to have been up here—on his climbs in 1994 and 1995. However, when I went to step across the cornice to reach the pillar, my foot plunged through into space, meaning I could not even safely reach the base of the pillar. Given the position, our fatigue, the cold, and the difficulty of the pillar even on this side, we decided not to risk trying to climb it. We instead placed the GPS on the highest solid ice of the highest cornice and let it run—approximately 3m below the highest point of rock on the pillar.

We downclimbed our 2,200m route in softening greasy snow, which proved exhausting and quite a mental trip, taking nearly as long as the climb up—38 hours in total. The women followed our tracks, avoided our route-finding error, and summited in around 16 hours to retrieve the GPS, which had recorded over 11 hours of data. They also had a slow descent, but we were all safely back in camp in the very early hours of December 30th. At least two of us experienced significant hallucinations during the climb, due mainly to fatigue, dehydration, and altitude, with both Pachi and me imagining an extra climber with us. For this reason we decided to name the route The Fifth Element.

With the data processed by AUSPOS via Iridium satphone and laptop, it eventuated that Epperly is in fact 4,508m—not counting the approximately 3m extra to the top of the rock pillar. That's 149m higher than the previous official height, making Epperly around the 6th highest mountain in Antarctica. No wonder it took us so long.

On New Year's Day we hauled sleds, via our cache at old Vinson BC, for 15km to a camp beneath the west face of Mt. Gardner and set up in cold, windy weather. Camilo and I had climbed Gardner back in December 2005 and our plan now, having ditched our original west face objective, was to repeat this route to high on Gardner then, as the Tyree first ascent team in 1967 had done, traverse high around the eastern side of Gardner using a high camp to launch a climb onto the connecting ridge to Tyree. In January 1967 Barry Corbet and John Evans had summited Tyree this way, in a 22-hour round trip from a tent placed by them and their team on the col between Gardner and Tyree. We would go somewhat lighter, with just a small tent and minimal food. All the bad weather meant that we extended our time on the ice with ALE and agreed to fly out around January 14th, ten days later than first planned. At this stage, with several days of poor weather forecast, Jarmila decided she needed to stick to our original itinerary and be on the January 4th flight home, so she left the team on the 3rd, returning to Vinson BC for an immediate plane to Patriots.

By Sunday January 6 blue sky returned, so Pachi, Camilo and, I headed up with a two-man tent and food and fuel for 48 hours or so. In good spirits, with the weather looking great, we climbed quickly up Gardner's normal route and found a nice flat place for the tent at 4,120m, high on the east side of Gardner. As we discovered, the 1967 team had also put a high camp here, the remains of which are visible nearby. We ate, drank and dozed for around eight hours, packed in the tent like three sardines with two sleeping bags. We reckoned it was game-on for sure. Unfortunately, as we were racking-up around 14:00 on Monday, the weather changed incredibly fast and clouds moved in from the west, totally smothering Tyree's upper-third and bringing more wind and snow. I'd never seen bad weather come in so fast in the Sentinel Range.

Before retreating, we did a brief recce of the passage from Gardner's slopes across toward the ridge for Tyree. Conditions up high worsened, though on our descent we diverted across the northern end of Gardner's upper plateau and made the first ascent of Mt. Ryan, a small peak newly-designated by the USGS in 2006. This was very easy from our side but is very steep and rocky to the north side, where it joins the south ridge from Mt. Shear. In very cold and blustery conditions we ran the GPS for just over an hour, then got moving. The winds had scoured the upper plateau of Gardner and now vast sections of blue ice were revealed, like walking on slippery glass. So, now getting plastered with rime, we had to actually do a near-horizontal rappel across one section to reach softer ice and the couloir down.

A couple of days later it cleared up again and we had to give it one more shot. We had no more food at this camp, our rescue insurance would run out in less than a week, so it was right now or never. Again the climb up Gardner's northwest couloir was straightforward in the sun, but wisps of snow over the crest signalled something else above. Sure enough, as we crested the plateau we saw a vast sea of gray cloud filling the eastern side of the range to the horizon. I'd said to Camilo that if we found something like this we would have to call it off, but we knew this was our last shot, so we just pushed on a bit more in case things got better. They didn't. Camilo and Pachi really wanted to stay, but I could not place both the Omega Foundation and ALE in a position where we might get into trouble, in such a difficult place, in such bad weather.

Lower down on the plateau we decided to get something out of our failure and made the first ascent of the rocky peak at the northwestern extremity of the Gardner plateau, west of Mt. Ryan. As we scrambled to the summit and placed the GPS, the cloud started flowing through the gaps in the range and over the plateau like water over a dam wall. Knowing we still had the blue ice to cross I called it off after less than 30 minutes and we made our way down one last time, gusts of spindrift chasing us down the upper couloir. Of course the sun came out the next day as we were leaving the mountain. Hauling full sleds out of camp on the 14th, we reached old Vinson BC a few hours later, spent one night there and were back in Punta Arenas for lunch on the 16th.

DAMIEN GILDEA, *Australia*

End of the Omega Foundation and new Vinson map. This expedition [above report] ends the GPS surveying work of the Omega Foundation in Antarctica. Since 2001, the Foundation has generously supported seven GPS expeditions to Antarctica—six of them to the Sentinel Range plus one to re-measure the highest mountain on Livingston Island, of which we produced a new map. In the course of this work we have made the first ascents of 17 previously unclimbed peaks, four second ascents, all by new routes, and numerous other climbs and traverses, most of them firsts, including new routes on both Vinson and Shinn, and ascents of five of Antarctica's seven highest mountains. All these points, and many more, have been surveyed with our Trimble 5700 GPS receiver and the resulting data processed by the Australian Government's AUSPOS facility. In keeping with the original aims of the Foundation, this data has been shared with the government Antarctic programs of the United States, Britain, and Chile in the interests of scientific co-operation and as a contribution to the greater body of Antarctic science. As of 2006, our data has been added to a specially-tasked, 4m resolution, cloud-free, IKONOS color satellite image mosaic, with contours generated from Aster imagery, which forms the basis of the new 1:50,000 Vinson Massif & The Sentinel Range map produced by Camilo Rada and me for the Omega Foundation. The map contains only official names— those recognized by the USGS Advisory Committee on Antarctic Names. Most of these names were suggested by the USGS for features newly identified from our work. I nominated three of my Omega team members for feature names in the resurveyed Craddock Massif, plus the eight previously unrecognized members of the 1966–67 Vinson first ascent team, so that their historical effort would be recognized on the Vinson Massif itself.

None of this would have happened without the incredibly generous support from the Omega Foundation, not only financially, but also in terms of constancy and flexibility. We have also had great support, beyond the call of duty or commerce, from all over the world, including the management and staff of ALE, specialists at AUSPOS and the USGS, and numerous friends, suppliers and colleagues, from Cambridge to Punta Arenas and all geodetic waypoints in between.

My teammates consider themselves very lucky to have been on these expeditions, and I consider myself fortunate to have been on the ice with them—Mike Roberts, Rodrigo Fica, John

Bath, Osvaldo Usaj, Steve Chaplin, Manuel Bugueno, Jed Brown, Pachi Ibarra, Jarmila Tyrril and particularly, Camilo Rada. Without Camilo our efforts would not have been nearly as successful or productive as they have been. But also with us every meter was the head of the Omega Foundation, Bob Elias, whose vision, patience and unprecedented generosity have made all this possible.

Damien Gildea, *Australia*

Antarctic Peninsula

Belgian second ascents, Spanish first ascent. An international team sailed aboard the yacht Euronav Belgica to visit the Peninsula for the 110th anniversary of the Belgian Antarctic Expedition 1897-99. Fittingly, one of the peaks they climbed this season, Mt. Allo (285m) on Liege Island, had been discovered and named by that expedition. Despite encountering difficult sea-ice and weather conditions, they also made the second ascent of Celsus Peak (1,375m) on Brabant Island, and the second ascent of the prominent Mt. Banck (675m) above Argentino Channel, near Paradise Harbor.

The Spanish brothers Eneko and Iker Pou visited Cape Renard at the northern end of the scenic Lemaire Channel. The Cape is better known as the location of Cape Renard Tower—or "Una's Tits"—a dual summited spire, one of the steepest mountain features on the Peninsula. However just south of the Tower is another steep massif with three peaks. The Spanish referred to these as "The Three Pigs" but named the one they summited Zerua Peak (Sky Peak). Their route Azken Paradisua (600m, 5.11 M6) is certainly one of the most technically difficult that has been climbed on the Antarctic Peninsula. See their report, below.

Damien Gildea, *Australia*

False Cape Renard, Zerua Peak, Azken Paradizua. From Cape Horn on December 10, my brother Iker, filmmakers Jabi Baraiazarra and Gotxon Arribas, and I sailed the legendary, harrowing, Drake Passage to Antarctica in the *Northanger*. Four long days from Argentina made it clear why no one wants to make this crossing by sailboat: nausea, dizziness, boredom, and anxiety—overwhelming anxiety when the waves crash over the boat, or when icebergs show up on the radar. Skippers Greg Landreth and Keri Pashuk call this crossing the "climber filter." Most mountaineers never even get on board. Of those who do, many arrive too weak to do anything. And those who aren't too weak are often too traumatized by the trip to climb. We reached Antarctica close to the latter group, but determined to stand our ground and fight.

Between Deception Island and Port Lockroy we saw many interesting concluding objectives for Iker's and my 7 Walls 7 Continents Project, but unfortunately, none where the *Northanger* could lay anchor. We weren't happy with what we saw at Port Lockroy, either, and decided to keep sailing southward. We finally found our objective at False Cape Renard: an awe-inspiring ensemble of three unclimbed peaks known to sailors as the Three Piggies. We set our sights on the one closest to the sea, which was the most accessible and the most beautiful, and landed on December 20 in good weather with low swell. Then the *Northanger* left in search of good anchorage. We had appallingly bad weather for the next four days and finally called the *Northanger* to bring more food. They arrived after four hours of sailing, but they could not stay

The Pou Brothers in Northanger, happy to have Zerua Peak behind them, the final climb of their "7 Walls 7 Continents Project." *Pou collection*

long at anchor because of the wind and icebergs pushing against the boat. After landing supplies in a rubber dinghy, a dangerous operation, we had a Christmas Eve party with plenty of drink. In the evening Iker went out to pee. This call of nature changed the course of the expedition. He asked me to come outside. We looked up at the sky: it was the best in the last four days. After five minutes of discussion, Iker and I rushed out to pack our backpacks. We were going up! Jabi and Gotxon still couldn't believe it. They said they'd wait in the tent until we reached the base of the wall, when we could call to tell them if we decided to go up. The forecast was still terrible, but we were in Antarctica and couldn't pass up a single opportunity.

It was very cold when we started to climb, but the light in Antarctica is incredible. With no night, we would be able to fight the cold by not stopping until we reached the summit and returned to base camp. Americans call this style "single-push." To shed all weight, we left behind our sleeping bags, bivouac sacks, tent, bolts.... If everything worked out and we didn't have to bivouac, the result could be perfect. But if we had to stop for any reason, at least some frostbite would be guaranteed.

The fourth pitch hit a snag: 7a with verglas. It was good this one was up to Iker, because in the cold I couldn't grip the rock and both my feet slipped on an ice sheet and I fell several meters into space. Higher, when I reached a ledge, I had to stop and warm my fingers because the pain was unbearable and my eyes were filled with tears. It hurt so badly that I arrived dizzy at the belay. My next two pitches were gorgeous 6a's. Iker led the pitch after that: verglased 6b+. The ice on the rock was giving us hell, but we were making it. After another couple of pitches we came to a snow ramp and then bad rock. Every so often, Iker repeated the same question: "How are we going to get down?" But after several pitches of shattered rock and steep mixed climbing up to M6, made harder by only having two axes between us, we embraced on the summit.

We still couldn't believe we had made it, that the 7 Walls 7 Continents Project was finally complete. The panorama up there was breathtaking, with hundreds of virgin mountains,

Azken Paradizua, the first route up Zerua Peak on the False Cape Renard. *Pou Collection*

channels of water packed with icebergs, and a solitude like nothing we have ever known. We felt fulfilled.

The rappelling was tense: the rock crumbled and we wracked our brains trying not to make mistakes. Problems flourished on the final rappels, including an anchor piton pulling out and a near-death escape during an overhanging rappel, a brush with disaster. After eight hours of dangerous rappelling, we felt overcome with tension and extreme fatigue when we finally embraced Jabi and Gotxon, who had fearfully watched the events play out. When we reached base camp we were too weak to celebrate anything. We had a bite and went to sleep. It had been 24 hours from camp to camp, and we could take no more.

ENEKO POU, *Spain*

SOUTH GEORGIA

Falklands War commemoration; South Georgia traverse with numerous ascents; Mt. Stanley, first ascent; quasi-crossings. In addition to the French expedition described below, the most notable climbing news was ascents of all four peaks that had been named after notable figures in the Falklands War. 2007 marked the 25th anniversary of the conflict, so it might be seen as appropriate that Sheridan Peak, Mt. Stanley, Mills Peak, and Ellerbeck Peak all received ascents.

French Alpinists Philippe Batoux, Manu Cauchy, and Lionel Daudet sailed to the island aboard Ada 2, skippered by the renowned French sailor Isabelle Autissier and two crew members. The team traveled along the island from northwest to southeast, using the yacht for support and repositioning between climbing and sections of sledhaulling. Ada 2 arrived at Grytviken on November 8, and on the 11th the climbing trio approached Mt. Paget (2,934m) up the Nordenskjöld Glacier. Climbing by a more direct variant of the 1995 northwest face route, all three summited on November 12, thus completing the sixth ascent of Paget, the island's highest peak. Shortly after, the three scored the first ascent of Sheridan Peak (955m). This small, sharp peak is named after Major Guy Sheridan of the Royal Marines who, on April 25, 1982, formally accepted the surrender of Argentine forces fighting on the island during the Falklands War. Sheridan himself had unsuccessfully attempted the peak in August 1999, retreating not far from the top. The French later made the third known ascent of another summit— Surprise Peak (ca 950m)—on November 18, by a 900m mixed route.

After more traversing, the team summited Mt. Worsley (1,104m), a small peak above the Esmark Glacier, via a long ridge, on December 2. Toward the end of the trip the team also attempted Mt. Sugartop (2,323m)—the only big peak aside from Paget to have had a second ascent—but retreated short of the summit in high wind and worsening weather. Ada 2 left

South Georgia on December 31 for the return journey to Ushuaia, having completed a very interesting and successful expedition to this historically unique and extremely challenging island of mountains.

Mills Peak was climbed on November 30. Andy Barker, Anjali Pande, and Less Whittamore were dropped on the coast of the Barff Peninsula and climbed the 627m peak, using snowshoes for the approach. Both Keith Mills, for whom the peak was named, and Guy Sheridan (above) visited South Georgia earlier in 2007 to mark the 25th anniversary of the end of the Falklands War.

The veteran Antarctic sailor and climber Skip Novak led a party of very experienced Italian climbers on a shorter crossing from King Haakon Bay to Stromness, making the first ascent of Mt. Stanley (1,263m) in the process. Novak, Anna Mattei, Romolo Nottaris, and Carlo Spinelli skinned up the Fortuna Glacier and onto the east ridge of Stanley, which they followed to the summit to top out early in the morning of October 23. After an enjoyable ski back to camp they rejoined Fabrizio Bernasconi, Sergio Brambilla, and Gianni Caverzasio to ski to a final campsite on the coast. They awoke the next morning to a giant cruise ship filling their horizon, before hauling into Stromness in the rain. An interesting aside is that it was Romolo Nottaris who filmed Erhard Loretan on his 1995 re-ascent of Mt. Epperly, mentioned above.

South Georgia now sees a number of short quasi-crossings, usually by commercially guided groups, that are marketed as relating to the celebrated crossing of the island by Shackleton, Crean, and Worsley in May 1916—even though modern visitors take a shorter and easier route, and have not just navigated 800 miles across the Southern Ocean in a 20-foot open boat, after escaping their ship being crushed in Antarctica. Traversing the long-axis of the island is significantly harder than these short crossings and has only been done once as a continuous journey, by Grant Dixon, Angus Finney, Pat Lurcock, and Jay Watson in October 1999, who pre-placed three caches along the route before starting. Their route was somewhat similar to that taken by the French this season. Most of the length of the island was also traversed, in separate sections, during the period 1951–56 by various parties under the leadership of the late British cartographer Duncan Carse, who did most of the exploration and mapping of the island during this time.

My additional sources for the above reporting on South Georgia: Grant Dixon, Pat Lurcock, Skip Novak, www.alpinist.com, http://yannick.michelat.free.fr/GeorgiaSat_News.htm, www.sgisland.gs.

DAMIEN GILDEA, *Australia*

Jordan

WADI RUM

New routes from 2006 and 2007. In October and November of both 2006 and 2007, James Garrett from the USA and Andreas (Res) von Känel from Switzerland (a mountain guide and brother of the late Jurg von Känel) climbed a number of new routes in and around Wadi Rum and Wadi Araba. Al Hasani is an impressive rock formation situated close to the little Bedouin village of Disi, and between Obeid's Bedouin Camp and the Camp of Lawrence in Sig Um Tawagi. Prior to 2006 it was unclimbed. In October of that year the American-Swiss pair put up Bedouin Camel Boys, a five-pitch route at 5c. The line is sustained and well protected, providing magnificent hand cracks leading to spectacular face climbing. While they were climbing, local camel boys cheered them on

One of the Camel boys standing before his namesake route, Bedouin Camel Boys, the first route on the formation Al Hasani, near Disi (5 pitches, 5c, Garrett–von Känel, 2006). *James Garrett*

and prepared some tea for their return. Parties repeating this route have found it very worthwhile, giving moderate but sustained climbing, purity of line, nice sequences, each pitch having varied climbing, and the route well protected yet not over-bolted. It appears to have the potential to be a popular classic, and the rappel line is direct, yet largely separate from the climb. They returned in November 2007 and added three short routes. Two hundred meters from Obeid's Camp, in the opposite direction to Al Hasani, they put up various one-pitch routes.

In November 2006, they visited Jebel Kharaz, situated to the left of the well-known tourist site of Kharaz Rock Bridge, where they put up various short face and crack routes to 6a, and then another new shorter route in the Abu N'Khala Towers just south of Rum Village. The pair then traveled to Petra and from there on to the Little Petra turn-off. From here they continued along the road toward Wadi Araba for six kilometers (from the Beidah-Little Petra junction), where there is a large rock formation that the local Bedouin call Sh'Karet M'Said. Many actually refer to it as The Face, due to a distinctive facial likeness of the West Face. Garrett and von Känel climbed up through the "mouth," then followed the left side of the "nose" and up past the right "eye," where they had to negotiate the overhanging "eyelid." The five-pitch line, christened The Face (5c: November 2006), gives enjoyable and well-protected climbing with some spectacular sequences and fine views up the Jordan Valley and toward the Dead Sea.

Walking a few hours through the valley in which Little Petra is situated, they found a fine formation with a blunt yet striking, north-facing arête. This gave the seven-pitch Bedouin Life (6a, 2006); from the summit an initial easy descent of the far side led to a series of rappels down the south face. The route was climbed on natural protection and is far from any tourist locations/ruins.

In November 2007 Garrett was introduced to the Siq Bajeah (a.k.a. Baaga or Ba'ja) by a local tribes-

High on the spectacularly featured rock of Bedouin Life. *James Garrett*

man who grew up in Little Petra. In this little known (to climbers) canyon he rope-soloed King Faisal (three pitches, 5a, named after the tribesman himself), an enjoyable route on excellent black sandstone, which followed hand cracks interspersed with overhanging features sporting huge patina holds. He installed bolted belay anchors, but from the top walked off west on a huge ledge before rappelling to the ground. He notes huge potential for new routes in this region of very good rock.

Garrett notes that none of these climbs was in any way near or part of the famous ancient ruins of Petra. He says that climbing in Petra where the ruins lie would be both inconsiderate and disrespectful, particularly as there is so much unclimbed rock left in Jordan. Nevertheless, these new routes lie within the Petra Archaeological Park, where currently climbing is not allowed. [See the following access report from Tony Howard.]

At the venues they climbed, it was as if they had stumbled on the best parts of Utah's Canyonland cracks combined with Nevada's Red Rock featured stone (though

Drilling threads to protect Jordan's highly sculpted sandstone. *James Garrett*

Wadi Rum is more featured and therefore even more "climber friendly"). Garrett noted that even just 10km from Rum Village it is still similar to the unclimbed American Southwest that greeted such activists as Harvey T. Carter and George Hurley in the 1960s. Garrett and von Känel found the local people the most gracious and generous imaginable, and the land gentle, friendly, and safe. [Some of these 2006 climbs were reported in the *AAJ 2007* based on information in the Guest House logs, but there were errors in the reporting, which we hope have been straightened out above.—Ed.]

LINDSAY GRIFFIN, *Mountain INFO Editor, www.climbmagazine.com*

Wadi Rum, various routes. Over the winter John was based in Amman, and between trips to Baghdad, Anne visited Jordan and we spent as much time as possible in Wadi Rum. We decided the place was fantastic, having world class everything (trad, sport, scrambling, camel-riding, ...). Our top ticks were: FFA of Towering Inferno, freeing 5 aid pitches to give an 8-pitch E6 6a; Rum's first headpoint: Rum Grit (E7 6b) right of Catfish Corner; onsight ascents of existing routes Rock Empire (8a; to after the crux pitches) and La Guerre Sainte (F7b; the best multi-pitch sport route imaginable!); and several new short routes. Anne returned to the U.K. earlier so John had chance to nip down for a couple more routes, both climbed onsight solo (probably the first solos of any long routes in Rum other than Bedouin routes): I.B.M., 13 pitches, F6b (about E3 5c); Inshallah Factor, 15 pitches, F6c (about E4 6a); both times descending Eye of Allah after reaching the East Summit and the Main Summit (by Hammad's Route) respectively.

ANNE *and* JOHN ARRAN, *U.K.*

Jordan, climbing access threat. Di Taylor and I discovered the climbing potential of Wadi Rum in 1984 and soon extended our explorations across the country, finding more climbing areas, treks, canyons, and caves. I wrote in Summit 26, 2002 about the problems faced by the Bedouin with regard to tourism development in Rum. This year, with the creation of new Nature Reserves throughout the country and the likely tightening of regulations in Petra, we realized that Jordan may be about to lose many of its traditional mountain freedoms. As a consequence we devoted a week of our time in Jordan this spring to discuss the issue with those concerned, armed with feedback from climbers, trekkers and national parks in the U.K., USA, and France, and based on the following extracts from the UIAA environmental objectives and guidelines adopted at their general assembly, 4 October 1997, in Slovenia:

"The UIAA believes that mountaineers can best meet their environmental responsibilities, as well as helping to safeguard mountain land and local communities, through a process of integration ... [by] Persuading decision makers that mountains and mountain people are important and responsible mountaineering is an activity deserving of the highest levels of support ... [and] Supporting the establishment of protected areas, such as national parks and reserves, to safeguard the finest mountain wildlife and scenery, so long as these are effectively managed, well integrated with local community needs and sensitive to mountaineering requirements."

Since Di, Al Baker, Mick Shaw, and I first climbed in Jordan in 1984, we and other mountain activists have discovered that Jordan is full of unexpected adventure tourism potential, including climbing, canyoning, trekking, mountain biking, paragliding, and (to a much smaller extent) caving. Simultaneously, the RSCN (Royal Society for Conservation of Nature) have, without consultation with activists, been creating their reserves and strictly regulating access that was, before the existence of the reserves, open to all. Ninety percent of each reserve is closed to the public "to protect the environment," the rest is controlled by the need to make advance bookings, use designated trails exclusively, and to have and pay for a compulsory guide. Additionally, numbers are severely reduced due to limited accommodation in campsites and hotels in the reserves; no overnighting is allowed other than in RSCN camps; entrance can only be at the specified entrance points, where a fee is charged. Climbing and other such activities are banned, with no reasons given. Long distance trails are frowned upon and discouraged from passing through the reserves, which are some of the most beautiful parts of Jordan.

Sabbah Eid, a Bedouin mountain guide, showing off his homeland. *Tony Howard*

Whilst the Petra Authority has taken the same stance with regard to climbing and other "adventure" activities, which are seen to be hazardous (due to lack of understanding on management's part), it has been less rigid in its approach to trekking and overnighting on the trails through the Archaeological Park. However, with the desire to further develop the commercial potential of the Park encouraged by consultants and funding from USAID, it now seems that bureaucrats with little or no understanding of mountain tourism are taking over. There was no consultation with mountain activists until the Petra National Trust contacted us for our views on designated trails and we subsequently presented our case for keeping the Petra Park open to trekkers and climbers. Sadly, we have been overruled on the climbing aspect, even where climbs already exist on the fringe of the Park; also, judging from the meetings we had with PNT since, it may not be long before Petra trekkers also lose their "right to roam."

Luckily the situation in Wadi Rum is, as yet, almost unchanged. Despite recent well-intentioned efforts by RSCN to protect the area from excessive environmental impact by closing large portions of it, the indigenous Bedouin were resistant to change—they had already grasped the opportunity to improve their economy back in 1984, and swiftly met the demand for services in trekking and climbing. Their traditional hunting routes had gained a reputation as among the world's best mountain adventures, and new and superb climbs and treks had been found, placing the area at the forefront of desert climbing and tourism. As a consequence, by the time others with commercial interests were attracted to Rum's financial honey-pot, climbing development, trekking, and adventure tourism were booming, and the opportunity for outside control had lessened, though the threat still remains.

It seems inevitable that Rum must have suffered environmentally due to the massive growth of tourism. However, when we were there this spring, even though there were scores of trekking groups enjoying multi-day walks in remote desert valleys and numerous climbers from around Europe enjoying the hot rock, all helped by Bedouin guides with transport, the trekkers were so dispersed and well organized that we only met two groups, and there were few if any signs of their presence. The main environmental impact seems to come from 4WD trips provided to day-trippers from nearby Aqaba and Petra, and is therefore limited to the "tourist circuit" in the RSCN's "intensive-use zone."

Consequently, the complaint that Rum is now "sinking" under 4WD tracks hardly seems justified. After one windy night this spring many of the tracks had already started to disappear under drifting sand. Even so, there are those who would like to control or curtail these activities by stipulating that access to all areas of Rum except the "intensive-use zone" can only be on foot or with horse or camel, and not by vehicle; this would not only make many climbs virtually unreachable, but would also make multi-day treks impossible as the necessary camps are serviced by 4WD; most importantly, it would also put numerous traditional Bedouin camps out of reach to their occupants. However, thanks to strong resistance from the Bedouin, Rum remains open and is prospering.

The north of Jordan is currently open as well, though there are plans to develop the Ajloun region for tourism. We have spoken to the Tourism Ministry, who informed us that they have no plans for designated trails, or closure of climbing and caving areas. Whilst few caves have been discovered there as yet, a number of quality single-pitch limestone cliffs are being developed for sport climbing, and trekking is becoming established in numerous Derbyshire-style limestone dales and forested hills. Just to the south, however, some of the awesome canyons above the Dead Sea, which offer spectacular canyoning, are already closed, or virtually closed, being in RSCN reserves. New reserves are opening and more are planned in the north; one already comes close to a climbing area—let us hope they do not encroach further.

With all this in mind, we gathered information on conservation and access from Roger Payne, the UIAA, and others in the world of climbing and conservation. This spring, with the support of Mark Khano of Guiding Star Tours, we presented it at meetings with the RSCN, PNT, Ministry of Tourism, USAID, and Jordan Tourism Development (SIYAHA). We did not get the opportunity to see the Aqaba Authority (ASEZA), but as Rum is currently suffering from minimal interference, it is probably best left to the local people to run their affairs unless they ask for support from the climbing and trekking community.

It rapidly became apparent that whilst some of the RSCN felt strongly that conservation was not just the prime, but sole priority of RSCN and were adamantly against all freedom of access within the reserves, there were others who were considerably more open in their approach to our stance that conservation and access can be compatible. So much so, in fact, that they made a goodwill gesture and invited us to trek with them in their proposed new reserve of Jebel Mas'uda, south of, and adjacent to, the Petra Park.

The two days we spent in the Mas'uda Reserve with Tarek abul Hawa, Laith al Moghrabi, and a local Bedouin, Mohammed Sa'idiyin, were worthwhile from everyone's point of view. Whilst in the reserve, we not only continued our discussions in more conducive surroundings than our boardroom meetings, but also repeated one of our own trekking discoveries through the Tibn Canyon, and descended an amazing series of Bedouin "ladders" and bridges down a vertical 100-meter cliff into a canyon with enough stunning rock scenery to make any climber's fingers itch. Thanks to Mohammed, we also saw numerous signs of wildlife, including a variety of birds, wolf spoor, hyena droppings, a venomous Painted Saw-scaled Viper, and a dead Blanford's Fox; ibex, he said, also inhabit this mountain wilderness.

Most of these species are endangered, and their long-term survival in Jordan would probably be in doubt were it not for RSCN and the creation of the new reserves, so we understand and respect the reasons for them. However, conservation and access have been proven to be compatible around the world, so let us hope it can be so in Jordan.

[Editor's note: Tony Howard and Di Taylor are the authors of *Treks and Climbs in Wadi Rum* and *Jordan: Walks, Treks, Caves, Climbs & Canyons*, and operates the tourism consultancy n.o.m.a.d.s., www.nomadstravel.co.uk.]

TONY HOWARD, *U.K.*

Egypt

Access issues. In the middle of 2007 the Egyptian Tourism Ministry announced that they were banning climbing in Sinai, which would have effectively stopped all climbing in Egypt. However, by late autumn this had been rescinded and Dave Lucas made a Sinai traverse without problem. In fact Lucas is being salaried for two years to lead treks and climbing trips, and to train the Jabaliya Bedouin in the St Katherines region in trek leadership and first aid, a project managed in Cairo and financed by the EU. Other British trips are planned for 2008.

The extensive mountainous area of the Red Sea Coast is rather different from the Sinai, and access still appears to be a no no, partly due to the exact line of the Egypt-Sudan border being in dispute and the discovery of oil offshore. Tony Howard and friends have been trying to go to this area on a yearly basis, their latest attempt in early 2008, but have been steadfastly refused by the Egyptian Army despite personal requests from local contacts. But there are others who suggest Egypt is incapable of banning climbing, as the regulators don't understand the concept, and in any case the Sinai is run outside Cairo's influence, with the mountain valleys full of opium farms that are operated, protected, or financed by the army and police chiefs, who certainly wouldn't listen to authorities in Cairo.

LINDSAY GRIFFIN, *Mountain INFO, www.climbmagazine.com*

Oman

Jabal Misht, Jabal M'Saw, Jabal M'Seeb, Jabal Kawr, Nadan Pillar; new routes. In December, I returned once again to the exotic limestone massifs of Jabal Misht and Jabal Kawr in Oman. My climbing partner on this trip was Richard Simpson, also from Christchurch, New Zealand. We found the people as welcoming as ever, and in the stable weather we were able to climb seven new routes. In all cases, we sought natural lines of weakness and climbed in traditional style using cams and nuts, as has been the norm in this area.

On the superlative Jabal Misht (2,090m), we found the cunning line Rock Vulture (505m, TD-, VI, 5.8R) near

The western end of Jabal Misht's south face, as seen from the "Beehive Tombs" at Al Ain. Rock Vulture takes a slanting ramp to the second tower right of the broad col. To its right is Madam Butterfly (700m, TD, 5.9, Chaudrey-Hornby, 2000) and to its left (taking the easier ground to the broad col), is the 1982 Davis-King-Searle Route. *Paul Knott*

Pitch 12 of Rock Vulture, above the crux at the start of the circling ledge. *Paul Knott*

Richard Simpson completing pitch 1 (IV) on Rock Vulture. *Paul Knott*

the western end of the south face. We accessed this neglected part of the face by scrambling up to an atmospheric hanging valley. The key to Rock Vulture is a broad ramp circling up and round the steep second tower. To reach this, we escaped from a deep cleft via two exciting crux pitches at British HVS and a short traverse and abseil.

We also climbed on the south side of Wadi Al Ain, opposite Jabal Misht. On Jabal M'Saw, a southwestern outlier of Jabal Misfah, we climbed White Knight (545m, D+, V+) on the buttress left of the existing White Magic. On Jabal Assala's furthest east tower (referred to by the friendly villagers below as "Lorbib"), we climbed the delightful Orange Roughy (383m, D, V+) on the main north pillar.

South of Jabal Kawr (ca 2,700m), we climbed two routes on the shaded and accessible north face of Jabal M'Seeb, adding to the three existing lines. Bloody Sunday (395m, TD-, VI-) was a varied and satisfying route sneaking through the overhanging head at the left side of the face. We named it for the havoc a dislodged flake caused to the back of my hand. Moonshadow (276m, D+, VI-) was a shorter, but still excellent line at the right hand end, featuring steep climbing up huge hollow blocks.

We climbed two easier routes on the adjacent sunny face of Jabal Kawr. Sunset Serpent (503m, D-, IV) takes a shallow buttress facing M'Seeb hamlet, and probably represents the easiest route to this end of the plateau. The hiss of a snake startled us on the entry pitches; at the top, we were surprised to discover a carefully wedged, faded cap sporting the coat of arms of the UAE. It may be that this marks the celebrated National Day Climb (500m, D-) climbed in 1984 by Bill Wheeler and friends, in which case their route must have taken the old watercourse right of Sunset Serpent, some distance from the line suggested by existing information. We made our final ascent on Christmas Day, weaving our way up AD+ (IV) slabs and stepped ramps to the summit of the Nadan Pillar, a striking feature rising 800m from the gorge that leads to the hidden cirque of Nadan. The pillar sports an alluring but somewhat inaccessible black and orange south face, from which our route would make an expedient descent. Below in the gorge, work continues on the improbable and somewhat destructive project to build a road through the ancient boulder choke to Nadan village. Despite the developing infrastructure in this part of Oman, we still met no other climbers during our stay.

PAUL KNOTT, *New Zealand*

Algeria

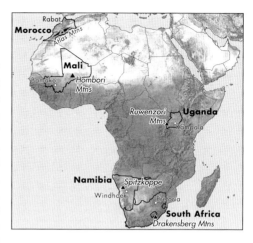

Hoggar Mountains, general notes and new route activity. Algeria is comprised of two big mountain ranges: the Atlas chain in the north, and the Sahara in the south, including the Hoggar, which has a surface area similar to that of France. Due to the altitude (an average of 2,200m, with Tahat at 2,918m), the temperatures are cool from November until March. Climbers have been coming from Europe to enjoy the winter warmth and the adventurous technical climbing since the 1930s, with ebbs and flows in popularity through the decades. The current trend is to open new routes using bolts, and to mark approaches and descents with cairns. This makes it easier for future climbers to just turn up at the route and start climbing. But it pays little respect to the past, when the routes were climbed using traditional gear, like pitons, friends, and nuts.

One of the benefits of this bolting trend, however, is that the level of climbs available in Algeria is now much wider and is open to a majority of climbers. All the new routes are around the 5.9 level, which suits the majority of climbers. Most of the routes have some bolts, but also require the use of cams and nuts. Unfortunately, some climbers have opened routes very near existing routes. This is not a good trend, as there are plenty of virgin summits available in the Hoggar. I think the future of climbing in the desert is in the Immidir Region and in the Tefedest. In these locations there is high-quality granite and a large choice of routes with a variety of features, from cracks to slabs.

In Algeria, particularly in the Atakor area, there is no danger of terrorism, at least not more than anywhere else. One must be wary of traveling in the deep south (700km south of Tamanrasset). There are gangs of thieves who operate from Mali and Niger that border Algeria. The main climbing areas are to the north of Tamanrasset, so it is quiet and safe. There is an anti-American feeling from the Arabic north in Algeria, but the Touareg people who populate the south of Algeria have no such prejudice. The best way to visit Algeria is to be respectful of the local culture and to be adaptable.

Here are the new routes in Algeria from 2007. In the Atakor Region, an Italian team in conjunction with the local Abalema agency, established various one- to three-pitch bolted routes. The Dutch team of Martin Fickweiler, Gerke Hoekstra, and Ronald Naar climbed in the Immidir Region on the T-in-Taouafa Massif. They established the 275m-vertical route graded 6c (5.11b) described in the following report. In the Tesnou region, a French team with the M'Zab agency climbed Le Cadeau de Neptoune, which was opened in January 2007 by J. Ala, Jean-Francois Gras, and J.F. Lignan. The route is graded 6a+ (5.10b) and is approximately 400m high. In the Tesnouu region, J. Ala, Jean-Francois Gras, and J.F. Lignan opened another 400m route, graded 5.

To see topos and learn more about Hoggar routes visit www.desert-dulac.com, which lists all the new routes. Also see my guidebook, *Escalade en Sahara* (the Hoggar Massif).

THOMAS DULAC, *France, Algeria*

Adrar Ti-n-Taouafa, southwest pillar. During a three-week stay in the Algerian desert, Gerke Hoekstra, Ronald Naar, and I explored an area southwest of the small town of Arak. Besides a couple of ascents on various mountains via classic lines, Gerke and I made the first ascent of the southwest pillar of Adrar Ti-n-Taouafa (N 24'416" and E 4'006") on March 28. The 275m vertical route is seven pitches, the crux being a 30m 5.11R pitch on questionable rock. The last three pitches

The southwest pillar route on Adrar Ti-n-Taouafa, the first route on this 275m formation. *Martin Fickweiler*

were off width, requiring Friends up to size 6. A total of five hand-placed bolts where used on the entire route. The Adrar Ti-n-Taouafa area has lots of potential for new, hard routes. It is 64km west of the more famous Tesnou, and can only be reached by 4x4. We found the Adrar Ti-n-Taouafa area when driving through the desert looking for mountains. We explained to the driver what we were looking for, and he took us to this beautiful place where one can just drive around and put up new routes on walls up to 300m in height. Most routes might need some bolts, but there are also lines that can be done clean. There is lots of crack and slab climbing.

Gerke Hoekstra enjoying friable rock on the crux pitch of the southwest pillar of Adrar Ti-n-Taouafa. *Martin Fickweiler*

It's best to fly to Tamanrasset and drive from there. As long as you organize your car with driver before you arrive in Algeria, it's no problem to travel around the country and climb lots!

MARTIN FICKWEILER, *Rotterdam, The Netherlands.*

Ethiopia

Tigray and Adwa regions, Nebelet, summary of new routes 2006–winter 2008. Ethiopia is a hard-core adventure-climbing destination where you have to take the rough with the smooth, and there can be more rough than smooth. The sandstone in southern Tigray is a bit soft, except where it is well weathered. On some of the towers we did (e.g. Sheba), the rock was good. I love

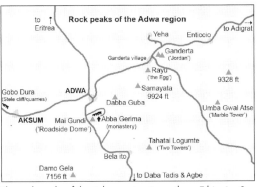

The rock peaks of the Adwa region in northern Ethiopia. See the text for peak and route identification. *Pat Littlejohn*

Rayu ("The Egg"). *Pat Littlejohn*

the climbing here because it's so challenging. It is at the adventurous extreme of rock climbing, and it won't appeal to the masses, that's for sure. There has to be a place like this now that so many African climbing areas have been bolted.

Further north in the mountains of Adwa, east of Axum, lie the mountains of Adwa, a superb range of peaks composed mainly of solid rock: basalt, quarzite, and, amazingly, marble. Many are technical peaks and towers with no easy route to their summits. Most summits have now been climbed, but there is still huge scope for serious adventure/trad climbing on many untouched faces. Protection is sparse, but so far this is a bolt-free and piton-free area, and long may it remain so!

See map for location of the climbing areas.

Gobo Dura: 4km west of Axum is the 100m cliff where the giant stele were quarried. This gives good climbing on very hard rock and has now been visited by several climbing teams. Good for a shorter/more relaxing day.

Damo Gela: An impressive formation towering 400m above the plains, having one easy route to the summit ("climbed in the time of Haile Selassie," according to locals) and a 10-pitch E1 taking the north buttress (Pat Littlejohn–Steve Sustad, 2006). The superb west face awaits an ascent.

Mai Gundi: 20 minutes from the road, with one route on the northwest face (5 pitches, E3, Littlejohn-Sustad, 2006) and another attempted. Easy route to summit via northeast ridge.

Abba Gerima cliff: Attractive and extensive crag overlooking the monastery (Ethiopia's equivalent of the Vatican). So far two five-pitch E4's climbed towards left side (Littlejohn-Sustad, 2006).

Dabba Guba: Striking dome set on a high mountain shelf and approached via gully bounding it on the west. Four-pitch E4 takes north ridge (Littlejohn-Sustad, 2008). Easy route to summit on S side.

Mt. Aftera: Not shown on the

Samayata (9,924 feet). *Pat Littlejohn*

map as I'm not sure where it is. Eight-pitch 5.10 climbed on the west face by Mark Richey and Mark Wilford 2007.

Ganderta ("Jordan"): Superb and very accessible double-summited peak close to the road. Long E1 takes east ridge to east summit (easy descent). Five-pitch E2 takes south face of west summit (abseil descent). Littlejohn-Sustad, 2007.

Tahatai Logumte: Twin towers rising 250m from the plains. One-hour walk-in. North summit climbed by three-pitch HVS taking north ridge. South summit by five-pitch E5 starting from notch between towers. Abseil descents. Littlejohn-Sustad, 2008.

Samayata (9,924 feet). *Pat Littlejohn*

Samayata: At almost 10,000 feet, the highest of the Adwa peaks. 1.5-hour walk-in to base of south face, which is probably the highest in the area at ca 600m. Only route so far climbs south crest of lower of two towers near left side of the main face: 11-pitch E1, nice "classic" climbing on great rock. Littlejohn-Sustad, 2008.

Umba Gwal Atse: Remarkable isolated tower of marble standing on the south side of the range. Two-hour walk-in. Six-pitch E2 wanders up shorter (200m) southwest side (Littlejohn-Sustad, 2007). The 300m northeast face is unclimbed and very challenging.

Tahatai Logumte ("Two Towers"). *Pat Littlejohn*

Rayu: Egg-shaped formation with easy route to summit on north side and big walls to south and west. Only route so far starts up southwest buttress, then veers left to a line of grooves and chimneys (8 pitches, XS, 6a, Littlejohn-Sustad, 2008). Scope for more superb extreme adventure routes.

Umba Gwal Atse ("Marble Tower"). *Pat Littlejohn*

Nebelet Tower: This spectacular twin-summited sandstone tower rises above the town of Nebelet (1.5 hours' drive north of Hawzien). Six-pitch 5.10 route takes steep line of cracks and chimneys on southeast side, then a long traverse right to gain summit. Abseil descent. Richey-Wilford 2007.

Bouldering can be found at Gobo Dura and a few km from the Italian Hotel in Hawzien (hundreds of round but featured boulders in pleasant setting, reputedly "world class").

PAT LITTLEJOHN, *Alpine Club*

Nebelet tower group, new routes. Ethiopia: the birthplace of humanity, coffee, Emperor Haile Selassie, and … climbing? Maybe. The people of northern Ethiopia understand getting vertical: they have churches carved into sandstone pinnacles. To get to one church, Abune Yemata, you have to climb 5.2 up a 150-foot face to get to the final three-foot wide gangplank walkway to the entrance. The country is covered with rock. On my first trip to Ethiopia, in October of 2006, I optimistically brought along a pair of rock shoes and a chalk bag; I returned three months later with a quadruple set of cams.

The Tigray region near Mekele. *Andrea Jensen*

My March 2007 expedition was inspired in part by Pat Littlejohn and Steve Sustad's trip (*AAJ 2006*, p. 305–307). Pat and Steve had spent time in the Gheralta, in the Tigray province of northern Ethiopia. They'd done a few impressive lines, and Pat sent me tantalizing photos of unclimbed massifs up to 1,500 feet tall and 1.5 miles long. Kristie Arend, Helen Dudley, Caroline George, Gabe Rogel, and I spent three weeks climbing around the area.

Scouting for continuous crack systems is the trick to climbing in Ethiopia. Pat and Steve had shot up a major chimney on Sheeba Tower, the primary tower in the Nebelet tower group northwest of Megab. We sought out other options, and ended up on a five-pitch route on a

Among Tigray's Nebelet Towers, Tewodros is the third major tower from the right. Burhardt and friends climbed the face in the photo. *Gabe Rogel*

Kristie Arend on Jewel in the Sand, on the Gheralta Massif. *Gabe Rogel*

tower we called Tewadros: Learning The Hard Way (III, 5.10). The route ascends a left-leaning crack on the south face, through a section of face climbing, to another wider crack to a large ledge on top of the second pitch. From here, scramble up and around to the west to the higher vertical wall; two pitches of exciting face climbing with intermittent cracks take you to the final summit mushroom, which we climbed on the west face.

The southwest buttress of Gheralta. Jewel in the Sand ascends a corner on the left, and Sandstorm is to the right of the lower pillar. *Gabe Rogel*

Other climbs of note include two routes on the Gheralta proper, both two to three pitches long. Our routes ended where the rock quality became suspect (read: friable, chunky, loose, unstable). Gheralta has potential throughout her flanks, though there is a persistent horizontal band at about 300 feet that tends to change rock composition. Many corners and cracks abound, the majority being wide (4–20 inches).

The volume of rock in Ethiopia is immense. There are towers, ridges, buttresses, canyons—everywhere. It is exploration at its greatest, with all of the perks and challenges along the way. The sandstone is quite soft and the face climbing is thus difficult. Because so little climbing exploration has happened to this point, it's hard to predict what all is possible for rock climbing in the area. One thing is for certain, however: you would be hard pressed to find a place with as balanced an offering of climbing and cultural experience. If you go to northern Ethiopia, you are climbing in the part of the country that was hit hardest by the famines of the 1980s and inspired "We Are The World." This is where the Derg dropped a napalm bomb on a market in 1988 and killed 2,500 people. Where endless terrace systems fight the ongoing battle against drought, rain, and short-harvests. This is not climbing to get away from it all. It's climbing within it all.

MAJKA BURHARDT, *AAC*

Tigray, Adwa, Nebelet, and Harrar; new routes and exploration. On November 30, Mark Wilford, my wife Teresa, and I flew from Addis Ababa to Mekele to explore the rock climbing of the Tigray region. We had learned of its climbing potential from Pat Littlejohn, who has made several successful trips to Ethiopia and was very helpful in supplying information on where and what to climb. In Mekele, we hired a four-wheel-drive vehicle and driver and headed north to the town of Hawzien, where spectacular sandstone towers

Mark Richey inside the Nebelet Tower during its first ascent. *Mark Wilford*

and walls, reminiscent of the American Southwest, stretch for miles. In addition to the climbable rock here, ancient churches and temples, some dating back to the 4th century, are found throughout the region. A few of these churches are located high on cliff walls and require moderate climbing to visit. Although very little tourist infrastructure exists in the Tigray region, we found in general the roads to be good, the food excellent, and the people incredibly helpful and friendly.

The rock quality was another matter. The sandstone around Tigray turned out to be soft and at times scary to climb. I started off the trip with a bad fall when a handhold broke on the first pitch of an unclimbed tower just outside of Hawzien. I landed directly on my tailbone, but besides a severely bruised butt (and ego), I was generally OK.

Next we traveled to Adwa, where we found a different type of rock, probably basalt and much harder and more featured than the Tigray sandstone. There are many cliffs, escarpments, and great boulders here with tremendous potential for

Approaching Nebelet Tower for its first ascent. *Mark Richey*

Mt. Aftera in the Adwa region. *Mark Richey*

exploration and new routes. On December 5 we made the first ascent of the west face of Mt. Aftera (6-7 pitches, 5.10R), which takes the prominent right-leaning ramp and crack system in the middle of the wall. We descended in the dark by a steep goat path on the east face, something we would never have found had it not been for a local guide who showed up at the top. On the climb we saw patches of an almost glass-like surface of bullet-hard rock, and gigantic Ruppels griffon vultures nesting on the route and landing a few meters from our belays.

After traveling around the Axum area and doing some great bouldering in the Axum quarries, on December 10 we made the first ascent of a spectacular sandstone tower that rises about 400 meters above the small town of Nebelet, which is about 1.5 hours' drive on a dirt road northwest of Hawzien.

Our route (6 pitches, 5.10R) followed a steep line of chimneys and cracks on the southeast side to a huge ledge between the two highest summits, where we made a long traverse right to a steep unprotected passage to the final summit. On top we were rewarded with spectacular views of the desert and the cheers of dozens of local villagers who'd turned out to watch the entertainment. After a long rappel from the summit block, we found a 3rd class descent that got us most of the way down the tower without ropes.

After the tower climb we discovered superb granite bouldering only a few kilometers from the Italian hotel in Hawzien, where hundreds of huge round and very featured boulders formed a long train in a lovely setting of small villages and cultivated fields. The local children where delighted to give us a tour and eager to impress us with their own climbing prowess. Next time I would bring some shoes and watch them really climb!

The last place we briefly visited was the region around Harrar in the extreme eastern corner of Ethiopia near the border of Somalia. In a place called the Valley of Mysteries, just above the main road, we found endless pinnacles and short, steep walls with many cracks. The rock appeared a kind of granite and much harder than in Tigray. Many of the wild-looking pinnacles would be a real challenge to surmount by even their easiest route. The intense heat and dust from major road construction in process discouraged us from climbing, but it would be worth returning during a cooler season after the road is complete.

MARK RICHEY, *AAC*

Kenya

MT. KENYA

My bouldering mate Pete Hoersy agreed to join me on Mt. Kenya. To minimize the walking distance, he used his rally experience to get his Land Cruiser stuck in the middle of the hiking pass right on some big rocks at about 3,400m. After hours of digging, jacking, and pilling rocks, the vehicle still did not move, and so we started hiking to reach Shipton's Camp just before midnight. On the next day we got a late start. We went up to the first good-looking rock faces. The best way (as we discovered during our second trip up the hill) is to follow the pass toward the Kami Hut and then take the left turnoff to the base of the north face Standard Route on Batian. The first tower on your right offers some good quality, steep climbing on an obvious orange face. We picked the central groove, which takes one pitch to reach and then another two to climb, with the first being the crux with some slightly overhanging layback climbing (Central Groove Line, 120m, 7a). The next day Pete discovered his climbing shoes missing, so we went back to the same face and climbed the overhanging pillar to the right of the previous line. This took four pitches of which two were seriously overhanging and boldly protected trad climbing (Hängender Pfeiler, 140m, 7a+/A2). It took me most of the day to lead those, and even though it was snow-storming, we did not get wet until we reached the easy exit and the summit just before sundown. Luckily we found Pete's shoes there. From the difficulty (especially the second pitch) and the character of the climbing (only the first route had some gear in place, and that was from a retreat by Alex Fiksman and me in 2005), we assume the routes to be first ascents.

The next day we were on the east face of Nelion, an impressive 400m wall, but due to thick fog it took us a long time to find a line to climb. We followed a crack system up the center, found some old bolts with new white slings, and finally had to retreat halfway up the face due worsening weather. On our fourth day we made an "all free" ascent (on sight and not using the bolts) of the central groove on the Kraft Rognon, a line put up by a German team a few weeks prior (200m, 6b+). Finally we had to get back down and dig out the car, which was hell of a lot of work.

The routes on Nelion are partly bolted, but we did not use the bolts. My dearest request: Please try to keep the mountains as clean as possible, no trash on the paths and on the cliffs, no fixed ropes, and no bolts or other metal in the rock as long as you can survive without them.

FELIX BERG, *Germany, Kenya Mountain Club*

Madagascar

Tsaranoro Valley, Tsaranoro Be, first ascent of Manara-Potsiny. We spent our summer in Madagacar's winter, climbing for the month of August in the Tsaranoro Valley. Our gang of four consisted of Felix Frieder, Benno Wagner, and myself from Germany, and Sandra Wielebnowski from Austria. Besides repeating a bunch of routes, we managed to do an incredible, beautiful first ascent, which beat all of our expectations: Manara-Potsiny (600m, 17 pitches, 8a) on the east face of Tsaranoro Be. After spending nine days drilling the bolts, we redpointed all the individual pitches in a three-day effort. After two rest days, Benno, Felix, and I climbed the whole route in an 11-hour day, and I managed to climb all the pitches without falling. The route is a "nonplusultra" [ultimate] when it comes to beauty and quality. In the total length of 600m, we encountered only six meters that wasn't perfect rock. The other 594m was iron-like granite, made for climbing. About the character of the route: In the lower 400m, a climber has to sneak through climbing of the French 7th grade, losing a lot of skin. The 13th pitch is the crux, with 30m of slightly overhanging climbing on small edges. This incredible pitch starts with a boulder-problem, has athletic moves in the middle, and finishes fingery. And the rest of the route? 200m of beautiful, exposed, and various climbing on spectacular rock, leading to the end of a pillar, from where another 100m of easier climbing leads to the top (the entire route is 700m to the top). Equipped with 160 bolts and abseil-belays, the route is a strong contender to be an extreme-classic in the Tsaranoro-Valley.

TONI LAMPRECHT, *Germany*

Benno Wagner on the perfect rock of Manara-Potsiny on Tsaranoro Be. *Toni Lamprecht*

The line of Manara-Potsiny on Tasranoro Be. *Toni Lamprecht*

Fast on-sight repeats of big walls. At the end of September and October 2006, a French-Polish team (Marie-Claire Hourcade, Pierre Muller, Denis Roy, and myself) was very active in Madagascar. During the first two weeks of our stay we repeated many of the most important routes on the big walls of the Tsaranoro Massif in the Andringintra National Park of southern Madagascar. The most impressive performance belonged to 42-year-old French Denis Roy. In my opinion, his climbs were some of the best ascents ever in the history of Madagascar climbing. In nine days, Roy climbed many serious big wall routes, always leading, on-sight and in the fastest time. Roy climbed the 21-pitch Gondwanaland (7c), on the highest (800 m) east face of Tsaranoro Be massive. Gondwanaland was opened in 1996 by a South Tyrolean team. The route was graded ABO+ and has been repeated only few times since then. It offers very delicate climbing on insecure slabs, with the potential for risky falls. A British team in cooperation with French-Polish team partly re-equipped the badly rusted old anchors on this line, which wouldn't have held long falls. After replacing those bolts, Roy (belayed by Pierre Muller) on-sighted the route in eight hours, leading all the pitches. The repeats of the route done before usually had taken two days.

Denis Roy redpointing Tafo Masina on the north end of Madagascar. *David Kaszlikowski/VerticalVision.pl*

His ascent was probably first on-sight of this serious route.

Then Roy, always accompanied by Pierre Muller, also climbed La croix du sud (300m, 6b ED-, on sight, 2–3 hours); Le crabe aux pinces d'or (320m, 7b+ ED+, on sight, 4 hours); Out of Africa (600m, 7a ED, on sight, 5–6 hours); Always the sun (400m, 7c+ ABO, on sight, 5–6 hours {most difficult last pitch}); Rain Boto (400m, 7b+ ABO-, on sight, 5 hours). It has to be stressed that granite in the Tsaranoro massive requires delicate, technical climbing on tiny and often breaking holds, so most of the climbers move up much more slowly than Roy.

Hourcade and I repeated Life In the Fairy Tale (500m, 7a RP), Le Crabe aux Pinces d'Or, Out of Africa OS, Rain Boto (rappel before the finish), and some other easier routes. Later on, we all moved to the north of the island where, apart from climbing many easy routes, Denis Roy onsighted Perfection (7c+/8a) and Ale Baba (8a/8a+). We all made a movie about climbing in Madagascar, produced by Denis Roy's Totem Pole studio (www.totempole.fr).

DAVID KASZLIKOWSKI, *Poland*

Iceland

Skardatindar, new route. In February Jean-Baptist Deraeck, Sébastien Ibanez, Sébastien Ratel, and I climbed what we think is a new route on Skardatindar (1,385m). We did not have any information on this mountain. We expected to find a route, but couldn't know in advance because it's a half-day walk to the foot of the wall. We did not need to climb to understand that the rock is rotten—to see it is enough! On the other hand, we saw that a beautiful line of ice and mixed climbing seemed doable. We had a bad night bivouacking in the moraines above the glacier due to the wind. The following day we climbed up the corridor 40–50°, then a sheet of 60°. We then found ourselves at the foot of a mixed passage of M4+, and finally, despite the bad rock and some stiff slopes, we climbed an arête in the face. Eventually the slopes of the center of the face led us to our line in the gulley itself. Ice and steep snow took us to the foot of the last M5 pitch. It was the hardest and certainly the most exposed part of the climb, and we were battered by a furious wind that knocked us off balance. Easy slopes then took us to the top. We descended along the edge (on the right when looking at the wall), then a little downclimbing and a rappel took us to the huge glacier below. Because of the high wind we hiked to the road, but the next day we regretted this because we could have climbed the beautiful waterfalls on the right side of the face. We called our route Jökullélé (500m, TD+, M5, WI4). Jökull means glacier in Icelandic.

The few days that remained did give us a little ice and some rock, but we couldn't climb the beautiful ice lines because of a rapid rise in temperature. This is a bit of a problem in Iceland: when it is cold, the days are very short, and when the days are longer, it can be too hot for the ice! But that is the chance you take when you try an alpine holiday in this lowland country.

During this trip Christophe Moulin climbed with Julie Gerber, Aurelie Leveque, Cecile Chauvin, and Laure Gaudin to open a route on the left side of the Porcelain Wall. And Patrick

Skardatindar, showing the Jökullélé route by Benoist, Deraeck, Ibanez, and Ratel. *Stéphane Benoist*

On the approach to Skardatindar. *Stéphane Benoist*

Pessi climbed with Basile Ferran, Mathieu Maynadier, Mathieu Detrie, François Delas, and Benoit Monfort on the right side of the Porcelain Wall, combining Doug Scott's route with a more recent route opened by Icelanders.

STÉPHANE BENOIST, *FFCAM, France*

Norway

SPITZBERGEN

Atomfjella Mountains, new German-Swiss routes. I first took note of Svalbard, as Spitzbergen is called in Norwegian, in 1999 when reading an expedition report about mountaineering in Atomfjella. Spitzbergen lies a mere 1,500km from the North Pole and, true to its name and unlike the flat Pole, promised to be a mountaineering paradise par excellence. Markus Stofer and I were delighted to be invited to join Gregor Kresal from Slovenia on the Atomfjella, the steepest mountain range of the island. Grega had been there twice before.

Spitzbergen is roughly as large as the Iberian Peninsula, and Longyearbyen, its capital, has a population of 1,500. A hundred years ago one would have set off from here with sledge dogs, but modern

Deutsch Slowenische Freundschaft on the "Triangle" northwest face. *Robert Jasper*

Norwegians, like the rest of us, rely on technology. And so when the snowmobile broke down just outside of town we had wait almost an hour in a -20°C whiteout for the mechanic to reach us. Sledge dogs wouldn't have given up so easily! Luckily in April the sun never sets, and 24 hours of daylight makes time seem relatively unimportant. After almost 18 hours we had to haul our gear and sledges over a long ice section to reach the upper basin of the Tryggvebreen Glacier, where we set up our tents for base camp.

The east face of Chadwickrüggen's Polar Pow(d)er.   *Robert Jasper*

Temperatures can drop seriously up here in the Polar circle, and we registered down to -28°C in the tents. The Slovenian Slibowitz drink warmed us from the inside; Klemen and Boris had managed to pack an astounding amount in just 20kg of flight allowance, but nevertheless the cold was almost unbearable, working away at our energy reserves and in doing so it became a life-determining factor. Up on the peaks and when climbing in the shade the thermometer even dropped to circa -40°C. Talk about life in the freezer!

The northern foresummit of Chadwickrüggen. The Slovenian route is on the left, and Knut is on the right.   *Robert Jasper*

We were immensely lucky with the weather. High pressure dominated the weather pattern over the next week, and we found out later that this was the best weather in 100 years. Though extremely cold, it the weather was stable, and we climbed every day. There were plenty of walls with fantastic mixed lines, so we realized our dream of establishing modern mixed and drytooling routes without bolts in an alpine environment.

The faces are similar to the

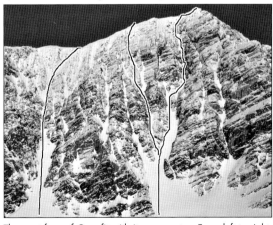

The west face of Ceresfjt with its new routes. From left to right: Norwegian, Slovenian, Northern Siesta.   *Robert Jasper*

Robert Jasper on Deutsch Slowenische Freundschaft.
Markus Stofer

north faces in the Alps, and almost all are virgin and circa 900m high. But we were so far out there that whenever the plane flew overhead toward the North Pole it kindled human warmth and a desire for civilization.

We were guests in the kingdom of the polar bears and we protected our camp with an alarm fence including a gun. We realized that this wasn't a game when we discovered fresh frying-pan sized footprints on the glacier close to our base camp. Luckily they led down and back out to the fjord. It seems climbers are less interesting than fat seals down on the ice pack.

Our complete expedition team was Anderj Erceg, Grega Kresal, and Boris and Klemen Zupanc from Slovenia; Markus Stofer from Switz-erland; and me from Germany. All routes were climbed alpine style without bolts and first ascended from the ground up. Only friends, nuts and pegs were used for protection.

The following are the first ascents put up by Markus Stofer and myself: Chadwickrüggen, northern foresummit, ca 1,600m, north face, "Knut" (600m, M5), possible first ascent (descent via east face to southern col 500m 40–45°), April 17; Ceresfjt, 1,677m (N 79°08.166', E 016°55.662'), west face, "Northern Siesta" (750m, M6), (descent from summit circa 500m east along the crest, down S face 40° to glacier, then west to the col, down west face 45°), April 19; Perriertoppen, 1,717m (N 79°09.237', E016°46.763'), south face, "Ich möchte kein Eisbär sein" (900m, M7), (descent across summit west-southwest to foresummit, then down to col, continue down east couloir 600m, 40–45°), April 20; Chadwickrüggen, 1,641m (N 79°05.787', E 016°47.890'), east face, "Polar Pow(d)er (700m, M6), (descent from main summit down via the S couloir 700m, 45°), April 22; "Triangle" NW Face, "Deutsch Slowenische Freundschaft" (450m, M7), (descent from main summit, abseil ca 80m down via north face into gully, then descend 400m 45°), by Andrej Erceg and me.

ROBERT JASPER, *Germany*

Atomfjella Mountains, new Slovenian routes. This was my third Svalbard expedition. There were so many things I had to learn about Arctic logistical problems and the secrets of these cold mountains. The experience you gain in Svalbard is unique, and my knowledge from other parts of the world just didn't work here in the beginning. As a matter of fact, at the end of the second expedition (2006) we climbed a very good route, The Partner (600m, M6+, Kresal-Zupanc). With that route I realized that the Atomfjella Mountains were worth coming back for to try the hardest needles.

It's true that the rock is usually quite bad around Spitsbergen, which is the main island of the Svalbard Archipelago, but there is one place where it's hard to the bone. This is Atomfjella. A little copy of the Alps. The place in one word is… amazing! Mixed climbing, which is usually a combination of snow and extremely hard rock with good drytooling cracks, can be awesome. A lot of peaks are still awaiting their first ascents, and even though people mostly think that Svalbard is a flat land, some of it is extremely steep. There are literally hundreds of walls facing all directions. The painful thing about climbing in Atomfjella is the temperature. I had never experienced such constant cold in over 23 years of climbing all around the world. When you're moving, climbing or skiing, it's still OK, but staying in your tent is sometimes pure torture. Bring only the best and warmest equipment!

The Slovenian part of the team (Andrej Erceg, Boris and Klemen Zupanc, and me) climbed 10 new routes. When we were not climbing, we were skiing excellent lines down numerous couloirs. We made roughly 15 first descents on

Little Bears Are Dancing. *Gregor Kresal*

skis. For our hardest climb we had to attack the so-called Arctic Needle three times. On the second try, after 12 hours of climbing, we had to stop just five meters from the top. The blizzard was simply too strong. We left some knifeblades and copperheads on the last pitch and were finally able to free the entire route a few days later. The top was so sharp we couldn't even stand on it. And the last two meters of rock were totally unstable, so we just put our hands on the top and that was it. Crazy climbing, extraordinary landscape! We all climbed in alpine style, without leashes and without placing bolts.

Partner. *Gregor Kresal.*

Our Slovenian routes: Arctic Needle, ca 1,450m, "The Little Bears Are Dancing" (500m, M7+, 90°), A. Erceg and G. Kresal, May 3; The Ridge Pallas—Ceres, ca 1,550m, "Besnica" (600m, M6), B. and K. Zupanc, April 27; "Mirkos Route" (600m, M5), B. & K. Zupanc, April 20; Chadwick Ryggen North, ca 1,580m, "Mis Usate" (600m, M5), G. Kresal and K. Zupanc, April 24; Ceres Fjellet, 1,677m, "Rocket Men" (750m, M4), A. Erceg and G. Kresal, April 19; Chadwick Ryggen Central, 1,641m, "Bulls Eggs" (800m, M4), A. Erceg, May 2; Broad Peak, ca 1,600m, "Kapucinsky" (700m, M4+), A. Erceg. May 1; "Bulldozer" (850m, M4), G. Kresal and B. Zupanc, May 2; "Sunny Couloir" (600m, III+/M), G. Kresal and B. & K. Zupanc, April 18; Pallas Fjellet, "Couloir Ideal" (700M, M3), G. Kresal, April 23.

GREGOR KRESAL, *Slovenia (adapted from www.planetmountain.com)*

Kyrgyzstan

TIEN SHAN

Jamantau and Fergana ranges, crossings and first ascents. On the 5th of July Katya Ananyeva, Dmitry Martynenko, and I left Osh, heading to explore the Jamantau and southern Fergana ranges. Neither place had any record of previous climbing activity, even during Soviet time. After a day-long drive from Osh, we started our trek from the small village of Jergetal. Hiking from west to east along the northern side of the Jamantau Range we acclimatized by climbing the snowy peak Chontash East (4,553m, N 40°54'59.64", E 74°25'48.60"), approaching the upper slopes via the small glacier coming through the gate between rock walls (III, 50–60°, Russian 3A). The bergschrund was still filled with snow. We tired of waiting for good weather under challenging Mt. Kamasu, but several days later we climbed rocky Mt. Kremen (4,351m, N 40°54'36.24", E 74°39'17.70") via the broad east ridge. This day-long route had a single 5.9 crux, with the rest rated 5.5/5.6. We had to belay the first four pitches up to the crux, and then moved simultaneously, placing pro every 10–20 meters. We descended along the same east ridge. All the mountains in the Jamantau Range are composed of good rock with a rough surface. The peaks are in the 4,500–4,800m range, with climbing starting around 3,700–3,900m. There are lots of small glaciers and smooth ice tongues, providing numerous moderate (50–75°) routes to the summits from their northern sides.

The northwest view of unclimbed Mt. Kamasu in the Jamantau Range. *Dmitry Shapolov*

Climbing one of them took Dmitry half a day. Eight pitches of 60–70° ice, followed by big crevasses, led two of us to the broad summit of Peak Ak-Jaman (4,488m, N 40°54'24.78", E 74°49'43.20"). One more hour of walking east down the scree slopes, and we were back to our tent. The southern side of the range doesn't have glaciers, instead consisting of rock faces and extensive fields of scree. The name "Jamantau" comes from the great difficulties of crossing seemingly simple passes. The valleys become narrow and canyon-like in the middle, while their lower parts are wide, flat, and green, with occasional summer yurts of Kyrgyz, happy to ply anybody with *kumis* (fermented mare's milk) until delirium sets in. After crossing the Jamantau Range, we found ourselves in the vast expanse of the Arpa Valley. We had to walk south for 50km to reach the Torugart-Too. As it sits near the border between Kyrgyzstan and China, a special "frontier spirit" makes the local population less friendly to visitors. Even with valid papers from the Kyrgyz border authorities, we had to argue for two hours with locals to continue farther. The mountains in the southern part of the Fergana Range consist of brittle schist, producing

Unclimbed peak 4,669m in the Torugart-Too, as viewed from the north. *Dmitry Shapolov*

large fields of scree and making rock-climbing out of the question. Luckily, there are lots of glaciers of different steepness and size, due to moist air masses regularly coming from the west. (We had rain every second day.) Standing on a crest of the range, one sees green hills of waist-deep grass on one side and brown dry desert of the Arpa Valley on other side. Profuse vegetation makes an unused trail soon disappear. We climbed only two summits here, the first being Peak 4,818m (on the Russian military map). The climb along the east ridge was an unroped walk in knee-deep snow, deposited the day before. We named the peak Haokan North (4,848m by GPS, N 40°32'51.84", E 74°37'26.70"). Then we approached Peak 4,893, which apparently is the highest in the Fergana Range and, according to a geographic encyclopedia, is named Uch-Seit. The glaciers were big and fat, reminding us of the Zaalay Range. We set up camp at the base of the icy north face (4,350m). There was a bridge over the bergschrund, then a strip of rocks that kept us from getting lost in the

View to the northwest from the summit of Peak Haokan, after fresh snowfall. The main crest of the Fergana Range runs from the left. *Dmitry Shapolov*

fog while we climbed seven pitches of 70° ice alongside it. The upper ridge was not steep, but crevassed, and I managed to fall through before reaching the corniced summit of Uch-Seit

302   THE AMERICAN ALPINE JOURNAL, 2008

(4,905m, N 40°42'26.04", E 74°21'14.10"). After crossing the Fergana Range by an easy pass (Russian 1B) to the north of Uch-Seit, we had to reach well-populated Oital Valley. It took five days and involved another two passes, and we built a suspension rope-traverse over the Karakulja River and a driftwood raft to cross Lake Kulun, whose rocky banks are too steep for walking. The raft held no more than two people, so we pulled it in shifts, with occasional rock

The makeshift raft in which they navigated Lake Kulun for the most harrowing part of the 26-day, 300km journey. *Dmitry Shapolov*

climbing up to 5.7 or swimming in 10°C water where the rocky banks overhung. This 5km took us a whole day and was the most difficult and scary passage in the entire 26-day, 300km journey.

DMITRY SHAPOVALOV, *AAC*

TORUGART-TOO

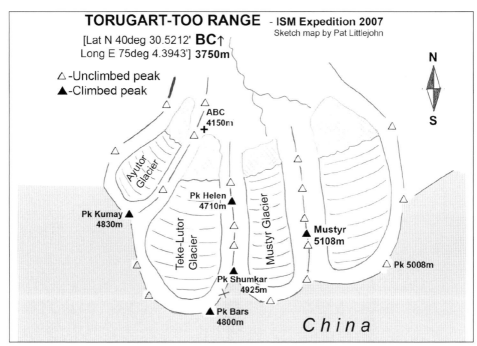

TORUGART-TOO RANGE - ISM Expedition 2007
Sketch map by Pat Littlejohn
[Lat N 40deg 30.5212' **BC↑**
Long E 75deg 4.3943'] **3750m**

△ -Unclimbed peak
▲ -Climbed peak

ABC 4150m +

N
S

Ayutor Glacier

Pk Helen 4710m ▲

Mustyr Glacier

Pk Kumay ▲ 4830m

Teke-Lutor Glacier

Mustyr ▲ 5108m △

△ Pk 5008m

Pk Shumkar 4925m

Pk Bars 4800m ▲

China

The central region of the Torugart-Too, as visited by the ISM party in September. *Pat Littlejohn*

Mustyr (5,108m), first climbed by Harford and Littlejohn. The central summit is the highest. *Barney Harford*

Piks Shumkar (4,925m, Falcon), Helen (4,710m), Bars (4,800m, Snow Leopard), Pik Kumay (Vulture, 4,830m), first ascents. Time flies. This was the International School of Mountaineering (ISM)'s 14th expedition to the Tien Shan, and it was as great as ever. This time we visited two virtually untouched areas, the Torugart-Too range, right beside the Torugart Pass into China, and the Western At Bashi, a very accessible range little more than a day's drive from Kyrgyzstan's capital city, Bishkek.

Torugart exceeded all expectations. On a map of the Tien Shan the range appears tiny, but it is nearly the size of the Swiss Valais, being 35km from end to end (and that's just the glaciated bits, not the "foothills" to either side, which contain many respectable peaks). The highest mountain in the range, and the glacier beneath it, have the Kyrgyz name of Mustyr, which means "snow pasture," a nice insight into the way local herdsmen perceive the mountains.

Access was easy compared to most previous trips. Base camp was just one hour's drive from the main road, and ABC three hour's walk above this. There were three glaciers we could reach easily, and plenty of superb objectives to keep us busy. Helen, Max, and I made a first recce to 5,108m Mustyr. We climbed a long snow/ice couloir for 400m before the altitude made us gasp a bit and forced a retreat. Next day was poor weather, but while some of us made an exhausting exploratory trek to the glacier to the east, Vladimir and Leif [all last names supplied near end of report] explored the next glacier to the west (Teke-Lutor) and climbed a good peak—Pik Shumkar (4,925m)—the first success of the trip.

Spurred by Vladimir's enthusiasm for this glacier, Max, Barney, Helen, and I made an early start next day to climb a neighboring peak, but after two hours climbing to a col, we looked the ridge above and saw that we had greatly underestimated the difficulties. On the other side of the col was a rocky peak that looked hard but shorter, so we attempted it instead. After three difficult pitches we succeeded on Pik Helen (AD+).

Next day two teams set off in different directions: Vladimir, Leif, and Pete to attempt a peak at the head of Teke-Lutor, and Barney and I for a more serious attempt on Mustyr (Helen and Max fancying a rest day). However, Pete, who had been feeling under the weather from the start, took a turn for the worse and retreated to base camp to recover from feverish symptoms. Vlad and Leif were also turned back after exciting ice climbing, but thanks to lucky route-finding and snow conditions that were just safe enough, Barney and I emerged exhausted on the summit of Mustyr at around midday. This was a fantastic peak and among the six best I have climbed in the Tien Shan over 14 expeditions.

Next day Vlad, Leif, and Helen climbed the big snow peak at the head of Teke-Lutor and were rewarded with an amazing sight: snow leopard tracks crossing the col! Some of these even continued to the summit. We have seen snow leopard tracks on just one other expedition. That settled the name for the first human ascent of the peak: Pik Bars, 4,800m (*bars* is Kyrgyz for "snow leopard".)

The priority now was to get down to BC and do something with Pete, who had recovered somewhat but had now suffered a retinal hemorrhage in one eye, causing a disconcerting blind spot. Despite this he had explored the glacier above BC and found a possible route up the big peak at the head of it. So in the morning we persuaded Natasha, our cook, to make a very early breakfast, and by 6 a.m. Pete, Max, Barney, and I were heading for the peak we later named Pik Kumay, 4,830m. It was a great effort by Pete. The summit was covered in footprints, which baffled us until we saw what had made them: a massive vulture!

There were wonderful-looking limestone crags above base camp, and we debated staying to climb for a day, but the lure of the next area, At Bashi, proved too strong and we were soon on the road again. [The At Bashi report is below—Ed.]

A list of first ascents in the Torugart-Too made by Max Gough, Helen Griffin, Barney Harford, Leif Iversen, Vladimir Komissarov, Pat Littlejohn, and Peter Mounsey:

Pik Shumkar (Falcon, 4,925m): northwest flank to north col, ridge to summit, PD, Iversen-Komissarov.

Pik Helen (4,710m): snow/ice couloir on west side to south col, steep couloir up buttress to summit, AD+, Gough-Griffin-Harford-Littlejohn.

Mustyr (Peak of the Snow Pasture, 5,108m): long couloir on west side to base of south ridge of south summit, long traverse north at ca 4,800m to snow/ice, AD, Harford-Littlejohn.

Pik Bars (Snow Leopard, 4,800m): to northeast col from Teke-Lutor Glacier, then snow/ice slope to easy summit ridge, PD+, Griffin-Komissarov-Littlejohn.

Pik Kumay (Vulture, 4,830m): from Ayutor gain northwest col, then snow ridge to first rock summit, second (highest) summit gained with more difficulty, PD (first summit), AD+ (second summit), Gough-Harford-Littlejohn-Mounsey.

PAT LITTLEJOHN, *Alpine Club*

Little Sister (4,206m), Middle Sister (4,341m), Big Sister (4,492m), Zeus (4,747m), Daisy (4,239m), Snow King (4,580m), first ascents; Rock Dragon (4,597m), attempt. Andy Barret from the U.K. and I from Cyprus arrived in Kyrgyzstan on September 23, hoping to explore the far west corner of the Western Kokshaal-Too Range, a region that climbers had not visited. But when we meet with our logistics provider in Bishkek (ITMC), we learned that there was no way to know if we would find horses when we reached the end of the 4x4 road, three days' walk from the valley we wanted to visit.

We spoke with Vladimir Komissarov, the president the Federation of Alpinism and Rock Climbing of the Kyrgyz Republic, as well as being president of the Association of the Central Asia Tour Operators. He had just returned from the first expedition to climb in Torugart-Too, on the border with China [see Pat Littlejohn's report, above]. He gave us lots of useful information about this range. We didn't want to spend too much of our limited time carrying gear to base camp, so we changed our plans to Torugart, with its easier approach.

Next morning, armed with an old Russian map (the only map of the area) that we borrowed from Vladimir, we loaded our powerful Russian 4x4 van with loads of food, gear, and

Base camp in the Torugart, with Mustyr on the left and mostly unnamed peaks. *Constantinos Andreou*

Looking from the west, from left to right: Little Sister (4,206m), Middle Sister (4,341m), and Big Sister (4,747m), all climbed in October. *Constantinos Andreou*

vodka, and left the capital with our good driver Alexander. After 30 minutes of driving we had our first breakdown, but Alexander didn't look worried, repaired the van in an hour, and had us on the move again. After three days and a cocktail of breakdowns, off-road driving, river crossings, dust, bad weather, and a big navigation exercise, we drove our 4x4 van up to 3,652m in a big valley on the north side of the range, with beautiful views of the Torugart peaks.

The weather was bad the next day, so we took the opportunity to acclimatize and plan our climbs for the next few days. Although the range is 35km long, only the glaciers in the center of the range had been explored by the previous expedition. This left the east and west sides untouched, with lots of unnamed and unclimbed summits to have a go at. Next morning we woke to a perfect blue sky. We grabbed our gear and walked up a peak close to BC on the east side of the valley. We went up the lower west slopes to get on the north ridge, which was a nice snow-covered ridge (up to 40°) running down from the summit of Peak 4,206m, which we named Little Sister (PD).

Full of energy from our first success, we made an attempt the next day on the north face of Peak 4,597m, west of BC, but we underestimated the difficulties, and after reaching 4,200m, turned back, as the climbing was getting harder than what we were ready for.

On October 1 we did a fast traverse of two peaks southeast of base camp. After crossing the frozen river on the east side of the valley, we climbed the west face of the first one, which was hard work in deep snow (40°). We reached the end of the north ridge that runs between

The north face of Rock Dragon (4,597m), which was attempted twice, reaching the 4,300m level on the north ridge. *Constantinos Andreou*

Little Sister and this peak. From this point we climbed the last rock section to the 4,341m summit of Middle Sister (AD). Despite clouds and wind, we then raced over to the summit of peak 4,467m, Big Sister (AD-).

After a much-needed rest day, on October 3 we walked to an unnamed dry glacier southwest of BC. On the east side of the glacier we discovered rocky peaks with amazing limestone formations, and at the head we found a beautiful snow-covered mountain that was waiting to be climbed. We started up a big 40°–50° gully running down the north ridge, and then worked our way up rock, snow, and ice, to 50°, to the summit of 4,747m Peak Zeus (AD). From this summit we had views west and south that unveiled a sea of unclimbed peaks.

A big storm consumed the next three days. During the storm we spent most of our time holding up our cheap Chinese tent, using our bodies to stop it from breaking in the strong winds. On the afternoon of October 6 the weather improved, and Andy left tent-holding duties to me, while he made a fast ascent of a 4,239m mountain close to camp that he named Daisy (F).

The next day the weather improved, and we went east into a big unnamed valley and then south into a small valley, with Little Sister and Middle Sister on the west side and Big Sister at the south end. On the east side was a nice snow peak with a long north ridge. We found a big gully that took us to 4,000m on the ridge, which we followed to the summit of Snow King, 4,580m (PD). From the top we had views east into an unnamed valley that was full of superb snow peaks.

On October 8 we made another attempt on the 4,597m peak looming over base camp, which by now we had named Rock Dragon. This time we attempted the north ridge. A 40° gully led us to the ridge at 4,100m. We tried to climb the ridge to the summit, but bad limestone got worse as we moved higher. The climbing was not hard (VD-S), but loose and unprotectable. We reached 4,300m, before deciding that the remaining ridge was too dangerous. We then said bye-bye to the amazing Torugart Range and left for the bars and cuisine of Bishkek.

CONSTANTINOS ANDREOU, *Cyprus*

AT BASHI

Topoz (Yak, 4,600m), Inek (4,560m), first ascents. On the drive from the Torugart-Too [see Littlejohn report, above] to At Bashi, we visited one of the most important historic sites in Kyrgyzstan: the Tash Rabat Caravanserai, a fortified "castle" high in the mountains. I was surprised to discover that it is located beside the most spectacular cliffs (up to 400m) I have yet seen at

Topozt (4,600m), the "Matterhorn" of the Orto Kaindy Valley in the At Bashi, climbed by Gough-Harford-Little-john. *Pat Littlejohn*

lower altitudes in Kyrgyzstan; one day this will be an important rock climbing destination.

A friend of mine, Andrew Wielochowski, had taken a novice group to climb in the western At Bashi just before our visit; otherwise there are no records of any mountaineering there. The peaks are lower, never reaching 5,000m, but the range is extensive, 100km from end to end. Our approach lay up a valley called Orto Kaindy, where Andrew had spotted an amazing "Matterhorn-like" peak that was too difficult for his team to attempt. We hired horses to get our gear up to a beautiful advanced base camp on a pasture below the glacier, overlooked by the awesome bulk of Topoz (the "Matterhorn"). A herd of semi-wild horses grazed around our camp, to complete this perfect cameo of mountaineering in Kyrgyzstan.

Our first attempt on Topoz was an exciting traverse over pinnacles on the south ridge, but we arrived at the summit dome too late in the day to attempt it. The following day a mysterious wind sprang up, building to gale force at times and threatening the tents, though all the time the sky remained clear. After 36 hours the wind simply died away. This meant we could make another attempt, this time via the west flank of the peak, which proved faster and got us to the summit dome by 11:30 a.m. An hour of rock climbing, and we were on top, gazing out at endless unclimbed summits receding into the distance to east and west, promising great future adventures.

On our last day at ABC Vlad and Leif climbed a nice little peak next to Topoz (Inek, 4,560m), while the rest of us read books in the sun, and then it was back to Naryn for sauna, feasting, and folk music.

First ascents in the At Bashi (2007) by Max Gough, Helen Griffin, Barney Harford, Leif Iversen, Vladimir Komissarov, Pat Littlejohn, and Peter Mounsey:

Topoz (Yak, 4,600m): south ridge to summit dome (traversing towers), then south face of summit dome, or summit dome by west flank and couloir, AD+ by south ridge, AD by west flank, Gough-Harford-Littlejohn.

Inek (4,560m): glacier ascent to Mamalik Pass, east scree and rock ridge to summit, PD, Iversen-Komissarov.

PAT LITTLEJOHN, *Alpine Club*

AK SAI – ALA ARCHA

Pik Box (4,242m), central buttress of east face, new route. Pik Box is popular for climbing. There are two classic routes: 4A on the northern wall (Aytbaeva, 1956), and 5B "The Balloon" (Mikhaylov, 1997) on the left side of the northern wall. In 15 hours of non-stop climbing, Vitalius Chepelenko and I ascended a new route on the eastern wall on September 16, proposed a difficulty rating of 4B. The vertical gain is 700m, and the length of the climb is 1,300m.

> IVAN PUGACHEV, *Kyrgyzstan, adapted from www.mountain.ru*

The new Chepelenko-Pugachev Route on the east face of Pik Box. *Ivan Pugachev*

WESTERN KOKSHAAL-TOO

Kizil Asker, southeast face, new route. Mikhail Mikhailov, Alexander Ruchkin, and I began climbing on September 5 and finished our two-day descent from the summit on September 14. We climbed in alpine style and mostly free, though we used aid on the overhanging sections. The wall itself consists of three bulwarks. The lowest is the simplest, with a grade of about 5A/5B. We climbed an ice couloir with no places to put a tent and had to chop into the ice to make a bivouac ledge. The second bulwark overhangs, with an average steepness of about 93 degrees. Between the second and the third bulwarks, instead of the expected nice ledge, we came across an ice "knife." The top of the wall—vertical monolithic granite—cannot be climbed directly. The average steepness of the route was 70–75°. We rated the 1,500m, 30-pitch route Russian 6B. The descent slope was dangerous from avalanches. To belay or rappel, we dug pits and fixed our ropes from buried sacks.

Overall, we were lucky with the weather. We had two or three days of comparatively bad weather and one whole day of sitting in camp, but otherwise it was fine. It was very cold at night. When it thawed in the mornings and in the afternoons, ice balls flew down. The rock on this wall is monolithic, with no loose stones.

The peaks here are wonderfully compact. In one tight area there are 8–10 mountains higher than 5,000m, and only one has a name—Kizil Asker. There are routes for all tastes: Himalayan, alpine, snow, ice, rock. However, the summer season is short--from the middle of August to the end of September, only 1.5 months. Before this the weather is unstable; two days of good weather in a row are nearly unheard of. Another feature of the region is its difficulty of access when the roads become impassable. The upper part of the valley is covered with grass growing on loam; when it gets wet, you cannot move except by helicopter.

> ALEXANDER ODINTSOV, *Russia; adapted from www.mountain.ru*

Kizil Asker's great southeast face, showing the line of its new route by Mikhail Mikhailov, Alexander Odintsov, and Alexander Ruchkin. Several attempts have been made on the spectacular ice couloir on the left [p. 349, *AAJ 2003*]. *Alexander Ruchkin*

Malitskovo Glacier; Pik 5,055m, Pik 4,975m, first ascents; Pik 4,995m, attempt. After a two-day drive from Bishkek into the Kokshaal region, Dave Swinburne and I were dropped off on July 20, having arranged to be collected at the same point on August 8. During this time we made two ascents of new peaks at the head of the Malitskovo Glacier. The peaks are marked 5,055m and 4,975m on the American Alpine Club's Kyrgyzstan map, but our GPS recorded 5,061m and 5,100m, respectively. Both peaks provided simple ascents of PD in grade. We found more interesting AD climbing during an attempt upon Pik 4,995m. The final summit ridge held unstable slush-like snow, and we found it unsafe to continue. We then spent several days on the adjacent Nalivkin Glacier. Several inches of fresh snow and daily squalls prevented further attempts.

Night temperatures rarely fell below freezing. With lots of sun, this made for poor snow conditions. We advise that a later period would be better for climbing in this area. This is supported by other trip reports, but we were governed by our work holidays.

STEWART HOWARD, *U.K.*

Camp on the Kizil Asker "knife," where the team had expected to find good ledges. *Alexander Ruchkin*

Nalivkin Glacier, Malitskovo Glacier; Pik 4,828m (Sigma Peak), first ascent; Piks 5,055m (Hidden Peak), 4,975m (Snow Dome), new routes; other ascents. We chose the western Kokshaal Too region for its potential for first ascents. Also called "The Forbidden Range," this was a closed military region until the late 1990s, when the first western expeditions arrived. It is still under military control, and permission to access the area has to be obtained from the military. Consequently, very few expeditions have visited this place, and many peaks remain unclimbed. We were given a map by ITMC, indicating climbed and unclimbed peaks in the area we intended to visit.

We drove with two vehicles, a 6-wheel drive bus and a smaller truck, from Bishkek via Naryn to the western Kokshaal Too Range. The trucks brought us to the slopes north of the Aytali River, opposite the Nalivkin Glacier, where we set up base camp next to a 3,860m lake.

The Fersmana and Malitskovo glaciers from the northern slopes of the Aytali Valley, more or less where the South African team parked their trucks. *Donovan van Graan*

Looking from Pik 4,968m to Pik 5,611m, with Byeliy, a.k.a. Grand Poobah behind.. *Ulrike Kiefer*

The view from Pik 5,055m (Hidden Peak) to Pik 4,975m (Snow Dome). *Ulrike Kiefer*

Patrick Black, Robert Cromarty, Linda Daffue, Willem Daffue, Greg Devine, Carl Fatti, Donovan van Graan, Dean van der Merwe, and I split into three groups, each exploring a different valley and assessing climbing possibilities there.

Patrick, Dean, Robert, and I went up the Nalivkin Glacier to look at Pik 5,055m, an apparently unclimbed peak high in the valley. We identified two possible routes, one over the west ridge and summit of 4,968m and the other via easy snow slopes leading from the west to the col between 4,968m and 5,055m. On August 14 Patrick and I climbed over the summit of 4,968m to the summit of 5,055m (Hidden Peak). Dean and Robert chose the other route.

Willem, Linda, and Donovan went into the Malitskovo Glacier basin. They came back confident that both 4,828m and 4,975m could be climbed and possibly 4,996m as well—all unclimbed peaks. On August 14 Willem, Linda, Donovan, and Carl climbed 4,828m (Sigma Peak). The point marked 4,975m turned out to be just a mark on the map. The summit lies south of this mark. On August 26 the same group summited this peak (Snow Dome) and measured its height as 5,105m by GPS. After a second reconnaissance to 4,996m we discarded our plans to climb it. There was not enough snow coverage to allow reasonable access, and the ascent seemed to involve some hectic rock climbing.

The third group, consisting of Carl and Greg, reported that the Fersmana and Sarychat glaciers had retreated far to the south, and the lower valleys were framed by sheer rock cliffs with no reasonable access to the summits.

Toward the end of the expedition Patrick and I walked far eastward, past the confluence of the Aytali and Sarychat rivers, in hope of being able to climb what we called "The Coloss," a massive cluster of peaks 4,671m, 4,879m, and 4,849m high, but we didn't have time. However, an ascent by the northeast ridge seems quite possible.

The following peaks were also climbed by the team: 5,156m, Obzhorniy, by Ulrike and Patrick via the northeast ridge; 5,156m, Obzhorniy, by Dean, Robert, Willem, Linda, Carl, and Donovan via the glacier and snow slopes to the north; 4,850m, Metel, by Greg, Dean, Robert, Willem, Linda, Carl, and Donovan; 4,656m, Peak Macciato, by Dean; and 4,578m, by Dean.

Pik 5,156m (Obzhorniy) at sunrise. *Ulrike Kiefer*

River crossings were major obstacles, especially in the afternoon. It was not easy to find a safe passage at times, and we had to help each other across. The weather, though, was kind; bad weather spells only lasted for only short times. The snow was firm and enjoyable early in the day and turned soft only after 11 a.m. We encountered deep, soft snow only on Snow Dome.

The mountain slopes are littered with ibex and Marco Polo sheep horns. We were privileged to watch ibex a number of times. We also saw eagles, lammergeyers, hundreds of marmots, and tracks of what we believe to be a wolf.

Happy with our achievements, we returned to Bishkek on the 25th. We left records of our ascents with ITMC, whose president is also president of the Kyrgyz alpine club. Later we learned of the British party [Stewart Howard and Dave Swinburne, above] who had been to the area just before us. They reported having climbed 4,975m (5,105m) and 5,055m, both from the Malitskovo Glacier. Thus, two of our "first ascents" turned out not to be such. Still, our two routes up 5,055m are new routes, approaching the mountain from a different valley. This discovery came as quite a shock. [Howard and Swinburne had returned just days before Kiefer's group left, and they had not yet sent their report to ITMC when Kiefer returned—Ed.] May this serve as a warning to others who are planning to scale an unclimbed mountain: Not even the best local information is necessarily correct. May this also serve as a reminder to pass on climbing achievements to local authorities, so they can keep the record straight.

ULRIKE KIEFER, *South Africa*

Central Kokshaal-Too, history prior to 2007. With the eastern (Dankova) and western (Kizil Asker) sectors of the Western Kokshaal-too having now been explored by a number of non-CIS climbing parties (beginning with a French-German team to the Dankova region in 1996 and an Anglo-American-German party to the Kizil Asker area in 1997), several recent teams have been investigating the little known central section. Exploration of this compact area of dramatic peaks along the Kyrgyzstan-China border has been dominated by Pat Littlejohn and his International School of Mountaineering (ISM) expeditions. In 2001 a splinter group from one of Littlejohn's expeditions traveled east to the valley leading up to the Malitskovo Glacier and climbed a 4,850m peak east of the entrance. Littlejohn was back in 2006, establishing a base camp below the Navlikin Glacier to the east, from where he hoped to attempt the first ascent of Pik Byeliy (Grand Poohbah, 5,697m). Byeliy has only seen one serious attempt. In 2000 Jerry Dodrill, Mike Libecki, and Doug and Jed Workman traveled to the Chinese side of the range and climbed 600m up the southwest ridge before being stopped by a lightning storm close to the summit. In 2005 the New Zealand-based team of Paul Knott, Grant Piper, and Graham Rowbotham hoped to climb it from the Fersmana Glacier east of the Malitskovo, but could see no safe lines on the northeast, east, or southern flanks. In 2006 Littlejohn's team tried to reach unclimbed Pik 5,611m, immediately north of Byeliy, but were stopped by heavy snowfall. Other members climbed peaks lower down the Malitskovo and made attempts on Piks 4,995m and 4,975m. On 4,995m they reached a forepeak but were stopped by the dangerously cor- niced connecting ridge, while on 4,975m they were turned back at ca 4,900m by the threat of avalanche.

September is generally considered the best month to climb in this area due to more stable weather, lower temperatures, and firmer snow conditions. Howard and Swinburne, judging by their own experiences, would also advocate September as the best time to visit the range.

LINDSAY GRIFFIN, *Mountain INFO, www.climbmagazine.com*

AK-SHIRAK RANGE

Pik 150th Anniversary of the British Alpine Club (4,836m), and four other first ascents; ski-moun- taineering. In 2006 I was asked to organize a ski-mountaineering expedition as part of the cele- brations of the 150th anniversary of the Alpine Club planned for 2007. In 2003 and 2006 I visited the Ak-Shirak Range in the Central Tien Shan and saw that there was plenty of scope for more exploratory mountaineering. Accordingly, on April 7, 2007 five Alpine Club members set

Ascending the Petrov Glacier on the way to "Pic 150th Anniversary of the British Alpine Club," with unclimbed peaks in view. *Dave Wynne-Jones*

Enjoying fine views from Pik 150th Anniversary of the British Alpine Club (4,836m) in the Ak-Shirak. *Dave Wynne-Jones*

out for three weeks in Kyrgyzstan: Stuart Gallagher, Gethin Howells, Adele Long, Gordon Nuttall, and I.

As we approached the Kumtor gold mine, however, I saw that conditions were hugely different from what I'd found in 2003. Though early in April, the road was clear, as were most of the slopes below 3,800m. Fortunately, Lake Petrov was still frozen solid, so 40 minutes and 2km after setting foot on the ice, we were setting up Camp 1 on a sandy beach beneath the snout of the Petrov Glacier. Camped at 3,730m, we had gained 2,000m in a five-hour drive; headaches were obligatory.

The next day we struggled up the convoluted glacier to leave a cache, and a day after, on a scout of the glacier, the snow cracked like a pistol as it settled in huge plates beneath us. Camp 2, almost 4,300m, had more stable snow conditions. The next day we mostly skied and occasionally climbed in crampons to a summit at 4,836m. Our first first ascent had to be named "Pik 150th Anniversary of the British Alpine Club" in the fine tradition of Soviet peak names. We then enjoyed carving turns all the way to the foot of the pass.

Our next peak was to the east and surprised us with fresh snow leopard tracks as we climbed up under its southwest face. Ice glinted under the snow, so we abandoned plans to skin up the face and left our skis at an ice boss on the west ridge. Trying to sneak past the ice boss, we found wind-polished armor plating, and we roped up for a short pitch. Higher, we roped again for more ice to the corniced summit at 4,887m. We called it Pik Ak Ilbirs (meaning "snow leopard" in Kyrgyz).

Over the next couple of days we headed east again to climb two more peaks from the pass at the head of the glacier. One was an icy whaleback rising to a narrow fin of snow and rock at the 4,720m summit (Pik Plavnik, or The Fin) from which we could see Khan Tengri and Pobedy looming majestically in the distance. The other was a heavily corniced ridge that dropped off steeply to the north, 4,815m, Pik Solidarnost (because it was the only one that we all got up). From there it was clear that our proposed route, linking several glacier systems, would take us far too low for safety in the prevailing conditions. We decided to break camp and head for the north-facing glacier bays to the south.

However, as we lost height snow conditions became increasingly difficult. We made heavy going of the descent and were lucky to find a good campsite on a medial moraine. Next day, while making an early crossing of the glacier to the south in an attempt on the peak opposite, we found the snow repeatedly collapsing under us with a resounding whump. A serac collapse from the flank of the mountain and plenty of evidence of avalanches from adjacent slopes led us to back off, instead climbing nervously but gradually up to scout the major pass to the east. That night we talked it through and decided we'd pushed our luck with avalanches far enough. The next day only Gethin reached our final summit, a rocky peak east of camp: Pik Mari (named after his mum).

After what had clearly been an exceptionally warm winter, we decided we'd just have to be satisfied with our five first ascents. I called in our transport on the sat-phone for two days hence, and we spent those days getting back down the glacier and across the lake. The mountains, of course, went on looking spectacularly beautiful, and it's clear that there is a lot more ski-mountaineering to do in the Ak-Shirak. Thanks are due to the team for their determination and good fellowship, and to the Mount Everest Foundation and Alpine Club Climbing Fund for financial support.

DAVE WYNNE-JONES, *Alpine Club*

TENGRI TAG

Temasek (4,374m), Singapura I (4,589m/4,550m), Ong Teng Cheong (4,743m), first ascents. The MacCoffee Tien Shan Expedition departed Singapore on July 20, 2005. [This report was filed two years late due to the expedition's exclusive media arrangement— Ed.] We were soon inserted by helicopter onto the Siemienova Glacier at 3,943m. On July 24 we climbed our first peak, 4,374m, via the snowy south-

Singapura I Peak (4,589m by GPS, 4,550m on the map) showing Rozani's Route. *David Lim*

east ridge. The peak lies on the Sigitova ridge, though it is not marked on our map (42°19.42' N 80°3.589' E). We named it Temasek Peak. We believe this is the first virgin peak to be climbed by any Southeast Asian climbers, and we named it after the first name our Singapore island nation was known by, Temasek. The route: Ramses Ridge (Russian 3A/French PD). On July 26 we climbed our second peak, 4,589m (by GPS), marked as 4,550m on our map, by the north face, after negotiating hidden crevasse fields and deep snow. The hardest part was the steep upper section at 55°, where Rozani executed a good lead to the corniced summit (42°18.49' N 80°0.788' E). We named this fairly tough mountain Singapura I Peak as it seemed to present the kind of challenges our nation faces. Rozani's Route (Russian 3A/French PD+). On July 28 we made an abortive attempt on the steep, rocky east face of our third peak, 4,743m. This peak is un-marked on the map, but listed as an unclimbed summit. Loose, dangerous rubble forced a retreat. On July 29 we tried again via the long Siemienova Glacier and Siemienova Pass, and then up the east ridge, reaching the corniced summit at 10:30 a.m. (42°20.188' N 80°0.1644' E). This 4,743m peak is the highest in the vicinity, and we named it Ong Teng Cheong Peak, in honor of our late President Ong. Mr. Ong was the Patron of the 1st Singapore Everest Expedition in 1998, and his support for this mountaineering quest was invaluable. We dubbed the route Wilfred's Ridge (Russian 3A/French PD). We called the aborted route from the east side Rabbit Gully.

DAVID LIM, *Singapore*

Ong Teng Cheong Peak (4,743m), named after the late president of Singapore. *David Lim*

Mohd Rozani on the steep face of Singapura I. *David Lim*

Pakistan

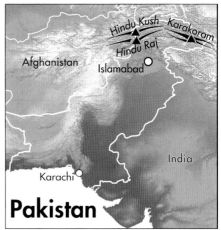

Pakistan

Overview. In 2007 Pakistani authorities received 91 applications to climb various peaks, of which 83 were approved, including 14 applicants who were granted permission to climb two peaks each, one three peaks, and another four peaks. Two expeditions were not granted permission to climb peaks situated close to the war zone near the Siachen Glacier, and six expeditions withdrew their applications. In all, 102 attempts on 22 permitted peaks were made, and 201 climbers, including 13 from Pakistan, were successful.

Eight climbers from a 26-member Austrian expedition, including the leader, Gerfried Göschl, reached the summit of Broad Peak to celebrate the 50th anniversary of the peak's first ascent, also by Austrians. Overall, 19 of 25 expeditions were successful on Broad Peak, putting 77 climbers on the summit.

Unlike the previous year, 2007 was successful for climbers on K2. Twenty-nine climbers from eight expeditions reached the top (out of 130 total climbers). The successful climbers included 11 members of the Russian expedition to climb a new route on the west wall. In contrast, it was an unsuccessful year on Gasherbrum II, as only one out of 14 expeditions reached the summit. There was one casualty on this peak, Jiri Danek, a member of the Czech expedition, who died after being hit by an avalanche. This avalanche affected much of the climbing route, and, when no safe route could be found, other expeditions abandoned their attempts. On Gasherbrum I, meanwhile, six of 10 expeditions were successful, putting 27 climbers on top. All five expeditions attempting Nanga Parbat were successful, putting 17 of 32 climbers on top without any accidents. There were 11 expeditions to Spantik Peak, of which 10 returned successfully, putting 44 climbers on top.

Two of this year's climbs are featured earlier in this *Journal*: the first ascent of Pumari Chhish South by two French climbers, Yannick Graziani and Christian Trommsdorff, and the first ascent of K7 West by an American-Slovenian expedition led by Steven House.

Winter attempts on Broad Peak and Nanga Parbat in 2007–2008 were unsuccessful. Expeditions to all other peaks requiring permits were unsuccessful, including Gasherbrum III and V, K6, Latok I, Khunyang Chhish Main and East, Pamri Sar, Masherbrum, Shispare, Diran, Ultar Sar, Rakaposhi, Beka Brakai, Kampire Dior, and Yeshcook. Some of these attempts are reported below.

SAAD TARIQ SIDDIQI, *Alpine Club of Pakistan*

Discounted peak royalties continue. During 2007 the Pakistan Ministry of Tourism maintained a 50 percent reduction on royalty fees for peak permits, and in November the government announced that these discounts and other concessions would continue in 2008.

The 50 percent discount applies to all peaks above 6,500m; there is no royalty on peaks below 6,500m. Furthermore, in Chitral, Gilgit, and Ghizar the royalty is only 10 percent of the published rate, except for Spantik. During the winter season (December–February), the royalty is only 5 percent of the normal rate. No liaison officer will be required outside of the Baltoro region. The Alpine Club of Pakistan publishes a list of current royalties at www.alpineclub.org.pk/peak_royalties.php.

KARRAR HAIDRI, *Alpine Club of Pakistan*

HINDU RAJ

Karka (6,222m), on the left, and Quinto Peak (5,684m) from the north, looking across the upper Chiantar Glacier. *Tarcisio Bellò*

Four climbers made the first ascent of Peak 5,519m by the north face and east ridge (TD, left), and then descended by the west ridge. The mountain was named Somerset Ski Club Peak after the club donated 8,500 euros to help build an aqueduct in Ghotulti village. *Tarcisio Bellò*

Karka and six other peaks in and near the Chhantir Valley. For the fourth time in 11 years, Franco Brunello led an expedition of the Alpine Club (CAI) Section of Montecchio Maggiore to the Hindu Raj for exploratory mountaineering and trekking. In August they placed base camp at 3,980m, two hours northwest of the village of Daudo Chat, north of Ghotulti in the Chhantir Valley. In addition to Brunello, expedition members Mara Babolin, Tarcisio Bellò, Roberta Bocchese, Andrea Caprara, and Bruno Castegnaro ascended various unclimbed peaks.

Of the expedition's seven ascents, the most difficult was Karka (6,222m). Babolin, Bellò, Bocchese, and Castegnaro climbed this beautiful peak over three days (August 12–14) via ice slopes on the northeast side (ED+), accessed by crossing Amin Pass (5,050m). Bellò returned to make the solo first ascent of Quinto Peak (5,684m, ED-) from the same side of the pass.

The expedition also climbed and proposed names for Aga Khan Peak (5,678m, TD-),

Vicentini Peak (5,750m, AD+), the Red Pillar (4,500m, ED-), and Belvedere Peak (4,520m, PD, possibly climbed before). In addition, they climbed Peak 5,519m (TD) and subsequently auctioned the name to raise money for an aqueduct in Ghotulti. The Somerset Ski Club (Sci Club Somerset) in Turin donated 8,500 euros to name the mountain Somerset Ski Club Peak.

Over four expeditions, Brunello and his teammates have climbed more than 30 peaks in this area of the Hindu Raj; they also have completed a number of innovative treks across high passes. A list of these peaks and their coordinates, along with Brunello's maps and additional photos, is available at the *AAJ* website: www.americanalpineclub.org/pages/page/47. The editors hope to prepare a comprehensive survey of the Italian exploration of this area for the 2009 edition of this *Journal*.

The impressive unclimbed southwest face of Karka (6,222m), at the head of the Chhantir Valley. In the foreground is Quinto Peak (5,684m) on the east side of Amin Pass (5,050m). *Tarcisio Bellò*

DOUGALD MACDONALD, *from reports by Franco Brunello and Tarcisio Bellò*

Chotar Zom (Dasbar Zom, 6,058m), south pillar; Nashran (5,200m), northeast ridge; Pois Chhish (4,400m). Our small French team—Eric Lantz, Didier Rognon, Arnaud Simard, and I, all from the BUC Alpin mountain club—spent July 22 to August 11 in the Dasbar Valley, south of Koyo Zom (6,871m). We explored the area and made three ascents.

Eric and Didier reached the summit of a 5,200m peak above the main valley via the northeast ridge. The climb followed an ice couloir with sections of 70° and ended with a snow ridge; they reached the summit after 800m of ascent. We named the peak Nashran, a combination of the names of our three Pakistani helpers. Nashran is a secondary summit of the beautiful Kachqiant (ca 6,000m), still unclimbed. The same pair later reached the summit of a small rock peak (4,400m) via a 700m

The French route up the south face of the peak they called Chotar Zom (6,058m GPS); they later came to believe this might be Dasbar Zom, climbed in 1968 from the north side by an Austrian team. The two climbers descended by the shadowed couloir just left of their ascent route, with ice up to 70°. *Florian Tolle*

The gorgeous, unclimbed ca 6,000m pyramid of Kachqiant, west of Dhuli Chhish (6,518m). The photo is looking south from Chotar Zom. *Florian Tolle*

face route of 19 pitches up to 5.10. They called the peak Pois Chhish and the route Lady Chatterley.

Didier and I also climbed the south pillar of a peak we called Chotar Zom ("small mountain," as it is far from the biggest in the area). We recorded an altitude of 6,058m on the summit by GPS. Subsequent investigation indicates this peak might be Dasbar Zom, climbed in 1968 by Austrians from the other side. Our climb began at a camp at 4,800m. The technical part consisted of two successive couloirs through loose rock bands, with ice to 55° and mixed rock at 5.4. These led to the upper snow slopes and a long, tiring plod to the top, which we reached at 4:30 p.m. To the north rose Koyo Zom, and all around we saw countless beautiful and technical climbs. Much of the descent took place during the night, with ice up to 70°, and we regained our bivouac at 11 p.m., having been on the go for 22 hours. We graded our route alpine D.

We went on this expedition, a first for all of us, to explore a seldom-visited area and to test our capacities on reasonable mountains while meeting great people. The mountains were not reasonable, but the adventure was great.

Editor's note: Florian Tolle has provided a map and photos of unclimbed peaks in this area. These may be found at the AAJ website: www.americanalpineclub.org/pages/page/47.

FLORIAN TOLLE, *France*

Buni Zom Main, attempt; Buni Zom South; 6MT, first ascent; 6MT West, attempt; Buli Zom, new route on north face and death. I had previously been to the Buni Zom range, northeast of Chitral in the western Hindu Raj, in 2002 and 2004. Our aim was Buni Zom Main (6,551m), but lack of information about the terrain and the route prevented us from reaching the peak's slopes. With the support of the Greek Climbing Federation, I organized an 11-member expedition to return in 2007; an independent climber, Nikiforos Stiakakis, also joined the expedition.

We set our base camp in the Kulakmali area (3,970m), a seven-hour trek west of Rahman village, in mid-July. [A map of this area may be found in *AAJ 2005*, p. 343—Ed.] Above base camp we climbed 100m of steep rock (V-) to gain access to the Khora Borht Glacier, west of the Buni Zom peaks; we put fixed ropes here to help us carry loads to higher camps.

We split into two teams of six, initially attempting the same objectives but one day apart. We set our first camp on the Khora Bohrt Glacier at 4,780m and a second camp at 5,430m, between Buni Zom's main and south peaks. On July 22 the first group returned to base camp and rested for two days.

The line of Vasilis (800m, ED 90°) on the north face of Buli Zom (5,909m). Dimitris Daskalakis and Vasilis Naxakis descended from the ridgeline without going to the unclimbed summit. During the descent, Naxakis fell to his death at the spot marked with an X near the bottom of the face. *Nikolas Kroupis*

Peaks above the southeastern bay of the Khora Bohrt Glacier: (1) The southern shoulder of Buni Zom South (6,220m). (2) 6MT (6,115m), with the northwest face marked. (3) 6MT West (ca 5,900m), with the start of the uncompleted route marked. (4) Bivouac site at 5,125m. *Nikolas Kroupis*

On July 25 we left base camp and reached Camp 2 early in the afternoon. Our plan was to climb the south face, likely by the same route that Dick Isherwood and Joe Reinhard followed in 1979 to make the third ascent of the peak. [Buni Zom was first climbed in 1957 and repeated in 1975 by a Japanese team that climbed the south face directly—Ed.] We started at 1:30 a.m., reached the col between the main and south peaks, and ascended the south face on its right side. At 5,800m we traversed left to a big couloir heading up to the northwest ridge. The avalanche danger increased above 6,000m, and at 9 a.m. we reached the northwest ridge (6,370m), where a giant cornice and unstable snow convinced us to retreat.

On the same day we met the second team, which, hearing our report, decided to attempt Buni Zom South (6,220m). They approached the peak from the northwest until they reached the west ridge at ca 6,050m. Only two members continued due to extreme cold. George Voutiropoulos and Akis Karapetakos summited Buni Zom South at 7 a.m. and enjoyed a magnificent view. The same day all of us returned to base camp.

We now split into smaller groups. George Voutiropoulos and I would attempt unclimbed 6MT (6,115m), while Manolis Mesarchakis, Vaggelis Zekis, and Nikiforos Stiakakis would go for a smaller, pyramid-shaped peak on the ridge west of 6MT, which we called 6MT West (ca 5,900m). Dimitris Daskalakis and Vasilis Naxakis would attempt unclimbed Buli Zom (5,909m).

Early in the morning on July 30 we left for 6MT, climbing past Camp 1 on the Khora Bohrt Glacier to 4,900m, where we headed east to a smaller glacier between Buni Zom South and 6MT. Around 3 p.m. we reached 5,125m and decided to bivouac. On July 31 Mesarchakis, Stiakakis, and

Zekis started their ascent to 6MT West by climbing snow and ice up to 65° toward the west ridge. They reached the ridge at about 5,600m, but rotten rock did not allow belays and they retreated.

On the same day Voutiropoulos and I continued up the glacier to 5,250m and then climbed an icy couloir on the north-northwest face of 6MT, moving together for speed; this couloir began at 45° and gradually increased to about 70°. We reached the north ridge and continued to the unclimbed summit, reaching it at 8 a.m. A large cornice protruded from the summit to the east, so we stopped 3m lower. We descended the steep face by many rappels with our 60m rope. The route was 900m, TD 70°.

On July 29 Naxakis and Daskalakis left base camp for Buli Zom, a peak on the south side of Phargam Gol. Buli Zom has a steep north face, and there is no record of previous ascents. On the first day the two climbers reached the face and bivouacked next to a serac at 5,000m. In the morning they started up the north face via a couloir and then exited to the west to make a long traverse across a 60° slope until they reached a water-ice passage through steep rock. At 5,700m they encountered dangerous fresh snow, so they traversed right again over mixed ground, and then climbed another steep ice pitch to reach the summit ridge at 6 p.m. Although they were very near the summit, they decided to descend while it was still light.

At about 9 p.m., near the middle of their descent, and having already rappelled 10 times, Naxakis didn't anchor himself sufficiently and slipped down the steep, icy slope to his death. Daskalakis continued rappelling to reach a system of crevasses and seracs where the body of our friend must have been lying. Unable to find him, Daskalakis returned to base camp early the next morning. During the next two days everyone in our expedition searched for Vasilis, with the precious help of two climbers from Denmark, Morten Johansen and Carsten Jensen, who had hoped to climb Buni Zom Main's east face. However, his body could not be found. The new route on the north face of Buli Zom is named for our friend: Vasilis (800m, ED 90°). In his memory we are collecting money to finish the school in Phargam village and support it with books, notepads, and salaries for the teachers.

NIKOLAS KROUPIS, *Hellenic Federation of Mountaineering and Climbing*

WESTERN HIMALAYA

NANGA PARBAT RANGE

Nanga Parbat, winter attempt. The Italian Simone la Terra and the experienced Pakistani mountaineer Mehrban Karim attempted Nanga Parbat (8,125m) via the Diamir Face. They reached the standard base camp on December 3 and established Camp 1 on the Kinshofer Route at 6,000m on December 10 in temperatures of –35°C. Strong winter winds were a constant hassle, and during the night of December 21 the base camp kitchen tent blew away with everything in it. At that point la Terra called off the expedition. The Diamir side of Nanga Parbat faces northwest and receives little winter sunshine; the team reported seeing the sun only once in December.

To date there have been several calendar-winter attempts on Nanga Parbat, the best by a Polish expedition to the Diamir Face, where, on February 11, 1997, Krzysztof Pankiewicz and Zbigniew Trzmiel retreated just 250m below the summit with severe frostbite.

LINDSAY GRIFFIN, *MountainINFO Editor, adapted from www.alpinist.com*

KARAKORAM

BATURA MUZTAGH

Baden Sar (5,455m), first ascent; Constanzia Sar (5,902m), first ascent; Har Sar (6,082m), attempt. As coleader of the Baden-Saxon Pamir-Karakoram Expedition 2007, which was supported by the DAV, I had the opportunity to spend time in the region where the Karakoram, Hindu Kush, and Pamir meet, an area whose exploratory history has fascinated me for years. After traveling from Bishkek, Kyrgyzstan, to Kashgar, China, then over Khunjerab Pass into Pakistan, we journeyed through the upper Hunza Valley and

Constanzia Sar (5,902m) is the easternmost peak in the Sakar Sar group. The expedition climbed the southern slopes and east ridge from a camp near the head of the East Sakar Sherab Glacier. The peaks on the right comprise the ridgeline north of Dehli Sang-i-Sar (6,225m). *Peter Metzger*

into the wild and romantic Chapursan Valley as far as Baba Gundi, the starting point of our expedition.

From here we trekked in one long day to our base camp in Buatar, located in the upper Chapursan at ca 4,000m, at the foot of the Chillinji Glacier and the entrance to the Har Valley, adjacent to the Afghan border. Our campsite was surrounded by many unclimbed 5,000m and 6,000m peaks. During the preparation for our expedition we had earmarked elegant 6,082m Har Sar as our first target. (Har Sar is also known Lupsuk Sar, but it is not the same peak as the Lupsuk Sar near Karambar Lake in the Hindu Raj.) Five of my teammates applied themselves to this task, but none was able to climb above 5,300m.

Meanwhile, I devoted myself to my personal goal, the reconnaissance of the practically unknown mountain regions of the Pamir-I-Wakhan. For acclimatization I made dayhikes from base camp to the Chillinji and Koz Yaz glaciers. Favorable conditions presented us at rather short notice with the opportunity to cross into the Wakhan Corridor in Afghanistan by the Irshad Uwin, a 4,963m border pass, which we planned to do in a small group composed of Martin Thaler, a guide, a cook, five porters, two horses with their horseman, and me.

At this time five of our teammates were trying an unnamed 5,455m peak in the extreme northwest corner of Pakistan, at the upper end of the Chapursan Valley. On August 13 Bernd Kern, Peter Metzger, Dr. Andreas Wegener, and Hans Wölcken reached the previously unclimbed summit and named the mountain after their homeland, Baden Sar.

On the 15th our small reconnaissance group left base camp in Buatar to head toward Afghanistan. In optimal weather we crossed the Irshad Uwin and descended the north side of the pass into the Lupsuk Valley. Our guide related to me how in 1935 his grandfather Isabad

Shah had accompanied R.C.F. Schomberg on the same route. The steep cliffs of the Karakoram changed gradually to the gentle slopes of the Pamir. Our route led us farther north to the Wakhan Darya, and then continued, always on the orographic left of the river, as far as Bozai Gumbaz. The first descriptions of these mountainous regions were provided by Chinese pilgrims in the fifth and eighth centuries, on their way to India with the aim of bringing Buddhist knowledge back to China. Marco Polo passed this way, and Britain and Russia squared off here in the Great Game at the end of the 19th century. From a mountaineering standpoint, the Pamir-I-Wakhan is almost virgin territory. Almost nothing has been climbed here since the 1970s.

We had fixed the 23rd of August as the time to rejoin the other members of the expedition in Baba Gundi, a deadline that precluded an extensive exploration of the Wakhan side valleys. In the interim our mountaineers had been active in the Sakar Sar region. On August 19, the Baden Sar team, plus Norbert Schaible, made the first ascent of the most easterly peak in the Sakar Sar group, at the head of the East Sakar Sherab Glacier. They climbed to the east ridge and followed it to the summit, which they named Constanzia Sar (5,902m), after their hometown of Constance.

WOLFGANG HEICHEL, *Germany*

Beka Brakai Chhok, attempt; Wahine (5,820m), first ascent. In June and July 2007, Lydia Bradey and I attempted the first ascent of Beka Brakai Chhok (6,940m) in the Batura massif. Arriving in Pakistan in early June, we spent four days walking into our base camp, situated at the head of the Baltar Glacier. We were accompanied by a cook (Javed), liaison officer/guide (Shulkar Allah Baig), and 35 porters.

By June 25 we had established three camps on Beka Brakai Chhok's south face, the highest on a col at 5,200m. This entailed a lot of moraine bashing and at times less than ideal snow. On June 28 Lydia and I left for our summit attempt. On July 3, after establishing two more camps, we reached a high point at ca 6,000m on a ridgeline beneath a 250m rock buttress. The climbing to that point had involved stretches of deep, unconsolidated snow, steep rock, and ice. We pitched most of the ground between camps 3 and 5, at times hauling the packs. Tent sites for camps 3 and 4 were on steep snow arêtes requiring some digging, but Camp 5 was atop a spacious ice blob attached to the main southeast ridge. At this point we realized we did not have the resources to reach the summit, so we descended to base camp over the next three days.

We were fortunate to share base camp with Italian climbers Lorenzo and Giampaolo Corona,

Lydia Bradey and Pat Deavoll teamed up with brothers Giampaolo and Lorenzo Corona to make a one-day ascent of Wahine (ca 5,820m) from a camp on the West Baltar Glacier. *Giampaolo Corona*

who were also unable to climb their chosen peak. The two teams combined and made the first ascent of a 5,820m peak above the West Baltar Glacier, southwest of Dariyo Sar. We named the peak Wahine. From a camp at ca 5,000m on the glacier, we reached the summit of Wahine in eight hours on July 10. The climbing was predominantly steep ice and snow with some rock. We took six hours to descend.

PAT DEAVOLL, *New Zealand*

Point 5,911m, attempt. During acclimatization for an attempt on Khunyang Chhish, Kazuo Tobita led a five-person team on an attempt on an unnamed 5,911m peak near Kilik Pass. This is northwest of the Karakoram Highway, near the northernmost point of Pakistan. From a base camp in the Kilik Jilga valley on the southeast side of the mountain, climbers reached a snow peak at 5,850m but did not reach the main summit.

TSUNEMICHI IKEDA, *Japanese Alpine News*

Peak 5,772m, attempt. Our three-man team (Wojciech Chaladaj, Jakub Galka, and Marcin Kruczyk) hoped to attempt unclimbed Purian Sar North (6,247m) in July. However, the bag containing the majority of our climbing gear was lost at Heathrow Airport in London. We waited for a week in Islamabad and then gave up. After borrowing some basic glacier equipment in Gilgit, we headed toward the Sath Marau (a.k.a. Sat Maro) Glacier. We drove to Bar village, north of Chalt, and then trekked three days to base camp (3,750m) on the moraine of the Rara Gamuk Glacier. (We highly recommend Shahid Alam Nagari, whom one can find in Bar village, as a guide and porter for trips in this area.) We placed advanced base camp (4,350m) in a meadow on the ridge separating the north and south Sath Marau cwms, and put Camp 1 below the east ridge of Peak 5,772m. After a serious and exhausting struggle in deep and

Unclimbed Sath Marau Tower (a.k.a. Sat Maro Tower, 5,967m) from the southeast. The north and south Sath Marau glacial cwms are surrounded by unclimbed rock and ice peaks of ca 6,000m. *Jakub Galka*

Enticing ice and mixed lines on the southeast face of Swat Maras (6,005m). The unclimbed peak is along the ridgeline between Sath Marau Tower (5,967m) and Gadeny (6,015m). *Jakub Galka*

unstable snow, we gave up at about 5,600m. Above us the ridge steepened into a rocky step that we would not have been able to climb without protection.

Most of the peaks above this glacier are still waiting for their first ascent. This is surprising because it is a relatively accessible area with many opportunities for climbs on beautiful ridges (Koran Peak, 5,577m–5,678m), stunning walls (Swat Maras, 6,005m, and Gadeny Peak, 6,015m), and 900m rock pillars and ice couloirs (Sath Marau Tower, 5,967m).

JAKUB GALKA, *Poland*

SHIMSHAL AREA—GHUJERAB MUZTAGH

Four first ascents in the Ganj'dur (Ganj-i-Tang) Valley. Before meeting Yannick Graziani to make the first ascent of Pumari Chhish South (featured in this *Journal*), Christian Trommsdorff led a small group of experienced clients to Pakistan's Shimshal region. Hoping to profit from spring snow conditions for first ascents and ski descents, the team visited Pakistan from April 21 to May 7. However, locals said the winter had been relatively dry and spring was about a month earlier than usual. The valley floors were almost completely dry, and the snowline was generally higher than 4,500m.

After hiring 20 porters in Shimshal, Bruno Dupety, Sylvain Granaud, Bruno Paulet, Philippe Yvon, and Trommsdorff made a two-day walk, first east along the main valley and then north to a base camp at 4,350m in the Ganj'dur (Ganj-i-Tang) Valley.

In six days the team made four first ascents of large peaks. They measured the first, due west of base camp, with GPS at 5,882m, but the summit was a large cornice and the team stopped 10m below the highest point. The second, northeast of camp, had a rocky top measured at 5,892m. Only Trommsdorff reached the summit of the third peak, due north; he recorded

a height of 6,050m on his altimeter. The fourth peak, immediately southeast of base, they dubbed Papy's Peak (5,544m measured by GPS).

Temperatures during the trip were mild at around –5°C at night. The lowest height at which the climbers donned skis and skins was 4,700m, and here the snow was extremely heavy and mushy, even in early morning.

The team completed the expedition by trekking back to Shimshal in one long and strenuous day.

LINDSAY GRIFFIN, *Mountain-INFO Editor, adapted from www.Alpinist.com*

Ski touring above the Ganj-i-Tang Valley, with Kanjut Sar (7,760m, left) and Yukshin Gardan Sar (7,530m) high in the distance to the south. French skiers led by Christian Trommsdorff made four first ascents of 5,500- to 6,000-meter peaks above this valley. *Bruno Paulet*

SHIMSHAL AREA—
SHUIJERAB GROUP

Shuwert Sar (6,152m), first ascent. I had only three weeks for my summer vacation in 2007, so I chose to try mountaineering in the Shimshal region, where it is relatively easy to approach the mountains. Guided by the panoramic photos taken by the 2002 Yokohama party (see *Japanese Alpine News* Vol. 3, pages 27–36) and talks with my colleagues in the Fukuoka Alpine Club, we picked a noble triangular peak east of Shimshal village and north of Shimshal Pass. This peak is

Shuwert Sar (6,152m GPS) seen from the southwest, above an arm of the Shuwert Glacier. Wataru Takasaki and Lehmat Raheem climbed the peak via its far (northern) slopes. *Tadashi Kamei*

one of those forming the divide between the East Shuijerab and Shuwert glaciers; its height was listed as ca 6,150m on the Yokohama party's map, and a GPS reading made at the top later showed 6,152m. A 6,429m peak is shown at the head of Shuwert Glacier on the map prepared by Jerzy Wala and published in Switzerland, but such a high peak does not exist here. We could find no record of any climbs surrounding the upper East Shuijerab Glacier, although a French party seems to have reached the northern fringe of the glacier in 2002, according to our high-altitude porter, Lehmat Raheem.

On July 30 we arrived at Shimshal village by driving two jeeps from Karimabad. After four days' march along the Pamir-i-Tang Valley with 23 porters, we reached base camp (4,533m) on August 2. The three other members of my party immediately left with the porters to continue trekking. Only Raheem, a guide, and a cook remained with me at the desolate valley basin. On August 3, in poor weather, Raheem and I trudged up a scree bed to the ice plateau at 5,150m, where we pitched Camp 1. The East Shuijerab Glacier, a wide, gentle snow slope, stretched into the far distance. We had started down to base camp when a triangular snow peak began to peep through the clouds. It must be our mountain—so beautiful but still a long way off!

On August 4 it was fine all day and I moved up to Camp 1 with Raheem in the afternoon. In the early morning the western sky was unusually dark, but we left camp anyway and tramped on hard snow up to the glacier head. I chose a roundabout route to bypass a steep headwall, and we reached the divide at 8:15 a.m. My GPS showed 5,950m. Across the ridge was the Shuwert Glacier, and beyond were the Pamir Mountains.

At 6,100m thigh-deep snow on the peak's northern ridge forced us to detour to the right, where Raheem led a steep pitch past a big crevasse to regain the ridge. We took turns breaking snow until we reached the top at 10:25 a.m. Strong winds blew, but we could enjoy the surrounding view and confirm this was the highest point along the divide. By 2:30 p.m. we were back at Camp 1 and immediately fell into sleep.

After returning home, I thought about a good name for this major peak in the heart of the Shuwert Glacier region and simply decided on Shuwert Sar (Shuwert means "black stone" in the Wakhi language), and so registered the name at the Pakistani Survey Office.

WATARU TAKASAKI, *Japan*

The south faces of Pumari Chhish South (7,350m, summit hidden in clouds) and Peak 6,890m. Yannick Graziani and Christian Trommsdorff made the first ascent of Pumari Chhish South via the snow ramp and mixed headwall on its left side. Steve Su and Pete Takeda attempted a complex rock and mixed route on the left side of unclimbed Peak 6,890m. *Christian Trommsdorff*

Yannick Graziani on the summit of Pumari Chhish South, after making the first ascent. To the west and north are: (1) Khunyang Chhish East (ca 7,400m, unclimbed); (2) Khunyang Chhish (7,852m); and (3) a shoulder of Pumari Chhish (7,492m). *Christian Trommsdorff*

HISPAR MUZTAGH

Pumari Chhish South, first ascent. On their third attempt over two years (2003 and 2007), Yannick Graziani and Christian Trommsdorff completed the first ascent of Pumari Chhish South (7,350m) over six days in June. The two men climbed the 2,700m south face alpine-style, with four bivouacs. Technical difficulties were concentrated between 6,400m and 7,000m, with sustained rock, mixed, and ice climbing up to 5.10- and M6; one 15m crack was aided. Graziani and Trommsdorff summited at noon on June 12; they descended over the next day and a half. Trommsdorff's full account of this climb may be found earlier in this *Journal*.

Peak 6,890m, attempt. On September 3, 2007, Steve Su and I began a nine-week expedition to Pakistan's Hispar region. We had a number of objectives, including Pumari Chhish (7,350m). Most expeditions gunning for 7,000m peaks tackle snow-covered terrain during summer, for the longer days and higher over-all temperatures. Thus they usu-ally leave by mid-August. My idea, based on past experience, was to wait for the traditional late-season weather window. What I did not anticipate was the intense cold.

After delays with British Airways—a common com-plaint—costing us a week, we arrived in base camp with sum-mer-like conditions almost im-mediately giving way to fall. Temperatures were no longer warm enough to melt new snow-fall, and the mountains were starting to show their winter

Steve Su cleans a mixed pitch on Peak 6,890m. Su and Pete Takeda climbed about 4,500' of the ca 8,000' face over six days. *Pete Takeda*

coats. We had 20 or so days of on and off snow showers before a significant weather window arrived. During this time we attempted several unclimbed 6,000m peaks, only to be driven off by avalanches and poor weather.

Eventually we settled on Peak 6,890m, a majestic summit with a steep rocky south face crowned with Peru-like snow flutings, guarded by hanging seracs, and offering no easy route. We decided to throw ourselves at the route with five or six days of supplies. We ended up spend-ing six days climbing 4,500' of very technical terrain—hard mixed, hard rock climbing, sus-tained post-holing, and sections of aid. We spent two nights in frigid open bivies. The final evening of climbing saw us well below any possible bivy, and well above our past bivy site. This meant the climb was over. We couldn't reclimb the technical terrain with our limited supplies, and we still had another 3500' to the summit. With one can of fuel and the temperature getting colder, we retreated on day seven, leaving almost every piece of our hardware for rappel anchors.

We were greeted at base camp by a very concerned liaison officer and cook, who were relieved to end what had become, in their words, "a winter expedition."

PETE TAKEDA, *AAC*

Khunyang Chhish, attempt. Kazuo Tobita (61) led a four-member party for his sixth attempt on Khunyang Chhish (7,852m), which has been climbed only twice. In July he unsuccessfully attempted the south face. Over 14 years Tobita has explored the mountain from all sides, mak-ing exploratory forays or attempts on the east face, north side and northwest ridge, west ridge, south ridge, and south face.

TAMOTSU NAKAMURA, *Japanese Alpine News*

"Madhil Sar"/Shifkitin Sar, clarification. After a conversation with Chris Clark of the 1986 British expedition to Shimshal Whitehorn, Lee Harrison has confirmed that the peak he called

"Madhil Sar" (ca 5,700m) in the 2007 *AAJ* (pp 321-322) was in fact Shifkitin Sar, climbed by a British team in 1986. This peak on the north ridge of Shimshal Whitehorn was subsequently climbed in 1996 and April 2006, as well as during Harrison's July 2006 expedition.

PANMAH MUZTAGH

Suma Brakk, first ascent; Latok I attempt; Choktoi Tower, new route to just below summit. On June 15 Doug Chabot, Steve Swenson, and I arrived in base camp on the Choktoi Glacier for an attempt on the unclimbed north ridge of Latok I and other peaks. After acclimatization with an ascent of the striking Biacherahi Tower, ca 5870m, directly behind base camp, we focused on the 6,166m triple-summited peak due west of camp, which we would name Suma Brakk, meaning "three summits" in Balti. This peak had been previously called Choktoi Peak and other names.

Leaving base camp on June 23, we descended the Choktoi Glacier to the southwest drainage off Suma Brakk and climbed to a glacial cirque at ca 5,000m, below the south face of the peak. The next morning, in three hours, we climbed a steep snow gully to a col on the south ridge and a perfect camp below a rock promontory at ca 5,600m. We left camp the following morning at 5 a.m. with daypacks and began a long, rising traverse across the south face, simul-climbing over moderate snow with passages of steeper ice and rock up to 5.8 or so. After about 500 meters of climbing we reached a saddle on the south ridge, where we continued through deep snow, arriving on a tiny summit perch at 9:30 a.m. With bad weather looming, we descended all the way to the Choktoi that day, arriving at base camp well after dark after 16 hours on the go.

Suma Brakk (6,166m, a.k.a. Choktoi Peak). Doug Chabot, Mark Richey, and Steve Swenson climbed the south face from a high camp at ca 5,600m. *Steve Swenson*

On July 5 we made our only attempt on Latok I with a midnight start, taking a line of snow and ice couloirs just left and east of the main rock ridge. We simul-climbed for 500m until it steepened and we had to belay three pitches of steep ice and mixed ground (about M4 A1) to reach the main ridge. From there, eight more pitches of steep snow and ice runnels on the west side led to the second horizontal ice ridge, where we placed a camp on a fine platform after 20 hours of continuous climbing. The next day we continued on the west side of the ridge across snow flutes and good ice to the third horizontal ridge, where we had considerable difficulty breaking through the cornice to find a spot suitable for a bivouac. The vertical, unconsolidated snow seemed bottomless and nearly impossible to protect. We carved out a small ledge below a mushroom atop the rock ridge, and I recognized it as the same place I had camped in 1997, nearly halfway up the climb, at 5900m.

Despite our rapid progress, the loose snow would soon seal our fate, and next morning, after several frustrating hours and less than a rope length of progress, we abandoned our attempt in impossible conditions. As Doug remarked, "You need a snow blower, not ice tools." We descended directly to the glacier on the west side of the ridge, reaching the Choktoi that day in about 26 rappels, considerably quicker than our descent along the main ridge in '97.

With Latok I out of the question and Doug heading back to the U.S., Steve and I looked around for another objective. We made one attempt on the southeast ridge of the Ogre, but again found deep and dangerous snow in the initial icefall. On July 20 we settled for a new-route attempt on the pointed Choktoi Tower, ca 5700m, the peak that forms an island at the head of the Choktoi Glacier. Steve and I climbed a long couloir on the north side of the tower to a rock col northwest of the summit. From there we traversed and ascended for eight or nine steep pitches on rock of increasing difficulty (to 5.11 A1), moving from one side of the ridge to the

other. We were stopped just 4m from the true summit by a short, blank wall. Nonetheless it was great climb, with superb position on the ridge. We descended through a tranquil night and reached our glacier camp by 9 a.m. after 27 hours of climbing, just as it started to snow. Unbeknownst to us, the peak had been climbed to the top by the opposite rock ridge the year before by a Canadian team (Relph-Walsh, 2006).

MARK RICHEY, *AAC*

The Bean Pole, first ascent; Latok I attempt. On July 12 Bean Bowers and I headed up the north ridge of Latok I to put in a cache and check out the bottom section of the climb. Skirting to the west the rock buttress climbed by many parties, we climbed 3,500' to ca 18,500' (5,639m) in seven hours. The climbing was mostly moderate and low-angle,

The Bean Pole (ca 18,500') on the north side of Choktoi Glacier. Bean Bowers and Josh Wharton climbed six long pitches (5.11+ A0) to the summit, starting on the southeast pillar and then moving right. *Josh Wharton* and despite the fact that there was obviously more difficult climbing to come, we both felt optimistic that given some good fortune with weather and conditions we had a chance to succeed. Unfortunately luck was not on our side. In 42 days at base camp we experienced only two truly good days, and the pressure never went more then a few points in either direction. Despite frequent desperate calls to our weather forecaster in Montana, the news was always grim.

On July 20 Bean and I climbed a small rock spire (ca 18,500') on the north side of Choktoi Glacier. The peak is obvious and aesthetic when seen from base camp below Latok's northern flank. We climbed six long pitches on the southeast pillar of the formation. The first 500' were surprisingly steep, with two pitches of 5.11 and a third of 5.11+ A0, which I was able to follow free at 5.12-. The remaining 500' proved relatively easy as we weaved around the peak to the east; Bean gained the summit with 40' of unprotected 5.8. We named the peak the Bean Pole in honor of Bean's first trip up an unclimbed peak. I recommend the route and encourage ambitious teams to bring a few pins and beaks to explore the thin splitters on the south face proper.

JOSH WHARTON, *AAC*

Peak 5,750m, the Outside Penguin; Latok II attempts. Backed by the AAC's Lyman Spitzer Award and Mountain Equipment Co-op, our team had chosen as an objective the unclimbed feature under and southwest of Latok II (7,103m). We facetiously named this gargantuan gendarme "Latok 11¾" (ca 6,300–6,500m); its southwest face presents a large wall of near-vertical unclimbed granite. Because of nearly continuous bad weather, this normally rock-climbable objective was shrouded in verglas and powder, rendering it too full-on for the likes of us.

Ryan Hokanson and Sam Johnson made two attempts on Latok II's northwest ridge, the first with Ken Glover. During their first try they climbed ice and mixed ground up to M7 (M6R) on the west face and then began a snow traverse to the ridge. They descended from 5,600m because of illness. On the second attempt, Hokanson and Johnson bypassed the mixed ground by simul-soloing a 900m ice ramp to reach a camp under a gendarme at 6,000m. They spent three nights here in a storm before descending amid dangerous avalanche conditions.

Ken Glover and I turned our attention to lower altitudes, and settled on Peak 5,750m, located two peaks down a ridge to the southwest of Latok II. Italians may have climbed the peak in 1977, and Americans Doug Chabot and Jack Tackle climbed it from the north in 2000. Its triangular south face rises 1,200m out of the talus-covered Baintha Lukpar Glacier and appears to have some of the best granite in the valley. On July 30, at the tail end of one of the few high-pressure systems of the season, we started up the rightmost of the twin buttresses with light alpine packs, carrying one sleeping bag, two down jackets, and a thin tarp as the extent of our bivy gear.

The face presented three steep headwalls. After an initial broken section, we reached the base of the first headwall, framed on its right by a ridge crest. By traversing two pitches, we reached the crest and followed it upward for a pitch before it stopped us at a blank overhang. A slab traverse right dropped us into a chimney, which we followed for three pitches to a sandy ledge atop the initial headwall. The second steep headwall loomed above. Searching for the line of weakness, we traversed two pitches to the right, where we climbed a ramp system before slipping behind a prow to find a hidden corner. Above the corner, moderate terrain led to a scree slope and a comfortable bivy.

Seven hundred meters up the face, we hoped for a quick, sun-bathed dash for the summit the next day. Instead, threatening skies and false summits made for a blue-collar finish. After soloing up moderate terrain past false summits, we reached the base of the third and final headwall. A long, broken pitch led to a steep cirque where our streak of luck appeared to end. Ken scouted to the right, then wisely retreated from an unprotectable face. Next I tried the left prow, which appeared to be blocked by an overhanging wart of granite. By stemming past an ice-chocked corner, I reached the base of the wart, and here our luck returned. A moderate ramp led to a crux pitch that gave way to the wart's top. Ken then led two mixed pitches with our one pair of crampons to reach the summit as snow began to fall.

The Outside Penguin (1,200m, V 5.10 A1 M3) climbs the south face of Peak 5,750m, above the Baintha Lukpar Glacier. The peak had been climbed at least once from the opposite side. *Jeremy Frimer*

Our first descent option, heading toward easy-looking gullies, appeared far more involved than we'd anticipated while scouting. Hence, we began rappelling our line of ascent; shortly thereafter, darkness and a powerful snowstorm descended upon us. At the first decent ledge we endured a miserable, sleepless bivy as the storm raged. On the third day, we continued rapping and downclimbing. We reached the base that afternoon in the pouring rain, after some 800m of rapping, overjoyed for having made the most of what the weather gods permitted: the Outside Penguin (1,200m, V 5.10 A1 M3).

JEREMY FRIMER, *Canada*

Peak 5,200m, the Partition, to subsummit. During the summer of 2007, Luisa Giles (British, 25), Sarah Hart (Canadian, 27), and I (Canadian, 28) established a 900-meter free climb in the Karakoram. The route is on a possibly unclimbed 5,200m granite peak on the south side of the Choktoi Glacier, near the base of Latok III. This is the westernmost of two similar north-facing rock buttresses joined by a high col and ice couloir. The eastern of these two peaks holds the Indian Face Arête, established by Doug Scott and Sandy Allen in 1990.

In mid-July a weather window allowed for a one-day reconnaissance, during which we spotted a left-trending line of corner and ledge systems on the east face. This face appeared to possess superior rock to the north-facing ridge crest. We climbed the first few hundred meters

The Partition (900m, TD 5.10b) reached a sub-summit atop the arête at ca 5,200m on the westernmost of twin rock buttresses below Latok III. The Indian Face Arête (Allen-Scott, 1990) climbs the left tower's arête line. The West Wall (Chinnery-Coull-Hollinger-Morten, 1999) starts 80m up the gully between the towers and joins the Indian Face Arête at half height. The 2007 party found evidence of a rappel line left by an unknown team on the right tower. However, it is not known if this tower has been summited beyond the arête top. *Jacqueline Hudson Collection*

before altitude sickness and gastrointestinal problems turned us around. A second single-day attempt was thwarted by bad weather, although we managed to further our high point.

During the next weather window we completed the route over three days, including a planned and an unplanned bivouac. We followed a series of cracks to a system of left-trending ramps, which ended as the face steepened. We spent the first night at this junction. The second day we followed a steep corner system on clean granite (200m of continuous, high-quality 5.10) to reach an upper groove on the east face. This groove kicked back and allowed for some fast simul-climbing over 300m of left-trending lower-angle slabs. The terrain steepened again and we followed face cracks and shallow corners to the ridge crest. Another 200m to 300m of ridge climbing on more fractured granite brought us to a sub-summit at ca 5,200m at 4 p.m. The true summit was a few hundred meters away, and would have required crossing a number of loose corner systems to reach. Due to lack of time and a perceived absence of quality climbing ahead, we stopped at this point and descended.

The descent roughly reversed the route. A stuck rope on an early rappel wasted the remaining two hours of daylight, and required cutting one of the ropes. A series of rappels aided by moonlight brought us back to our stashed bivy gear by 11 p.m., and at this point we decided to stay on the wall for a second night. After finishing the descent, we devoured a breakfast of fresh bread, jam, boiled eggs, tea, and coffee brought to us by our worried base camp cook.

During the climb we found two old pieces of rappel tat (one low on the route, the other about two-thirds of the way up). It is possible that a previous party had reached the summit of this peak by another line, but it is unlikely that our line had been climbed before.

The route went free with 19 full 60m rope lengths, including many fantastic pitches of 5.9 and 5.10 climbing and roughly 300m of simul-climbing over moderate terrain. The Partition (900m, TD 5.10b) was named in honor of the 60th anniversary of Pakistan's independence, and also because the Indian Face Arête is situated on the adjacent peak—a metaphor for the geography and politics of India and Pakistan.

We also made several attempts on Peak 5,700m, whose northeast ridge was our original objective. However, early reconnaissance showed the rock quality to be generally poor, with exfoliating loose granite.

JACQUELINE HUDSON, *Canada*

BALTORO MUZTAGH

ULI BIAHO AND TRANGO GROUPS

Great Trango Tower, northwest face, completion of Ukrainian route (2003) and new variation to Azeem Ridge; Broad Peak, attempt. In the summer of 2007 the Krasnoyarsk Federation of Alpinism, with support of the administration of the Krasnoyarsk Region, organized a Karakoram expedition. The goals were to ascend Great Trango Tower via technically complex new routes and to ascend Broad Peak by the classic route. Eleven climbers, a trainer, and a doctor, all from Krasnoyarsk, took part in the expedition.

We formed two teams: one for the Ukrainian route of 2003, the other to try a line right of the Russian route of 1999. The first team included Vladimir Arkhipov, Sergei Cherezov, Yuri Glasyrin, Oleg Khvostenko, Andrei Litvinov, and Aleksandr Yanyshevich. The second was made up of Evgenni Belyaev, Aleksei Komissarov, Igor Loginov, and Aleksandr Mikhalitsin.

The teams started at about the same time, on the 6th and 7th of July. On the Ukrainian route, we climbed capsule-style with portaledges and a large reserve of provisions. We had a precise description of the route, and at the end of every pitch we found a bolt with a rappel carabiner.

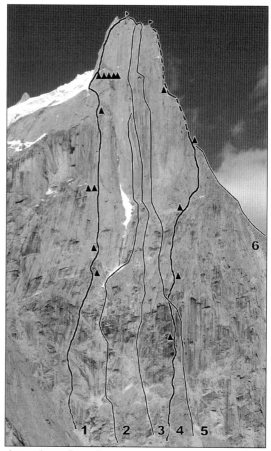

The northwest face of Great Trango Tower (ca 6,250m). (1) Ukrainian route to ca 6,050m (2003), completed to southwest summit (left flag) in 2007 by Krasnoyarsk expedition. (2) Lost Butterfly (Berecz-Nadasdi-Tivador, 1999), to 60m below ridge. (3) Parallel Worlds (Lowe-Ogden-Synnott, plus film crew, 1999), to summit ridge. (4) Krasnoyarsk variation to Azeem Ridge (Belyaev-Komissarov-Loginov-Mikhalitsin, 2007), to right flag on ridge. (5) The Russian Way (Koshelenko-Odintsov-Potankin and cameraman, 1999), to southwest summit. (6) Azeem Ridge (Cordes-Wharton, 2004), to southwest summit. *2007 Krasnoyarsk Karakoram Expedition*

Meanwhile the second team moved upward, crossing the Russian route. On the fourth day they emerged onto a shelf at the base of the steep upper wall. A band of severely broken rock awaited them. Not finding a sufficiently safe passage, the guys began to exit to the right, deviating from their planned line. Toward the end of the fourth day they emerged onto the Azeem Ridge (Cordes-Wharton, 2004). They required another $2^1/2$ days to ascend the upper part of this ridge. On July 12 they reached their high point at one of the towers along the summit ridge. The weather began to worsen, and the prognosis for the coming three days was not consoling. The team decided to descend via their ascent route.

By this time on the Ukrainian route we had reached our final bivouac and climbed another 150m on the summit tower. We estimated there remained about 200m to the summit. During the night a storm started. The next day, in abominable weather, we succeeded in climbing another 50m and reached the point from which the Ukrainian team had retreated in 2003. On July 14, with the storm continuing, we climbed three more ropelengths and emerged onto the ridge. The summit was very close, but the next day the storm did not allow us to leave our portaledges. On July 16 the storm took a respite, and at 11 a.m. we reached the southwestern summit of Great Trango Tower. We quickly descended via the route of ascent, once again in a snowstorm. On the evening of July 17 our friends met us at the foot of the wall, and at base camp a celebratory dinner awaited us.

On Broad Peak, having acclimatized sufficiently, we immediately ascended to Camp 3 at 7,100m and cached our equipment at Camp 4, at 7,500m. The next day the weather was outstanding, and many climbers went from Camp 3 to the summit, but we descended for a rest. After our rest, when the forecast promised great weather, we went up. Unfortunately the prediction did not come true. After three days of waiting for an improvement in Camp 3, we were forced to descend to catch our plane. Thus our expedition ended.

OLEG KHVOSTENKO, *Russia (translated by Henry Pickford)*

Shipton Spire (Hainabrakk), Fragments of Freedom. Our team of four climbers from the Moscow Karakoram Expedition— Denis Savelyev (leader), Evgeny Korol, Andrew Muryshev, and Sergey Nilov— ascended a new line called Fragments of Freedom on Hainabrakk's southeast face. Although there were already several routes on this face, we found a completely new line, not joining or crossing the others. Our

The line of Fragments of Freedom (VII A4 6b+) on Shipton Spire's southeast face. Silvia Vidal's solo new route, Life is Lilac, ascends the northeast pillar, on the right side of the wall. *Denis Savelyev* route is just to the left of the 2001 Italian route (Women and Chalk) and right of the 1996 and 1998 American routes.

Climbing capsule-style, we tried to follow the most direct line we could. As a result, the route has lots of artificial climbing up to A4. Several pitches were completely free, but dirt and grass in wet cracks limited the free climbing. We began climbing on July 18, and all four climbers reached the summit on July 30. We descended the route, removing all ropes and gear except belay bolts, and reached the base on July 31, after 14 days on the wall. The 1,450m route went in 33 pitches and was graded VII A4 6b+.

We had lots of problems organizing the trip and during our trek to base camp, but we solved them all. As for me, I am very happy. There's nothing more exciting and pleasurable than making something new.

DENIS SAVELYEV, *Russia*

Shipton Spire, Life is Lilac, solo new route to shoulder. In the summer of 2007 I went to Shipton Spire and soloed a new route to the first needle atop the northeast pillar (870m, A4+ 6a, 17 pitches to 5,300m). It was almost all hard aid (because I was looking for it), with some A4+ and A4 pitches. I followed a non-natural line on the right side of the wall, with some pitches turning to the north side, and finished at the last belay on Prisoners of Shipton (2005).

I set advanced base camp at 4,450m; from there I carried my stuff for eight days to the base of the wall, two and a half hours away. I fixed the first 200m and then spent 21 days (August 10–30) on the wall, with 20 bivvies in three camps. It was a great experience.

My goal from the beginning was to reach a high point at 5,300m. To reach the summit of Shipton (5,852m) from here, you must climb Ship of Fools (Ogden-Synnott, 1997), and there are many traverses with hard climbing; going alone was for me not a good idea, because of the danger of cleaning and rappelling traverses.

I rappelled the route. At belays there's at least one bolt (8mm), except at the first belay. During the rappels I had problems because of the haulbags' weight, and because I'm very small. During one diagonal rappel I had problems reaching the lower belay, and spent an extra night in the middle of this rappel, at 5,000m, in between two rocks, with no portaledge, no food, and little water. During one of the upper rappels my rope stuck, and after an hour I cut it. I know that's garbage on the wall, but it was my only dynamic rope and I had no other one with which to climb the pitch again.

At the base I carried down my gear right away because at noon the next day porters were coming

Sílvia Vidal takes a break during the descent from her new route on Shipton Spire. With porters arriving the next day, she dragged all of her gear down to advanced base camp, by herself, in one day. It had taken her eight days on the way up. *Sílvia Vidal*

to advanced base camp. What I carried up in eight days, I carried down in one. Dragging it.

I had no radio or phone, and no other people at advanced base camp. Totally alone. I called the route Life is Lilac. My life had this color at that moment.

SÍLVIA VIDAL, *Spain*

Cat's Ears, Epica Direct. In mid-August Cedar Wright and I realized a wild line that corkscrewed around the Cat's Ears towers (ca 18,250'). We climbed in alpine style over two days from a high camp, with one nauseous, headachy shiver bivy 500' below the summit, and reached the unclimbed of the two "ears."

The first day was characterized by two headwalls split by an 800' traverse along mixed snow, ice, and choss. During the simul-climb through choss-land I lost communication with Cedar and desperately called for a belay before committing to a section of frozen, overhanging talus. After the second headwall, we traversed another 400' to the third and final overhanging granite headwall. We were now on the backside of the tower, which was unnerving because of avalanches ripping off Hainabrakk 300' across the gully. As the sun set I led a nasty No. 4 Camalot groove and descended, wet, to a bivy ledge with not even enough room to man-spoon.

After a night without sleeping bags, our feet were lifeless blocks of ice, and the uncertainty about our line was overwhelming. The final 600' was the most difficult and dangerous part of the route, with huge pull-and-pray death blocks, overhanging off-widths, and tricky aid moves through awkward roofs. We both pulled out the full bag of tricks, making use of the entire rack, from No. 6 Camalot to No. 00 TCU. Cedar and I took turns climbing the final needlelike summit block. I think we both were misty-eyed after overcoming our doubts and reaching a tiny virgin summit in the middle of this awe-inspiring valley. Also on the summit was the skeleton of a raven, which had auspiciously made the true first ascent of the tower.

Descending our route meant reversing two huge and tricky traverses, now in a delirious dehydrated state. It's not over until it's over with this kind of climb, and one pitch before we touched down our ropes stuck. Cedar sucked it up and jumared the 6mm tagline, held in place by a mystery knot.

Our summit appeared to be the higher of the two Cat's Ears, but I don't consider our climb the first ascent of the formation. The

Renan Ozturk and Cedar Wright spiraled around the Cat's Ears towers (ca 18,250') to make the first ascent of the southwest "ear." *Renan Ozturk* other summit, the northeast ear, had been climbed twice, by lines totally different from ours. It's a complex formation, and I would say we did the third ascent of the formation and the first to the southwest ear.

We named our climb the Epica Direct (V 5.11+ C2). Epica was the nickname of our good friend Erica Kutcher, who was buried in an icefall collapse just above Shipton base camp. Erica was one of the most promising female Yosemite climbers ever to roll through the scene. She earned the nickname Epica because she was never afraid to go for it and often the results were epic. I think Erica would appreciate the sarcastic "Direct" name for our route.

RENAN OZTURK, *Yosemite, California*

Hainabrakk East Tower, alpine-style link-up. Ko Imai and Hiroki Suzuki made the probable second alpine-style ascent of this ca 5,650m formation, linking the American route (Copp-Pennings, 2000) and the Slovak route (Kolarik-Rabatin, 2005) on July 11-12. Their climb was 1,100m (31 pitches) and 5.10 A2.

TAMOTSU NAKAMURA, *Japanese Alpine News*

La Reina Roja, southwest face. I first visited the Trango group in 2000 to try the Slovenian route on Nameless Tower. Our expedition was unsuccessful, and it took me seven years to return to Pakistan. There are not many big-wall climbers in Mexico, and fewer who share the goals and could afford the expense of climbing in Pakistan. So I traveled alone and asked my friend Ali Muhammad to be my partner and guide for this expedition. I had met him as a guide and cook for our expedition in 2000. He was interested in learning the techniques of big-wall climbing. I taught him the basics, and we chose a wall 300m up from the Nameless Tower base camp on the Trango Glacier, by the trail to Shipton base camp. After studying the line with a telescope, we started up the left skyline and fixed the first two pitches. Over four days of bad weather we carried everything we'd need to the base of the wall and hauled one bag up the first two pitches.

On June 19 we started up, prepared to head to the top. We bivouacked at the end of the fifth and eighth pitches, with two pitches fixed above our second bivy. On June 21 we left the pig atop the eighth pitch, thinking it would only be four more pitches from the top of our fixed lines to the summit. After seven pitches we reached the top just before sunset. We'd forgotten headlamps, so the descent was epic. The rope got stuck three times. We reached our bivy gear at 1 a.m. on June 22, and then continued down the next morning after some sleep.

We called our route Estrella de la Mañana (or Morning Star or Skarchan): 936m, 5.10b A1, 17 pitches.

LUIS CARLOS GARCÍA AYALA, *Mexico*

Editor's note: At the beginning of their route, Luis Carlos García Ayala and Ali Muhammad followed portions of an existing climb called Sadu (350m, 6b+ A1, Antoine and Sandrine de Choudens, 2003). Above the small point at 4,400m (Sadu Peak), where the de Choudens ended their climb, García Ayala and Muhammad continued for nine pitches to another summit, which they called La Reina Roja. Sadu was repeated in 2005 by a Slovenian expedition, which also added a route (Piyar, Piyar, 6b+ A0) left of the original line.

The Russian route on the west face of K2 gained ca 3,000m from advanced base camp, with the crux rock wall ascending from 6,500m to 7,850m. The Russians placed seven camps en route, the highest at 8,400m. *K2 Russian Expedition Direct West Face Collection*

BALTORO MUSTAGH – OTHER

K2, west face. Applying the tactics they used successfully on the north face of Jannu in 2004 and the direct north face of Mt. Everest the same year, a Russian team made the first ascent of the west face of K2 (8,611m). After a siege of two and a half months, an extremely strong team completed what is almost certainly the hardest route on the world's second-highest peak.

Arriving at their 5,000m base camp on June 7, 16 climbers, most of whom had taken part in the Jannu and Everest expeditions, began fixing ropes and establishing camps on a previously unattempted line left of the west ridge. After initial snow slopes above the Savoia Glacier, the meat of the route is formed by a mixed rock buttress that rises from 6,500m to 7,850m. Although a prominent curving couloir skirts the buttress on the left, the Russians chose to tackle a direct and far more difficult line up the center. They established Camp 2 immediately below the buttress and set to work on the steep rock wall above. The initial section was as hard as Jannu; above, the angle was not as extreme but the difficulties were still sustained. Operating in small, close-knit teams without recourse to supplementary oxygen, the expedition battled through inclement weather to reach the top of the bastion on July 30. Here, they placed Camp 6.

Bad weather stopped activity for a few days, but then Alexey Bolotov, Gennady Kirievsky, and Nikolay Totmjanin moved back up the mountain, spent four days in Camp 5 waiting for a weather window, and on August 10 left Camp 6 for a summit push. Deep snow, at times up to their chests, slowed them considerably, and at 8,500m they hit an unexpected vertical rock step. Unable to find a way through, the exhausted trio retreated.

On August 21 the weather allowed the Russians another shot. On the previous day they had established a seventh camp at 8,400m, and in the morning Andrey Mariev and Vadim Popovich found better snow and took a different line to reach the summit. The next day nine other members followed them: Bolotov and Totmjanin, and then Gleb Sokolov, Eugeny Vinogradsky, the three-man team of Vitaly Gorelik, Gennady Kirievsky, and Victor Volodin, and finally Pavel Shabalin and Ilias Tukhvatullin. This was a particularly notable effort for Popovich, who had never climbed an 8,000m peak, and for Shabalin and Tukhvatullin, who spent three nights at or above 8,150m before reaching the summit. Shabalin and Solokov both became grandfathers during the climb.

The team descended via the same route, leaving most of their fixed ropes and camps on the mountain. Two climbers were evacuated by helicopter because of injuries or illness, in mid-July and early August.

LINDSAY GRIFFIN, *MountainINFO Editor,*
adapted from www.alpinist.com

Rappelling steep ground on the 1,350m rock wall that formed the crux of the west face. The Russians worked in four-man teams that moved up and down more than 50 fixed ropes to advance the line and to descend to lower camps for rest. *K2 Russian Expedition Direct West Face*

K2 west face interview. The Russian magazine *Verticalniy Mir* (No. 68) interviewed K2 west face expedition leader Viktor Kozlov in September 2007, shortly after he returned to Russia from K2. Following is an excerpt.

Q. How much useful information did you get from the reconnaissance expeditions you completed? Of course, they did not and could not provide a full map of the route. From under the rock wall, the upper part of the face is completely invisible. However, in 2005 we were lucky with the weather and could study the wall. Underneath there weren't any rocks, which means they aren't falling from the wall. The upper part, I repeat, we didn't see at all.

Q. How did the team form? I return to our reconnaissance. When we approached the wall, we set ourselves a question: Is this suicide or a real possibility? And we answered: If we have a strong team and work constantly with two four-man groups, replacing each other, then it is a real possibility. And of course the usual requirements—excellent equipment and sufficient financial backing. The skeleton crew came together during the previous two expeditions—Lhotse Middle (2001) and the northern wall of Everest (2004)—and the four group leaders recommended the remaining members.

Q. Were there assigned roles for the groups—some handled the technical challenges of the route, some brought up the equipment? First of all, we had five high-altitude porters who brought our provisions to advanced base camp. Early on, we decided that after advanced base camp there would be no high-altitude porters. Secondly, there was the question of using the oxygen equipment. Not everyone was as decisive as Bolotov, Shabalin, Tukhvatullin, Mariev, and

Totmjanin, who answered the question categorically: We will climb without the use of oxygen equipment. There were people who said: If we don't make it without oxygen, then let's use the medical supply. But during the ascent, despite the risk, the idea took shape in everyone's head that we would not use oxygen. And we did not use it. We understood that, although we had a considerable reserve of time in case of bad weather, there awaited a huge amount of work on the wall and above. For that reason everyone labored hard, spelling each other. Indeed, during work on the wall some people had better weather, some people had worse, some people did more, some less, but everyone was working on a common project. There were leadership duties, groups spelled each other, and who would climb to the summit no one knew.

Q. *Were there any surprises on the route?* The beginning was technically very difficult. The same guys who were on Jannu and other difficult rocky routes, for instance on Aksu, they said: "Yes, this is extreme, we've never had anything similar, certainly not on an 8,000er." When we talked about this in base camp, the guys came to this conclusion about the western wall of K2: This is the wall of Jannu plus the northern wall of Everest. Of course it may have been possible to go farther left, circumvent the extreme part via the snowy couloir, and then go up onto the wall—this is simpler, although more dangerous in terms of avalanches. But on principle we went up the center.

Q. *Now that the route is done, you can evaluate—would it have been better to organize anything differently?* Well, look, the weather forecast is for at most five days. And the approach to the fourth or fifth camp—this is a minimum of three, or even four days. For that reason the guys went up to work in any weather. We weren't able to wait for a 10-day prognosis—no one will give you one. And there were occasions when guys sat in the fifth camp for four days. They arrived there and we got a forecast for a window for the next day, and suddenly it changes to four days away—and one had to wait. But when all the expeditions on K2 and neighboring summits were sitting in base camps, our guys were working. They climbed, waited, fought.

Q. *The weather conditions were severe, but this is typical for K2. Can one say that you were not lucky with the weather?* No, I wouldn't say that. If we had had bad luck with the weather, we would not have reached the summit. June was sufficiently stable, and our altitude then was not that great; therefore we paid no attention to the caprices of the weather. In July our altitude increased and the weather deteriorated. August was completely bad. For example, a Pole and two Slovenes, who wanted to climb the left couloir in alpine style, turned back having decided the situation was hopeless.

Q. *When Totmjanin's group worked for several days above 8,000 meters and nonetheless was unable to make the summit, what thoughts arose?* I was certain that on August 10 they would reach the summit. When they reached the end of the fixed ropes (7,850m), they climbed alpine style. And there turned out to be an awful lot of snow. In the video they took, I saw that in places they were climbing up to their chests in snow. But there was no avalanche—the Lord protected us all. The guys put up the sixth camp at 8,150 meters, spent the night in it, and went on toward the summit. While considering the route we believed that it was not necessary to immediately go out onto the ridge that divides the western and the southwestern walls. But the snow forced them onto this ridge. And after a short while the guys came up against a rock face of about 50 to 70 meters. They had no special equipment, and they didn't risk climbing without it. They looked to the left, to the right. Altitude: 8,500 meters. Ultimately they understood that their strength was nearing an end, and they turned around and descended. They did the right thing.

Q. Mariev, Popovich, and the others who ultimately summited, they went along the snow-field, not out on the ridge? Yes, but this is not a field, it's a slope with an average steepness of 45°, and in places reaching 60°. The condition of the snow was better—more compact—than it was for Totmjanin, Bolotov, and Kirievsky.

Q. Would you say that the successful expedition on K2 is your greatest achievement as an organizer of similar projects? I won't say "I." We had a powerful team. Of course I would like to organize something again, gather a great team. But for the time being there's no answer to, "What's next?"

Interview by ARTEM ZUBKOV *and* ILIA KAZARINOV,
translated from the Russian by Henry Pickford

K2, north face attempt, north ridge ascent. After abandoning their dreams of an alpine-style new route on the north face of K2 because of severe weather and poor climbing conditions, Serguey Samoilov and Denis Urubko succeeded on the rarely climbed north ridge on October 2. The Kazakh climbers' rapid ascent, in difficult conditions and with no supplementary oxygen, was the latest in the year that K2 has ever been climbed.

After arriving at base camp in late August, Samoilov and Urubko acclimatized on K2's north ridge, reaching 8,300m on September 16. Back in base camp, they rested for their attempt on a direct route up a shallow spur on the north face, left of the north ridge route. But persistent poor weather loaded the face with snow, creating dangerous avalanche conditions.

The two climbers approached the face on September 27, but a blizzard that night scrubbed any hope of an attempt on the new route. Instead, they traversed to the north ridge, reaching Camp 2 on that route on September 29 in poor weather. They next day was clear, though windy and cold, and they continued to Camp 3, and on October 1, despite a new storm, they climbed to Camp 4. On October 2 they reached the summit and returned to high camp.

The north ridge of K2, first climbed by a large Japanese expedition in 1982, has seen only a handful of repeats. Until now, the latest autumn ascent of K2 was a 1978 American team's summits on September 6 and 7, via the northeast ridge.

DOUGALD MACDONALD, *adapted from*
www.climbing.com

Broad Peak, winter attempt. Italian Simone Moro led a small team to attempt the first winter ascent of Broad Peak (8,047m). His partners were Leonhard Werth and accomplished Pakistani 8,000m climbers Qudrat Ali and Shaheen Beg, from Shimshal. In the winter of 2006–07, Beg and Moro had managed

Denis Urubko and Serguey Samoilov made the latest ascent of K2 in history, summiting October 2 by the north ridge (center). They had hoped to climb a new route on the shallow spur to the left of the north ridge, between two enormous serac bands. *Steve Swenson* to reach the site of Camp 3, despite huge logistical and administrative difficulties delaying their approach to base camp. In 2007–08 Moro once again was plagued by logistical problems and didn't arrive at the 4,800m base camp until near the end of January, by which time Werth, fed up with the delays, had left for home. By February 3 the remaining three had reached the site for Camp 2 at 6,200m on the original 1957 route, fixing some 5mm static rope. During the month they made a couple of attempts to go higher but were always beaten back by high winds and –35°C temperatures.

In early March, with their permit due to expire on the 10th, they got a break. Reaching Camp 3 at 7,200m, they set out at 6:30 a.m. and by 2 p.m., in great weather, had reached 7,800m. Although Moro felt strong enough to continue to the summit, he realized it would mean a night out during the descent, something all the climbers would be unlikely to survive. They retreated.

LINDSAY GRIFFIN, *MountainINFO Editor, adapted from www.alpinist.com*

Gasherbrum IV, west face to south ridge, attempt. My desire to visit the Baltoro dates from long ago, but many things had to fall into place before it could happen. One night, after a few too many drinks, I managed to convince Jordi Corominas. I had always dreamed of Gasherbrum IV, Bonatti's mountain, and Jordi was also excited about an alpine-style attempt on the west face. The municipality of Vall de Boi gave us financial support, and by early June we were there.

The Baltoro is spectacular, including the approach from the desert, Concordia, and everything along the way. Except for the mega-expeditions with lots of porters. I wasn't too happy about them.

To acclimatize we climbed partway up the American-Australian route on the northwest ridge. We took only a 100m length of 5mm rope and perched our tent in a col at 6,500m. From there we managed to climb to 6,900m, right below a big serac. After descending to base camp, I went across to Broad Peak base camp to visit Spanish friends and climbed to 7,000m to further my acclimatization.

After a week of constant snowstorms, we finally gave our objective a try. On July 18 we started late and by the following day had reached the top of the serac, where we set up our tent. We used the rope only on the glacier and to overcome the serac. The second day dawned with mist and wind, but we charged on and at 7,100m found traces of passage from previous attempts to climb the south ridge. We reached 7,200m and pitched our tent on the crest of the ridge. However, the weather took a turn for the worse. We had to stay in the tent for the rest of the afternoon and all the following day. It wasn't until the morning of the third day that the weather improved. We climbed a couple of pitches but soon realized that with limited food and gas we would not go far. We could see Camp 1 across from us on Gasherbrum II, and it looked inviting, so we headed down that way.

After more than a day's rest in Camp 1 we made an attempt on Gasherbrum II. I started from camp after dinner with friends from Spain, while Jordi waited until 8 a.m. I turned around at 7,600m with cold feet and a number of other excuses. However, Jordi went on to reach the summit in a single push, joining our friend Jordi Marmolejo, who had slept at Camp 3.

The experience was very gratifying. To try a mountain like Gasherbrum IV in alpine style and with such a good partner was a treat. What I did not like was all the garbage on the normal

The west face of Gasherbrum IV (7,925m). (1) Northwest ridge. An American-Australian team first climbed the complete ridge in 1986. (2) Central spur of west face (Koreans, 1997). (3) West face (Kurtyka-Schauer, 1985). In this historic alpine-style ascent, the pair reached the summit ridge but did not go to the highest point. (4) West couloir and south ridge attempted by a Spanish pair in 2006. B1, B2, and B3 mark the bivouacs, with two nights spent at 7,200m. *Oriol Baró*

route on Gasherbrum II and the peakbaggers' fixation with fixed rope. They charge on without much planning and with little thought for the descent. It is a surprise that there are not more accidents. The guardian angel must work overtime above 7,000m. [Editor's note: This report was accidentally omitted from the 2007 *AAJ*. The attempt took place in 2006.]

ORIOL BARÓ, *Spain (translated by Rolando Garibotti)*

MASHERBRUM RANGE

Honboro Peak West, first ascent; "Bukma Peak," ascent by south ridge; Mirkasia Peak, first ascent. The Honboro Group and Shimshak (Mango Gusor) Mountains are located on the other side of the deep Hushe Valley from the better-known Charakusa and Nangma valleys. Andrzej Gluszek, Wojciech Kozub, and I visited these mountains from July 20 to August 25. Our main target was the highest summit in the range, Honboro Peak (6,454m), which is likely still unclimbed.

For access to the massif, we chose the Thalle Valley, running along the western flanks of the range, and established base camp in Olmo village at the mouth the Bukma Valley, which leads to the north and west slopes of the mountain.

During acclimatization we visited the Thalle Glacier and ascended a nameless and probably unclimbed peak (ca 5,800m). After passing the difficult front edge of the glacier, we camped in a cirque at about 5,200m. A steep 300m gully led us to a wide pass on the west side of the mountain, 400m below the summit. An easy snow ridge followed by three pitches of 60° ice and mixed (M3+) on the summit pyramid brought us to the snowy top. We called the mountain Mirkasia Peak.

Now we turned to our main target. After two days' walking we put our tent on Bukma Glacier below the amazing 1,600m north face of Honboro Peak. Our plan was to climb the left side of this wall, to a wide pass between Honboro and the 6,000m peak to its left. We estimated this section of the wall to be 900m high.

After four days of waiting for good weather, we climbed the wall (M4 60°) in eight hours. Because of great danger from falling rocks and ice, we climbed most of the route unroped. From the pass, at 5,700m, the rest of the route did not look as straightforward as we'd expected. In full sun, snow conditions were too bad to continue, so we decided to wait for evening. At 2 a.m. we began to climb toward the summit, but at 7 a.m., in beautiful weather, horrible snow and lack of protection 300m below top, along with a huge threatening cornice, forced us to retreat. In late afternoon, as consolation, we climbed for two hours in poor snow to the summit of Honboro's 6,200m neighbor. A sling on top informed us that the peak was not virgin, but the views of K2, Gasherbrum IV, and numerous other mountains rewarded our effort. After seven rappels and a lot of scary downclimbing, we returned to our tent the next day.

A Polish trio climbed Honboro Peak West (6,430m, right) in a 53-hour round trip from a high camp below the peak's west face, above the Khasumik Glacier. After climbing 500m of mixed ground, they followed the 2km southwest ridge to Honboro's west summit. Previously they had attempted Honboro's main peak by climbing 900m up the north face to a saddle between Honboro and the ca 6200m "Bukma Peak" to its east (left). When snow conditions halted the attempt on Honboro at ca 6,150m, the trio climbed "Bukma Peak" instead, finding slings on top indicating a prior ascent. *Lukasz Depta*

Our last option was the southwest ridge. It appeared to be rocky, which seemed safer than the poor snow we had been climbing. The shortest approach was from Khasumik Glacier. After six days of bad weather, avoiding the Khasumik Icefall to the left, we reached the edge of the Khasumik cirque. We established camp at 5,200m on the

The Polish team made the first ascent of Mirkasia Peak (ca 5,800m), above the Thalle Glacier, during acclimatization. *Lukasz Depta*

opposite side of the glacier from the west face of Honboro. A large serac threatened the beginning of our route; 200m of steep ice and 300m of mixed ground would gain the pass, and then about 2km of unforeseeable terrain would lead to the top. Because of the unstable weather, we planned to climb as quickly as possible without bivouac gear.

We began the climb after a day's rest. After climbing a cone-shaped ice field beyond the reach of the serac, we faced difficulties up to M5. Long sections of bad rock make this route not recommended for future ascents. After nine hours of climbing we reached the ridge. A steep icefield led to the first subpeak in three hours. From here, finally, we could see the rest of the route. In our way were two crags and the steep summit pyramid. We passed the first obstacle easily by snow on its right side. As we were climbing the next one, darkness fell. Poor rock in M5 terrain significantly slowed our climbing. When we reached the base of the summit pyramid, it was midnight. We stopped for a few hours of rest, melted some snow, prepared soup with couscous, and shivered in thin down jackets for four hours until dawn. The remaining 200m was not difficult, but our fatigue made it seem a long way. Finally, we stood on Honboro Peak West (6,430m). The east summit was 200m from us and no more than 20m higher, but the corniced snow ridge between the peaks was not inviting. We decided that the west summit was the logical end of our route on the southwest ridge. Dark clouds were gathering, and we had a long way to descend. Strong winds prevented us from stopping to brew up, and darkness fell as we built our first rappel station near the pass. At daybreak, after 53 hours (including our rest stop), we stood back on the glacier in heavy snowfall. A huge avalanche rolled down from the serac across our approach line before we had returned to the tent.

This area holds the possibility for many interesting first ascents. However, the best time for activity is probably in autumn or spring rather than in summer. During our climbs, the 0°C isotherm jumped to 6,000m, a major factor in causing the fractured rock.

LUKASZ DEPTA, *Poland*

CHARAKUSA VALLEY

Vince Anderson, Steve House, and Marko Prezelj completed the southwest ridge of Naisa Brakk (ca 5,200m, right), attempted by Jeff Hollenbaugh and Bruce Miller in 2004. They returned to attempt the long ridge west of Naisa Brakk, climbing about 2km before descending. *Marko Prezelj*

K7 West, first ascent; Sulo Peak, probable new route; Naisa Brakk, southwest ridge; spire below K7 West. In August and September, Americans Vince Anderson and Steve House and Slovenian Marko Prezelj spent nearly six weeks in the Charakusa Valley. They acclimatized by climbing the northwest face of Sulo Peak (a probable new route) and by making the first ascent of the southwest ridge of Naisa Brakk. [Editor's note: Naisa Brakk has been incorrectly called Nayser Brakk; according to House, the

Alpine Club of Pakistan says Naisa is the preferred spelling.] They then made the first ascent of K7 West (6,858m), via the southeast face. While waiting for conditions to improve on unclimbed K6 West (ca 7,100m), they climbed 2,000m along a rock ridge west of Naisa Brakk, crossing two summits, with difficulties up to 6a+, before descending to the west. With K6 West still out of condition, Prezelj and Maxime Turgeon climbed a rock spire on the east side of the south face of K7 West. [See Turgeon's note below.] House's full account of this expedition appears earlier in this *Journal*.

The Ski Track (400m, 5.11, Favresse-Stefanski-Villanueva) on Iqbal's Wall, the rock face opposite the lower west side of K7 West. The face likely got its first ascent in 1998 by Luca Maspes, Galen Rowell, and Natale Villa, who climbed a prominent dihedral on the left side. *Adam Pustelnik*

Badal Wall, new route to shoulder; Nafees' Cap, first ascent; Iqbal's Wall, new route. After failed attempts on three new routes, the team of Nicolas and Olivier Favresse (Belgium), Adam Pustelnik (Poland), and Sean Villanueva (Belgium) succeeded on a new route called Badal (1,200m, 5.12+ A1) on the huge rock wall on the west side of K7 West, all free except for 5m of icy cracks. They then made a single-push, all-free first ascent of Nafees' Cap, a spire at the base of K7's south face, by a new route called Ledgeway to Heaven (1,300m, 5.12+). Before leaving the valley, Nicolas Favresse, Jerzy Stefanski (Poland), and Villanueva returned to one of the lines they had failed to climb earlier and made the first ascent of the Ski Track (400m, 5.11) on Iqbal's Wall. Nicolas Favresse's story about this expedition appears earlier in this *Journal*.

K7, attempt. Thanks to the Lyman Spitzer and Shipton-Tilman awards, in late summer Scott DeCapio and I, traveling with our Canadian friends Max Turgeon and Louis-Philippe Ménard, tried some climbs in the Charakusa Valley. First we got horribly off-route trying to repeat No More Tasty Talking—yes, that dead-obvious prow on Naisa Brakk. We wandered too far left, climbing 1,500' of virgin terrain (probably 5.10R), so crappy and un-fun that it's not worth elaborating on, and then descended from the midway notch.

In mid-September we attempted a new line on K7. (The south-facing clefts between buttresses that we'd hoped to climb on K7 West were melted out and rubbly.) We got about halfway up K7 (22,743'/6,934m), starting from the east with a previously unclimbed (we think) ice and mixed couloir of about 3,000' vertical. This is the next couloir to the right of the Japanese route's start. The climbing was mostly moderate, with a short crux of maybe WI5 M6, and brought us to a junction with the Japanese route at the end of our first day. The next morning we got another 500'–1,000' higher, passing relics of the Japanese first ascent and reaching the Fortress formation, which looked hard. Thinking ourselves clever, we tried to traverse around it to the left. A man wiser than us once said there's a fine line between clever and stupid, and indeed there is. We dead-ended and, wilting under our too-heavy packs, gasping under too-thin air, and melting under too-warm temps—in other words, suffering from simple lameness—we retreated from about 19,000' and descended the basin to the west (where Steve House's 2004 solo goes).

We realize that opinions vary on what constitutes a new route (such as joining an existing line or reaching prominent landmarks), but we do have some standards. As we whimpered back to camp, it seemed quite clear to us who got the better of our little exchange with K7.

Of note, farther right on the east face were some spectacular-looking ice lines. The bottom portions, however, were gushing waterfalls while we were there, and though we stayed in the valley another 10 days or so after our attempt, a ton of snow fell and we never ventured back up to the east face.

KELLY CORDES, *AAC*

Farol East, solo first ascent; spire below K7 West, first ascent. Louis-Philippe Ménard and I had big plans for the Charakusa Valley, but LP was injured when we attempted the south buttress of Farol Central during acclimatization, and he had to depart for home on September 8. With nothing better to do, I stayed to see what the weather would bring.

On September 11 I returned to the tent we had left at the base of Farol more than a week earlier. My goal was a narrow ice line on the southwest side of unclimbed Farol East (ca 6,350m). Due to the orientation of the route, I had to stop in the extreme afternoon heat and bivy as soon as I reached the summit ridge. After an early start the next day, I stood on the highest summit I'd ever been on by noon, alone in the middle of the Karakoram under a sky without even the sign of a cloud.

Over 1,300m above the glacier, with only 50m of 6mm cordelette for rappelling, I didn't have any time to lose. At 9 p.m., soaking wet from an extended session of canyoneering, and with barely half of the cordelette left, so frozen it could have stood by itself, I was back to the security of my tent.

On the 17th, a day before the porters were to arrive for Vince Anderson, Steve House, and Marko Prezelj, Marko still had energy to burn. I joined him to go see what the pillars on the south face of K7 West had to offer. Without having previously scoped any particular line, our attention was caught by a shallow dihedral and crack system that sliced through the south face of the farthest east pillar. [See photo on p. 74 for the location of this pillar.]

At 7:30 a.m. we were throwing on rock shoes. After about 100m of unroped climbing, we did 15 pitches of interesting steep rock. Perfect overhanging hand cracks, steep dihedrals, mostly 5.10 or 5.10+. At 5 p.m. the summit was still a few rope lengths ahead, but it seemed so close that there was no way we were bailing. At 8:30, after three more pitches and a few meters of aid, we were on the top of the buttress (900m, 5.11 A0). We hadn't reached any real summit, and the formation that we climbed hasn't got a name. But we left in the morning with the goal of reaching the top of that pillar with only a single light pack between the two of us, and we had attained our goal—and that was as satisfying as reaching any other summit of the Charakusa or any other valley.

MAXIME TURGEON, *Québec, Canada*

(1) The summit of Farol Central (ca 6,350m), likely first climbed by the south pillar, just out of view to the left (Hoehlen-Mitterrer, 2005). (2) Maxime Turgeon (inset photo) soloed an ice gully to make the first ascent of Farol East (ca 6,350m), with one bivouac. (3) Unclimbed Farol Far East (ca 6,200m) was attempted by Raphael Slawinski and Steve Swenson via the prominent gully line right of the sharp peak, also in 2005. *Maxime Turgeon*

Haji Brakk, attempt on west face. From June 28 to July 17 the small Polish expedition of Jerzy Stefanski and I climbed in the Charakusa Valley. We acclimatized with a night at 5,000m and an ascent of Sulo Peak (ca 5,950m) by its southwest couloir, and then we had a week of bad weather. During this time we made plans to try the west face of Haji Brakk (ca 5,985m). Our proposed line was to the right of the Steve House route (2003, first ascent of the peak). It followed a mixed dihedral, then snow slopes to a small ridge, and then a 150–200m headwall. After four hours of approaching we made a bivy at the base of the wall. However, there was rain and snow-fall that night, and the next morning we went down to base camp all wet.

We got a forecast for good weather for several days, so we packed our gear and went back to the base of the wall. We decided to bivy higher than before, just below the dihedral. Unfortunately, we discovered that during repacking we had forgotten the gas. It meant defeat at the beginning, but in spite of this we decided to climb. About 3 a.m. we woke, ate a little, and had a cold drink. We quickly climbed the huge dihedral, where the rock was far from perfect and there was mixed climbing up to Scottish VI. The most problematic pitch was a chimney with a waterfall. Because of technical difficulties (about VI+/VII-), Jerzy led with rock shoes; I followed with two backpacks. We got very wet, but at 2 p.m. were on the snow slope. The weather was perfect—too perfect. The snow became heavy. We had to stop and bivy.

When we woke at 1 a.m., the snow was frozen. Above a 65° snow-ice slope, we reached an 80m mixed wall up to 85°. Climbing this was difficult (at least Scottish VI), with only psychological protection. The ice and snow became less safe minute by minute. After three hard pitches, we reached the small ridge at midday. To reach the headwall we would have had to rappel to a 60° snow couloir and climb it for two pitches. Because of bad snow, we first would have had to bivy and wait for the freeze. Because we were dehydrated and out of food, and I was afraid my wet toes were freezing, we decided to retreat. We rappelled to our last bivy, then started downclimbing the couloir Steve House had climbed. It was risky because of stone falls and the bad condition of the snow and ice. About 6 p.m. we reached our first bivy, and the next day we went down to base camp. My toes were frostbitten, but fortunately I lost just nails. However, my climbing in the valley was over.

After several days Jerzy soloed the south couloir of Beatrice (5,800m) in 4½ hours up and down. At the end of the expedition he climbed a new route called the Ski Track on the 400m Iqbal's Wall, with Nicolas Favresse and Sean Villanueva from Belgium. [See summary above.] Without the Polish Climbing Association (PZA), this expedition wouldn't have taken place.

JAN KUCZERA, *Polish Climbing Association*

Jikji (6,235m). In July and August a Korean expedition made the possible first ascent of a 6,235m peak they called Jikji, above the South Charakusa Glacier. This peak is connected to Drifika (6,447m) by a long ridge extending to the south, and is just south of Poro Peak (6,187m), which was climbed in 1988 by a British expedition. It is hidden by the bulk of Poro from the Charakusa Valley. The Koreans appear to have climbed the long south ridge of Jikji with three camps. The name Jikji is from the oldest book printed with metal type in existence, made in 1377 in Korea.

DOUGALD MACDONALD

A Korean team made the probable first ascent of Jikji Peak (6,235m), just south of Poro Peak (6,187m), by climbing the south ridge from the South Charakusa Glacier. *Korean Jikji Expedition*

NANGMA VALLEY

Shingu Charpa, east face. While planning our expedition back home, I could not get over the fact that it seemed prudent to plan 20 days for our new route on Shingu Charpa's east wall. But looking at the photos, that's what my experience suggested. This wall is strongly defended not by one crux but by a set of hard problems. Perhaps for that reason our predecessors did not reach the top. They solved some problems but were not ready to solve the following ones. And we do not blush to say that it was not easy for us either, psychologically or physically.

Mikhail Davy, Alexander Shabunin, and I spent 21 days on the climb, and another three days descending; we had 11 different bivy sites. Our route gained 1,600m, with a mix of free climbing and aid on rock, as well as pitches of ice and mixed. We graded it ABO 7a (6c obl) M5, but this is just one indication of the difficulties.

For one, we had a small team, and each climber had no time to recover his breath, notwithstanding his position on the rope. For another thing, although the wall pretended to be silent during our reconnaissance, it revealed a cruel temper during our first night in the portaledge. A thousand tons of rock (I do not exaggerate) flew by, brushing the portaledge's edge. And that happened not just once or twice. Night rockfalls similar to the collapses on the Petit Dru and falling ice after the morning sun's appearance forced us to adapt if we did not want to be ground to dust. The seconds usually jumared with heavy packs so we could avoid hauling bags that might dislodge rocks, and we had to search with great care for protected bivy sites. Sometimes we raced all day to reach the next sheltered corner.

Although we free climbed a lot, this route is not suitable for a pure free ascent.

Alexander Shabunin, Alexander Klenov, and Mikhail Davy (from left to right) below the east face of Shingu Charpa (5,600m). The three men spent 24 days on the face. *Sergey Porodnov*

We found a layer of sand on the edges and huge, hanging loose blocks. The cracks are muddy and grassy or covered with a crust of burr-shaped crystals. Indeed, such rock is hard for aid climbing too.

The weather was horrid. Either we are losers or it is the general rule for the area now, but we dealt with much cold and snow. It was always about 0°C, the most tiring temperature. In winter, at –30°C, you can wear enough clothes and heavy boots to keep dry and warm. But we climbed in rock shoes or light boots that were all the time soaked.

I believe I understand why the Ukrainian and American teams did not get to the summit by the north ridge. [Editor's note: Both attempts were in 2006.] It was so distant and they faced ice and mixed terrain when they felt their moral and physical strength was on the wane. We only managed to win the summit on our second push. During the first one we climbed five pitches from a bivy where we thought the summit was close, but then realized we did not have time to return before nightfall. It wasn't easy to force ourselves to repeat an attempt early the next morning. We were almost out of food—our daytime menu had been reduced to tea in the morning and a package of soup for three men in the evening. We faced the sad prospect of a starving descent. But finally we did it! It was time well spent.

ALEXANDER KLENOV, *Russia/Kazakhstan*

Anne Arran leads 5.11+ splitter cracks on the 14th pitch of Bloody Mary on Denbor Brakk. *John Arran*

Denbor Brakk, Bloody Mary, mostly free ascent; Zang Brakk, Welcome to Crackistan. Seeking free-climbable routes in the rock spire wonderland of the Nangma Valley, we first examined the left side of Shingu Charpa's east face, but when poor weather made free climbing unlikely we turned our attention to lower, steeper walls that would hold less snow. We hoped to warm up and acclimatize with a three-day free-climbing attempt on the slabby left-hand side of Zang Brakk (4,800m), but a stream swollen with glacial run-off proved uncrossable, so we focused our binoculars on the closer Denbor Brakk (4,800m).

After scoping the southwest face we chose to attempt the Czech route Bloody Mary (Jonak-Satava, 2004), which already had free pitches up to UIAA IX- (5.12c). We repeated the 500m climb in a seven-day capsule-style ascent. Of the route's two aid pitches, the first (A1) went on natural gear at E6 6b (5.12c), just left of the original offwidth roof; the other (A2) we freed on top-rope at 5.12d, initially somewhat right of the knifeblade aid line. Although we did not want to add bolts to an existing aid pitch without the consent of the first ascensionists, John feels the addition of two more bolts to the pitch would be in keeping with the nature of the other hard pitches, and would make the climb one of the best, hardest, and most varied free lines in the region.

We then returned to Zang Brakk, looking for a free-climbable line up the southeast pillar. An Austrian team had free-climbed to half-height at 5.12d (now thought to be 5.12c), before running into blind seams. By opting for a variant line and climbing two pitches of E6/7 (5.12d), we onsighted all-free almost to the top of the pillar. However, hampered by five days of unsettled, snowy weather, we ran completely out of food and water, and thus did not have time to free the crux pitch, which we had aided on tiny knifeblades and beaks at A3. John worked the moves on top-rope and said the pitch would likely go free at around E7 6b (5.13b), and might need a bolt or two for protection. We pressed on to the summit on day nine. As nearly all of the 500m route's 17 pitches involve hard crack climbing (including six pitches of 5.12), Welcome to Crackistan must rank as one of the most continuously hard jamming routes on any big wall, and now awaits a completely free ascent.

ANNE *and* JOHN ARRAN, *UK*

Zang Brakk, Czech Start Canadian Pinish. I was coming to the end of my summer guiding season in the Alps when I applied for the John Lauchlan Award to pursue my dream of exploring new routes in the Karakoram. After Lilla Molnar—a good friend and solid climber—agreed to join me, we began thinking about an objective. Sean Isaac bestowed his knowledge, and we decided on the Ladyfinger and Hunza Peak.

However, after we arrived and trekked for a long day in the remarkable area of Ultar Meadows, we decided to abandon Ladyfinger and Hunza for safer and quicker approaches in the Hushe Valley. We were fortunate to find a conveniently located and spectacular base camp up the Nangma Valley, above which many talented climbers have left a legacy of hard aid and spicy free climbs. We stumbled upon the unfinished east face of Zang Brakk (4,800m), where a Czech team had abandoned a line earlier this summer. [See note below.] The objective seemed to fit our window of weather, ability, and motivation.

The first day of our ascent, September 19, was blessed with sunshine, and we added two pitches to the Czechs' initial three. Lilla won the day's crux with a tricky A2 butt-crack pitch. After waiting out a couple of bad weather days, which provided rest and a chance to scope the summit ridge and descent route, we charged back up to our

The east face of Zang Brakk (4,800m), showing the Czech start (1) and Canadian start (2) to the route Czech Start Canadian Pinish (500m, TD- 5.10 A2). The circle marks the Czech high point. The new route Welcome to Crackistan (500m, TD- 5.12d A3) ascends the right side of the prominent pillar on the left. *Jennifer Olson*

previous high point in deteriorating conditions on September 22. Wearing everything we had, we climbed mostly 5.10 A1 for the next six pitches. Actually, we didn't climb so much as extricate plants and harvest dirt. If extreme gardening were an Olympic sport, we'd be medal contenders. The rock itself was brilliantly clean, slightly featured granite. The cracks have the potential to be just as remarkable, with rigorous cleaning.

As we neared the summit ridge it snowed and got dark. We had to traverse the ridge in rapidly deteriorating conditions, climbing up and rappelling down several times before we were able to put the rope away. From the top we descended slowly, with a bit of backtracking, and arrived at base camp 16 hours after we began.

Lilla coined the name Czech Start Canadian Pinish for our route (500m, TD- 5.10 A2, 11 pitches) because our guide, Imran, was not used to the small appetites of picky white girls and would often ask if we had "pinished our dinner." This route would go free at 5.11-. You could replace the A2 pitch with a 5.10+ offwidth with a steep exit.

JENNIFER OLSON, *Canada*

Drifika, completion of southwest ridge to west summit; other ascents and attempts. The Czech expedition of Ondrej Baszczynski, Martin Klonfar, Ondrej Martinek, Petr Novosad, Martin Simunek, and Jiri Splichal spent most of August in the Nangma Valley. Three climbers repeated

Hasta la Vista David (2004) on Zang Brakk, and then Klonfar and Splichal climbed the 10-pitch Trihedral Route (450m, VII A2) on Denbor Brakk. Later they discovered that much of their line followed the German route Haulbag, Du Arschloch (Häbel-Sauter, 2006), with variations on the first and fourth pitches. In mid-August, four climbers attempted Drifika (6,447m), reaching 6,250m.

On August 23 Klonfar and Splichal completed the southwest ridge to the western summit of Drifika, calling their line Babba's Dead Cam (V M4, loose rock). From a camp at 5,300m the two climbed steep ice on the southwest face to reach the southwest ridge. This icefield had been climbed in 2004 by a Slovenian quartet, which retreated at 6,300m. From the cornice atop the ridge, Klonfar and Splichal climbed several pitches of icy loose rock to reach Drifika's western summit.

Baszczynski and Novosad started a route on Zang Brakk's east face that was completed a few weeks later by Lilla Molnar and Jennifer Olson (Czech Start Canadian Pinish, see note above.)

Dougald MacDonald, *from a report at www.vsak.net*

Martin Klonfar and Jiri Splichal completed the southwest ridge to the western summit of Drifika (ca 6,440m). A Slovenian quartet had climbed the southwest face to reach this ridge in 2004. The Czechs added several pitches of icy rock climbing to gain the west summit. *Jiri Splichal*

From the crest of the southwest ridge of Drifika, the Czech duo climbed a loose rock traverse and M4 icy corners to reach the western summit. *Jiri Splichal*

Igor Brakk, Inshallah. In July, Toni Caporale, Maurizio Felici, Alessandro Palmerini, and I opened Inshallah (610m, ABO- VII A0, ice 70°) on Igor Brakk (5,010m) in the Amin Brakk group of the Nangma Valley. The initial goal of our Abruzzo-based expedition was the ascent of a virgin peak in the Charakusa Valley, followed by an attempt on Broad Peak, but once in the region we found it would be impossible to travel to or from the Charakusa through Gondogoro Pass, and so we had to make a virtue of necessity.

We decided to visit the Nangma Valley, which we knew only through photos shared by friends. We had to be at the Broad Peak base camp by July 15, and time was tight. After six days in the Nangma Valley, five of which passed in the rain, we had only four days to climb. With our initial ideas for a big-wall route wrecked, we were forced to climb in alpine style, light and fast, although the peaks that surrounded us are not the best for this style.

After a sleepless night because of Toni's intestinal illness, which forced him to stay behind,

Inshallah (610m, ABO- VII A0) on Igor Brakk (5,010m) in the Amin Brakk group. Hidden behind a rock pinnacle low on the face was a pitch of 70° ice, "protected" with cams placed between rock and ice. *Agostino Cittadini Collection*

we approached our chosen climb. We had already cached some of our equipment at the base. The first 200m were inside a winding gully with short steps up to V+, interspersed with unstable boulders that we took care to leave in place. Finally we were under the main wall.

The steep climbing began with a frozen channel of black ice covered with debris, protected with cams placed between rock and ice. Cracks that appeared inviting were filled with gravel and wet sand. In subsequent pitches, after passing an overhang with aid (A0), the inclination of the wall decreased, but lack of holds and blind cracks made progress uncertain. The pitches followed with constant difficulties. The precariousness of the protection was discouraging, and we alternated leads to let the tension diminish from the pitch just led.

Finally, exhausted by the altitude, we touched the summit at 5:30 p.m. We dedicated our ascent to our lost friends Stefano Imperatori and Alberto Bianchetti, and installed a commemorative plaque entrusted to us by CAI dell'Aquila. The descent by rappel lasted until 9 p.m. We decided to call our climb Inshallah, which means in one sense "to hope"—above all the hope of returning soon to the Nangma Valley's Eldorado of granite.

Agostino Cittadini, *Italy*

India

HIMALAYA

Overview. The year 2007 saw reduced mountaineering activity in the Indian Himalaya. An important reason was the stiff charge enforced by two state governments whose states contain large numbers of peaks, i.e. Sikkim and Uttarakhand (formerly Uttaranchal). In addition to expedition fees imposed by the Indian Mountaineering Foundation, these two states insist on additional fees and stiff conditions, which have put off many climbers. As a result there was not a single expedition to the east (Sikkim and Arunachal Pradesh) and few expeditions to the Uttarakhand area. [Things are improving in Sikkim, as described by Roger Payne in his article about Sikkim starting on page 112 of this *Journal*—Ed.]

There were 113 IMF-reported expeditions (61 Indian and 52 foreign). Of these, about 70 were to routine peaks. For example, Stok Kangri, a peak which can be climbed in about three days from Leh, received as many as 25 expeditions in 2007. This peak has often been climbed illegally, but now the IMF has opened a branch office in Leh, so expeditions register here and are more likely to pay the requisite fees.

The requirement for having "X-Visa" stamped on one's passport has been done away with in the case of 113 peaks (a list is available on the IMF website). For these peaks the IMF has a single-window clearance and will even collect fees for paying the state governments. For all other peaks old requirements and formalities continue.

Three expeditions visited the eastern Karakoram, which takes much organizing and clearances. With much fanfare the Siachen area was declared open for trekkers, but Pakistan immediately registered a strong protest. At present only one team, consisting of military cadets, has visited the most sensitive parts of Siachen. No trekking is yet allowed in the area. However, the practice of allowing joint Indian and foreign expeditions to the Siachen Glacier continues.

Expeditions to Kalanka and Changabang were beaten back by freak storms in September and October. However, expeditions to difficult peaks like Arwa Spire and Arwa Tower were successful during May. Some notable climbs were the ascent of Kulu Makalu, Mukut Parvat East Peak, Manirang, and Menthosa, all by Indian mountaineers. The west ridge route on Nilkanth, pioneered by Martin Moran in 2000, was repeated by a Himalayan Club, Kolkata, team. It was an energetic climb, with members proceeding from the last camp to the summit and back with two bivouacs. They had excellent weather and made full use of it. The cryptic message on reaching the summit, as agreed earlier, was "The Himalayan Club is smiling," which it was!

The Indian Mountaineering Foundation organized seven expeditions. Two were ladies' teams. The IMF expedition to Changuch, an unclimbed mountain rising above the Pindari Glacier, ran into extremely bad weather. After waiting for a few days after the first clearing, the team decided to climb along the Pindari Icefall to a higher camp. An avalanche landed on their camp, killing two Sherpas. A third Sherpa was rescued, but will spend at least one year recuperating. Similarly, an Indian-Australian expedition to a 6,350m peak rising above Col Italia could not get far, as the Thangman Glacier was in flood and impossible to cross. The same glacier had earlier been crossed, with great difficulty, by an Indo-American expedition that climbed Chong Kumdan I. Nearby Mamostong Kangri was climbed by two teams: an Indo-French expedition,which climbed it by the normal route, and the Vikas Regiment of the Indian Army, which made a variation approaching from the east. For the first time there was an Indo-Bangladesh expedition, which climbed Rubal Kang.

Several trekking agencies, particularly those that take students to the mountains, are unregulated in India. This year two deaths of young people on routine treks have raised controversy. On the initiative of one of the parents, the High Court in Mumbai has ordered the government to frame rules for such agencies. This could be a welcome step that Indian mountaineers have been waiting for.

Many changes are evident in the Himalaya directly due to global warming. Lower villages are receiving less snow, and villagers complain that there is not enough snowmelt for irrigation. At certain villages flowers and fruits now have to be planted a thousand feet higher than before because of rising temperatures. And glaciers, such as the Chong Kumdan, are certainly receding.

A trekking team including myself was permitted, for the first time, to trek near the tri-junction of India, China, and Burma—the easternmost point of India. Considering its sensitive nature, as Indian and Chinese forces had clashed here, this was a significant development. We located Chinese inscriptions on a huge rock that was mentioned in the *Geographical Journal* in 1910 by Ronald Kaulback, who was a member of F. Kingdon-Ward's party. Further research is needed to completely decipher these writings, but it is an important discovery.

During the year two notable books were published. *Heights of Madness* by Myra MacDonald considers the war on the Siachen Glacier. She was a reporter with Reuters who flew over the glacier in poor weather, met army officers, and talked with those involved in the war. Later she did the same on the Pakistan side. The other book is by leading British author Charles Allen. *Kipling Sahib* illuminates Rudyard Kipling's life in India. It was released at JJ School of Arts in Mumbai, where Kipling was born.

Finally, the (British) Alpine Club's 150th anniversary was celebrated in the Indian Himalaya by organizing a small expedition to the Kagbhusandi Valley. The team climbed two peaks, despite plenty of snow on the ground. One of the peaks was named "AC 150," fitting to the occasion (see Dave Wynne-Jones' report later in this *Journal*). On the way to the mountains we stopped at Auli, a ski resort above Joshimath. From there, in front of Nanda Devi, Mark Higton called the London police. To avoid penalties—it was the last day to do so—Mark provided his credit card number to pay the fine for a traffic violation in London. The operator murmured in amazement at the end of it all, "No one has paid us traffic fines from high Himalaya, Sir!"

HARISH KAPADIA, *Honorary Editor, The Himalayan Journal*

EASTERN KARAKORAM

Siachen Peace Park, dead or alive? The 23rd anniversary of the Siachen conflict was marked by another disappointment. The last round of talks between the Defence Secretaries of India and Pakistan ended in April 2007 without an agreement. This was the third time that an agreement had seemed to be within our grasp, and hopes were high; it was the third time that the two countries backed off at the last minute, as if suddenly frightened at the prospect of an agreement. Five months later, in mid-September, the Indian Army announced that, subject to certain conditions, it was opening the Siachen to trekkers and climbers. This sounded like the death knell of the Siachen Peace Park (SPP).

The SPP was proposed primarily as a conservation effort; it was also hoped to ease the problem of defining boundaries. As there were no inhabitants in the area, the boundaries would be those for a park rather than for national territory. An agreement on Siachen could pave the way to a settlement of the whole Kashmir problem.

Instead, the Indian move seems to assert that the Siachen area is Indian territory and non-negotiable. As might have been expected, Pakistan reacted angrily. It would need a remarkable optimist to claim that the SPP is still alive.

The Himalayan Club has invested a great deal of effort in the SPP proposal. The concept of a transboundary park was first floated in an article in the *Himalayan Journal*, Vol. 50, 1992-93. The HC co-sponsored a meeting in Delhi in 2001 that endorsed the proposal and sent an appeal to the Prime Minister of India before his meeting with the President of Pakistan. (The meeting ended in disarray.) The Editor of the *HJ*, in his many travels, seldom failed to promote the idea of an SPP; in general, it met a favorable response everywhere, abroad and in India. The HC participated in a joint Indo-Pakistan climb in the Alps, organized by the UIAA (World Mountaineering Federation) to promote the proposal. The 75th anniversary of the Club in 2003 included a series of talks on the Siachen Peace Park in Mumbai, Bangalore, and Chennai. Together with *Sanctuary* Magazine, the HC held a seminar in Mumbai; the Chief Guest was Prof. Saleem Ali, an American of Pakistani origin; he has written and spoken about the SPP in Pakistan, America, and elsewhere. A special brief was prepared, at his request, for a senior official associated with the Indo-Pakistan talks.

It is sad that India and Pakistan have not been able to agree on a transboundary park or on a withdrawal of troops, especially when we see other countries which have difficult political problems managing to cooperate on conservation issues. Thus the Balkan Peace Park, a grassroots project associating Kosovo, Montenegro, and Albania, seems to be moving ahead, the Mt. Elgon Regional Ecosystem Programme associating Kenya and Uganda likewise. The idea of a transboundary peace park for the Golan Heights between Israel and Syria has been floated; that is surely one area that presents even more intractable problems than Kashmir.

Our main interest must be to protect the Siachen from further degradation and to restore it to the greatest extent possible to the status it enjoyed for millions of years, until war broke out in 1984. The name "Siachen Peace Park" has gathered resonance over the past 15 years, although in the early stages, other names were used, such as International Park of the Rose, Siachen Glacier Park. If a transboundary park seems impossible at present, there is still no reason why efforts to clean up and protect the area should not be pursued. The Siachen Peace Park can be a national park for the present.

Since the Army is responsible for the area and is authorizing trekkers and climbers, it should ensure that visitors adhere to the codes we already have. One assumes that the Army has plenty of people there well-versed in environmentally correct behavior; they can organize training courses for visitors, including porters. Such courses have been conducted by Mountain Wilderness in India, Pakistan, and Afghanistan; the Army has acquired immense experience in organizing training in mountaineering and in protecting the environment.

Surely the need for a military presence will not endure forever. When that happy time comes, and the Siachen is free of permanent human presence, the area could then be turned into a national peace park. Then the glacier can be given whatever time is needed to recover from the rude treatment it suffered while it was in the front line of battle.

AAMIR ALI, *Himalayan Club, adapted from The Himalayan Journal*

Chong Kumdan I (7,071m), southeast ridge. On August 20 at 4 p.m., Marlin Geist, Donald Goodman, Chris Robertson, and I, with Sherpas Nima Dorje, Pemba Norbu, and Ming Temba, completed a new route on Chong Kumdan I. Our route climbed the southeast ridge to its intersection with the main east ridge, which we followed to the summit. This was the second ascent of the peak. The first was made in 1991 by an Indo-British expedition, jointly led by Harish Kapadia and Dave Wilkinson. We appear to have been the first expedition to this area since 1991.

The approach to Chong Kumdan is from the Nubra Valley, which lies north of the famous Khardung La. This region is sandwiched between Pakistan-occupied Kashmir on the northwest and the Aksai Chin area on the northeast. The approach to the mountain is along the historic Silk Route to Yarkand over the famous Saser La (pass), a route known as the "Skeleton's Trail." We used 50 horses to carry nearly two tons of equipment and rations across the Saser La (5,375m) and two major glaciers (Aqtash and Thangman). The horsemen from Ladakh were of tremendous assistance in finding a way across the glaciers' ice and rocks. The Shyok River ("river of death") brought the expedition to a halt at the other end of the Thangman Glacier. The river blocked the route for the horses, so we carried loads from here.

Our main ambition had been to climb the virgin peak of Chong Kumdan II (7,004m). On reaching base camp, we explored a route through the South Chong Kumdan Glacier, only to be faced by huge gaping crevasses, towering seracs, and penitents. The top snow layer had disappeared, due to global warming. The ice was bare and exposed, and it was dangerous to travel the glacier with the equipment and rations required. So we shifted focus to Chong Kumdan I, which minimized glacier travel. The route on Chong Kumdan I involved 45° to 55° ice for 400m to the crest of the southeast ridge. We fixed 500m of line on this section. We then followed the crest of the southeast ridge for a few hundred meters to 6,450m, where we established Camp 2. The 20° to 30° slopes were underlain by hard ice. We spent nearly four hours excavating tent platforms. From Camp 2, we climbed the remainder of the ridge to where it intersects the east ridge near 6,800m. Above Camp 2 we fixed four ropes and continued the route past several gendarmes, passing a cornice on the right at the top of the slope. This part of the climb could be made without fixed lines, as the slopes were moderate: a maximum of about 45° near the intersection with the east ridge. Due to poor snow, it took more than five hours to negotiate the last section to the summit.

One of our Kumauni support staff, Anand Ram, passed away on August 10 due to altitude sickness at the Saser Brangza Army Camp. Our Sherpa Sirdar, Ang Tashi, took ill on August 15 at Camp 1. He was accompanied down to ABC by expedition members on the 16th. When there was no improvement in his health, despite being provided bottled oxygen and medication, he was evacuated by helicopter and hospitalized at Hundar, where he recovered. Tashi had been climbing regularly at high altitude, had climbed Everest, and was one of the fittest Sherpas around.

DIVYESH MUNI, *Honorary Secretary, Himalayan Club, India*

Mamostong Kangri (7,516m), new approach and ascent. This Indian Army expedition with 30 strong members was led by Col. Ashok Abbey in October-November. Following a new approach route, they climbed the peak as autumn cold and snow was settling in. After crossing Saser La, they turned north along the Shrok and turned further west in the Thangman Valley leading toward Mamostong Kangri. Climbing a ridge directly, they avoided the Hope Col. Several members reached the summit (numbers and names are not known). Mamostong Kangri lies south of the Chong Kumdan massif and features a 2,000m face that must be one of the greatest unclimbed snow and ice walls in the Indian Himalaya; it will be a super-route if a safe line can be found. While camped nearly a mile from the bottom of this face in 1991, a British team was buffeted by spindrift from a large serac avalanche. The 2007 Indo-French team climbed the opposite side, repeating the original route via the southeast ridge to the upper northeast ridge, first climbed in 1984 by an Indo-Japanese expedition led by Balwant Sandhu (who made the first ascent of Changabang). This was a strong team, with experienced Japanese such as Ogata and Yamada, and Indians such as Chauhan, PM Das, and Rajiv Sharma. This high mountain has received about half a dozen ascents by several routes, but the 2007 ascent appears to be the first since 1992.

HARISH KAPADIA, *Honorary Editor, The Himalayan Journal, and* LINDSAY GRIFFIN, *Mountain INFO, www.climbmagazine.com*

Rimo I (7,385m), route unknown. In July-August, an Indian Mountaineering Foundation team led by Major K. S. Dhami claims to have reached the summit of Rimo I, a difficult peak in a side valley to the east of the Siachen Glacier. Bad weather and porter trouble hounded the expedition from the start. Kalyansing (an instructor at NIM) drowned in the Terong River in the first days of the expedition. Major Dhami suffered serious frostbite. The weather was said to be poor on the summit day, but we await further details and photographs. Rimo I was only climbed once previously, in 1988 by an Indo-Japanese expedition jointly led by Hukam Singh and Yoshi Ogata, via the southwest ridge. Prior to the first ascent the mountain had defeated very capable climbers such as Victor Saunders and Stephen Venables (1985) and Peter Hillary (1986).

HARISH KAPADIA, *Honorary Editor, The Himalayan Journal, and* LINDSAY GRIFFIN, *Mountain INFO, www.climbmagazine.com*

JAMMU & KASHMIR

Nun, northwest face, attempt. In September Jean-Marc Challandes, Sebastien Gerber, Andreas Hutter, Berhard Spack, and we established an advance base camp at 5,400m on the big plateau that lies at the foot of the 1,700m-high northwest face of Nun. In three days we equipped the first part of the face with fixed ropes. We planned to install a small bivouac in a crevasse at about 6,100m. The plan was to continue from there in alpine style and descend the northwest ridge to an altitude camp (C1) that had been previously set up at 6,680m.

However, on September 18, when Jean-Marc was climbing above Josep and Andreas at 6,000m, he heard a loud noise underneath his crampons, and the big ice slab they were on dropped a few centimeters. At this point, considering the bad ice conditions, they gave up the northwest face attempt.

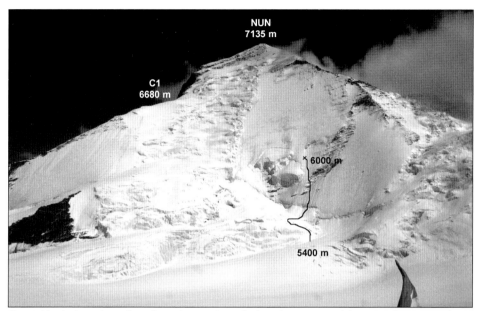

The 1,700m-high northwest face of Nun (7,135m). Marked are the attempt and the point where ice conditions become critically bad. On the left, the northwest ridge with C1. *Team NUNzero7*

At the same time, the other three climbers were acclimating at C1 on the northwest ridge. On September 19, in good weather conditions, Simon, followed by Bernhard, reached the summit (7,135m), while Sebastien stayed at C1 (6,680m) because of altitude sickness. Then early winter and heavy snowfall prevented the rest of the climbers from reaching the summit by the northwest ridge. For more information, see www.nun007.ch

SIMON PERRITAZ *and* JOSEP SOLA I CAROS, *Team NUNzero7, Swiss Alpine Club*

LADAKH & ZANSKAR

Shafat Fortress, Colorado Route. From August 8 to 12 Jonny Copp and Micah Dash made the first ascent of the Shafat Fortress (ca 19,500'), via the east face. The 21-pitch Colorado Route is 1,000m, VI 5.11 M6 C1, and merits a feature article in this *Journal [pp. 64–71].*

Peak 5,200m (Golden Sentinel). This small peak near Gulmotonga (Kargil) was summited on August 20 by an expedition led by Italian Mourizio Orsi. They followed the east face and north ridge. They propose naming the peak Golden Sentinel.

HARISH KAPADIA, *Honorary Editor, The Himalayan Journal*

Pangong Range reconnaissance; Peak 6,342m (Mt. Maan). The Pangong Range is just a one-day drive northwest from Leh, crossing Chang La (5,250m). This range includes more than 10 peaks over 6,000m, some of which are still unclimbed. The one problem is getting permission from Indian authorities to enter the Ladakh district of Jammu & Kashmir, so close to the sensitive border with China. Fortunately, in July the Japanese Alpine Club Ishikawa Section obtained climbing permission from IMF after four months of trying, and a traffic permit to the prohibited Pangong Tso area, the first ever given to foreigners, from the local Security Office.

The Pangong Range extends its main crest along the southern shore of Pangong Tso, and the northeast side of the lake gives a good approach to the mountains. Major peaks are Kangu Kangri (6,724m, climbed by an Indian Army Party), Kakstet Kangri (6,461m, probably also climbed by the Indians), Spangmik (6,250m, climbed by Chukyo Alpine Club, Nagoya, Japan), unclimbed peaks such as Mari (6,587m), Harong (6,210m), Tangtse (6,096m), and 12 unnamed peaks. Of these peaks Mari looked the most attractive in shape, altitude, and imagined technical difficulty; therefore we picked it as our target.

On August 3 our seven-member party left Leh, crossed Chang La, and arrived at Maan village on the shore of the Lake Pangong. It was only a half day of driving on a paved road, but due to four time-consuming checkposts, it was midnight when we arrived at the village.

The next day we looked up into the mountains for a good place for our base camp. Because we were the first foreigners, we had no information besides the map, nor any photo identifying our objective. From the map we knew Mt. Mari was out of sight behind the main divide. Gentle scree slopes ran up for some distance and then abruptly steepened. There the wall was cut by seven gorges, some guarded by waterfalls. Judging from the map, Mari seemed located above the fourth glacier from the right, which was hidden behind huge terminal moraines. We pitched base camp at 4,250m on the pasture facing this valley, and Camps 1 (4,746m) and 2 (5,653m) on up the glacier.

On August 11 I went alone to reconnoiter the upper part of the glacier. After several hours of hiking I saw striking twin triangular peaks standing far ahead. Immediately I recognized them as Mt. Mari! I climbed farther and stood on a ridge that divided two valleys. Above a snow flat stood a rock mound 20m high, shaping the 6,342m unnamed peak that we later named Mt. Maan after the village at its foot.

A glance at the sheer ridge connecting the east summit of Mt. Mari with its main west summit (6,587m) made me abandon the idea of following it. Attempting the west summit would require going down to the western glacier basin, then climbing 800m back up its west face. Giving up the idea of climbing Mt. Mari, we changed our plan to bringing all seven of us to the summit of Mt. Maan, which we did on August 14 and 15. On the 16th we sent five porters to C2 to carry all the gear down to BC.

Notes: Maan is a village consisting of approximately 30 families. It is marked "Mari" or "Mun" on some maps, but "Maan" or "Man" is considered correct. *Maan* means "medicinal herb." *Mari* means "red mountain": Ma means "red," and *Ri* means "mountain." Maps: LADAKH/ZANSKAR (Centre)1/150,000/Geneve/2005; LEOMANN MAPS INDIAN HIMALAYA MAPS, Sheet-9, Rupsh, Tso Moriri, Pangong Tso 1/200,000/England/2000; INDIA AND PAKISTAN EDITION-2-ANS, NI-499, Pangong Tso 1/250,000/Washington DC/1962.

RENTARO NISHIJIMA, *Japanese Alpine Club (translated by Tamotsu Nakamura, Japanese Alpine News)*

HIMACHAL PRADESH

LAHUL & SPITI

Gangsthang, lower west face; Thirot Shivling (5,324m). Our team of nine climbers met with cold, variable weather but discovered a magnificent new valley for mountaineering, the Thirot Nala in the Lahaul district of Himachal Pradesh. Initial reconnaisances of unclimbed Nainghar Choti (6,094m) were hampered by heavy snowfall and poor visibility. However, the splendid pyramidal peak of Gangsthang (6,162m) offered a more accessible objective, and at 4:30 p.m. on September 30 six of us stood on the tiny summit, having made a new route up the west face before finishing up the normal southwest ridge. Peter Ashworth, Gustavo Fierro-Carrion, John Leedale, Arun Mahajan, Luder Singh, and I were the lucky summiteers, who then witnessed the kaleidoscope of a Himalayan sunset during the descent. The climb rates alpine D-, with pitches of Scottish III and IV in the 600m couloir used to access the final ridge. On September 28 Allan Clapperton, David Geddes, Frank Johnstone, Arun, Luder, and I reached the subsidiary rock peak of Thirot Shivling (5,324m), at PD-.

The team also enjoyed a superb journey into the area, the night sleeper from Delhi, the amazing narrow-gauge railway to Shimla hill station, beautiful roads through the verdant valleys of Kullu and Manali, and a breath-taking drive over the 13,000-foot Rohtang Pass into the spectacular Chandra-Bhaga valley.

MARTIN MORAN, *Alpine Club*

Gangsthang (6,162m) and Thirot Shivling (5,324m). The new route is on the west face, where it joins with the normal southwest ridge route. *David Geddes*

Pangi Valley, Sersank Peak, attempt; Peak 5,027m, first ascent. A small British expedition explored the upper Tiaso Nala and the area of the Sersank Pass in late June and early July 2007. The team, consisting of Rob Ferguson, Graham Little, Jim Lowther, and I, with a support team provided by Rimo Expeditions, left Delhi by road on June 17 and reached Manali after a 16-hour drive. On June 20 we crossed the Rohtang Pass to reach Chery in the Chandra Baga Gorge, some distance beyond Kilar. The road had been swept away by a major landslip and looked as if it would be some time before it was rebuilt. The gear was ferried across in the dark, and the next morning two jeeps took the team to the roadhead by the village of Tajana Adwar, a beautiful campsite.

Sersank Peak, showing the northwest ridge attempt. *Chris Bonington*

Two easy days of walking took us to base camp in the Hangrung Nala. There seemed two possible routes up Sersank Peak (Shib Shankar): the south ridge by a series of glaciers and snow slopes, or more directly up the northwest ridge, whose lower slopes were guarded by a steep rock buttress. We chose the latter, and established an advance base at the top of a moraine ridge below a gully that led to a ramp that reached up to half the height of the buttress. The ramp was fixed with rope by Rob and Jim, supported by our two Sherpas, Ang Tachei and Samghyl. Then the weather broke, and after four days of rain and snow the team dropped back to base camp.

On July 3 Graham, Jim, and Rob returned to the fray, while I went for a smaller, easier peak on the ridge to the northeast of base camp. On July 4 Graham, Jim, and Rob established Camp 1 at the head of the ramp on a large snow mushroom overlooking the northeast face and started climbing the steep rocks above. After three terrifying pitches on very loose rock, reaching 5,500m, they decided the route was too dangerous.

Meanwhile, Raj Kumar and I established a camp on the ridge above base camp at 4,674m, and on the following day scrambled to the highest point of the ridge, an elegant little peak at a height of 5,027m.

The team reunited at base camp that evening, and since there was no time to reconnoiter an alternative route, we started back toward the roadhead, reaching it on July 7. Heavy rain on July 8 caused over 20 major landslips on the road beside the Chandra Bhaga river, forcing us to walk out, covering 65km to Udaipur in two days. Raj Kumar, Samghyl, and Manbahadur did a magnificent job carrying loads of up to 40kg each. It was an eventful and enjoyable trip up a beautiful unspoiled valley. The local people were particularly friendly and helpful.

CHRIS BONINGTON, *Alpine Club, from the Himalayan Club Newsletter*

MIYAR VALLEY

Point 5,930m (Rachu Tangmu), central summit, Secret of Thin Ice. Two Slovak mountaineers, Andrej Kolarik and Juraj Svingal, climbed a new route to an unclimbed peak in the massif of Pt. 5,930m. This peak is situated on the other site of the main river in Miyar Valley, opposite Castle Peak. They called the massif "Rachu Tangmu" (Cold Horns) because the main summit looks like two horns. The first ascent of the main summit of Rachu Tangmu was made in 2005

The Secret of Thin Ice, which climbs to the central tower of Rachu Tangmu (Pt. 5,930m). *Andrej Kolarik*

by Oriol Baro and Oscar Cacho. The Slovak route, Secret of Thin Ice, climbs to the central tower of Rachu Tangmu (1,340m, ED+, 850, M6+ A1). They climbed this route in three days from September 29 to October 1. Until noon of the first day they were on the lower, easier part of the face, then they continued up the steep part on dangerous bad ice and snow. After a cold bivy, they traversed a bit to the right. They reached the edge of a couloir in the dark and climbed until midnight. After four hours of rest they finished their route and reached the central summit of Rachu Tangmu. The main summit was far away, with two broken and hard towers on the ridge. With no food or water, they decided to descend, reaching base camp at 22:30.

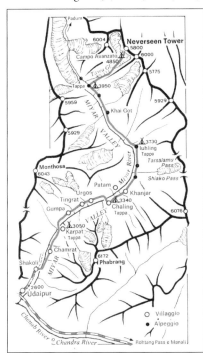

Miyar Valley, Garhwal, Uttarankhand, India

This was the third Slovak expedition to Miyar Valley. In 2002 Igor Koller, Dodo Kopold, Vlado Linek, and Ivan Stefansky did a new route, Sharp Knife of Tolerance (500m, F7a+ A3) to the ridge of Iris Peak in the massif of Castle Peak in 11 days. In 2003 Kopold and Stefansky returned to Miyar and made the first ascent of Last Minute Journey (900m, ED) via the south face of the Three Peaks Mountain massif. They called this peak Mt. Mahindra (5,845m).

VLADO LINEK, *Jamesak, Slovakia*

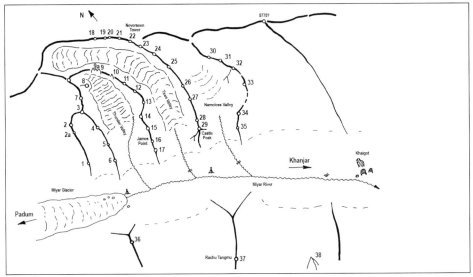

The peaks near Neverseen Tower in the upper Miyar Valley, with names collected by Vlado Linek. Please send comments, additions, corrections, and other changes to vlado@linek.sk and aaj@americanalpineclub.org. Originally published in *Jamesak. Igor Koller and Vlado Linek Andrej Kolarik*

1) Lammergeier Spire (Small Chamonix Tower), 5,350m (Jangpa Glacier)
3) Point 5,960m 4) Peak with window on summit
5) Goya Peak, 5,300m
7) Two Peaks Mountain
8) Peak with snow plateau
9) Three Peaks Mountain
9a) Mt. Mahindra
10) Thunder Peak, 5,990m
12) Veneto Peak, 5,850m
13) Point 5,650m
14) Yellow face from Dali Glacier (Thunder/Dali Glacier) (Premsingh Peak)
15) Big face from Dali Glacier
16) James Point, ca 5,500m
17) Small face from Dali Glacier (Toro Peak)
19) Paola's Peak

20) Peak 5,700m
21) Peak 5,750m (Grandfather Enzo Peak)
22) Neverseen Tower, ca 6,000m (Chhudong/Tawa Glacier)
23) Lotus Peak, 5,630m
23a) Point 5,650m
24) Geruda Peak, 5,640m
29) Castle Peak, ca 5,900m
29a) Iris Peak
29b) David 62's Nose
32) Ogre 33) Mont Blancu
34) Walker Spur
35) Brouillard Pillar, 5,240m
36) Lorena Peak
37) Rachu Tangmu, Point 5,930m
37a) Point 5,800m
38) Winter Matterhorn

Miyar Nala, Toro Peak, Toro Ridge; Korklum Gou (Window Peak), Shangrila Ridge; Premsingh Peak, Trident Ridge; Castle Peak, south face, David's 62 Nose tower, Lufoo Lam. My wife Tanja and I took the public bus to Tingrit, a small village at the end of the road. After a two-day approach on foot, with two horses for our stuff, we came to base camp under Castle Peak in a mix of rain and snow. Over the next three weeks we had much unstable and bad weather, but also two nice spells. On September 16 we climbed the east ridge of a rounded mountain we called Toro Peak (ca 4,850m) for acclimatization. We called our route Toro Ridge (300m vertical, 450m long, V+). The peak had already been climbed, and could even be hiked up.

We went for another acclimatization climb after a day of rest. We made an afternoon approach to the base of the mountain and made a brief bivouac under a boulder. During the

The 300m vertical Toro Ridge on a 4,850m previously climbed summit the Grmovseks called Toro Peak. *Andrej Grmovsek*

Andrej Gmorsek climbing Loofo Lam on Castle Peak, with Korklum Gou–Window Peak (ca 5,600m) in the background, showing the 600m-vertical Shangrila Ridge route. *Tanja Gmorvsek*

night we climbed 500 meters of a loose gully and, with the first sun, started climbing maybe the most aesthetic peak in the area. A perfect right-angle ridge led to the summit, with a huge window below an arch of rock that formed the top of the peak. After 500 meters of climbing, we were surprised by old slings, as we thought we were climbing an untouched line. A bit sad, we continued. The last pitch to the arch was seriously rotten and loose and was the crux. In early afternoon, we happily lifted our hands on a perfect summit. We were even happi-er when we didn't find rappel slings. After returning home, we read a new *AAJ* report about an unfinished attempt on more or less the same line, leading us to believe that we were the first people on this summit. So we named the peak Korklum Gou (Window

Trident Ridge (500m vertical, 1,000m long) on a virgin peak they called Premsingh Peak (ca 5,200m). *Andrej Grmovsek*

Peak, ca 5,600m) and the route Shan-grila Ridge (600m, 900m long, VII R).

We then spent five rainy and snowy days in base camp with Slovak climbers Andy and Juraj. The temperature dropped significantly, and a lot of snow accumulated on the upper walls. After the weather improved we decided to move to the Tawa Glacier side valley, to an advanced base camp under Neverseen Tower. The approach to this ABC involved almost 1,000m of altitude gain, half of it wandering on an unstable glacial

David's 62 Nose (ca 4,950m) on Castle Peak's south face, showing 350m-vertical Lufoo Lam–Windy Way. *Andrej Grmovsek*

moraine. Fresh snow on moving and slippery stones made walking hard and dangerous. Even south-facing, steep walls like Neverseen were plastered with snow. We stopped on the glacier to wait until the walls cleared of snow.

So as not to lose time in nice weather, we decided to climb a nice three-tower east ridge opposite our temporary camp. But it snowed all night, and we waited one more day for the ridge to dry. Then, on September 29, we climbed Trident Ridge (500m, 1,000m long, VII/VII+) on a virgin peak we called Premsingh Peak (ca 5,200m). Even in the sun it was cold for rock climbing, and it became clear that Neverseen was not a suitable option. With only a few days left, on October 1 we climbed our last route on the rock tower David's 62 Nose (ca 4,950m) on Castle Peak's south face. We called our route Lufoo Lam (Windy Way) (350m, 400m long, VII+). This tower had already been climbed, by Italians.

Climbing in this remote, uncrowded valley was a great adventure. It was nice to deal with hospitable local Buddhist people. The climbing itself was enjoyable because of the featured migmatite rock, which is something between granite and gneiss, and solider than it looks. We used only removable protection and left only a few rappel slings, to keep the area as adventurous as possible. We enjoyed our four new routes, on two virgin peaks, but our wish of climbing something on Neverseen remains a dream. I suggest that late summer is probably not the best time for rock climbing there because of low temperatures. There is still a lot worth exploring in this region.

ANDREJ GRMOVSEK, *Slovenia*

Mahindra, middle summit, Ashoka's Pillar; Peak 5,960m; Orange Tower. After long and crazy travel days, including a ride from a fellow named Happy, Freddie Wilkinson, Pat Goodman, and I thankfully found the end of the road in the small Himalayan village of Tingrit. In preparation for the months when the sturdy stone houses will be buried in meters of snow, bushels of straw lay stacked upon the flat roofs. Sweet peas, for which this valley is known, were starting to ripen. From Tingrit we hiked for three days to our base camp below Castle Peak, passing through open

Peak 5,960m, which was climbed via its west ridge. *David Sharratt*

Mt. Mahindra, showing 700m Ashoka's Pillar, which yielded sustained and superb 5.11 climbing. *David Sharratt*

grasslands and fields of wildflowers, fields populated by sheep and shepherds, horses, cattle, and small villages. After traveling through Delhi's chaos and lack of infrastructure, I reflected on India's many contradictions as we passed well-maintained schools in each tiny community. There is even a helicopter pad in Tingrit, so that medicine and supplies can be flown in to help the people endure austere winters. With base camp established, we headed up the Jangpar Glacier with our sights set on the pyramid-shaped Peak 5,960m. To get our groove on and acclimatize, we first climbed the Orange Tower. This previously unclimbed peak does resemble a tower from one vantage point, but is really more of an elongated fin, and hosts much potential for short multi-pitch cragging on generally solid and well-featured rock. We climbed the Tower by a six-pitch route, featuring a memorable pitch of overhanging climbing on wind-sculpted pinches. After some bad-weather tent time we set out on Peak 5,960m via the west ridge. To gain the ridge, we climbed 500m of low-angle alpine ice and a few pitches of choss-aneering. We climbed the ridge to the base of a steep 350m buttress that led to the summit, but retreated as snow flurries turned to an all-out slush storm. As the gods continued to puke mashed potatoes on us, we rappeled through the night onto the Dali Glacier. Having not previously explored the Dali Glacier, we found ourselves cliffed-out and hunkered down on the ice for a short shivery sleep. At first light we made our way down to base camp. A few days later Freddie and I returned to summit Peak 5,960m, while Pat endured severe stomach pain in base camp. The ridge was moderate, with generally solid rock on its crest, and the final buttress had fun 5.9 climbing. From the ridge to the summit is about 700m vertical, or about 1,000m of climbing.

Lured by entrancing views of Mt. Mahindra's clean walls at the head of the Dali, we decided to keep a camp on the Dali Glacier. We scouted our route with binoculars in the late morning and climbed the first two pitches of our envisioned line. Pitch one was steep, technical, and tricky-to-protect 5.11. It shared the belay with a route that Italians had established to a broad ledge about halfway up the peak. Our route shared pitch two with the Italian route. We rapped and left ropes fixed for our next climbing day, when we climbed to the broad ledge where the Italian route ends, sharing a pitch or two of it, but generally staying to its right. The climbing was sustained 5.11 and great; we got to the ledge early and traversed 150m right to the base of Mt. Mahindra's middle summit. Freddie deftly led the way through discontinuous cracks and pods—the kind of run-out face climbing where you don't know if you are going to get more pro. He got it done, and I took the final few pitches to the summit, feeling guilty for getting a clean, steep, well-protected 5.10 glory corner, with a fun roof to cap it, just below the middle summit. We named the route Ashoka's Pillar (700m, 5.11R). To the best of our knowledge ours was the first ascent of Mt. Mahindra's middle summit. During this ascent Pat got a break from his stomach malaise and free-soloed a new 5.9 route to the top of Peak 5,300m. We climbed all routes free and onsight without bolts or pins. The trip was supported by a grant from Mountain Hardwear.

DAVID SHARRATT, *AAC*

Miyar Glacier, Pangi Valley, Zanskar, Kishtwar, exploration; crossings of Kang La (5,440m), Poat La (5,500m), Dharlangwala Jot (5,086m), Shopu Pass (3,400m). For many years I have been trying to connect the entire length and breadth of the Himalaya on foot. In 2007 I put together an inexperienced but tough, eager team from the Navy, and on August 10 our rickety bus groaned over Rohtang Pass. Next morning we hiked into one of the greenest, loveliest valleys in the entire western Himalaya. Village children and women gathered around, while the men offered us peas and potatoes. Three days later we reached the Miyar Glacier, and the day after that we topped Kang La, where the panoramic view extended into Zanskar. Kang La is crossed by trekkers going from Miyar to Padam, and we spied a group of hikers ascending from the other side. This pass took us across the Great Himalayan Axis, into the Zanskar range.

The next day as we hiked up the Tidu Glacier, my eyes riveted to the trio of peaks, 5,995m, 6,294m, and 5,935m (from west to east), which girdled the glacier. Each is virgin and would give even the best

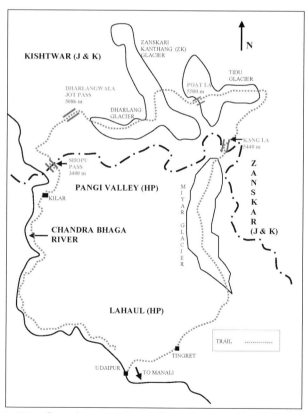

In 17 walking days, Lt. Cdr. Satyabrata Dam's expedition covered 156km, crossing Kang La (5,440m), Poat La (5,500m), Dharlangwala Jot (5,086m), and Shopu Pass (3,400m) in the Himachal (Miyar, Pangi), Zanskar, and Kishtwar. *Satyabrata Dam*

A virgin peak on the Zanskari Kanthang Glacier. *Satyabrata Dam*

A virgin wall at the confluence of the Kanskari Kanthang and Dharlang glaciers. *Satyabrata Dam*

Admiring ridges along the Dharlang Glacier. *Satyabrata Dam*

climbers a hard time. The icefall below Peak 6,294m was horrifyingly rotten. Up toward the cwm of the glacier lay two superb peaks, 5,609m and 5,763m, both virgin.

On August 18, we climbed steeply over rock and ice flutings toward Poat La, which looked deceptively close. Navigating through colossal obstacles we finally reached the little-known Zanskari Kanthang Glacier. On the side opposite, two rock walls reared up like sentinels; they would be a rock climber's delight. About 15km long and 1km wide, the Zanskari Kanthang Glacier has rock and ice problems strewn from one end to the other, several topping the magical 6,000m mark, all unclimbed and never before photographed from nearby. One might be a miniature Trango Tower. If we had had climbing gear, I would have stopped there. One could spend a month on this small glacier and climb more than dozen adrenaline-pumping peaks in true alpine style.

This may be the prettiest sight I have seen in the Himalaya. Our camp was perched on a tiny grassy ledge at about 4,800m on the right bank of Dharlang Glacier, just at the junction with ZK Glacier and another icefall. To my south, peaks 6,072m, 5,698m, and 5,615m (east to west and all unclimbed) spread out like a Japanese fan, coming down to the glacier in outrageously oversized falls of ice and rock. It was an unusually narrow gorge, filled with glacier ice, rocks, and frozen pools with towering rock and ice walls rearing into a brilliance that simply took my breath away.

That day we waded through the Bodh Nullah and descended to a grassy meadow. Sheep and yaks dotted the green field, and a few horses loitered. The mountain slopes on either side bustled with flowers, butterflies, bees, and birds. It was paradise after so many days of rock and ice. We camped next to a stream; I could reach my hand out of the tent to touch the freshest

Peak 6,294m rears out of the Tidu Glacier. *Satyabrata Dam*

Peak 5,995m on the Tidu Glacier. *Satyabrata Dam*

Peak 5,935m at the head of the Tidu Glacier. *Satyabrata Dam*

water in the world. At 6,002m, Shiv Shankar is the giant in that area. As far as I know, it is still virgin, but this region is so rarely visited by climbers or hikers, and so little has been written about these mountains, that nothing can be known with certainty.

Our next objective was the dreaded Sersank Pass. What we heard from local shepherds was not encouraging. The glacier leading to the pass has broken down, with steep icefalls and huge crevasses opening up. It was impossible to cross this pass without climbing equipment, and certainly not with such a large group as ours. We had two options for leaving this narrow valley. We could walk due west, along the Dharlang Nullah, come out at Machel, and go by road to Kishtwar and Jammu. Or we could cross the high, rarely used pass of Dharlangwala Jot and enter the remote Huram valley of Kishtwar. From there we could loop back across the Shipu Ridge into the Pangi Valley of Himachal and Killar. According to the shepherds, this trail was well-marked and the pass had little ice, so this would be our route.

Tien Singh and I started early, to find the base of Dharlangwala Jot. Eventually we came across a group of severe-looking nomad women, unruly and dirty kids, and a very old man. They spoke in pure Kashmiri, and we barely understood a word. The inevitable dog bared its teeth and strained at its leash. A kilometer later we came across a muddy hut in the middle of nowhere, tended by a woman and her children, with three of the fiercest dogs I have seen in the Himalaya. She offered buttermilk that we gulped down.

Around another cliff, we crossed a rickety bridge filling the chasm over the rushing waters of Dharlang Nulla. We pitched our tents and waited for the others to catch up. The next day was long and stressful, as we crossed a high pass, so we spent the morning of the 23rd relaxing, drying our clothes and sleeping bags before descending to the Huram Glacier. Typical of Kishtwar, the ridges were decked with gravity-defying hanging glaciers and massive waterfalls. Soon we reached plush meadows and green pastures. The vista was so exotically beautiful that I could have stopped at every step and stayed there forever. Farther ahead, the stream dropped away, turning toward the villages of Tun and Bhatwas. I stopped often to gaze awe-struck at nature's handiwork, musing that if this did not prove God's existence, then nothing will.

The next day we descended into the immense grazing ground of Sanyot Adhwari, where the Billing Nullah united with the Huram. Typical Tibetan houses with flat roofs and black-framed doors held snot-nosed kids and red-cheeked women, who welcomed us heartily. Sonam, our only Ladakhi member, finding his brethren, beamed from ear to ear. Only seven families and around 30 folks populated Tun. They were clearly Tibetan and Ladakhi in origin. None of them knew how their people reached here across the high passes, nor when or why. We rested on the open roof of the village chief and then walked down through the villages of Alya, Khizrauni, Muthal, and Chag finally camping on the Chaund next to the gurgling Sansari Nullah. A group of young Kashmiri women visited our campsite in the evening and, showing none of the restraint or coyness that they are normally known for, visited each of our tents and even entered our kitchen tent looking for male company.

On the 25th we crossed Bhatwas and a bridge across the Sansari Nullah. The trail went through a thick wood of pine, deodars, and chinars littered with generous amount of bear droppings.

Camping at the base of the Poat La. *Satyabrata Dam*

Looking back from the Poat La. *Satyabrata Dam*

The icefall leading to Sersank La. *Satyabrata Dam*

Then we had to climb over the Shopu Pass to return to the Himachal's Pangi Valley. From the village of Dharwas we managed a lift on a tipper to Killar, the main village in the valley. The rest of the journey to Manali would be in buses, and I thought that all dangers were over. But when the bus (if it could be called one) flew like a maniac around blind turns on the worst road I have ever seen, I realized that our troubles were far from over. All 60 passengers were threatened with a watery grave in the foaming waters of Chandra Bhaga River. Then the bus shuddered to a halt just inches from the chasm at the edge of a landslide. We had to walk across the kilometer-long landslide and get into another bus on the other side.

It was the evening of August 27 when we reached Manali after a wonderful journey that stitched together four remote valleys. We had explored some of the last blank spots in the Himalaya. My only regret was that we lost one porter. Just before we reached Shopu Pass, a stone zipped out of the woods and struck young Min Bahadur Thapa, who died on the spot. The boy had taken leave from his apple picking job at Manali and came along with us, hoping to make some extra money for his old parents back home. There was no reason why he should die that day, at that spot. We were out of all dangers on easy ground, on the last day of our hike. But he died. As long as men go into the wild, there will be some who will not return. I wish to dedicate this expedition to the memory of the young man who did not return. May his soul rest in peace.

Expedition Summary: 17 walking days, covering 156km. Passes crossed: Kang La (5,440m), Poat La (5,500m), Dharlangwala Jot (5,086m), Shopu Pass (3,400m). Regions covered: Himachal (Miyar, Pangi), Zanskar, Kishtwar. Maps: 52 C, 52 C/16, 15, 11, 12, 8 and Trekking Route map of Himachal Pradesh Sheet No I (First edition, which can be bought from DMAS Manali).

LT. CDR. SATYABRATA DAM, *India*

UTTARANKHAND (FORMERLY UTTARANCHAL) GARHWAL

Changabang, north face and west ridge attempts. In August, Kester Brown, Craig Jefferies, Marty Beare, and I, all from New Zealand, with Adam Darragh from Australia, traveled to the Bagini Glacier to attempt the north face and the second ascent of the west ridge of Changabang (6,864m). After jointly establishing a camp (ca 5,000m) at the head of the Bagini Glacier's west branch, the west ridge team of Beare, Darragh, and me fixed 300m of rope up 50° snow and mixed terrain to the col (ca 5,800m) at the base of the west ridge, where we established a camp. After acclimatizing here and fixing another 200m of rope up 60° ice and mixed terrain, we descended to Base Camp intending to climb alpine-style above this point.

Meanwhile Brown and Jefferies spent time acclimatizing on peaks above base camp. Noticing that the right side of the face was in good condition and less prone to spindrift, on 16 September they started up the north face of Changabang via the line pioneered by the British 1996 attempt. After three days, they established themselves on the top of the buttress. Climbing to this point involved ice up to 90°, often covered in insubstantial snow. After a rest day the pair traversed the icefield to join the line of the British 1997 ascent (Cave-Murphy) and in doing so climbed a few hundred meters of new ground. Difficult, steep ice gave access to the upper icefield, and here they endured an open bivy on the ice arête, at 6,200m, under the headwall. Heavy snowfall overnight and into the next day forced them to retreat down the left side of the buttress in 16 rappels. They descended from high on the face in under five hours. Previous parties who have reached the summit ridge via the British 1997 route have descended south to the Changabang Glacier, in both cases with fatal consequences.

In the meantime, the west ridge team moved into the col camp. A week-long storm arrived on 24 September, dumping over half a meter of snow at base camp and forcing an epic retreat. After the storm cleared, we only had time to climb back to our high point and retrieve our gear, a feat possible only with snowshoes for glacier travel. The west ridge still awaits a second ascent and is an obvious candidate for an alpine-style attempt.

BRIAN ALDER,
New Zealand Alpine Club & AAC

Kalanka, north face attempt. This 2,000-meter face has only a single route, climbed by a Czechoslovakian team using fixed ropes in 1977 during the mountain's second ascent. Several teams have failed to climb the north buttress, a line in the middle of the face. This buttress is one of the great prizes in the Garhwal, as are other untried lines on Kalanka's north face. The left side of the north face was the line that most interested Kenton Cool and me. We guessed the snow slope to be about 800-900m long, and we hoped to climb in a single push through the night and the next day to the shoulder. We guessed the upper ridge to be approximately the same length but more technical and that it would take two days to climb. Descending would probably take two days, making the overall time on the face of five days. This turned out to be a little optimistic.

Adam Darragh at the base of the west ridge of Changabang. The original Boardman-Tasker (1976) route follows the mixed terrain before skirting the large roof on the right and exiting the headwall near the obvious corner. *Brian Alder*

Our chosen line did not feature much rock, but did pass through two bands low on the face and around gendarmes on the shoulder, all granite. What rock we encountered was very compact

The north faces of Kalanka and Changabang, showing the route taken by Nick Bullock and Kenton Cool. *Kenton Cool*

and didn't offer the chance for gear. In four days of climbing the only rock gear we placed was two wires and two pegs. The initial easier-angled section of the snow slope was relatively firm snow covering ice. Runnels carved by spindrift were firmer, but constantly poured powder. The section passing the first rock band was steep and gave unprotected climbing on insecure snow. The middle section of the face gave a mix of deep unconsolidated snow, hard ice, névé, and powder. The upper snow ridge leading to the shoulder was deep, bottomless powder following deep flutings with no chance of protection. On the ridge the snow was knee-deep and heavy, though, when we dropped onto the north face to climb beneath gendarmes, the snow was bottomless and nearly vertical. The whole face had a covering of ice beneath the snow that proved a problem when attempting to dig bivouac sites, as we could not dig deep enough to make comfortable ledges.

Nick Bullock near the high point of their north face attempt, showing the unclimbed upper ridge above. *Kenton Cool*

On September 15, the fourth day of our climb and following several poor bivies, we started with the final wallow up deep unconsolidated snow to the crest of the ridge (6,300m). We followed the crest to a gendarme, which we turned on the right by dropping down onto the north face. This proved insecure, as numerous flutings had to be dug through; levitation proved the best technique for coping with the bottomless powder. After we passed the gendarme, the ridge to the right looked dangerous and insecure and would no doubt take a long time to climb. But the left side of the ridge was overhanging rock, making the thought of trying it on that side unappealing also. Beyond the final gendarme the ridge leading to the summit looked technical and time-consuming. Given that we were on the last day of food and faced with another two to three days of climbing and two days of descent, we decided to go down. The descent took the rest of that day, and after a horrible night at our first bivy site, continued until we reached the moraine on the afternoon of the 16th. All of the approximately 25 rappels were from ice-screw v-threads, which, given the amount of ice on the face were often difficult to construct.

Weather: In hindsight arriving at BC as early as August 24 was a good move, although at the time we thought that maybe we had made a mistake, as the monsoon was still active. Rain and heavy mist were prevalent for two weeks, making acclimatization forays and time at BC uncomfortable, but never bad enough to stop us from getting ready for a settled period. The weather then settled to the most stable period I have experienced in India, giving warm, sunny days with only a small amount of precipitation in the afternoon. Arriving early meant that we were ready to take advantage of the settled spell. The weather remained stable for approximately two weeks, until a storm hit after we had left BC, dumping one meter of snow at BC and two meters at ABC.

Waste: We carried all trash from the climb and from ABC to BC. From BC porters carried out the waste, which was taken to Joshimath for disposal.

Logistics: This was the first time I have had weather reports sent via e-mail while I was on an expedition, but for climbing such a big face it is certainly worth the cost. Our agent was C. S. Pandy of Himalayan Run and Trek (www.himalayanruntrek.com). I found Mr. Pandy to be extremely professional and the service he gave without fault, though somewhat more expensive than what I was used to. Our LO was perhaps the most affable and approachable LO I have encountered. The bureaucracy was the usual hassle, as once again there appeared to be no dialogue between the IMF and the Indian Embassy in London, resulting in stress getting X-visas. I sent my passport to a company called Travco, who arranged the visa and did a good job, even though the Indian Embassy was, as usual, unhelpful and misinformed.

NICK BULLOCK, *Alpine Club*

Arwa Tower (6,352m), north face, Lightning Strike. From May 31 to June 8, the team of Denis Burdet, Thomas Senf, and Stephan Siegrist made the first ascent of the north face of Arwa

Tower (6,352m), via the route Lightning Strike (900m, VI M5 5.9 A3). They accomplished this climb in capsule style after earlier climbing seven pitches over four days, leaving three ropes fixed for their final push. The climb is the subject of a feature article in this *Journal.*

Peak 6,400m (Miandi Peak), first ascent; Kharchakund, attempt; Yeonbuk (5,953m), attempt. On October 5 Bruce Norman, from Scotland, and I made what may be a first ascent of a 6,400m peak in the Garwhal region. The ascent was the culmination of a process that began earlier in the year, when Bruce and I tried to get a permit to attempt the first ascent of Jankuth (6,805m), a fantastic peak at the head of the Gangotri Glacier. Marty Beare and I had tried unsuccessfully to climb the peak in 2004, and it was unfinished business.

Lightning Strike on the north face of Arwa Tower. *Visual Impact/* Denis Burdet

However, though our permit request was acceptable to the Indian Mountaineering Foundation, it was denied by the Uttaranchal state government, so we changed our objective to the unclimbed east ridge of Kharchakund, also on the Gangotri. We were granted the permit, and Shelley and Paul Hershey, from Dunedin, joined our venture, with the unclimbed southwest ridge of Kharchakund as their goal.

Two weeks of great weather prevailed, during which we spent four days acclimatizing on non-technical Kedar Dome, and put in food dumps at the base of Kharchakund. By October 23 we were ready to go, and the four of us set up an advanced base camp on the lateral moraine under the east face. Next morning we went for a scout, the main result of which was Paul and Shelley deciding to attempt Yeonbuk (5,953m) instead of Kharchakund, because of the serac fall on the southwest ridge.

The Gangotri Glacier. Peak 6,400m (Miandi Peak) was climbed by Pat Deavoll and Bruce Norman in 2007. Jankuth (6,805m) was attempted in 2004 by Marty Beare and Pat Deavoll. *Pat Deavoll*

Bruce and I headed off on the 25th, establishing ourselves on the east ridge after climbing several bulletproof pitches of 60° ice. We woke next morning to a snow storm (the same one that thwarted the Changabang team). After some dithering, we decided to come down, and just as well, as the storm lasted six days.

We headed back up the glacier when the fine weather reappeared. Bruce and I intended to try the southwest ridge, as the east ridge was now snowed up and out of condition. Paul and Shelley were still looking at Yeonbuk. However, when Bruce and I got to the bottom of the route a day-and-a-half's walk from basecamp, we concurred with Paul and Shelley's earlier assessment: too much serac danger.

"Enough of this damn mountain," we thought. "Time is running out and if we are going to salvage anything from this trip we need to look at something else." Up glacier was a good-looking peak I had noticed on the 2004 Jankuth expedition, and if the weather stayed promising, we thought we had a chance of climbing it in the limited time we had left. We headed up glacier to the base, then spent a day climbing the 600m icefall that took us into a pleasant cwm on the west face. At this point we started to doubt the weather and decided if we were to have any chance of summiting, we would have to climb the remaining 1,100m in a single push (not so difficult for Bruce, who four weeks previously had climbed K2 without oxygen, but for me something of a challenge).

We left camp at 4 a.m. the next morning and by 1 p.m., by alternate ice and snow pitches, had reached the summit ridge. By this stage it was really cold and windy and beginning to whiteout. Pushing on, we made the summit at 3 p.m. after a final 60° pitch of superb ice. The weather abated a bit and we got sketchy views of the line Marty and I had taken on Jankuth, to the south, and of the massive Satopanth (7,075m) in the opposite direction. We stared hard at

Yeonbuk but saw no sign of Paul and Shelley. It turns out they had decided the avalanche threat was too high and headed back to base camp the day before.

"Ok, good, we've climbed something," we said, before heading down. By the time we got back to our camp in the cwm at 9 p.m. the weather had packed in, and descending the icefall the next day was a little fraught. Walking back down the glacier in a whiteout/thunderstorm my hat started to smolder! We propose the name Miandi Peak for the previously unclimbed 6,400m mountain, because it sits above the Miandi Barmak.

PAT DEAVOLL, *New Zealand*

Arwa Spire and Kalanka, attempts. In June a Korean team led by Park Heungsoo attempted Arwa Spire but was defeated by bad weather and snowfall. In August and September a Dutch team led by Mike Van Berkel failed on Kalanka because of bad weather, and in September and October a Czech team led by Petr Masek failed at 5,200m on the north face of Kalanka, also because of continuous bad weather.

HARISH KAPADIA, *Honorary Editor, The Himalayan Journal*

Panpatia Glacier, exploration. The trail from Badrinath to Kedarnath Valley, as followed by the team of Shipton and Tilman, is a fascinating piece of history. Their trail via the Gandharpongi Valley was followed by a British team led by Martin Moran. There was a route from the nearby Panpatia Glacier to cross a pass toward the southern valley, giving an easier exit to the Kedar Valley. The exploration was completed this year by a team led by Tapan Pandit, from West Bengal . In June they entered the Khirao valley and reached its head where the Panpatia Bamak (glacier) lies. Following the northern edge of the glacier, they crossed Parvati Col to reach the upper plateau. Traversing southwest on this plateau they crossed Panpatia Col and descended to Kachni Tal and Madhyamaheshwar. Previous parties had tried this crossing from both directions and failed. With this historic crossing the routes of earlier explorations are now joined.

HARISH KAPADIA, *Honorary Editor, The Himalayan Journal*

Kagbhusandi Tal, Peak AC 150 (5,030m), Dhanesh Parvat (5,490m), Kankul Peak (5,080m). To celebrate the links between the Alpine Club and the Himalayan Club in the year of the AC's 150th anniversary, Harish Kapadia organized an expedition to the Kagbhusandi Valley, which he had first entered in May and June of 2006. Hathi Parvat and Otika Danda had been climbed, but other peaks around the valley had not been touched. Harish's interest in the climbing potential of the area was shared by Atul Rawal and four British alpinists: Chris Astill, Mick Cottam, Mark Higton, and I.

The approach involved taking the night train from Delhi to Haridwar and a day's drive to Joshimath, where we spent a couple of days acclimatizing at Auli while we obtained permits. A further drive along the Badrinath Road brought us to Govindghat, the popular starting point for Hemkund and the Valley of Flowers, where the walk-in began. On the first day's trek we had a timely reminder of the Alpine and Himalayan Clubs' links with tradition by a chance meeting with Nanda Sinh Chauhan. Now ninety-four years old, he was with Frank Smythe in 1931 and 1937 when Smythe discovered the Valley of Flowers. Leaving the main trail at Bhuidhar, we trekked up the Kagbhusandi Valley in three days to a base camp at Chhaiyan Kharak (3,815m), with Hathi Parvat (6,727m) towering to the north.

First impressions were clouded by the weather. Days of monsoon-like rain on the approach had delivered at least 30cm of soft snow at 4,000m, despite the heat of the sun, when it appeared. This was unusual, but not unprecedented. In 2006 Harish had been turned back from the Kankul Khal pass by deep snow in early May. Scheduling the 2007 expedition for the last week of May should have overcome the problem but hadn't. Climbing was exhausting, when each step sank us knee-deep in snow. Even the proposed trek out over the Kankul Khal around June 12 proved impossible, since snow remained too deep for porters to carry loads over the pass.

Despite the difficult snow conditions, Mick and I made an early ascent to the Kankul Khal, recording a GPS reading of 4,665m,

Mick Cottam on the summit of Danesh Parvat after the successful first ascent via the west ridge, north face, and east face. *Dave Wynne-Jones*

and Mark joined us for a night out on the upper Barmal Glacier, where we obtained good views of the peaks at the head of the glacier and the Barmal Khal, a newly discovered pass of over 5,000m. Our whole team made several forays up the steep flanks of the valley, hoping to spot likely lines to climb. Many ridges and couloirs attracted attention, but looked to be tough propositions in the conditions, with the ridges plastered with snow and the couloirs avalanching. When conditions improved, we climbed three peaks, all first ascents.

We approached the first from a camp at 4,300m below the Kankul Khal. The mountain lay immediately west of the pass, and we climbed it by its northeast flank. A wide stone chute enabled us to access the first snowfield, which we crossed to a 50m wall, where a line of weakness up crumbling rock led to a second snowfield. This narrowed to a broad ridge with a distinctly steeper spur toward the top. At the spur Mick and Chris took to the couloir flanking the ridge to the east, then gained the crest of the ridge from the top of the couloir, but owing to a concern about avalanche danger in the couloir, Mark and I took the spur directly, in four pitches of about Scottish 3. We all joined for the east ridge and face, climbing four more pitches of mixed ground to gain a massive granite block that we originally took for the summit. The true summit lay 60m along a narrow snow ridge beyond and gave a GPS reading of 5,030m.

Consensus graded the route at alpine AD, and we decided to recommend the name Peak AC 150.

We next tackled Dhanesh Parvat, by a glacier approach from the south. We established Camp 1 at the confluence with the main Barmal Glacier and Camp 2 at 5,000m on the tributary glacier. Mick and I left Camp 2 at 1 a.m., yet still found ourselves postholing in soft snow at 2 a.m. The glacier headwall led to a narrow snow ridge running north to a broader saddle below the west ridge of Dhanesh Parvat. The west ridge rose steeply to a narrow crest of snow and rock running into the sheer face of the granite summit block. For two hours we probed cracks choked with snow, overhanging flakes, and a chimney full of unstable semi-iced-in blocks, before conceding defeat and retreating down the ridge. Then, from below, we spotted a narrow snow ramp rising under the overhanging north face of the summit monolith. Two pitches of doubtful

Mick Cottam leading the first pitch on the east face of the summit block of Danesh Parvat (5,490m) in the Central Garhwal's Kagbhusandi Valley. *Dave Wynne-Jones*

snow that seemed on the verge of sliding into the void led to the east face of the summit block. Sun-warmed rock just the right side of vertical rose in cracks and narrow ledges towards a summit that we reached in two pitches with moves of V/V+. We rappelled to the west ridge. We estimate the grade at D.

The third peak, which lies to the east of the Kankul Khal, was climbed by Chris and Mark from a camp below the pass. They ascended a couloir falling west from the north ridge of the main summit, then, finding the ridge holding wet snow, traversed into a rocky couloir on the east face. The couloir more or less paralleled the ridge, below it, to the summit. The map indicated the peak's elevation as 5,080m, though the GPS reading was lower than for AC 150. They graded the route at about AD and recommended Kankul Peak for its name.

Having run out of time, we retraced our steps to Bhuidhar, where we celebrated the 150th birthday with a memorable party, complete with cake. The expedition was a superb way of celebrating the roots of both clubs in exploratory mountaineering. Thanks are due to Harish for proposing the trip and making the Indian arrangements, and to Mark for coordinating the UK end. Thanks are also due to the Alpine Club climbing fund for financial support.

Dave Wynne-Jones, *Alpine Club*

Nepal

KANTI HIMAL

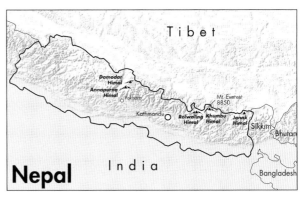

Rongla Kangri attempt; Pk. 5,984m and Pk. 5,930m, first ascents. Our permit for Nyegi Kangsang, a peak on the Indo-Tibetan border, was withdrawn just one week before we were due to leave for Kathmandu en route to Lhasa. A number of factors contributed to an increased level of paranoia from China's regime in Tibet [This report was written well before the run-up to the 2008 Olympics—Ed.]: (1) 2006 video footage of a Buddhist nun and another Tibetan being shot dead on the Nangpa La, taken by foreign climbers on Cho Oyu; (2) the unfurling of a "Free Tibet" banner at Everest base camp during April 2007, when a Tibetan-American and three other Americans were arrested and detained, causing Chinese authorities to send troops to the Nepal border at Zhangmu and close the border for three days; (3) the possibility of demonstrations against the Chinese occupation of Tibet during the run-up to the 2008 Olympic Games. Issuing permits for border areas, such as ours on the already sensitive McMahon Line, was taken out of the hands of regional civilian governors and placed under the control of army commanders. We presume that when these commanders were asked by the Chinese-Tibetan Mountaineering Association to grant us our permit, they were not prepared to consider the possibility of any problem on their patch. This decision was plainly over the heads of the CTMA. Moreover, the Congressional gold medal given to the Dalai Lama in New York caused celebrations by Tibetans in Lhasa, which caused the authorities to impose a 9 p.m. curfew in the city for several days and cancel visas for low-cost tourist groups from Nepal to Tibet. Since the opening of the Lhasa Railway, 92% of Tibet's tourism is now Chinese, so the authorities have little to fear from economic implications alienating Western tourists; Although peak permits seem to be

The southwest face of unclimbed Rongla South (6,516m) on the Nepal-Tibet border in the remote Kanti Himal. *Julian Freeman-Attwood*

Looking northwest from above advanced base to peaks in the remote Kanti Himal on the Nepal-Tibet border. (A) Pk. 6,275m (unclimbed). (B) Pk. 5,930m climbed via the south ridge (left skyline) by the British expedition. (C) Pk. 5,984m climbed via the north ridge by the British expedition. (D) Part of Rongla South (6,516m). The col crossed to reach the upper Rongla glacier lies between A and B. *Julian Freeman-Attwood*

obtainable for eastern Tibet (Nyanqen Tanglha), it appears that border areas will be difficult to access in 2008 at the time of the Olympics.

We therefore asked the CTMA for permission to climb a peak on the Tibet-western Nepal border called Rongla Kangri (known in Nepal as Kanti Himal, 6,647m). Only three peaks in this area had previously been climbed: Kaqur Kangri (6,859m), the highest summit in the Rongla Range (2002), and two smaller peaks of 6,328m and 6,159m, climbed from the Nepal side in 1997. We knew a Japanese team had already obtained a permit for the Changli Himal, west of Rongla Kangri [in September they made the first ascent of the highest peak in this group, 6,721m Kubi Kangri—see elsewhere in the *Journal*]. Unfortunately, the Chinese commander in charge of permits for this area was away and we had no alternative but to give up on Tibet for 2007. However, we had already paid airfares, and our equipment was in Kathmandu, so we were lucky to obtain, on short notice, a permit from Nepal to access the Kanti Himal.

Nick Colton, Luke Hughes, Phil Wickens, and I, with our LO, Manohari Baral, and two cooks/helpers, Phurba Tamang and Prem Tamang, flew to Jumla and on September 13 set off on our long trek north toward the border. We passed through Gamgadhi and Mugu, finally discovered a route up the Koji Khola, and established base camp on the 23rd at 4,650m. In the 16 days we were at or above this camp, it snowed on 10, leaving us only six days for activity. We later found that this was one of the worst post-monsoon periods in years.

Heading northeast toward the 5,495m border pass named the Koji La, we placed an advanced base at 5,170m, northwest of a lake, occupying it on October 1. The following day we moved northwest to the border col, giving access to the previously untrodden upper reaches of the Rongla Glacier on the far side, where we dumped loads at our proposed site for Camp 1. Above, to the east, rose a 200m granite face of 45-50°, leading to the northwest ridge of the 6,516m Rongla border summit (Rongla South). From there it would be a relatively straightforward ascent to the 6,647m main summit a little farther north.

On the 3rd Luke and I made a foray to the Koji La. According to local yak herders this was an ancient but little-used trade route. Now no yaks can cross the rocks on the Nepalese side, rocks that have been exposed by recent glacial recession, so it is only passable on foot. We got the impression that a few smugglers use the pass in summer, and we found prayer flags at 5,300m. The areas immediately north and west of this pass are the sources of the great Bramaputra River.

On the 4th Luke, Nick, and Phil left advanced base and established Camp 1 at 5,750m. Relentless winds and heavy drifts of snow were the norm for the next few days, but the three managed to climb the main snow gully in the granite face of Rongla South to 5,810m and deposit equipment. On the 6th the weather worsened and Luke took advantage of being the only member with skis to return to advanced base for more supplies. We decided that while Nick and Phil retreated over the col, Luke would rescue the gear from the face. Having done this Luke took the opportunity to solo Pk. 5,984m on the frontier ridge west-southwest of Rongla South. He climbed the north ridge over relatively compacted snow with some rocky bands. On the summit he was pummeled by strong winds. The following day, the 9th, the three woke to perfect conditions and, making an early start, climbed back to the col and up the icy south ridge of Pk. 5,930m, another border peak just south of Pk. 5,984m. I came up from base camp the same day and with Phurba and Prem removed advanced base. We left the area the following day, reaching Gamgadhi on the 14th. From here we were able to get a Twin Otter flight on the 17th to Nepalgunj, followed by a scheduled flight to Kathmandu. It had proved to be an exceptionally worthwhile exploratory expedition into little-known territory.

JULIAN FREEMAN-ATTWOOD, *Alpine Club*

KANJIROBA HIMAL

Shey Shikhar, first ascent. The 41-year old Japanese mountaineer Katsuhito Fujikawa made the first ascent of Shey Shikhar (6,139m), an elegant peak in the Dolpo region immediately southeast of the Kanjiroba Group. In 1995 American Geoff Tabin was offered a permit for Shey Shikhar from Tso Karpo Lake to the north. However, on entering the Tso Karpo valley above the large lake of Phoksumdo, he found that an approach to the mountain (marked as Junction Peak on some maps) would be suicidal from this direction and instead turned to the highest peak in the valley, Tso Karpo Kang (6,556m). This peak directly north of Shey Shikhar had first been climbed from the south by two Japanese in 1971 (though it was not added to the official list of permitted peaks until 2002). Tabin's expedition made the second and third ascents, via the southwest ridge and via a more direct route up the southeast face. The team also made the probable first ascents of a mountain to the southwest they called Bahini Kang (6,100m) and, to the east, Kang Yaja (5,962m), via the south ridge.

The well-traveled Japanese explorer Tamotsu Ohnishi reached the Tso Karpo Lake in 2003 but was not able to make a serious attempt on Shey Shikhar due to bad weather. He planned to try the east ridge from a base camp at a little over 4,200m, noting that there was a 200m rock wall that looked steep and loose.

Katsuhito Fujikawa reports setting up base camp at 4,700m on August 20. He climbed directly from this camp to the crest of the east ridge at 5,500m, overcoming a loose rock face at an angle of around 50-60°. The crest above was steep, narrow and about one kilometer in length, with precipitous drops on both sides, before he reached the summit. Fujikawa appears to have made the climb in one push on the 23rd, leaving base camp at 3 a.m. and returning at 9:30 p.m.

LINDSAY GRIFFIN, *Mountain INFO, www.climbmagazine.com*

UPPER DOLPO

PANZANG REGION

Chamar Kang, probable first ascent. After a long trek around northern Dolpo following in the footsteps of the great Japanese explorer Ekai Kawaguchi, a seven-member Osaka Yamanokai (Osaka Alpine Club) party, led by Tamotsu Ohnishi, arrived at Tinkyu in the Panzang Khola and on September 19 set up base camp at Kangtega Sumna (4,550m), between the 5,564m border pass of Chukang La and, to the south, the 5,466m Kella La.

The next day they traveled west into the valley known as Tinje, from where they planned to attempt Chamar Kang (a.k.a Changmar Kang or Kang Tega, 6,060m, N 29°14'10", E 83°21'48"). From here they climbed to the crest of the north ridge at 5,886m but then descended to a col at 5,720m to set up a high camp for the night.

On the 21st Toshitsugi Irisawa, Koichi Kato, Ohnishi, and Chhepa Sherpa left the camp at 6:15 a.m. and set off up the northeast face. They climbed this snow-and-ice slope of 45-55° in nine pitches by front-pointing, using double ice tools and 60m ropes. A further four pitches led to the summit, which they gained at 2 p.m. By 3:30 p.m. all four had regained the high camp, and they returned to base camp just after 7 p.m. Worsening weather accompanied them as they climbed down the route of ascent [Ohnishi originally believed that this peak had been climbed previously, but there are no reports of this, nor did he find any evidence—Ed]. The next day Kaori Inaba and Koji Mizutani repeated the ascent.

TAMOTSU OHNISHI, *Japanese Alpine Club*

ANNAPURNA HIMAL

Varaha Shikhar (The Fang), second ascent, east face to south ridge. [Photo on page 4.] Gangwon University Korean Expedition made a new route up the Fang (7,647m), via the 1,400m east face to the south ridge. The only previous ascent of this difficult mountain on the rim of the Annapurna Sanctuary southwest of Annapurna I was made in 1980 from the west, outside the Sanctuary, by an Austrian expedition. Connecting the east face to the south ridge from inside the Sanctuary had captured the attention of Korean teams since 1986. Gangwon University expeditions attempted this route unsuccessfully in 1991 and 1997.

The expedition left Korea on September 1 and spent seven days beginning September 4 acclimatizing in the Langtang, where they climbed Naya Kanga (a.k.a. Kangja Chuli, 5,844m). After this the team of Choi Chan-gyu, Hong Seong-wook, Kim Yong-gil, Lee Jong-heon, Lee Hak-young, Park Bong-ha, Park Hong-gi, Park Su-seok, Song Il-ho, Yu Hyun-jong, Yu Jae-hyeong, and Sherpas Dapjen, Geljen, Swana, Tshering, and Wangdi was helicoptered to a 4,600m base camp below the Fang, arriving on the 17th. Due to over a meter of fresh snow and a large crevasse, it was necessary to establish a temporary camp before eventually siting Camp 1 at 5,400m on the 30th, after 12 days hard work. Camp 2 (5,900m), about half way up the east face, and Camp 3 (6,400m), on the crest of the south ridge, were established in the next week and Camp 4 at 6,900m on October 11. On the 16th a final camp was placed on the ridge at 7,200m.

Yu Hyun-jong and three Sherpas stayed at this Camp 5, while Kim Yong-gil and Park Hong-gi stayed at Camp 4 to support Yu and Park Su-seok in a summit attempt on the 17th. However, the final 200m to the top turned out to be far more difficult than expected, with sections of 80°. The lead climbers retreated so as to retrieve more rope to fix on this final section, to ensure a safe ascent and safe return [reportedly 6,600m of rope were fixed intermittently from base camp to summit, with the whole section from Camp 1 to 4 fixed—Ed.]. Everyone descended to base camp, a particularly trying event for Yu and Park, the former having been badly frostbitten (some Sherpas high on the mountain also contracted frostbite). On October 22 the team began to move up the mountain for their final attempt, but on the 24th Park Bong-ha fell from the fixed ropes below Camp 3. He was injured, and two members descended to him with food and a sleeping bag, then dug a small snow cave for shelter. He was nursed there for some time until able to move, when a group helped him back to the ridge and then down to Camp 1.

On the 27th Choi Chan-gyu was also injured in a fall, though not so badly. Finally, on the 29th, Park Su-seok and Sherpas Wangdi and Tshering stood on the summit. All members were back at base camp on the 31st. The route has been named Dalgwa Yeohoon (which translates to "Yeo-hoon with the Moon") after Korean Kim Yeo-hoon who lost his life in a fall during the 1997 attempt.

LEE YOUNG-JUN, *Corean Alpine Club (translated by Peter Jensen-Choi)*

Editor's note: The Fang had been attempted eight times before the Korean ascent. In 1979 it was being billed as the highest unclimbed mountain in Nepal, and during the spring of that year Sepp Mayerl's Austrian team tried the very steep west ridge, approaching from the north flank and fixing 3,000m of rope before establishing Camp 5 at 6,600m. But after a member lower on the mountain slipped and fell 2,000m to his death, the expedition was abandoned. In the autumn of the same year Arturo Bergamaschi's Italian expedition tried the mountain from the Annapurna Sanctuary, on the opposite side. They attempted the southeast ridge, which they abandoned at 6,350m because it was far too difficult and dangerous. Mayerl returned the following spring, this time focusing on the south flank of the west ridge. The Austrians reached the crest at ca 5,700m, after climbing a wall similar to the Matterhorn north face. They then fixed the ridge to 6,450m. Leaving a camp there, Mayerl, Hermann Neumair, and Ang Chhopal Sherpa, reached the summit after a night at 7,040m. In 1982 French attempted the east ridge to the south ridge, climbing a couloir on the east flank to reach the east ridge at 6,800m. The way above looked similar to the south face of Annapurna, but bad weather prevented them from attempting it. In autumn 1984 Scott Fischer and two companions followed the line attempted by Mayerl's 1979 expedition; the west ridge from the north. Fischer and Wesley Krause reached a high point of ca 7,300m before bad weather forced retreat. Autumn 1986 saw the first of four Korean expeditions. Kim Jong-Duk and five others attempted the east face, but after fixing 2,600m of rope over difficult terrain had still only reached 5,450m. When avalanches wiped out 1,000m of their rope, the team gave up their attempt. The next Korean attempt took place during the first weeks in December 1991, when Yu Jae-Hyung's 11-member team tried the Italian line on the southeast ridge. They found the route technically very difficult, and at 6,350m retreated due to high winds. Yu returned in the autumn of 1997 and tried the east face direct to the south ridge. The team reached 7,300m on the ridge before Kim Yeo-Hoon fell to his death.

Annapurna I, south face, new route attempt. Ueli Steck of Switzerland wanted to complete a route on Annapurna I's vast south face that had been started in the autumn of 1992 by French climbers Pierre Beghin and Jean-Christophe Lafaille. These two Frenchmen had been attempting an alpine-style ascent of the great face by a new line in the couloir slightly to the right (east) of the 1970 British route and had reached 7,400 meters, when they were forced to retreat in the face of snow and wind. During the descent a rappel anchor failed and Beghin fell to his death.

   In May, Steck went to complete this line alone, but he was defeated at only 5,850m on the 21st when he was hit by a falling stone that smashed his helmet—though not his head. He fell to ca 5,500m on the glacier, was knocked out, and has no memory of what happened. He staggered away with bad bruising on the back of his head and his spinal area, but no blood flowed. As he wandered around not knowing where he was, Robbi Bösch, a member of his support team, found him. With a badly bruised body and his only helmet shattered, Steck abandoned the idea of climbing the south face of Annapurna for the moment. "This route is climbable," he said, but didn't know whether he still wanted to be the one to climb it.

ELIZABETH HAWLEY, *AAC Honorary Member, Nepal*

Annapurna East, first solo ascent. One of the main events of autumn was the solo ascent, by Slovenian mountaineer Tomaz Humar, of Annapurna East via the south face to the east ridge. Humar selected the far eastern end of the face because there are not as many falling stones as elsewhere. After arriving in the Annapurna Sanctuary, Humar first acclimatized by climbing the popular trekking peak Tharpa Chuli (a.k.a. Tent Peak, 5,663m) via the northwest face. After this his first major problem was to find a feasible way to get to Annapurna's south face among confusing rock towers and wide crevasses. It took him five days to find the key, a small hidden plateau near the foot of the face. He then rested at base camp and waited for a snowstorm to end before going for his climb.

   On October 24, with a Sherpa companion, Jagat Limbu, he crossed the South Annapurna Glacier and climbed up to a glacial terrace below the east rib of Annapurna, where the pair camped for the night at 5,800m. To this point the route followed the line taken by previous attempts and ascents of Annapurna's long east ridge and features a section of complex ground, including a tricky rock buttress through the icefall. Prior to this, Humar had not slept above 5,300m and decided to spend the next day furthering his acclimatization by staying put in camp. He spent three hours looking for a way to cross the plateau to access the face and during that day a fierce wind moved his tent 20m while he was inside, but no damage was done. On the 26th he set off at 6 a.m. Jagat Limbu would wait at this camp until Humar returned.

   The Slovenian began climbing the south face of Kangsar Kang (a.k.a. Roc Noir, 7,485m) to the right of Annapurna's east rib. He took food for five days, a stove and two gas cylinders, a bivouac sac, a small sleeping bag, two ice screws, two Prussiks, and an ice axe, but no helmet nor oxygen. At first the face was bare rock, then covered with snow, then rock, again snow, and his second bivouac at 7,200m was in a snow hole he dug out of deep snow. He stayed there for two nights while rocks fell beside his snug hole; he was not hit.

On the 28th he resumed his climb. He left his snow hole with the "absolute minimum" of gear. He started up at 6 a.m. despite strong wind and his not having slept, while pondering what to do. It was very cold. After two hours he had gained the east ridge and began to move along the ridge to the east summit; most of the way he traversed a few meters below the crest on the north face, moving carefully, conscious of the danger of cornices breaking under his weight. Furthermore, he had strong wind to contend with, and often had to lie down on the snow and crawl on hands and knees between gusts.

He had expected to reach the east summit at noon, but it was 3 p.m. when he got to the 8,026m top. (The main summit of Annapurna had been Humar's first 8,000m peak, which he climbed via the north face in 1995.) He soon began his descent, Radioing to Jagat Limbu that he was on his way down the way he had come up. But this also was not easy. The wind had obliterated his tracks, and after it became dark, the light from his headlamp lasted only briefly. He had to wait for the moon to rise at about 7 p.m. to give him sufficient light to climb over the mini-peaks on the ridge. At 8:25 p.m. he was back at his second bivouac, in the snow hole. He brewed hot drinks and slept until 2-3 a.m. on the 29th before completing his descent. His toes had become slightly frostbitten, but he had scaled the face and next day descended to Limbu in four hours. The piar then continued down to base camp, reaching it that night.

ELIZABETH HAWLEY, *AAC Honorary Member, Nepal, and* LINDSAY GRIFFIN, *Mountain INFO,*
www.climbmagazine.com

Editor's Note: Tomaz Humar's climb was the first solo ascent of Annapurna East, an 8,000m summit originally ascended in 1974 by Spaniards, Jose Manuel Anglada, Emilio Civis, and Jordi Pons, via the north ridge. Prior to 2007 it had only been climbed twice since. Humar climbed to the right of Annapurna's east rib, the line ascended in 1988 by legendary Poles, Artur Hajzer and Jerzy Kukuczka, who climbed the 1,500m snow and ice spur to the east ridge and then continued up to the east summit. The south face of Kangsar Kang was first climbed alpine-style in 2000 by a three-man French party, but their ascent was not widely reported at the time and until recently remained largely unknown. Humar believed he was climbing new ground, though in fact he followed the 2000 line, the most logical on this section of the face (being exposed to serac fall for only 20 minutes near the bottom of the wall, at ca 6,000m, while the Polish route is objectively more dangerous and for a greater length).

The French acclimatized by camping on the summit of neighboring Singu Chuli (a.k.a. Fluted Peak, 6,501m) for three nights, from where they had a good view of the line. After a rest at base camp they returned with just a tent inner, one 50m rope, and no sleeping bags. They then climbed the face with a bivouac at 6,800m, exiting onto the east ridge of Annapurna, just 200m left (west) of Kangsar Kang's summit. The climbing involved snow and ice to 60° but no difficult terrain. After a second miserable night just below the crest, the three then attempted to reach Annapurna East, but the wind was strong and, fatigued, they traversed to the north ridge, on which they bivouacked. During the night a storm broke the tent poles and the next day, the worse for wear, they descended the north ridge of Annapurna East and eventually picked up fixed ropes belonging to a French expedition attempting the classic 1950 route. They used these to descend to the north-side base camp.

Annapurna II, first winter ascent. The main success winter success in Nepal was the first winter ascent of Annapurna II (7,937m). Philipp Kunz (German) employed three Sherpas from east Nepal: Lhakpa Wangel, Temba Nuru, and Lhakpa Thinduk, the latter two with no real previous high-altitude experience. The team followed the route of the first ascent from the north, establishing base camp on January 16 at 5,000m. Strong winds and heavy snowfall stopped activity for a while, but the then Sherpas forced a route to a site for advanced base on the glacier below Annapurna IV, at 5,800m. Kunz joined them there on the 28th. The Sherpas fixed more rope and the whole team camped at 6,600m on the 31st. They spent another night there while working on the route above, then moved up on February 2 to a camp at 7,400m. Next day they camped at 7,600m and on the 4th reached the summit. The crux of the route was a 55° section of mixed rock and snow above 7,100m. In all the Sherpas fixed 2,500m of rope, a hard job in the very cold weather and one which Kunz realizes would have been much easier with a bigger team. They had planned to have six camps above base but found this was not possible, due to lack of available sites. Only one other party had previously attempted the peak in winter: a 1983 British expedition, which failed to make any real progress because of deep, unconsolidated snow.

Annapurna II has only had five confirmed ascents. The summit was first reached in 1960 by the British-Indian-Nepalese Services Expedition led by Jimmy Roberts. They placed camps up the north face/northwest ridge of Annapurna IV (7,525m), following the route of the first ascent of that mountain by Germans in 1955. By the middle of May they established Camp 5 on a shoulder of Annapurna IV, where the long west ridge branches off to Annapurna II. After a slight loss of altitude, they found a place for Camp 6 near the base of the summit pyramid at 7,200m. Two Sherpas established this camp while Chris Bonington, Richard Grant, and Ang Nyima started out from Camp 5 and climbed all the way to the summit. The route up the final pyramid followed a 45-50° rock rib interspersed with boulders and perched slabs, giving difficult rock climbing. Yugoslavians from Slovenia repeated this ascent in 1969, also climbing Annapurna IV. In 1973 Japanese shortcut the route by climbing directly up the north face between IV and II before continuing along the west ridge. Katsuyuki Kondo reached the top in a remarkable solo performance. Koreans may have repeated the original route in 1989. Some of the expedition climbed Annapurna IV, and later two members radioed that they were close to the summit of Annapurna II on the west ridge and would have to bivouac on the descent. They disappeared but are generally credited with having reached the top. The only ascent that has not taken place from the north was in 1983, when a strong Australian team climbed the south face.

LINDSAY GRIFFIN, *Mountain INFO, www.climbmagazine.com,* and RICHARD SALISBURY,
The Himalayan Database

DAMODAR HIMAL

Chako, first ascent. A 10-member Kanagawa Alpine Federation party, led by Tatsumine Makino (62), made the first ascent of Chako (6,704m), via the southwest ridge. The team approached via Nar Gaon and Phu Gaon, making their base camp on July 9 at 5,100m below the snout of the glacier south of the Lugula Himal. This site has running water and is conveniently situated for attempts on both Bhrikuti Shail and Chako. Above the snout, with its ice cave, the team moved up the glacier, passing a clean stream and a three-stepped waterfall, then more moraine, to place Camp 1 at 5,500m on July 13. Sixty to 90 minutes above this camp was a triangular rock and above this, at ca 5,900m, the party began to fix rope. At 6,000m they reached a snow plateau and at 6,200m, on the southwest ridge, found a small space below a large ice block, on which they could situate two tents. They established this Camp 2 on the 16th. Above a rock

Chako (6,704m), a remote border peak in the Damodar Himal, remained unattempted until last year, when it was climbed via the southwest ridge by a Japanese expedition. Seen here is the west face, bounded on the right by the ridge climbed by the Japanese and on the left by the northwest ridge leading toward the Lugula Himal *Lindsay Abbotts*.

barrier from 6,500m to 6,550m the ridge became narrow and quite steep, at one point forming an exposed section of vertical rocky terrain. The climbers continued fixing rope all the way to the summit, which Kazuhisa Kamisaka and Akio Omura reached at 11.50 a.m. on the 24th, accompanied by Hari Bahadur Chaulagai and Ang Phuri Lama, the latter a 60-year-old Sirdar from Beni. Chako lies on the Tibetan border, and the summiteers noted that the Tibetan side was a steep pyramidal rock face. The party descended to Camp 2 by 4 p.m., but at around that time an avalanche destroyed one of the tents. No one was hurt, and the two Sherpas continued their descent, past Camp 1 and all the way to base. The Japanese slept in the remaining tent and reached base camp the following day. This was the first attempt on the high Damodar summit.

The team then planned to climb Bhrikuti but after reaching 5,800m on the south ridge, decided it was too avalanche-prone and descended. The expedition now began a trek towards Khumjungar (a.k.a. Khamjung or Khumjung, 6,759m), which lies northwest of Chhiv. It has no recorded ascent, though it may have been climbed by Japanese in 1982. However, the Lapso Khola was too swollen to cross, and any attempt to reach the mountain was abandoned. (Earlier in the year Khumjungar had been reconnoitred by Pete Athans and Renan Ozturk.) The two Americans reached the Chame valley in March but found the snow too deep to make progress toward the peak). The Japanese then moved south and on August 7 climbed the trekking peak of Chuli West by the west ridge. After this they crossed the Thorong La to Muktinath and continued to the base of their next objective, Gaugiri. By that time they were too tired to make an attempt and instead walked to Lho Manthang, where on the 27th they found that their proposed route to Arniko Chuli in West Mustang (6,034m, climbed by Ohnishi and a Sherpa couple in 2002) was not feasible. Locals were harvesting their crops and believed that if foreigners entered the area, the crops would be ruined. The team gave up on the peak, its final goal, and trekked back down the Kali Gandaki to Beni, where they took the bus out to Kathmandu.

TAMOTSU NAKAMURA, *Japanese Alpine News;* ELIZABETH HAWLEY, *AAC Honorary Member, Nepal; and* RICHARD SALISBURY, *The Himalayan Database.*

MANSIRI (MANASLU) HIMAL

Himalchuli, from the north. The Ukrainian National Himalayan Expedition climbed Himalchuli (7,893m) from the Lidanda Glacier to the north. Jointly led by Mstislav Gorbenko and Sergey Pugachev, the eight-member team arrived at the 3,600m base camp on April 13. They established an advanced base at 5,100m on the Lidanda Pass, which marks the start of the huge northeast ridge, on the 19th. From there six members worked the route ahead, which would eventually involve ca 15km of climbing before they reached the summit. They used no local help beyond base camp, took no oxygen on the route, and used a minimum amount of fixed rope (ca 250m). They placed Camp 1 (5,900m) and Camp 2 (6,500m) on the plateau east of Lidanda Peak (6,693m, formerly known as Rani Peak) and on the south ridge of Lidanda Peak, respectively. From there the team outflanked Lidanda and descended to the glacier plateau northeast of Himalchuli, where on May 10 they established Camp 3 at 6,200m. They placed Camp 4 two days later at 6,800m on the northeast face. Slanting up across this face in a couloir, which was 60° in places, with a section of hard ice at 80°, the climbers reached the northwest ridge, where they set up Camp 5 in a bergshrund at 7,250m. The ridge leading back toward the summit was not technical but comprised poor rock and snow. Instead of following the crest, the climbers climbed down the right flank for 100m, and then slanted across 65° terrain for 800m before rejoining the crest. They placed their final camp on the 17th at 7,680m, and all six climbers left for the summit at 3:30 a.m. on the 19th. At 9:30 a.m., after negotiating 40° slopes, Sergey Bublik, Yuri Kilichenko, Andrey Kiyko, Maksim Perevalov, Pugachev, and Vladimir Roshko reached the top. They had left no sleeping bags at the top camp, and when they arrived back at Camp 5, they found it crushed by snow, so all had to descend to Camp 4. The following day, the 20th, they were back in Camp 3 and reached base camp on the 22nd.

Himalchuli, the 18th highest peak in the world, has now been attempted 26 times but only six teams had summited prior to the Ukrainians. Some of the earlier attempts concentrated on the long northeast ridge, though a small British team in 1953 reached 5,600m from the south. Japanese got to 6,400m from the north side in 1958; another Japanese team made a spirited effort in 1959, getting to 7,400m on the northeast face before being defeated by steep ice. Italians climbed slightly higher in 1974, finding the climbing very hard. Later in 1974 another Japanese expedition tried the same route but was defeated at 7,050m. Japanese tried again in 1977, and two members reached the northwest ridge, progressing to ca 7,800m before a climber was killed when a falling cornice hit him. A British team reached 6,400m in 1978; Americans reached 5,800m from the south in 1979. After 1979 no other expedition attempted the route until the Ukrainians in 2007.

Most climbers, certainly in later years, have approached from the south. Himalchuli was first climbed in the spring of 1960 by Yiro Jamada's Japanese expedition via the southwest face. The team reached the gently sloping saddle between Himalchuli West (7,540m) and the main top, then continued up the southwest ridge to the summit. Unusually for an attempt on a sub-8,000m peak at that time, the climbers used oxygen. In 1978 Yoshio Ogata's Japanese team climbed a hard new route up the south face to southwest ridge and, after visiting the main summit, made the first ascent of Himalchuli West. As this was not then on the permitted list, the famous and prolific Ogata was banned from Nepal for five years. In 1984 Americans made the first ascent of the southwest ridge integral, traversing the south flank of the west summit to join the Japanese route in its upper reaches. This was repeated in spring 1985 by Hungarians (the first Hungarian ascent of any major Nepalese mountain), while in autumn of that year Japanese appear to have repeated, more or less, the 1978 route. Yet more Japanese appear to have repeated the 1978 route in the autumn of 1986, the last time the mountain was climbed from the south.

Himalchuli West has been climbed twice since 1978: in 1989 by a multi-national, commercially organized expedition via the southwest ridge, which they found long and hard and on which they fixed 3,500m of rope, and on December 19, 1990, again by the southwest ridge, by Koreans who were making a winter attempt on the main peak. Lidanda Peak (6,693m) was first climbed in 1970 via a Dutch team via the south ridge, a route that was repeated again by two members of the 1978 British Himalchuli expedition.

LINDSAY GRIFFIN, *Mountain INFO, www.climbmagazine.com*

GANESH HIMAL

Punchen Himal North, first ascent. After the expedition to Dolpo, reported elsewhere, Tamotsu Ohnishi's Osaka Alpine Club expedition returned to Kathmandu, and some members flew home. The remaining six left for a trek up the Buri Gandaki on October 7. Before Nyuk (Ngyak) they turned right and headed up the Shyar (or Shar) Khola valley, which runs northeast, behind and north of the Ganesh Himal. On the 18th they set up base camp at 4,124m, just north of the Shyar Khola. The following day Irisawa, Kato, Mizutani, Ohnishi, and Chhepa Sherpa placed a high camp at 4,850m (N 28°40'21", E 85°06'96") at the start of the northeast ridge of their chosen objective, the unclimbed Punchen Himal (6,049m, N 28°39'40", E 85°08'48"). This previously unattempted peak lies on the Tibetan border north of 6,247m Pashuwo.

On the 20th all started climbing up the ridge at 5 a.m. The ridge was mainly rock, with occasional icy sections, to 5,700m, where they moved onto the northwest face and fixed 250m of rope, reaching the crest of the northwest ridge at 5,900m. Above, a 60° slope, then breakable crust over deep soft snow that they however climbed without ropes in an hour, led to the north summit at 5,962m. It was only 11:30 a.m., but the way to the main summit led along a knife-edge ridge. There wasn't enough rope for all members to continue, so Ohnishi and others went down. After three hours on the saw-tooth ridge, the remaining members had gained no altitude above the north summit and were still half a kilometer from the main summit. Although not technically difficult, the route had been a tiring succession of loose rock and unconsolidated snow, and the team decided to retreat. On the way down they took a more direct route from 5,700m, rappelling straight down the face to a small lake above high camp. On the 21st they returned to base camp and left for a trek over the Larkya La and around the northwest side of Manaslu to inspect other peaks they hope to attempt in the future. They returned to Kathmandu in November.

ELIZABETH HAWLEY, *AAC Honorary Member, Nepal;* RICHARD SALISBURY, *The Himalayan Database; and* TAMOTSU OHNISHI, *Japanese Alpine Club*

Gorilla Peak, Ganesh, first ascent. Ganesh V (6,770m) lies at the eastern end of the Ganesh Himal, visible from Kathmandu. The northern flanks, technically in Tibet, were climbed by a large Japanese expedition in 1980, while later the south face was climbed by a Slovenian team

Ganesh V from the southeast showing the route followed by the French team along the east ridge to make the first ascent of Gorilla Peak. Bivouac 1 is at 6,200m. *Aymeric Clouet*

En route to the first bivouac on the east ridge of Ganesh V (6,770m). The main summit is the most distant snow-capped top, while Gorilla Peak (6,741m GPS), reached by the French team, is the second pointed rocky pinnacle to the right. *Aymeric Clouet*

[Editor's note: In 1980, 12 members of Yoshio Nagao's expedition summited via the north face and northwest ridge. In 1987 Haruo Makino's Japanese expedition put four members on the summit via the south ridge, a route that was more or less repeated in 1994 by a Slovenian expedition, after the latter had given up the idea of a new route on the southwest face. Four Frenchmen, who had a permit for Paldor, attempted the south face and northwest ridge in 2006 but were killed, probably in an avalanche from high on the peak. Aymeric Clouet was one of the party who later that season went to search for the bodies.] Before 2007 these were the only routes on the mountain. Our recent climb established a new route to a subsidiary summit.

At 4 p.m. on November 15, Frederic Degoulet, Julien Dusserre, Mathieu Maynadier, and I reached the top of the third point (6,741m by GPS) of Ganesh V, having climbed the east ridge. We named the virgin aiguille Gorilla Peak, because we could see the face of a gorilla in the summit rocks when looking from the east. Our route from base camp was 6.5 km long, with a vertical interval of 2,700m (1,240m of technical ridge climbing). Difficulties encountered included 3-4km of cornices, 75° snow, mixed climbing to M5 and rock to 6a.

After a 15-day acclimatization trek along the paths of Gosainkund Lake (the sacred lakes of Shiva), we met our team of 10 porters and cooks in the village of Tatopani. Buildings were grouped around thermal hot springs, and the place is a pilgrimage destination. It was the last village we would see for 23 days. Our acclimatization was uneventful, other than our change in diet to Dal Bhat, a traditional Nepalese dish that caused intestinal problems. Following a pattern of three days at altitude, then three days rest, we established our advanced base camp at 5,500m, sheltered by a small cliff. Our first bivouac was at 6,200m, where we left a cache of bivouac equipment, food, and gear. After one final rest at base camp we decided to "put to sea" and try for the summit. The expression is fitting, as a marvelous sea of clouds accompanied us, as though we were sailing on an ocean of cotton. However, these clouds eventually began to transform into wet cumulus, dropping snowflakes in the afternoon. The change in weather forced us to adapt, as the climbing became more mixed and was swept by small snow slides. Sometimes we had to stop for a few hours to wait for a clearing, in order to get oriented. On the evening of the fourth day, when we bivouacked at ca 6,500m, we were informed that 100 km/hour winds were forecast for the following day till evening The temperature was already low, each night dropping to –20 or –25°C, and we realized a further drop would prove unbearable.

Knowing that we would not have a second chance, we set our hearts on the most easterly of the three summits of Ganesh V. This was the rockiest and in our opinion the most beautiful. On the fifth day we climbed 250m of granite (mixed and 6a) to the top, about 30m lower than the main summit. The forecast allowed enough time for a quick descent, and the immense joy of successfully reaching the top made us forget, during the bivouac that followed, the cold and the fear of being ripped off the wall by the wind. It was late on the sixth night that we reached base camp, where we were greeted warmly by Kamal and Rai, our cooks, who were happy to join in our celebrations.

AYMERIC CLOUET, *France*

JUGAL HIMAL

Gurkarpo Ri, first known ascent. Paulo Grobel organized two commercial expeditions for Nepal's post-monsoon season. On October 2 Grobel, two Sherpa companions, and five French clients reached the summit of Saribung (6,328m) in the Damodar Himal. This, the fourth ascent of the mountain, more or less followed the original route up the northeast face and northeast ridge, pioneered in 2003 by Jim Frush and Steve Furman. The leader then returned to Kathmandu to collect a new group, for a more demanding ascent of Langtang Ri (7,205m) in the Langtang Himal, a peak which has been attempted at least seven times, four times successfully.

Grobel established his base camp, near the foot of the Langtang Glacier, at a spot known as Pemthang Karpo. [Also referred to as Morimoto Peak Base Camp—6,150m Morimoto Peak, officially named Bhemdang Ri, lies to the northwest—the site is immediately below and north of 6,412m Langshisha Ri—Ed.]. A quick probe north convinced the French team that with all the fresh snow on the moraine-covered glacier, just reaching the foot of the mountain would take too long and would be particularly difficult for their porters. It was time for a rethink.

The weather forecast, which predicted clear skies but winds up to 60km/hour at 6,500m, made the west ridge of Gurkarpo Ri (6,889m) seem the best alternative. However, Grobel knew nothing of Gurkarpo Ri's history, had no idea whether it was on the government's list of permitted peaks, and was unaware that it had never been climbed. Time was getting on, and calculating that he only had around 10 days left to make the ascent, Grobel realized the climb would have to be made in a more or less continuous push.

The summit of Gurkarpo Ri (6,889m) seen from the high glacier plateau lying between the mountain and Langshisha Ri (6,412m). Marked is the upper section of the first ascent route. Camp 3 is at ca 5,800m to the left of the prominent Arête des Rapiettes. Camp 4 is at 6,200m and the point where the route above gains the upper section of the west ridge is 6,600m. From here the route follows relatively gentle slopes on the far (southern) side. *Paulo Grobel*

He and his team quickly established Camp 1 at 4,800m on a side glacier, and Camp 2 on a huge flat glaciated col between Langshisha Ri and Gurkarpo Ri. Realizing that two more camps would be needed, Grobel had 800m of static line and 25 snow stakes air-dropped, something of an (expensive) novelty in Nepal but necessary in order to give his clients the best chance of success. The sharp snow and ice spur leading up the northwest flank of the west ridge was dubbed the Arête des Rapiettes. The team placed Camp 3 to the left of the arîte at 5,800m. As a training/acclimatization exercise, they climbed this arîte to a small summit at a grade of PD+. Grobel and his two Sherpas, Cho Temba and Zangbu, climbed and fixed the broad glaciated couloir left of the arête. The 400m snow/ice slope led to a plateau and the site of Camp 4 at 6,200m. On October 31, while the other members rested in this camp, Grobel, Cho Temba, and Zangbu fixed rope on the 45-50° slopes above, leading to a vague col on the upper west ridge at 6,600m.

The next morning, November 1, Cho Temba awoke with a bad headache, and Grobel thought it wise for him to descend to Camp 2, accompanied by Zangbu. The remaining five climbers continued. One member stopped before the ridge due to a bronchial infection, but the other four, Pierre-Oliver Dupuy, Marc Kia, Jean Francois Males, and Grobel, reached the crest and were surprised to find the southern slopes quite gentle. They made good progress, finding only one short section of 40° surmounting a bergshrund, before reaching the summit in excellent if cold weather. The descent went without incident, and three days later all members were back at Kyanchin Gompa in the Langtang valley. They named the route Some More Rice?, grading it alpine D.

From information supplied by PAULO GROBEL, *France*

Editor's note: Gurkarpo Ri had been attempted at least five times prior to the French ascent. The first known attempt was by Koreans in the winter of 1993. They reached 6,100m on the west ridge but gave up due to technical difficulty. Japanese tried in the autumn of 1998 by what they refer to as the northwest ridge, but gave up at 6,150m. A German expedition the following year was prevented from coming to grips with the west ridge due to deep snow. A Korean team tried in the winter of 2001 but gave up low on the south face due to avalanche and cold. In autumn 2003 another

Korean team the southeast face but gave up low due to avalanche conditions. The peak had gained a reputation for difficulty, but it seems that all except the Japanese approached the mountain up the Langshisha Glacier to the south, rather than the northerly approach used by the French.

ROLWALING HIMAL

Dingjung Ri South, first authorized attempt from Nepal. Three members of Japan's Kwansie Gakuin University Alpine Club, Mayuto Demoko, Kenro Nakajima, and Naoki Tenaka, made the first authorized attempt on the east ridge of Pt. 6,196m, which might be described as Dingjung Ri South. Arriving early in the year, they approached via Thame and the normal route toward the Nangpa La, then established a 4,950m base camp on the Meluka (Pangbuk) Glacier on March 3. They placed a higher camp below the southeast face of the peak at 5,435m. Neither Demoko

Dingjung Ri South (6,196m) seen from the east. In March 2007 Mayuto Demoko and Kenro Nakajima reached a point about 60m below the summit via the line shown. Nakajima returned in March 2008 and completed the same route to the summit with Hiroki Yamamoto—the first authorized ascent of this peak on the Nepal-Tibet border. *Kenro Nakajima*

nor Tenaka had previous altitude experience, so the team fixed 500m of rope up the southeast face and onto the crest of the east ridge. On March 12 they made their first summit attempt, but it was late by the time they reached 6,000m, so they retreated. Their second attempt took place on the 18th. At 5,700m Tenaka slipped on the fixed ropes and bruised himself, so he retreated. The other two continued to 6,132m but saw that the way involved a difficult traverse leading to a snow/ice face below the summit. Fatigue and lack of rope for fixing forced a decision to descend.

A little to the north, Dingjung Ri (6,249m) lies on the Tibetan border south of 6,625m Pangbuk Ri and north of the Menlung La. It has had no known recent ascent. But there is ambiguity when it comes to the naming of Pt. 6,249m and Pt. 6,196m. On the new list of permitted peaks announced in 2002, Pt 6,249m, as designated on the HMG-FINN map, is Dingjung Ri. In fact neither 6,249m nor 6,196m are named on this map. The old Schneider Rolwaling map has the heights of these peaks as 6,320m and 6,249m respectively, naming the latter (Pt. 6,196m on the FINN map) Dingjung Ri. This is the terminology used on Japanese maps, and the Japanese climbers refer to Pt. 6,196m as Dingjung Ri. It is unlikely the authorities know which is the true Dingjung Ri.

Pt. 6,249m was first climbed as long ago as 1955 during Alf Gregory's productive Mersey-side Himalayan expedition, which climbed many peaks in the Rolwaling region and made a reconnaissance of Gauri Shankar. Peter Boultbee and Denis Davis, who crossed the Menlung La west into Tibet and made an ascent of Ripimo Shar (6,647m) from the north, also moved north up the Menlung valley and climbed Dingjung Ri from the west. They were hindered from reaching the summit of this then unnamed peak by a crevasse, over which they executed a big jump. As Kang appears in so many peak names, they felt it apt to name the peak after one of the world's great jumpers, the kangaroo, and called the peak Kangkuru, a moniker that stuck for many years and appears on the Japanese maps.

In March 2008 Kenro Nakajima returned and completed the route with Hiroki Yamamo-to. The two climbed to the summit from a high camp at ca 5,430m and their climb, which appears to be the first authorized ascent of the peak, will be reported in *AAJ 2009*.

KENRO NAKAJIMA, *Japan;* ELIZABETH HAWLEY, *AAC Honorary Member, Nepal*,
RICHARD SALISBURY, *The Himalayan Database;*
and LINDSAY GRIFFIN, *Mountain INFO, www.climbmagazine.com*

Likhu Chuli I, north ridge, attempt. Japanese Koichi Ezaki and Hiroshi Kudo made the first official attempt on the north ridge of Likhu Chuli I (6,719m). The well-known trekking peak of Parchamo (6,279m) is the northerly extension of this ridge. On November 24 the pair climbed the steep and technically difficult east (Khumbu) flank of the ridge towards the crest, fixing rope to 5,950m. Above, they felt the need to fix more rope. They had cached ropes earlier in the month, after Ezaki led a larger expedition to Parchamo, but when they returned they found the ropes had been stolen. Not wishing to progress without more fixed rope, they abandoned the expedition.

In 1960 a French team, led by Robert Sandoz, that had Chobuje (Chobutse, 6,686m) as its original aim, climbed a number of peaks from the Rolwaling, including Parchamo and Pimu. After abandoning Chobutse due to ice fall, they turned to Likhu Chuli I (then known as Pig-pherago Shar). After establishing camps at 5,500m and 6,150m, Cécile Barbezat and Nawang Dorje reached the summit on October 21 via the steep, difficult west ridge. To the west, Likhu Chuli II (Pigpherago Nup, 6,659m) has no known ascent. Both summits were officially opened to foreign climbers in 2003.

ELIZABETH HAWLEY, *AAC Honorary Member, Nepal, and* RICHARD SALISBURY,
The Himalayan Database

Kwangde Lho, north face in winter. In January 2008 Vladimir Belousov and Alexander Novikov made a calendar-winter ascent of Kwangde Lho (6,187m) via a new route on the Hungo face. The Russians' original aim was a line between the Breashears-Lowe December 1982 route (ED2, WI6, 1200m) and the Lorenzo-Munoz 1985 route, Mandala (1150m, little information on difficulty). However, when they arrived below the north face, they found very dry conditions, and the only possible line they felt they could climb without resorting to aid was the wall beneath the Kwangde Lho–Kwangde Nup col.

Belousov and Novikov started on January 8, carrying two small rucksacks, one sleeping bag for both climbers and a Bibler tent. Their route slanted left across the lower section of

The north or Hungo face of Kwangde in relatively dry winter conditions. (A) Kwangde Shar (6,093m), (B) Kwangde Lho (6,187m) and (C) Kwangde Nup (6,035m). (1) The start of Mandala (1,150m, Lorenzo-Munoz, 1985) and (2) Chicory (5.7 WI4 M4 40-50°, 1,200m, Belousov-Novikov, 2008), with the bivouac sites B1 and B2 marked. A photo showing all the remaining routes on this face appears in AAJ 2007. *Vladimir Belousov*

Kwangde Nup's north face, climbing a couloir and rock band to reach the northwest spur descending from the summit of Lho. Below the central rock barrier, near the point where Mandala comes in from the left, they made a horizontal traverse right. The crest above had looked difficult, probably requiring hard rock climbing and aid; to the right lay icy mixed walls that could be climbed free. The Russians chose these and eventually reached the southwest ridge 100m below the top, where they made their second bivouac just short of the summit. It was -20°C, very windy, and they were unable to pitch the tent. They sat up all night trying to keep warm and the next morning reached the summit in clear weather at 9.30 a.m. They named their route Chicory. Although it is hard to say whether the new route shares common ground with Mandala, Chicory is mostly 40-50° snow and ice with five difficult pitches: three (M4, WI4, M3) through the rock band above the narrow couloir on the first day, one the exit pitch onto the southwest ridge (M3 and 5.7), while the last was on the south side of the mountain just below the second bivouac (M2/M3 and WI3). On the first four the leader led without a pack, the second jumaring while carrying both packs.

From the summit the pair descended the original route (Ishikawa-Iwahashi-Ogawa-Sherpas, 1978), making several rappels to reach the south ridge, which was hard ice. They descended to the Lumding Valley, walked across the frozen lake, and made the long, arduous climb back north across the Lumding La, finally reaching Phakdingma on the Dudh Kosi on the 12th. Although the vertical gain on the north side of the mountain is 1,200m, Chicory has an estimated climbing distance of 2,110m. It is probably the easiest way to reach the summit ridge via the Hungo face.

VLADIMIR BELOUSOV, *Russia, and*
LINDSAY GRIFFIN, *Mountain INFO, www.climbmagazine.com*

The north face of Kwangde Lho. Alexander Novikov leads the pitch of WI4 through the rock band above the initial couloir of the new Russian route Chicory. *Vladimir Belousov*

Editor's note: a four-man Japanese expedition is reported to have made a calendar winter ascent of the mountain in 2007 via the south ridge, reaching the summit on January 5.

MAHALANGUR HIMAL–KHUMBU SECTION

Jasmaba Goth, west ridge attempt. Jasamba Goth is the name given to the 6,730m shoulder toward the end of the long northwest ridge of Pasang Lhamu Chuli, where the ridge splits into two branches; one falling north of west and the other south of west. The peak was named by Tamotsu Ohnishi in 1996, when his Japanese expedition climbed the southerly branch of the ridge, over the summit, and up the northwest ridge of Pasang Lhamu Chuli to make this mountain's second ascent. (The first, by a Japanese party in 1986, was made from Tibet, and it is not clear where they reached the northwest ridge.) They were followed the same season by a French expedition. The northwest ridge marks the frontier between Nepal and Tibet, and its continuation reaches the Nangpa La. There are rumors that Pasang Lhamu Chuli was climbed by climbers preparing for fast alpine-style ascents of lines on Cho Oyu, and it seems unlikely that the accessible Jasamba Goth was still virgin when it was climbed by the Japanese.

The peak was attempted again in September by a three-member American team led by Dan McCann. They appear to have followed the Japanese route to a high point of 6,500m on the 22nd. The following day McCann and Bob Merrill reached the 6,540m west summit of Friendship Peak (6,592m).

LINDSAY GRIFFIN, *Mountain INFO, www.climbmagazine.com*

Pasang Lhamu Chuli, first ascent of southwest face and south pillar. After attempts in 2005 and 2006, Hans Kammerlander finally climbed the southwest face and south pillar of Pasang Lhamu Chuli (7,351m), a peak immediately southwest of Cho Oyu. It was formerly Jasamba but officially renamed after the death in May 1993 of Pasang Lhamu, a Sherpani who was the first Nepalese women to climb Everest but perished during the descent. The peak forms the most westerly summit of the Nangpai Gosum group and had been climbed at least four times previously.

In October 2004 Slovenians Rok Blagus, Samo Krmelj, and Uros Samec made a highly underrated ascent of the south pillar, reaching the upper crest at 6,650m via a difficult ice and mixed climb (ED M5) up the southeast face. They used no fixed ropes but first climbed the face to 6,100m, slept there for acclimatization, and fixed rappel anchors for the descent. They next climbed to 6,400m and did the same. On their third foray they left their advanced base at

Nils Nielson close to the summit of Phari Lapcha East after the first ascent of The End of the Beginning. (A) Dzasampa Tse (6,295m). (B) Pasang Lhamu Chuli (7,351m) with the south pillar climbed by Kammerlander and Unterkircher in profile. (C) Nampai Gosum I (a.k.a. Cho Aui, 7,321m). (D) Nampai Gosum I South (7,240m). (E) Nampai Gosum II (a.k.a. Chamar, 7,287m). (F) Nampai Gosum III (7,488m). (G) Cho Oyu (8,188m). (H) Ngojumba Kang I (7,916m). *Halvor Dannevig*

5,450m and climbed the whole southeast face in 14 hours, slanting left onto the crest at 6,650m. There the angle eases, and they spent two nights at that altitude before going for the summit. The first narrow corniced section above proved difficult, but above 7,000m they found the route straightforward.

In spring 2005 Kammerlander, with fellow South Tyroleans Luis Brugger and Karl Unterkircher, attempted the south pillar integral from the "saddle" between Pasang Lhamu Chuli and the 6,295m Dzasampa Ri. The "saddle" is actually a long, quasi-horizontal ridge, studded with rocky pinnacles and towers. Italians had reached it at its northern end via steep snow and ice slopes on the southwest face. They progressed part way up the steep mixed crest above over snow and poor rock before retreating in high winds. In 2006 Brugger and Kammerlander returned, following the same line, fixing rope and reaching the end of the steep section, where the Slovenian route comes in from the right. As they were returning to base for a rest before the final push, Brugger became detached from a fixed rope and fell down the southeast face to his death.

Kammerlander, with Ernst Brugger (brother of Luis) and film maker/cameraman Hartmann Seber, arrived at their 5,200m base camp immediately south of the mountain on May 2, 2007. Unterkircher arrived the next day and with Kammerlander set about establishing Camp 1 at ca 6,050m on the crest of the south ridge. To reach this point the two reclimbed their old line up the southwest flank, fixing a few ropes. They spent a couple of days and nights at this camp, to aid their acclimatization, and worked on the route above, before returning to base camp on the 12th in heavy snowfall. They returned a few days later and climbed the difficult pillar above, fixing ropes to 6,700m, where the main technical difficulties ease and the angle relents. This high point was the same reached by Brugger and Kammerlander in 2006 when,

The south pillar of Pasang Lhamu Chuli (7,351m). (1) The original 1986 Japanese route up the northwest ridge. (2) The southwest face and south pillar integral (Kammerlander-Unterkircher, 2007). (3) The southeast face and south pillar (Blagus-Krmelj-Samec, 2004). *Karl Unterkircher*

due to inaccurate altimeter readings, they thought they were over 7,000m. At 6,500m a steep, difficult rock band bars the route, and the pair was forced off the crest, making a quasi-horizontal traverse to the right before they could slant back left up a line of weakness to regain the ridge at 6,650m. This line of weakness appears to be the same snow/ice couloir that was climbed in 2004 by the Slovenians. Throughout their time on the mountain the weather was less than clement; by late mornings the sky had become cloudy, and from then on snow showers would occur. On the 18th they descended to base camp to rest and wait for a good spell during which to make their summit attempt.

Good weather never really arrived, but the pair decided to set off on the 21st and later that day regained Camp 1. After resting there, they started climbing again at 1:30 a.m. on the 22nd, jumaring their fixed ropes to the high point and then embarking on the final 650m to the summit, which had been climbed by the Slovenians in 2004. Although less difficult, it was not straightforward, and the final 120m lay on a particularly sharp and exposed crest. The pair reached the summit at 3 p.m., after a climbing time from base camp of around 20 hours and a vertical gain from the moraine of almost 2,000m. They regained Camp 1 at 9 p.m. During the descent the following morning they found that a section of rope on the southwest face a little below camp had been swept away by avalanche; the slope they had ascended a couple of days before was now smooth and clean. They had a couple of ice screws and a length of Kevlar for emergencies, and managed to set up a series of delicate rappels and arrived in base camp at 2 p.m. Kammerlander, who after the ascent called it the most difficult of his career, felt the climbing on the ridge to be of the same order as the north face of the Eiger but at a much higher altitude. This was the first of Unterkircher's two notable ascents in 2007. He later made the first north-to-south traverse of Gasherbrum II (see Climbs and Expeditions, Pakistan), climbing a new route on the Chinese face.

LINDSAY GRIFFIN, *Mountain INFO,*
www.climbmagazine.com, and www.kammerlander.com

Phari Lapcha, second ascent of north face, Japanese variant to Bonfire of the Vanities. Fumitaka Ichimura and I climbed the north face of Phari Lapcha (6,017m). In the lower section we followed new ground but traversed to the original French route for the upper part of the face. We graded our 1,000m, 24-pitch line ED1 AI4 R. We left Gokyo village on November 22, climbed onto the snow band that traverses the bottom of the face just above its base, moved right, and bivouacked below the start of our line. Next day we climbed the narrow gully above. The terrain was mostly hard snow, so placing ice screws proved impossible. At times the rock was loose. By evening we had reached a small icefield, where we enjoyed a sitting bivouac on a small ledge. On the third day we hoped to climb directly toward the summit, but the ice turned out to be thin, so we slanted up right on an obvious ramp and joined the French route. [The French route, which represented the only prior ascent of the north face, was put up in November 2003 by Seb Constant and Jérome Mercader at ED1 M5 WI4. Named Bonfire of the Vanities, they climbed the route in 27 pitches, with one bivouac at 5,670m and a second at the exit point on the summit ridge at 5,970m. The Japanese reached the French line just above the site of the first

French bivouac—Ed.] We continued up the French route, reaching the summit ridge after dark, where we bivouacked on a good ledge beneath a rock pinnacle. On our fourth day we continued up sugar snow to the spectacular summit and descended to the southwest. Because snow and ice were so thin, we could not go down the gully that forms the easiest ascent route on this side of the mountain; it was too loose and dangerous. [The first official ascent via this gully and the upper northwest ridge took place in spring 2003 by a 10-member multinational team including a group of

The north face of Phari Lapcha (6,017m). (1) The Ichimura-Nakagawa variant (ED1 AI4 R) to (2) Bonfire of the Vanities (ED1 M5 WI4, 1,000m, 27 pitches, Constant-Mercader, 2003). The three Japanese bivouacs are marked and both parties reached the main summit. *Hiroyuki Nakagawa*

Sherpas—Ed.] Instead we descended the French route [The Bridge of Lost Desire, climbed in November 2003 by Constant and Mercador to give a 350m line at WI3 and M4—Ed.], reached the glacier in the evening, and continued down to bivouac for a fourth time. On the 26th we walked down to Machermo village.

HIROYUKI NAKAGAWA, *North Japan Climbing Team*

The northeast face of Dawa Peak (5,920m) showing the line of Snotty's Gully (700m, WI5 M5+, Bracey-Bullock, 2006), repeated in 2007 by Dannevig and Nielsen. This peak was named by the owner of the Machermo Lodge after his daughter. The main north face of Phari Lapcha lies just to the left. *Halvor Dannevig*

Nils Nielsen on the crux pitch of Snotty's Gully, northeast face of Dawa Peak. *Halvor Dannevig*

Dawa Peak, Snotty's Gully, second ascent; Phari Lapcha, The End of the Beginning, first ascent. Halvor Dannevig and I traveled to the upper Khumbu, hoping to find interesting climbing on "not too high" peaks. We consider how we do it to be more important than what peak we climb, so for us snow-plodding up fixed ropes on famous peaks is not interesting. As I was a Himalayan novice, the peaks around Gokyo seemed a perfect start to my Himalayan climbing. Our main objective was an unclimbed line on the north face of Phari Lapcha (6,017m).

Staying at the Gokyo Resort Lodge, we had a perfect view across the lake to the north face. The more we looked through binoculars, the more we realized that it was not ice, but snow, that was plastered to the face. For acclimatization we tried to climb a new line on the unnamed 5,906m peak between Dawa Peak (5,920m) and the Renja Pass. Standing in a cave underneath a thin ice curtain, after climbing 200m of powder snow and really bad ice, we were not optimistic. I continued, and in half an hour managed 15m of snow-covered M5. With no protection in sight above and no ice, I rappelled and found myself two meters outside the cave.

The only place we saw ice on the north side of the Phari Lapcha massif was in Snotty's Gully (WI5 M5+, ca 700m but 1,000m of climbing), a line climbed by the accomplished British alpinists Jon Bracey and Nick Bullock in 2006. With so many unclimbed lines around, it didn't feel right walking to

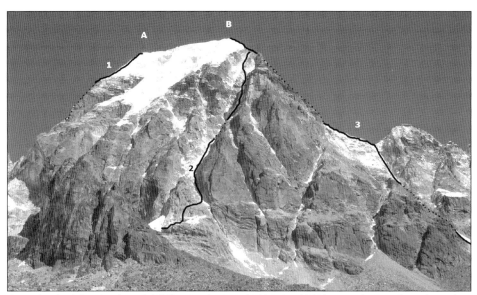

The south side of Phari Lapcha with (A) Phari Lapcha Main (6,017m) and (B) Phari Lapcha East. The rocky peak on the right edge of the picture is Machermo (5,766m). (1) The Bridge of Lost Desire (350m, WI3 M4, Constant-Mercader, 2003). (2) The End of the Beginning (ca 900m, M4 WI3, Dannevig-Nielsen, 2007). (3) The line of descent followed by Bremond, Constant, Degonon, and Thomas after their ascent of the east face in 2006. This was also the line used in descent by Dannevig and Nielson in 2007 after climbing The End of the Beginning. *Nils Nielsen*

the base of this climb. But we had traveled to Nepal to find good climbing, so it didn't really matter that much. We started climbing at 5 a.m. the next day, carrying chocolate in our pockets and one small pack with water and two down jackets. Being from Norway, we like to think we have the best ice climbing in the world. But when we stood on the summit at 2:40 p.m. that day, we realized that some of the pitches of perfect water ice would have been super-classics in any of our home-country's valleys. We rappelled and downclimbed to the Machermo Glacier, hoping to have a look at the south side of Phari Lapcha to see if there were any interesting lines. Due to afternoon cloud, we were unable to see this side of the mountain, but stumbling into the village of Machermo at 6:30 p.m., happy in the prospect of dinner and a warm bed, we had already decided to try something else up there after a couple of rest days.

Pitching a tent at 5,250m, close to the Machermo Glacier, we saw a gully of snow, ice, and rock on the southwest side of Phari Lapcha. Starting at 3 a.m. the next day, we climbed 100m of rock to get into the gully, then 300m higher, after having climbed snow and perfect ice up to WI3, we found ourselves at the crux: two long pitches of verglassed rock. Although not too difficult to climb (M4), these pitches proved interesting to protect. After three more mixed pitches, we arrived at the upper part of the gully, safe from rockfall and on easier ground. Two hundred meters higher, after climbing steep snow with short sections of rock, we joined the southeast ridge. At 9 a.m. we stood on the summit of Phari Lapcha East. We believe this route to be new and have named it The End of the Beginning (ca 900m, M4 WI3). It was climbed in the same light style as Snotty's Gully, with just one small pack. We found the route similar to the Eugster Direct on the north face of the Aiguille du Midi, Mont Blanc Massif.

NILS NIELSEN, *Norway*

Ama Dablam (6,812m), showing the line of the Korean attempt on the northeast face to north ridge. The 5,200m ABC lies at the start of the northeast spur. Camp 1 is at 5,700m and Camp 2 at 6,100m, with the high point on the north ridge reported to be ca 6,400m. The 1985 Buhler-Kennedy route climbs the central rib to the left, forcing a way through the huge capping seracs before traversing right to finish via the final section of the north ridge. The left skyline is the east ridge climbed by Georges and Hubert in 1983, while the right skyline is the northwest ridge climbed by Cartwright and Cross in 2000. The north ridge descends toward the camera before slanting down right from a point a little higher than the level of C1. *Lee Young-jun collection*

Ama Dablam and Himalayan conditions. The Himalaya appear to be getting drier, so relatively easy mountains are becoming technically more difficult with more exposed rock and more danger from unusual avalanching. Ama Dablam (6,812m) is no longer the mountain it was before November 2006, when a huge mass of ice broke away at ca 6,500m, above Camp 3, swept six climbers in their tents hundreds of meters down the mountainside, and buried them in a mound of avalanche debris.

According to Giampietro Verza, a mountain guide who knows the area well and who led a small Italian team to Ama Dablam during the spring, the ideal area for Camp 3 is still exposed to ice avalanches, and the large serac on the final ice slope is dangerously fractured. Sherpas are refusing to camp under it, and to scale the mountain directly from Camp 2, without the usual third high camp, makes the final summit climb not only too long for many climbers but also more dangerous. "The mountain remains the desired one for many climbers, but now you have to consider that this beauty is demanding more," Verza remarked.

Fourteen teams attempted Ama Dablam's standard southwest ridge during the pre-monsoon season. For the first time since the spring of 1996, not one succeeded. Too many days of snowfall was the explanation given by some, but more said that bad snow conditions on the route caused them to abandon their climbs at altitudes between 5,900m and 6,100m.

The only success on Ama Dablam this spring was achieved by two Americans who were looking for difficulty. Aric Baldwin and James Cromie found it on their ascent of the northeast spur and north ridge without Sherpas. They slept on the summit, waiting for daylight so they could see if anyone had made the top via the southwest ridge, with which they weren't familiar. No one had, but they managed to descend safely.

In the autumn there were 56 teams on the standard route. Some skipped Camp 3; others pitched what they called Camp 2.7 or 2.8. Still other teams established a camp at the traditional altitude, 6,300m, but as far to the right of the avalanche path as possible.

The leader of a commercial expedition who used the old Camp 3 site was Luis Benitez, an American leader of a multi-national group. He explained that if his clients had tried to summit from Camp 2, a large proportion of them would never have made it. They were not strong enough to go that distance up and back in one day. A Korean team did skip Camp 3. They left Camp 2 at 6,100m at 3 a.m. and were on the summit 15 hours later. They stayed there half an hour and did not get back to Camp 2 until 1 a.m. the next day.

Benitez, who has led groups on Ama Dablam before, was not happy about the continuing danger of falling debris. Not all leaders agreed with the degree of his concern, but he felt "the hazard level is now significantly higher," even if Camp 3 is skipped. He believed that "clients need to be made aware of the increased hazard because of the seracs threatening the route." There was an ice avalanche while his members were in Camp 3. They were far enough to the right of the seracs' path not to get hit, but they "felt the blast" from the falling ice. "The whole Dablam is calving, and eventually all of it will come off," he said.

In the meantime, until all of it has fallen off, perhaps the southwest ridge should not be used by commercial teams. But another route will require a higher degree of technical skill. Pumori, also in the Everest region, used to be included in commercial organizers' offerings, but its southeast face came to be widely regarded as avalanche-prone, and there were fatalities. Few venture on it now. The mountain's safer ridges present technical challenges not suitable for commercially organized groups.

In the spring some climbers returning from Cho Oyu, the least difficult of the world's 8,000m mountains and for that reason an extremely popular one, reported that it too is becoming harder technically. The mountains, like their glaciers, are changing.

ELIZABETH HAWLEY, *AAC Honorary Member, Nepal*

Editor's note: Ama Dablam's rarely attempted northeast spur to north ridge was first climbed in 1981 by Australians Lincoln Hall, Andy Henderson, and Tim McCartney-Snape, after an attempt by an ill-fated British expedition in 1959. It was possibly not repeated until 2000. In their alpine-style ascent Baldwin and Cromie climbed from base camp to ca 5,850m, the point where the northeast spur joins the north ridge, on April 12. On the 13th they climbed to 6,100m and on the 14th, in poor weather, to 6,150m. On the 15th they bivouacked at 6,250m and on the 16th, when they met some technically difficult terrain, at 6,350m. On the 17th they fixed climbing ropes through the crux pitches above and returned to their bivouac site for the night. On the 18th they made it to 6,450m, 6,500m on the 19th, 6,590m on the 20th, and 6,700m on the 21st. On the 22nd they bivouacked on the summit. Two days later they reached the site of Camp 2 on the Normal Route and the following day reached the valley. Both were slightly frostbitten after their prolonged effort.

Ama Dablam, northeast face to north ridge, new route attempt. A Corean Alpine Club expedition led by Cho Yu-dong, with Cha Gyeong-ryeol, Choi Dong-ryeol, Choi Young-sik, Jang Byeong-wook, Kim Dong-gyu, Park Seok-hee, and Yang Byeong-ok, reached base camp on October 26 at 5,000m below the northeast face of Ama Dablam. They established advanced base on the 29th at 5,200m. Choi Dong-ryeol and Park Seok-hee pushed the route to 5,800m, and the team placed Camp 1 at 5,700m on November 3. The following day Cha, Choi Young-sik and Jang reached 6,000m, and later Choi Dong-ryeol, Kim, Park and Yang climbed onto the crest of the north ridge at 6,100m, where they discovered a old deadman of French manufacture. All members descended to base camp on November 10 due to deteriorating weather. They rested here for four days, then on the 15th Choi Dong-ryeol, Jang, and Kim set off for a summit attempt. They made Camp 2 at 6,100m on the 16th, and on the 17th Jang and Kim reached the expedition high point on the north ridge at 6,400m. Due to their lack of provisions and fuel and a weakening physical state, base camp requested that they abandon further progress and descend.

LEE YOUNG-JUN, *Corean Alpine Club (translated by Peter Jensen-Choi).*

Editor's note: There has only been one ascent of the 1,400m northeast face, a magnificent alpine-style push from December 1–7, 1985, by Carlos Buhler and Michael Kennedy. The pair climbed the snow-fluted central rib and then weaved through the large capping serac barrier to gain the summit slopes and the final section of the north ridge. The climbing was on snow of varying consistency, steep and sustained throughout. The Korean line starts up the 1985 route but then takes the obvious funnel to the right that terminates on the crest of the north ridge, the latter an elegant line first climbed in 1979 by a large French expedition for the fourth overall ascent of the mountain, via its third route.

Lhotse south face, winter ascent, correction. In *AAJ 2007*, p. 394, it was stated that the old fixed rope found by the Japanese in the upper part of the couloir came from past Polish expeditions. In fact, it originated from the 1990 Soviet expedition that made the first ascent of the central pillar on the south face.

From October 11–13, 1990, Russians Klinetskij, Totmijanin, Tarasov, and Obihod tried to reach the summit via the final section of the central pillar. They reached an altitude of 8,460m on the crest but were then defeated by difficulties. The key to the eventual success was found by Sergey Bershov and Vladimir Karatayev. Leaving the top camp at 8,300m on the 15th, they made a traverse across the left flank of the ridge and then a 40m descent into the couloir. They climbed and fixed the bed of the couloir for a further 80m before returning to camp for the night. Next day they returned to their high point and, with their oxygen finished, Bershov led the final 60m headwall, at one point using a hook for crucial protection. The two had to move together before Bershov could reach a good anchor, after which they progressed slowly to the main summit.

WOLFGANG BÖTTCHER, *Germany*

MAHALANGUR HIMAL–MAKALU SECTION

Makalu, winter attempts. Five of the six 8,000m peaks still to be climbed in winter lie in the Pakistan Karakoram. The sixth, Makalu (8,485m) lies in eastern Nepal. Two teams were on the mountain together this winter. One was the tried and tested Italian trio of Romano Benet, his wife Nives Meroi (together with Gerlinde Kaltenburnner the leading women's 8,000m peak collector), and Luca Vuerich (Benet and Nivoi had only recently returned from a post-monsoon attempt on Makalu). The other was a strong four-man Kazakh expedition comprising Gennady Durov, Sergei Samoilov, Eugeny Shutov and Denis Urubko. If anyone could overcome winter conditions on Makalu it was likely to be Samoilov and Urubko. The Kazakhs flew into the lower (4,800m) base camp on January 9, 2008, a few days prior to the Italians. They found the normal route up the west flank and northwest slopes in good condition, with snow rather than ice. After a number of aborted attempts thwarted by bad weather and high winds, they reached the

Makalu La (7,400m) and at the start of February set out for a summit attempt. However, they only gained a short distance, reaching an altitude of ca 7,500m before, once again, being battered by ferocious winds. Retreat, even for the likes of Urubko, was the only option.

The Italians didn't get quite as high but stuck it out for a few more days after the departure of the Kazakhs, until on February 9 storm-force winds destroyed their upper base camp (5,400m). Subsequently, on the long walk down the difficult moraine to lower base camp, Meroi was blown over by the wind and broke her right ankle. The others carried her down to camp, where despite continued high winds, all three were evacuated by helicopter on the 12th.

Before their arrival, Makalu had received about 11 attempts in winter, starting with Renato Casarotto's 1981 expedition to the southeast ridge. The most memorable in recent years took place during the winter 2005-06 and resulted in the disappearance of the celebrated mountaineer, Jean-Christophe Lafaille. The Frenchman left his tent at 7,600m on January 27, 2006, for a summit push; how high he got is unknown, as his body has yet to be discovered. Previously, several climbers had reached heights of around 7,500m on both the normal route and the southeast ridge.

LINDSAY GRIFFIN, *Mountain INFO, www.climbmagazine.com*

KUMBHAKARNA HIMAL

Merra, second known ascent, new route. During their acclimatization for Jannu, Valery Babanov and Sergey Kofanov made an ascent of 6,334m Merra in the Anidesh Himal directly north of the Kumbhakarna Glacier. The mountain received its first known ascent in October 2006, by Thejs Ortmann and Claus Ostergaard from Denmark. From an advanced base at 4,700m on the Kumbhakarna Glacier, they followed the left (west) flank of a moraine-covered glacial valley leading northwest towards Merra. They placed their first camp at 5,450m, below the start of a rocky arîte splitting the glacier beyond into two flows. The easterly flow leads towards the upper section of the east-northeast ridge and was the one followed. Ostergaard climbed the southeast flank of the east-northeast ridge solo to reach the crest at around 6,200m, above which a sharp crest led back left to the summit (see *AAJ 2007*).

The two Russians followed the bed of the moraine-covered glacial valley, crossing the Danish approach below the rocky arîte and continuing on the westerly glacier flow. There was much snow on the mountain, and the weather was poor, with snow every afternoon. On October 5 they pitched a small tent at 5,700m and the next day took it with them on their summit attempt. Continuing up the glacier, they climbed the southeast face directly below the main summit to reach a small shoulder on the east-northeast ridge at 6,200m, where they pitched the tent. Their arrival point on the ridge was much closer to the summit than Ostergaard's the year previous. The Russian pair then continued to the top and returned to the tent for the night. The final 300m was sharp and had to be climbed carefully. The total time for the ascent from the 5,700m camp was nine hours. The climbers regained base camp on the 7th.

From information supplied by SERGEY KOFANOV

Merra, third known ascent. A month after the Russians summited Merra (6,334m), the mountain was climbed again, this time by a French party that appears to have more or less followed the Russian route. Lionel and Vincent Palandre, Nicolas Rosset, and Pasang Phutar Sherpa set up an advanced base at 4,700m, most likely at the same point as the Danes in 2006 (see above). They appear to have made a higher camp in the moraine-covered glacial valley at 5,200m on November 3, after which Pasang Phutar reconnoitred the way ahead and decided to follow the west bank of the westerly glacier flow. On the 4th the team climbed up the left side of the glacier and then crossed it diagonally to the right to place a second camp at 5,800m. Pasang Phutar then fixed 15m of rope above this camp and on the following day all four climbers set out for the summit at 3 a.m. They climbed the 50° south face directly to the east-northeast ridge and then on up the crest (35°, but sharp and tricky where corniced) with good snow conditions, to the final 25m, where a rocky aríte led to the highest point. The time was 7:10 a.m. They returned safely to advanced base on the 6th.

ELIZABETH HAWLEY, *AAC Honorary Member, Nepal and* RICHARD SALISBURY,
The Himalayan Database

Jannu (7,711m) seen from the northwest. (1) The line soloed by Jordi Tozas with (H) his high point of 6,800-6,900m. (2) Original 1976 Japanese route on the northwest face to northeast ridge. (3) 2004 Russian route on the true north face. (4) 2007 Russian route on the west pillar. *Lindsay Griffin*

Jannu, northwest face, attempt. Toward the end of September, I made a discreet attempt on a new line up the left side of the northwest face of Jannu (7,710m). There were many difficulties for me and my trekking partner, Antoni, to overcome before we reached the village of Ghunsa: transport difficulties due to Maoist activities and difficult trekking due to a late end to a vigorous monsoon. With us were a guide and two porters. My baggage for Jannu weighed just 25kg.

I spent a week in Ghunsa, acclimatizing up to 6,000m in the surrounding mountains. On September 23, after a non-stop walk of 20 hours, I reached our previously established equipment cache on the moraine of the Kumbhakarna Glacier. My original idea had been to try the virgin Jannu East, solo, but I could see immediately that there was too much snow on the mountain and decided instead on a fast, light ascent of Jannu by a partial new line.

One morning I set off at 1 a.m., heading for the steep rib that defines the left side of the face [Tozas left his 4,500m base camp and took only two hours or so to reach the glacier plateau below the north face. Avoiding most of the rock buttress normally followed, he climbed the more dangerous but faster icefall alongside—Ed.] Starting well left of the original 1976 Japanese route and a little left of the fallline of the giant seracs that characterize the lower section of this route, I climbed snow and ice couloirs to a rib that gave access to the objectively threatened terrain at the left edge of the large serac barrier. From there I bypassed the seracs on the left and continued on steep snow slopes to join the Japanese route. At an altitude between 6,800-6,900m, after almost 1,900m of new climbing at Alpine ED (the grade reflects objective dangers and conditions, as well as technical difficulty), my general fatigue, grave avalanche danger, and excessive quantities of deep snow made me give up. I made a delicate descent of the Japanese route, having close shaves when the mountain shrugged off large powder snow avalanches. On my return to Kathmandu I found I had lost six kilos in body weight.

JORDI TOZAS, *Spain*

Jannu, west pillar. After their ascent of Merra Peak, reported above, Valery Babanov and Sergey Kofanov made the first ascent of the west pillar of 7,710m Jannu. The pair left base camp at 4,700m on October 14 and reached the summit on the morning of the 21st, after an alpine style ascent. They took only a small tent and a sleeping bag for two. Their route followed previous attempts into the upper glacier basin below Jannu's north face but reached the Yamatari La (the 6,350m col between Jannu and Sobithongie) by a line to the right [A French expedition reached the col in 1994 by slanting right up the 80° ice face below it, where they fixed 500m of rope. They continued up the west pillar to 6,900m before being forced down by the difficulty, cold, and wind. A French expedition in 1998 also began fixing rope on the face below the Yamatari La but abandoned the attempt 150m below the col when they decided the line was too threatened by falling seracs—Ed.]

From the col Babanov and Kofanov climbed directly up the crest of the west pillar, making their sixth bivouac 100m below the west shoulder at 7,300m. On the 20th they took minimal equipment (caching the sleeping bag but taking the tent) for the last part of their ascent, which joined the 1983 French route (the French reached this point via the southwest ridge) for some technical pitches on mixed rock and ice. They slept at 7,600m and next day woke at 4:30 a.m., because they were very cold after spending the night without a sleeping bag. They completed the ascent of the summit ridge and at 9:45 a.m. reached the highest point. This lay slightly beyond a false summit, a 20m-high lower point which at first they thought was the top. He found it more demanding than his ascent of the south face of Nuptse East in 2003, where he fixed a considerable amount of rope, but the climbing on Nuptse was technically harder. The total height gain on Jannu was around 3,000m and the difficulties WI4+ M5 80°. The pair spent two more nights out while descending their route, although they didn't stop the second night but continued downclimbing to arrive at base camp, totally exhausted, between 2:00 and 3:00 the following morning. For a complete account see Sergey Kofanov's article, "The Magic Pillar," earlier in the *Journal*.

LINDSAY GRIFFIN, *Mountain INFO, www.climbmagazine.com*

JANAK HIMAL

Ghhanyala Hies, attempt. A five-member ski expedition, which comprised Yan Andre (leader), Stephane Dan and Pierre Alexis de Postestad (French) and Thor Husted and Nathan Wallace (Americans), was the first officially to attempt Ghhanyala Hies (6,744m). This is a remote peak, on the Tibetan border northwest of Janak, that was brought onto the permitted list in 2002. It is believed this was only the second group planning to attempt the mountain, the first being two Americans who failed to reach it around 10 years previously.

The five made the normal Kangchenjunga north-side trek as far as Lhonak, arriving on October 10th. From there they branched left to reach the Lhonak Glacier, where on the 13th they established base camp at ca 4,980m. Over the next few days they followed the main Chijima (Tsisima) Glacier northeast to 5,500m, where on the 17th they established a higher camp. On the 21st they left this camp and climbed Chijima II (Tsisima II, 6,170m) via the northwest face [Editor's note: This is the most northerly of the three Chijima peaks, the highest, on the far side of a 6,000m col to the southwest being 6,196m and the lowest, a little southeast of the highest, being 6,126m. The American-French team most likely followed the west branch of the Chijima Glacier and climbed northeast-facing slopes to the upper northwest ridge/face]. De Postestad turned back at 5,900m, but the remaining four continued to the summit and then skied back down (45-50°, excellent powder).

On the 23rd all members left the 5,500m camp and continued northeast up the main Chijima Glacier to its head at 5,850m, where de Postesdad and Mingma Tamang waited, while the others skinned across the horizontal glacier to the base of Ghhanyala Hies. All four climbed a 50-55° icy couloir to 6,150m, where the face above rose directly to the west-southwest ridge. Here they moved left but found more icy conditions. Their aim had been to ski down the mountain, but now they decided the slopes were too icy and the way ahead looked too difficult to climb up and down with their heavy packs, which included skis. They descended.

ELIZABETH HAWLEY, *AAC Honorary Member, Nepal and*
RICHARD SALISBURY, *The Himalayan Database*

JONGSANG HIMAL

Drohmo south pillar, major variation; Drohmo East, first ascent; Pathibhara Chuli, southwest face; Kirat Chuli west face and Chang Himal north face, attempts. The Slovenian Alpine Association organized an expedition to the Kangchenjunga region, situated in the remote northeastern part of Nepal. Leadership was given to veteran expedition leader Tone Skarja, a man with much Himalayan experience. The team also comprised alpinists Tine Cuder, Matej Kladnik, Ales Kozelj, Boris Lorencic, Mitja Sorn, and I, accompanying by expedition doctor Damijan Mesko.

The main objective was an ascent of Kangbachen, at 7,902m the fifth highest summit in the Kangchenjunga Massif. However, the moraine of the Ramtang Glacier was so shattered that it was not possible for porters to reach the proposed base camp. Instead, we established base camp farther north at Pangpema (4,940m) and attempted nearby peaks.

To acclimatize for attempts on the difficult north face of Chang Himal (Wedge Peak or Ramtang Chang, 6,802m) and an ascent of Kirat Chuli (Tent Peak, 7,362m), Kozelj and Sorn made an ascent of the south pillar of Drohmo's central summit. They found good snow conditions and climbed largely to the right of the crest of the pillar, joining the 1998 route, climbed by Roger Mear and Doug Scott, in only a few places. They took two days from the 6,000m col at the foot of the pillar, reaching the small summit at the top of the crest on October 16. [Editor's note: Mear and Scott continued a short distance west along the summit

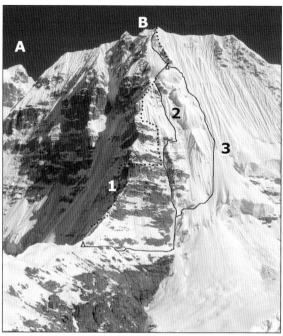

Part of the Drohmo massif seen from the south. (A) Drohmo (6,881m). (B) Drohmo Central (6,855m). (1) Original route up central spur of south face (Mear-Scott, 1998). A steep slope of snow and rock leads up from the glacier to the left in about five pitches to reach the ca 6,000m col at the foot of the spur. (2) Slovenian route (Kozelj-Sorn, 2007). (3) Descent used by Kozelj and Sorn. *Mitja Sorn*

ridge to reach a possibly higher corniced top, which they registered as 6,855m. The main summit of Drohmo is 6,881m and situated a considerable distance to the west. It remains unclimbed.] From the col the 800m-high route averaged around 60°, with steeper sections up to 80°. Due to good snow conditions, the two were able to descend a largely independent route, completely on snow, to the east of their line of ascent. They then tried the north face of Chang Himal, but were forced to bail after one bivouac, at a point less than half way up the face, because of terrible conditions: considerable amounts of soft snow over rock. An attempt on the unclimbed west face of Kirat Chuli was abandoned at the bottom, when they found it to be deep in snow and avalanche prone. [This face had been climbed to 6,700m, seemingly above all technical difficulties, in 2002, by another Slovenian team—Ed.]

Starting a leftward traverse through snow-covered rock slabs high on the first ascent of Smrdljiva sled (Stinking trail), South Face of Drohmo East. *Tine Cuder*

The north face of Chang Himal (a.k.a. Wedge Peak or Ramtang Chang, 6,802m) seen from Drohmo. Marked (with bivouac site) is the attempt by Slovenians Ales Kozelj and Mitja Sorn, who were defeated by terrible snow conditions. This peak has only been climbed once: an unauthorized ascent in 1974 from the Ramtang Glacier to the south by three Slovenians. *Mitja Sorn*

The south face of the Central (6,855m) and East (ca 6,695m) summits of Drohmo, showing the two 2007 routes. On the left the Kozelj-Sorn route on the central spur and on the right the Cuder-Kladnik-Kozelj route, Smrdljiva Sled (Stinking trail). *Miha Valic*

Cuder, Kladnik, and Kozelj then made another ascent of the south face of Drohmo (Sorn staying at base camp with a toothache), this time to the previously unclimbed east summit (ca 6,695m). After a bivouac at the foot of the face, the three climbed their new route in eight hours, largely on snow and ice, reaching the summit ridge just left of the highest point. Again, they found good conditions and were able to summit and descend to base camp the same day, October 25th. They called the 900m route Smrdljiva Sled (Stinking Trail) and rated the difficulties TD+, VI/4+, M4.

Lorencic and Valic acclimatized with an ascent of Pangpema Peak (6,068m) and then climbed Pk. 6,630m on the southeast ridge of Pathibhara Chuli (Pyramid Peak, 7,140m). The route followed snow slopes up to 45° on the southwest ridge, the summit being reached on the 16th [most likely the first ascent of this summit—Ed.]. They returned to base camp after three days, well acclimatized. However, they were unable to examine the southwest face of Pathibhara Chuli, their next objective, because it was obscured by cloud each afternoon.

After they rested a few days, the weather stabilized, and they set out for the remote basin beneath the virgin southwest face of Pathibhara Chuli. The next day they climbed to the glacier plateau below the wall and examined their proposed route, spending the night at 5,900m. The day after they climbed 50-60° snow slopes to a narrow shelf below a rock band, where they spent the night at 6,900m. The following morning, the 24th, they climbed through the rock band (UIAA IV, 20m) and reached the summit. This was the first ascent of the mountain from Nepal and only the second overall ascent. [Pathibhara Chuli was first climbed in the spring of

Pathibhara Chuli (7,140m) on the Nepal-Sikkim border. Marked is the Lorencic-Valic route on the southwest face, which was followed to make the first ascent of the mountain from Nepal. The right skyline is the unclimbed south-east ridge. On the far right of the picture are the convoluted ice slopes of Pt. 6,630m, a subsidiary summit climbed for the first time by the Slovenian pair prior to their ascent of Pathibhara Chuli. The left skyline is the west ridge, attempted in 1996 and '98 by Australian and New Zealand teams. In the left distance is Langpo (6,965m), first climbed by Alexander Kellas in 1909. *Miha Valic*

1993 from Sikkim by an Indo-Japanese expedition via the northeast ridge, over the Sphinx. The 7,090m northeast summit has been reached twice from Nepal: in 1949 by Swiss and in 2006 by Slovenians—Ed.] They descended the same route, reaching base camp in a round trip of five days. The team found walking on the convoluted shattered glaciers of the area very strenuous, but the weather and climbing conditions were good.

MIHA VALIC, *Slovenia*

No fatalities post monsoon. In the autumn of 1967, when only two expeditions attempted Nepalese Himalayan peaks over 6,600m, there were no climbers' deaths. Every autumn since then there have been deaths—until 2007, when none of the 183 teams suffered fatalities. Why none now, after 40 years of fatal falls, pulmonary edema and other kinds of illness, and climbers freezing to death at high altitudes? Certainly there has been increased understanding of the causes of high-altitude sickness and what to do about it, and this knowledge is more widely shared. Clothing, sleeping bags, tents, ropes, and other gear have improved and become more widely available, notably in Eastern Europe. But do these factors fully account for the difference? The weather has gotten no kinder. Has it been all of the above, plus climbers' better judgment and better weather forecasts on which to base their judgment—plus sheer good luck? Whatever the reasons, it's a nice surprise.

ELIZABETH HAWLEY, *AAC Honorary Member, Nepal*

China

Xinjiang Province

Pt. 4,976m (Kichinekey Tagh), first ascent; Chiatuk (5,582m), northwest face; Pt. 5,485m (Tiltagh), west face route; Yilpiz (ca 5,315m), north face. From Bishkek our organizers on the ground (Novino-mad—very good) arranged overnight accommodation and road transport to Torugart Pass on the Kyrgyzstan-China border. (Be warned: if you are getting Kyrgyz double entry visas at the airport, do not allow them to issue you a group visa: it causes a hassle at the border. Get individual visas for every member of the party. It doesn't cost extra.) Two days of hard road travel took us to Kashi, then a further day to Subax, the starting point for the walk to base camp. Three days' walk to base camp was extended to four because of difficult terrain on the 9km up the north side of the glacier. We helped the porters as much as we could, but their Chinese bosses helped very little. Local Kyrgyz porters were excellent: experts with pack animals (camels and donkeys) and hardworking; we formed good relationships with them, especially those from the village of Chiatuk.

A donkey fell and was badly injured on the first day on the glacier. It was bleeding heavily from a wound to its cheek. Fortunately, Joe Howard is a farmer, and he applied pressure and then expertly stitched up the wound using our sewing kit. The porters were amazed and grateful, as was the donkey!

We arrived at base camp at 4,500m on July 25, where it snowed. On the 27th Kevin, Isobel, Richard Taylor, Joe, and I crossed the glacier to the central rognon, and all climbed Pt. 4,976m for acclimatization, except Isobel who was feeling the altitude. We climbed it by a broad snow couloir due east of the summit, followed by the summit rocks. We named the peak Kichinekey Tagh (Kyrgyz for "small mountain") and graded the route PD. It had two pitches of Scottish III toward the top of the couloir.

On July 18 Dave and I headed for the far side of the glacier to attempt Pt. 5,582m, the peak immediately west of Kala Peak, while the others aimed to climb the north face of Kala. All camped together by river on the south side of the glacier. On July 29 we established a high

John Allen, David Barker, Joe Howard, and Richard Taylor made the first ascent, via the line marked, of the north face of Yilpiz (5,313m), which rises from the Kuksay Glacier basin immediately east of Muztagh Ata. *John Allen*

The northwest face of Chiatuk (5,582m), showing the route of ascent. *John Allen*

camp at 4,900m on Pt. 5,582, and the following day we summited after about 11 pitches, up to Scottish IV, through the rock ban. The last four pitches on the headwall were relatively unprotected due to unconsolidated snow. Chiatuk (5,582m), northwest face route, 700m, TD Scottish IV 70°.

On August 2 Dave, Richard, Joe, and I headed back to the broad glacier basin below Chiatuk to attempt new routes on the "Barrel," a rocky buttress not given a height on the map, and Pt. 5,496m. Kevin, Neil, and Isobel headed down the glacier to

John Allen on the summit of Chiatuk, admiring the east ridge of Mustagh Ata. *John Allen Collection*

attempt Pt. 5,485m, the fourth summit marked with a height on the map up from the snout on the south side of the glacier.

At 2 a.m. Richard and I headed for 5,496m, Dave and Joe for the Barrel. We quickly encountered poor snow conditions—a thin crust over bottomless sugar snow. This made progress arduous and caused avalanche concern. We abandoned our attempt and joined our comrades on the Barrel, climbing it in 10 pitches, plus moving together, with excellent snow and ice except for the last few ropelengths. We summited around 10 a.m. and were back in high camp just after 1 p.m. Yilpiz (Kyrgyz for "snow leopard"), ca 5,315m, north face, TD, Scottish III sustained, 60°.

August 4-6: heavy snowfall each night, with snow continuing through the day, only easing in the afternoons. By the 6th we were concerned because Kevin, Neil, and Izzi had not returned from Pt. 5,485m, but on the afternoon of the 7th they returned. They had had a minor epic, but summited the peak. They had to surmount 500m of hideous scree to gain the tongue of the glacier, which they followed to the top. Tiltagh (Kyrgyz for "tongue mountain"), 5,485m, west face route, PD.

The weather continued to be poor, but on the 7th Joe, Richard, and I put up Kuksay's first trad rock routes, on the buttress to the east of base camp. Come To Daddy was two pitches at HVS 5a; it takes the obvious diamond-shaped buttress via a central line. You're Mine Now is a 40m HS 4a that follows cracks on the large slab uphill and right from Come to Daddy.

Other Comments: Our ground organizer in China was Kong Baocun, president of the China Xinjiang Mountaineering Organization (CXMO). We found him to be dishonest, difficult to deal with, and manipulative. We would certainly not recommend him to an expedition visiting Western China.

When the team members who climbed Tiltagh traveled down the south side of the Kuksay Glacier, they noted that it might be easier to establish a base camp on that side of the glacier. A base camp on that side would be in alpine meadows and free of objective dangers, such as rockfall (though our site was reasonably safe).

We were sponsored by the Mount Everest Foundation, the British Mountaineering Council, DMM, and Mountain Equipment

JOHN ALLEN, U.K.

KUN LUN

Mt. Manse (6,355m), Mt. God Tang (6,013m), Mt. Ye Zi (6,046m), Mt. Lazio Tagh (6,045m), first ascents. Our Finnish Kun Lun Expedition set off with a donkey caravan from a Tadjik village on August 4, for a 24-day journey to attempt virgin peaks of the Kunlun massif. Our team consisted of Henri Arjanne, Kalle Berg, Andrey Ershov (expedition manager), Lauri Hämäläinen, Veli-Matti Helke, Mikko Piironen, Rauno Ravantti, and me (leader). We set up base camp at 4,500m and spent six days on nearby glaciers, spotting possible lines to climb in alpine style on the area's 6,000m peaks. While our main objective was the first ascent of Point 6,355m, our reconnaissance revealed vast first-ascent possibilities throughout the massif.

We climbed four previously unclimbed peaks in the vicinity of base camp. We have searched all databases known to us and have

Mt. Lazio Tagh (6,045m), showing the line of its first ascent. *Lauri Hämäläinen*

Mt. Ye Zi (6,046m), showing the line of its first ascent. An attempt was first made on the foreground ridge, but it ended at 5,700m because of a giant chasm that is not shown on the map. *Mikko Piironen*

Mt. Manse (6,355m) on the left, and Mt. God Tang (6,013m), showing the lines of their first ascents. *Lauri Hämäläinen*

found no prior claims to these peaks. Also, Kong Baocun assures us that these peaks had not been climbed. In addition to the climbs, the expedition (Berg and Saarikivi) explored the Salawor and Qongtan glaciers. This was probably the first time these glacial valleys had been explored in depth. Below are listed the peaks we summited. All were formerly unclimbed, and all names are our proposals:

Mt. Manse (6,355m): 38°11'19" N 75°11'26" E. Route: Karakul Gringos (12 hours, 900m, D+, Arjanne, Hämäläinen, August 13). Distance from BC to climb start: 2 days (1 day hiking, 1 day glacier climbing).

Mt. God Tang (6,013m): 38°10'43" N 75°10'43" E. Route: Petite Mountain Sickness (8 hours, 500m, D+, Arjanne, Berg, Ershov, Hämäläinen, Helke. Piironen, Ravantti, Saarikivi, August 14). Distance from BC to climb start: 2 days (1 day hiking, 1 day glacier climbing).

Mt. Ye Zi (6,046m): 38°10'13" N 75°07'22" E. Route: A Man Who Dances Like A Tibetan (10 hours, 950m, TD-, Arjanne, Hämäläinen, August 22). Distance from BC to climb start: 1 day hiking.

Lazio Tagh (6,045m): 38° 11'06" N 75°05'06" E. Route: Island Couloir, 14 hours, 950m, AD, Helke, Piironen, Ravantti, August 23). Distance from BC to climb start: 1 day hiking plus difficult glacier crossing (Koktay).

Our base camp location was at: 38°08'14" N 75°06'06" E. The start of our trek was at: 38°05'12" N 75°00'16" E. Our local climbing organizer and permit issuer was China Xinjiang Mountaineering Organization Director Kong Baocun, Xiyudadao 6, Kashgar, Xinjiang, China. Email: climbing@126.com, climbing@xj.cninfo.net. Tel/Fax: 0086-998-2902678, Mobile: 0086-(0)13899111222.

TEEMU SAARIKIVI, *Finland*

KARAKORAM

Gasherbrum II, north face, first north-south crossing of the mountain, alpine style. We left Italy for Pakistan in early June, reaching Islamabad and then Kashgar, China in the following days. After waiting two days for the trucks coming from the Karakoram Highway, which had been blocked by a landslide, we left for Ilik, the last village reachable by motor vehicles. Two or three days later, crossing the storied Aghil Pass, we entered the wild Shaksgam Valley with our caravan of camels. In a further three days of trekking we reached the Gasherbrum North Glacier and then spent two weeks crossing the glacier and attempting to find a good location the base camp, and also a route for the camels carrying our equipment. On June 24 advanced base camp was finally set up, and we were all in our tents.

The north spur of Gasherbrum II was climbed in alpine style by Daniele Bernasconi, Compagnoni-Unterkiercher alpine-style ascent. The black buttress right of the icefall was the technical crux and was fixed with rope. *Daniele Bernasconi*

Trying to take advantage of the good weather, Karl, Michele, and Spaniards Mikel Zabalza, Josu Bereziartua, and Juan Vallejo (the "Al filo de lo Imposible" team) inspected the mountain, finding two climbing lines. The Spaniards wanted to retrace and complete the path of Kari Kobler's 2006 Swiss expedition along the east ridge, while we decided to try the northern spur that rises vertically to GII's summit: an absolutely elegant line noted in 1983 by Agostino Da Polenza and Kurt Diemberger.

To reach the spur, which rises above an icy plateau at about 5,800m, we climbed a 1,000m rock pillar (UIAA 5+, 6) next to huge collapsing overhanging seracs. This is the only place where we put fixed ropes, but we considered this pillar part of the approach, not part of the climb, which begins at the plateau. Within a few days we overcame the pillar and placed an advanced camp on the upper plateau. The weather had been unstable since the beginning of July, and we spent weeks in acclimatizing climbs on the surrounding peaks, waiting for a better weather forecast from our contacts in Innsbruck. These climbs also allowed us to assess our climbing line from various points of view, confirming that climbing the spur in alpine style would be possible. On July 18 we learned that a brief good-weather window was coming, and we went quickly up to the advanced camp. The next day we climbed for over 12 hours on the spur to an "eagle's nest" at about 6,900m, where we put the bivouac tent. The route so far had been exposed and mixed, predominantly on ice slopes of 50° to 70°. The wall was dangerous because of seracs and threatening avalanches, which sometimes fell only a few hours after we passed. On July 20 we decided to leave before dawn, but when we glanced out of the tent, the sky was overcast, and the wind cut our faces. So we waited, trusting in a forecast that said the weather should be good for a day and a half. We started climbing at 9 a.m.; fortunately, the wall here was less exposed to the seracs, even if it was increasingly steep.

Karl and I were worried for Michele, who had been unable to drink and eat anything for two days. We were together when we left the spur, at about 7,500m. Then Karl and I headed toward the top while Michele followed more slowly. From this point the snow was harder, and the wind finally eased. At 8 p.m. we arrived on top—8,035m. But we weren't finished yet. We decided not to return down the ascent route, as it was too dangerous. We preferred the Pakistani side, even though it was loaded with deep snow and unclimbed this season.

After phone and radio calls with home and with Juan Carlos Tamayo at base camp, where the Spaniards had returned after failing on the northeast ridge, we called Michele. He had reached 7,850m, but it was late, and we decided to meet him on the col between GII and GIII. So we didn't take the normal route, but descended from the west ridge to about 7,500m. In the dark we met Michele and together started down under the light of a few stars. We traversed the south face in deep snow searching for the normal route. We got it but suddenly lost it again, entering a couloir that led to the edge of a huge serac. At about midnight we biviede without tents at about 7,000m. In the morning, with a series of rappels and traverses, we reached the normal route and then Camp 3, strangely deserted. Later we learned that the mountain had been abandoned because of an avalanche that a few days earlier had claimed victims near Camp 2.

People were waiting for us at Camp 1. After a refreshing break, we left for base camp. Just above there we met Italian friends who welcomed us with "luxury goods." Special thanks to the Ev-K2 Cnr Committee, Autogrill, Mico Sport, and Montagna.org.

DANIELE BERNASCONI, *Italy*

SICHUAN PROVINCE

SHALULI SHAN

Peak 5,600m, first ascent; Dangchezhengla (Bongonzhong, 5,830m), north side. Steve Hunt, Dick Isherwood, Peter Rowat, and I spent October in Western Sichuan, exploring the northern

approaches to Yangmolong (6,066m) and attempting to climb it. In good, though never totally clear, weather we entered the Sanchu River valley and stayed with villagers, before establishing base camp at 4,400m in a tributary valley. From there we stocked an advance base camp at 4,900m at the foot of the westernmost glacier descending from the northern side of Yangmolong. Dick found himself suffering from breathing problems, which meant that he was unable to climb above 5,000m. To acclimatize, the rest of us made the first ascent of a fine 5,600m snow peak to the

Walking around the range on the southeastern approach to Dangchezhengla (left, 5,830m) & the central summit of Yangmolong (6,066m). *Dave Wynne-Jones*

From the southwest, Danchezhengla (5,830m) is on the left, and Yangmolong (6,066m) on the far right. *Dave Wynne-Jones*

southwest of ABC and south of Peak 5,850m, at about PD in difficulty. After a day's rest, we climbed a new route on the north side of Dangchezhengla, first climbed by a Japanese team in 2002. Our ascent climbed through a rocky buttress to the south of the main glacier to gain a

High on Dangchezhengla (5,830m). *Dave Wynne-Jones*

snow ridge leading to a steep foresummit, where we joined the Japanese route up the difficult summit ridge. After a steep 70m pitch of deep unconsolidated snow to a shoulder, climbed largely via my burrowing efforts, we flanked the corniced ridge on unconsolidated snow, sometimes crusted over but hollow to a depth of a foot. At one point we tiptoed along the cornice breakline with axes planted in the ridge crest for support. Estimated grade: D. [Dangchezhengla is referred to locally as Bongonzhong—Ed.]

The weather then became very cold and windy, with frequent snow showers, which put a stop to climbing for about a week. Peter managed a reconnaissance of the shattered saddle to the northeast of the main summit, and we established a camp at 5,100m on the easternmost glacier descending north on Yangmolong. Steve and I attempted the steep north spur, which falls almost directly from the main summit, but were forced to turn back at 5,400m. It was extremely cold, and snow conditions were difficult, with an inch or two of crust over unconsolidated snow. A threatening storm finally blew in around 2 p.m. and lasted until after dark.

With just a few days left, we decided to pack up, descend to the valley, and walk around the mountain to reach Dangba, while the base camp team supervised the return of equipment by the original route in from the north. We believe ours was the first Western party to make this trek through beautiful and varied country. So it was a good trip despite not climbing Yangmolong.

DAVE WYNNE-JONES, *U.K.*

Yangmolong (6,066m), Dangchezhengla (5,830m), historical notes. Yangmolong is the highest of a small group of snow peaks in the middle of the Shaluli Shan, north of the Genyen massif and immediately east of Batang on the Sichuan-Tibet Highway. Three other main peaks make up the group: Dangchezhengla (referred to locally as Bongonzhong); Pt. 6,033m (unnamed on maps, though local people refer to it as Makara), on the ridge connecting Dangchezhengla with Yangmolong; and an unnamed Pt. 5,850m, northwest of Dangchezhengla.

The only previous attempt on Yangmolong also was made from the north, in 1991 by a Japanese expedition that was thwarted by avalanche-prone slopes. Kiyoaki Miyagawa and Junta Murayama made the first ascent of Dangchezhengla in June 2002. This pair was part of a four-man Japanese team that approached the south side of the mountain from Batang and fixed ropes through the icefall to the 5,565m col between Dangchezhengla and Pt. 6,033m. Most of the Japanese members were not in the full flush of youth (Miyagawa was 61) and decided that attempting either Pt. 6,033m or Yangmolong over the top of 6,033m, would be too difficult. Instead they concentrated on Dangchezhengla. After climbing a 500m face of steep ice on the right (north) side of the east ridge above the col, they rejoined the corniced summit ridge and followed it to the highest point.

The second ascent was made in March 2007 by a Chinese team. Although it is believed they approached from the south, it is not certain which route they followed. However, what is known is that during the descent from a successful summit bid, lead climber Liu Xinan fell 300 meters and died of his injuries. Although largely unknown outside his own country, Liu Xinan was one of China's top climbers and winner of China's national sport climbing competition in 2000. Among other climbs, in 2005 he had made the third ascent of the difficult Celestial Peak in Siguniang National Park, by a new route.

LINDSAY GRIFFIN, *MountainINFO Editor, adapted from www.alpinist.com*

Garrapunsum (Jarjinjabo, 5,812m), Man Chu Gangri (5,434m), first ascents. Originally we had planned to attempt a first ascent of Kawaluori (Kawarani) near Ganze. However, it proved impossible to secure permission due to religious celebrations and the need to avoid disturbing the delicate political balance in the region. We believe the monks, who refused permission to climb the mountain to a 2005 expedition, were never approached on this occasion. On consultation with Lenny (Chen Zhenglin), our liaison officer and base camp manager, we switched our objective to Garrapunsum, an unclimbed peak in the Jarjinjabo range farther south, that was formerly called Jarjinjabo, probably based on the Chinese PLA map (see naming note, below). Our main goal was for all six team members to make a joint first ascent, and route

The south face of Garrapunsum from Zhopo Pastures. This peak has been called Jarjinjabo, but Garrapunsum is the correct local name. *Hamish Rose*

The route on Man Chu Gangri (5,434m) as seen from Garrapunsum. *Charles Kilner*

choices revolved around this goal.

As we had intended to climb a different mountain, we had not researched Garrapunsum and had little information about our new objective. We had a single photograph of the south side and the Chinese PLA 1:100,000 map of the Jarjinjabo, Xiashe, and Hati Massif as found in Tamotsu Nakamura's book, *East of the Himalaya: the Alps of Tibet*, and other articles written in the *Japanese Alpine News* by the same author. We established base camp at 4,200m in the Zhopo Pastures (30.5430N 99.4571E) under the west end of Garrapunsum on September 26. We reached this point in 4x4 vehicles, thus avoiding a long walk. The mountain has three main summits, from which it gets its name, meaning "three blacksmith brothers." These form a long ridge running southwest-to-northeast, with subsidiary summits at the west end. The sketch map suggested that to the east of the main summit the ridge splits in two, forming a V and connecting to adjacent peaks to the northeast and southeast. Glaciers flow into the heads of both north and south valleys, and we guessed these led to the eastern ridges. The flanks of the mountain consist of impressive buttresses, hanging glaciers, and gully systems. Although several lines stood out on both the north and south sides, only one appeared to be suitable for our group. This involved a large but reasonably angled north-facing buttress, with a number of possible routes through mixed snow and rock, followed, we presumed, by snow to the summit out of sight. Total height from the valley floor: somewhere around 1,200m.

On September 30 Hamish Rose and Simon Mills scrambled up the lower buttress to a good bivy at 5,200m. The following morning they made two attempts to forge routes through loose mixed ground that proved steep, precarious, and prone to rockfall, finally conceding that it was too dangerous to continue.

Meanwhile the rest of us took on an acclimatization peak across the valley and gained the summit of an unnamed 5,434m peak (referred to here as Man Chu Gangri—see naming note, below). Our route followed the obvious deeply cut river gorge on loose moraine, until we could gain the glacier, and then threaded through crevassed but generally easy-angled snow to the summit. This gave us a good view back to our main objective, where we spotted a possible alternative route that was not obvious from the valley.

With the new route in mind, we hired horses and a handler from the local nomadic people to move kit for five days, and on October 3 established an advance base camp at the head of the north valley, at 4,600m. We then made an exploratory climb, following the easy-angled slopes of the main glacier up into the heart of the massif until we could get a clear view of the route to the main summit, which appeared to be a reasonable snow climb all the way, then we retreated to ABC.

We made the final climb from ABC on October 6, leaving at 4 a.m. and summiting around 1 p.m. The route followed the main glacier to a short steep snow slope (50°-55°) on the north side of the southeast ridge. We climbed this directly through a cirque and then followed the ridge to the summit. Half of the party remained at the access point to the ridge, while the remainder of the team continued 150m to the northernmost of the "three blacksmith brothers." The central brother was distinctly lower than the main summit, while the southwestern brother was slightly lower. Because of dangerous snow conditions on the connecting ridge, we did not cross to the far west summit, which is still unclimbed. All team members reached one or more of the summits. Theresa Booth, Charles Kilner, Evelyn Mullins, and Basil Thomson climbed Man Chu Gangri on October 1. Charles, Simon Mills, and Hamish climbed Garrapunsum on October 6. Theresa, Charles, Evelyn, and Hamish are members of the Rockhoppers Mountaineering Club.

We had consistently good weather, with clouds in the mornings and only light winds. Apparently three days after we left base camp it snowed down to below 4,000m, which would have stopped us had we still been climbing.

Notes on mountain names: Garrapunsum is the phonetic spelling of the Tibetan Khamba name. *Garra* means "blacksmith," *Pun* means "brother," and *Sum* means "three." The Chinese character phonetic spelling has been recorded as Kalabingsong, Galabison, or Garapinsung. We used *Man Chu* for the unnamed 5,434m peak, as that is the name of the river (chu meaning "river" in Tibetan) and the ridge in front of the peak. *Gangri* was added, meaning "snowy peak" in Tibetan. Kawaluori is the phonetic spelling of the Chinese name. Grid references: Kawaluori: 31.4525N, 100.2167E; Garrapunsum: 30.5783N, E99.4940E; Man Chu Gangri: 30.6062N, 99.4677E.

THERESA BOOTH, *Rockhoppers Mountaineering Club, U.K.*

The highest peak is Hati (5,524m), as seen from the southwest across the Zhopu Valley. The route of the first ascent by Gerrard and Sykes roughly follows the left skyline. *David Gerrard*

The southern aspect of Haizi Shan Ja-Ra (Zhara or Yala Peak, 5,833m). Gerrard and Sykes intended to attempt the left-hand gully on the face, which leads to the top of the southwest ridge. *David Gerrard*

Hati (5,524m), first ascent. It was early May, and within minutes of embarking from the jeep in the Zhopu Pasture, David Sykes, our L.O. Lenny, and I were surrounded by local families on their annual caterpillar-fungus hunting holiday. These ground-dwelling grubs are frequently infected with a parasite fungus, which sprouts from their bodies in springtime. The resulting growth is harvested by the locals, who live above 4,000m and earn a healthy portion of their yearly income selling the grubs for Chinese medicines. The resulting influx of people into the hills at this time of year meant plenty of opportunity for baggage transportation, but also maximum charge as a penalty for taking them from caterpillar-fungus hunting. After a day pottering up the foothills to get a good view of our intended mountain, Hati (Nazdenka), we observed that it was getting warmer. On our arrival the nights had been a reassuring −5°C, but now they were just above freezing at 4,300m. The beautifully clear days meant the beating sun cooked everything to a crisp. We watched the mountain's snow cover wearing thinner and thinner, and wondered whether our route options were also disappearing. Two days later David and I awoke at 2 a.m. in our bivy tent on the moraine below the route, stumbled across a boulder field onto the snow, and began an ascent of the west face, cursing the warm temperatures with every step we sunk up to our thighs. As I sat at one of the belays, two eagles, of which we had seen many over the preceding days, glided through a notch in the ridge and followed our creeping progress. From here more soloing brought us to the summit snowfield and very shortly the top. We relaxed, duvet clad in the −8°C heat, and soaked in the view. To the south lay the impressive Xiashe, recently climbed by Pat Deavoll and Karen McNeill, with Ed Douglas and Duncan Tunstall hot on their heels for a second ascent by a different route. Surrounding this peak were other imposing summits, all unclimbed. Looking west, the triple peaks of Garranpunsum, the three blacksmiths, appeared in the distance past the spires of the Jarjinjabo rock towers. The far distance was a continuum of white peaks, most of which are unclimbed. Our route on Hati was rather short and sweet, at 500m and AD-ish.

We were back at BC the following day, charged up for the next first ascent. Unfortunately, our buoyant optimism was deflated by an amazingly bad weather system, which came and sat in silence on our valley, getting wetter and colder day by day, until we woke one morning in six inches of damp snow and decided enough was enough. Thoughts of an early return home to family impelled a decision to hightail back for an early flight, but stunning weather on the return bus journey prompted a rethink. A couple of days later (May 23) we were at another base camp, intending a second ascent of stunning Haizi Shan by the unclimbed south face. This peak had presented to the highway a breathtaking view of snow-filled gully lines and white buttresses, and we couldn't resist. We didn't pick the optimal approach, though, and the ascent to the approach pass, a valley descent, and the subsequent huge slog up a 45° talus field also took our breath away. The mountain gods had obviously not been heeding our pleas, and we were greeted by ominously warm temperatures that reduced our gully to a waterfall. Further attempts at optimism were set back by three avalanches, one of which made us scramble to our feet. Then came a storm full of thunder, lightning, and heavy rain. And finally came the snow. My impression is that we were perhaps a month too late for good snow/ice. Our feelings about future projects in this area are that Garrapunsum would offer cracking lines, and the south face of Haizi Shan would be spectacular in cold, snowy conditions. The slabs and buttresses of Hati were of rough, compact, good-quality limestone, which bodes well for the quality of climbing on the southeast aspect of Hati (approach via next valley to east from our approach). We recommend visiting the area a month earlier (in April) for snow/ice routes, as the night freezing level went from 4,000m to 5,000m in the first week.

DAVID GERRARD, *U.K.*

QONGLAI SHAN

Bawangshan (5,551m), Susunshan (5,183m), first ascents. Our expedition went in commemoration of the 10th anniversary of the Japanese Alpine Club, Hiroshima Section. Though Bawangshan belongs to the Qonglai Mountains, the area surrounding this peak was unfrequented by climbers until I reconnoitered it in 2006. It is located at 102° 41' E, 31° 27' N in Sandowangdi of Xiaojin County, Aba Prefecture. There are no other mountains exceeding 5,300m in the vicinity of Bawangshan, but these shorter precipitous peaks surround the 5,551m Bawangshan as if guarding a king (*bawang* means "king," *shan* means "mountain"). Bawangshan has three eminent ridges. The south ridge has a series of summits called the "nine peaks"; the northeast ridge is 15km long and

Bawangshan (5,551m), showing the line of its first ascent, on the south ridge. *Minoru Nagoshi*

reaches the main vehicle road, G317; and the west ridge reaches Hoangtsuliang Pass.

Hiroshi Matsushima, Chiharu Yoshimura, and I set up base camp at 3,750m (Tongnyop-ungzi), and advance camp at 4,700m. On October 3 we climbed from advance base to Bawang-shan's summit in 12 hours, using ropes for 300 vertical meters, providing us with 10 pitches of climbing up to 5.9. On the descent we bivouacked on the spur of the south ridge, but we could not sleep, as the temperature dropped to –8°C. From advance camp on October 4 we climbed Susunshan (5,183m, west of Bawangshan) for another first ascent.

MINORU NAGOSHI, *Japanese Alpine Club,*
Hiroshima Section

The first ascent route on Peak 5,965m. *Joseph Puryear*

Genyen Massif, Peak 5,695m, first ascent, Inglis-Puryear. In mid-October, Julie Hodson, Peter Inglis, Jay Janousek, Michelle Puryear, and I made our way toward Mt. Genyen (6,204m). Following the extensive research of Tamotsu Nakamura, our objective was the unclimbed peak of elevation 5,965m—the second highest peak in the Genyen area—just west of Mt. Genyen. Peter and Julie were good friends of Christine Boskoff and Charlie Fowler,

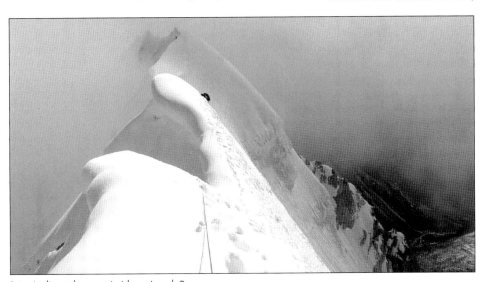

Peter Inglis on the summit ridge. *Joseph Puryear*

who were killed on Mt. Genyen the previous fall, and we all wanted to pay tribute to them.

After a bumpy three days' ride by hired van from Chengdu, we arrived at the small town of Sanla, southeast of the Genyen massif. Being already acclimatized from earlier weeks of attempting peaks, we made quick progress and established base camp three days and 30 miles from Sanla. Our base camp was set up at 4,200m on October 19. The next day Peter, Julie, and I left for high camp, which we established at 5,000m below a glacier on the mountain's southeast aspect. On October 21 we made an attempt up what appeared to be the path of least resistance, but eventually a cliffy sub-summit impeded progress.

The next day Peter and I left high camp early. Temperatures were cold, and the weather was unsettled but not necessarily threatening. We headed for a large mixed couloir directly above camp, which appeared to bypass the sub-summit. Most of the chossy lower gully was frozen in place, and we quickly gained elevation. Just past mid-height, fifth-class rock and moderate mixed climbing provided entertainment, until steep snow led us to the crest of a ridge. This ridge led to a steep snow headwall that led to the final east-trending summit ridge. We continued up over a large snow hump but were forced to downclimb exposed 60° snow on its backside. This led to a flat col.

We continued up an avalanche chute to the bergschrund below the upper south-facing headwall. Snow conditions on the entire climb had been absolutely perfect, so we continued unroped up the 55° headwall for 200m to the ridge crest. The summit ridge was quite a surprise; it was very sharp and slightly corniced to the other side—very Alaskan. We got out the rope and traversed another 200m to the small summit, arriving just before noon. We said a prayer for Charlie and Christine before the uneventful descent. Once back in high camp, we hurriedly packed, so we could reach base camp before dark. The climb was a tribute from all of us to Charlie and Christine. As Peter said on the summit, "They died in the most beautiful place in the whole wide world. And we miss them dearly."

We spent another four days exploring around the north side of Mt. Genyen and visiting the 600-year old Lengo Monastery, before returning to the town of Lamaya. The whole trip was absolutely amazing, as we explored a vast wilderness, made friends with nomadic people, and took a step back in time in this distant region of the Tibetan Plateau.

JOSEPH PURYEAR, *AAC*

SIGUNIANG NATIONAL PARK

BIPENG VALLEY

Dragon's Tooth/Longya Feng (5,250m), east ridge attempt; Peak 5,138m, north face attempt; logistical notes. Jon Otto, China's greatest first ascensionist, tipped me off about the potential of the Bipeng Valley. My initial foray into the valley was in the winter of 2005, to scout ice-flow potential. Once immersed in the valley, I looked past the waterfall ice and up at the untouched rocky peaks. I have since been to the valley on four trips, with varying success and experiences on each trip. Some logistical notes are at the end of this report.

The local Chinese rock climber Liu Yong and I met in Chengdu on September 20 and went straight to the local market to stock up on food. By the 24th we were poised at the base of our target peak. From the Bipeng Valley side the striking Dragon's Tooth resembles the

Dragon's Tooth (left), Queen's Tower and Queen's Peak (right). *Jon Lane Sullivan*

The attempted route on Peak 5,138m's north face. *Jon Lane Sullivan*

Matterhorn. From the Changping Valley side the peak looks like a rocky mass. Our goal was to climb the aesthetic line up the northeast ridge in a long day.

We pitched our tent on a sloping hillside at 4,228m and set out at 4 a.m., bound for the ridge. By daybreak we were roping up at the base of the wall. We were quickly sobered by the mixture of loose rock and Scottish-style moss holds, reaching 4,600m before encountering the first rock pitch of quality. Liu Yong took the lead up a 5.10 hand crack that curved into an overhang. He jammed his way up and dead-ended at the overhang, looked around for a long time, and lowered back to the belay ledge. I was in disbelief, so I climbed to the roof to see if I could find a route. The hand crack dissipated into 100% featureless terrain; it was like trying to escape from a racquetball court. From our belay perch we could look left down the east face and right toward the north face. The east face was a series of blocky overhangs with seemingly featureless rock in between, similar in scope to the Diamond on Long's Peak. The north face had more handholds and ledges, but was caked with snow and loose blocks leading to more overhangs. Neither looked possible. We made several rappels to the ground, using pitons and cordalette.

The Dragon's Tooth is still unclimbed from the Bipeng Valley side. The rock quality is good up high, but difficult. We gave the peak the name Dragon's Tooth while back in Yang'er Ge's cabin (see below). When I'm in Bipeng Valley I have to describe peaks by elevation and appearance, or with photos. We decided to name the peak to alleviate further confusion. After several rounds of green tea, beer, and moon cakes, the locals and I decided Dragon's Tooth would be a fitting name for this beautiful sharp-featured peak.

Liu Yong on the only good rock of the climb, just before being shut down on the Dragon's Tooth. *Jon Lane Sullivan*

The next day we decided we'd hike farther up the valley of scree and try to climb several pitches of rock on the Dragon's Tooth's east face, so we could gain the south ridge and then the summit. As we neared the east face, we were again disappointed by loose snow and blocky overhangs. Our attention turned to Peak 5,138m, just south of the Dragon's Tooth:. This peak is an obtuse rocky mass, but we could see a line winding up to the summit. I was excited to climb it and gain a better view of other peaks in the area. We were at the base of the north face, which was coated in snow, ice, and wet rock, but the angle was only about 45–55°. We did not have boots, crampons, or axes, just a light rock rack, rope, helmets, and a bit of food and water.

The snow was soft but held together well. We kick-stepped easily in the snow and scrambled up 5th-class rock. The terrain got more difficult at 4,600m, so we roped up and used a running belay with occasional rock protection. Our thin gloves and approach shoes were completely soaked, but we pushed on to 4,900m by about 3 p.m., by which time a sleet storm began, and we turned around. By the time we reached the tent the weather had cleared, and we were looking at stars. Bipeng Valley has a tendency to morph from summer clear, to winter blizzard, to spring monsoon in a 24-hour period.

We decided to pack up and return to Shanghaizi to replenish our spirits.

This expedition was made possible by support from the McNeill-Nott Climbing Grant sponsored by the American Alpine Club and Mountain Hardwear.

Jon Lane Sullivan, *AAC*

Logistical notes on reaching Shanghaizi from Chengdu. The public bus leaves the Chadianzi station early in the morning. It is wise to buy tickets the day before and have a local call to confirm about bus schedules beforehand. The bus ride itself has taken me anywhere from five to eight hours to Lixian. From Lixian I negotiate a minivan to take me to the trailhead at Shanghaizi; the price of this ride can vary depending on your Chinese bargaining skills. It is about 1? hours' drive on paved road with plenty of rockslide potential. Lixian is a tacky trucker town, but does offer dingy accommodations. I prefer getting all the way to Shanghaizi and acclimating in the fresh mountain air.

Shanghaizi is essentially a dirt parking lot with several guesthouses catering to Chinese escaping big city life. I always stay with Yang'er Ge and his family in the cabin near the river. He has lived and worked in Bipeng Valley for most of his life. His family has cold but quaint gue-strooms and will cook three square meals a day. Shanghaizi is at an elevation of 3,417m, which is good for acclimatizing. I take hikes up-valley scouting peaks for several days. Yang'er Ge can also arrange horses or porters to help ferry gear to base camp. Prices vary depending on weather and your language skill. [For further notes on logistics, see Joseph Puryear's notes below—Ed.]

Jon Lane Sullivan, *AAC*

Shuangqiao Valley

Hunter's Peak (5,360m), northeast face, attempt. Ahn, Chi-young, and I attempted a new route on the northeast face of Hunter's Peak, a.k.a. Lieren Feng. A Japanese-authored photograph book with English text (The Goddess on the Mountains in Southwestern China, by Kenzo Okawa) names the peak Shourengfeng and gives its elevation as 5,472m. However, our guide called it Lieren Feng, at 5,362m, and other sources have it as 5,360. The peak may have been ascended by Japanese teams by the ridges to the left and right of the northeast face, but we are not certain. Ahn, Chi-young, and I established base camp at 4,106m on August 3. We left the next morning at 8:45 a.m. under gorgeous blue skies and made a small deposit of gear and pro-visions by noon at 4,484m. From here we climbed seven pitches, until conditions deteriorated enough to halt our progress at 4,713m. The only protection from the drizzling rain and falling rock was a small one-man cave that Chi-young slept in, while I slept half sitting and lying on a small platform with my legs dangling over the edge.

We started climbing again when the rain ceased the following morning at 9 a.m. The rain began to come down again at noon, just as we reached a couloir that branch-ed up to the right. We found shelter on the left wall of the couloir and remained shel-tered at 4,847m until three o'clock, when we grew restless and decided to continue on,

Hunter's Peak (Lieren Feng, 5,360m), showing the rain-plagued line of attempt on the northeast face by Ahn Chi-young, and Peter Jensen-Choi. *Peter Jensen-Choi*

despite the heavy drizzle. Chi-young continued to a small ledge of precariously loose slabs, with sitting space for no more than one. In continuing drizzle, he remained on a tiny ledge at 5,000m, while I stayed where I was through the night. The drizzle continued off and on with an occasional break in the fog. Morning arrived, and I traversed up to Chi-young. To my shock, the traverse consisted of enormous, unstable boulder flakes. At his belay stance we assessed our circumstances. The drizzle was not enough to provide drinking water, and we had only a few gulps left. We had our fill of falling rock, rain, and less than ideal conditions. We had been terribly misinformed of this peak's conditions, and were ill-prepared from the start. We pulled out our Kevlar rappel line and made our way back to BC as the rain began to pick up immensely. We arrived at BC shortly after 7 p.m., drenched to the bone after 500m of rappelling.

PETER JENSEN-CHOI, *Corean Alpine Club*

CHANGPING VALLEY

Peak 4,764m, first ascent, southeast pillar, Xie Xie route. Giovanni Moretti, Riccardo Redaelli, Silvestro Stucchi, and I arrived from Italy and set up base camp at the head of the Changping Valley, between great nameless, unclimbed mountains that present wonderful granite walls of between 400 and 900 meters. After looking around, we chose the virgin Peak 4,764, with its 450m wall. On August 22, after giving up on one attempt due to bad weather, we reached the top in 6.5 hours of climbing up the

The Xie Xie route follows the skyline above the arrow on the northeast pillar of Peak 4,764m. *Silvestro Stucchi*

southeast pillar (400m, 10 pitches, VI A0). We called the route Xie Xie, which means "thank you" in Chinese. We descended the northwest face, with downclimbing and one 60m rappel to reach a gully and walk to camp. We left pitons and one bolt at belays (not all are equipped) and one piton on a pitch.

ELENA DAVILA MERINO, *Italy*

Barbarian (5,592m), Savage Sister (ca 16,390'), attempts. Josh Butson and I returned to the Changping Goa Valley in late September searching for another remote adventure. From the previous year's experience, we knew our objective: the mountain locals call "The Barbarian." But when we arrived at the mountain's base, we gave up on our big wall gear as we watched

The Barbarian (left center) and Putala Peak (right). *Jon Lane Sullivan*

The 16,390' peak Butson and Clark called Savage Sister. Their attempt stopped approximately 150m shy of the summit via the northeast face (the large snowfield on the left skyline of this photo). *Ben Clark*

bus-sized blocks tumble from the large amphitheater above the great east wall. Underestimating the valley is one thing, hiking for a week to this seeping chosspile was another feeling altogether. Steep overhanging roofs and polished granite made up the lower reaches of the wall, with enormous stretches of featureless granite. Having no bolts, we searched the cirque only to find that there was no "good" way up the mountain. Our ethos of alpine style and "leave no trace" would have no place here. It would take a lot of juice and time to drill the wall—a Warren Harding-sized effort. To the left there was little hope in 2007, but in 2006 there had been a ramp above a serac band that could have provided easy access to the upper mountain. The valley would be a dangerous place in the winter, but I suspect that there could be a 1,000m ice climb right up the heart of the east face.

After retreating from below the Barbarian, we attempted an innocent-looking pyramid adjacent to the Four Sisters group of peaks, where a mixed route took us from base camp at 16,500' to an estimated altitude of over 18,000' before stopping us short on a wind lip that settled like a hippopotamus rolling over. Many days of freezing rain had destroyed the last of a consolidated summer snowpack. On our descent we narrowly avoided considerable rockfall on a talus slope. We called the mountain the Savage Sister.

Josh and I have climbed on several peaks in the Changping Goa Valley, where we succeeded in sending hard onsight gound-up mixed, rock, and ice climbs with little more than pins and the occasional pinky-sized hex. The climbing here is runout, very heady, and chances for a rescue are slim to none. If you stick to peaks like Pumio, The Falcon, and Siguniang, the rock is granite with some splitters, and the new route potential is enormous. There are also easier objectives for the classic mountaineer, including moderate snow climbs accessible in a few days.

BEN CLARK, *AAC*

Changping, Shuangqiao, and Bipeng valleys, mapmaking. After my attempt on the Dragon's Tooth, I trekked around the Changping, Shuangqiao, and Bipeng valleys for about nine days, hiking up hillsides, over passes, and up subsidiary valleys trying to get a concept of the valley. There have been many intrepid climbers in these valleys, but it is still hard to figure out which peak is which. Each peak may have a Chinese name, a Tibetan name, a name given by the first Western team to climb it, or no name. Some peaks can be seen from different valleys; locals in different valleys have different names for the same peak.

My mission was to use my local knowledge and language skills to unravel the mystery of this new climbing destination. I interviewed local horsemen, Chinese mountaineers, the Sichuan Mountaineering Association, and foreign climbers such as Jon Otto, Tom Nakamura,

Lara Shan (5,700m, left) and Mt. Siguniang (6,250m, right). *Joseph Puryear*

and Ben Clark. The result is a hand drawn map with 51 of the most prominent peaks that rise from the Bipeng, Changping, and Shuangqiao valleys. This is the most accurate and useful map of the region. Enjoy. The expedition was made possible by support from the McNeill-Nott Climbing Grant sponsored by the American Alpine Club and Mountain Hardwear.

JON LANE SULLIVAN, *AAC*

Chad Kellogg and Jay Janousek on the summit of Lara Shan. *Joseph Puryear*

SIGUNIANG

Lara Shan (Peak 5,700m), first ascent, American Standard. Chad Kellogg and I were to make our second attempt on Mt. Siguniang (6,250m) in April. After reaching base camp at just under 12,000' in the Changping Valley, we decided on an unnamed, unclimbed 5,700m peak for our acclimatization climb. Our friend Jay Janousek joined us for this ascent. We spent three days approaching our high camp at 15,200', hiking up into a narrow hanging valley due west of the peak. These were relatively short days as we adjusted to the altitude. After another day of unsettled weather, we started the final ascent early in the morning on April 18. A 700-foot narrow snow couloir beside a jumbled glacier icefall provided a perfect keyhole to reach the main face. From here we navigated an easy but steep glacier, with several hanging seracs threatening various parts of the route (hence the name of the route: American Standard is a brand of toilet, and you'd better be careful or you might get flushed). Several steep-but-short ice steps provided fun cruxes. After topping out on the main headwall at just under 18,000', we followed a large plateau, with one major crevasse problem, to the summit pyramid. This consisted of a little more slogging and two pitches of glacial ice. We reached the summit in the early afternoon on April 18, a perfectly clear and windless day. So clear, in fact, that we could just make out Gongga Shan (7,556m , the highest peak in Western Sichuan) in the far distance. We started our descent and made 12 full 60m rappels, plus much downclimbing, and reached our camp just as the sun was setting.

After our descent, a few days of unsettled weather allowed us to rest and prepare for our bid on Siguniang, but we learned that Chad's wife Lara died in the Alaska Range. Chad departed immediately, and our expedition ended. We suggest the name Lara Shan for the 5,700m previously untrodden summit, after our good friend Lara Karena Kellogg.

Chad and I thank the American Alpine Club for presenting us with the McNeill-Nott Award for our attempt on Siguniang.

JOSEPH PURYEAR, *AAC*

Notes on logistics for climbers. Climbing permits for Sichuan Province are relatively easy to acquire. Contrary to previous reports, no one has ever been declined a permit. Certain parties just refused to pay the fee and hence were "denied." The climbing fee for peaks under 7,000m is $700, payable only in US dollars (this includes Mt. Siguniang). The permit process takes approximately 30 minutes and is easily accomplished in person at the Sichuan Mountaineering Association in downtown Chengdu, with no prior notice necessary. Once in Rilong, the small village that is the jump-off point for the Qionglai Mountains, there are a few more additional fees. Because the mountains are within the Four Girls Mountains Nature Reserve, there is an entrance fee and a per-day camping fee. The entrance fee was 70 Yuan (about 9 USD), and the camping fee was 12 Yuan (about 1.60 USD) per person, per day. There is a separate permit for low-elevation rock and ice climbing that costs around 30 USD. This permit can be obtained in Rilong.

Chengdu is a full-service city, and it is easy to purchase most of your food here at a number of large grocery and multi-department stores. There are several gear shops where you can purchase camping gear, but climbing gear is limited. In Rilong there are shops where you can buy enough food for a shorter trip, but expect the selection to be limited. Transportation from

Chengdu to and from Rilong can either be by public bus or by private vehicle. For public transportation, expect to pay around 100 Yuan (about 13 USD) per person, plus an extra per-bag fee. The bag fee is usually negotiable but can be upwards of 50 Yuan (6.50 USD) per bag. For a private van that can easily hold four climbers plus gear, expect to pay 1,800–2,000 Yuan (240–266 USD). Horses can also be hired in Rilong and run from 200–300 Yuan (about 26–40 USD) per horse. It is feasible to take a single load or ferry loads up to base camp as well. Contrary to what foreign climbers might think, the first "pure alpine" ascents (those climbs that left from the trailhead without the use of horses) were made long ago by the likes of Charlie Fowler, and before him by local climbing guides. Also, yaks pose no threat in the valley and are quite afraid of humans.

Climbing in the Qionglai Mountains of Sichuan Province is going to change dramatically over the next couple of years. The Chinese government is actively promoting the area for tourism, and Rilong is undergoing major changes. The small mountain road from Chengdu to Rilong is being overhauled and widened into a superhighway of sorts in order to handle the expected onslaught of visitors. Many of the residents of Rilong are being evicted from their homes in the main area of town, where the government wants to build hotels and other large tourist facilities. Some of the residents' families have lived in these homes for over 300 years. (Tibetans have resided in the valley for over a thousand years.) Compensation for their homes is minimal. In addition the government plans to build a gondola to a sacred hilltop where there are several stupas that look out toward Mt. Siguniang. Other changes already implemented include the reconstruction and expansion of a 3km boardwalk system that leads into the main Changping Valley. It would not be surprising if this boardwalk one day extended all the way (17km) to the meadow at the main base camp area. The Shuangqiao-gou Valley, just west of the Changping, a few years ago received a paved road that leads several kilometers to its head. It remains to be seen how the Chinese will manage the environmental and social impacts of a large influx of visitors to such a small and delicate alpine area. [For further notes on logistics, see the last paragraph of Jon Lane Sullivan's notes above—Ed.]

JOSEPH PURYEAR, *AAC*

YUNNAN PROVINCE

HENGDUAN MOUNTAINS

Deep Gorge Country ("Three Parallel Rivers": Salween, Mekong, Yangtze), exploration. My many voyages of discovery to what I call "East of the Himalaya–Alps of Tibet" were triggered by reading the enchanting narratives of Frank Kingdon-Ward, in which he chronicles his travels to the remote Tibetan regions of

The caravan crossing the Yu Qu at Gebu. *Tamotsu Nakamura*

The east face of unclimbed Mukong Xueshan. The left (south) peak is 6,000m, and the right peak is 6,005m. *Tamotsu Nakamura*

Circa 5,700m peaks from the Yu Qu–Salween Divide. *Tamotsu Nakamura*

Circa 5,700m peaks from the Yu Qu–Salween Divide. *Tamotsu Nakamura*

northwest Yunnan and southeast Tibet in the early 1900s. A paradise for plant-hunters, this land is also attractive to mountaineers because numerous stunning peaks are still unclimbed. Throughout the entire East of the Himalaya region, I count 255 unclimbed 6,000m peaks on the map: 200 in Nyanchen Tanglha East, 30 in the Kangri Garpo Range, 20 in the Deep Gorge Country of the Hengduan Mountains, and five in the Sichuan West Highland of the Hengduan Mountains.

The Deep Gorge Country has especially fascinating scenery. The Tibetan Plateau has been eroded by some of Asia's longest rivers, which sculpted the high plateau not merely into a land of steep mountains, but of deep valleys with gloomy shadows and forbidding gorges. This Deep Gorge Country was intensively explored by Kingdon-Ward, and I have been tracing his footsteps since 1990.

In this time I have seen a wave

of change rushing through China, even reaching the isolated frontiers in Yunnan. The Deep Gorge County, which the Chinese call Three Parallel Rivers (Salween, Mekong, and Yangtze), was registered as a world UNESCO natural heritage site in 2002. Taking advantage of the famed Shangri-La in James Hilton's *Lost Horizon*, the Chinese government is highlighting the Meili Snow Mountains on the Yunnan-Tibet border and the Mekong River Valley for tourism development. Still, there remain many unfrequented and little-known mountains and valleys to attract an old explorer. I have that good fortune.

This is the first known photo of the south side of challenging and unclimbed Damyon (6,324m). It was taken from Do Village. *Tamotsu Nakamura*

In autumn I led an expedition of six members—Eiichirou Kasai (67), Tsuyoshi Nagai (75), Ms. Sonoe Sato (48), Tadao Shintani (64), Lu Weidong (58), and me (72)—to the Gorge Country to revisit an isolated borderland of my particular interest and sentiment.

The expedition was rather hard and uncomfortable. Our original plan was to go up the Salween River (Nu Jiang) northwestward from Tsa-warong, but the muleteers refused, as the trail was too narrow and dangerous for pack animals carrying loads. We were forced to choose an alternative route along Yu Qu (Wi Chu), a tributary of the Salween that I had already followed twice. Extraordinarily heavy snowfall in mid-November closed high passes, including two (4,900m and 5,300m) that we'd wanted to cross. In addition, all six members caught serious colds from the heavy smoke in the Tibetan houses where we slept.

Nevertheless, we were satisfied to unveil two 6,000m massifs and a 5,700–5,800m massif. These peaks are in the following mountain ranges:

Baxoila Ling: The northern part of this large range is on the Lohit Parlung Tsangpo–Salween Divide. The southern part is on the Irrawaddy-Salween Divide in Tibetan Autonomous Region. Its name is Gaoligong Shan in Yunnan Province. There are three outstanding mountain massifs: Yangbayisum (6,005m), Chagelazi (6,146m), and Mukong Xueshan (6,005m). Xueshan means "snowy mountains."

Salween-Yu Qu Divide: There are three massifs: Geuzong, a massif of 5,700–5,800m peaks, a central massif of 5,700m peaks, and a northern massif of 5,400–5,600m peaks.

Nu Shan/Taniantawen Shan: This is a large range on the Salween-Mekong Divide. Nu Shan, in the southern part, includes the famous holy peak of Meili Snow Mountain (6,740m) with well-developed glaciers, while Taniantawen Shan, stretching north of Nu Shan, has the rocky massifs of Damyon (6,324m) and Dungri Garpo (6,090m), with no eminent glaciers.

A couple of years ago, as part of the ambitious West Development Plan, a vehicle track was opened 56km as the crow flies from Bingzhonglou to Tsawarong on the left bank of the

The east face of unclimbed Geuzong (5,770m). *Tamotsu Nakamura*

Salween River. On November 8, thanks to this new road, we reached the administration center of Tsawarong in six hours from Bingzhonglou, whereas the old path required three or four days on foot. Tsawarong is a warm, fertile land to Tibetans, who normally live on the arid and cold high plateau. Kingdon-Ward loved the people and culture of Tsawarong, and visited there three times, in 1911, 1913, and 1922. Here we arranged for a 16-horse caravan to take us along the Yu Qu Valley.

On November 10 we started walking.

It is said that Yu Qu is the most beautiful pine-forested valley in Eastern Tibet, and we were overwhelmed by the grandeur of the first bend of the Yu Qu gorge. All along our route we were welcomed in Tibetan houses. On November 13 I left Razun village in the predawn dark, because at last I could take a picture of Mukong Xueshan. Twice before I had tried to view this mountain: first from the pilgrimage trail around the Meili Snow Mountains in 1996 and again in 2003, when I traversed the gorge country from Zayu to Mekong. However, the mountain had remained veiled in clouds, and I never saw it. In 2007 the gods finally blessed me, and I could photograph the magnificent and precipitous northeast face. The north peak is the main summit (6,005m), while the south peak is 6,000m high.

On November 13 our caravan departed from Do village (3,350m) to reconnoiter the Damyon massif from the west. We ascended through primeval conifer forest along the Do Chu, a tributary of the Yu Qu, and camped at 3,560m. On the following day we reached a summer yak pasture at 4,140m, which was surrounded by outstanding lofty rock peaks of ca 5,800m, south of Damyon's main peak. If we had come in summer, we would have found a fairy meadow. But it had snowed heavily lately, and we returned from the pasture to escape the snow.

Damyon (6,324m) has long been worshiped by local Tibetans and the Nashi minority. The Damyon and Dungri Garpo massifs are in the southern end of the Taniantawen Range, which is 50km long from south to north, with five unclimbed 6,000m peaks. According to an old villager, to reach the west face of the main peak, one must cross a 4,850m-high pass called Zeh La near the headwaters of the Do Qu, which is beneath the south face. There is a pasture just north of a lake called Uke Tso, where camping is possible. A trail passes northward from the Uke Tso to a 4,000m pass near Chaka, where the Sichuan-Tibet Highway crosses the Mekong River.

The old man also explained that each rock peak south of Damyon has a name. From north to south the names of the 5,800m–5,900m peaks are Lamyon, Gonmyon, Nachamyon,

Suzemyon, and Kashonmyon. Myon means "goddess." The other Goddess Mountains, sisters of Damyon, have their own legend and continue peak after peak to the north of Damyon.

In 1998, also in mid-November, I crossed Di La (4,581m), adjacent to Beda La to the northwest, and saw the panorama of the mountains on the Yu Qu-Salween Divide. One of our objectives in 2007 was to gather as much information as possible on the mountains between Salween and Yu Qu. This range is little known and receives little attention, because there are no peaks exceeding 6,000m, and only a few tiny glaciers. The Russian topo map (1: 200,000) tells us there are many 5,300m–5,800m peaks ranging from northwest to southeast. They break down as follows:

Geuzong massif (5,700m–5,800m): West of Jino to Do villages. Many outstanding rock peaks in northern part.

Central massif (5,300m–5,700m): West of Bake to Jomei villages. Many lofty peaks.

Northern massif (5,400m–5,600m): West of Zayi to north. Few attractive peaks.

The path along the Yu Qu Valley was too close to the mountains to have good views. I could only manage to take pictures of the Geuzong massif from near Do Village, on the way back, after reconnoitering Damyon and the central massif from the Ge La (3,960m), between Bake and Meila villages. I took pictures of the northern massif in 1998, on the way to a 4,000m pass west of Zayi.

This deeply eroded country of southeast Tibet is most beautiful in the Yu Qu Valley. The river flows in a narrow gorge between two snow-clad ranges of the Salween–Yu Qu and Yu Qu–Mekong divides.

Our quest to see unknown mountains ended in Jomei, where muleteers from Jino and Do villages held a farewell party for us. This was the first such festivity in my 17 years of traveling in "East of the Himalaya." We were deeply moved by the event and felt the warmth of the people of Tsawarong. In a Tibetan house at Jino, the family remembered my stay in 1998 and rendered the best services. At Meia Village, I met an old man whom I interviewed nine years ago about the former slavery system in Tibet.

Even here we could see the rapid changes sweeping through western China. In Pitu, which was an old center of Tsawarong, two new guesthouses had been constructed and the main streets were rebuilt. Cars and motorbikes were gradually replacing pack animals for local transport. In Jomei we were invited to a primary school and welcomed by seven teachers and 150 pupils.

On November 26, we left Jomei by three Land Cruisers for the return journey. I thank two old friends for their support on our expedition: Weidong Lu, who joined us as an interpreter from Kunming, and Shaohong Cheng (Tibetan name: Gerong), a guide from Deqen who traveled with me several times to the Gorge Country since 1996. Cheng arranged everything for our journey. I proudly recommend him as the best and most reliable guide for trekking in the Hengduan Mountains.

TAMOTSU NAKAMURA, *adapted from Japanese Alpine News*

Tibet

NORTHWEST TIBET

Lungkar Shan, Tachab Kangri (6,704m), attempt. In August we visited the northern end of the Lungkar Shan in northwest Tibet. Our peak, Tachab Kangri, lies southeast of Marme village and Tsa Tso lake. Marme lies roughly 60km southwest of the county town of Gertse (Lumaringpo), from which it can be reached by road. Our party consisted of Kevin Clarke, Mike Dawber, and Richard Sant from Scotland, and me from England. We left Kathmandu on July 31 and traveled by Land Cruiser via Zhangmu, Nyalam, Saga, Tsochen, and Gertse to reach our base camp on August 6. We placed camp by a nomad encampment at 5,000m at the foot of the narrow Tachab Valley, which runs southwest, terminating in the Tachab Glacier and the northeast face of the peak. With the help of yaks we established advance base at 5,670m on the 11th, at the foot of the glacier 8km up the valley. We occupied Camp 1, on the glacier at 6,017m, on the 14th. A final push on the 16th to establish a last camp on the col to the southeast of the summit was halted by a large snow slide on

the slopes above the route. We explored an alternative route via the northwest col, but abandoned it when an even larger slide devastated the entire slope below. Our final high point was about 6,300m. The route appeared to consist mainly of straightforward snow slopes without significant technical difficulties. The weather was mixed throughout the expedition, with frequent thunderstorms, perhaps reflecting severe monsoon conditions in India at this time.

JOHN TOWN, *Alpine Club*

The northeast face of Tachab Kangri (6,704m) from advanced base camp. *John Town*

NYANCHEN TANGLHA EAST

Yigong Tsangpo, Shashim Valley, reconnaissance. In November Stuart Holmes and I made a further exploratory sortie into the Nyanchen Tanglha East. The original plan, to reconnoiter the valleys south of Niwu, in the heart of the main chain, rapidly fell foul of the infamous Lhari–Niwu road. (The road is being reconstructed in its entirety, reflecting the boom in the local economy on the back of medicinal grass and caterpillar fungus. The new road is wide and fast, and the 110km journey should be possible in three hours at any time of year after January 2008.) Instead, we were deposited at the settlement of Shing Sham, at 4,050m in the main

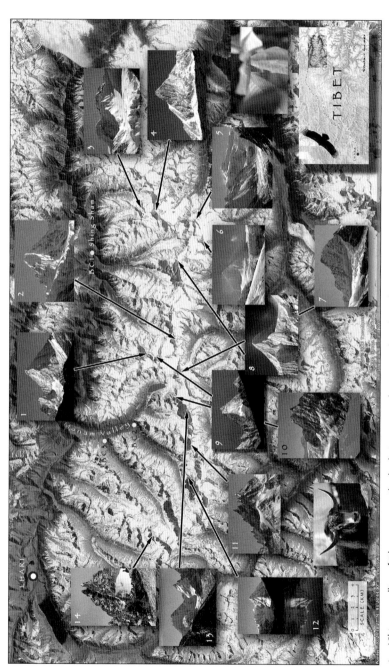

1) Kajaqiao (Chinese spelling of Tibetan name, Chachacho), 6,447m, showing north and east faces (Fowler-Watts, 2005). 2) Champaponga, ca 6,200m, directly south of Manamcho. Unclimbed. 3) P6,008m from the north, with the rocky P6,230m behind. 4) Mandingcho, 6,230m. Unclimbed. Taken from NW at 6,008m. 5) Yashimcho, 6,502m, at the head of the Yasham Valley, due south of BC1 at Shing Sham. Unclimbed. 6) Chomo, 6,434m. Unclimbed. View of east and north faces from the slopes of 6,008m. 7) P6,088m. Unclimbed. Showing the north face from head of Manam Valley. 8) P6,432m. Unclimbed. View of east and north faces from the slopes of 6,008m. 9) Manamcho, 6,264m, from BC2 in upper Manam Valley (Fowler-Ramsden, 2007). 10) Unnamed and unclimbed peak, ca 6,000m, above the moraine-dammed lake at head of Manam Valley. 11) Unclimbed granite spires, ca 5,800m, with north side of P6,066m and P6,146m behind. 12) P6,182m. Unclimbed. View from NE, up valley from BC2. 13) P6,146m (left) and P6,066m (right). Both unclimbed. North faces viewed from upper Manam Valley. 14) Unclimbed granite peak, ca 5,900m at the head of valley above BC3. Mountain heights are from Chinese map data compiled by Tamotsu Nakamura; mountain names are from local villagers. *Map compilation and all photographs by Stuart Holmes and Bruce Normand from November 2007. A color version of this photo montage is available on www.americanalpineclub.org/AAJ*

valley of the Yigong Tsangpo, 10km east of Kajaqiao and almost exactly halfway between Lhari and Niwu. The friendly local farmers/herders invited us to camp in a walled field that gave protection from wind and yak horns. Like everywhere in the deep, hanging valley systems of eastern Tibet, only a wooden footbridge gives evidence of easy livestock trails to yak pastures higher in the side valleys. This one, the Shashim Valley, gives direct access to two valley forks, each with summer settlements at 4,500m at the feet of short but steep glaciers. The Shashim Valley is dominated by pointed, fluted Peak 6,432m, for which no other name was found. The western fork is a cirque consisting of a north-facing wall extending from Peak 6,432m to Peak 6,278m and predominantly west-facing slopes on a ridge capped by rocky 5,000m summits. Although the locals spoke of a pass, Hongka La, leading directly south to Upper Niwu, the entire cirque appeared to be guarded by icefalls. The eastern fork is longer, stretching back to massive Yashimcho (6,502m), the highest peak in the Kajaqiao part of the chain, and to the shapely Chomo (6,434m). The eastern side of this glacier is dominated by steep, rocky Mandingcho (6,230m) and the western side by Peak 6,432m. While acclimatizing, we also walked 4km up-valley to the next bridge and hanging side valley, which is the end of a large glacier descending from the east side of Kajaqiao. The peaks around this glacier are Peak 6,278, shapely Champa-ponga (ca 6,000m), Manamcho (6,265m), and the commanding pyramid of Kajaqiao (6,447m, known locally as Chachacho). The early November weather was unstable and showery, with dark clouds blowing over the summits from behind (southwest) on most days. Total snow accumulation was below 5cm in the 4,500m pastures, but did not melt. On one of the better days we hiked to a rounded snow ridge at 6,008m directly north of Mandingcho and affording excellent views in all directions except straight south. After 10 days the weather pattern broke, being replaced by blue skies and cool temperatures, with occasional solid afternoon cloud, for the remaining two weeks. However, the transition was accompanied by a windstorm, which deposited large amounts of snow on north and east faces. This allowed us plenty of time to re-explore the two valley systems with excellent visibility, Holmes choosing the north side of the Yigong Valley to see the chain in full perspective, and me choosing to re-ascend both the Kajaqiao Valley and Pt. 6,008m. Fresh footprints on a snow ridge photographed in the former were identified instantly by the locals as "yeti," presumably a type of small bear. Pt. 6,008m yielded a full panorama of the Sepu Kangri Range and views over the original target peaks south of Niwu.

With time to spare, we chose to complete our exploration of the chain by accessing the part west of Kajaqiao via the Manam Valley. This wide, flat valley is reached by a steel bridge at km 26 from Lhari and descends from a pair of glacial lakes almost directly beneath the west face of Manamcho. Rising directly out of the lakes are the extremely steep, rocky peaks 6,088m, 6,146m, and 6,066m. The ridgeline running northwest from Manamcho contains many rocky summits and towers in the high 5,000m range, and Kajaqiao looks over the scene from the neighboring cirque. Joining the Manam Valley from the southwest are two further valley forks, both 10km long, straight, flat, and easily accessed by yak-grazing trails. While the more northerly fork is dry and notable for a number of vertical granite faces, the more southerly leads to further shapely peaks, such as 6,186m and 6,056m, the first in particular with a number of potentially excellent mixed lines on its northern and western aspect.

BRUCE NORMAN, *Switzerland*

The first ascent line on Manamcho (6,264m) as seen from high on Peak 5,935m, Steve Burns climbing. *Ian Cartwright*

Manamcho (6,264m), Peak 5,935m, first ascents. When I was climbing Kajaqiao in 2005, neighboring Manamcho looked so good that I had to go back to the Nyanchen Tanghla East. It's not so much that the climbing is top quality, but that the overall mountaineering experience is. The combination of soft snow and deep bureaucracy is enough to put most people off, which preserves a sense of solitude. Out of the 160 or so 6,000m peaks here, only about four have been climbed. And the peaks are spectacular. It must be a bit like the early Alpine Club pioneers found the Alps. A virtually untouched range, with Matterhorns still unclimbed. Here, though, there is the added touch of exotic cultural interest. Local people commented to us that they had only seen white people on their satellite TVs. It's a strange place. One month's caterpillar fungus (Chinese medicine) hunting gives the men enough money to spend the rest of the year as idle rich, revving motor bikes along dirt tracks 250km from the nearest tarmac.

Our team of four—Steve Burns, Ian Cartwright, Paul Ramsden, and I—intended to climb Manamcho and explore to the northwest, which we knew contained spectacular peaks that had not been clearly photographed. Previous teams had visited in September–November, but we chose pre-monsoon in April. Winter snow was still prevalent, and our 2005 base camp was choked with ice. However the mountains appeared to hold less snow than post-monsoon. Ankle-deep snow in Lhasa shortly after we left did not bode well, but in fact the weather was primarily fine, although during one week out of the four we were in Tibet there was heavy snowfall every day. On balance, the months of March and September are probably best.

Learning from our mistakes in 2005, we brought snowshoes, which proved invaluable. After acclimatizing, Paul and I crossed an extensive snow plateau. A reconnaissance led us to focus on the northwest ridge, which had been attempted by Phil Amos and Adam Thomas in

Paul Ramsden leading on day three during the ascent of Manamcho. *Mick Fowler*

2005. They had retreated from 5,880m in the face of strong winds and heavy snowfall. We were initially blessed with better air conditions, and passed their high point on our third day out from base camp. Thereafter, the climbing was mainly snowed-up rock, at about Scottish grade IV. We bivouacked two more times before reaching the summit area. By now the weather had deteriorated badly, and we spent a miserable night on a nose-to-tail ledge, enduring two feet of snowfall during the night.

Morning brought frighteningly strong winds and made the final 75m the most challenging on the route. It was a pity not to be able to see the magnificent view that there must be on a fine day. Instead, we got the hell out as soon as we could by rappelling non-stop back down the route of ascent and wading through waist-deep new snow to a gear dump we had left on the glacier. A further day of knee-deep wading on snowshoes took us back to base camp seven days after leaving.

Steve and Ian had less luck. Having acclimatized and decided to have a go at point 5,935m to the north of Manamcho, they reached 5,700m before Steve began to feel ill. Frustration turned to elation as the ensuing descent and recovery occupied the bad weather period; by the time they were ready to climb again, glorious blue skies had returned. Two days from base camp took them to a good tent platform, and from there snow slopes and mixed pitches of AD or so brought them to the summit, from which they enjoyed a panoramic view. Manamcho and Kajaqiao dominated the eastern horizon, while to the west were the unclimbed peaks surrounding the Manam Valley. Paul and I had a few days to explore at the end. Our main interest was the Manam Valley, which is dominated by Manamcho (meaning "Buddha of Manam"). The valley was one of the most beautiful we have visited, and sports several spectacular 6,000m peaks.

MICK FOWLER, *Alpine Club*

KANGRI GARPO

Ata Glacier, reconnaissance. The Alpine Club of Kobe University (ACKU) has been pursuing unexplored mountains for the past several decades. Our new target is the Kangri Garpo Mountains. More than thirty 6,000m peaks in this range remain unclimbed. In 2002 we found an approach to the main peak of the Ata Glacier, Mt. Ruoni (6,805m), the highest point in the 280km Kangri Garpo Range. In 2003 ACKU sent a climbing party led by Kazumasa Hirai (the first summiter of Chogolisa, in 1958) to attempt Mt. Ruoni from the Ata Glacier, but the party failed at 5,900m on the northeast flank because of bad weather and dangerous conditions.

[Editor's note: See *AAJ 2002* p. 429 and *AAJ 2007* p. 429 for more history of the Kangri Garpo].

Ever since the ACKU made the first ascent of Que-er Shan (6,168m) in a joint expedition with the Mountaineering Association of the Chinese University of Geosciences Wuhan (MACUGW) in 1988, both parties have maintained a good partnership, not only in mountaineering, but also in academic collaboration. In May 2007 ACKU and MACUGW agreed to hold joint expeditions to unexplored areas of Tibet. They focused on the Kangri Garpo mountains, which are close to the heavily restricted border between India and Myanmar. Our 2007 reconnaissance party intended to find possible climbing routes on Ata 3-Sisters (KG-1, Mt. Ruoni, 6,805m; KG-2, 6,703m; and KG-3, 6,724m). These peaks were discovered on the southwest bank of the Ata Glacier during past ACKU expeditions, which were sent to survey peak heights. For example, Mt. Ruoni (Bairiga) has different recorded altitudes: 6,805m on the USSR map, versus 6,610m and 6,882m on old rough Chinese maps. KG-4 (6,290m) and KG-5 (6,300m) are not shown on existing maps but were discovered by these explorers. Positioning and height identification are still pending. We do not know whether the Chinese authorities have made an aerial survey. The Chinese Army supposedly keeps the up-to-date and precise maps of this area, but these are not open to the public. Even though we tried through the Chinese University of Geosciences, we were not granted permission to view the maps. We have also failed to get permission from the Chinese Academy of Science to see surveys of peaks in this area.

On October 3, in unsettled weather, seven members of the joint party—three from ACKU led by Takeru Yamada, and four from MACUGW led by Niu Xiao Hong—with ten yaks left Lhagu and headed to the Ata Glacier via Kogin and Chutsu. Because the stream flowing from the Ata Glacier is blocked by two lakes and a gorge above Chutsu, they detoured and followed a yak trail crossing over the Hyona flat.

The Ata Glacier has unique topography, in that it flows southeast from the divide of the Kangri Garpo mountains and splits into two branches. The south tongue descends into a tributary of the Kangri Garpo Qu. The north tongue drops into a glacier lake, Cuo Cho Hu (4,265m). Our base camp was sited on the east bank of the glacier near the lake (29°13'12.1" N, 96°49'11.2"E ±13m, 4,291m).

One of challenges of a joint party involving different cultures is to overcome cultural gaps and differences in climbing style. On the first day at BC part of the team practiced rope work on the glacier. Meanwhile, others reconnoitered the route to advanced base camp (ABC). Since ACKU had reached the Ata Glacier in 2002 and 2003, we knew just where to put ABC despite the cloudy weather: on the break point of the glacier (29°12'3.2" N, 96°48'42.9" E ±7, 4,391m).

On November 5 we three Japanese members sited Camp 1 on the upper crevassed area (29°11'36.3" N, 96°47'17.3" E, 4,588m). We put on Japanese-style snowshoes to avoid sinking deeply into the snow.

On November 8 a half day of fine weather gave us our only chance to take pictures and look for climbing routes on the south flank of the northeast divide of the Ata Glacier, the highest point we reached in this reconnaissance (4,797m). Three days of snowy weather erased our tracks in the crevasse-labyrinth, as over two feet of fresh snow covered the crevasses. Takeru Yamada decided to return to the base camp on the tenth in dense fog. We had only a few meters of visibility, but we safely returned to ABC without falling into crevasses, thanks to our GPS track-back function and flags.

We tried to measure the height of Three Sisters from the point 29°12'47.9" N, 96°46'39.9" E ±6m, 4,725m, on the Ata Glacier. We used a simple level, scale, and a GPS to get a vertical view angle on each peak. The heights of the 3 Sisters, calculated using the measured data, as well as the Google Earth peak position, are KG-1 (Ruoni), 6,900m; KG-2, 6,650m; and KG-3, 6,700m.

While we were in the mountains, a large cyclone hit Bangladesh, and a week later, an unusual snowstorm ravaged eastern Tibet and Shangri-La (Zhong Dian). We had expected good weather during the first week of November, but this year it did not happen. [Editor's note: We were unable to secure photos of publishable resolution in time for the *AAJ 2008*. However, we have posted Takeru Yamada's original report with photos and a map at www.ameri-canalpineclub.org/AAJ.]

TAKERU YAMADA *and* TATSUO INOUE, *Alpine Club of Kobe University, Japan*

HIMALAYA

Everest, exotica. Centuries ago European theologians debated the question of how many angels can dance on the head of a pin. The modern equivalent might be how many climbers can stand on the summit of Everest. We may soon find out, as the numbers rise dramatically. The authorities in Beijing said last November they would limit the number on the mountain this spring and raise their fees. They raised the fees, all right, by $1,000 per climber, but as to numbers, they allowed hundreds to move up and down throughout the season, even while a very large Chinese team made a trial run to the summit with Olympic-style torches and tested the torches' performance at 8,850m. Only one climber is known to have been turned away: the mayor of Prague, Pavel Bem, was refused entry into Tibet at the Nepalese border because he displayed a Tibetan flag in front of the Chinese embassy in Prague and met the Dalai Lama several times. So he and his teammates went around to the Nepalese side, and he climbed it successfully from there.

A vast number of men and women did summit Everest this spring: 597 compared to 458 last spring and 305 the spring before that. An experienced leader of commercial expeditions on the north side, Russell Brice, attributes the large number of successes on his side this season— 287 climbers—to the fact that the trail was very fast, which enabled so many climbers to move up and down rapidly, in some cases to descend all the way from summit to advance base camp on the same day, and many unskilled climbers to reach high altitudes and even to succeed. The route was fast because it was stamped down by Brice's Sherpas when they were fixing the ropes to the top at the end of April; then light snowfall froze the route. When climbers came along after the Sherpas, they moved on top of a thin layer of snow covering the frozen trail.

Among the astonishing total 597 who managed to summit Everest was the newly crowned oldest person, Katsuske Yanagisawa of Japan, who was 71 years and 63 days old when he climbed to the top on 22 May. He dethroned another Japanese, Takao Arayama, who was a mere 70 years, 225 days old last year.

A Briton, David Tait, who intended to make a double traverse with a Sherpa—up the north side, down the south, back up the south side and down the north—found he was too tired after descending the south side and would need a long rest before going back up again; he stopped there. He explained later that in his training for Everest, he had neglected to train for his descent, and his knees felt it. Anyway, his single traverse was "great, fantastic."

A party of three Filipinas and three Sherpas followed Tait the next day in their own north-south traverse. Now traversers are boasting of being first from their country, just as occasionally someone is still declared to be the first to the summit of his or her nationality. And in the case of these three women, Janet Belarmino, Carina Dayondon, and Noelle Cristina Wenceslao, they are correctly claiming to be the first females to make the crossing. They are also the first, unluckily, to be charged an extra fee of $3,000 per person for the privilege of making a traverse from the Tibetan side, as per a sudden demand by the authorities in Beijing in mid-April. This was on top of the $11,500 per traversing member they had already paid, in addition the normal payment to their Kathmandu trekking agency for permission to be on the mountain and for other agency services. (No traversing extras were charged for Sherpas.)

Among those who did not reach the summit this spring were an Austrian couple, Wilfried and Sylvia Studer, who made their 11th attempt without using artificial oxygen, reaching 8,700m together, and declaring they would not come again; a Dutchman, Wim Hof, known as the Iceman, who planned to go without bottled oxygen to 7,250m wearing only shorts, socks and high climbing boots—"climbing in the cold gives a very powerful feeling," he explained—reached 7,400m before he reported to his teammates that his legs had started to freeze and he turned back. (In Kathmandu he said he was completely satisfied.)

The 2007 season's death toll of seven was well below spring of 2006's near-record of 11, and even further below it in terms of percentage of people on the mountain. The body of one of last year's climbers, David Sharp, whose lonely death drew a large amount of outraged commentary at the time, was moved away from the trail this spring at his family's request. (The 1996 Indian body known as Greenboots, a macabre landmark when not covered by snow, was not removed; it was underneath the snow this season, and anyway it is so solidly frozen in place that earlier efforts to move it failed.)

ELIZABETH HAWLEY, *Honorary Member, AAC, Nepal*

Everest, north side, Second Step free climb. On June 14 at 6:15 a.m. Leo Houlding and I free-climbed the Second Step on the North East Ridge of Chomolungma. Prior to the ascent a team of four high-altitude Sherpas led by Phurba Tashi Sherpa of Khumjung, Nepal, removed the ladder placed by the 1975 Chinese expedition. I led the pitch traditional style (ground up and setting my own gear), for protection placing a four-inch cam with a wood block stack to accommodate the wide crack. After an offwidth move, the climbing followed face holds. Besides the large cam, I placed two other cams and clipped two in-situ pitons. Given the altitude, exposure, and climactic consideration, the Second Step is approximately 5.10 in difficulty. We reached the summit at 9:55 on the same morning.

This is likely the highest technical free climb in the world. Not having the ladder in place makes the climb more demanding and replicates the situation that Mallory and Irvine would have encountered in 1924.

Previous climbers (Oscar Cadich, 1985, and Theo Fritsche, May 22,2001) have free-climbed the Second Step with the ladder in place. This was my second go to free climb this formidable barrier. In 1999 I matched feet on the next to last rung, having climbed the crack. Our climb in 2007 was filmed by Altitude Productions for a documentary titled *The Wildest Dream*. After our free ascent of the Second Step, Phurba Tashi Sherpa and team replaced the ladder at the request of the Chinese Mountaineering Association.

CONRAD ANKER, *AAC*

Everest, north side, Second Step history. A big Chinese team reported in 1960 that they had reached the top after scaling the Step by one man standing on another's shoulders—and getting badly frostbitten in the process. At the time there was widespread disbelief in the West, and when in 1975 another Chinese expedition climbed the same route, they put a ladder up the Step to make it easier to climb. Ever since, all summiters on this route have used it or its recent replacement.

As Anker and Houlding showed that the Step can be surmounted without ladder and ropes, it is theoretically possible that Mallory and Irvine did so too.

But Anker does not believe Mallory or Irvine could have gotten to the top in 1924. There were no fixed ropes, let alone any ladder, in place for them; their clothes were too thin for the extreme cold at the highest altitudes—Conrad wore such clothes at 7,500m and had no desire to climb in them—and the gear available in 1924 was not nearly as good as it is today. He could have added another reason: climbing skills had not been developed to today's higher standards. He feels it's amazing that they got to the Yellow Band above 8,100 meters, where Irvine's ice axe was found in 1933. All the way? Not likely.

ELIZABETH HAWLEY, *Honorary Member, AAC, Nepal*

Kubi Kangri (6,721m), first ascent; glacier measurements. The Kubi Tsangpo Headwaters Expedition 2007, which I headed, made the first ascent of Kubi Kangri, the highest peak in the Kubi Tsangpo headwaters, without the assistance of Sherpas. Our climbing leader, Atushi Senda, and six students reached the summit from C2 via the east ridge and descended to C2 via the north ridge. Beside the main objective of the first ascent, we attempted two unclimbed peaks—Absi (6,254m) and Langta-chen (6,248m)—surveyed glacial shrinkage; retraced the steps of a Japanese Buddhist monk, Ekai Kawa-guchi, who traveled through this remote borderland in 1900; and studied the relation between psychology and high altitude. We saw many wild animals around our base camp, including wild yaks, Tibetan wild donkeys, a snow leopard (just 20m from camp), and the tracks of a Himalayan brown bear (also known as the Yeti).

The headwaters of the great Yalung Tsangpo (which turns into the Bramaputra before joining the Ganges) is split between two branches at 82°54'E 30°20'N: the Kubi Tsangpo and the Chema-yundung. In 1907 Sven Hedin surveyed each river by volume and length and concluded that the Chema-yundung was the main stream.

The local Tibetan name of this mountain range is Chang-la Himal or Asja Himal. The Nepalese name is Chang-la Himal or Gorakh Himal; the range continues into the Ronglei Himal and Kanti Himal, including Kaqur Kangri (6,859m) east of this area. All peaks surrounding the headwaters of Kubi Tsangpo are called Kubi Kangri, and most of these peaks have no proper names. Access is difficult, either

Kubi Kangri (6,721m), the highest peak in the headwaters of the Kubi Tsangpo, one of the two main forks of the Yalung Tsangpo. The peak was climbed via its east ridge. *Toyoji Wada*

from Tibet or Nepal. In 1983 the Japanese Northwest Nepal Women's Expedition, headed by Kyoko Endo, failed on Kubi Kangri, the highest peak of the Chang-la Himal, largely due to the difficulty of access.

Nepalese locals are not well acquainted with Kubi Kangri, because other peaks on that side block their view of the peak, and so they don't have an individual name for it. However, as our Tibetan guides call this peak "Dong Dong" or Kubi Kangri, we applied the name Kubi Kangri to the highest peak (6,721m) in the range. The Tibetan side is easier to access, because the glacier complex is more stable. But only recently have bridges spanned the Yalung Tsangpo and its tributaries, which previously could only be crossed in winter. We owed our success on Kaqur Kangri (6,859m) in 2002 (*AAJ 2003*, p. 418) to this easier access.

There are many unidentified 6,000m–6,500m peaks around Kubi Kangri. On the border, from north to south, are Chang-la (6,563m), Kubi Kangri (6,271m), Langta-chen (6,248m), Asja (6,265m), Absi (6,254m), and Ngomo-dingding (6,133m). On the Tibetan side are yet more beautiful mountains, including Anro, Cnema-yundung, Gave-ting, and Mukchung. They are all virgin peaks, except for Kubi Kangri.

These mountains have gentle, heavily crevassed glaciers in the headwaters of Kubi Tsangpo. Some of the glaciers have glacial lakes at the terminus that can easily be reached by four-wheel-drive vehicles, except when it's raining hard, and the streams swell. The tracks run through yak and sheep pastures, utilized from April to August.

Foreigners are prohibited from entering this region without permission. In 2007, because of preparations for the 2008Olympic Games and the prevalence of chicken flu, the Chinese authorities were particularly nervous before giving permits.

We spent six days, from August 18 to 24, driving from Kathmandu through Zangmu, Nieram, Saga, New Tongpa, and Paryan to base camp at 4,800m on the shores of the Kubi Tsangpo. It was rainy and cloudy until we reached base camp, when it turned to sunshine.

Twelve kilometers of route finding through moraines to C1 at 5,600m was exhausting. It only got worse to C2, and we had to fix ropes. At 6 a.m. on September 14 we left C2 and reached the east ridge of Kubi Kangri. We had to fix ropes on 15 more pitches because of steepness. At 12:40 all seven members stood on the summit in bad weather. Soon after taking pictures, we descended the north ridge.

After Kubi Kangri we tried to climb two other peaks. Huge crevasses and icefalls stopped us low on Langta-chen. On Absi, after fixing ropes, we gave up at about 6,000m on its rock-and-ice northwest ridge. This peak would be suitable for alpine-style climbing.

There is lots of information about the glaciers of Nepal, but little on those of the Tibetan side of the Himalaya. In 1907 Sven Hedin made invaluable observations on the glaciers. In 2007 we could use Hedin's work to find evidence of receding glaciers in the last 100 years. We measured the termini of the Langta Glacier and the Absi Glacier. A picture that Hedin took in 1907 shows no glacial lake on either glacier. Soviet maps of 1946 also show no glacial lakes. But now there are. Comparing Hedin's picture to our observations leads us to estimate that in the last 100 years the Langta Glacier has retreated by 1,500m to 2,000m, and the Absi Glacier by 1,200m. [Editor's note: the *Japanese Alpine News Vol. 8*, May 2007 features articles on climate change and fast-melting glaciers in Bhutan, Central Tibet, Tien Shan, Altai, and Yunnan in China.]

TOYOJI WADA, *Japan*

Monda Kangri (6,425m), West Peak (6,292m), first ascents. Two Japanese parties have visited the Monda Kangri massif. The second party, consisting mainly of Hida Mountaineering Club members, made the first ascent of its main peak in 2007. The first party, in 2004, reached 6,100m by climbing its west glacier (*Japanese Alpine News Vol.6*) but were stopped by insuperable crevasses. Because the glacier is so complex, routes up the long but stable ridges seemed key to a successful climb.

Monda Kangri is only 140km south of Lhasa, and base camp near Lake Phulma can be reached in a day's drive. The 2007 party arrived at their 4,950m BC on September 9 and left on the 19th. They climbed the west ridge, which led to the 6,292m peak west of the main summit—West Peak or Peak III. From here they followed the main ridge to the top of Monda's main summit.

Lower parts of the west ridge were guarded by steep rock bands, but the team placed 200m of fixed rope and set C2 at 5,500m. On the 14th eight members made the first ascent of the West Peak from C2. On September 18 two members of the Hida Mountaineering Club connected the West and main peaks. I know no further details of the ascent. I came to know of this party's ascent of Monda Kangri through an account written by a member of the party, Shigeo Tamichi, who had joined the team from the Fukui Section of the Japanese Alpine Club and reported the ascent in the JAC monthly bulletin Yama No.753. I contacted the Hida Mountaineering Club, but they were reluctant to give information because of trouble with payment of the climbing fee. It is disappointing that a mountaineer would hide what he has done. If the Hida MC thought the fee unreasonable, they might not pay it, but they should announce their reasons and publish the records. If reasonable, they should pay the fee.

KEI KURACHI, *Japan*

Yalaxianbo (6,635m), first ascent. The Yamagata Mountaineering Federation (northern Japan) made the first ascent of Yalaxianbo, near the border with Bhutan, to commemorate its 50th anniversary in 2007. This peak is located at 28°45'N, 91°50'E, 135km south of Lhasa in the Shannan Prefecture of the Tibetan Autonomous Region. Among the local Tibetan people Yalaxianbo means "a holy peak" where the gods abide. It is the highest mountain in the headwaters of the Yarlung Valley.

A party from the federation headed by Yoshiki Itoh first attempted Yalaxianbo via the north ridge in August and September 2001. They were stopped by bad weather. In May 2006 Inaizumi and Takahashi made a reconnaissance of the east face from the Gayue Valley. The 2007 expedition was comprised of Masahiko Inaizumi (leader), Toshinori Kasuya (deputy leader), Makoto Takahashi (climbing leader), with six other Japanese members and four Nepalese Sherpas.

The team reached Lhasa from Xining by the Qinghai-Tibet Plateau Railway, and on September 20 arrived at Chudagong village at the foot of Yalaxiabo. On September 23, after the Sherpas arrived, they started ferrying loads to base camp. No pack animals (donkeys) were available. BC was established at 4,750m, and C1 was set up at 5,250m, from which route-fixing commenced. On October 6 C2 was placed at 5,600m on the rocks, C3 at 5,850m on the snow plateau. [The route climbs the northeast aspect of Yalaxianbo to the snow plateau, then bears left (south-southeast) to a steep snow wall, then sharply right (west-northwest) to the main summit—Ed.] On October 16 Takahashi, Yoshida, and Phunuru Sherpa stood on the summit, before returning to C3. On October 18 they left BC for Lhasa, and on October 22 the China

Mountaineering Association held a party in Beijing to celebrate the first ascent.

TAMOTSU NAKAMUA, *Japanese Alpine News*

Cholong Kangri (6,182m), first ascent. On September 30, 2007, John Deans (U.K.), Greg Vernovage (U.S.), Kurt Wedberg (U.S.), and I summited an unclimbed Tibetan peak located by GPS at N 28°82, E 90°30. Leaving base camp at 3:30 a.m. we ascended from 16,045' (N 78°79, E 90°32) to a cache at 18,110'

The northwest face of Yalaxianbo (6,635m). The first ascent followed approximately the peak's left skyline. *Yamagata Mountaineering Federation*

(28°81, E 90°31) on the south ridge. We roped up and with crampons ascended the southern ridgeline, staying to the west side of the cornice, and arriving at the summit ridge at 2 p.m. From there we traversed to the northwest, to the true high point on the ridge. The descent followed the same route along the south ridge, and we arrived into base camp in darkness by 8p.m.

In 2006 we had visited the region to reconnoiter this cluster of four peaks. The locals named this one Cholang Kangri; it is two peaks to the east of the peak named Jangsung Lhomo on the 1:100,000 scale topographic map by Mi Desheng. Our peak is unnamed on the map and given an elevation of 6,182m (6,234m GPS). We chose the route along the southeasterly ridge because keeping to the ridge on the approach avoided crevassed glaciers on either side.

CHRISTIAN BERGUM, *AAC*

Christian Bergum, John Deans, and Greg Vernovage climbing the southeast ridge on the first ascent of Cholong Kangri (6,182m). In the background (looking south) is Kula Kangri (7,554m) and peaks along the Tibet-Bhutan border. *Kurt Wedberg*

AMERICAN ALPINE CLUB GRANTS

The American Alpine Club provides resources for climbers and explorers to attempt new challenges, conduct scientific research, and conserve mountain environments. The AAC awards nearly $40,000 annually, although the size and number of awards vary from year to year. In 2007, the McNeill-Nott Award was created in honor of Karen McNeill and Sue Nott; the award is cosponsored by Mountain Hardwear. For more information on all the grant programs, please visit www.americanalpineclub.org.

    Grant recipients' original objectives for 2007 are reported below; in some cases, they may have decided to attempt other objectives. Expeditions labeled with an asterisk (*) are reported in this Journal.

LYMAN SPITZER CUTTING EDGE AWARDS (2007)

Jonny Copp and Micah Dash, Boulder, Colorado*
Unclimbed Shafat Fortress in the Zanskar Mountains of India
$3,000

Scott DeCapio, Estes Park, Colorado*
Attempt on K7 West in Pakistan
$2,750

Samuel Johnson, Anchorage, Alaska*
Big-wall route on unclimbed "Latok II 3/4" in Pakistan
$1,000

Cory Richards, Canmore, Alberta
Southeast face of Huantsán in Peru
$1,500

Dave Turner, Sacramento, California*
Solo attempt on new big-wall route on Cerro Escudo, Chile
$1,000

Josh Wharton, Rifle, Colorado*
North ridge of Latok I in Pakistan
$2,750

MCNEILL-NOTT AWARDS (2007)

Jessica Drees, Seattle, Washington*
New routes in Fox Jaw Cirque, Greenland
$3,000

Joseph Puryear, Leavenworth, Washington*
New route on Mt. Siguniang in China
$1,500

Jonathan Sullivan, Castle Rock, Colorado*
Unclimbed 5,000-meter-plus peaks in China
$1,500

MOUNTAIN FELLOWSHIPS (FALL 2006)

Michael Bromberg, Crested Butte, Colorado*
New routes and ski descents near the "Backside Glacier" in Alaska
$400

Kyle Dempster, Salt Lake City, Utah*
Big-wall climb in the Gran Sabana area of Venezuela
$800 (REI Challenge Fund)

Jessica Drees, Seattle, Washington*
New rock routes in southeastern Greenland
$800

Colin Haley, Mercer Island, Washington
New route on Cerro Torre, Patagonia
$400

Benjamin Venter, Truckee, California
Climbs in Patagonia
$800

Erin Whorton, Seattle, Washington*
New rock routes in southeastern Greenland
$800

MOUNTAIN FELLOWSHIPS
(SPRING 2007)

Brad Cabot, Seattle, Washington*
Unclimbed peaks in western Greenland
$850 (REI Challenge Fund)

Ian Nicholson, Seattle, Washington*
*New route on the Blade in British Columbia's
Waddington Range*
$800 (John R. Hudson Fund)

Matt Othmer, Philadelphia, Pennsylvania*
East face of Cerro Aratiyope in Venezuela
$850 (John R. Hudson and Rick Mosher
funds)

Althea Rogers, Troy, New York*
Unclimbed peaks in western Greenland
$850 (REI Challenge Fund)

Kelly Ryan, Port Potter Valley, California*
Unclimbed peaks in western Greenland
$850

Eli Stein, Los Angeles, California
Youth meet in Dolomites of Italy
$340

ZACK MARTIN BREAKING BARRIERS
GRANT (2007)

Fabrizio Zangrilli, Boulder, Colorado
*Attempt on a new route on K2 and work on a
new girls' school in Khane, Pakistan*
$1,765

2007 RESEARCH GRANTS

*The Arthur K. Gilkey Memorial Research
Fund, the William Putnam Research Fund,
and the Bedayn Research Fund*

Teresa Chuang, Berkeley, California
Shifts in species ranges as a result of climate change
$1,500

Julie Crawford, Mancos, Colorado
*Continuing work on the Global Observation
Research Initiative in Alpine Environments
(GLORIA)*
$1,400

Jennifer Geib, Columbia, Missouri
*How alpine plants' pollination "niche
breadth" may affect their response to
pollinator density*
$1,000

Jeanette Hagan, Santa Barbara, California
*Evolution of the central Sierra Nevada frontal
fault zone*
$1,000

Timothy Jang, Sylmar, California
*Injury and treatment patterns of Southern
California climbers*
$500

Phillip Keating, Bloomington, Indiana
*Mapping high-elevation polyepis forests in
Cayambe-Coca Ecological Reserve in north-
eastern Ecuador*
$750

Stephen Matter, Cincinnati, Ohio
*Rate of tree-line rise on Jumpingpound Ridge
in Alberta, Canada*
$1,000

Ryan McKeon, Bozeman, Montana
*Relationship between Quaternary glaciation
and modern topology in the San Juan
Mountains of southwestern Colorado;
implications for an arid "glacial buzz saw"*
$1,000

Erich Pietzsch, Bozeman, Montana
*Wet slab avalanches in Glacier National Park,
Montana*
$1,500

Jeremy Shakun, Corvallis, Oregon
*Developing a cosmogenic chronology of
tropical glaciation in the Peruvian Andes*
$750

BOOK REVIEWS

EDITED BY DAVID STEVENSON

Yosemite in the Sixties. GLEN DENNY. SANTA BARBARA, CA. PATAGONIA AND T. ADLER BOOKS. 2007. 106 BLACK AND WHITE PHOTOS. 144 PAGES. HARDCOVER. $60.00.

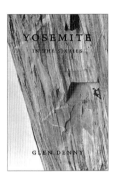

If you take a chunk of the real world and shove it through a lens, *voila*, you have a photograph. Some would say you have "captured" the moment or "recorded" the event. Perhaps, but we shouldn't treat all photographs the same. Some represent but others illustrate while still others evoke. The impact of some photos depends in part on the artistic decisions made by the photographer and also on what the viewer brings to them, and the more this is so, the more reality recedes.

For those of us who were lucky enough to throw down a sleeping bag in Camp 4 in the 1950s and 1960s, Denny's pictures serve as reminders of the contradictions of our youth. We sought freedom through the construction of iron ladders on big walls; we went one up on the material world by deciding we could do without; we were fierce individualists (as, I think, Denny's photos reveal) and at heart loners who formed friendships that (usually) survived the grab bag of quirks, tics, phobias, and neuroses that shaped our personalities.

For those who came to Yosemite later (or have yet to come), Denny's pictures will have to stand on their own. While they can be viewed as mementos from a bygone era, they also transcend time as much as they attest to it. The cubist geometry of Yosemite's walls hasn't changed. Denny sees the rock as found sculpture and takes delight in the play of light and shadow (in two photos, he sees a climber as shadow). Almost half of the photos show climbers climbing. In many of them the climber is small and the rock vast, and, since we can't see the antiquated gear being used, we might imagine that the pictures were taken at any time in Yosemite's climbing history.

In other photos the tools of the time are on full display—a shot of Chouinard sorting gear for a big wall, other shots in which bongs and Lost Arrow pitons and aluminum oval carabiners crowd picnic tables, and shots on climbs that show the use of Goldline rope and curious footwear.

Also specifically of the time are the portraits of climbers, about a third of the collection. It's hard to imagine that Denny managed to photograph everyone who was doing significant climbs in the 1960s, but it seems that way. Chouinard, Roper, Robbins, Harding, Kor, Pratt, Frost, Rowell, Bridwell, Sacherer, and Schmitz appear more than once, and a number of other climbers can regard themselves as duly memorialized. In an extended essay in the book, Steve Roper remarks on Denny's ability to capture not only the faces of these climbers but also their personalities. In most of these shots, if the climber was aware of Denny's lens he didn't show it, and so the face is more interesting, more revealing, than if the climber had been asked to say "cheese."

In the 1960s, climbers camped in the upper part of Camp 4, an area now out of bounds, and Denny offers about 15 photos depicting life in the camp, including a classic shot of a bear head down in a garbage can. There are also photos of a wedding in the meadow and a series on winter climbing.

Rounding out the collection are several peopleless photos, shots that remind us of the Valley's beauty, both as a whole and in its parts, and that could give some people the notion that being up on one of those walls would be an exceptional experience. Some of these pictures have led others to mention Ansel Adams, and this is quite understandable. In the 1950s and 1960s, Best's Studio in the Valley exhibited many photos by Adams, including one on the front porch that was four or five feet high and showed Salathé and Nelson on their epic 1947 ascent of the Lost Arrow. Denny includes an almost identical photo with Harding and Bob Swift replacing the pioneers. But there are significant differences between the two photographers. Adams rarely photographed people, and he used a large format camera mounted on a tripod. Denny used a hand-held 35mm camera. That said, both photographers approach their subjects with a strong esthetic sense. Although Denny loves the marriage of climber and rock, his photographs could easily impress someone with no interest in rock climbing.

The book is handsomely produced and would grace any coffee table. In fact, that is a good place for it since it will repay repeated visits. Already the book has won the National Outdoor Book Award for Design and Artistic Merit and the 2007 Banff Mountain Book Festival award as Best Book—Mountain Image.

JOE FITSCHEN

Forever on the Mountain. JAMES M. TABOR. NEW YORK: W.W. NORTON & COMPANY LTD., 2007. BLACK AND WHITE PHOTOS AND TWO SCHEMATICS, A THOROUGH INDEX, AND A RECOMMENDED READING SECTION. 400 PAGES. $26.95.

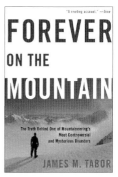

In 1967 three Colorado climbers, led by Howard Snyder, joined forces with a team of nine Pacific Northwest climbers, led by Joe Wilcox, because the National Park Service in charge of Mt. McKinley required parties to be at least four in number. The fourth member of the Colorado team had to drop out at the last moment, which thrust together these two teams who did not know each other. It was not to be a happy marriage and would end in tragedy when seven of the Wilcox party died from exposure some days after they (six of them; one stayed in high camp) attempted to climb to the summit from their 17,900-foot camp during a lull in a fierce storm. From the evidence later gathered, it seems they persevered on their descent until the elements overcame them and their high-camp companion. Their desire to gain the summit and their relative inexperience were surely the key elements that clouded their judgment and precluded their doing the prudent thing, which would have been to descend from high camp. This decision was theirs, not, as suggested years ago, that of their leader, Joe Wilcox.

Over the past 40 years, my assumption regarding the causes was similar to most of my peers: a mountaineering disaster that was the result of inadequate leadership (Joe Wilcox), expertise, and conditioning, exacerbated by a one-two punch of severe weather events. Many of us relied on our personal experiences on the mountain, mine being a 45-day climb of the East Buttress with five others in 1963. We also read the report and analysis written in the journal I now edit, *Accidents in North American Mountaineering*. Shortly thereafter, Howard Snyder's book, *The Hall of the Mountain King*, laid the blame solely on Joe Wilcox' doorstep. Wilcox' book, *White Winds*, not published until 1983, did not change many opinions. But James M. Tabor's thoroughly researched book has certainly done so—with one exception.

In chapters often titled with a variation on well-known phrases and titles—e.g., "Lone Man Walking," "Divided We Falter," and "Pictures of an Expedition"—there are references to historical climbs including anecdotes from other mountaineering disasters, scientific analyses of such conditions as hypothermia and hypoxia, and portraits of individuals who have contributed to our understanding of mountains, exploration, and the human animal. One of the book's great strengths is how these details make the story interesting to an audience broader than just seasoned mountaineers.

Two Alaskan mountaineering icons, Bradford Washburn and bush pilot Don Sheldon, are scrutinized for their roles in this saga. While Tabor provides a balanced view, acknowledging their positive contributions, it becomes clear that these men were significant antagonists to Joe Wilcox in particular, and to the expedition in general, throughout the drama. The two chief administrators of Denali National Park do not fare well in Tabor's analysis, primarily because of their indecision, even though Tabor points out that they "…cannot be faulted for not doing a job they did not know how to do."

This is where my exception lies. Tabor lays considerable blame on the NPS for not attempting to make airdrops and not inserting rescue personnel. Daryl Miller, the current South District Chief Ranger stationed in Talkeetna, who has been intimate with the mountain for more than 20 years, said to me in an e-mail, "That particular storm would have prevented any outside help for days, and the seven climbers, including the one left at the 17,900-foot high camp, would have perished regardless of any rescue effort assembled anywhere from anyone. I disagree with Tabor regarding his assumption that the National Park Service could have prevented this terrible accident." Wayne Merry, the one ranger on hand at the time with climbing experience, put it another way: "… an over flight by a capable aircraft during one of the brief windows of clear weather might just possibly have identified the situation and dropped supplies. Very unlikely, but possible. But we didn't know the situation. So if there was a failing, *it is that we didn't try to find out.*"

About 30 very well known mountaineers are mentioned as reference points for particular details relevant to the climb, such as avalanches, falling into crevasses, surviving difficult bivouacs, and being affected by fatigue, cold, and altitude. In addition there are unlikely references to individuals such as J.D. Salinger, Malcolm Gladwell, Ferdinand Magellan, Napoleon I, Martha Stewart, and Elisabeth Kubler-Ross. The reader will enjoy learning why they appear.

We learn much about each expedition member. Tabor brings those who perished back to life and gives us a full picture of the survivors, including a final chapter that describes his recent encounters with them. In the end one can only conclude that this expedition, comprised of two disparate groups, came to a bad end not so much because of leadership and personalities, though they play their roles, but because (1) after one team had summited, six of the remaining Wilcox contingent decided to go for the summit instead of descending, and (2) they were nailed by the kind of perfect storm that would have leveled the best of climbers.

This book won the Banff Festival Award for good reason. If you decide to do so, best to set aside the time it takes you to read 400 pages in one sitting.

JED WILLIAMSON

Woman on the Rocks: The Mountaineering Letters of Ruth Dyar Menden-hall. EDITED BY VALERIE MENDENHALL COHEN. BISHOP, CA: SPOTTED DOG PRESS, 2006. 352 PAGES. $18.95.

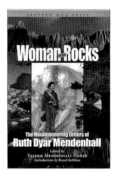

In 1937 two young cousins joined the Sierra Club, and so, apparently, began a lifelong joyous romp through an Arcadian landscape: where bright voices of companions echoed like the calls of birds; where the touch of lichen-covered granite felt like an ecstatic revelation; where a single turn filled the mind with a burst of notes; where a climber might suddenly leap into the air, dodging the whistling rockfall that swept below him, to the "great amusement" of his partners; where a girl discovering an old shoe with human bones might declare, "All my life I have hankered after finding a corpse"; and where everyone would hurry off to bed as a great golden moon overflowed the sky, brimming with visions of the next day's pleasures.

A realm of golden laughter and play flowing in a ceaseless allegro, scarcely interrupted by reminders of death, with all the force of life itself—these are the origins of California climbing as one young woman depicted them. Soon after their first outing, the cousins Ruth Dyar and Phoebe Russell became the editors of the *Mugelnoos*, the Sierra Club's ski-mountaineering newsletter. For Ruth it was the beginning of a life dedicated to alpine climbing and skiing—and to a voluminous correspondence about her pursuits. By the time she died in 1989, she had written thousands of letters to her family and friends. She also kept carbon copies for a future memoir.

Woman on the Rocks: the Mountaineering Letters of Ruth Dyar Mendenhall represents the youngest daughter Valerie Mendenhall Cohen's efforts to compile an approximation of this unwritten book, with passages selected from the more than nine hundred pages her mother left behind. The result is a series of lyrical—and highly personal—echoes from a now scarcely imaginable world. Eight years before he met Ruth at Tahquitz, Ruth's future husband, John Mendenhall, may have been the first Californian to belay and pitch out a climb (on Laurel Mountain in 1930). As the couple wandered through what was still largely a vertical wilderness, the Mendenhalls put up numerous North American first ascents that included the southeast face of California's Mt. Whitney, the north face of Wyoming's Teewinot, and Canada's Mt. Confederation. Ruth continued to edit the *Mugelnoos* until 1978, while publishing books on climbing techniques and backcountry cooking and eventually joining the American Alpine Club's board of directors.

As a pre-pioneer of California female climbers, Ruth performs a dual role; to her climbing partners she is both a "manly" comrade and a lady: "It is odd how they [male climbing partners] might know a wench can charge up a 14,000-foot peak with great stamina, but regard her as unable to fetch a cup of water from a lake two feet away." Her early prose is almost self-consciously girlish, with the sort of gushing ebullience that one of Jane Austen's more vivacious heroines might use, mentioning a hat "that excited much comment" or a climb during which "as soon as one [man] got out of sight around a corner of rock, the other would begin to flirt."

Over time another voice emerges, with a deeper, more mature consciousness of the wild. Of her journey back from her first attempt on Mt. Confederation with John in 1940, she writes, "We had seen the mountains, not as a pretty scene to be looked at through a glass window…. We had lived the mountains—the cold and the snow and wet; we had slept on the rocks, smelled them, eaten smoke and ashes without food, climbed over the downed timber, shivered, drank the rivers and the lakes; they would be a part of us, not postcard scenes."

Throughout her life, climbing remained for the letter writer a means to experience the "highpoints of existence," the "peaks of exaltation." Lowpoints are brushed over with a puzzling innocence about accidents and consequences. "In the mountains," she writes on the top of Mt. Whitney, when she learns that World War II has begun, "the youngest, the strongest, the most skilled, the bravest win—in war they die." That the best may die in the hills as well is something the letters hardly acknowledge.

For the most part, the book is a wild, continual shout of joy. What it isn't, as a result, is a gripping narrative. And the reader may well wonder whether the true story might lie in those moments of real commitment that Ruth downplays as she tries to reassure family members. Or else it lies somewhere between that transcendent life she found in the heights and the daily struggles of her domestic existence. Glimpses appear in the editor's notes of untold family conflicts and climbing near-misses, and of one daughter's ultimate rejection of the lifestyle her parents chose.

But as its editor writes, the book is not its author's polished creation: "This is a human story. This is not the story Ruth would have produced for publication." So why, the reader might ask, should anyone other than a historian keep turning the pages? For the reason that Royal Robbins praises Ruth in his introduction: because she had, in her own manner, "the heart of a mountaineer"—a conviction that climbing might offer a pure source of mental, physical, and spiritual beauty. And because today Ruth's belief in the sheer enjoyment of adventure seems far more radical and eccentric than it should.

Among her papers, Ruth's daughter found the introduction to the unwritten book, in which Ruth justifies it best: "Climbing used to be such fun, old climbers so good to new ones.... Now is a time of specialization, foreign expeditions, and public interest in climbing. But then were the great beginnings, and the best climbing friends one could have had. Nowadays the climbers swarm over the earth—but in our heyday, the new routes, the unclimbed summits, lay closer at home, and perhaps were even harder to reach."

KATIE IVES

Brotherhood of the Rope: the Biography of Charlie Houston. BERNADETTE MCDONALD. SEATTLE: THE MOUNTAINEERS BOOKS, 2007. HARDCOVER $34.95; PAPERBACK $18.95.

Most contemporary climbers know the name Charles Houston, but many aren't sure where or when they've heard it, and fewer still can recall his achievements. Until you bring up K2—high and wild K2. K2 was the scene of one of the most remarkable mountaineering tales of all time: that of the 1953 American K2 expedition and the dramatic fall while the team of climbers was lowering Art Gilkey.

Having grown up in Los Alamos, where George Bell lived for much of his life, I was very aware of the significance on the 1953 expedition from my early high school years, and in the early 1980s, borrowed *Savage Mountain* from a friend's father, Eiichi Fukushima, himself part of the Mount Vinson first ascent team.

The 1953 trip was the epitome of friendship—a group of friends, some quite new to each other, deciding to evacuate another of the brethren from a dangerous mountain together, as a team, and possibly the most cohesive team of climbers that has ever existed. *Savage Mountain* is a good entré into the lives of a remarkable group of American mountaineers whose important climbing activities spanned many years, but in *Brotherhood of the Rope: the Biography of Charlie Houston*, Bernadette McDonald has given us the long view of perhaps one of the more significant members of that 1953 brotherhood: Charlie Houston.

Brought up in a setting of wealth and privilege, Houston stands out not so much for what he accomplished, but for how he did it—with grace and humility and diplomacy, and a continual questioning of his own self-worth and achievements. Indeed, McDonald so focuses on Houston's insecurities that a non-climber-type reader might think he was some kind of insecure neurotic. To me, his story is remarkably like the stories of all climbers—the insecure-while-bold, navel-staring, ponderous bunch that climbers are.

But the story's a good one, and it overshadows McDonald's apparent qualms about Houston's personality. After an apprenticeship in the Alps, he joined Brad Washburn's expedition to then-unclimbed Mt. Crillon in southern Alaska in 1933. It was with Washburn, Bob Bates, Ad Carter, and Terris Moore that Houston became part of the legendary Harvard Five, a group of 1930s mountaineers whose climbing adventures would span the globe and several decades. Although they were unsuccessful on Crillon, Houston learned a great deal from Washburn, a true master of Alaskan expeditioneering.

"…Charlie learned from Washburn the critical importance of sound leadership," McDonald notes. "Potential for a power struggle existed between the two, since both had strong personalities. Washburn recalled a small misunderstanding over some routefinding when he had to struggle to retain control of the situation. Despite the disagreement, Washburn contended that Charlie was the strongest climber in the group—much stronger than Bates. But Charlie insisted that he took a subservient role on Crillon, absorbing what he could from Washburn."

The following year, Charlie's father Oscar—something of an adventurer himself—suggested an attempt on Foraker, the fourth highest mountain on the continent, and one that "had not yet been mapped; few people had been near it, and none had described it." Yet somehow Oscar had procured a sketch of the mountain. Charlie took what he'd learned on Crillon, and, with T. Graham Brown, Charles Storey, Chychele Waterston, Carl Anderson, and Oscar headed to the Yukon, where they climbed Foraker. Although Washburn, who was not invited, returned and climbed Crillon that year, he and Houston would never climb together again.

In 1936 Houston and several American youngsters joined forces with a handful of famed British mountaineers, including Noel Odell, Bill Tillman, Peter Lloyd, and T. Graham Brown, to climb Nanda Devi, the highest peak that would be climbed until Annapurna, in 1950. Although Houston and Odell managed to establish a high camp at 25,000 feet, Houston ate contaminated meat, and had to descend the next day. Tillman and Odell continued to the summit.

Houston's next major climb was his almost-as-famous 1938 attempt on K2, with Bob Bates, Dick Burdsall, Paul Petzoldt, Bill House, and Briton Norman Streatfield, in which Houston and Petzoldt reached 26,000 feet. The failure was not entirely without achievement, as the climbers cracked the nut on a route that would, ultimately, become the standard route on the peak.

The 1953 expedition is also documented in detail, but thankfully does not distract from Houston and Bates' own book on the subject (*K2: The Savage Mountain*), nor from the other sections of Houston's life that are so well documented in *Brotherhood*.

Most readers will be interested in the other important aspect of Houston's life: his research into altitude's effects on the human body. Beginning early in his career, in WWII, Houston played a leading role in researching how oxygen and lack of it affected pilots, and then mountaineers, and pretty much anyone else whose life required them to get high.

In 1967 Houston got involved with the high-altitude physiology study (HAPS) on the upper slopes of Canada's Mt. Logan, an ongoing series of summer experiments that would last until 1979. By 1975 Houston and his research team had identified and described acute mountain sickness (AMS), pulmonary edema, cerebral edema, and retinal involvement, four of the basic conditions considered standard for high-altitude mountaineers to know today.

"He always backed [his observations] up with research," McDonald writes. "He offered up countless examples of preventative and coping measures for the debilitating effects of HAPE. His findings were used by climbers around the world, particularly those going to the highest range—the Himalaya. They changed the way climbers planned their acclimatization programs and how they treated and reacted to the early symptoms of high-altitude sickness. His research firmly established Houston as one of the world's leading authorities on the subject—he undoubtedly saved lives in the mountains."

His devotion to altitude research was a theme throughout, and, eventually, in 1980, Houston started work on *Going Higher*, a groundbreaking book that brought together medicine and altitude in a carefully woven balance. Self-published, it wildly outsold his expectations, has become the standard resource on the subject, and is currently in its fourth edition.

Houston was also an advocate for drug rehabilitation programs, and for community and family medicine, His devotion to his family is well-documented in this biotome. In *Brotherhood*, readers will find a treasure of American mountaineering's most famous ascents, stories, characters, and periods, all told from the perspective of one of American mountaineering's most noble sons.

CAMERON M. BURNS

The Eiger Obsession: Facing the Mountain That Killed My Father. JOHN HARLIN III. NEW YORK: SIMON & SCHUSTER, 2007. 283 PAGES. $26.00.

For more than 20 years I've known John Harlin III, not really well, but not simply casually either. During all that time I never got up the nerve to ask him what it was like to be the son of *the* John Harlin, the Blond God, probably the finest American alpinist of his day, the first American to climb the Eiger Nordwand, and of course the martyr of the Eiger Direttissima. Yet I had a strong sense that father and son were utterly different kinds of people. The John Harlin I knew seemed soft-spoken, sensitive, a good listener, a patient and skillful editor, and the farthest thing imaginable from an egomaniac. I only met John Harlin *père* once, when he was the surprise speaker at an AAC annual banquet in Boston in the early 1960s, where he gave a slide show that had the audience gasping. Everyone, however, knew the Harlin of legend: impossibly tough, fanatically driven, movie-star handsome, with a steely calm in the face of impending disaster.

To climb the Eiger in homage to one's lost father, with IMAX filmmakers in attendance and a book contract in hand, could have amounted to little more than a stunt. Neither book nor film would have been produced to celebrate what would have been merely the umpteenth ascent of the 1938 route without that connection—even though the climber was a man in his late forties. But it turns out that *The Eiger Obsession* is a moving, surprising, deeply introspective, and altogether splendid work. In our vast literature of mountaineering, there is no other memoir quite like it.

John Harlin III was only nine years old when his father's fixed rope broke and he plunged to his death in 1966. With disarming honesty, the son writes, "I wish I knew my father. All my life people have asked me how much I remember him, and the answer is that I really don't know." (I guess other friends were less reticent than I about asking the key question.) Because of that distance and uncertainty, *Obsession* is as much a work of biographical research as it is a memoir. Yet the personal strands of the story add a trenchant testimony to a kind of mountain writing that is just beginning to be explored, most notably by Maria Coffey: the impact of death on the loved ones left behind.

Harlin's book goes deepest when he plumbs the sorrows of his long-suffering mother and of his devastated younger sister. The book becomes almost shocking as Harlin unblinkingly recounts the less-than-admirable behavior of some of his father's closest but most difficult partners, especially Gary Hemming and Dougal Haston. (With role models like that, who came to the ends they did, it is a wonder that the younger Harlin climbed at all!)

Finally, as Harlin does battle with his mountain nemesis, freely acknowledging the spasms of fear and doubt that climbing writers all too often suppress, the book becomes a rattling good adventure tale.

When John Harlin III won the AAC Literary Award last year, the honor was long overdue. Year after year, as chairman of the selection committee, Harlin refused to allow his name to be put in nomination, despite the ardent pleas of his colleagues. When he finally stepped down, the committee could pin the medal to his jacket lapel. And if anyone in the climbing world still wonders why Harlin so richly deserves the award, the answer is simple: read this powerful and utterly genuine book.

DAVID ROBERTS

Higher than the Eagle Soars: A Path to Everest. STEPHEN VENABLES. LONDON: HUTCHINSON, 2007. 370 PAGES. HARDCOVER. $49.95.

Don't be scared by the clunky title—*Higher than the Eagle Soars* manages to be both thrilling and introspective. It is a rare climbing retrospective that can hold my interest from first to last, but this one did. The retrospective is a daunting genre, because it draws lines of connection from youth's telling impulses—the tree that needed climbing in the front yard—to adulthood's raging struggles—that ice-choked crack in the Karakoram. But Venables pulls it off, engaging the reader from early music lessons, through the mountaineering club at Oxford, all the way to Everest.

Stephen Venables is a familiar name to most climbers, first thanks to his resumé of hard, lightweight ascents in the big mountains of Asia, and second because of the award-fetching books documenting those climbs. *Higher* offers an overview of this one climbing life, and delves deeper into the man behind the frostbite. Venables is an accomplished writer, and readers warm to his affable, understated style. For instance, before a hard first ascent in Peru he observes, "Some basic climbing ability is always helpful when pioneering new routes in the world's greater ranges, but what really counts is making yourself comfortable and having a good night's sleep." He proceeds to sketch this climb, like the others in this book, with a satisfying portrait of physical risk and emotional response. It is Venables' ability to put the reader in his own quaking boots that makes him a master of the climbing narrative.

The book's climbing tales rub elbows with lions of the British 80's scene—Dick Renshaw and Lindsay Griffin, Alex MacIntyre and Peter Boardman—and takes us from the Lake District to the Highlands, from the Alps to Pakistan, to Nepal and back. Throughout, Venables dramatizes the joy of exploring other countries when climbing is your entrée—you meet another culture in the intense focus of the trip, and thereby break through to something more than a tourist's jaded comfort.

One psychological dynamic most of us can identify with is the rat whose gnawing Venables can't help but feed. Climb, no matter the cost in comfort, relationships, career, or digits. He captures that familiar agony that drives an otherwise sane person to take beautiful scenery on a beautiful day and focus it all into one line's grim contest with gravity. "I cursed the immaculate weather, and wished there were some way of avoiding my self-imposed destiny…. Fear of future regret outweighed fear of the risks." This is vintage Venables: honest, accurate, and bold, without being proud. On a lighter note, the book's color photographs offer a minatory lesson in the history of British glasses, from bad rectangular frames, to worse round peepers.

In sum, the climbing stories are engaging, and in many cases able retellings of epics familiar from his eight previous books. What distinguishes *Higher* is what distinguishes Venables himself—the range of interests. For example, these thoughts on Yorkminster Cathedral: "entranced by the pale gleam of its Tadcaster stone and the eclectic mishmash of styles, from the restrained lancets of the north transept to the floral exuberance of the great west window, all of it somehow adding up organically, in the way that those great Gothic cathedrals do, to something huge and timeless and emotionally uplifting." We don't generally get architectural rhapsodizing in climbing books. But like Ruskin before him, Venables brings the alpine aesthetic back to the city. Moreover, he is always keen to talk about classical music and opera, offers anecdotes from his days as thespian and set-designer, and slides references to canonical literature into his stories, in a humble, welcome manner.

This book ends in 1988 on Everest's Kangshung Face. This brilliant ascent is the conclusion to *Higher* and the culmination of Venables' many alpine adventures. The action of a four-man team pushing a new route up Everest without oxygen is powerful and engaging. What is more, the final ascent offers hallucinations that bring back many of the characters and experiences from his earlier life. Thus the narrative comes full circle, and the final chapters function like one of Venables' beloved symphonic codas—this conclusion restates the major theme, prolongs it enjoyably, and finally pushes it to a vigorous end. So, to mountain readers I say, get out your reading glasses, don your symphony frock, and enjoy the grand narrative Venables orchestrates on these pages.

JEFF McCARTHY

High Infatuation, A Climber's Guide to Love and Gravity. STEPH DAVIS.
SEATTLE: THE MOUNTAINEERS BOOKS, 2007. 224 PAGES. BLACK AND WHITE
PHOTOS. $16.95

High Infatuation, Steph Davis' collection of memoirs and essays, is a
journey through her climbing career, starting at age 18 on the cliffs of
the Potomac in Maryland. Davis quickly fell in love with climbing and
moved to Colorado for grad school, learning to trad and alpine climb in
places like the Diamond, Indian Creek, and Yosemite. After school she
lived in her grandmother's old station wagon with her dog, following
the seasonal cycles on the dirtbag climbing tour and returning to Moab, Patagonia, and Yosemite
year after year.

Written more like a journal, chapters range from climbing stories to personal vignettes
and are not all connected in chronology or theme. By the book's end though, Davis has grown
and found her passions through climbing. Numerous black and white photos add character
and context. During travels to Patagonia, Baffin Island, Kyrgyzstan, and Pakistan, she accepts
challenges and her own insecurities, finally learning to trust herself: "Pummeled by doubts,…
I craved the uncertainty of knowing that success or failure was entirely up to me," she writes,
before rope-soloing Peak 4,520m in Kyrgyzstan. In Baffin, Davis spends a month on a wall with
two friends, and her writing becomes calmer as time under the midnight sun ticks by without a
clock. There, her landscape descriptions are more creative: "I sit for hours…watching low clouds
creep like dragons along the ice corridors below."

As her world-view widens, the writing becomes richer with descriptions of people and
interactions, humor and humility. In Pakistan, Davis' team befriends a military general, who
allows them access to the remote Kondus Valley where they hope to climb. There, close to the
war-ravaged Kashmir region, she connects with local Muslim women.

Between climbs and expeditions, Davis ruminates on her complex relationship with
climber Dean Potter, whom she eventually marries. While their emotionally charged relationship is trying, they do come together for some incredible climbs, including the first one-day
ascent of Torre Egger in Patagonia.

When Davis moves away from expedition climbing to harder free routes, she encounters
a new set of challenges. At first, she admits, she preferred the risk of real physical danger on big
routes to the artificial pressure of failing on a sport route. Overcoming this, she free-climbs El
Cap, first by way of Freerider, then Freerider in a day, and finally on the Salathe. She realizes her
strongest tools are her determination and strategy and uses them to her advantage on the route.
"It took all my drive and more discipline than I knew I had to free the Salathe," she says.

Davis has been visible in the U.S. climbing community in the past 10 years and has not
escaped criticism, which she discusses: "After all the years I'd spent as a climber, trying to get away
from being judged as a young woman," she says, "I realized I'd been judging myself that way."

Davis' writing is at times eloquent, woven with lovely metaphors, and the stories are very
personal, giving the reader insight into her perspective. Some of these, like the essay in which
she explains her reasons for being vegan, are more intimate than some readers may like. This is
a double-edged sword, though, because the same qualities of honesty and humanness are Davis'
strongest suits as a narrator.

EMILY STIFLER

Mountain Rescue Doctor: Wilderness Medicine in the Extremes of Nature. CHRISTOPHER VAN TILBURG. NEW YORK: ST. MARTIN'S PRESS, 2007. 304 PAGES. HARDCOVER. $24.95.

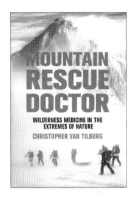

Few titles dramatize with greater flair the nervy, adrenalin-driven world of mountain rescue than Christopher Van Tilburg's new memoir. Packed with detail about the anatomy of these operations, the book runs at a break-neck pace, quickly bringing readers into this world of primary surveys, intubation, and resuscitation, without the hysterics that sometimes accompany such accounts.

The book opens with a description of treating an injured hiker who had fallen from a trail in the Columbia Gorge National Scenic Area. "As Jim lowers me into the abyss, I also have to haul down the stretcher and medical bag, as the brush is too thick and entangled to drop the gear down on a rope. So in addition to keeping myself upright, bushwhacking backward down the hillside, and trying to watch for the upcoming cliff edge, I am dragging the stretcher. Wiry vine maple branches reach out, grab the stretcher, and pull it back up the hill. As I tug, the vine maple fights back and tears my shirt. Finally, I yank the stretcher with all my might. It pops free, slides another ten feet, and nearly bowls me over. The rope goes taut again: Jim's got me."

This tense, active opening leads immediately to background about emergencies, adventure sports, and descriptions of the rugged landscape around Hood River County, Oregon, where the author lives. An emergency room physician and a member of the Crag Rats (the first official volunteer mountain rescue group in the nation), Van Tilburg details his mountain rescue work season by season, describing operations he participated in, such as skiers floundering in tree wells, hikers falling off cliffs, mountain bikers soaring off hillsides, cliff jumpers suffering back fractures.

The account includes detailed information about how mountain rescues are conducted, neatly inserting this information into the narrative so that it feels nothing like a text book or a how-to. Each of these operations requires flexibility, training, judgment, and caring. The reader comes away impressed with the dedication of Van Tilburg and his colleagues, as well as the toll it sometimes exacts on their family and professional lives. The book highlights the tensions of fitting mountain rescue work into the rest of his life, taking time away from his daughters, his wife, his career, and his own outdoor adventures, while giving his life a meaning and purpose that is compelling.

The book's seasonal organization doesn't provide much in the way of narrative direction. You don't feel that the rescues, emergencies, and personal challenges will add up to something greater or will yield deeper insights. Instead, the book seems embedded in the point of view of the author himself, who reacts to these emergencies and doesn't seem to have time to put them into a wider context, because his beeper keeps going off.

The exception to this is the chapter on the most recent Mt. Hood tragedy, in 2006. Van Tilburg participated in the rescue and gives a clear, informative account of its progress, much more analytical and reflective than the overheated hyperbole that appeared in newspapers, magazines, and television. Though he doesn't directly criticize the three men's decision to climb a difficult route on the north side of the mountain with a storm coming in, he makes it clear that their fast and light approach didn't leave much margin for error, especially given the severity of the storm.

When he returned from the rescue, his daughters, six and eight, bombarded him with questions about it and its aftermath: three men dead, one of them, Kelly James, leaving four children behind. The author answered them simply and directly. "The mountains are not necessarily dangerous," I say to them. "You just have to learn to be careful. You have to respect nature and the mountain."

There is much distilled wisdom in that answer. Moments like this give the book its authenticity and poignancy. You come away impressed with Van Tilburg's knowledge, practicality, sensitivity, and appreciation for the pleasures as well as the dangers of mountaineering, convinced that he's the kind guy you'd want to call if you ran into trouble in the mountains.

NICHOLAS O'CONNELL

Soul of the Heights—50 Years Going to the Mountains. ED COOPER. GUILFORD, CT: FALCON PRESS, 2007. 224 PAGES. $39.95.

Ed Cooper's *Soul of the Heights* is a beautiful collection of photographs and stories spanning his 50-year "vision quest" in the mountains. Beside offering a portfolio of magnificent images, it is a work of historical merit, especially of the Pacific Northwest climbing scene that helped shape American mountaineering.

Although Cooper's name is long-familiar to those who read photographic credits in calendars, postcards, and magazines, it is probably a measure of your longevity as a mountaineer if you remember him as a climber, much less as one of the most prolific alpinists of his generation. Herein, however, lies the book's greatest surprise. From the moment he climbed Mt. Rainier at age 16, he recalls, "I realized that mountains would be my raison d'être."

Cooper's legacy as a climber, although it lasted scarcely a decade, is noteworthy. Between 1953 and 1963 he may have accomplished more first ascents than anyone but Fred Beckey, with whom he sometimes shared a rope. While still a teenager, he graduated from mass ascents of prominent Northwest volcanoes, led by the Mazamas or the Mountaineers, to climbs up ever-more-difficult routes with smaller groups of friends and new acquaintances—many of whom became pillars of the Cascades climbing community. In the summer of 1955, when he was just 18, he climbed most of the major volcanoes stretching between mounts Baker and Shasta, including a difficult route on Rainier and six ascents of Mt. Hood. Thereafter he kept upping his ante, sometimes solo. The list of his achievements is impressive, including the second ascent of the West Buttress of Denali; new routes in the Bugaboos; the Grand Wall of the Chief near Squamish, British Columbia; the horrifying then-forbidden Willis Wall on Rainier, and finally, his first ascent of the Dihedral Wall on El Capitan, which was only the fifth ascent of the Captain, and the first by a "Valley Outsider."

Cooper's love of photography predated his passion for climbing, beginning in high school. Starting with his very first climb, he carried simple 2^1/$_4$ by 2^1/$_4$ format cameras, larger than those carried by most, and he returned with striking images of the mountain environments he loved. Although he was slow to publish, these were part of an evolving "master plan" that would shape the rest of his life and forever limit his ability to "get a real job." Over time he augmented his 2^1/$_4$

equipment with larger formats, inspired in part by Ansel Adams, a great influence on his work. In turn Cooper's own mastery of the medium inspired many other young mountain photographers beginning their careers in the late sixties and early seventies, including myself. Even 40 years after viewing some of his first photo essays in the Sierra Club's legendary *Ascent*, I still recall my own astonishment at his skill working with light, contrast, and detail.

Not surprisingly, Cooper's photography is the best part of *Soul of the Heights*, rich in magnificent shots, both in black and white and in color, which eventually became a more saleable medium for him. Many of these images correspond directly to adjacent text in the 22 chapters, and others are clustered into three portfolios in which he chose pictures primarily for their aesthetic majesty. My favorites are his black and whites, some of which rank right up there with a few captured by Adams. With notable exceptions, however, I don't think his color images fully measure up. Similarly, Cooper's landscapes are generally more powerful than his actual climbing pictures. While his landscapes transcended the standards of his time, his pictures of people in action were outpaced by others, including Galen Rowell. In that respect the action images in his book are more powerful for their historical significance than their aesthetic beauty. I suspect, however, that even Cooper would acknowledge this, and it does not reduce from the visual majesty of his work. Simply put, at a time when climbing photography began leaping to new levels, he turned his keen eyes to the landscapes that dominate *Soul of the Heights*. For those with an interest in technical details, Cooper provides an appendix outlining what camera, film, and lens he used to create each picture, including extensive input about his new-found love of the "digital darkroom" that has helped him either rescue or bring new life to images that had faded over time.

Cooper's extensive text is a readable and compelling autobiography of a young climber and his later struggles as a mountain photographer. He is at his best when he devotes all or most of a chapter to a single mission, such as the weeks he and Jim Baldwin spent puzzling their way up the Chief, a climb that created traffic jams similar to those of Warren Harding's first ascent of El Capitan. His storytelling is similarly good in describing rigors on the Willis Wall, where he and various companions and rivals encountered a gripping mix of intrigue, scarcely tenable danger, and National Park Service bureaucracy. For those interested in a photographic career, the later chapters paint a realistic picture of the rigors of survival in that difficult trade—a period during which Cooper graduated from mountaineering toward "topping" (and often bivouacking on) mountains as a means to create images composed of angles and lighting a non-mountaineer could never achieve.

My only complaint is that Cooper's writing is uneven, the words occasionally not measuring up to his imagery. This is an admittedly tall order, but periodically he falls into half-told, episodic recollections about expeditions, places, and other climbers that leave the reader hanging. This is especially evident in his development of certain characters (although he does a good job with Beckey) and sometimes with his own true motivations. Twice, for example, he fleetingly describes his estrangement from the Yosemite climbing community, summing it up in the following sentences:

"In Chris Jones's book, *Climbing in North America*, he writes that, disgusted with the treatment by local climbers, I retreated back East. This story seems to have been repeated in other publications. The fact is that economic necessity drove me to move. Less than three years later, I returned to the West Coast for good to pursue photography. Had I wished to continue technical climbing, nobody would have driven me away or stopped me." Obviously, there is a story behind the scenes here, and Cooper should either have told us more, or simply not raised the subject. Similarly, he writes often about his undying love for the mountains—a truth that glows from nearly all his pictures—but in his prose a certain detachment borders on the clichéd.

Nitpicking aside, the photography alone will keep you turning pages and dreaming of new places to explore, photograph, or climb. *Soul of the Heights* tells an entertaining and informative story, especially for those interested in a key evolutionary period of North American mountaineering. It is a worthy addition to any mountain lover's library.

GORDON WILTSIE

Night Driving, Invention of the Wheel & Other Blues. DICK DORWORTH. FOREWORD BY JACK TURNER. LIVINGSTON, MT: FIRST ASCENT PRESS. 2007. 254 PGS. $25.00.

Dorworth, 1975. As an impressionable twenty-one-year-old living in my native Midwest I was dreaming of making a life in the mountains. Then I read "Night Driving" in *Mountain Gazette*. Within two months my car was loaded, and I was driving into the sunset to make it happen. Okay, maybe I can't claim a one-to-one, cause-and-effect relationship, but Dorworth's influence is clear in hindsight. If "influence" is not quite the right word I'll just say that "Night Driving" made me aware of some of the possibilities.

Now, well over 30 years later, here it is collected in book form, the title essay along with a half dozen others. I was hesitant to revisit it, fearing embarrassment for my former self: the kid who thought this stuff was the real goods might be revealed for the unworldly unread naïve waif that I actually was. I fear returning to Castañeda and Hesse for the same reasons.

In Dorworth's case, I'm happy to say, my fears were unfounded.

Among Dorworth's non-literary mountain deeds: holding the world's record for speed on skis, first person over 105 m.p.h.; his six-month "Funhog" road trip with Chouinard, Jones, Tejada-Flores, and Tompkins, on which they put up the Californian Route on Fitz Roy; and two years later with Robbins, the first ascent of Arcturus on Half Dome. This book is officially categorized as "Memoir: Mountaineering," so we hear the stories of those events in these pages, right? Wrong. Although we do read about driving on the Funhog trip, during the almost 10 pages he devotes to it there's no mention of summiting Fitz Roy. So where's the mountaineering? Where's the skiing?

There are glimpses, of course, but Dorworth is writing about the life that he's made *around* those activities. In his foreword Jack Turner calls "Night Driving" "a memoir of a well-spent epic youth on the ski-racing circuit." Turner, as usual, gets it right, but it's a hard essay to summarize. It's an essay about energy and movement, about velocity, and it embodies those characteristics—thus hard to pin down. "Europe: Fourth Time Around," which, in nearly 70 pages, closes the book, is much the same. Both describe a life to which the mountains and skiing are central, both portray a large cast of characters, succinctly and lovingly. Many of the cast I'd never heard of before: skiers or friends of Dorworth. Others are more familiar, for example the crew of a Bev Clark film, *The Skiers*: Dougal Haston, Mick Burke, Rick Sylvester, Jim Bridwell, Wayne Poulsen, Jr., and Ginger. I've read hundreds of pages about Haston, but Dorworth's single page undoubtedly gets to his essence. Of Ginger (first name? last name?), all that Dorworth says is that he was a Brit who once bivvied on the Bonatti Pillar for a stormy week with a group of Japanese who didn't speak English; that, and that he skied with an Aspen influence. What else do we need to know?

As a youth reading Dorworth I trusted his take on places, believing (correctly) I'd one day make my own lists: "The resort of Verbier, and the mountains which give it life, had once again treated us well. It is, along with Sun Valley, Portillo, La Parva, Chamonix, Aspen, Cervenia and Slide Mountain, a special place for me—a place of magical spirits, friendly, protective, harsh…."

My descriptions of his work have thus far neglected Dorworth's single most salient feature: he's *thoughtful*, what educators call a "reflective practitioner." This thoughtfulness might be directed inward: "I was having some strictly personal reactions to 'skiing' which were making me acutely aware that the majority of my energies, for the past 23 years, had been put into one or another aspect of sliding down a snowy hill, on a pair of upturned sticks."

Or his gaze may be directed outward, as in this spot-on take on the 1950s: "Truman gave way to the blandness of Eisenhower and his distasteful vice president; Stalin dies; the Korean police action ended; Marilyn was both vamp and victim of our society; Hemingway got his Nobel; Bill Haley rocked around the clock…and my family periodically rose before dawn to watch the atom bombs light up the horizon of my childhood."

Between the first and last essays are five more, each tightly focused. One is on vegetarianism, one is a meditation on Ecclesiastes and coyotes, and one is an instructive illustration of instinct in the mountains.

I've admitted there isn't much actual climbing described here, and yet Dorworth's three-paragraph description of his climb of the North Buttress of Mt. Morrison in the Sierra is, to my mind, as perfect a description of a climb as is possible. Dorworth is said to have an unpublished manuscript about ski racing—I'd love to read it, and I would hope for one too about his climbs, whether it's written yet or not.

It's natural to compare *Night Driving to On the Road*. Turner does it; the back cover blurbs do it. Somewhere in *Night Driving* Dorworth himself writes of reading *On The Road* for the second or third time. I too once loved *On the Road*, but I have to admit that I can't block out the mental image of a bloated, alcohol-soaked Kerouac living with his mother and dead before the age of 50.

Dorworth must be around 70 now, and he's still living the life to which we all aspire. I know, intellectually, that shouldn't make his words any more or less resonant and true. But, for me, it does.

DAVID STEVENSON

IN MEMORIAM

EDITED BY CAMERON M. BURNS

PETE ABSOLON 1960–2007

On August 11, a hiker trundled a rock that killed Pete Abosolon, 47, as he was climbing a new route in Leg Lake Cirque in the Southern Wind River Mountains.

Pete Absolon. *Courtesy of NOLS*

Though born in St. Paul, Minnesota, Pete spent his childhood in Texas and Maryland, and graduated with a BA from George Washington University in 1983. He promptly put his geology background to work, becoming a climbing guide at Seneca Rocks, West Virginia. There he met his future wife, Molly Armbrecht, while climbing. Pete was known as "the first climbing guide" at Seneca Rocks. Pete established a number of difficult, bold routes at Seneca including The Viper (12b, PG), Projected Futures (12b), Icing on the Cake (11d, PG), and Terminal Atrocity (10c, X).

Molly and Pete married in 1988. They moved to Lander, Wyoming, in 1990 and began full-time work as National Outdoor Leadership School (NOLS) field instructors. The following decade was filled with journeys of all kinds. Pete climbed and traveled extensively: from Alaska to the Karakoram, the desert southwest to Yosemite, and across the Canadian and U.S. Rocky Mountains. There was hardly a place he didn't explore with a rope, in a boat, on a bike, or on foot. Accompanying him on many of these trips was Molly, an accomplished writer, skier, climber, and mountaineer.

Pete helped shape wilderness education throughout his adult life, first as a mountain guide and climber and later as a NOLS instructor. His reach in outdoor education grew substantially when he took on broader, supervisory responsibilities; he was the director of NOLS Rocky Mountain when he died.

Pete was a dedicated and talented climber. He trained hard and climbed often. Needing a training facility in the small town of Lander, he convinced his local climbing partners to "invest" in his 20-foot high garage gym. Pete did the research and planning to give each of his adventures the best chance at delivering the most climbing for the time available, and he was generally the source of motivation in any partnership. He was safe and deeply experienced. When you climbed with Pete, you always climbed at your best. He bred confidence.

In September 2000, Pete and Molly embarked on their greatest adventure yet: parenthood. Avery Absolon, almost seven years old at Pete's death, brought awe and joy to Pete's life every day. Even as a toddler, Avery was an enthusiastic and skilled participant in the family outdoor pursuits. She loved skiing, climbing, fishing, hiking, and biking with her Dad. She also drew Pete into her own special world where he happily participated in elementary school activities, and put on his dancing shoes for special father-daughter dance recitals and practices. Days at the crags now included entire worlds for the woodland fairies and Avery's imagination. Having Avery did not slow down or alter the Absolons' joyful, active lives. They continued to pursue their dreams and interests and simply expanded their incredible world to include this bright, energetic, and beautiful daughter. They became an ever-closer unit. The name Absolon conjured up not one face, but three, like a wonderful team.

In addition to Avery and Molly, Pete leaves behind his parents, Mary and Karel Absolon of Rockville, Maryland; sister Mary Absolon of Edina, Minn.; sister Martha Delahanty of Long Valley, New Jersey; and brother John Absolon of Rockville, Maryland; as well as an extended family who loved him very much. Pete was preceded in death by his brother, Fritz Absolon, of Rockville, Maryland.

LIZ TUOHY, AILEEN BREW, *and* PHIL POWERS

ROBERT G. ALLISON 1928–2007

Robert Allison at the Ranch. *Courtesy Robert E. Hyman*

Bob Allison died April 22, at the age of 78, after a long struggle with cancer. He was serving at the time of his death as chair of the AAC's Grand Teton Climbers' Ranch Committee. He had previously served for many years as president of the Kansas City Climbing Club.

When I first met Bob he was already past 70, and my entire experience with him thereafter was at the Climbers' Ranch in Wyoming. Bob's principal qualities, as they struck me, were his excellent health, his wry sense of humor, and his good heart. That first June, just five or six years ago, while we were in the Tetons together, Bob was also planning another of his many trips to the Wind River Mountains for later that summer. His objective was again to climb Gannett Peak, 13,804 feet, the highest mountain in Wyoming. If I recall, that was to be the seventh or eighth time he climbed that mountain. Of course, the "difficult" part of the climb only begins after a 22-mile approach carrying a 60-pound pack. I was impressed with his physical stamina and strength, and the happiness he found among the mountains.

During one of Bob's trips to the Wind River Range he and his group came upon a large, obviously man-made pile of rocks. Skeletal remains of a horse stuck out from the bottom of the pile. Bob paused to study the scene, as if in meditation, then wondered aloud, "Didn't they know that if you pile a bunch of rocks on top of a horse you'll kill it?"

At the Climbers' Ranch, Bob was always a quiet presence. Though always sociable, ready to laugh and exchange stories, he was just more inclined to listen than to talk. It is a tribute to his easy-going manner and openness to friendship that people who met him at the Climbers' Ranch enjoyed his company whether they were in their 20s and had just met him for the first time or were older and had known him for years. He was universally regarded with affection and respect. His knowledge of the Teton Range and other mountains was well-known, and we were often entertained by descriptions of his journeys to the Russian Caucasus, to Mexico, China, and the old British base camp at Mt. Everest.

When Bob was diagnosed with cancer two years ago he reacted with a perfect balance of acceptance and determination. He even found humor in the situation. When the American

Alpine Club waived the costs of his stay at the ranch that August, he told me afterward that it was a good deal, because if he outlived the prognosis of the doctors he might have free room and board in Wyoming for years to come.

Last June Bob was back at the Climbers' Ranch, and was, as usual, an active participant in Work Week. One day from across the ranch common I saw him carrying a heavy load of building lumber. I walked over to give him a hand and said, "Bob, why don't you leave that for the young guys?" Bob paused and gave me that wry grin. "It's late in the afternoon," he said, "the young guys are all tired."

My favorite recollection of Bob concerns an event at which I was not even present, but serves very well to illustrate his love of family and friends, his love of the mountains, and his celebration of physical vitality even as, after a debilitating year of cancer and chemotherapy, his physical vitality was steadily waning. Bob told me last June that he thought he might try to climb up to the Lower Saddle, between the Middle Teton and the Grand Teton. The ascent from the Climbers' Ranch to the Lower Saddle is more than five miles and 5,000 vertical feet, and ends with the challenge of surmounting an 80-foot headwall. When Bob told me he wanted to go up there he didn't present it as a major goal or as the last ambition of a man in failing health. He just said it casually, as if the excursion might make a nice day, maybe in June, maybe later in the season. Bob seemed happy simply to have the prospect before him, the thought itself a pilgrimage into the future, a connection to the past, and a triumph over the constrictions of fate. In my heart, I did not think he could make it, that week or later. Yet he did make it, accomplishing the climb in August. It was an extraordinary achievement for anyone his age, and much more so with his advanced illness. When I spoke to him afterwards he expressed his joy with quiet humility and gratitude.

My journal notes the event: "In August Bob Allison returned to Wyoming with his daughter, Shawna, and friends from Missouri and Colorado. He went along with everyone to the Garnet Canyon Meadows, at 9,200 feet, and camped. The next day he went where he wanted to go, reaching the Lower Saddle in the lee of the Grand Teton at 11,600 feet. He camped there with his daughter and friends, watching the Shadow Range on the floor of Jackson Hole at sunset, enjoying again the marvelous view out across Wyoming to the east, across Idaho to the west, range after range of snow-crested mountains, radiant in the late golden sunshine, slowly fading in the long blue light of dusk."

The last time I talked to Bob, early in April, he was cheerful and warmly asked about my daughter, who he recalled was leaving for Latin America with the Peace Corps this spring. He was looking forward to visiting the Climbers' Ranch again in June, he said, though I sensed that he knew very well he was not going to make it.

Bob lived with sensitivity to the resplendence of the earth, with fidelity to his family and friends, with kindness and generosity of spirit. He was modest and gentle and tough as Teton granite. In these last two years he showed us how to live with serenity and resolve "in the long blue light of dusk." I will miss him, as will many others from throughout the country who shared with him his happy visits to the Climbers' Ranch.

WILLIAM A. FETTERHOFF

ROBERT HICKS BATES 1911–2007

Bob Bates and I were close friends for more than 70 years. We began climbing together in the 1930s in the quarries around Boston and in Northern New England under the tutelage of some of the best climbers in the Northeast. Then we went to Alaska, where we learned about expeditions from Brad Washburn, and in 1938 and 1953 Bob and I worked together to organize and lead the American expeditions to K2. Afterward, together with other members of both teams, we wrote two books, *Five Miles High* (1939) and *K2: The Savage Mountain* (1954). As many people have found, collaboration in authorship is a test of friendship, and Bob and I passed happily.

Robert Bates in 1985. *Ulugh Muztagh archive*

If I were to use a few words to describe Bob, I would say that he had a sunny, cheerful disposition. I am confident that Bob never met a person he did not like or who did not like him. He was equally at home with students, Peace Corps volunteers, sherpas, ambassadors, and kings, and one might meet any one of these in the hospitable home he and his wife Gail kept in Exeter. Bob also had many stories of Alaska and his experiences in WWII, but his great talent was the huge collection of songs and ballads he committed to memory. He could produce the right song for any occasion, and I have a vivid memory of him standing in front of a battered tent, high on K2, singing his heart out in a furious wind. What his voice lacked in quality he made up for in enthusiasm. I can also remember him sitting

Robert Bates and Nick Clinch (right) singing for supper in China, with Tom Hornbein (left) and Pete Schoening in support. *Ulugh Muztagh archive*

high on a rock overlooking the Baltoro Glacier singing to the stupendous Trango and Baltoro towers across the glacier. He was singing and laughing and clearly in his element. Bob even had the grace to joke as I nervously extracted his abscessed tooth at 19,000 feet! I remember seeing Bob angry only twice: first when he missed a shot at a sleeping goat when we were on a mountain hunting for meat, and, second, when he thought he had irretrievably lost his favorite gun in a Russian stream. In good days and bad, Bob brightened the day for all of those around him.

On our two expeditions to K2 we met with triumph and disaster and treated them both the same. In both years, the members of each party quickly became friends and remained so for the rest of their lives. It was this brotherhood of the rope that helped us to survive the long ordeal during our 1953 retreat from near the summit of K2.

Bob was a strong and sturdy climber, wise about the weather and snow conditions, and a great voice in making hard decisions. Bob was an amusing spectacle on skis, but often the first to reach camp in the afternoon and the first to start out in the morning, although his pack often came undone! He was a fast walker, and we had to be careful not to let him get too far ahead of the party when he carried the day's lunch.

I don't know much about Bob as a teacher, but as a tent mate, in good weather or bad, no one could be better. He was truly a wonderful friend and I miss him more than I can say.

CHARLES S. HOUSTON

ROBERT HICKS BATES

Bob Bates, teacher, author, mountaineer, and first Peace Corps director in Nepal, died on Thursday, September 13, in Exeter, New Hampshire. He was 96. As an instructor in English at Phillips Exeter Academy from 1939 to 1976, Bob encouraged and inspired countless students with his warmth, energy, and optimism. In addition to teaching in the classroom, he introduced many students to rock climbing and winter survival in the White Mountains of New Hampshire, sharing his great enthusiasm for the outdoors.

Bates climbed during the "golden age of mountaineering," a time when few of the world's highest peaks had been reached. The 1938 team to K2 trekked more than 350 miles, finishing up the Baltoro Glacier to the base of the mountain, ferried supplies to eight high camps, and reconnoitered several possible summit routes. They reached a height of 26,000 feet before limited supplies forced the team to turn back. In 1953, a massive storm forced the expedition's eight climbers to descend while attempting to save the life of a seriously ill member. A fall by one climber at 25,000 feet resulted in a tangle of ropes and bodies as each pair of roped climbers fell in turn, all miraculously held by Pete Schoening [obituary in *AAJ 2005*] in what has rightly been described as the most famous belay in mountaineering history.

Bob was born on January 14, 1911, in Philadelphia, and was introduced to some of the traditions of mountaineering by Dr. James M. Thorington, who would become our Club's 12th president [obituary in *AAJ 1990*]. He absorbed from his parents an early fascination for exploration, an interest in other cultures, and a love of reading that lasted throughout his life. His father, William Nickerson Bates (1867–1949), was a distinguished classicist at the University of Pennsylvania. Both he and Bob's mother, Edith Newell Richardson, were descendants of Minutemen from Cambridge, Massachusetts, who were killed on the first day of the American Revolution. Bates attended the William Penn Charter School in Philadelphia before graduating from Phillips Exeter Academy in 1929. He earned an undergraduate degree, magna cum laude, in 1933, and a master's degree in 1935 from Harvard University. His education interrupted by World War II, Bates earned his Ph.D. from the University of Pennsylvania in 1947. His thesis on the literature of the mountains was published 53 years later under the title *Mystery, Beauty, and Danger*.

Early in his career at Harvard, Bates made friends in the Harvard Mountaineering Club who became known as the "Harvard Five": Brad Washburn [*AAJ 2007*], Ad Carter [*AAJ 1996*], Charlie Houston, Terry Moore [*AAJ 1994*], and Bob Bates—climbers who became major players in American mountaineering for many years. With Washburn, who became a renowned cartographer and director of the Museum of Science in Boston, Bates explored some of the largest unmapped areas of North America, in Alaska and the Yukon Territory, making several first ascents between 1932 and 1942. The story of their survival, after walking close to 100 miles across crevasse-filled glaciers in the Yukon and summiting both Mt. Lucania (the highest unclimbed peak in North America at the time) and Mt. Steele, is an epic of alpinism (the full story was published in 2002 as *Escape From Lucania*, by David Roberts).

By the time the United States entered World War II, Bates had acquired considerable experience with the limitations of the cold-weather clothing, boots, and equipment. He entered the U.S. Army in 1941 and was assigned to the Office of the Quartermaster General as a captain in charge of testing clothing and equipment for use by the army's mountain troops. He coordinated the successful third ascent of Mt. McKinley in 1942 as part of the Army's Alaska Test Expedition, a test of army food, clothing, and equipment conducted jointly with the American Alpine Club. For further testing in combat and for training mountain troops in effective protection in cold weather, Bates was sent to Anzio, Italy, in 1944. His work there resulted in significant decreases in casualties from frostbite and trench foot. He was discharged in 1946 as a lieutenant colonel, having been awarded the Legion of Merit and a Bronze Star.

After the war, Bob returned to teaching at Phillips Exeter, continuing to travel and climb. In 1954, he married Gail Oberlin, the first staff member of the American Alpine Club and sister of our late past-president, John Oberlin [*AAJ 2007*]. Gail is an avid traveler who survives Bob. During the 1962–1963 academic year, they lived in Kathmandu, where Bates had been recruited by Sargent Shriver to be director of the first group of Peace Corps volunteers, with Willi Unsoeld as his associate director. One outcome of this experience was for Bob and Gail to bring a Tibetan refugee from Lhasa to study at the University of New Hampshire, a young woman who became a member of his extended family. After returning home to Exeter, they continued to welcome countless students, climbers, Peace Corps volunteers, and friends from around the world, always imbuing them with a sense of excitement about the possibilities in life and the belief that they could accomplish whatever they set out to do.

Remaining active after his retirement from teaching, Bates, in 1985 at age 74, led, with Nick Clinch, the first joint Chinese-American climbing expedition to Ulugh Muztagh, the so-called "great ice mountain," a previously unclimbed peak in remote south-central China. Bates recounted the experience in his autobiography *The Love of Mountains Is Best* (1994).

Besides his mountaineering interests, including the presidency of the American Alpine Club and honorary membership in the 10th Mountain Division alumni (and later, honorary presidency of the AAC), Bates was also very involved in civic affairs in the town of Exeter. The preservation of the Dudley House in its present location in the center of town and the adjacent "Town Common" owes a great deal to his efforts, as does the historical integrity of Water Street. He was an active member of the Exeter Historical Society, chairman of the Historic District Commission, and, as a committed outdoorsman, worked with conservation organizations to save the open land surrounding Exeter. Always engaged with other people, Bob was modest about his own accomplishments, often dismissing admiring comments such as "You've had such an amazing life!" with a smile and the simple reply, "I've had an interesting one."

In addition to Gail, Bob's survivors also include two nieces, Edith B. Buchanan of Denver, Colorado, and Elizabeth T. Bates of Philadelphia, Pennsylvania, three great-nieces, two great-nephews, two great-great-nephews, and Tsering Yangdon with her son Nima Taylor. Bob's older brother, William N. Bates, Jr., predeceased him. Burial was in the final resting place of many notable Yankees—Mt. Auburn Cemetery, Cambridge, Mass. Here he lies only a few rope lengths from the grave of our Club's first Honorary President, Henry Snow Hall, Jr.

It has been my sad duty, as Bob's successor in the Honorary Presidency of the American Alpine Club, to compile these reminiscences about the most popular climber in the Club's more than century-long life. And so I will close with the reporting of Greg Todd, one of Bob's former students, who attended his memorial service in Exeter on October 27:

"Among the 250 or so gathered in Phillips Church were Charles Houston and Bob Craig, surviving members of the 1953 K2 expedition; Tom Hornbein, from the first traverse of Everest (via the west ridge, with Willi Unsoeld); and Nicholas Clinch, who had led the first-ascent parties on Mt. Vinson and Hidden Peak [Clinch and Craig are both past AAC presidents]. After many stories about Prof. Bates's absolute and total unflappability, Charlie Houston shuffled up to give an impromptu story about how 'no one today has said a thing about it, but Bob could, on occasion, lose his temper. As his climbing partner over so many years, I had occasion to see it. It happened once, back in 1931...' (laughter). They were lost in Alaska, trying to get back to civilization after their plane radioed that it could not return to pick them off the glacier. They had tired of squirrel. Then they saw some goats, on the mountain slopes below. Bates climbed up some rocks high above, took careful aim, and *fired*. A goat got up and yawned. He aimed again, and *fired*. A second goat got up, and ambled away. Bob Bates aimed again and *fired*...but this time all the goats got up and started slowly walking—in their direction! Bates threw down the gun, hit the stock hard, and said, 'Gosh, dang it!' (Or something like that.) So, Bob Bates did lose his temper. At least that once.

"Clinch gave a gripping talk about their travels to western China in 1985 to climb the Ulugh Muztagh, a deeply remote mountain in Tibet, then-unclimbed and a possible 8,000-meter peak. When they returned to Urumchi, all the Chinese provincial dignitaries had gathered to celebrate the American mountain team, in a gala welcoming event. The Communist Youth Orchestra of Western China played suites of music in salute. Dozens of dancers in native costume performed regional dances. There were acrobats, other musicians, and many songs accompanied by curious instruments. Many speeches and toasts were made, which they could not understand.

"Then everything stopped. There was no motion. Only silence. Nick Clinch turned to the local chairman of the Communist Party, and asked: 'What's wrong?'

"'Nothing is wrong. Now, it is your turn to entertain us.'

"Bates and Clinch looked at each other. Bates, then in his 70s, and Clinch moved slowly toward the stage, perhaps thousands watching, and agreed on their plan. They took a microphone and broke into 'The Wreck of the Old '97,' a song Bates had sung so many times on so many mountain expeditions that by now Clinch knew all the words as well. As they sang verse after verse, the Chinese audience exploded in applause.

"To end the memorial service, Clinch brought Hornbein up to the podium. And the two of them sang five verses of that song for us right then and there! The last verse was especially memorable:

Oh all you ladies, you had better take a warning,
From this time on, and learn,
Never speak harsh words to your true-lovin' husband,
He may leave you...and never return!

"That brought the assembled crowd to their feet, in both cheers and tears, for Mrs. Bates, who rose in the front. And with that began the organ recessional, and the service was over. It was a great moment."

WILLIAM LOWELL PUTNAM

EDMUND PERCIVAL HILLARY 1919–2008

"Sir Edmund described himself as a person of modest ability; in reality he was a colossus.... He was our hero," New Zealand's Prime Minister Helen Clark said in her tribute to him at his state funeral in Auckland. Referring to him as Sir Ed, as he is generally known in his native land, she added, "Above all, we loved him for what he represented—a determination to succeed against all odds." It was she, not his family, who announced his death to the world.

The prime minister of India spoke of him as one who "drew our attention to the grandeur of Mother Earth." (The street in New Delhi where the New Zealand diplomatic mission is located was renamed in 2003 as Sir Edmund Hillary Marg.) Nepal's premier stated that, "The government and people of Nepal shall always cherish fond memories of his selfless devotion to the cause of development of the Everest region, his humane qualities and courageous spirit, as well as his contribution to make Nepal known to the world."

The saga of Hillary's ascent of Mt. Everest has been recounted innumerable times. The story I like best is Hillary's recent description of how he felt when he and Tenzing Norgay had finally "knocked the bastard off" by fighting their way up the difficult rock feature known ever since as the Hillary Step. "[Tenzing] really had a greater desire for success than I did. When we actually got to the top, he was overwhelmed. I wasn't overwhelmed at all. In fact, when I got to the top of Everest, I

Edmund Hillary in India. *Courtesy Capt. M. S. Kohli*

looked around, and across the valley is another great mountain [Makalu] and, instead of doing anything particularly dramatic, I looked at this mountain and I mentally picked out a route by which the mountain could be climbed. I didn't climb it, it was climbed by a French expedition [led by Jean Franco two years later], but even when I was on the summit of Everest I was still looking for challenges across the valley."

Hillary was constantly looking for challenges throughout the prime of his life. His famous adventures after Everest included making the first visit to the South Pole overland since 1911, by driving across the continent on a Massey Ferguson tractor in 1957; searching unsuccessfully in Khumbu for the yeti in 1960 (he hadn't expected to succeed—he didn't believe the creature existed); chugging up the length of the Ganges River in a jet boat in 1977; and becoming the first person to visit the world's three poles (South, North, and the summit of Everest) in 1985, when he landed at the North Pole with Neil Armstrong, the first man on the moon.

He served as New Zealand's high commissioner (the title for ambassadors amongst Commonwealth nations) to India, Bangladesh, and Sri Lanka, and ambassador to Nepal, from 1985 to 1989. The New Zealand mission in New Delhi had been closed in 1982 by a prime minister who disliked Indian Prime Minister Indira Gandhi, but when a new government came into office in Wellington, Hillary was chosen to reestablish New Zealand's presence in South Asia. He was the ideal person for the job: he acknowledged that he was not a professional diplomat and so left the diplomacy to his staff, but he also knew that he could open doors for them because of his fame from Everest and from his jetboat trip up the Ganges River from sea to source, which lasted for several weeks and was witnessed by millions of Indians—four million at Calcutta alone—who lined the river banks and considered his trip a religious pilgrimage up their holy river.

Hillary was a man who took glory from Nepal, but was one of the very few who returned to give something back, to contribute to the well being of its people. A few others, like Doug Scott, have made similar contributions elsewhere in Nepal, but not nearly on the same scale. Hillary built the Lukla airfield, which became the gateway to Mt. Everest. He founded his small aid agency, the Himalayan Trust, and in Nepal's Solukhumbu district built 27 schools, two hospitals, 12 clinics, and numerous foot bridges; his Trust continues to maintain, repair, reequip, and expand the schools and hospitals four decades later, and to send from Kathmandu all the supplies they require to function properly. He was instrumental in getting the Everest area's

Sagarmatha National Park established and staffed; his trust has financed tree nurseries in and just outside the park to counteract the serious deforestation that had been taking place. He organized and raised considerable funds for the rebuilding of the fire-gutted Thyangboche monastery.

He was revered by the Sherpa people, who were profoundly grateful for his decades of helping them help themselves. They refer to him and they addressed him as "Bara Sahib" (literally "great master"). When they held their Buddhist memorial services in January, they prayed for him to be reincarnated as a human being who would return to them in his next life and carry on his work.

Hillary's and his Trust's contributions to the well being of the local people helped to create an area in the north of Nepal which is by far the most prosperous remote area in the country. This is because the people are educated, have good health care, and can speak English and thus earn a good living as trekking guides, climbers, and lodge owners. The Khumbu part of Solukhumbu, the northern area of the district, did not have a single local Maoist during the ten-year Maoist uprising. As it did throughout the Maoist rebellion, his Himalayan Trust will continue its work despite its founder-chairman's death. Last November he designated his wife, the former June Mulgrew, who has been intimately involved in its work for years, as his successor.

He was rewarded for these efforts during the celebrations marking the 50th anniversary of the first ascent of Everest by being made an honorary citizen of Nepal (no one else has received that accolade). He and his summit partner are being honored posthumously by Lukla airfield's officially becoming the Tenzing-Hillary Airport.

He was a truly modest man, as Prime Minister Clark mentioned at his funeral service. An editorial in an Auckland paper noted, "His modesty was as legendary as his mountaineering achievements. If ever there was a man who could—in the words of a famous poet of British imperialism—walk with kings without losing the common touch, Sir Ed was he."

He was the finest man I have ever known. He lived by his very high ethical standards. He did an immense amount of good for other people—and he greatly enjoyed doing it. He was a warm family man who was devastated by the death of his first wife and child in 1975 in a plane crash at Kathmandu airport while he was building a hospital at Phaphlu in Solukhumbu. He loved a good laugh, enjoyed his Scotch and ginger ale, was endlessly patient with people wanting him to pose with them for a photo or asking him for his autograph. (Some years ago, his face was engraved on the New Zealand five-dollar bill—he was the only living person except the Queen to appear on New Zealand currency—and he was often asked to sign one, thus taking a number of them permanently out of circulation.)

He had firm ideas on a number of topics, and when he was asked a question, he would often come out with some pretty blunt answers. He became outspoken on his views about commercial climbing expeditions on Everest, and how they cause great crowding on the standard routes by people who are not real mountaineers. He was convinced that mountains should be left to mountaineers, and there should be a strict limit on the number of climbers on the mountain in the same season; he believed that "the commercialization of the mountain" was "something of a disaster in the sense that you would have a small group of experienced guides who would conduct frequently inexperienced people up the mountain" and dangerously clog the main routes with their numbers. As he remarked to me several times, "I'm only glad we were there when we were, when we had the mountain all to ourselves, and we were accomplishing something with our own skill and determination."

In one of his last formal interviews, Hillary was asked last year how he would like to be remembered after his death. "If remembered at all, I would like to be remembered for the schools and hospitals and bridges and all the other activities that we did with—not 'for'—the Sherpas. Unquestionably, they are the things I feel were the most worthwhile of everything I was involved in."

Do you think about dying now? At this stage of your years? "No, I don't spend a lot of time thinking about dying, but I like to think that if it did occur that I would die peacefully and not make too much of a fuss about it."

He died quietly on the morning of January 11, 2008. His body had worn out. His heart stopped beating.

ELIZABETH HAWLEY

Editor's note: A much longer version of this memorial is available at www.americanalpineclub.org

LARA-KARENA BITENIEKS KELLOGG 1968–2007

Lara Kellogg photographed by a Tibetan nun. *Courtesy Chad Kellogg*

Lara Kellogg died last April in a fall she suffered while descending Mt. Wake in Alaska's Ruth Gorge. She was two weeks shy of her 39th birthday. News of the accident immediately fanned out across her vast network of friends in Seattle and beyond. Sadly, her husband, Chad Kellogg, was one of the last to know. A lone horseman carried word of the accident involving Lara to his base camp in China's Qionglai Range, but he had to hike out to Rilong to receive the full report of what had happened. Days before her death, Chad and his partners, Joe Puryear and Jay Janousek, had summited an unnamed 18,900-foot peak in the Chang Ping Valley. They subsequently christened it Lara Shan— Lara's Peak [p. 435].

It was Lara, not Laura—something new acquaintances tended to get wrong. Her parents were Latvian immigrants who settled in working-class West Seattle. Her father, Robert, introduced her to the mountains at age nine with a foray partway up Mt. Rainier. Even more than most Seattleites, she loved that mountain. She loved mountains, period. Still, she didn't become a climber until her mid-twenties. By then she had been a bike messenger, a bike racer, a kayak guide, a snowboarder, a skateboarder, but not a climber. That changed quickly. After she got a job at Marmot Mountain Works, a Seattle-area climbing shop, she started disappearing every chance she got. Along with her legendary dogs, Greedy and Chavez, and various partners in crime, she started ticking off classic climbs in the Cascades, the Olympics, the Coast Range, the Sierra. I was privileged to be an occasional sidekick. One of the finest memories of my life, in fact, is topping out on North Dome with Lara as the full moon rose over Yosemite.

After I moved to San Francisco, I saw Lara less often. She always made a point, however, of swinging through town on her way to the Valley. I was trying to make my way as a journalist then, and Lara was trying to make a go of climbing. She was succeeding, too, landing guiding gigs with Cascade Alpine Guides and Mountain Madness, and a stint as a climbing ranger on Rainier. Her adventures became farther-flung. Postcards started arriving from distant corners—Nepal, Peru, Alaska. She was out climbing harder and harder routes. Among the accomplishments that studded her climbing resume were the Ferrari Route on Alpamayo, Tangerine Trip on El Capitan, the West Ridge of Mt. Hunter, and the first ascent of Luk Tse in the Nyanchen Tanglha Range in Tibet.

Lara never called attention to these feats, choosing instead to shower kudos on poor low-landers like me. I remember she called me from some airport on the way back from Nepal and she wanted to congratulate me on an article I landed in *Smithsonian*. I was like, "Wait, didn't you just climb Ama Dablam?" But, no, it was all about me. I was the cool one. She was that way with everyone.

Lara's development as a climber was mirrored by her development as a scientist. When I first met her she was a college dropout, but she soon re-matriculated and finished her degree, eventually enrolling in the masters forestry program at the University of Washington. Work she did on spatial analysis of forest fires was published posthumously in a peer-reviewed ecology journal.

Lara always believed she would die young, and she lived life accordingly. Her days started early and ended late, the waking hours a whirlwind of non-stop action. Somehow she managed to fit in more friends, more adventures, more laughs, more of everything than the rest of us could ever manage. And when I picture her now, she's cloaked in an aura of positive energy—a sun the rest of us merely orbit.

According to all reports, she was apprehensive about the trip to the Ruth Gorge. Some friends read it as stress, others as something more ominous—a premonition of doom. Who knows? All that's certain is she's gone. Gone, but never forgotten.

Her Latvian grandmother used to plead with her: "Lotty, don't go to the mountains, Lotty. You're nothing in the mountains." But of course, she was always something special—in the mountains and out of them—something very special indeed.

PAT JOSEPH

CHARLES FREDRICK KROGER 1946–2007

"I've been thinking, Clay. Maybe I don't have much time left, so what should I do? Try to find a cure for pancreatic cancer? I don't think I could do as well as lots of other people trying to solve that problem. But I could go down to the shop and work on finishing the bed."

It was my one of my last "good" days with Chuck. He had salvaged some incredible clear fir beams off a house here in Telluride. He had them all stacked in storage, so we drove out in his yellow truck and sorted through them. The beams were long

Charles Kroger in Telluride. *Ben Knight*

and heavy and I was sure he would "bust a nut," or worse, burst the feeding tube the doctors had just put in, but we picked out two "real nice ones." Straight grain, golden-colored. Not a knot the whole way. We got them on the truck and got them in the shop and Chuck started tinkering.

A few days later I went over and we planed them. Aaron had said, "Yeah, that thing will never be used…" referring to one of a dozen immense steel machines in Chuck's shop. Well, I used it with Chuck, on that one day, our last real good day. We planed and planed and fed and pushed these immaculate pieces of wood through again and again until they were perfect.

They had to be. Chuck was building Kathy their "wedding bed" (as the design bible *A*

Pattern Language would call it). It was the last item in the house, the culmination not of just their 30 years building in Telluride, but the final touch to Chuck's house. I didn't tell Chuck the Chinese Proverb: "When a man finishes his house, he will die." But I knew it was time. And he did too. And this was the only way to finish the house. Finish the wedding bed. The core. The soul.

It was close, I'd say, down to the wire. But he "got 'er done" just in time. Just like the six times he finished the Hard Rock 100-mile footrace that traverses through the San Juans and goes right by his front door. Ten minutes to spare his first time—47:50—and still couldn't win the Caboose Award!

We all ponder, does climbing make the man or does a man define his climbing? Chuck's mastery of building and welding, his ability to find "relentless forward motion" in his running, were these the products of, or the reason for, his mastery of climbing? I would have to guess both, however I never had any idea to what extent Chuck had climbed.

This is because Chuck was a man of doing. "Well, let's just go get 'er fixed up," or "Hey, I have a great idea, anybody want to go climb so and so?" Chuck didn't care about what was behind him and he never looked anywhere except to a "can do" future.

That certainly must have been his attitude toward El Cap in 1969 and 1970. He did not only the third ascent of the West Buttress and North America Wall, but put up the Heart Route. In one season he had climbed five of the seven routes on the wall. "Been there, done that," he moved on to put up one of America's first wilderness Grade VI big wall on Tehipete Dome. A wall so remote 30 years passed before its second ascent. When I wanted to hear about the wall route he climbed on Boboquavari, all he wanted to do was talk about meeting Ed Abbey on that remote peak's descent route.

But wall climbing was just a quick diversion for Chuck. Altitude was what he wanted, and despite a lack of funding he pursued it around the globe. In 1972 he led a successful trip up the Pioneer Ridge on Denali, making the third ascent and walking all the way in and out. Later, in 1978, he would lead an American exchange to Russia, where he climbed three peaks including the first ascent of a 6,242m peak, and was on the summit party for the first ascent by western-ers of Peak Communism, 7,495m.

And yet, despite Chuck being my friend and mentor for 12 years, I never really knew about any of this until after his passing on Christmas Day. I guess I should have asked him for more stories when I could. Stories about his tenure as president of the Stanford Mountaineering Club, and Freedom of the Quad, and Hoover Tower. Stories about sailing to Hawaii, and the Maldives, and getting cast about in big storms. Stories about his six trips to Antarctica, or about Chile, or Peru.

Because in those stories would have been pearls of wisdom now lost to the world. Windows into the mind of a great thinker and adventurer who always thought outside the box, and who taught us the priorities that count most in climbing and in life.

"You know, Clay, I was thinking. I bet it would be a pretty good idea to go down to the Vilcanota [in Peru] and buy a burro. Then you could carry all your stuff and you could trade cigs and lighters for potatoes and really meet some neat people."

I guess in the end it was about the people after all. Rest in peace my good friend, we will all miss you more than you ever imagined.

CLAY WADMAN

J. ALEX MAXWELL 1910–2007

J. Alex Maxwell, better known as "Lex," was born in Yakima on July 26, 1910 to Mary Murphy Maxwell and Alexander James Maxwell. His first job after graduating from the local community college was as a bookkeeper in a local bank, followed a few years later by taking the same position at Yakima Federal Savings & Loan in 1936. He retired there in 1972 as the president. He remained on their board until his death in 2007. His only time away from that institution was for three and a half years during World War II, when he served as a captain in the Air Force. He was married to Mary Burns, his wife of 71 years. They had five children, and many of his trips were with his family, whether hiking, climbing, or skiing.

Lex Maxwell in the Cascades.

Lex's impact on mountaineering in the Northwest will be remembered long beyond his lifetime. He is best known locally for the authorship of his local hiking classic *Hither, Thither and Yon*. He was also referred to as a "noted mountain chef" with his famous "Glue Stew" before the days of instant freeze-dried foods. The recipe is one of those selected for the book *Gorp, Glop & Glue Stew* (reprinted as *Beyond Gorp*). Lex climbed in Mexico, the Rockies, the Tetons, the St. Elias Range, the Bugaboos, the Olympics, and, of course, throughout the Cascades. Among his first ascents are: Ulrichs Couloir (July 1933) and the West Ridge (August 1935) of Mount Stuart; Northeast Face of Little Tahoma (August 1959) and South Face of Kay's Spire (September 1956) on Mt. Rainier; the Southeast Face (June 1956) of North Peak in the Stuart Range; and the West Ridge (July 1963) and South Klickitat Glacier Icefall (July 1962) on Mt. Adams.

Lex, the first Washington member of the American Alpine Club outside of the Seattle area (1958), was one of the founders of Central Washington Mountain Rescue in Yakima, in about 1953. In addition to training local climbers in rescue techniques, Lex went across the Cascade Mountains to the monthly board meetings of Seattle Mountain Rescue (MRC in those days) representing the embryo group in Yakima. Then he would come back to Yakima and pass on the information he had picked up. Going to the meetings involved a 300-mile round-trip evening drive over Snoqualmie Pass, famous for its many feet of snow each winter. He was almost always at the fore of mountain rescue missions in the Eastern Cascades.

In his "History of CWMR," Lex wrote: "Our early needs were many-fold. We had to train our personnel in techniques of evacuation for injured people, in first aid, in teamwork and how to cooperate with the civil authorities as well as other rescue units. We needed money to buy bergtragas, litters, ropes, first aid supplies, climbing equipment and radios. We raised the money, we trained our people, and it was long, hard, and sometimes thankless. Yet along the way, a call for help would come and as everything cranked into gear, it gave a new stimulus to our efforts."

Lex was a leader in most of the business and civic organizations in Yakima, both during and after his active business life, but when a call for a rescue came, he would drop whatever he was doing to go out into the field, whatever the weather or the time of day, to help whoever was in trouble.

Lex had a lifelong interest in skiing and won many slalom events as a ski racer. This led to his involvement in developing the American River Ski Bowl between 1936 and1940. He also helped in the construction of the hut at Camp Schurman at 9,500 feet on Mt. Rainier. He was an avid skier who had a hand in discovering and developing the White Pass Ski Area and impressed his children by ascending Mt. Rainier with the express purpose of skiing down it. He hiked the mountains with his wife, family and friends until he turned ninety-five, a goal to which we can all aspire.

Lynn Buchanan

Richard E. McGowan 1933–2007

I first became acquainted with Dick McGowan more than 50 years ago when the climbing world in the United States was a small village spread across the country, connected by gossip and rumor and not the Internet. If we didn't know another climber personally, we certainly knew his reputation. I probably met Dick at that time and I certainly knew about him.

Dick McGowan on Everest in 1955.
International Himalayan Expedition

Dick started climbing in 1950 and quickly began going on major expeditions to Alaska, making first ascents of King Peak, Mt. Augusta, and Mt. Cook. He also climbed extensively in the Cascades, making many first ascents and new routes. Dick rapidly gained a reputation as an extremely strong mountaineer and probably the leading snow and ice climber in the country. He went to Everest in 1955 on Dyhrenfurth's International Himalayan Expedition where he was the first American to climb the Khumbu Icefall. He must have like it the experience because he did it 24 times on that expedition. When he returned he took over the Mount Rainier Guide Service. During his climbing career he did 11 major expeditions. He also led the first guided climb of Denali, in 1961.

He was running the Guide Service in 1959 when I spent the summer in Seattle. I had returned from Europe with a lag screw that a Swiss friend showed me to illustrate the principle of the ice screw. I had a prototype made, Pete Schoening got some other samples from Europe, and we went to Rainier to use one of Dick's climbing classes for our test. We had perfect conditions, a warm day. When we pulled directly on the ice pitons they all shot out with a big slurp. Then we put in the ice screws. We pulled. They held. We put the entire class on the rope and they still held. Dick had not seen ice screws before, and I will never forget the look on his face, as he said, "This is going to revolutionize ice climbing." Not only was he right, but later that summer he led the revolution by using them to make the difficult ascent of the entire Nisqually Icefall.

I really got to know Dick on Masherbrum (25,660 feet) in the Karakoram. George Bell and I wanted the finest climbers on rock and ice in the country. Dick was one of them. Moreover, George had been with him on Everest in 1955 and knew his capabilities. The climb took a tremendous team effort by everyone. We were lucky to get up and to have survived. Although he did not reach the summit, Dick was a major factor in our success. From the very beginning we used Dick's unique talents to push forward. We found 16 Balti men willing to carry loads to Camp I through the Serac Glacier. As a former middle school geography teacher, and with his Rainier guiding experience, Dick was the perfect man to handle the Baltis in this exercise in mass mountaineering. They were so effective that in a week almost everything had been moved to Camp I and we practically abandoned Base Camp for the rest of the expedition.

Dick was always in the vanguard until we reached Camp VII at 25,000 feet on the great southeat face. Dick and Willi Unsoeld made the first attempt on the summit, where they reached 25,000 feet and found a site for Camp VII. A snowstorm came, and on the retreat from Camp VI, Dick, Willi, Tom Hornbein, and George Bell were hit with a surface slide, which swept them down the slope. Somehow they managed to stop before going over an ice cliff. For a moment they seemed all right, then Dick pitched head first into the snow. He had inhaled a large quantity of ice crystals into his lungs, which produced a wild delirium. Fortunately, he pulled himself together a little, the snowing stopped, the sky cleared, and Dick managed to get to Camp V. He recovered sufficiently during the night to make it down to Camp III the next day. Although Dick rapidly improved, he never got back to his old form, but his drive and strength were such that when the weather finally cleared he was in the second summit team with Tom Hornbein and Jawed Akhter. But his lungs had not fully recovered and he had to return.

Despite everything the expedition managed to climb the mountain, the last climber got off the peak on July 12th, Dick's birthday, and we had what must have been one of the more meaningful birthday celebrations in his life.

The qualities of strength, courage, and character that Dick showed on Masherbrum were displayed all his life and especially in coping with the various health problems that beset him in his later years. The man was strong, both physically and mentally.

Dick was more than a mountain climber. He was a pioneer businessman in the outdoor industry. In the early 1950s when REI decided to expand from the room it had in downtown Seattle presided over by Jim Whittaker, Dick became the manager of its first store until he went to Everest in 1955. In 1963 he opened the Alpine Hut chain of mountaineering stores in Seattle and Portland, followed the next year by an outdoor equipment manufacturing plant making tents, backpacks, sleeping bags, and clothing. It moved to Wenatchee in 1967 and grew to include more than 180 employees by 1974, when Dick sold it. In 1977 he became one of the owners of Mountain Travel, and later became its CEO. He retired from Mountain Travel in 1996. But he couldn't be still. Two years later he founded Next Adventure, now managed by his daughter Kili.

Dick cared about people. He considered his employees part of an extended family. He cared about family and especially his children, the three he had with the late Elizabeth Whisnant: Richard Jr, Devi, and Michaele, who predeceased him in 1995, as well as Kili, his daughter with Louise Summer, his wife of 35 years. Dick also served for many years on the Board of the American Himalayan Foundation, which is helping to provide a better life for the people who live in the Himalaya. Everyone who had a relationship with Dick, whether it was close or remote, is better off for having it.

There is an old Islamic saying, "How do you know he is your friend? Is he your neighbor or have you gone on a long journey with him?" I cannot say Dick and I were neighbors, but I can say I did go with him on what seemed like a very long journey. Dick died on February 27 in Berkeley, California. He was a good man and a good friend. I was privileged to know him, and I will miss him.

NICHOLAS CLINCH

Mike Strassman 1960–2007

Mike Strassman, prolific first ascentionist, writer, and video maker was found dead at home in Lone Pine on July 1. He was 47 years old. Mike was best known for directing the 1988 video *Moving Over Stone*. But as his friends and climbing partners began comparing notes after his death, we realized that no one could count all the new routes Mike had done, because they are scattered across so much of the West. From Cochise Stronghold to the Idaho panhandle, and out obscure dirt roads in Nevada. But mostly up and down the Eastern Sierra. I'm thinking 200, but at this point that's just a wild guess.

Mike Strassman. *Courtesy Judy and Steve York*

Mike had first ascents on every one of the Mt. Whitney Needles, just for starters, a project that lasted decades and face-tiously spawned the "East Face Club." He counted nine Needles marching southward from Whitney, gave some of them trademark goofy names and eventually put FAs on each. The climbs themselves are often outstanding and serious. Like the proud Aiguille Junior (10a), and "the finest route I have done in the Whitney Region," the South Face of Aiguille Extra. Like a solo FA on Keeler Needle that took eight days. On the face of Mt. Whitney itself, seven attempts finally led to a runout 5.11 crux. Name? "If at First…"

Strassman's Greatest Hits in Arizona would have to include Ides of Middlemarch (5.9+) and Magnas Coloradas (5.11a) at Cochise Stronghold, and discovering the Wall of the Trundling Trolls on Mt. Lemmon. In the Sierra, there's Malletosis (10b) in Tuolumne and well as Switch Hitter (10d) and He She (10b) in Rock Creek. Mike was a pioneer in the Owens River Gorge—try Nucko, Pride of the North (11b) and Steel Monkey (12c). And in the Alabama Hills you could choose from Strassman routes literally "too numerous to mention."

When I met Mike in 1986 he was fresh out of UCLA film school and quickly inspired me with the dream of a video that became *Moving Over Stone*. We had no idea what we were getting into. Mike had produced nothing bigger than a five-minute student video, and I had never worked in the medium. Over the next year, with support from Patagonia and Austin Hearst, we filmed from Yosemite to Smith Rock, from Indian Creek to the Needles, with rock stars like John Bachar, Lynn Hill, Dale Bard, and Peter Croft. In between, our crew of three was often crammed among camera cases and tripods in my tiny VW Sirocco for long night drives criss-crossing the West. Leasing a shoulder-top TV camera, we quickly discovered that its old-school tube technology was delicate. Not built for dangling shots hundreds of feet up. One time it quit on us in Indian Creek, which led to the novel scene of Mike in a desert phone booth with a technician on the line trying desperately to repair it with a Swiss Army Knife. Half-shot sequences were adroitly salvaged by fine editing on Mike's part. *Moving Over Stone* was the sec-ond-ever climbing video to hit the market. It went on to become the best selling "rock video" of all time.

Mike formed Range of Light Productions, which became well-known for snowboard and mountain bike videos, like *Kamikaze*, featuring deadly speed wobbles careening down Mammoth Mountain. Mike also wrote *The Basic Essentials of Rock Climbing*, *Climbing Big Walls*, and the first-ever guidebook to the Alabama Hills.

The sardonic way Mike treated his own life could become abrasive, even erupting into flame wars. But then he would turn generous and surprisingly civic-minded. Like the weekend in the Alabama Hills when he organized rock stars to teach disadvantaged kids to climb, then everyone built trails alongside the BLM ranger. And as Kevin Kleinfelter pointed out, "He was also a legendary entertainer. A Strassman party was not something to miss. Anyone who's attended one of these events will know what I mean."

Mike had been battling for years with crystal meth. Last spring he wrote a song about it, "Sorry Ass Tweaker." which Peter Mayfield used to introduce a video warning to teenagers www.chromadynamics.com/lifeormeth.html. It's powerful. And poignant.

Mike, I have a bottle of your ashes right here. Next spring I'm taking you with me up Birch Mountain again. We always talked about climbing that long, Dark Star–like buttress together. Our project deteriorated into wrangling over naming it after your dead friend or mine. Now it's gonna be you.

DOUG ROBINSON

SADAO TAMBE 1916–2007

Sadao Tambe, born in Kyoto, Japan, learned climbing as a member of the famous Keio University Alpine Club. After earning his degree in economics in 1939, Sadao started his career in management with Nippon Yusen Kaisha, one of the largest shipping companies in Japan, which blessed him with the chance to travel to many foreign countries until his retirement. Sadao earned fame as one of the foremost translators of mountain books in Japan, and he published many books, especially about Himalayan expeditions, which led to strong friendships with Nepalese, Indian, Pakistani, and Chinese mountaineering authorities. He also translated *Americans on Everest*, by James Ramsey Ullman, which allowed him to meet and befriend Bill Putnam, then president of the AAC. Bill invited Sadao to the General Assembly of the UIAA and introduced him to board members from around the world.

Sadao was a member of the Japanese Alpine Club from 1965, served on the board of the Japanese Mountaineering Association starting in 1970, and was vice president of JMA from 1975 to 1984. He was elected to the board of the UIAA in 1976, where he served for eight years. Among his diplomatic achievements were active behind-the-scenes negotiations that led to a unanimous UIAA vote to accept mainland China into the UIAA. Sadao was also a long-time member of the AAC. Sadao is survived by his wife Tsukiko, three children, and four grandchildren. We miss Sadao and will always cherish his memory in our hearts.

TAKEO YOSHINO

Brief obituaries of other AAC members may be found at www.americanalpineclub.org

NECROLOGY

Peter Absolon	Eaton Cromwell, Jr.	Ed C. Holt	Duane McRuer
Robert G. Allison	Curt Dempster	Lara Kellogg	Chris Nolen
Robert Hicks Bates	Joshua Fonner	Chuck Kroger	Thomas C. Russler
Kurt G. Beam	John Kevin Fox	J. Alex Maxwell	Michael A. Strassman
David L. Blockus	Walter T. Haswell, III	Richard McGowan	Sadao Tambe
Rev. Harold O.J. Brown	Douglas L. Hoffmann	Russell McJury	Bradford Washburn

CLUB ACTIVITIES

EDITED BY FREDERICK O. JOHNSON

ALASKA SECTION. It was a busy year in the most northern of AAC sections. We officially purchased and signed the lease agreement with the State for the Snowbird Hut on the lateral moraine of the Snowbird Glacier in the Talkeetna Mountains—the first hut for the AAC. Originally built for backcountry skiing access, the hut is also situated in close proximity to multi-pitch alpine climbs, but is in dire need of a rebuild. To finance a new hut, the Section hosted a slideshow at the Bear Tooth, a favorite local theater pub, which generously donated the proceeds from the door. With good attendance from the Anchorage outdoor scene, the event not only raised needed monies but also provided good exposure to the Alaska AAC. The rebuild of the hut is slated for summer 2009.

The slideshows in Anchorage have been a great way to bring our members and others from the outdoor community together and provide an excellent forum for networking and public outreach. In 2007 we hosted a diverse series of shows that ranged from the Marmolata in Italy to remote Aleutian peaks, from Kyrgyzstan to Patagonia, and even included a mountain geology lesson!

Kicking off our spring series, we enjoyed an artful slideshow from club member/biologist/photographer James Brady on climbing in Croatia, the Italian Dolomites, and the Tien Shan range of Kyrgyzstan. Joe Stock lectured on the first ski traverse of the Neacola Mountains (Aleutian Range), which encompassed over 100 miles and 20,000 vertical feet through whiteouts, icefalls, and deep powder. In March, Club member/geologist Peter Haeussler delivered a fascinating presentation on the mountain forming processes of the Alaska Range, the 7.9 earthquake that rocked the Denali area, as well as other active faults and earthquake activity in the Alaska Range. In April we had a showing of "Fun Hogs," a classic 1968 film featuring Yvon Chouinard and cohorts on their adventure from Ventura, California, in a Ford Econoline van to Patagonia in three-and-a-half months and 16,500 miles. In our fall series, Scott Darsney gave a captivating presentation on his climb of Manaslu (8,163m) in Nepal, followed by an interesting adventure climbing and exploring in the Aleutian chain via sailboat. Our November slideshow was the benefit for the Snowbird Hut, with Jim Donini and Freddie Wilkinson presenting "The Good, the Bad and the Ugly," which awed the sold-out theater by contrasting young and old, modern and traditional, Alaska and Patagonia. In December local climbing legend Carl Tobin gave an inspirational presentation titled "Climbing with My Mentor," featuring images of his climbs with George Lowe from the East Face of Everest to the Dolomites. The Alaska Section gratefully acknowledges the BP Energy Center for providing the modern facility for our slideshows.

In 2008 our goals are to organize more fund-raisers for the Snowbird Hut rebuild, to design another hut, to co-sponsor climbing events, and to increase conservation efforts and public outreach.

HARRY HUNT, *Chair*

OREGON SECTION. Keith Daellenbach along with Kellie Rice were the super-achievers of the Oregon Section on the Madrone Wall Preservation Project. One mile south of the City of Damascus along the Clackamas River Bluffs resides an amazing civic treasure. The Madrone Wall is a publicly owned 44-acre Clackamas County site which has been closed to public access since 1997, when the County pursued an ill-conceived rock quarry that would have destroyed these splendid bluffs. Over a quarter million dollars were wasted studying how to blow up the cliffs. In 2000 the County dropped plans to quarry the site with "County forces." With the help of Mazama Club funding and the climbing community, a study by the Madrone Wall Preserva- tion Committee showed the County why it was uneconomical, even under the most favorable circumstances, to reduce these beautiful cliffs to aggregate, thus destroying their unique water- shed, natural habitat, and recreational and educational resources. Keith and Kellie have worked diligently on the Madrone Wall Project along with other members of the MWPC (Mazamas and AAC) to create a climbing park in the suburbs of Portland. Kellie is an active Portland climber who also works with the Access Fund. Long-time AAC member and exploration geolo- gist Richard Bence hosts the Madrone Wall Web site.

On a Columbia River Gorge Service Project, Christy Hansen, myself, and others worked on the rescue litter shelter at Broughton's Bluff. The Oregon Section has had good success with the rescue litter station program and will collaborate with Al Schumer and the Cascade Section to create more such structures in the North Cascades.

In September Christy Hansen and I made a number of ascents testing concepts for the Space Mountaineering Analogue Project (SMAP). The idea is to learn from each discipline to bring new ideas to space exploration as well as mountaineering. A brief abstract of our work may be found in "Earth and Space 2008" in the Proceedings of the ASCE. Members of the Oregon Section will be testing ascending mechanisms and techniques in space tether climbing.

ROBERT MCGOWN. *Chair*

SIERRA NEVADA SECTION. We had an active year hosting climbing, social, and conservation events for AAC members and the climbing community. In February we hosted our second Ice Climb-munity based out of the off-the-grid Lost Trail Lodge in Coldstream Canyon near Truc- kee. The Climb-munity events are intended to get both AAC members and nonmembers out climbing together, foster climbing community, and promote AAC membership. Warm and wet weather ended up foiling the ice climbing, but those attending enjoyed skiing and snowshoeing in the beautiful canyon below the Sierra crest. That, along with great meals, a warm fire, and live music at the lodge kept spirits high.

In an effort to connect the AAC locally with younger climbers, the Section created the Annual Meeting Attendance Grant. In March we awarded our inaugural grant to young big- wall ace and AAC member Dave Turner from Sacramento. We paid Dave's way to attend the AAC Annual Meeting in Bend, Oregon, where he received a Lyman Spitzer grant to support his attempt on a new route on Cerro Escudo in Torres del Paine in Chilean Patagonia [pp. 24–31]. As a spring and fall resident of Camp 4, Dave is a great ambassador to younger climbers in Yosemite.

In April Section members began their annual volunteer support for the climbers inter- pretive program in Yosemite. This wonderful program of Saturday evening free public presen- tations by climbers is part of Linda McMillan's ongoing effort in leading the AAC's work to promote the interests of climbers and preserve the historical importance of climbing in Yosemite Valley.

Members and friends gathered for the Donner Summit Climb-munity in June to enjoy superb granite cragging. We camped within walking distance of the climbs on undeveloped property owned by our member Bela Vadasz of Alpine Skills International and enjoyed a barbeque and campfire. This low-key climbing event provides a great way for climbers who haven't yet joined the AAC to check us out and experience the Club at a local level.

The July Climb-munity attracted over 50 climbers to Tuolumne Meadows and Tioga Pass. Our member Tom Burch secured a group campsite in the Meadows, which we (over)filled and shared with some climbers who were shut out of the full campground. Word got out in the campground, and we had many friends wander over to our site to share a beer and campfire. August featured the sequel to our Donner Summit Climb-munity. The weather was splitter, and everyone enjoyed great climbing and another fun barbeque and campfire on Bela Vadasz's beautiful Donner Pass property.

The Section kicked off its series of fall events with the ever-popular Pinecrest Climb-In, graciously hosted by Royal and Liz Robbins and Tom Frost in mid-September. Members and guests gathered for cragging at Gianelli Edges and a wonderful party at the Robbins cabin. It's worth noting that while the Sierra Nevada Section has a tradition of strong membership and leadership from women climbers, no doubt the presence of Liz Robbins and the inspiration of her first female ascent of the Northwest Face of Half Dome resulted in 25 women attending this year's Climb-In.

In late September our members also participated in the tremendous effort of the annual Yosemite Facelift cleanup organized by the Yosemite Climbers Association with support from the AAC and the Sierra Nevada Section. Check out these numbers and you can't help but be inspired by the power of grassroots effort: 2,945 volunteers contributing 18,335 person-hours; $344,148 Park Service–value of work done; 132 miles of roadway cleaned; 80+ miles of trails cleaned; 42,330 pounds (over 21 tons) of trash collected, with everything recycled that could be. The AAC and the Section contributed 300 T-shirts featuring graphics designed by our own Scott Sawyer. We also sponsored one of the evening slideshows, with Royal Robbins and Tom Frost describing their ascent of the West Face of Sentinel Rock.

In November the Section hosted the second annual Fall "High Ball" in Bishop. About 50 climbers joined the party Saturday night at Mill Creek Station. Thanks to Roger Derryberry for opening the shrine to Warren Harding for our event. Jerry Dodrill and Kevin Jorgenson presented an electrifying multi-media show featuring insights into their creative collaboration with still photography and video from their diverse climbing experiences, and, of course, there were the wicked highball boulder problems. The gear raffle was a great success. On Sunday a number of us joined local BLM ranger and climber Scott Justham for climber's coffee at the Happy Boulders trailhead, followed by a work session repairing the trail into the Happies and collecting trash. The explosion in the popularity of bouldering obviously comes with consequences for the surrounding environment and demands responsibility from us.

Later in November, noted climbing photographer Giulio Malfer passed through the San Francisco Bay area on a visit to California, and we coaxed a few notable Section members to sit still for his large-format portrait camera. Thanks to Steve Roper, Irene Beardsley, and Nick Clinch for making themselves available. And thanks to Giulio for giving the AAC permission to use his portraits of our members in promotional materials and at the Bradford Washburn

American Mountaineering Museum.

On December 9th the Sierra Nevada Section wrapped up the year with our traditional Annual Holiday Dinner at Spenger's Fish Grotto in Berkeley. Members and guests enjoyed drinks, a dinner buffet, a recap and photos from this year's Section events, and a gear raffle. About 100 members and guests attended and were treated to a heartfelt presentation by John Harlin III, editor of the *American Alpine Journal* and author of the recent book, *The Eiger Obsession: Facing the Mountain that Killed My Father*, which was featured in the IMAX film, The Alps. To commemorate the evening, each attendee received a complimentary copy of the last issue of the climbing anthology, *Ascent*, co-edited by Allen Steck, who was in attendance. Coincidentally, that issue included an article by Harlin. Other notable members attending were Lou Reichardt, a member of the first American ascent of K2, and long-time Sierra Nevada guide, author, and filmmaker Doug Robinson.

DAVE RIGGS, *Chair*

CENTRAL ROCKIES SECTION. The year started out with a bang in January, when the Central Rockies Section sponsored the 13th Annual Ouray Ice Festival. We provided a station and the CRS Tent, a volunteer staff, and swag. Our members Ryan McCombs, Chris Kellner, and JP Parsons, plus Ellen Stein, Trevor , and Dario from Chile were provided with a group motel room by the CRS in exchange for staffing the table for three days, promoting the AAC, and serving hot chocolate. Spirits were high, and despite the unseasonably cold temperature, the crew was still successful in signing up 17 new AAC members. AAC staff members Phil Powers and Charlie Mace were in attendance to support the CRS crew and add that extra level of oversight and polish that all good volunteers appreciate. Ouray area local Danika Gilbert developed and hosted the Women's Base Camp Breakfast. Twenty-two women attended, aged 14 to their mid-70s, and talked about everything from training techniques and networking with other women, to peeing methods while out adventuring! The catered breakfast was great (Sara from Secret Garden catering). Danika stated "we felt specially honored that Eve Nott and Julie Johnson joined us."

In February the Section helped sponsor the 9th Annual Cody Ice Festival in Cody, Wyoming. Billed as the "Friendliest Little Ice Festival in the Northern Rockies," it boasts nearly 100 routes, most of which are multi-pitch ice and all of which are in a very remote, beautiful area.

In June the CRS Chair put out a call for grant ideas, with over $3,000 available from CRS shirt sales, banquets, auctions, and donations over the last 10 years. Two $1,000 grants were awarded based on the numerous letters that our members provided. The Colorado Avalanche Information Center received a grant to further efforts in "wet avalanche" research. New communication equipment will allow retrieval of real-time analysis and use it to run snowpack models and provide information to their public Web site. The second grant went to the Colorado 14er Initiative for the Mt. Massive ascent trail, which must be re-routed around wet or steep fall-line areas.

This year I confronted the human waste problem that many popular crags face. Partnering with Restop® I designed an oak "BagBox" for use at trailheads to dispense these small backcountry bags. Rocky Mountain National Park was sufficiently excited to put two Bag-Boxes into immediate service. Seven other National Parks are looking at this box design.

In October the 7th annual Lumpy Trails Day at Lumpy Ridge in RMNP was held in conjunction with the Access Fund's Adopt-a-Crag program. It was amazing that 37 volunteers showed up in a full-blown, early-season wet blizzard. Although this was less than half of the original group of volunteers, it was nevertheless a proud showing. Rock stair construction was abandoned for safety, but access trails were reclaimed, and over 500 native plants were plugged in where a parking lot once was. Breakfast, lunch, and great swag were provided by local businesses and the CRS.

The year ended with a sad note on a high point. After 10 years of leading the Central Rockies Section, I resigned my position as Chair. My tenure spanned five AAC presidents and dozens of directors and included chairing the original Huts and Sections committees. I felt honored to receive the Access Fund's Sharp End Award in 2002 and the AAC's Angelo Heilprin Citation in 2004.

Greg Sievers, *former Chair*

New York Section. The year 2007 was a particularly active and interesting one for the New York Section. We reached a record 750 members by year's end, aided by a special outreach to younger members by the national AAC and by continuing to provide a variety of appealing indoor and outdoor programs. Our recent programming alliance with the Rubin Museum, whose state-of- the-art theatrical facility makes it one of New York's premier venues, once again proved its value. In April, Mark Richey held the sold-out audience in rapt attention with scenes and video from his expeditions to the Himalaya in 2006. In the fall another historic and perhaps "only in New York" show featured first ascents, almost 20 years apart, of Thalay Sagar in the Gangotri. John Thackray and Roy Kligfield talked about their pioneering first ascent in 1979, while Andy Lindblade discussed his historic north face direttissima in 1996, for which he won a coveted Piolet d'Or.

On the outdoor front, both our Spring and Winter Outings, held in the High Peaks of the Adirondacks, sold out quickly. One of the venerable traditions of both outings is a Happy Hour and sit-down dinner with the slideshow provided by member volunteers. These are particularly welcome after a hard day on the ice or rock. Dan Lochner talked about his success on Chapuyeva (6,731m.) in the Khan Tengri Massif in Kyrgyzstan, while Jack Jefferies, who is a 5.12 climber as well as a former world champion skydiver, discussed the intricacies and challenge of the latter sport.

Finally, on October 27 our Fall Annual Dinner, now in its 28th consecutive year, featured Geoff Tabin, M.D., as special guest speaker. Geoff, who was the fourth person to climb the Seven Summits and a member of the 1983 Everest East Face Expedition, is perhaps best known as a co-founder of the Himalayan Cataract Project. HCP, through its facilities and remote mobile camps, has had great success in pioneering very low-cost cataract surgery for the afflicted in Nepal, Tibet, and other parts of the Third World. Geoff is one of those climbers who is truly making a difference in the lives of people. Accordingly, the event was run as a fundraiser for HCP.

At the Dinner we welcomed the return of the NY Section Flag. In January, Dr. Sam Silverstein brought it with him to Mt. Vinson for the 40th Reunion of the American Antarctic Expedition. Sam was an original member of the AAC team that in 1966–67 made first ascents of peaks in the Ellsworth Range. Finally, Edgar Walsh showed photos of the 150th anniversary celebration in June of the (British) Alpine Club, in Zermatt, where he and his wife Linda ably represented the NY Section.

None of the above would have been possible without the support of a dedicated corps of volunteers, including, among others, Mike Barker, our Membership Chairman, and Jon Light and Richard Ryan, our cinematography and A/V experts, respectively. Thanks also go to our webmaster Vic Benes, who has made www.nysalpineclub.org an attractive and informative forum for stories, photos, and "partners wanted" notices. Among those who were paired thanks to this service were Clif Maloney and Bob Street. Clif and Bob, who are 70 and 68, respectively, set a new American age record for their successful climb of Vinson this past December with guide Marty Schmidt.

PHIL ERARD, *Chair*

NEW ENGLAND SECTION. In 2007 we lost Bob Bates, our famed AAC Honorary President, one of the great "Harvard Five" mountaineers (Bates, Carter, Houston, Moore, and Washburn) portrayed by David Roberts in his January 1981 *Harvard Magazine* article, "Five Who Made It to the Top."

In February Bill Atkinson, Rick Merritt, John Kascenska, and others were at the Club's annual meeting in Bend, Oregon. We hiked to the top of the cinder cone in Bend, where we happened to meet Dee Molenaar. At 82 and the oldest on the cliffs, Bill trailed rope-gun Tom Thrall up some 5.6s at Smith Rock.

Sixty-three members and guests attended the Section's 11th annual gala dinner on March 24 in Weston at the Henderson House, a mansion now owned and operated by Northeastern University as a conference center. Here we shared conviviality and fine dining amid an exhibition of Jeff Botz's large-format Himalayan photos. We learned of the accomplishments in Nepal of special guest Dan Mazur, who also gave a stirring account of the rescue of Lincoln Hall on Everest in 2006. Mark Richey delivered an elegant and heartfelt remembrance of our own late, great H. Bradford Washburn. Barbara Washburn was in attendance. Also at this meeting we welcomed our new member Jack Hadock.

The June Basecamp at Nancy Savickas's refuge in Albany, New Hampshire, by now a tradition, brought out 28 of us to quaff, stoke the grill, and air outrageous falsehoods around the campfire. The Fall Outing, also at Nancy's, was a great success and our biggest bash yet. Here for the first time were such notables as Jed Williamson, Bruce Franks, and Bob Hall.

Various individual activities: Mark Richey achieved the summit of Suma Brak (20,230') in Pakistan for a first in alpine style. Nancy Savickas and Yuki Fujita bearded the awesome ice at Rjukan, the site of the infamous Nazi heavy-water plant in Norway. To celebrate his 50th anniversary of joining the "NH 4,000-Footer Club," Scott Skinner repeated all 48 summits in 2007. Ben Townsend and team climbed the five-pitch "Wild, Wild Life" (5.10) in Katahdin's northwest basin. At the AAC Board meeting in Asheville, North Carolina, Sam Streibert reconnected with Dennis Merritt for climbing on Table and Looking Glass mountains. With a combined age of 110, Eric Engberg with Ed Ward bested several 5.10s in Tuolumne Meadows, and Eric climbed a 23-pitch 5.12 with his son Zeb at El Potrero, Mexico. In Yosemite Chad Hussey's highlights were Cathedral's "Mordor Wall" and "Crest Jewel," and 10 pitches of desperation on North Dome. Dick Tucker, Dick Traverse, and Bob Dangel completed the noteworthy Ptarmigan Traverse and ascended Dome Peak (8,786') in Washington's North

Cascades. After 30 years unroped, Malcolm Moore returned to the rocks of the Cascades and also skied the backcountry of Italy's Ortler group.

BILL ATKINSON, *Chair, and* NANCY SAVICKAS, *Vice Chair*

BLUE RIDGE SECTION. Section events in 2007 included a number of slideshows held at the Rhodeside Tavern in Arlington, Virginia. Dimitry Shapovalov gave two very interesting talks about climbing in Russia and Central Asia, with expeditions to the Pamirs, Kyrgyzstan, and the volcanoes of the Kamchatka Peninsula. John Heilprin (grandson of Angelo of the AAC's Angelo Heilprin Citation) described his participation on an expedition to the north ridge of K2 in 2000 and, as a journalist himself, shared his experiences of participating in a media-oriented climb. Section Treasurer Phil Boyer provided an introduction to climbing in the Cascades from many years of trips when he lived in Seattle.

In addition to these meetings, in March 2007 we had our annual not-so-black-tie dinner at the home of Jeanette Helfrich, former chair of the Section. This was attended by around 50 climbers from the AAC and other local climbing groups, with attire ranging from tuxedos to pile jackets—ironed, of course.

In October, in conjunction with the local Potomac Mountain Club, we hosted a public talk by Fred Beckey at the National Cathedral School. Fred reminisced about more than 60 years of first ascents from Alaska to the desert southwest.

Section members climbed widely through North America in 2007, from summer bouldering on the East Coast to winter ice routes in the Canadian Rockies. Our members attended a number of AAC events, including the annual meeting in Bend, Oregon, in March and the September meet hosted by the Southeast Section at Table Rock, North Carolina. We were also active in local climbing access and conservation issues, including participation in events hosted by the Access Fund at Great Falls and Carderock, two local climbing areas. Section members, as part of a coalition of local climbers, were active in discussions with the National Park Service to ensure continued access to climbing at Great Falls as part of the proposed NPS management plan.

SIMON CARR, *Chair*

SOUTHEAST SECTION. Despite geographic and demographic obstacles, 2007 witnessed a significant renaissance in AAC activity in the Southeast Section. Historically, development of a sense of AAC community within the Southeast has proven difficult. This has been due to the lack of a strong AAC tradition in the region, the Section's thousand-mile, eight-state sprawl, and a widely dispersed AAC population.

When it announced the new volunteer position of AAC Ambassador in early 2007, the Club provided the means for the Southeast Section to begin to address these challenges effectively. Prototypical implementation of the Ambassador role has significantly strengthened the local AAC presence in several Southeastern communities. With the support of the section chair and the AAC staff in Golden, our vanguard of Ambassadors in 2007 initiated successful local events in Louisville, Charlotte, Chattanooga, and Raleigh.

In June Dr. Martin Klapheke hosted a Louisville dinner for the AAC membership residing in the lower Ohio Valley. AAC president Jim Donini joined members and their guests from Kentucky, Ohio, and Indiana. While well versed in the perils of mountaineering, Jim learned a few new lessons in the risks of tight itineraries as he managed to miss both of his flight connections on his journey from Colorado to Louisville. He did arrive in time for dessert and delivered a superb presentation on his climbing partnerships with Tackle, Crouch, and other mature climbers.

One of the best examples of the contribution a committed AAC Ambassador can make was a project initiated by Max Poppel in Chattanooga. In October Max and a small team of local members produced "Chattanooga on the Rocks," an AAC-sponsored weekend of climbing, films, and pizza. Saturday featured bouldering at The Stone Fort, one of the premier bouldering sites in the Southeast. On Saturday evening over 75 members and guests gathered for pizza and a screening of the Reel Rock Tour. Gear raffles and auctions raised over $400 for the AAC general fund. On Sunday frigid temperatures led to a change in plans with a second day of bouldering substituting for the planned day of trad climbing at Sunset Rock. Max has only recently joined the AAC, yet he is committed to seeing that it is visible, viable, and relevant to climbers in the Chattanooga region. He's a great model for an AAC Ambassador as well as a terrific example of the power of the youth movement in the new AAC.

Also in October, Rick Gromlovits hosted a small barbecue at his home in the Charlotte area for the membership in western North Carolina.

The high point of the year was the September climbing meet at the Table Rock, N.C., Outward Bound Camp. The AAC Board of Directors joined the southeastern AAC community for a well attended weekend of meetings, rock climbing at Table Rock and in the Linville Gorge, and evening dinner presentations. On Friday evening Mark Richey and Steve Swenson shared engaging perspectives on leisure time in the Karakoram. Local climber and humorist Pat Goodman was the featured speaker on Saturday evening. I would like to thank former Director of Operations, Charlie Mace, for his initiative and support in bringing the Board of Directors meeting to the Southeast and the N.C. Outward Bound School for their superb event management.

The Third Annual Eastern North Carolina AAC Barbecue was moved from November to January 12 in order to accommodate members' fall climbing plans. Thirty-odd (yes, some were exceedingly odd) members and their guests gathered at my home in Raleigh for socializing and good old Carolina barbecue. Dr. Amer Adam, a local member, delivered an entertaining slide show featuring his September visit to the Cordillera Blanca, which resulted in a new route on Nevada Shaqsha with his partner, Shy Rohani.

I would like to formally thank all of the AAC staff, from Phil Powers on down, for their terrific support for the Southeast Section. In 2007 we succeeded in overcoming years of inertia. Our Section's focus in 2008 will be to build upon our 2007 successes, recruit additional AAC Ambassadors, and continue to build a strong sense of AAC community throughout the Southeast.

Finally, on behalf of the membership, I would like to congratulate North Carolina member Barry "The Gangsta" Myers on his paradigm-shifting, 52-hour solo of the North Wall of Rum Doodle, August 22–24. Wicked, Barry, wicked!!

DAVID THOENEN, *Chair*

INDEX

COMPILED BY RALPH FERRARA AND EVE TALLMAN

Mountains are listed by their official names. Ranges and geographic locations are also indexed. Unnamed peaks (eg. Peak 2,340) are listed under P. Abbreviations are used for some states and countries and for the following: Article: art.; Cordillera: C.; Mountains: Mts.; National Park: Nat'l Park; Obituary: obit. Most personnel are listed for major articles. Expedition leaders and persons supplying information in Climbs and Expeditions are also cited here. Indexed photographs are listed in bold type. Reviewed books are listed alphabetically under Book Reviews.

SUBMISSIONS GUIDELINES

The *American Alpine Journal* records the significant climbing accomplishments of the world in an annual volume. We encourage climbers to submit brief (250-500 words) factual accounts of their climbs and expeditions. Accounts should be submitted by e-mail whenever possible. Alternatively, submit accounts by regular post. Please provide complete contact information, including e-mail address, postal address, fax, and phone. The deadline is December 31, through earlier submissions will be looked on very kindly! For photo guidelines and other information, please see the complete Submissions Guidelines document at www.americanalpineclub.org/AAJ. Please address all post correspondence to: The American Alpine Journal, 710 Tenth Street, Suite 100, Golden, CO 80401 USA; tel.: (303) 384-0110; fax: (303) 384-0111; aaj@americanalpineclub.org; www.americanalpineclub.org